barbri®

The Conviser Mini Review: Illinois

Table of Contents

To be used in conjunction with the Summer 2010 and Winter 2011 BAR/BRI Bar Review Courses

CM

AGENCY

TABLE OF CONTENTS

AGENCY

I. CREATION OF AGENCY

A. INTRODUCTION

Agency refers to the legal relationship whereby an agent is authorized to represent a principal in business dealings with third parties.

B. CREATION OF AGENCY RELATIONSHIP

Agency is consensual. Not all contractual formalities are necessary to create an agency relationship.

1. Capacity

a. Principal Must Have Contractual Capacity

A principal must have contractual capacity. Thus, a minor's appointment of an agent is voidable, and incompetents and most unincorporated organizations cannot be principals. (However, in many jurisdictions, partnerships and other organized business entities can be principals and appoint agents.)

b. Agent Needs Only Minimal Capacity

One may be an agent even though he has no contractual capacity. (*Exception:* If the agent has literally no mental capacity, he cannot act for the principal.)

CMR Exam Tip Notice the different capacity requirements: A principal must have contractual capacity but an agent need not. Thus, a minor can be an agent but not a principal.

c. Disqualification of Agents

An agent may be disqualified for representing both parties or failing to have a required license.

2. Formalities

a. Consent

Consent of both parties is required.

b. Consideration Not Required

No consideration is necessary.

CMR Exam Tip Remember that no consideration is required to establish an agency relationship; *i.e.,* one may agree to serve as an agent gratuitously and be saddled with the duties of an agent.

c. Writing

Generally no writing is required, but many states require a writing when the contract the agent is to enter into with a third party is within certain provisions of the Statute of Frauds, most notably land transactions.

3. Modes of Creating Agency Relationship

The agency relationship may be created by an act of the parties or by operation of law.

a. **By Act of Parties**
Parties may create an agency by agreement between the principal and agent (*i.e.,* actual authority), holding out by the principal (*i.e.,* apparent authority), or ratification.

b. **By Operation of Law**

1) **Estoppel**
An agency may be created through estoppel. Estoppel is virtually the same as apparent authority (*see* II.A.3., *infra*) in that it requires third-party reliance on the principal's communication.

2) **Statute**
Statutes creating agencies are usually designed to accomplish a limited purpose (*e.g.,* statute appointing secretary of state as out-of-state motorist's agent for service of process for damages arising from driving in-state).

CREATION OF AGENCY—ELEMENTS

For a valid agency relationship to exist, check for the following:

☑ *Capacity* — Principal must have full contractual capacity
— Agent must have at least minimal mental capacity

☑ *Consent* —— of both parties

☑ *Writing if required* —— by Statute of Frauds (equal dignities rule)

Note: Consideration is **not** required.

C. RIGHTS AND DUTIES BETWEEN PRINCIPAL AND AGENT

1. **Agent's Duties**
In addition to any express contractual duties that the agent owes the principal, fiduciary duties of loyalty, obedience to reasonable directions, and reasonable care under the circumstances (including duty to disclose all relevant information) are owed. (While a gratuitous and a compensated agent may owe the same duty of care, the measure of "reasonableness" may vary because compensation is a proper circumstance to consider.)

2. **Principal's Remedies**

The principal's remedies against the agent include contract actions (against compensated agents), tort actions, actions for secret profits, equitable actions for an accounting, and withholding of compensation for intentional torts or intentional breaches of fiduciary duty. The principal may recover the actual profits or properties held by the agent whether or not the agent's profit has caused the principal any loss.

3. **Subagents**

   a. **Liability of Agent**

   An agent has absolute liability to the principal for breaches by a subagent.

   b. **Duties**

   If appointed with proper authority, the subagent owes the principal the same duties as the agent. If the subagent is unauthorized, he owes no duties to the principal, but does owe duties to the agent.

4. **Principal's Duties**

The principal owes the agent all of the duties imposed by their contract, reasonable compensation, and reimbursement for expenses. The principal also generally should cooperate with the agent and not unreasonably interfere with the agent's performance.

CMR **Exam Tip** Remember that if the agency agreement is silent regarding compensation, the agent is entitled to *reasonable* compensation. Also remember that a principal generally owes no duty to compensate a subagent even if the agent had authority to hire the subagent.

5. **Agent's Remedies**

A compensated agent has the usual contract remedies against the principal (but has a duty to mitigate damages). Also, an agent has a right to a possessory lien for any money due from the principal, including compensation owed for services.

6. **Real Estate Brokers' Contracts**

   a. **Nonexclusive Contracts**

   Nonexclusive contracts generally entitle the agent to compensation upon his production of a ready, willing, and able buyer, even though the sale is not consummated.

   b. **Exclusive Contracts**

   Exclusive contracts enable the broker to get his commission if *anyone* produces a ready, willing, and able buyer.

DUTIES OF PRINCIPAL AND AGENT	
Principal's Duties	**Agent's Remedies for Principal's Breach of Duties**
Compensation Cooperation Indemnity/reimbursement Express contractual duties }	{ Contractual remedies Possessory lien
Agent's Duties	**Principal's Remedies for Agent's Breach of Duties**
Reasonable care Loyalty Obedience Express contractual duties }	{ Contract remedies (if agent compensated) Tort remedies Constructive trust Action for secret profits Withhold compensation

II. CONTRACT LIABILITY—AGENCY POWER

A. ACTUAL AND APPARENT AUTHORITY

When deciding whether a principal will be bound on an agent's contract, it should first be determined whether the agent had *actual authority*. If she did not, look to see whether *apparent authority* was present.

CMR **Exam Tip** The most important of all agency concepts for bar exam purposes are those involving actual and apparent authority. A very high percentage of questions will require you to display your understanding of this area.

1. Actual Authority

Actual authority is authority that the agent reasonably believes she possesses based on the principal's dealings with her. It may be express or implied.

a. Express

Express authority is that which is actually contained within the four corners of the agency agreement. It is effective even if it was granted mistakenly or because of misrepresentation.

b. Implied

Implied authority is that which the agent reasonably believes she has as a result of the principal's actions. It includes authority:

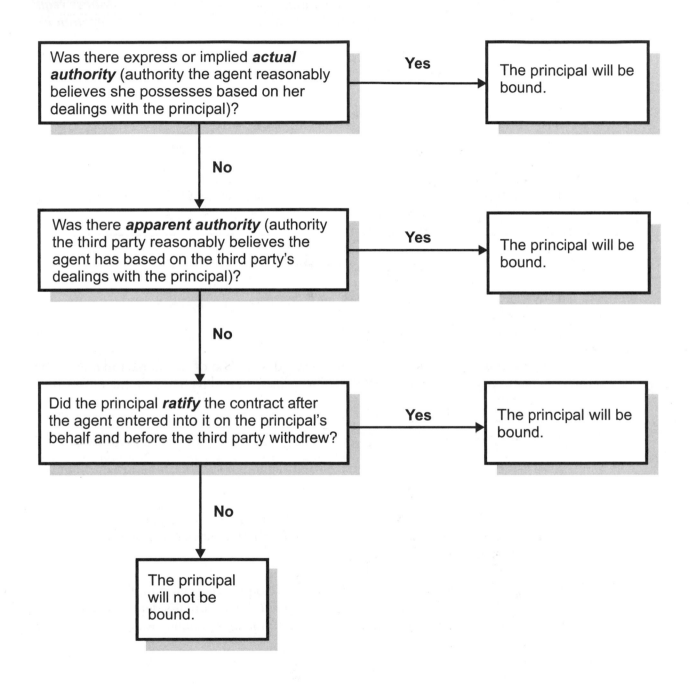

CMR APPROACH CHART

WILL AGENT'S ACTS BIND THE PRINCIPAL?

Was there express or implied *actual authority* (authority the agent reasonably believes she possesses based on her dealings with the principal)?

Yes → The principal will be bound.

No ↓

Was there *apparent authority* (authority the third party reasonably believes the agent has based on the third party's dealings with the principal)?

Yes → The principal will be bound.

No ↓

Did the principal *ratify* the contract after the agent entered into it on the principal's behalf and before the third party withdrew?

Yes → The principal will be bound.

No ↓

The principal will not be bound.

1) *Incidental to express* authority;

2) *Arising out of custom* known to the agent;

3) *Resulting from prior acquiescence* by the principal;

4) *To take emergency measures*;

5) *To delegate authority* in cases of *ministerial acts*, where *circumstances require*, where *performance is impossible* without delegation, or where *delegation is customary*;

6) *To pay for and accept delivery of goods* where there is authority to purchase;

7) *To give general warranties* as to fitness and quality and grant customary covenants in land sales, *collect payment*, and *deliver* where there is authority to sell; and

8) *To manage investments* in accordance with the "prudent investor" standard.

2. Termination of Actual Authority

If you have determined that actual authority was created, you must then consider whether that authority has been terminated.

a. How Termination May Occur

Termination of actual authority occurs by:

1) *Lapse of a specified or reasonable time*;

2) *The happening of a specified event*;

3) *A change in circumstances*, including destruction of the subject matter of the authority, insolvency of the agent or principal, and a change in the law or business conditions;

4) *Agent's breach of fiduciary duty*;

5) *Either party's unilateral termination* (although such termination may constitute a breach of contract); or

6) *Operation of law* (*e.g.,* death or loss of capacity of either party except where a durable power of attorney—written authority that says it will not terminate on the principal's disability—is present).

CMR **Exam Tip** The bar examiners sometimes try to play on your emotions by making it seem unfair to terminate the agent's authority at the principal's death. Answer with your head and not with your heart—death terminates an agency unless the agency is irrevocable (*see* below).

b. Irrevocable Agencies

Neither an agency coupled with an interest nor a power given as security may be unilaterally terminated by the principal if the agency was given to protect the agent's (or a third party's) rights and it is supported by consideration. Neither will such agencies be terminated by operation of law.

3. **Apparent Authority**

   a. **Basic Theory**
   Apparent authority arises from reasonable beliefs of third parties. If a principal directly or indirectly holds out another as possessing certain authority, thereby inducing reasonable reliance by others on that authority, the person so held out has apparent authority, even though as between himself and the principal such authority has not been granted.

   CMR | **Exam Tip** | Be sure to remember that in an apparent authority situation, you need to discuss what transpired between the *principal and the third party*. This differs from an actual authority situation, where you would be discussing what transpired between the principal and the agent. In discussing apparent authority, ask yourself what the principal did to indicate *to the third party* that the agent had authority.

   b. **Types of Apparent Authority**

      1) **When Agent Has No Actual Authority**
      There are certain situations in which, at the time the agent acts, he has no actual authority, yet the principal may be bound.

         a) **Impostors**
         Where the principal negligently permits an impostor to be in a position to appear to have agency authority, the principal will be held liable for the impostor's actions undertaken with such authority.

         b) **Lingering Apparent Authority**

            (1) **Notice May Be Necessary**
            Where an agent's actual authority has terminated (unless due to death or incompetence), he will have apparent authority to act on the principal's behalf as to all third parties with whom the principal knows he dealt unless and until the third parties receive either actual or constructive notice of the termination.

            (2) **Writing Manifesting Authority**
            Where an agent's actual authority has been terminated but third parties rely on a written authority of the agent, the agent's apparent authority is not considered to be terminated.

            (3) **Death or Incompetency**
            Death or incompetency of the principal terminates *all authority* of the agent without notice to either the agent or third parties. There is a limited exception for a bank honoring transactions for a customer's account until it learns of the customer's death or incompetency and has a reasonable time to act.

2) When Agent Exceeds Actual Authority
There are situations where the agent exceeds his authority, yet the principal is still bound.

a) Prior Act
Where the principal previously permitted the agent to exceed his authority and knows that the third party is aware of this, the principal is bound by the agent's unauthorized act.

b) Position
Where the agent is in a position that customarily carries with it certain responsibilities, the principal is liable for the agent's acts that come within these customary responsibilities. (A general agent has considerably broader apparent authority here than a special agent, who is engaged in specific transactions rather than a continuity of service.)

3) Inherent Authority (Inherent Agency Power)
Inherent authority results in the principal being bound even though the agent had no actual authority to perform the particular act. This occurs because courts wish to protect innocent third parties rather than a principal who gave some actual authority to the agent. Examples of inherent authority include:

a) Respondeat Superior
Under the doctrine of respondeat superior, the principal is held liable for the torts of her employee committed within the scope of employment.

b) Conduct Similar to that Authorized
Where an agent exceeds his actual authority, but the conduct is similar to acts authorized, the principal will be held liable.

c. Improper Disposition of Goods
The principal will be held liable for the disposition of her goods by an agent possessing them if the agent was given some indicia of ownership, or if the goods disposed of were sold by an agent who is a dealer in the particular goods.

B. RATIFICATION

1. Effect of Ratification
An agency relationship is created by ratification when an "agent" purports to act on behalf of a "principal" without any authority at all, but the "principal" subsequently validates the act and becomes bound. Ratification gives the transaction retroactive effect unless the "principal" lacked contractual capacity at the time the "agent" entered into the unauthorized transaction (in which case the "principal" is deemed to have "adopted" the contract), or unless retroactivity would interfere with intervening third-party rights. Upon ratification, the "agent" is relieved of liability for breach of his implied warranty of authority (*see* C.2.a., *infra*).

2. Prerequisites of Ratification
For ratification to occur, the "principal" must know (or have reason to know) all material facts, accept the entire transaction, and have capacity (be competent and of legal age). Ratification is a unilateral act of the "principal" and requires no consideration.

3. **Methods of Ratifying**

Ratification may be express or implied through the conduct of the "principal." Such conduct would include acceptance of the transaction's benefits, silence if there is a duty to disaffirm, and suing on the transaction.

4. **What May Be Ratified and by Whom**

Generally, a "principal" may ratify anything she could legally do, unless performance was illegal at the time of ratification, the third party has withdrawn, or there has been a material change in circumstances. Only a disclosed or partially disclosed "principal" may ratify. An "agent" may not treat the contract as his own.

C. LIABILITIES OF THE PARTIES

1. **Third Party vs. Principal**

The principal will be liable to the third party on a contract entered into by her agent if the agent had valid authority to act.

2. **Third Party vs. Agent**

The agent's liability depends on whether the principal was disclosed.

a. **Disclosed Principal**

A disclosed principal (existence *and* identity known to the third party) is always liable on the contract, and the agent generally is *not liable*. *Exceptions:* An agent is liable if the parties to the contract intended the agent to be liable, and an agent may be liable to the third party under his implied warranty that a principal with contractual capacity exists, and that he, the agent, had authority to contract for the principal.

b. **Partially Disclosed and Undisclosed Principals**

A partially disclosed principal (one whose existence is known but whose identity is withheld) or an undisclosed principal (neither identity nor existence is disclosed) results in liability for both the principal and the agent. The majority of courts permit a third party to file suit against both the principal and agent but, upon objection of either defendant, the third party must elect prior to judgment which party he wishes to hold liable. If the third party obtains a judgment against the agent without knowledge of the principal's identity, he can later sue the principal when her identity is discovered if the judgment has not been satisfied.

CMR **Exam Tip** Remember that the type of principal (disclosed, partially disclosed, or undisclosed) is relevant only when you are considering whether the *agent* is liable. Do not discuss the type of principal when analyzing the principal's liability. Any type of principal will be bound as long as the agent had authority.

3. **Third-Party Liability to Principal and Agent**

a. **Disclosed Principal Situations**

When the principal is disclosed, *only the principal*, not the agent, may enforce the contract and hold the third party liable.

b. **Partially Disclosed and Undisclosed Principal Situations**

When the principal is partially disclosed or undisclosed, *either* the principal or agent may enforce the contract and hold the third party liable. Note that if the agent enforces

the contract against the third party, the principal is entitled to all of the rights and benefits thereunder.

1) **When Principal May Not Enforce Contract**
The principal may not enforce the contract if there has been an affirmative fraudulent misrepresentation of the principal's identity or if there is an unforeseen increased burden to the third party due to the fact that performance is due to the principal and not the agent.

CMR SUMMARY CHART	**LIABILITY ON CONTRACT**
Principal	Bound if valid authority existed (actual, apparent, by ratification)
Agent	Bound unless principal's existence *and* identity are disclosed (also can be liable for breach of the implied warranty of authority)
Third party	Bound to principal if valid authority existed; bound to agent if principal partially disclosed or undisclosed and agent enforces contract, but principal entitled to contract benefits

III. TORT LIABILITY—RESPONDEAT SUPERIOR

A. IN GENERAL

The doctrine of respondeat superior imputes joint and several liability to the employer-principal for torts committed by the employee-agent within the scope of the employee's employment. The derivative nature of this liability means that if the employee is not liable, the employer generally cannot be held liable. However, personal defenses of the employee not going to liability do not bar recovery from the employer. Note that in addition to liability under the doctrine of respondeat superior, an employer may be liable for *her own negligence* in hiring or retaining an employee or in supervising or entrusting an employee with specific responsibilities.

B. EMPLOYER-EMPLOYEE RELATIONSHIP

To establish the liability of the principal under respondeat superior, the first determination must be that an employer-employee ("master-servant" under old terminology) relationship existed.

1. Independent Contractor or Employee?

As a general rule, a principal is liable only for torts committed by agents who are employees, not for torts of agents acting as independent contractors.

a. Right to Control

The determinative distinction between the independent contractor and the employee is that with the independent contractor, the principal has *no* right to control the manner and method in which the job is performed, while with the employee, the principal does exercise such control.

CMR
APPROACH
CHART

LIABILITY OF PRINCIPAL FOR AGENT'S TORTS

Is the agent an *employee* or an *independent contractor* (look chiefly to the extent of the principal's *control* over the manner and method of the agent's performance)?

Employee

Independent Contractor

Was the act *within the scope of employment* (*i.e.*, was the employee where she was supposed to be, doing what she was supposed to be doing, with the purposes of the employer in mind)?

Was either the activity involved *inherently dangerous*, the duty *nondelegable*, or the principal *negligent* in selecting the independent contractor?

Yes

No

Yes

No

The principal is liable.

The principal is not liable.

The principal is liable.

The principal is not liable.

    1)   **Factors to Consider**

In determining the existence of the right to control, consider: (i) the characterization by the parties; (ii) whether the business is distinct; (iii) the customs of the locality regarding supervision of work; (iv) the degree of skill required on the job; (v) whose tools or facilities are used; (vi) what the period of employment is (definite and/or short, more likely to be independent contractor; indefinite and/or long, more likely to be employee); (vii) what the basis of compensation is (if on time basis, more likely employee; if on job basis, more likely independent contractor); (viii) what the understanding of the parties is; and (ix) whether the person was hired to further the principal's business (nonbusiness purpose, *e.g.,* mowing lawn, more likely independent contractor).

2. Liability for Acts of Subservants

The doctrine of respondeat superior also applies to duly authorized subservants. Authorization to hire subservants can be express or implied. Implied authorization can arise from: past practices, emergency situations, or a reasonable necessity to achieve an authorized result. The employer is generally not liable for the torts of a subservant engaged without authority.

3. Employer-Employee by Estoppel

Where a principal creates the appearance of an employer-employee relationship upon which a third party relies, that principal will be estopped from denying the relationship and will be liable under the doctrine of respondeat superior.

4. Liability for Acts of Borrowed Employees

The original employer will normally be liable for the tortious acts of a loaned employee. However, the key issue in determining liability for the loaned employee's torts is whether the borrowing principal or the loaning principal has the ***primary right to control*** the employee's actions.

5. Liability for Acts of Independent Contractors

A principal will incur direct liability for the acts of an independent contractor where: (i) inherently dangerous activities are involved, (ii) nondelegable duties have been delegated, or (iii) the principal knowingly selected an incompetent independent contractor (if the principal was merely negligent in selecting the independent contractor, the principal is liable only for her own negligence in selection, not for the contractor's negligence).

C. SCOPE OF EMPLOYMENT

If an employer-employee relationship existed, the employer will be liable for the employee's torts if they were committed within the scope of the employee's employment.

1. Same General Nature as Job

To be within the scope of employment, the employee's conduct need not be actually authorized. Nor does prohibition by the principal necessarily remove the conduct from the scope of employment. If the nature of the employee's conduct is similar or incidental to that which was authorized, the conduct is probably within the scope of employment. However, serious criminal acts are normally considered to be outside the scope of employment.

2. Frolic and Detour

Consider whether the employee's conduct was within the time and place of the authorized employment. A detour or small deviation from the employer's direction is within the scope of employment, while a frolic or major deviation requiring a substantial departure from employment is beyond the scope. Once it is shown that the employee has left the scope of employment, there must be proof of return before the employer will be held liable for the employee's tort.

Note: The employer's ownership of the vehicle driven by the employee at the time the employee commits a tort does not automatically impose liability upon the employer for the tort.

3. Motivation to Serve Employer
Finally, consider whether the employee's conduct was actuated, at least in part, by a purpose to serve the employer.

a. Passengers
The employee's invitation to passengers, unless expressly authorized by the employer, is generally held to be outside the scope of the employment relationship, and the employer would not be held liable for injuries sustained by such passengers.

b. Unauthorized Instrumentalities
The employer is not liable for torts caused by the use of substantially different instrumentalities from those authorized (*i.e.,* those creating a greater risk of harm).

c. Trips with Two Purposes
If the employee makes a trip with two purposes, it will be within the scope of employment if any substantial purpose of the employer is being served.

4. Intentional Torts
Intentional torts are not normally within the scope of employment unless a natural incident of the employee's duties (as where force is authorized), where the employee is promoting the employer's business, or where the nature of the work gives rise to hostilities. A principal is liable for an agent's misrepresentations if the agent had actual, apparent, or inherent authority to make statements concerning the subject matter involved.

5. Ratification
An employer may ratify an employee's torts if the normal requisites of ratification are met. In tort ratification situations, pay particular attention to the requirement that the employer must have knowledge of all material facts.

CIVIL PRACTICE AND PROCEDURE—ILLINOIS

TABLE OF CONTENTS

CIVIL PRACTICE AND PROCEDURE—ILLINOIS

I. ILLINOIS COURT SYSTEM

A. INTRODUCTION
Civil procedure in Illinois courts is governed by the Illinois Constitution, the Illinois Code of Civil Procedure, and the Illinois Supreme Court Rules.

B. COMPOSITION OF ILLINOIS COURT SYSTEM
There are three levels of courts in Illinois—circuit courts, appellate courts, and the supreme court. The circuit courts comprise the trial-court level. The appellate court hears appeals from final decisions of the circuit courts, with exceptions for those cases that may be directly appealed to the supreme court and with many exceptions to the final judgment rule, as discussed in XII., *infra.* The supreme court has general administrative authority over all Illinois courts, and it generally hears appeals only from the appellate court (either "as a matter of right" or as a discretionary appeal), except in limited cases in which it has original jurisdiction or cases in which direct appeal from the circuit court is allowed.

II. FORUM NON CONVENIENS

A. ILLINOIS APPLICATION FAVORS PLAINTIFF'S CHOICE
A circuit court with subject matter jurisdiction of a case may refuse to exercise it on the ground that there is a more convenient forum available to the parties. Courts will consider the ***convenience*** to the plaintiff and defendant, and ***the public's interest*** in keeping the case in Illinois. Usually, a motion for forum non conveniens dismissal will be granted if the parties have no relationship to Illinois and no property within the state.

if no relationship + no property — granted

B. CONDITIONAL DISMISSAL
There are two mandatory conditions on forum non conveniens dismissals. If the plaintiff files the action in another forum within six months of the dismissal order, (i) the defendant ***must accept service of process*** from that court, and (ii) if the statute of limitations has run in the other forum, the defendant ***must waive the statute of limitations defense.*** If the defendant does not abide by these conditions, the cause will be reinstated. Similarly, if the court in the other forum refuses to accept jurisdiction, the plaintiff may, within 30 days of the final order refusing jurisdiction, reinstate the action.

III. JURISDICTION OVER THE PERSON AND OVER THINGS

A. JURISDICTION OVER THE PERSON—GENERAL AND SPECIFIC JURISDICTION
For a forum state to exercise jurisdiction over a person without violating due process, that person must have had such "minimum contacts" with the forum state that requiring him to defend there would not "offend traditional notions of fair play and substantial justice." It is further required that the person receive reasonable notice.

must

1. General Jurisdiction—Traditional Common Law Bases
Illinois has four traditional common law bases of personal jurisdiction:

a. Consent
Consent may be express (by filing suit or entering a general appearance in Illinois court) or implied (*e.g.,* suits arising from the defendant's use of Illinois highways).

b. Presence of Individual in Illinois at Moment of Service
The two exceptions to this basis are enticement and immunity. A defendant cannot be enticed into Illinois by force or fraud to obtain jurisdiction. A person subpoenaed to testify before a grand jury or in a criminal case in Illinois is immune from civil process. A criminal defendant who is extradited or waives extradition to Illinois to stand trial is only immune from process for civil actions arising out of the criminal transaction.

1) Service of Process

a) Commencing the Action, Summons, and Service
Filing a complaint with the clerk of the circuit court commences a civil action for statute of limitations purposes. The clerk then issues a summons, which is typically valid for 30 days. Thereafter, the summons and a copy of the complaint must be promptly placed with a process server (usually the sheriff, deputy sheriff, county coroner, or some private person who is 18 years or older and not a party to the action) for service on the defendant. After service is made or attempted, the process server completes a "return," stating either that service was made or the reason why service was not made. If service was not made, the plaintiff must have another summons (an "alias summons") issued for service. Note that if the plaintiff fails to exercise reasonable diligence in obtaining service on a defendant, the action *as to that unserved defendant only* may be dismissed without prejudice, with the right to refile the action if the statute of limitations period has not run.

CMR | **Exam Tip** | Don't let statutory language and timing differences in the service of process rules for federal and state courts throw you for a loop and cause you to spend valuable time studying what are *very similar rules*. Both rules require the plaintiff to exercise care in having the defendant served promptly. The only real difference is that in federal court, a plaintiff need not show "good cause" (or what would be called "reasonable diligence" in Illinois) until after the 120-day service period has expired, whereas *an Illinois state court could look at the plaintiff's "reasonable diligence"* (or what would be called "good cause" in federal court) in serving process *at any time.*

b) Waiver of Service
The plaintiff may send the defendant a copy of the complaint and a form, which the defendant may return, requesting that the defendant waive service. The defendant's waiver of service does not waive personal jurisdiction or venue issues.

2) Service on Individuals

This includes (i) personal service and (ii) substituted service—leaving a copy of the summons at the defendant's abode with a family member or a person residing there (13 years or older), informing that person of the contents, and then mailing a copy to the defendant at that address.

c. "Doing Business" in Illinois

To "do business" in Illinois, a corporation must register and have an agent and an office in Illinois for receiving service of process. If a business does not register, it may still be subject to Illinois court jurisdiction if it "does business" in the state.

CMR | **Exam Tip**   On the bar exam, you should use the terms *doing business* and *transacting business* in accordance with common usage. "Doing business" refers to a series of business activities in Illinois sufficient to give an Illinois court *general* jurisdiction over a foreign corporation or other entity. "Transacting business" refers to business activity, which may consist of a single transaction, sufficient to give an Illinois court *specific* jurisdiction (*i.e.*, jurisdiction over the defendant in a case arising from that transaction) over a corporation or other entity under the long arm statute.

1) Interpretations of "Doing Business"

a) Single Transaction—Not "Doing Business"

A single transaction is not sufficient to constitute "doing business."

b) "Mere Solicitation" Rule—Not "Doing Business"

A business entity or individual that sends agents into the state simply to solicit orders that must be accepted out of state is not "doing business" in Illinois.

c) "Solicitation Plus" Rule—"Doing Business"

Any activity of the business entity or individual in addition to sending traveling salespeople or maintaining resident salespeople will be taken to imply "presence."

d) Relevant Time Period

The relevant time period for determining whether a defendant is "doing business" in Illinois begins on the date that the cause of action accrues and extends to the date the defendant was made a party.

e) Implications of "Doing Business"

A business entity or individual "doing business" in Illinois is subject to service of process upon an officer or agent on any cause of action, even a claim that has nothing to do with the business being done in Illinois.

2) Service on Corporations

a) Illinois Corporations and Registered Foreign Corporations

Personal jurisdiction over Illinois corporations and registered foreign corporations is obtained by serving the registered agent or any corporate officer or agent found anywhere in the state. Where the registered agent cannot be served, the secretary of state becomes the agent for service of process. Service on an agent is effective to confer jurisdiction, even if the agent

neglects to notify the responsible officers, unless the agent has a relation to the lawsuit that is adverse to that of the principal.

b) Unregistered Foreign Corporations
If an unregistered foreign corporation is "doing business" in Illinois, it may be served in the same manner as an Illinois corporation or registered foreign corporation.

3) Service on Partnerships

a) Partnership Sued in Firm's Name
Personal service on any partner or agent of the partnership is effective.

b) Partner Sued for Partnership Liability
Personal jurisdiction may be obtained either by (i) personal or abode service on the partner himself, or (ii) personal service on any other partner and mailing a copy of the summons to the sued partner's abode.

4) Unknown Owner
Where the owner of a business has failed to register the business name, personal jurisdiction may be obtained by personally serving an agent of the business or by publication as provided for in in rem and quasi in rem actions.

5) Service on Voluntary Unincorporated Associations
A voluntary unincorporated association may be sued in its own name by personally serving an officer or agent of the association or by publication and mail in like manner as for service on individuals.

d. Domicile or Residence in Illinois
An Illinois domiciliary or resident may be served inside or outside the state. If jurisdiction is based on consent, corporate presence, domicile, or long arm jurisdiction, proper service outside Illinois yields in personam jurisdiction, just as if the defendant had been served inside the state. Otherwise, out-of-state service yields only in rem jurisdiction, and a resulting judgment can only affect property. Service outside Illinois must be made like in-state service and may be made by any person over age 18 who is not a party to the lawsuit. Return must be by affidavit and must state the time, place, and manner of service.

2. Specific Jurisdiction—Long Arm Statute
Section 2-209 of the Illinois Code of Civil Procedure provides four broad bases for jurisdiction over persons who are not currently residents or domiciliaries of Illinois (*see* long arm chart, *infra*).

a. Specific Acts
The statute lists 14 specific acts that will subject a person to jurisdiction in Illinois with respect to causes of action *arising from the doing of those acts.*

b. Other Bases
The statute lists four other bases that will subject a person to *general jurisdiction* in Illinois based on current or past "presence" in Illinois as defined in the statute.

c. **Foreign Defamation Judgment**

A court may exercise personal jurisdiction over a person who obtained a judgment in a defamation proceeding outside the United States against any person who is an Illinois resident or corporate entity that has its principal place of business in Illinois for the purpose of rendering declaratory relief with respect to the Illinois resident's liability for the judgment or determining whether Illinois would recognize the judgment.

d. **"Catch-All" Basis**

A "catch-all" provision allows Illinois courts to exercise jurisdiction on any constitutionally permissible basis.

JURISDICTION UNDER THE ILLINOIS LONG ARM STATUTE

Specific Acts—A person who does any of the following acts submits to the jurisdiction of the Illinois courts as to any cause of action arising from the doing of the act. The act furnishes the minimum contacts necessary to satisfy due process.

☑ Transaction of business within Illinois. *transaction*

☑ Commission of a tortious act within Illinois. *tort*

☑ Ownership, use, or possession of real estate in Illinois. *property*

☑ Contracting to insure persons, property, or risks located in Illinois at the time of contracting. *insuring in state*

☑ With respect to marital actions, maintaining a domicile in Illinois at the time the action arose or committing an act in Illinois giving rise to the cause of action.

☑ With respect to actions under the Illinois Parentage Act, engaging in sexual intercourse in Illinois during the possible period of conception.

☑ Making or performing any contract or promise substantially connected with Illinois.

☑ Engaging in sexual intercourse in Illinois that is claimed to have resulted in the conception of a child who resides in Illinois.

☑ Failure to support a child, spouse, or former spouse who has continued to reside in Illinois.

☑ Acquisition of ownership, possession, or control of any asset or thing of value within Illinois.

- ☑ Breach of fiduciary duty within Illinois.

- ☑ Serving as a director or officer of an Illinois corporation. ✓

- ☑ Owning an interest in a trust administered in Illinois. ✓

- ☑ Exercising fiduciary powers granted under the authority of Illinois.

Other Bases—The statute also lists the following bases upon which an Illinois court may exercise jurisdiction over persons as to actions arising in or outside of Illinois. Jurisdiction on these bases is general (as opposed to jurisdiction based on the above enumerated acts, which exists only as to actions arising out of the acts).

General

- ☑ As to natural persons, presence within Illinois when served.

- ☑ As to natural persons, domicile or residence within Illinois when the cause of action arose, the action was commenced, or process was served.

- ☑ As to corporations, being organized under the laws of Illinois.

- ☑ As to either persons or corporations, doing business in Illinois.

Foreign Defamation Judgment—The statute authorizes jurisdiction over a person who obtained a foreign judgment in a defamation proceeding.

"Catch-All" Basis—Finally, the statute provides that an Illinois court may exercise jurisdiction on any other basis now or hereafter permitted by the Illinois or United States Constitution.

CMR **Exam Tip** While you should be familiar with the specific grounds listed in the Illinois long arm statute as bases for jurisdiction, you should also be aware that, reduced to its simplest form, the statute provides that *almost any activity connected with the state* is sufficient, under either the specific grounds or the catch-all provision, for jurisdiction with respect to an action arising from the activity.

3. **Fiduciary Shield Doctrine**
   Under the fiduciary shield doctrine, if an individual is in Illinois to act on behalf of a corporation or other entity, those acts cannot later be used as the basis for jurisdiction over her individually.

B. **JURISDICTION OVER THINGS**

1. **In Rem Jurisdiction** — *fight over specific property*
   An action in rem adjudicates the rights of all persons with respect to specific real or personal property located in Illinois. It does not bind the parties personally.

2. **Quasi In Rem Jurisdiction**

   a. **Quasi In Rem—Type I**
   Quasi in rem type I actions determine the rights of specific persons in specific property in Illinois. Only the interests of named parties are affected by the judgment.

   b. **Quasi In Rem—Type II**
   Quasi in rem type II actions involve the exercise of jurisdiction over an out-of-state defendant by seizure of property having no relation to the plaintiff's claim. The minimum contacts requirement has essentially eliminated this type of action.

3. **Incidents of In Rem or Quasi In Rem Jurisdiction**

   a. **No Limited Appearance**
   No limited appearance is permitted in quasi in rem or in rem actions. The defendant who desires to avoid in personam jurisdiction must either default, thereby forfeiting the property if proper in rem jurisdiction was obtained, or appear generally, submitting to jurisdiction over his person.

   forfeit

   b. **Attachment**
   Where such jurisdiction is appropriate, one method of obtaining it is to seize the in-state property of the nondomiciliary, nonresident defendant. The Illinois attachment statute also allows prejudgment attachment as a security device to prevent dissipation of the property.

4. **How Notice May Be Given**

   threshold

   In in rem and quasi in rem actions, if the defendant cannot reasonably be served, notice may be by publication. The plaintiff must file an affidavit with the court clerk stating that the defendant is inaccessible, and the defendant's address, if known. The court clerk then has the notice published in a newspaper in the county at least once a week for three weeks. A copy of the notice must be mailed to each defendant whose address is known.

5. **Opening Defaults in Cases of Service by Publication**

   if no notice,

   A defendant who has not received a copy of the complaint or the mailed notice may, within one year, open a default judgment obtained pursuant to service by publication. If he receives written notice of the judgment, he has 90 days to open it.

C. **APPEARANCE**

1. **General Appearance**
   A general appearance constitutes consent to jurisdiction, even if it is made inadvertently. It cannot be revoked unless it was entered fraudulently by an attorney who was not authorized to appear on behalf of the defendant. An appearance may be made by a defendant or his attorney. A corporation can appear only through an attorney. An appearance is usually made by the plaintiff or defendant filing the proper papers. In actions requiring no answer, a physical appearance in court by a defendant or his attorney will suffice.

2. Objections to Jurisdiction Over the Person

a. Grounds

Prior to the filing of any pleading or motion other than a motion for an extension of time to answer or appear, a party may object to the court's jurisdiction over the party's person, either (i) because the party is not amenable to process in Illinois, or (ii) for insufficiency of process or insufficiency of service of process.

b. Motion

A party may object to personal jurisdiction by filing a motion to dismiss or a motion to quash service of process. The motion *may be made singly or included with others in a combined motion*, with each motion clearly identified. The motion must be supported by an affidavit setting forth the facts that constitute the basis for the objection, unless those facts are apparent from papers already on file.

c. Waiver If Responsive Pleading Filed First

If the objecting party files a responsive pleading or a motion (other than a motion for an extension of time) prior to a motion challenging personal jurisdiction, that party is deemed to have waived *all* personal jurisdiction objections.

d. Preserving Objection to Jurisdiction After Court Rules

1) Contesting Merits Waives Objection for Defects in Process or Service

Where the objection to personal jurisdiction is based on an irregularity in the summons or service of the summons, the objection is waived if the party proceeds to trial on the merits after his objection is overruled. The party may decline to contest the merits and allow a default judgment to preserve his objection to jurisdiction. However, if the appellate court rules against him, he will have suffered a final judgment on the merits with no opportunity to defend. The judgment is res judicata, immune to collateral attack, and entitled to full faith and credit.

2) No Waiver of Objection for Nonamenability to Illinois Process

A party's objection that he is not amenable to Illinois process is not waived by contesting the merits of the case after the court overrules the objection. The party can preserve this objection as a ground for appeal from the final judgment of the court. This objection is not waived because it is an objection to personal jurisdiction (as opposed to an objection for a technical defect in process or in service). It usually arises under the long arm statute, where the party denies committing any of the enumerated acts giving rise to jurisdiction.

CMR **Exam Tip** The operation of the "nonamenability to Illinois process" provision is best understood using examples. In the first example, suppose that an out-of-state defendant's objection to personal jurisdiction is that service of process was improperly made to his neighbor's 10-year-old daughter instead of to the defendant personally at his home. The defendant faces the dilemma described: he may either defend on the merits and thus waive his jurisdictional objection, or he may take a default and risk that the appellate court will find that service was adequate. In the second example, suppose that the defendant's objection to personal jurisdiction is that he did not engage in any of the long arm activities, has no other contacts with Illinois, and is therefore not amenable to Illinois process. The defendant can choose to defend the action in Illinois and, if he loses, still raise the jurisdictional objection in the appellate court.

IV. VENUE

A. GENERAL RULE

Venue is proper in the county of residence of any defendant or the county where some part of the cause of action arose. If all defendants are nonresidents of Illinois, suit may be tried in any county. Improper venue may be waived by the defendant, and is waived unless objected to at the proper time.

1. **Corporations**

   With respect to Illinois corporations and registered foreign corporations, a corporation is a resident of any county where it is doing business or where it has any office. An unregistered foreign corporation is a nonresident; thus, venue is proper in any county, if the corporation is the sole defendant.

2. **Partnerships**

   A partnership sued in the firm name is a resident of any county where it is doing business, has an office, or where one of its partners resides. Where a suit is brought in the name of the partners individually, venue is proper where any sued partner resides. Defendant partners cannot be sued in a county just because the partnership does business in the county, unless the cause arose from the activity of the partnership in that county. Where no partner is an Illinois resident, there is no Illinois office, and the partnership does not do business in Illinois, the partnership is a nonresident, and venue lies in any county if the partnership is the sole defendant.

3. **Voluntary Unincorporated Associations**

   A voluntary unincorporated association is a resident of any county in which the association has an office or, if no office can be found, of any county in which any officer of the association resides. A voluntary unincorporated association sued in its own name is a nonresident of Illinois if all its members are nonresidents and it does not have an office or do business in Illinois. Thus, venue is generally proper in any county.

B. SPECIAL RULES

1. **Title to Real Estate**

   Suits involving title to real estate must be filed in the county where the real estate is located.

2. **Governmental Corporations**

   Suits against governmental corporations must generally be filed in the county where the principal office is located or where the transaction (or some part of it) occurred.

3. **Libel**

   In an action for libel against a newspaper or magazine (or persons connected with it), if the defendant resides or the article was composed or printed *in Illinois*, venue is proper in the

Illinois county where: (i) the defendant *resides*; (ii) the defendant has *its principal office*; or (iii) the article was *composed or printed*. If the defendant resides or the article was printed *outside of Illinois*, venue is proper in any Illinois county where *the libel was circulated*.

4. Insurance Companies

Suits against insurance companies incorporated or doing business in Illinois, in addition to any county of proper venue under the general rule, may be filed in any county where the plaintiff resides.

CMR **Exam Tip** An action against an insurance company is the only instance in which the plaintiff's county of residence, without more, is a proper venue.

C. OBJECTIONS TO VENUE

1. Procedure

An objection to venue must be made by a motion to transfer to a court of proper venue on or before the date on which the defendant is required to appear, or within any extended period of time granted to him to answer. The only exception is when the plaintiff moves to dismiss a defendant upon whose residence venue depends. Any remaining defendant may then promptly move to transfer to a proper venue.

2. "Dummy Defendants"

Sometimes a defendant is joined for the sole purpose of allowing the action to be brought in the county of his residence. A co-defendant in such a case may make a timely motion to transfer to a court of proper venue on the grounds that the "dummy defendant" was joined for improper reasons. If this motion is made and overruled, it must be renewed at the close of all the evidence in order to be preserved for review.

D. MOTION TO "CHANGE" VENUE

A motion to "change" venue is a motion to transfer an action to a new county because the inhabitants of the county are prejudiced against the defendant or his attorney (or an adverse party has an undue influence over the minds of the inhabitants). The motion must be supported by the affidavits of two inhabitants of the county and must be established at a hearing. Moreover, the petition must be presented before trial or hearing begins and before the judge to whom it is presented has ruled on any substantial issue in the case, except that if grounds for change of venue occur later, a petition may then be filed on such grounds. Transfer is to any other convenient county.

E. TRANSFER OF VENUE DUE TO INCONVENIENCE OF CHOSEN FORUM

Don't have to

A trial court has the discretionary right to *transfer* cases from one *Illinois* county of proper venue to another proper *Illinois* county under the doctrine of forum non conveniens. If the more convenient forum lies in *another state*, a *dismissal* of the action is the appropriate remedy.

CMR **Exam Tip** Be sure to use appropriate terminology on your exam. Remember that venue refers to the geographic *location* of a court that may hear the case; jurisdiction refers to the *power* of a court to hear a particular case.

F. CHANGE OF JUDGE

An unlimited number of challenges to a judge for cause are allowed. A party is also entitled to one substitution as of right. An application for substitution as of right is made by motion and must be granted if it is presented before the trial or a hearing begins and before the judge has ruled on any substantial issue in the case. Thereafter, the parties may consent to a change of the judge.

V. STATUTES OF LIMITATIONS AND REPOSE

A. IN GENERAL
The statute of limitations is not jurisdictional; it is waived by the defendant if not asserted as an affirmative defense. The date of filing the complaint is the significant date for determining whether an action has been commenced within the applicable period provided by the statute of limitations.

1. Statute of Limitations May Be Subject to Statute of Repose
Although all claims are subject to a statute of limitations, some claims (*e.g.*, medical malpractice) are also limited by a statute of repose. A statute of repose provides an outermost time for the filing of a lawsuit, which begins to run on an event. Illinois, by statute, frequently allows for statutes of repose to be tolled for disabilities.

B. JURISDICTIONAL TIME LIMITS
Distinguish time periods within which actions must be commenced (unless waived by defendant) from time limits that are jurisdictional and thus cannot be waived. The latter category includes wrongful death (two years) and Dram Shop Act (one year); these jurisdictional time limits *cannot be avoided by* the general statutory provision for extending time limits because of *infancy or disability.*

C. TIME PERIODS
The periods of most interest to the bar examiners include:

(i) *Twenty Years:* Real property actions; revival of a domestic judgment.

(ii) *Ten Years:* Mortgage foreclosures; non-U.C.C. actions on indebtedness and written contracts.

(iii) *Five Years:* Foreign judgment enforcement; non-U.C.C. unwritten contracts; real or personal property injury; all other civil actions not specified by statute.

(iv) *Four Years:* U.C.C. contracts (*i.e.,* contracts for sale of goods).

(v) *Three Years:* Actions against officers or carriers or for fraudulent devises.

(vi) *Two Years:* Abduction; contract to make will; contribution among tortfeasors; criminal conversation; false imprisonment; malicious prosecution; personal injury; products liability (with various statutes of repose); seduction.

(vii) *One Year:* Libel; privacy torts; slander; claims against local public entities.

1. Medical Malpractice
Generally, any suit for damages for injury or death against a physician or licensed hospital

arising from any "patient care" (broadly construed) must be brought within two years after the date the plaintiff knew or should have known of the injury or death, but no later than four years after the act or omission causing the injury or death. If the plaintiff is under a disability *other than infancy* at the time of the act or omission, both periods do not begin to run until the disability is removed. If the plaintiff is a minor, the statute of repose is eight years (with no tolling), but in no event may the plaintiff file suit after her 22nd birthday. If the plaintiff is a minor and has another disability, the four-year statute of repose, with tolling for the other disability, applies.

D. REFILING AFTER DISMISSAL OR REVERSAL

If (i) a case is reversed on appeal after judgment was entered for the plaintiff for reasons other than on the merits; (ii) a motion in arrest of judgment is granted after judgment was returned for the plaintiff; or (iii) an action is dismissed voluntarily by the plaintiff, involuntarily by the court due to a lack of prosecution by the plaintiff, or involuntarily by a federal court due to a lack of jurisdiction or improper venue, the plaintiff is allowed to refile the action within the longer of the remaining limitations period or one year from the date of the dismissal or reversal. The original action must have been timely filed, and the plaintiff is allowed *only one* such refiling.

E. DEATH OF PLAINTIFF OR DEFENDANT

If the *claimant dies* and the cause is one that survives, the representative can bring an action within the limitations period or within one year of death, whichever is later. If the *defendant dies* and the cause survives, the action can generally be commenced against his representative after expiration of the limitations period and within six months after the defendant's death.

F. DISABILITY OF PLAINTIFF

In case of disability at the time the cause accrued, the time is extended for two years after the disability is removed. Disability can be due to infancy, insanity, total incompetence to manage one's affairs, absence from the United States, or military service.

G. DISCOVERY RULE

Illinois follows the "discovery rule" in cases where the plaintiff may not reasonably be able to discover his injury within the limitations period (*e.g.,* medical malpractice cases). The discovery rule tolls the statute of limitations until the plaintiff *knows or reasonably should know* that he has been injured and that his injury was wrongfully caused. However, the discovery rule does *not* toll the statute where a *sudden traumatic event* (*e.g.,* an explosion or accident) causes the plaintiff's injury, regardless of whether the plaintiff is immediately aware of the injury. Note that the statute still may be tolled if the sudden traumatic event disabled the plaintiff.

H. STATUTE TOLLED FOR ABSENCE, INJUNCTION, OR FRAUDULENT CONCEALMENT

The statutory period does not run (i) during the absence or concealment of the defendant from the state unless both parties were nonresidents when the cause accrued, (ii) when the action is stayed by an injunction, (iii) when the defendant fraudulently conceals the cause of action from the plaintiff, or (iv) when, as to childhood sexual abuse cases and sexual assault cases, the defendant intimidates the plaintiff from bringing an action.

I. REVIVAL

Revival arises where there is payment or a new written promise made after the full statutory period has run.

J.　RELATION BACK
The defendant may plead a set-off or counterclaim otherwise barred by the statute of limitations to a cause of action owned by the plaintiff before the defendant's claim was barred.

K.　OUT-OF-STATE ACTION
If a claim arose outside of Illinois, at a time when the parties were not residents of Illinois, it cannot be timely brought in Illinois if it could not be timely brought in the state where it arose.

L.　CLAIMS AGAINST LOCAL PUBLIC ENTITIES
Action must be commenced within *one year* from date of injury or accrual of action. However, this limit is not applicable to minors.

VI.　PARTIES—MULTIPARTY LITIGATION

A.　PRELIMINARY MATTERS

1.　Designation
The misnomer of a party is not a ground for dismissal.

2.　Assignments
An assignee may sue in his own name but must allege that he is the bona fide owner of a nonnegotiable chose in action and set forth how and when he acquired title.

3.　Wage Assignments
Wage assignments are valid in Illinois.

4.　Subrogation
The subrogee (insurer) must be disclosed and identified in an action by the subrogee. In Illinois, collateral estoppel does not apply in the second action brought by the subrogor (insured) if the first action was brought and conducted by the subrogee (insurer). Illinois does not have a "real party in interest" statute.

B.　JOINDER

1.　Joinder of Plaintiffs
Plaintiffs may join if: (i) their right to relief arises from the same series of transactions, and (ii) a common question of law or fact would arise if they sued separately.

Joinder of *multiple plaintiffs* who have all dealt with the defendant at *separate times,* signing separate contracts, or upon whom fraud has been perpetrated separately is *not permitted,* even though the separate transactions appear to be part of a repeated pattern.

a.　Necessary Parties
A party is necessary if the determination of the case will necessarily affect his interests. If any plaintiff, counterclaimant, or third-party plaintiff who is a necessary party refuses to join, he may be made a nominal defendant, cross-defendant, or third-party defendant by issuance of service upon him.

b. Class Actions

1) Prerequisites

A class action may be brought if: (i) the class is so ***numerous*** that joinder of all members is impracticable; (ii) there are ***questions of fact or law common to the class*** and these questions predominate over any questions affecting only individual members (Illinois courts frequently find this requirement not satisfied in mass tort class actions); (iii) the representative parties will ***fairly and adequately protect the interests of the class;*** and (iv) the class action is an ***appropriate method*** for the fair and efficient adjudication of the controversy.

2) Opting Out

Any class member may "opt out" of the action. The case may not be dismissed or settled without court approval.

2. Joinder of Defendants

The joinder of defendants, except for necessary parties who must be joined to satisfy due process, is permissive and not mandatory. Any person may be joined as a defendant who is alleged to have an interest in the matter, who must be joined for the complete determination of the matter, or who is alleged to be liable either jointly, severally, or in the alternative. Illinois further requires that potential liability be based upon a ***common question of law or fact***. Two or more defendants may be joined in the alternative where the plaintiff is unsure which of the defendants is liable or to what extent.

3. Joinder of Joint Obligors

Joinder of joint obligors is always permissive. An unsatisfied judgment against fewer than all the joint obligors will not bar subsequent suit against those not sued, but only one satisfaction is permitted. In subsequent actions, a joint obligor not originally sued is liable only for the unsatisfied portion of the obligation.

4. Actions Against Partnerships

Actions against partnerships may involve joining any or all of the partners. If the judgment is in the firm name, it may be executed only against partnership assets. If its assets are inadequate, later suits against individual partners may be prosecuted.

5. Misjoinder and Nonjoinder

Misjoinder of an impermissible party is not a ground for dismissal of the action. Failure to join any necessary party ("nonjoinder") is not a ground for dismissal of the action until reasonable opportunity has been given to add him as a party.

6. Interpleader

Any party may join persons whose claims against him (arising out of the same or related subject matter) may otherwise subject him to multiple liability and require the joined parties to interplead. This device is available in Illinois by complaint or counterclaim if jurisdiction can be obtained over the adverse claimants.

C. THIRD-PARTY PRACTICE

A defendant, by filing a third-party action, may bring into the lawsuit as a third-party defendant anyone who is or may be liable to him if he is found liable to the plaintiff. A third-party complaint may be filed as a matter of right within the time for answering, and thereafter only by leave of court.

1. **"Liable to Him"**

   Illinois permits ***contribution among tortfeasors*** so that one joint tortfeasor may bring in the other wrongdoer in order to secure equitable apportionment of damage based upon degree of fault. A third-party complaint will be dismissed unless such liability to the original defendant exists.

2. **Available Defenses**

   The third-party defendant has all the ***rights of the original defendant*** and also may file any defense to the main action that the original defendant could.

3. **Severance**

   The judge may ***sever*** the actions to avoid complication or prejudice.

4. **Exclusion of Liability Insurers**

   A liability insurer may not be made a third-party defendant.

D. **INTERVENTION**

Intervention involves the situation where a person not joined wishes to become a party.

1. **As of Right**

   A person must be allowed to intervene where a statute confers an unconditional right to intervene or where one may either be (i) bound by the judgment in a case where one's interest is inadequately represented, or (ii) adversely affected by the court's disposition of property.

2. **Permissive Intervention**

   A person may seek leave of court to intervene where a statute gives a conditional right to intervene or the person's claim and the main action have a common question of law or fact.

3. **Procedure**

   The intervenor must petition the court, setting forth both the grounds for intervention and his proposed initial pleading. Denial of a petition to intervene is a final judgment that is immediately appealable by the would-be intervenor. The granting of such a petition is an interlocutory order that is not ordinarily appealable.

4. **Nature of Intervenor's Interest**

   To intervene, a person must have a legal right to protect, by which Illinois courts probably mean a pecuniary or property interest.

E. **ABATEMENT**

If a party dies and the action survives, and the case has already been filed, his personal representative may be substituted by order of the court upon motion.

VII. PLEADING

A. IN GENERAL

No further pleading is required beyond a complaint, answer, and reply (which must be filed where an answer sets up a new matter). Pleadings are liberally construed.

1. Insufficient Pleadings

Where any pleading is insufficient, the court may order a fuller or more particular statement.

2. Untrue Statements

Untruthful pleadings may subject the pleader to the costs of the other side (including attorneys' fees) in disproving them.

3. Supplemental Pleadings

By leave of court, a party may be permitted to file supplemental pleadings setting up matters arising after the original pleadings are filed. Unlike amendments, these do not relate back to the date the original pleading was filed.

4. Defects Not Objected to Are Unreviewable

Defects not objected to are unreviewable. The one exception to this is an objection that a pleading fails to state a cause of action, which may be raised for the first time on appeal.

5. Nonwaiver by Filing Reply

Filing a reply that denies affirmative matter in an answer *does not admit* that the facts pleaded as an affirmative defense are sufficient to constitute a legal defense.

6. Extensions of Time for Good Cause Shown

For good cause shown on motion after notice to the opposite party, the trial court may extend the time for filing any pleading or doing any act that is required *by the rules* to be done within a limited period, either before or after the expiration of the time.

B. PLEADINGS THAT STATE A CLAIM

1. Fact Pleading

Illinois is a fact pleading jurisdiction. Facts upon which the cause of action is based (not evidence or conclusions of law) must be pleaded. Facts of which the court may take judicial notice need not be pleaded. If facts are adequately stated in one part of the pleadings, they may thereafter be incorporated by reference. The plaintiff need not plead facts in anticipation of an affirmative defense.

2. Joining Causes of Action and Separate Counts

A plaintiff may join any number of causes of action, legal or equitable, against properly joined defendants in a single complaint, but such joinder is not compulsory. A count is a section of a complaint that fully states a cause of action and that could stand alone as a complete complaint. Each cause of action that would support a separate recovery must be stated in a separate count and must be separately numbered. Alternative theories of recovery, whether consistent or inconsistent, may (but need not) be presented in separate counts.

3. Alternative Pleading

When a plaintiff does not know which of two or more statements of fact is true, she may plead them alternatively in the same or in separate counts *regardless of their consistency or inconsistency.* Likewise, alternative legal theories, whether consistent or inconsistent, can be joined. The alternative theories may be supported by inconsistent allegations of fact. Furthermore, this situation does not involve election of remedies, even when submitted to the jury.

4. **Claims Based on Written Instruments**
   If a claim or defense is founded on a written instrument, so much as is relevant must be recited in or attached to the pleadings as an exhibit. Any attached written instrument will be considered part of the pleadings. Where the instrument is unavailable to the pleader, she must attach an affidavit stating the facts that made the instrument inaccessible to her.

5. **Prayers for Relief**
   Every complaint and counterclaim must contain specific prayers for relief that may be asked in the alternative. The court may grant relief other than that prayed for in the complaint but must protect against prejudice by surprise.

   a. **Default by Failure to Appear**
      In a case of default by failure to appear, or where an order has been entered holding a defendant in default for failure to plead, relief is limited to that in the complaint's prayer for relief. If the plaintiff amends her prayer for relief, notice must first be given to the defaulting defendant, who may then be allowed to appear.

6. **Declaratory Judgments**
   Declaratory relief, which involves a binding declaration of rights having the force of a final judgment, may be requested as a part of any complaint, counterclaim, or other pleading requesting relief. It may be the sole relief requested or it may be accompanied by other requests. The court will refuse to give declaratory relief if there is no actual controversy or if giving it would not terminate the controversy. Declaratory judgment action is neither legal nor equitable.

7. **Verified Pleadings**
   Any pleading may be verified by oath. If verified, all subsequent pleadings must be verified. A nonparty may verify a pleading.

C. **RESPONSIVE PLEADINGS**
   Once the defendant is presented with a formally proper complaint, three options are open to him: challenge its legal sufficiency, deny an essential allegation, or assert an affirmative defense. All three or any combination of these tactics may be used.

1. **Admission or Denial**
   Every answer and subsequent pleading must contain an explicit admission or denial of each allegation of the pleading to which it responds. General denials are not permitted. All *facts* alleged that are *not denied are admitted*, except where there are allegations as to damages, where the responding party has no knowledge sufficient to form a belief, and where there was no opportunity to deny. Denials must be explicit but can be based on no knowledge (if an affidavit of no knowledge is attached).

Note, however, that failure to deny does not admit the allegations where the party making the allegations (who could have taken advantage of the failure to deny) introduces evidence in support of the allegation. Note also, failure to deny *admits only well-pleaded facts*, not legal conclusions, and *does not admit that the undenied facts are sufficient to constitute a good cause of action or legal defense*.

2. Defenses

A party may plead as many defenses as he may have. Each should be separately designated and numbered.

a. Alternative Defenses

A party in doubt as to which of two or more statements of fact is true may, regardless of consistency, state them alternatively or hypothetically in the same or different defenses. A bad alternative does not affect a good one.

b. Affirmative Defenses

Any affirmative defense must be pleaded in the answer to be available at trial. These include payment; release; satisfaction; discharge; license; fraud; duress; estoppel; laches; Statute of Frauds; illegality; instrument or transaction void, voidable, or contrary to statute; nondelivery; and want or failure of consideration.

3. Counterclaims (Including Cross-Claims)

"Counterclaim" is the generic term used in Illinois to describe claims asserted in a responsive pleading, including all cross-demands in the nature of recoupment, set-off, and cross-bills in equity, and cross-claims against co-defendants.

a. No Distinction Between Permissive and Compulsory Counterclaims

In Illinois, all counterclaims are considered permissive. However, res judicata (claim preclusion) may prevent a defendant from bringing a counterclaim as a separate action in a later suit if a successful prosecution of the later action would nullify the earlier action.

b. Connection with Plaintiff's Claim Not Required

Illinois does not require any connection between the plaintiff's claim and the counterclaim. However, the court may order separate trials to avoid delay, embarrassment, or undue complication of the trial.

c. Pleadings and Service of Process

Counterclaims are considered part of the defendant's answer, and they are governed by the rules for pleading. Service of process on parties already before the court is unnecessary, but additional defendants not already before the court must be joined by service of process.

d. Timing

A counterclaim may be filed after judgment when a judgment by confession has been entered. Additionally, a claim may be asserted in a counterclaim even though barred by the statute of limitations if it was not so barred when the plaintiff's cause of action arose.

4. Verification

A denial that a written instrument was duly executed or assigned must be verified to be effective. If not made by the person alleged to have executed or assigned the instrument, the verification may be on information and belief only.

D. AMENDMENTS TO THE PLEADINGS

At any time before final judgment, amendments to the pleading are in the discretion of the court but are very liberally permitted. Amendments include introducing parties who should have been joined as plaintiffs or defendants, changing the cause of action or defense, or adding new causes of action or defenses.

1. Conforming Pleadings to Proofs

Amendments to conform the pleadings to the proof can be made at any time, *before or after judgment*. They are not allowed unless the proof admitted was *material to the issues* in the original pleadings.

2. Amendments After the Statute of Limitations Has Run

Notwithstanding the statute of limitations or private contractual limitations on the time for instituting any action, a claim or defense set up in the amended pleading is not barred by lapse of time if it is deemed to relate back to the date of filing of the original pleading as amended. Two conditions must be satisfied: (i) the original pleading was filed in time; and (ii) the added claim or defense arose from the same transaction or occurrence.

3. Cases of Mistaken Identity

An amendment adding a defendant after the statute of limitations has expired relates back to the date on which the original pleading was filed if:

a. The original action was *filed within the limitations period*;

b. The defendant, *within the time that the action might have been brought plus the period allowed for service of process* (*i.e.,* the plaintiff filed suit *before* the limitations period has expired, but served the defendant, using the "due diligence" required by the Rules, *after* the limitations period has expired):

    1) *Received such notice of the commencement of the action* that the defendant would not be prejudiced in maintaining a defense on the merits; and

    2) Knew or should have known that, *but for a mistake concerning the identity of the proper party*, the action would have been brought against him; and

c. The amended cause of action *grew out of the same transaction or occurrence* set up in the original pleading.

CMR **Exam Tip** For your exam, remember that the rules for "relation back" of pleadings *are essentially the same in Illinois state courts and federal courts.* It's just the timing of service of process that is a little different.

E. BILL OF PARTICULARS

If a party believes his opponent's pleading is deficient in particularity, he may demand of him a bill of particulars specifying the details desired. The adverse party must then either object to the demand or file a bill of particulars. Once filed, the bill becomes part of the pleadings.

VIII. MOTIONS BEFORE TRIAL

A. SECTION 2-615 MOTIONS

Section 2-615 motions relate to *defects on the face of the pleadings.* All objections to pleadings must be raised by a *single motion* rather than in responsive pleadings. The motion must point out specifically the defects complained of and ask for appropriate relief.

1. Kinds of Objections Authorized

a. Pleading or Portion Thereof Be Stricken for Insufficiency at Law

With regard to a complaint, the motion to strike for insufficiency at law requires the court to answer the question whether the pleader can prove any set of facts in support of the allegations of his complaint that would entitle him to any kind of judicial relief. If there are no such facts, the action is subject to dismissal. If the claimant alleges only conclusions, the pleading will be stricken.

1) Effect of Dismissal

If the action is dismissed for failure to state a cause of action, that decision is on the merits and res judicata applies unless the dismissal order specifies otherwise.

b. Pleading Be Made More Definite and Certain in a Specified Particular

The question on a motion to make more definite is whether the pleading is sufficiently informative to allow the movant to frame a response.

c. Designated Immaterial Matter Be Stricken Out

An opponent can raise at this early stage the issues of relevancy and materiality.

d. Necessary Parties Be Added

e. Designated Misjoined Parties Be Dismissed

2. General Rules as to Section 2-615 Motions

a. Defects

Defects must be *specified.*

b. Prior Pleadings

Prior pleadings will be considered.

c. Successive Motions

All section 2-615 objections should be consolidated into a single motion.

d. Pleading Over After Denial of Motion

Where a section 2-615 motion is denied, the moving party waives error in the denial by pleading over. When a party wishes to stand on his motion, he must submit to a default or summary judgment and appeal from it.

e. Judgment on the Pleadings

Where no factual issues are presented by the pleadings, any party may move for judgment on the pleadings. If issues of fact are presented by the motion, it may be treated as a motion for summary judgment. Since failure to state a claim on which relief can be granted is a defect that can be raised at any time, even for the first time on appeal, this defect can be raised by motion for judgment on the pleadings even though no motion to dismiss was filed.

B. SECTION 2-619 MOTIONS

A section 2-619 motion is a pre-answer dispositive motion used to attack any claim or defense on a wide variety of grounds.

1. When the Motion Must Be Made

The motion must be filed within the time for answering, which can be extended by court order or by the filing of other motions. Section 2-619 grounds may also be raised as alternative defenses in the answer, in which case a summary disposition before trial could be sought by means of a motion for summary judgment.

2. Grounds for Motion

a. The court *lacks subject matter jurisdiction* and transfer to another court will not remove the defect;

b. The plaintiff *lacks legal capacity* to sue or the defendant lacks capacity to be sued;

c. There is *another action pending* between the *same parties* for the *same cause;*

d. The cause of action is *barred by a prior judgment;*

e. The action was *not commenced within a limitation period;*

f. The claim has been *released, satisfied of record, or discharged* in bankruptcy;

g. The claim is *unenforceable under the Statute of Frauds;*

h. The claim is *unenforceable because of the defendant's disability;* or

i. The claim is *subject to a valid affirmative defense* avoiding the legal effect of, or defeating, the claim.

3. Motion Decided on Merits or Denied Without Prejudice

Where the motion is contested, the court may take proofs and then either grant or deny the motion. If a material and genuinely disputed issue of fact is presented, however, the court may deny the motion without prejudice to the defendant's right to raise the same defense in his answer. The question of fact will then be decided at trial, rather than in a hearing on the motion.

a. Jury Cases

If a jury demand has been filed in a law case by the party opposing the motion, the trial judge must deny the motion so that the parties may have a jury trial on the factual issues, if there is any genuine issue of fact with respect to the defense.

b. Motion Decided on the Merits

If the judge denies the motion, the defendant may later raise the same issues and defenses unless the judge has stated that he has disposed of the motion on the merits.

CMR SUMMARY CHART	PRETRIAL MOTIONS		
Motion	**Purpose**	**Examples of Application**	**Procedure Notes**
Section 2-615	Motion attacking defects *on face of pleading*	Used to: strike pleading insufficient at law (*e.g.,* for failure to state a claim); strike immaterial matter; make pleading more definite; add necessary parties or dismiss misjoined parties	All objections to pleadings should be consolidated in one motion before making responsive pleading. May combine with 2-619 defenses. Movant's pleading over after denial of motion waives error, except as to failure to state a claim.
Section 2-619	Pre-answer dispositive motion to dismiss on variety of grounds other than defects on face of pleading	Used when: P lacks capacity; cause is barred by res judicata, Statute of Frauds, or statute of limitations; claim has been released, satisfied, or discharged	D must file this motion before answering, but may instead raise defenses in answer. D's pleading over after denial of motion does not waive error.
Section 2-1005	Motion for summary judgment	Parties agree on facts to extent that there is no genuine issue of material fact, and moving party alleges he is entitled to judgment as a matter of law	P may move after D has appeared or time to appear has expired. D may move at any time. Motion may be accompanied by affidavits, discovery products, and testimony.

    c.   **Effect of Denial**

If the judge rules for the plaintiff on a section 2-619 motion, he will order the defendant to answer.

    d.   **Pleading Over After Denial**

A party who files a responsive pleading after his section 2-619 motion has been denied on the merits does not waive any error in the denial of the motion. The error may be raised on appeal without further assertion of the defense at trial.

C. SUMMARY JUDGMENTS

Summary judgments are used when the pleadings state a cause of action on their face, but in reality, there is no genuine issue of material fact to be tried.

1. When Motion Can Be Made

A plaintiff cannot move until the defendant has appeared or the time for him to appear has expired. A defendant may move at any time.

2. Partial Summary Judgment

The court may grant summary judgment as to some counts or demands but not as to others. When a summary judgment will not dispose of all the issues, the court, in granting the motion, may either enter judgment at that time, postpone entry of judgment, or enter judgment and stay enforcement until the remaining issues have been determined.

3. Affidavits

    a.   **Requirements**

Affidavits in support of a motion for summary judgment should be made on the ***personal knowledge*** of the affiant and should state facts with particularity.

    b.   **Bad Faith**

If affidavits are presented in bad faith or solely for the purpose of delay, the court may require the guilty party to pay the opponent's reasonable expenses, including attorneys' fees, and may hold the offender or his attorney guilty of contempt.

4. Genuine Issues of Fact

The court must not deprive parties of a jury trial if there is controverted evidence on material issues. If a genuine issue exists, the motion must be denied.

IX. DISCOVERY

A. SCOPE OF DISCOVERY

Any matter generally related to the subject matter of the lawsuit may be discovered. Discovery is not limited to information that would be admissible in evidence at trial.

1. Relevance

    a.   **Materials**

A party may obtain information as to the existence, description, condition, and location of any documents or tangible things.

b. Persons Having Knowledge
A party may obtain from other parties and nonparties full disclosure of the identity and location of persons having knowledge of relevant facts.

c. Witnesses
A party must furnish the identity and addresses of witnesses who will testify at trial.

d. Insurance
A defendant may be required to disclose the existence and amount of his insurance coverage.

e. Reports of Experts
Reports of experts prepared for trial are subject to discovery unless disclosure would reveal the attorney's theories, mental impressions, or litigation strategy.

f. Not Limited to Opponent's Case
Full disclosure of relevant matter is required whether it relates to the claim or defense of the party seeking disclosure or of any other party.

g. Limited and Simplified Discovery
A limited and simplified system of discovery is also available for certain cases involving potential money damages of $50,000 or less and for cases falling under the mandatory arbitration procedures, but excluding small claims actions and some family law matters.

A uniform disclosure statement as set out in Rule 222 requires disclosure of certain basic information regarding the action. The duty to provide disclosure is a continuing duty, and each party must seasonably supplement or amend disclosures whenever new or different information or documents become known to the disclosing party. Under this procedure, each party is permitted up to 30 interrogatories, including supplemental interrogatories and subsections. No discovery deposition may exceed three hours, absent agreement among the parties. Discovery depositions may be taken only of parties, treating physicians, and opinion witnesses.

h. Discovery Before Suit
A person who needs to identify those who may be responsible to him for damages may bring an independent action for discovery before filing suit.

2. Limitations

a. Privileged Information
All privileges applicable at trial are applicable here. The two privileges most applicable to discovery are the ***work product*** privilege (material prepared by or for a party in preparation for trial is subject to discovery unless it contains or discloses the theories, mental impressions, or litigation plans of the party's attorney) and the ***attorney-client*** privilege. The identity, opinions, and work of a consultant is discoverable only on a showing of exceptional circumstances.

b. Time Limitation
No discovery can be initiated before all the defendants have appeared or are required to appear, without leave of court granted upon good cause shown.

3. **Judicial Control**

    On its own initiative or on motion of any party or witness, the court may at any time make a protective order denying, limiting, conditioning, or regulating discovery to prevent unreasonable annoyance, expense, etc.

4. **Sanctions**

    a. **Refusal to Answer**

        If a deponent, whether or not a party, declines to answer questions, any party may ask the court for an order compelling answers and the court may assess costs against the offending party or deponent if the refusal to comply was unreasonable.

    b. **Failure to Comply with Order or Rules**

        If a party refuses to comply with the discovery rules or a discovery order, the court may impose sanctions upon the party that can include (i) staying the proceedings; (ii) prohibiting the offending party from filing additional pleadings; (iii) barring a witness from testifying about that issue; and (iv) entering a judgment by default or an order dismissing his action, with or without prejudice, against the offending party as to the claims or defenses asserted in any pleading to which that issue is material. However, the sanction should bear some relationship to the party's violation.

    c. **Abuse of Discovery Procedures**

        The court may suppress information obtained through abuse of discovery procedures. Where such abuse is willful, it may impose any of the above-listed sanctions.

B. DEPOSITIONS

Depositions may be either evidence depositions or discovery depositions. If the type of deposition is not specified, it may be used only for discovery. If the evidence deposition of a witness is to be taken within 21 days of trial, a discovery deposition is not permitted absent stipulation by the parties or court order.

1. **Any Party May Depose Anyone**

    A deposition may be taken of any person without a court order. Service of a notice is sufficient to require attendance of a party at the taking of his deposition, and his production of documents or tangible things named in the notice. Nonparty deponents must be served with subpoenas, but service can be by mail. Subpoenas are generally available to compel attendance of nonparty physicians only by court order.

2. **Where**

    Without leave of court, depositions may be taken only where the deponent resides, is employed, or transacts business. *Exception:* Nonresident plaintiffs, their employees, and real parties in interest can be required to come to Illinois to have their depositions taken. By stipulation or court order, a deposition may be taken by telephone, video conference, or other remote electronic means.

3. **Use of Oral Depositions**

    a. **Discovery Depositions**

        A discovery deposition may be used only:

1) For *impeaching* the deponent, as with an inconsistent statement made by him as a witness;

2) As an *admission*, against a deponent who is a party;

3) As an *exception to the hearsay rule*, if otherwise admissible (*e.g.,* a statement against interest);

4) In *substitution* for an affidavit; or

5) *As evidence,* on reasonable notice to all parties, if:

   a) The deponent (i) is not a party or a retained opinion witness, (ii) is unavailable because of death or infirmity, and (iii) has not given an evidence deposition;

   b) The party against whom the deposition is being offered appeared at, or had been given proper notice of, the deposition; *and*

   c) The court finds that admitting the deposition would "do substantial justice between or among the parties."

b. Evidence Depositions
In addition to the above uses, all or part of an evidence deposition may be used by any party for any purpose if any of the following conditions exists at the time of trial:

1) The deponent is dead or *unable to testify* because he is senile, sick, infirm, or in jail;

2) The deponent is *out of the county* unless the absence was procured by the party offering the deposition, with further exception that a party who is not a resident of Illinois may introduce his own deposition if he is absent from the county;

3) The attendance of the deponent *cannot* be procured by service of *subpoena*; or

4) The court, by reason of *extraordinary circumstances*, finds use of the deposition desirable.

c. Partial Use
Where only part of a deposition is used at trial by a party, any other party may introduce any other portion that in fairness should be heard in connection with the part used.

4. Procedure for Oral Depositions

a. Scope of Examination
The deponent may be examined regarding any discoverable matter as if under cross-examination.

b. Unfairness
A deponent or party may object that the deposition is being conducted in bad faith, in

which case the deposition is suspended for the court to decide on a request for an order suspending or limiting the deposition.

    c.   Objections

    Objections to procedure or evidence are included in the deposition.

    d.   Signature

    Unless waived by the deponent and all parties represented at the deposition, the deponent has the right to examine the transcript and record any changes. The transcript is then signed by the deponent.

5.   Procedure for Deposition on Written Questions

The party requesting the deposition serves the written questions on the other parties, stating who is to answer them and before whom the deposition is to be taken. A party may serve cross-questions within 14 days; within seven days later, redirect questions may be served; and within seven days after that, re-cross questions. Objections to written questions are waived if not served in writing within the time for succeeding questions.

C.   WRITTEN INTERROGATORIES TO PARTIES

Written interrogatories may be served on any other party to the lawsuit. The party served must either answer each interrogatory or object to it. Answers or objections to questions are due in 28 days. Objections to answers or to refusals to answer are heard by the court on motion.

1.   Option to Produce Documents

If answers may be obtained from documents of the interrogee, it is sufficient answer to produce those documents responsive to the interrogatory.

2.   Identity and Testimony of Witnesses

If asked in an interrogatory, a party must disclose the identities and addresses of lay, "independent expert," and "controlled expert" witnesses who will testify at trial. For lay witnesses, the party must also disclose the topics on which the witnesses will testify. For independent expert witnesses, the party must also disclose, to the best of his ability, the topics on which the expert will testify and the opinions held by the expert. For controlled expert witnesses, the party must disclose the topics on which the expert will testify, the conclusions and opinions held by the expert, the bases for the conclusions and opinions, the expert's qualifications, and any reports prepared by the expert.

3.   Supplementation of Interrogatories

A party has a duty to seasonably supplement or amend any prior answer or response whenever new or additional information subsequently becomes known to that party.

4.   Use of Answers

Answers may be used only in the same manner as a discovery deposition. Answers are not pleadings and do not constitute judicial admissions or evidence unless and until they are read into evidence.

D.   DOCUMENTS AND TANGIBLE THINGS

Any relevant document or physical evidence may be examined on request served on any party. The party seeking production of documents or tangible things, access to real estate for purposes

of inspection, or surveys or photographs need not show good cause; the party resisting must object on grounds that the matter sought is outside the scope of discovery. Items sought must be sufficiently specified.

E. PHYSICAL OR MENTAL EXAMINATIONS

Physical or mental examinations may be made of any party whose physical or mental condition is at issue in the lawsuit. Normally, the party requesting the examination suggests the identity of the examiner and sets forth the examiner's specialty or discipline. If the suggested examiner is refused by the court, the court will permit the moving party to suggest other examiners. The examiner's fee and the examinee's loss of earnings are paid by the moving party.

F. ADMISSIONS OF FACTS

Requests for admissions of facts may be served on any other party. All facts not denied under oath within 28 days are admitted, unless the court has extended this deadline for good cause.

G. DEPOSITIONS FOR PURPOSE OF PERPETUATING TESTIMONY

A person who wishes to perpetuate his own testimony or that of another person may file a petition in the circuit court of the county in which the action might be brought, or in which one or more of the persons to be examined resides. Notices are served on all those named; if that cannot be done, service by publication may be ordered. If the court is convinced that the perpetuation of the testimony may prevent a failure or delay of justice, it will grant the petition, or as much of it as is merited.

H. PRETRIAL CONFERENCE

Generally, the court must hold an initial case management conference within 35 days after the parties are at issue and in no event more than 182 days following the filing of the complaint. Counsel *familiar with the case and authorized to act* must appear at the conference.

1. Agenda
The matters to be considered are:

    a.   The nature, issues, and complexity of the case;

    b.   Simplification of issues and amendments to pleadings;

    c.   The possibility of obtaining admissions of fact and documents that will avoid unnecessary proof;

    d.   Limitations on discovery;

    e.   The possibility of settlement;

    f.   The advisability of alternative dispute resolution;

    g.   When the case should be ready for trial;

    h.   Whether additional management conferences are needed; and

    i.   Any other matters that may aid in the disposition of the case.

2. **Pretrial Order**

At the conclusion of the conference the judge will enter an order reciting the agreements reached by the parties, and any action taken by him. In a very real sense, the order may replace the pleadings as the official statement of issues for purposes of rulings on evidence and later res judicata determinations.

X. TRIALS

A. DOCKET MANAGEMENT

1. **Consolidation**

A circuit court has broad discretionary powers to consolidate for trial various actions pending on its docket. The court must balance considerations of efficiency against possible prejudice to parties and undue lengthening and complication of the trial.

2. **Severance**

The court possesses broad discretionary powers to sever for separate trials separate claims in an action, or separate defenses, and different parties. However, the bifurcation of liability and damages within a single action generally should not occur.

3. **Extensions of Time**

Convenience of the parties, the court's docket, and the diligence or lack thereof shown by the parties will determine whether requests to postpone will be granted. Since the matter lies in the judge's discretion, a stipulation between the parties for a continuance is not controlling.

4. **Order of Proceeding**

The order of proceeding ordinarily accompanies the burden of proof. A court commits prejudicial error if it denies the privilege of opening and closing to the burdened party.

B. VOLUNTARY DISMISSAL

Before trial or hearing, a plaintiff may dismiss her action without prejudice if she (i) notifies every party who has appeared and (ii) pays costs. Under this section, a trial begins when opening statements are made in a nonjury trial or when voir dire begins in jury trial; a "hearing" means the equitable equivalent of a trial. A dismissal at this stage does not result in dismissal of a pending counterclaim or third-party complaint. After a trial or hearing has begun, a plaintiff may dismiss only on stipulation with the defendant or on motion supported by affidavit; the plaintiff also must abide by any conditions the court sets. The court may hear and decide a motion filed prior to the plaintiff's motion for voluntary dismissal if that prior motion could result in a final disposition of the action. Under certain circumstances, the plaintiff may refile (*see* V.D., *supra*).

C. MANDATORY ARBITRATION SYSTEM

Illinois requires arbitration of civil actions in which each claim is for money only and does not exceed the monetary limit (excluding interest and costs) of the circuit or county court in which the case is brought.

1. **Discovery and Hearings**

Limited and simplified discovery is used, and the established rules of evidence are used at

the hearing. Documents such as the records of health-care providers, itemized repair bills, and sworn statements from witnesses are, however, presumptively admissible at the hearing. If the opposing party wishes to cross-examine the author of a document made admissible, she must subpoena the author and bear the costs.

2. Failure to Attend or to Participate

A party must attend the arbitration proceedings and participate in good faith. If the party fails to attend or participate in the proceedings, she forfeits her right to reject the award (*see* below), unless the court, in its discretion, vacates the judgment and orders a rehearing.

3. Award and Rejection of Award

An award must dispose of all claims, and it may not exceed the monetary limit of the applicable circuit or county court. If a party wishes to reject an award, she must file with the clerk of the court a written notice of rejection and certificates of service on all other parties, along with paying the proper fee. Once the award is rejected by one party, it is rejected for all (except those parties who are barred from rejecting the award). At the later trial, an arbitrator may not be called to testify about the arbitration proceedings.

D. JURY CASES

1. Right to Jury Trial

Under the Illinois Constitution, there is a right to a jury in cases at law but not in cases in equity. There are also statutory rights to jury trial.

2. Joinder of Legal and Equitable Matters

With cases involving matters of equity and law, the court will determine if the matters are severable, and if so, whether they should be tried together or separately and in what order. If severable, law issues are tried first before a jury when a jury has been properly demanded.

3. Jury Demand

A jury trial will be waived unless a timely demand is made. However, a court *may* grant a tardy demand for a jury trial, even though the demanding party can no longer demand a jury as of right.

(i) *The plaintiff* must file his jury demand when the case is filed.

(ii) *The defendant* must file his jury demand by the time he answers. If the plaintiff has filed a jury demand, the defendant need not. If, thereafter, the plaintiff waives a jury, the defendant may promptly demand one. A third-party defendant can similarly rely on a jury demand filed by the plaintiff or defendant. If that demand is withdrawn, the third-party defendant may file his own.

If a case is *transferred from the equity to the law docket*, the plaintiff has three days and the defendant has six days to demand a jury.

4. Jury Size and Alternate Jurors

Where the claim for damages does not exceed $50,000, the cause will be tried before a jury of six unless either party demands a jury of 12. The court may impanel one or two alternate jurors to replace jurors unable to perform their duties.

5. **Voir Dire**

The judge initiates the questioning of prospective jurors, which may be supplemented by the attorneys within reasonable limits. No questions on law or instructions are allowed.

6. **Challenges**

   a. **Challenges for Cause**

   Each party has the right to unlimited challenges for cause based on disqualification, interest, or bias of the prospective juror. Denial of a challenge for cause is not reversible error unless the party's peremptory challenges are then exhausted.

   b. **Peremptory Challenges**

   Each side has five peremptory challenges and up to three more may be granted for each additional party on a side with the qualification that both sides must have an equal amount.

   c. **Additional Challenge**

   Where the court directs the impaneling of alternate jurors, each side is entitled to one additional peremptory challenge to be used only against alternate jurors. Any of the unused peremptory challenges may also be used on alternate jurors.

7. **Evidence**

   a. **Examination of Adverse Party**

   Any party, or the officers, directors, managing agents, or foreman of any party, may be called and examined as if under cross-examination at the instance of any adverse party. The party calling may impeach by prior inconsistent statements.

   b. **Examination of Hostile Witnesses**

   If a court determines a witness is "hostile," he may be examined by the party calling him as if under cross-examination.

   c. **Business Records**

   The business records rule does not permit introduction of medical records or police accident reports.

8. **Instructions**

Unless the parties agree on oral instructions, the court must give the instructions to the jury in writing. They must be limited to the law of the case. After the instructions have been given, they may be clarified, modified, or explained only in writing, unless the parties agree otherwise.

   a. **Submission of Instructions**

   At the close of the evidence, each party submits to the court the instructions it wishes to have given. The court then holds a conference to settle the instructions.

   b. **Objections to Instructions**

1) Failure to Give an Instruction

A party may not object on appeal that the court failed to give an instruction unless he tendered it before the conference.

2) Given Instruction Was Erroneous

Only objections to instructions that are interposed at the conference are preserved as grounds for motions for a new trial, or on appeal. The instruction must have been clearly objected to and the reason it is objectionable specified.

c. Illinois Pattern Instructions

Trial courts must use any applicable Illinois Pattern Jury Instructions unless the court determines that on a particular subject the pattern instruction does not accurately state the law.

9. Directed Verdicts

If, at the close of evidence and before the case is submitted to the jury, any party moves for a directed verdict, the court may: (i) grant the motion, (ii) deny the motion, or (iii) reserve its ruling and submit the case to the jury. No assent by the jury is needed.

If the court denies the motion or reserves its ruling and submits the case to the jury, the motion is waived unless renewed in the post-trial motion. Note that the motion is not waived by failure to make it before the jury verdict is returned.

a. Standard for Directed Verdicts and JNOV

A directed verdict may be granted at the close of *all* the evidence, if *all* the evidence, when viewed in the aspect most favorable to the opponent, so overwhelmingly favors the movant that no contrary verdict based on that evidence could ever stand. [*Pedrick* rule]

b. Standard for New Trial Compared

A substantially stronger case is required for a directed verdict than for a new trial. A new trial may be granted when the evidence supports the verdict to some extent, but its manifest weight is against the verdict.

10. Verdicts

a. General Verdicts

The jury will render a general verdict with or without answers to special interrogatories. Illinois does not employ special verdicts unless there are exceptional circumstances.

b. Separate Counts

When a complaint or counterclaim contains separate counts upon which separate recoveries might be had, the jury must find a separate verdict on each demand when so requested by any party.

c. Grounds for Recovery Defectively Stated

If several grounds for recovery of a single demand are pleaded alternatively in one count or in separate counts and one or more of them is legally defective, a general verdict in favor of the claimant will not be set aside if one or more other grounds is sufficient to sustain the verdict.

d.   **Grounds Not Proven**

When more than one ground of recovery has been pleaded in support of the same demand, in one count or in separate counts, a general verdict in favor of the claimant *will not be set aside* because the evidence in support of any one ground is insufficient to support recovery, *unless:*

1)   Before the case was submitted to the jury, the defendant moved to withdraw that ground from the jury on account of *insufficient evidence; and*

2)   It appears that denial of the motion was *prejudicial.*

11.   **Special Interrogatories**

The jury may be required by the court, or must be required on the request of any party, to find specially upon any material question of fact stated to them in writing.

a.   **Conference**

The special interrogatory is tendered and ruled on at the same time and in the same manner as an instruction.

b.   **Error on Appeal**

On appeal, the submission of a special interrogatory to the jury is a ruling of law subject to review. Error in submission of a special interrogatory must be preserved by timely objection as in the case of instructions. One need not object to the court's refusal to submit an interrogatory requested by him; his submission is deemed a request for a correct ruling.

c.   **Special Findings Control General Verdict**

When a special finding of fact by the jury is inconsistent with the general verdict, the special finding controls and the court may enter judgment accordingly.

d.   **New Trial**

When an answer to a special interrogatory is actually inconsistent with the general verdict, a new trial should be ordered *only* if the inconsistent special finding is against the manifest weight of the evidence. If the answers to the special interrogatories are inconsistent with each other, and one or more is inconsistent with the general verdict, the court may not enter judgment. Unless it sets aside the inconsistent answers, it must order a new trial.

e.   **No Instruction or Argument on Consistency**

The jury may not be told of the necessity for consistency or what answers are consistent with the verdict.

12.   **Single Post-Trial Motion**

All post-trial relief must be sought in a single post-trial motion filed within 30 days of judgment or discharge of the jury where no verdict is reached. Any relief not requested in the post-trial motion and any ground for relief not stated is waived, but the trial judge has the power to grant a new trial on his own motion.

a. **Grounds for Granting New Trial**

1) *Prejudicial errors* committed by the judge;

2) *Misconduct* by a party, attorney, court official, or juror;

3) The *verdict is contrary to the preponderance of the evidence* (contrast the *Pedrick* standard for JNOV);

4) *Damages* awarded are so *excessive or inadequate* as to indicate passion or prejudice on the part of the jury; and

5) *Manifest error by the jury,* or disobedience to instructions.

b. **Conditional Requests and Conditional Rulings**
JNOV and a new trial may be sought in the alternative. If so, the judge must rule on both, even if he grants the JNOV.

c. **Timing, Stay of Execution, and Time to Appeal**
Where judgment is entered on the post-trial motion, the party against whom judgment is so rendered may file his own post-trial motion within 30 days of the entry of judgment. A party against whom JNOV has been entered need not then move for a new trial in order to preserve the alleged error as a ground for appeal. The filing of a post-trial motion stays execution, and the time for appeal does not begin to run until it is decided.

d. **Remittitur**
Remittitur involves a judge's conditional denial of a motion for a new trial grounded on the excessiveness of the jury's award of damages. The judge may offer to deny the defendant's motion on the condition that the plaintiff remit the excessive amount. A party who consents to a remittitur as a condition to denial of a new trial is not thereby precluded from asserting, on appeal by the opponent, that the amount of the verdict was proper.

E. NONJURY CASES

1. **Defendant's Motion for Judgment**
No express findings by the judge are required in nonjury cases. If the defendant moves for judgment at the close of the plaintiff's case, the court may weigh the evidence in determining if the plaintiff has sustained his burden of proof. If the motion is denied, the defendant proceeds to present his case.

2. **Post-Trial Motion**
A post-trial motion may be filed within 30 days of judgment or decree to request (i) rehearing of an issue, (ii) retrial of the entire case, or (iii) modification or vacation of the decree or judgment or other relief therefrom. The filing of the post-trial motion stays execution and the time for appeal. Failure to file one does not waive any error for purposes of appeal in nonjury cases.

XI. JUDGMENTS

A. CONTRIBUTION AND INDEMNITY JUDGMENTS IN PRINCIPAL ACTION

If relief is granted against a party who, upon satisfying the judgment, will be entitled by operation of law to be reimbursed by another party to the action, the court may determine the rights of the parties as between themselves and thereafter, upon motion and notice, render a final judgment against the party ultimately liable.

B. JUDGMENT BY CONFESSION

If a party confesses judgment, no process or notice is required. The judgment is void unless entered where the defendant resides or has property or where the note was executed. A judgment by confession may be opened if, by affidavit and verified answer, the defendant shows he has a good defense or a valid counterclaim.

C. JUDGMENT BY DEFAULT

If a defendant fails to appear or answer, a default judgment will be entered against him. Failure of the clerk to give notice of judgments by default to all parties does not impair the validity of the judgment. The plaintiff or defendant may demand a jury on the issue of damages. Upon motion filed within 30 days of entry of default judgment, the court may set aside the judgment upon any reasonable terms and conditions.

D. RELIEF FROM FINAL JUDGMENTS AND DECREES

Section 2-1401 is a device by which judgments may be opened after 30 days and before two years have elapsed from their entry. It enables a party to bring before the court that rendered the judgment matters of fact which, if known to the court at the time judgment was entered, would have prevented its rendition. It cannot relieve a party from the consequences of his own mistake or negligence. One major use of section 2-1401 is to vacate a default judgment. Time during which the person seeking relief is under legal disability or duress, or during which the grounds for relief are fraudulently concealed, does not count. The petition procedure does not affect other methods for obtaining relief from a void order, judgment, or decree (*e.g.,* by collateral attack showing lack of jurisdiction, or an independent suit in equity).

CMR **Exam Tip** Note that if fewer than 30 days have passed since entry of a default judgment, the defaulting defendant may move to have the judgment set aside, and the court in its discretion may do so under section 2-1301 (the code section governing default judgments).

E. RES JUDICATA AND COLLATERAL ESTOPPEL

1. **Res Judicata (Claim Preclusion)**

   Once a *final* judgment *on the merits* has been rendered on a particular cause of action, a claimant cannot assert the *same* cause of action (usually one arising out of the same transaction) in a later lawsuit. If the claimant lost the first lawsuit, the claim is *barred*. If the claimant won the first lawsuit, the cause of action *merges* with the judgment. This is known as *res judicata*.

2. **Collateral Estoppel (Issue Preclusion)**

   A judgment for the plaintiff or defendant is conclusive in a subsequent case on a different cause of action *as to issues actually litigated* and *essential to the judgment* in the first case.

This is known as *collateral estoppel*. In Illinois, a party may assert collateral estoppel if:

a. The issue decided in the first case is *identical* to the issue presented in the second case;

b. There was a *final* judgment *on the merits* in the first case;

c. The party *against whom* collateral estoppel is to be applied was a party, or in privity with a party, in the first case; and

d. The application of collateral estoppel is not *fundamentally unfair*.

XII. APPELLATE PRACTICE

A. WHEN APPEAL MAY BE TAKEN
All final orders, including any contempt sanctions, are appealable within 30 days of the entry of final judgment. There are a number of exceptions to the final order rule.

1. Interlocutory Orders Appealable as of Right
Interlocutory orders that have immediate impact upon the parties, or that may allow a situation to become irremediable, are appealable within 30 days of entry.

2. Partial Final Judgments

a. With Certificate
In actions involving multiple parties or multiple claims, the trial judge may enter a final judgment as to one party or cause of action. To do so, the judge must certify that there is no just reason to delay enforcement or appeal. In the absence of such a finding, any partial judgment remains interlocutory, unenforceable, unappealable, and subject to revision at any time before entry of a final judgment that disposes of all of the claims and the rights and liabilities of all of the parties. The plaintiff's complaint presents multiple claims most clearly when it presents demands for separate and cumulative relief, as to which judgment on one would not bar judgment on the other.

b. Without Certificate
Rule 304(b) provides that rulings on section 2-1401 motions, proceedings to collect from judgment debtors, or rulings which determine the rights or status of a party in estates, guardianships, conservatorships, or receiverships, etc., are appealable without certification. The appeal must be filed within 30 days (*see* B., below).

3. Appeals from Certain Circuit Court Orders
By rule, a party may also petition the appellate court for leave to appeal from a circuit court order that grants a *new trial*; grants or denies a motion to transfer venue based on *forum non conveniens*; denies a motion to dismiss based on a *lack of personal jurisdiction*; grants or denies a motion for a *transfer of venue* based on the defendant not being a resident of the county in which the action was commenced, and that no other legitimate basis for venue exists; grants a motion *to disqualify a party's attorney*; or grants or denies a *certification of a class action*. The petition must be filed within 30 days after the order in question was issued, and the answer must be filed 21 days thereafter.

4. **Interlocutory Appeals by Permission**

An immediate appeal may be sought from an interlocutory order if the judge finds (i) that the order involves a question of law as to which there is substantial ground for difference of opinion, and (ii) that an immediate appeal from the order may materially advance ultimate termination of the litigation.

B. **PROCEDURE**

The jurisdictional act is the filing of a notice of appeal in the trial court. The notice of appeal must be filed within 30 days after the entry of the judgment appealed from. Enforcement of judgment for money may be stayed pending appeal upon filing of an approved bond, while other judgments and orders may be stayed by order of court.

COMMERCIAL PAPER

TABLE OF CONTENTS

COMMERCIAL PAPER

I. IN GENERAL

A. INTRODUCTION

Commercial paper (*e.g.,* checks and promissory notes) is governed by Article 3. To facilitate a freely transferable but safe substitute for cash, a central theme of Article 3 is the holder in due course ("HDC") rule: If an instrument is in a special form (called "negotiable") and is transferred in a special way (by "negotiation") to a person who takes the instrument for value, in good faith, and without notice of any defenses to or claims on the instrument (*i.e.,* an "HDC"), the HDC will be able to force someone to pay the money due under the instrument unless the person from whom payment is sought has available one of the very few so-called real defenses provided by Article 3.

B. TERMINOLOGY

The two basic instruments of commercial paper are the note (*e.g.,* promissory note) and the draft (*e.g.,* a check). The U.C.C. does not apply to money.

1. Note

A note is a promise to pay. Two basic parties are involved: the party promising to pay (the "maker") and the party to whom payment is promised (the "payee" or "bearer").

a. Certificates of Deposit

A certificate of deposit is like a note. It is an instrument made by a bank containing: (i) an acknowledgment of money received; and (ii) a promise to repay.

2. Draft (Bill of Exchange)

A draft is an order to pay. Three basic parties are involved: One party (the "drawer") orders another party (the "drawee," often a bank) to pay money to a third party (the "payee") or to bearer.

a. Check

A *check* is any draft payable on demand and drawn on a bank.

CMR | **Exam Tip** | When answering a Commercial Paper question, you should pay particular attention to the parties involved on the instrument so that you can determine whether the instrument is a note or a draft. Remember, there are only two parties on a note (a *maker* promises to pay a *payee*) and there are three parties on a draft (a *drawer* orders a *drawee* to pay a *payee*).

II. FORMAL REQUISITES OF NEGOTIABILITY

A. NEGOTIABILITY DEFINED

Whether an instrument is negotiable depends on its form. To be negotiable, an instrument must be a written and signed:

1. *Unconditional*

2. *Promise or order*

3. *To pay a fixed amount of money* (with or without interest) that:

a. Is payable *to order or bearer* when issued or first in possession of a holder;

b. Is payable *on demand or at a definite time*; and

c. *States no unauthorized undertaking or instruction* by the person promising or ordering payment.

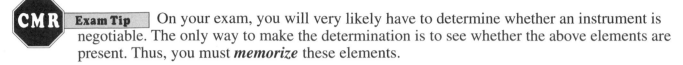 On your exam, you will very likely have to determine whether an instrument is negotiable. The only way to make the determination is to see whether the above elements are present. Thus, you must *memorize* these elements.

B. UNCONDITIONAL

An instrument is conditional (and not negotiable) if: (i) it *expressly states a condition* for payment (*e.g.,* "I promise to pay to the order of Alex $500 if the Bears or Saints win the Super Bowl"), or (ii) it states that the promise or order is *subject to or governed by* another writing. A promise or order is *not* conditional merely because it: (i) refers to another writing regarding collateral, prepayment, or acceleration; (ii) limits payment to a particular source or fund; (iii) requires a countersignature of a specimen signature (*e.g.,* traveler's checks); or (iv) contains a statement required by law that the holder is subject to claims and defenses of the original payee.

1. Effect of Reference to Separate Writing

Mere reference to another writing is irrelevant to negotiability and rights of HDCs, but as between the two parties, the writing modifies or controls the terms of the instrument.

CMR **Exam Tip** Bar examination questions frequently deal with an instrument that recites the consideration out of which the instrument arose. Remember that such recitation does not make the instrument conditional.

C. PROMISE OR ORDER TO PAY

A note must contain a promise to pay (*e.g.,* "I promise to pay"). A draft must contain an order to pay (*e.g.,* "First Bank, pay . . ."). The U.C.C. rules are liberal as to what constitutes a writing or signature.

D. FIXED AMOUNT OF MONEY

Money is any medium of exchange authorized or adopted by the government (*e.g.,* "currency"). Requiring foreign currency payment does not destroy negotiability, but requiring payment in something other than money (even as an alternative, *e.g.,* "$300 or an ounce of gold") makes an instrument nonnegotiable.

1. What Is Fixed?

To be negotiable, the *principal* due under the instrument must be fixed. Variable or indexed interest rates are acceptable. The "judgment rate" will be applied if the instrument states that it is payable "with interest" but the rate is not specified.

E. PAYABLE TO ORDER OR BEARER

1. To Order

An instrument is payable "to order" if it is payable to the order of an identified person (*e.g.,* "pay to the order of Becky") or to an identified person or order (*e.g.,* "pay to Becky or her order").

2. **To Bearer**

An instrument is payable to bearer if it: (i) states that it is payable to "bearer" (*e.g.,* "I promise to pay bearer"), "order of bearer," "order or bearer," "order and bearer," or otherwise *indicates the possessor is entitled to payment*; (ii) *does not name* a payee; or (iii) is *payable to "cash"* or otherwise indicates that it is not payable to an identified person (*e.g.,* "I promise to pay to the order of Mickey Mouse").

3. **Identification of Payee**

The person to whom an instrument is payable is governed by the *intent* of the maker or drawer (*i.e.,* a check payable to "John Smith" is payable to the particular John Smith the drawer intended). A payee may be identified by any means, and more than one payee may be named.

F. ON DEMAND OR AT A DEFINITE TIME

1. **Demand**

An instrument is payable on demand if it fails to state a time for payment or states that it is payable "on demand," "at sight," etc.

2. **Definite Time**

An instrument is payable at a definite time if it is payable: (i) on a fixed date; (ii) after elapse of a specified period after sight; or (iii) at a time *readily ascertainable* when the instrument is issued. Events that will occur on an uncertain date (*e.g.,* "after my death") are not "readily ascertainable."

a. **Acceleration and Extension Clauses**

Acceleration clauses (*e.g.,* "pay bearer $5,000 on April 15, 3000, or at my death if I should die sooner") do not destroy negotiability. *Extensions* at the option of the maker, and extensions that are automatic on the happening of an event, are acceptable if the extension is to a *further definite time* stated in the instrument (*e.g.,* "pay bearer $5,000 on August 12, 2005, but if a Uranus mission has been launched, payment may be made on August 12, 2015"). An extension at the option of the holder is always permitted (but he may not exercise it if the maker objects and tenders payment).

G. NO UNAUTHORIZED UNDERTAKING OR INSTRUCTIONS

Only three undertakings or instructions are authorized by the U.C.C.; any other undertaking or instruction will destroy negotiability:

1. An undertaking or power to *give, maintain, or protect collateral*;

2. An authorization or power given to the holder to *confess judgment* or to realize on or dispose of collateral; and

3. A *waiver of the benefit of a law* that protects the obligor.

H. MISCELLANEOUS

1. **Rules of Construction**

Some rules of construction concerning instruments are: handwriting controls type and print; type controls print; and unambiguous words control figures.

2. Opting Out

Except in the case of checks, negotiability is destroyed by a conspicuous statement on the instrument that it is not negotiable.

3. Two or More Signers in Single Capacity

Two or more signers in a single capacity are generally jointly and severally liable in that capacity.

4. Incomplete Instruments

An incomplete instrument may be enforced according to its incomplete terms or as augmented by an *authorized* completion. If the instrument is completed without authority, it is treated as a fraudulently altered instrument. (*See* VII. F.2., *infra.*)

ELEMENTS OF NEGOTIABILITY

To determine whether an instrument is negotiable, be sure that the instrument has the following characteristics:

☑ *Unconditional* (does not state a condition for payment and is not subject to or governed by another writing)

☑ *Promise* (note) *or order* (draft) *to pay* (written and signed)

☑ *A fixed amount of money* (with or without interest)

☑ *Is payable to order or bearer*

☑ *On demand or at a definite time*

☑ *Contains no unauthorized promise or undertaking*

III. NEGOTIATION—BECOMING A HOLDER

A. THE NEGOTIATION PROCESS

Recall from the introduction that a central theme of Article 3 is to provide a safe alternative to cash for persons who qualify as HDCs. To become an HDC, one must first become a holder (essentially, a person in possession of an instrument with a right to enforce it). A person becomes a holder through a transfer that qualifies as a negotiation. The steps needed to negotiate an instrument depend on whether the instrument is payable to bearer or to order.

1. Bearer Instruments

Bearer instruments are negotiated by *transferring possession* of the instrument (*e.g.,* Yolanda gives Zack a bearer note; there is a negotiation).

2. **Order Instruments**

    a.   **Negotiation to Specific Payee**

        An instrument payable to an identified person (the payee, such as John Smith) is negotiated by *transferring possession along with the identified person's indorsement* (*e.g.,* John Smith may negotiate a check payable to his order by indorsing the check and delivering it to a transferee).

    b.   **Payee's Indorsement Must Be Valid**

        Generally, the right to enforce will not pass unless the payee's indorsement is *authorized* and *valid*. In most cases, forging the payee's name breaks the chain of title, and generally no subsequent possessors of the instrument can qualify as holders.

CMR **Exam Tip** Keep in mind that the right to enforce will pass only if all necessary signatures of all payees and special indorsees are on the instrument.

    c.   **Multiple Payees**

        An instrument may be payable to more than one payee, either *jointly* (*e.g.,* "pay to the order of Becky *and* Cindy"), in which case *each* must indorse, or severally (*e.g.,* "pay to the order of Becky *or* Cindy"), in which case any *one* may indorse.

    d.   **Location of Indorsement**

        An indorsement must be written on either the instrument or an allonge affixed to the instrument.

    e.   **Effect of Transferring an Order Instrument Without Indorsement**

        The delivery of an order instrument without required indorsements may transfer possession but is not a negotiation.

        1)   **Rights of Transferee Without Indorsement**

            Unless and until she obtains the indorsement, the transferee does not have the status of a holder.

        2)   **Different Rules for Banks**

            A depositary bank that takes an instrument *for collection* becomes a holder if the customer was a holder at the time of delivery. This is true even if the customer has not indorsed the instrument.

        3)   **When Indorsement Obtained Later**

            Upon obtaining the transferor's indorsement, title is vested in the transferee, who now becomes a holder—having both the right to enforce and possession.

3. **Types of Indorsements**

    Every indorsement can be described by certain qualities: special or blank, qualified or unqualified, *and* restrictive or unrestrictive.

a. Special or Blank

1) Special Indorsement
A special indorsement names a particular person as indorsee, *e.g.*, "Pay John Smith [signed] Peter Payee." The indorsee (*i.e.*, John Smith) must sign in order for the instrument to be further negotiated. Words of negotiation (such as "pay to the order of") are *not* required in indorsements, and extra words generally do not impair negotiability.

2) Blank Indorsement
A blank indorsement is a signature that is not accompanied by the naming of a specific indorsee (*e.g.*, the indorser merely signs his own name, probably the way most people indorse their paychecks). Blank indorsements create bearer paper, which may then be negotiated by delivery alone.

3) Indorsements of Names Not Necessary to Chain of Title
Forgery of names *not* necessary to the chain of title will not keep later takers from becoming holders.

4) Forgery of Drawer's Name
Forgery of the drawer's name does *not* break the chain of title, and thus subsequent transferees may qualify as holders. This is because the forgery operates as the genuine signature of the *forger*.

5) Multiple Indorsements—Last Indorsement Controls
If an instrument has been indorsed several times, the last indorsement controls what is necessary for further negotiation.

b. Qualified Indorsements
An indorsement with the words "without recourse" is a qualified indorsement and limits the contract liability imposed on indorsers. (*See* VII.B.2., 3., *infra,* for further discussion.)

c. Restrictive Indorsements
Any other language added to an indorsement creates a restrictive indorsement. Restrictive indorsements generally are *ineffective* to limit transfer or negotiation (*e.g.*, a check indorsed "pay Pete Payee only" may be further negotiated to anyone) or to condition payment (*e.g.*, a check indorsed "pay John if he fixes my car" may be further negotiated even if John has not fixed the car). However, an instrument with words requiring bank collection (*e.g.*, "for deposit," "for collection") must be paid consistently with the indorsement by any person or the first bank into which the instrument is deposited (*i.e.*, the depositary bank) or it will be deemed to have been converted.

d. Anomalous Indorsements
An anomalous indorsement is an indorsement made by a person who is not a holder of the instrument, usually for accommodation (*i.e.*, suretyship) purposes. The anomalous indorser becomes liable on the instrument.

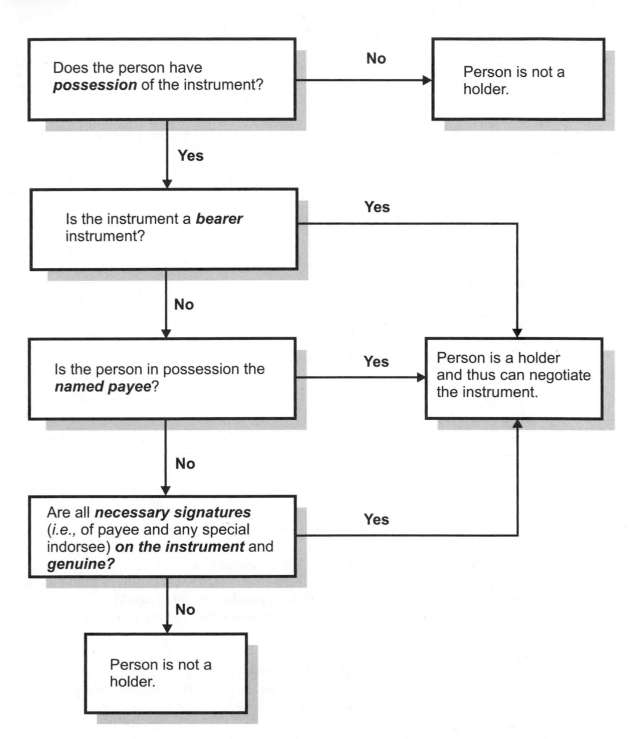

HOLDER STATUS = POSSESSION AND RIGHT TO ENFORCE

Does the person have *possession* of the instrument?

No → Person is not a holder.

Yes ↓

Is the instrument a *bearer* instrument?

Yes → Person is a holder and thus can negotiate the instrument.

No ↓

Is the person in possession the *named payee*?

Yes → Person is a holder and thus can negotiate the instrument.

No ↓

Are all *necessary signatures* (*i.e.*, of payee and any special indorsee) *on the instrument* and *genuine?*

Yes → Person is a holder and thus can negotiate the instrument.

No ↓

Person is not a holder.

IV. HOLDERS IN DUE COURSE

A. INTRODUCTION

Once again, recall that a central theme of Article 3 is the HDC rule: If a negotiable instrument is negotiated to a holder in due course, the HDC takes free of most defenses. Thus on the exam, it is very important to determine whether the holder trying to enforce an instrument is an HDC. Determining HDC status is a two-step process: (i) Is the person a holder? (ii) Does the person hold in due course?

B. HOLDER

A holder is a person in possession of an instrument with the right to enforce the instrument. The instrument must be payable to bearer or to the person in possession and free of forgery.

C. DUE COURSE

"Due course" requires the holder to take for *value*, in *good faith*, and *without notice*.

1. Value

Any one of the following constitutes value:

(i) Performance of the agreed *consideration*;

(ii) Acquisition by the holder of a lien or a *security interest* in the instrument (other than a judicial lien);

(iii) Taking the instrument as *payment of* or security for an *antecedent debt*;

(iv) Trading a *negotiable instrument* for another instrument; or

(v) Giving the instrument in exchange for incurring an *irrevocable obligation* to a third person by the person taking the instrument.

Note: An executory promise is *not* "value," unless it is an irrevocable obligation to a third party.

CMR **Exam Tip** Do not confuse value with consideration for the underlying contract. For example, an antecedent debt is value, but not consideration.

a. Value Need Not Be Equivalent to Face Amount

The value given in exchange for an instrument need not be equivalent to the face amount of the instrument. An instrument purchased at a discount (*e.g.,* a $1,000 promissory note purchased for $900) is sold for *full value* as long as the full price agreed upon has been given.

1) Compare—Partial Failure of Consideration

If one pays less than the agreed-upon value, one becomes a partial HDC in proportion to the percentage of the value paid.

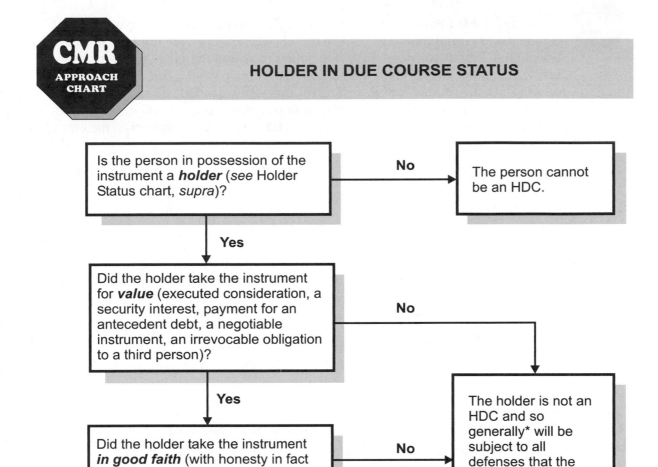

CMR
APPROACH
CHART

HOLDER IN DUE COURSE STATUS

Is the person in possession of the instrument a **holder** (*see* Holder Status chart, *supra*)?

→ **No** → The person cannot be an HDC.

↓ **Yes**

Did the holder take the instrument for **value** (executed consideration, a security interest, payment for an antecedent debt, a negotiable instrument, an irrevocable obligation to a third person)?

→ **No** →

↓ **Yes**

Did the holder take the instrument **in good faith** (with honesty in fact **and** compliance with reasonable commercial standards)?

→ **No** → The holder is not an HDC and so generally* will be subject to all defenses that the maker or drawer may have concerning the instrument.

↓ **Yes**

Did the holder take the instrument **without notice of any claims or defenses** at the time(s) the holder gave value **and** took possession?

→ **No** →

↓ **Yes**

The holder is an HDC and can enforce the instrument subject only to real defenses.

*If the holder does not qualify as an HDC but was a transferee of an HDC, the holder will have the rights of an HDC unless the holder was a party to a fraud involving the instrument.

Exam Tip It is important to understand the difference between a purchase at a discount and partial failure of consideration (which makes the holder a proportional HDC). In the discount case, the holder pays less than the face value of the instrument (*e.g.,* pays $5,000 for a $6,000 note) but pays the *full agreed consideration* ($5,000). The holder is an HDC for full value ($6,000). However, if the holder pays only *part of what he agreed to pay* (*e.g.,* pays $2,500 of the agreed $5,000 for a $6,000 note), the holder is an HDC only *in proportion* to the consideration paid ($3,000—half value).

2) **Time of Payment**
The time of payment can be important because good faith and notice are determined at the time of negotiation or the time of payment, whichever is later.

b. **Bank Deposits**
The bank becomes a holder for "value" to the extent that it permits withdrawals of the amount credited to the depositor's account—using the "first-money-in, first-money-out" rule to determine whether the particular item credited has been reached.

2. **Good Faith**
To be an HDC, the holder must take the instrument in good faith. Good faith means honesty in fact (a subjective test) *and* observance of reasonable commercial standards (an objective test).

3. **Notice to Purchaser**
The holder must purchase the instrument without notice of certain things. Notice includes both actual notice and *reason to know* from facts surrounding the transaction.

a. **Facts Constituting Notice**

1) **Instrument Overdue**
A purchaser has notice that an instrument is *overdue* if: (i) any part of the principal is overdue; (ii) an acceleration has been made; or (iii) more than a reasonable time has elapsed after issue of a demand instrument (for checks, 90 days).

2) **Unauthorized Signature or Alteration**
A person will not be an HDC if she takes the instrument with notice of alterations or unauthorized signatures.

3) **Claims to the Instrument**
Notice of claims to the instrument prevents HDC status. A claim is a property or possessory right to the instrument. Notice that a fiduciary has negotiated the instrument for his own benefit also prevents HDC status.

4) **Defenses or Claims in Recoupment**
Notice of defenses (*e.g.,* infancy, duress) or claims in recoupment by the obligor (which reduce the amount payable) prevent HDC status.

5) **When and How Notice Must Be Received**
To be effective, notice must be received in such time and manner as to give a reasonable opportunity to act on it.

b. Facts Not Constituting Notice

Knowledge of the following facts does not of itself give the purchaser notice:

1) The instrument is *antedated, postdated, or undated*;

2) The instrument was issued in return for an *executory promise*, unless the purchaser has notice that a defense or claim has arisen from the terms thereof;

3) Any party signed for *accommodation*;

4) An *incomplete instrument has been completed*, unless the purchaser has notice of any improper completion;

5) Any person negotiating the instrument was a *fiduciary*, unless the purchaser also knows that the negotiation constituted a breach of trust;

6) That there has been a *default in payment of interest*;

7) There is a *public filing or recording* of a document (*e.g.,* security agreement) concerning the instrument;

8) The instrument was *sold at a discount*; or

9) *Notice of discharge* of a party, other than a discharge in an insolvency proceeding.

4. Transaction Precluding HDC Status

A holder does not become an HDC of an instrument taken by: legal process or purchase at a judicial sale; acquiring it as a successor in interest to an estate or other organization; or purchasing it as part of a bulk transaction not in the regular course of business of the transferor.

5. Time at Which HDC Status Determined

HDC status is determined at the moment the instrument is *negotiated* to the holder *or* when she gives *value*, whichever occurs later. Thus, if the transferee acquires notice of a claim or defense prior to negotiation or the giving of value, she will not qualify as an HDC.

6. Holder of Security Interest

If the holder merely has a security interest in the instrument and the person obligated to pay has a defense or claim against the person who created the security interest, the holder is an HDC only to the extent of the unpaid portion of the secured obligation.

7. Payees as HDCs

A payee might qualify as an HDC, but generally because the payee is involved in the transaction giving rise to the instrument and has dealt with the person he wishes to sue (the maker or drawer), the payee will be subject to that person's defenses. In rare circumstances, a payee could be treated as an HDC, but on the bar exam you generally should assume that the payee is not an HDC.

8. Successors to Holders in Due Course

a. Shelter Rule

A transferee acquires whatever rights her transferor had and thus is said to take "shelter"

in the status of her transferor. The purpose of this rule is to protect the free negotiability of commercial paper.

b.   Exception to Shelter Rule
No HDC rights are given to persons who were *parties to fraud or illegality* affecting the instrument.

c.   HDC Rights and Remote Transferees
Once a person qualifies as an HDC, all subsequent transferees will acquire the same HDC rights, unless they are transferees after the holder failed to obtain HDC rights because she was a party to fraud or illegality.

V.   CLAIMS AND DEFENSES ON NEGOTIABLE INSTRUMENTS

A.   IN GENERAL
An HDC can enforce an instrument subject only to real defenses (*i.e.,* the HDC takes free of personal defenses and claims). Thus, whether an obligated party such as a maker, drawer, or indorser will be forced to pay depends on whether the holder is an HDC and on the nature of the obligated party's defenses. If the holder is not an HDC, the obligated party may assert any of the ordinary contract defenses (*e.g.,* failure of consideration). If the holder is an HDC, the obligated party is limited to so-called *real defenses*.

1.   "Claim" Defined
A claim is an affirmative right to a negotiable instrument because of superior ownership.

B.   REAL DEFENSES
Real defenses may be asserted against both HDC and non-HDC transferees of a questioned instrument.

1.   Forgery

a.   Forgery of Names Necessary to Title
If the signature of the payee or any special indorsee was forged, generally no subsequent taker can be an HDC because no one can obtain the right to enforce necessary to qualify as a "holder." However, if the person whose name was forged ratifies the unauthorized signature or is estopped from denying it, subsequent takers can qualify as HDCs.

b.   Forgery of Names Not Necessary to Title
The forgery of any name other than the payee or a special indorsee (*e.g.,* maker, drawer, acceptor, or indorsers on a bearer instrument) does not affect the right to enforce; subsequent takers may qualify as HDCs if they meet the usual tests. Even so, a party whose name was either forged or placed on the instrument by a nonagent has a real defense of unauthorized signature unless he has ratified the signature or is estopped from denying it.

2.   Fraud in the Factum (Real Fraud)
Fraud that causes the obligor to sign an instrument *without knowledge or reasonable*

opportunity to learn of its character or essential terms (*e.g.,* obligor signs what he thinks is an autograph book, but which is really a promissory note) is a real defense. Other fraud (most types, such as when the obligor gives a promissory note in exchange for a fraudulent promise) is only a personal defense.

3. Alteration of Instrument
In certain circumstances, an HDC may be able to collect only the original amount (*i.e.,* not the altered amount), so that the alteration is a partial "real" defense. In other situations, the HDC may be able to collect on the instrument as altered. (*See* IX.K., *infra.*)

CMR **Exam Tip** Remember that there is a difference between alteration (changing the terms that the maker or drawer inserted in the instrument) and unauthorized completion (filling in blanks left by the maker or drawer). Generally, the maker will not be liable for the altered amount but will be liable for the full amount of the unauthorized completion.

4. Incapacity to Contract
If under state law the party lacks capacity to contract (*e.g.,* persons declared incompetent by judicial proceedings), and the contract is thus rendered *void*, the incapacity constitutes a real defense. If the obligations of the incompetent are merely voidable at the option of the incompetent, the incompetency is a personal defense and cannot be raised against an HDC.

5. Infancy
Infancy is a real defense if it is a defense in a simple contract action under state law. If the state does not make such contracts *void or voidable*, it is only a personal defense.

6. Illegality
If illegality in the underlying transaction renders the obligation *void*, it is a real defense, even if the HDC was not involved. If the contract is merely voidable, the defense is personal.

7. Duress
It is a real defense if one party acts involuntarily in a contract situation under *extreme duress*, *e.g.,* a gun pointed at one's head.

8. Discharge in Insolvency Proceedings
Discharge of debt in any proceeding intended to liquidate or rehabilitate a person's estate is a real defense.

9. Statute of Limitations
The running of the statute of limitations is a valid defense against an HDC. ***Three years*** applies to actions: (i) on unaccepted drafts (after date of dishonor; *see* VII.B.6., *infra*); (ii) against issuers/acceptors of cashier's checks, certified checks, etc. (after demand); (iii) for conversion; (iv) for breach of warranty; and (v) to enforce other Article 3 rights (after accrual). ***Six years*** applies to actions: (i) on notes payable at a definite time or on demand (after due date or demand for payment); and (ii) on certificates of deposit (after demand for payment, but the period does not start to run until the stated due date).

10. Accommodation (Suretyship) Defenses

An accommodation party is, in effect, a surety. By signing the instrument, she incurs liability without being a direct beneficiary. If an HDC knows of the accommodation, he takes subject to the surety's defenses (*i.e.,* discharge to the extent of loss caused by: (i) extension of due date; (ii) material modification of obligation; or (iii) impairment of collateral).

11. Discharges Known to HDC

An HDC takes subject to any discharge of which he had notice. "Discharge" means discharging events named in Article 3 and other acts that would discharge an obligation to pay under a simple contract. If the HDC has no notice of discharge (from the face of the instrument or otherwise), discharge is a personal defense.

CMR | **Exam Tip** | The real defenses can be remembered by using the mnemonic "FAIDS": *F*orgery, *F*raud, *A*lteration, *A*djudicated incompetency; *I*nfancy, *I*llegality, *D*uress, *D*ischarge (by insolvency proceedings or that otherwise are known by the HDC); *S*tatute of limitations, and *S*uretyship.

C. PERSONAL DEFENSES

Personal defenses cannot be asserted against one having rights of an HDC, but any transferee of a negotiable instrument without HDC rights takes the instrument subject to all personal defenses, which include every defense available in simple contract actions.

CMR | **Exam Tip** | Probably the most common personal defense on the bar exam is that the contract out of which the commercial paper arose was not properly or fully performed. Remember that this defense cannot be used against an HDC, but it can be used against a non-HDC.

1. Consideration and Negotiable Instruments

Negotiable instruments must be supported by consideration, and the lack thereof is a defense, except against an HDC. In cases of partial failure of consideration, the failure is a pro tanto defense.

2. Claims or Defenses of Another

Generally one must rely on one's own defenses and cannot use the claims or defenses of a third party as a defense. Under the "payment rule," the liability to pay is discharged by payment to a person entitled to enforce the instrument unless another person has an enforceable claim to the instrument and: (i) payment is made with knowledge that it is prohibited by an injunction; (ii) the paying party has received indemnity from a person with a claim to the instrument for refusal to pay the person entitled to enforce (inapplicable to cashier's checks, certified checks, etc.); or (iii) the paying party knows that the instrument is stolen and that the person paid is in wrongful possession.

a. Theft Exception

A defense that the non-HDC acquired the instrument by theft and the person holding the instrument is in wrongful possession must be raised if known by the person paying, or payment will not result in discharge of liability.

COMMERCIAL PAPER DEFENSES	
<u>REAL DEFENSES</u>	<u>PERSONAL DEFENSES</u>
May be raised against HDC	May *not* be raised against HDC
(Mnemonic "FAIDS")	
F } Fraud in the factum Forgery	Simple contract defenses (*e.g.,* lack of consideration, failure of consideration, breach of warranty, fraud in the inducement, etc.)
A } Alteration Adjudicated insanity	
I } Infancy Illegality	
D } Duress Discharge through bankruptcy Discharges known by HDC	Must be one's *own* defenses except the payor must raise the defense of theft if known
S } Suretyship defenses Statute of limitations	

(CMR SUMMARY CHART)

VI. TRIAL PROCEDURE

A. IN GENERAL
Article 3 specifies the trial procedure to be followed in negotiable paper cases.

B. WHO MAY ENFORCE?
An instrument may be enforced by: (i) a holder; (ii) a nonholder in possession with rights of a holder (*e.g.,* a subrogee); or (iii) a person not in possession but entitled to enforce (*e.g.,* lost, stolen, or destroyed instruments).

C. BURDEN OF PROOF
A prima facie case requires proof that: (i) signatures are genuine; and (ii) the person presenting the instrument is entitled to enforce it.

1. Proof of Signatures—Presumption of Validity
Validity of a signature must be specifically denied or it is admitted.

2. Proof of Defenses

A plaintiff who proves a prima facie case is entitled to payment unless the defendant raises a defense or claim. If a defense or claim is raised, the plaintiff can cut off defenses by establishing HDC status.

3. Where Instrument Is Lost, Destroyed, or Stolen

If a check is lost, destroyed, or stolen, a person entitled to enforce may maintain an action if she can prove ownership, terms, and the facts that prevent production of the instrument, but the court has discretion to require protection (such as a bond) to indemnify the defendant against other claims.

D. ACTION FOR CONVERSION

A person entitled to possession may bring an action for conversion of the instrument, except for issuers, payees, and indorsees who never received delivery.

E. VOUCHING IN

It is possible to "vouch in" parties to an instrument who may be liable to the party sued. If a defendant to a suit on an instrument has a right of recourse against someone else if he is required to pay, then he may give that third person written notice of the litigation. If, after receiving notice, the third person fails to appear and defend, he will be bound by any determination of fact common to a suit against him by the party giving the notice. A person "vouched in" may also "vouch in" persons liable to him.

VII. LIABILITY OF PARTIES

A. INTRODUCTION

A number of parties to a negotiable instrument may be held liable simply because their names appear on the instrument. Generally, no one may be held liable unless her signature or the signature of an authorized representative is on the instrument.

 Exam Tip   Many bar exam questions deal with liability of the parties on an instrument. You should first identify the status of each party (*e.g.,* maker, indorser, etc.), and then discuss each party's liability. If the fact situation is complex, chart the transfer chain.

B. PARTIES WHO MAY BE LIABLE ON AN INSTRUMENT

1. Maker of Note, Issuer of Cashier's Check

By signing her name, the maker of a note makes a contract to pay the instrument according to its terms at the time it is issued. The promise is unconditional, but proper defenses may be raised. Similar liability is imposed on the issuer of a cashier's check.

2. Indorser—Secondary Liability

An indorser may sign an instrument (usually on its backside) for any of a number of purposes: (i) negotiating the instrument; (ii) restricting payment; or (iii) incurring indorser's liability. An indorser is considered to be secondarily liable (*i.e.,* a person entitled to enforce the instrument looks first to the drawee or maker). Indorsers may be held liable on contract or warranty theories.

a. **Basic Obligation—Indorser's Contract**

The indorser's contract—the basic obligation to pay according to the terms of the instrument at the time of indorsement—arises merely from the indorser's signing her name on the instrument, although the obligation may be negated if the indorser includes the words "without recourse" with her indorsement. However, before a holder can look to an indorser for payment, the holder must fulfill three prerequisites: presentment, dishonor, and notice of dishonor.

1) **Presentment**

Presentment is a demand for payment made by a person entitled to enforce the instrument. Presentment is usually made on the drawee of a draft or the maker of a note. Presentment may be made by any commercially reasonable means.

a) **Checks**

An indorser's liability on a **check** is discharged unless the check is presented for payment or given to a depositary bank for collection within 30 days after the indorsement.

b) **When Presentment Excused**

Presentment is excused if: (i) the person entitled to present cannot with reasonable diligence do so; (ii) the maker has repudiated the obligation to pay or is dead or insolvent; (iii) by the instrument's terms, presentment is unnecessary; (iv) the obligor has waived presentment; or (v) the drawer instructed the drawee not to pay or the drawee was not obligated to pay.

2) **Dishonor**

Dishonor occurs when the maker or drawee does not pay within the allowed time after presentment. Generally, demand instruments other than checks are considered dishonored if not paid on the date presented.

a) **Time Instruments**

Most time instruments (*i.e.,* instruments payable at a particular time) payable at or through a bank are dishonored if not paid on the date they become payable or on the date of presentment, whichever is later. Time notes not involving a bank are dishonored if not paid on the date they are payable.

b) **Checks**

If a check is presented for other than immediate payment over the counter (*e.g.,* when you deposit your whole paycheck into your checking account without receiving cash back), it is dishonored if the bank returns the check or sends written notice that it is dishonoring **before**: (i) **final payment** (which usually occurs after settlement through a clearinghouse) or (ii) the bank's **midnight deadline** (*i.e.,* midnight of the next banking day after the day the instrument is deposited).

3) **Notice of Dishonor**

An indorser is not liable on an instrument unless she is given timely notice that the instrument has been dishonored. **Notice of dishonor** may be given by any commercially reasonable means, and generally must be given **within 30 days** after

dishonor (or 30 days after a collecting bank's midnight deadline if the instrument was taken by the bank for collection). *Note:* Notice of dishonor need not be given to the maker of a note or the drawer of a draft.

a) When Delay in Giving Notice Is Excused
Delay in giving notice is excused if caused by circumstances beyond the control of a notifier who exercised reasonable diligence after the cause of the delay ceased to exist.

b) When Notice Entirely Excused
Notice of dishonor is excused entirely if: (i) the terms of the instrument make it unnecessary; or (ii) the obligor waives notice.

4) Multiple Indorsers
If there are several indorsers, any one indorser is liable to any holder or later indorser of the instrument for the *full amount* that the instrument stated was payable at the time the indorser indorsed.

b. Warranty Liability of Indorser
When an indorser transfers an instrument for consideration, the indorser becomes liable as a transferor. (*See* below.)

3. Transferor—Five Transfer Warranties
Warranties are made by any person who (i) transfers (*i.e.,* any movement except issuance or presentment) the instrument (ii) for consideration. Warranties run to *all subsequent holders if the transfer is by indorsement*, but run only to the *immediate transferee if the transfer is not by indorsement*. Presentment, notice of dishonor, etc., are *irrelevant* to warranty liability. Other than on checks, warranty liability can be negated by a transferor if she places words to that effect on the instrument. In general, a transferor warrants that:

a. She is *entitled to enforce* the instrument (*i.e.,* that all indorsements necessary to the chain of title are genuine and that the transferor is a proper person, in her own right or as agent, to make presentment and obtain payment);

b. All *signatures are authentic and authorized*;

c. The instrument has *not been altered*;

d. *No defense* or claim of any party is good against her; and

e. She has *no knowledge of any insolvency proceedings* that have been instituted against the maker, acceptor, or drawer.

CMR **Exam Tip** Don't forget that consideration is important here. A transferor who gratuitously transfers the instrument warrants nothing, although this does not shield her from the contract liability of an indorser if she indorses (*i.e.,* the obligation to pay the instrument according to its terms when the indorser signed if there is presentment, dishonor, and notice of dishonor).

CMR **Exam Tip** When an exam question requires you to consider the liability of an indorser, don't forget to discuss **both** her **contract** liability **and** her **warranty** liability and **why** either or both are applicable or inapplicable. Show the examiners you know the presentment-dishonor-notice of dishonor trilogy **and** the applicable transfer warranties.

4. Drawer—Secondary Liability

Generally, if a draft is dishonored, the drawer is obliged to pay according to the draft's terms when the drawer signed (or if incomplete, according to its terms as completed). A drawer, like an indorser, has secondary liability. However, if a draft is **accepted by a bank** (*see* 6., *infra*), the drawer is discharged and cannot be held liable if the bank fails to pay.

5. Drawee

The drawee of a draft cannot have any liability unless and until she signs the instrument (and thus becomes an acceptor; *see* 6., *infra*). Thus, a **holder generally cannot force a drawee to pay** out on a draft.

a. Duties of Drawee Bank to Customer

When a bank is the drawee (*e.g.*, checks), the bank may be **liable to its customer** for failure to accept the draft, because a contractual relationship exists which imposes duties on both bank and customer. A bank is obliged to honor its customer's check if sufficient funds are on deposit to cover the draft. A bank may choose to honor a check even if the customer has insufficient funds, in which case the customer is liable to the bank for the overdraft. If a bank wrongfully dishonors a draft, the customer may collect damages for harm proximately caused by the wrongful dishonor. Banks may refuse to pay checks over six months old, unless again ordered to pay by the drawer.

1) When Bank Cannot Charge the Account

The bank must honor a check as drawn. Therefore, it cannot charge the account: (i) if there is no order by the depositor (where the drawer's signature is forged); (ii) for more money than the original order (where a third party altered the amount); (iii) if the bank pays the wrong person (*e.g.*, the forger of the payee's or indorsee's signature); or (iv) if the item is postdated and the customer notifies the bank of the postdating (the bank cannot pay it before the stated date). If the bank violates these principles, the customer is entitled to a recredit on her account.

b. Duties of Customer to Bank

The bank can successfully charge the customer's account if it can show that it suffered a loss because the customer negligently failed to discover, and notify the bank of, any unauthorized payments on his bank statement resulting from an alteration or forgery of his signature. The customer may answer such proof by showing that the bank was negligent in paying the item. The loss will then be **allocated** between the bank and the customer **in proportion to the fault of each**. (*See* E.4., *infra*, for further discussion.)

c. Death of Customer

The customer's death does not revoke the bank's authority to pay a check until the bank (i) knows of the death and (ii) has a reasonable time to act on the knowledge. Even with such knowledge, the bank may continue paying checks for **10 days** after the date of death unless someone claiming an interest in the account orders that payment be stopped.

d. Subrogation

A bank that pays a check is subrogated to the rights of the person it pays against the customer. Thus, if a bank pays an HDC, it can assume the position of an HDC in attempting to charge its customer's account.

e. Stop Payment Orders

Under the U.C.C., an *oral stop payment order* is effective for *14 days* and then lapses unless confirmed in writing within that period. A *written stop payment order* is binding for *six months*. The bank must be given reasonable time to act and is not obliged to honor stop payment orders on cashier's checks. If the bank pays an item in spite of a stop payment order, the *customer* has the burden of proving that a loss has occurred and the amount of the loss. Thus, if there is an HDC in the chain of transferees of the item, the customer cannot recover—since even if payment had been stopped, the customer would have had to pay the HDC.

f. Bank's Right to Recover Payment from Party Paid

If the bank erroneously pays out on a forged instrument to an HDC, it generally may not recover back from the party paid unless there has been a breach of a transfer warranty (*see* 3., *supra*) or a presentment warranty (*see* VIII.C.1., *infra*).

6. Acceptor

An acceptor (usually, but not necessarily, a drawee bank) signs a draft and thereby becomes primarily bound to pay the instrument. In essence, the acceptor contracts to pay the draft when due in accordance with its terms when accepted. Accepted drafts are often required when the payee does not want to rely on the credit of an unfamiliar drawer. The draft is usually presented to the acceptor, which signs the draft (and usually charges its customer's account at that time) and returns it to the presenting party. This process is called *presentment for acceptance*. Acceptance may be sought at any time by any party entitled to enforce the instrument.

a. Certification of a Check

Certification is the acceptance of a check by the bank on which it was drawn. Certification *discharges the drawer and all prior indorsers*. The bank does not have to certify a check, absent some special agreement with the customer, but if the bank chooses to certify, it puts its own credit on the line. A bank will therefore charge its customer's account immediately upon certification, rather than waiting for the check to be paid. Failure to certify may constitute a dishonor.

7. Accommodation Parties

An accommodation party signs an instrument to lend his credit to another party to the instrument. He is, in essence, a surety. The accommodation party may sign in any capacity (*e.g.,* as a co-maker or as an indorser). If an accommodation party pays the instrument, he will have an action on the instrument against the party accommodated, irrespective of the parties' formal positions on the instrument.

a. Liability

An accommodation party is never liable to the party accommodated. He is liable to other parties in the capacity in which he signed. An HDC's awareness of accommodation status allows the accommodation party to raise his suretyship defenses, but does not release him from his liability as maker, indorser, etc.

b.   Proof of Accommodation Status

A person signing an instrument is presumed to be an accommodation party, and there is notice of accommodation status, *if* the signature is anomalous (*i.e.,* by a person who is not a holder) or otherwise indicates that the signer is acting as surety or guarantor. To give the accommodation party the benefit of any discharge relating to his character as surety, parol evidence is generally allowed to show accommodation, *except* when the holder is an HDC without notice of the accommodation.

c.   Collection Guarantee

"Collection guaranteed" means the signer will be liable *only if*: (i) the person entitled to enforce has reduced his claim to judgment against the maker or acceptor and execution is returned unsatisfied, or (ii) seeking judgment would be futile (because of insolvency, etc.).

CMR SUMMARY CHART

LIABILITY OF THE PARTIES

Party	Liability to Holder	Notice of Dishonor Required?
Maker	Primary	No
Drawer	Secondary*	No
Drawee	None*	No
Acceptor (including certifier of a check)	Primary	Yes, if acceptor is a bank
Indorser	Secondary	Yes
Transferor	Secondary	No
Accommodation Party	Depends on capacity in which party signed	Depends on capacity in which party signed

*If the drawee signs the instrument, the drawee becomes an acceptor and is primarily liable on the instrument. The drawer's liability is discharged.

C. EFFECT OF PERSONS SIGNING JOINTLY

If parties to an instrument sign jointly, they have *joint and several* liability on the instrument, and thus either one or both can be sued for the entire amount due. If one party pays more than his share, he generally has a right of contribution against the other jointly liable party. A release of one jointly liable party by a third party does not affect the right of contribution.

D. EFFECT OF REPRESENTATIVE OR AGENT SIGNING

Generally, no one is liable on an instrument unless her signature or the signature of an authorized agent appears on the instrument.

1. Liability of Represented Person ("Principal")

If a representative ("agent") signs her own name or the name of the principal, the principal is bound if the agent had authority to sign. The principal may be bound even if the agent lacked authority in cases of: (i) *ratification* (where the principal adopts the signature, appropriates benefits, or fails to deny the signature's validity); or (ii) *estoppel* (where the principal's negligence contributed to the making of the unauthorized signature). Estoppel operates in favor of one who is otherwise an HDC or one who pays the instrument in good faith, applying reasonable commercial standards.

Note that a principal can be held liable even if her signature does not appear on the instrument.

2. Liability of Representative ("Agent")

Liability of the agent depends on whether the agency and the principal's identity were disclosed.

a. Agent Signs Principal's Name Only

If the agent signs only her principal's name, the principal will be liable if the agent was authorized, but the agent is not liable because neither her name nor her authorized agent's name appears on the instrument.

b. Agent Signs Own Name But Discloses Principal

If the agent signs her own name with the principal's authority, the agent is not bound if the signature shows it was made on behalf of the principal identified in the instrument (*e.g.,* signature "Blue Corp., by Joan Smith, Treasurer"; Smith not personally liable).

c. Agent Signs Own Name But Does Not Disclose Principal's Name and/or Agency Relationship

If the signature does not show it was made in a representative capacity or the principal is not identified in the instrument, the agent is liable to HDCs who take without notice (but not to non-HDCs if she can prove the original parties did not intend her to be liable).

d. Check Cases

An agent with authority who signs her name to her principal's check is not liable if it is drawn on the principal's account and indicates the principal's identity.

E. EFFECT OF UNAUTHORIZED SIGNATURES

Generally, an unauthorized signature is ineffective as the signature of the person whose name is signed but is *effective as the signature of the signer*. The unauthorized signer therefore assumes

all obligations to any party who gave value for the instrument. However, the Code specifies *five* circumstances in which a forgery or unauthorized signature will be **validated** because the person whose name is used has done something to preclude her from raising the issue.

1. **Fictitious Payee**

   Carelessness of a maker or drawer in issuing an instrument may make forgery of the payee's name likely. In such cases, the resulting forgery is effective to pass the right to enforce the instrument to later transferees.

   a. **Issuance to Imposter**

   If a person pretends to be someone else (or pretends to be an agent) and induces the drawer or maker to issue an instrument, the forgery of the payee's name (or a name substantially similar to the payee's) will pass the right to enforce against the drawer or maker.

   b. **Issuance to Payee Not Intended to Have Interest in Instrument**

   If an instrument is payable to a fictitious payee (*i.e.,* someone who does not exist) or to a person to whom payment was not really intended (*e.g.,* where an employee dupes an employer into signing a check payable to a supplier to whom no money is owed): (i) any person in possession of the instrument is a holder; and (ii) an indorsement in a name similar to that of the named payee is effective as an indorsement as to anyone who takes in good faith and for value.

   c. **Requirement of Ordinary Care**

   Persons paying or taking fictitious payee instruments must use ordinary care in doing so. Otherwise, they are liable to the extent that the failure to exercise care contributed to the loss.

2. **Fraudulent Indorsements by Employees**

   If an employer entrusts an employee with responsibility for an instrument (*e.g.,* an employer's cashier) and the employee fraudulently indorses, the indorsement is effective. (Again, the taker or payor must exercise ordinary care.)

3. **Failure to Exercise Ordinary Care—Negligence Rule**

   If a person fails to exercise ordinary care and that failure substantially contributes to an alteration or forged signature, that person is precluded from raising the alteration or forgery against a person who paid the instrument in good faith or took it for value or for collection.

   a. **What Constitutes "Negligence"?**

   Negligent actions include: (i) leaving blanks or spaces on the instrument; (ii) mailing the instrument to someone with the same name as the payee; and (iii) failing to follow internal procedures designed to avoid forgeries.

   b. **Later Parties Not Completely Protected**

   A prior person's failure to exercise due care does not relieve later parties from the same standard. Loss may be allocated between the parties based on the share of the loss resulting from each party's negligence.

4. **Bank Statement Rule**

   a. **Customer's Duty to Examine Statement**

   Failure to examine one's bank statement is a form of negligence that can preclude the

defenses of forgery and alteration. The customer must examine her own signatures and the amount of each check. If the customer fails to promptly report a forgery or alteration, she is precluded from complaining that the item was not "properly payable." Moreover, if the statement has been available for a reasonable time (not more than 30 days), and she fails to report the forgery or alteration, the customer is estopped from demanding recredit on other items forged or altered by the same wrongdoer and subsequently paid (until notice is given).

b. Result Where Bank Is Also Negligent
If the bank fails to exercise ordinary care in paying a check, the loss is allocated between the bank and the customer, but if the bank did not pay in good faith, the bank bears the entire loss.

c. Time Limits
A customer may not assert an alteration or a forgery of his signature if he does not notify the bank within *one year* after the bank has made the instrument available to him. A customer may not assert a forged indorsement more than *three years* after the cause of action accrues.

5. Estoppel by Certification
Because a bank has the opportunity for checking identification and bona fides if it certifies a check, it is estopped from claiming that the named payee was not the original payee as against subsequent parties.

UNAUTHORIZED SIGNATURES

General Rule: Forged signatures are valid only as the signature of the *forger* and are invalid as the signature of the named payee.

Exceptions: Forgery will be valid as the name forged when:

(i) *Fictitious payee's signature forged*—issuance to impostor or to a payee not intended to have an interest in the instrument.

(ii) *Entrusted employee forges signature*—includes agents, not just employees.

(iii) *Negligence contributes to forgery*—for example, leaving blank spaces or mailing to person with the same name as the intended payee.

(iv) *Bank statement rule violated*—failure to discover forgeries and alterations within a reasonable time after receiving bank statement.

(v) *Bank certifies*—estoppel by certification.

However, if the taker fails to exercise ordinary care, the loss generally will be shared according to the negligence of each party.

F. EFFECT OF ALTERATION AND INCOMPLETE INSTRUMENTS

An alteration is an unauthorized change that purports to modify the obligation of any party. Its effect depends on whether the alterer's intent was fraudulent or nonfraudulent.

1. Nonfraudulent Alteration

Nonfraudulent alterations do not discharge parties, and the instrument may be enforced according to its original terms.

2. Fraudulent Alteration

Unless the party assents or is estopped from asserting the alteration, a fraudulent alteration discharges all parties, *except* that a payor bank, a drawee paying a fraudulently altered instrument, or an HDC may enforce the instrument: (i) according to its original terms; or (ii) in the case of unauthorized completion, according to its terms as completed.

VIII. PAYMENT

A. INTRODUCTION

General issues are: (i) When can the maker or acceptor safely pay? (ii) What if the maker or acceptor pays by mistake? and (iii) What if an acceptor finds she should not have accepted?

B. WHEN CAN MAKER SAFELY PAY AND AVOID FURTHER LIABILITY?

1. Determine If Party Seeking Payment Is a Holder

The maker must first determine that the party seeking payment is a holder. If he is, the maker may safely pay him, even if the maker knows that a third party has a claim to the instrument. If the maker pays someone who is not a holder, she will have to pay the true holder when he comes along.

2. Actions of Third Party to Protect Claim

For a third party to protect his claim to the instrument, he can (i) offer to indemnify the maker or acceptor in an amount deemed sufficient by the maker or acceptor while the other two parties fight it out or (ii) seek an injunction in an action in which the maker or acceptor, the holder, and the third party are parties.

3. Do Not Pay Where There Has Been a Theft

The maker or acceptor may not safely pay the holder of an instrument if she knows that the holder acquired the instrument by theft or that he holds through one who acquired it by theft. If the holder is an HDC, the maker may pay him.

C. FINALITY OF PAYMENT—RECOVERY FOR INSTRUMENTS MISTAKENLY PAID OR ACCEPTED

Payment of a negotiable instrument is final, except that: (i) the payor can pursue those who breach transfer warranties; and (ii) the rule of finality operates only in favor of persons who took for value and in good faith and those who in good faith change their position in reliance on the

payment or acceptance. Thus, if the person who receives payment is not one of the persons described in (ii) above, an action to recover the payment can be maintained.

1. Presentment Warranties

As noted, the "payment is final" rule does not affect a payor's right to sue for breach of a presentment warranty. There are two sets of presentment warranties: (i) those made to drawees on unaccepted drafts; and (ii) those made to payors of other instruments.

a. Presentment Warranties on Unaccepted Draft

A drawee (*e.g.*, a bank) can recover for breach of a presentment warranty, even from HDCs and persons who detrimentally relied on payment. On unaccepted drafts, persons obtaining payment and previous transferors warrant that:

(i) The warrantor is *entitled to enforce* the draft or is authorized by one who is (in essence a warranty of "good title"—that there are no unauthorized or missing indorsements);

(ii) The draft *has not been altered*; and

(iii) The warrantor has *no knowledge that the drawer's signature is unauthorized*.

Note that a forged indorser's signature destroys "good title," but a forged drawer's signature does not.

CMR **Exam Tip** Note the difference in result between a forged drawer's signature and a forged indorser's signature. If a bank pays out on a forged drawer's signature, payment is final and the bank cannot recover the money back from the party paid because no presentment warranty is broken (the forgery is treated as a valid signature *of the forger* and thus the presenter had the right to enforce the forger's instrument as against the forger). But if the bank pays out on a forged indorser's signature, a presentment warranty is broken (the presenter did not have the right to enforce against the drawer because of the forgery).

b. Presentment Warranties on Other Instruments

On other instruments presented to a party obligated to pay, only the warranty that one is entitled to enforce (or represents one who is) applies, because the drawer, maker, or acceptor should know if his signature is forged or if the instrument is altered.

c. Who Makes the Warranties?

The warranties are made by: (i) any person who obtains payment or acceptance, and (ii) any prior transferor. Note that these warranties on presentment are similar, but not identical to, the transfer warranties made by an indorser. The warranties are made to any person who in good faith pays or accepts.

CMR
COMPARISON
CHART

COMMERCIAL PAPER WARRANTIES

The Transfer Warranties	The Presentment Warranties	
	Unaccepted Draft	**Other Instruments**
1. Entitled to enforce	1. Entitled to enforce	1. Entitled to enforce
2. Signatures are authentic and authorized	2. No knowledge that drawer's signature is unauthorized	
3. No alteration	3. No alteration	
4. No defenses are good against the transferor		
5. No knowledge of insolvency proceedings (against maker, acceptor, or drawer of unaccepted draft)		

IX. DISCHARGE

A. IN GENERAL

An instrument itself never dies by discharge because discharge *of a party* is a personal defense, which an HDC can cut off. No discharge of any party is effective against a subsequent HDC unless the HDC has notice of the defense when he takes the instrument.

1. Effect of Instrument on Obligation for Which It Was Taken

a. Certified, Cashier's, or Teller's Check Generally Discharges Obligation
If a certified, cashier's, or teller's check is given to fulfill an obligation, the obligation is *discharged* as if cash were given, but this does not affect any indorser liability of the obligor.

b. Other Instruments Generally Suspend Obligation
If any other negotiable instrument is given to fulfill an obligation, the underlying obligation is *suspended* until the instrument is paid or certified (which results in discharge) or is dishonored. If the instrument is dishonored, the person seeking payment can sue on the instrument. If he is the obligee on the obligation for which the instrument was given, he may choose instead to sue on the underlying obligation.

    c.   **Lost, Stolen, or Destroyed Instruments**
If the obligee is entitled to enforce the instrument, but is no longer in possession because of loss, theft, or destruction, the obligation remains ***suspended*** to the extent of the instrument, and the obligee is limited to enforcement of the instrument.

    d.   **Tenders "in Full Satisfaction"—Accord and Satisfaction**
If a claim is unliquidated or subject to dispute, the claim can be discharged in full if the person against whom the claim is asserted in good faith tenders an instrument that conspicuously states that it is tendered in full satisfaction of the claim (*e.g.,* the memo line says "Payment in Full") and the claimant obtains payment of the instrument. However, if the claimant is an organization, it can, by notice sent before the instrument is tendered, require that such instruments be tendered to a designated person, office, or place to be effective. If the claimant sends no such notice or is not an organization, the discharge will not be effective if the claimant returns the payment within 90 days.

B.   **DISCHARGE BY PAYMENT**
The liability of a party is discharged to the extent of her payment (or satisfaction) even if made with knowledge of a claim of another person to the instrument, ***unless*** the claimant indemnifies the payor or enjoins the payment. On the holder's request, payment may be made prior to maturity, and need not be made in good faith and without notice that the title of the holder is defective, ***but*** there is no discharge if the payor knows the instrument is stolen and pays a person she knows is in wrongful possession.

C.   **DISCHARGE BY TENDER OF PAYMENT**
The effect of tender is governed by contract law principles. Tender of the amount due on an instrument discharges any duty to pay interest after the due date. Any person with a right of recourse against the tendering party is discharged to the extent of the amount tendered.

D.   **DISCHARGE BY CANCELLATION OR RENUNCIATION**
Even without consideration, persons entitled to enforce may discharge a party through: (i) intentional voluntary acts (*e.g.,* surrendering or destroying an instrument or striking out a signature); or (ii) renouncing rights in a signed writing. But note that such discharge is not effective against a subsequent HDC without notice.

E.   **DISCHARGE BY IMPAIRMENT OF RECOURSE OR COLLATERAL—SURETYSHIP DEFENSES**
Discharge of an obligated party does not discharge an indorser or accommodation party with a right of recourse against the obligated party, but impairment of collateral, extension of the due date, or other material modification of an obligation discharges such parties to the extent of the impairment or the loss caused by the modification. In cases of impairment of collateral or time extension, the loss must be proven. For other modifications, loss is presumed.

    1.   **What Constitutes Impairment?**
Collateral is impaired if: (i) a security interest is not perfected or otherwise filed; (ii) collateral is released without obtaining substitute collateral; (iii) there is failure to perform acts required to preserve the collateral's value; or (iv) there is failure to dispose of collateral as the law requires.

2. **Limitations on Discharge**

An accommodation party is not discharged unless the person entitled to enforce knows of the accommodation. Parties who consent to the basis of the discharge or who waive suretyship or impairment defenses are not discharged.

F. DISCHARGE BY REACQUISITION

Upon reacquisition (transfer to a former holder), the reacquirer may cancel indorsements made between the time she formerly held the instrument and the present. Cancellation discharges such indorsers as against subsequent holders, including HDCs. Reacquisition automatically cancels the intervening indorsers' liability to the reacquirer.

G. DISCHARGE BY ANY ACT THAT WILL DISCHARGE A SIMPLE CONTRACT

Parties are discharged from liabilities to other parties on an instrument by acts or agreements that would discharge obligations to pay money under a simple contract.

H. DISCHARGE BY DELAY IN PRESENTMENT OF A CHECK

If a check is not presented for payment or given to a depositary bank within 30 days after the indorsement, the *indorser* is discharged. If a check is not presented for payment or given to a depositary bank for collection within 30 days after its date and the delay deprives the drawer of funds to pay the obligation (*e.g.,* bank goes bankrupt), the *drawer* is discharged to the extent of the loss if he assigns his rights against the drawee to the party entitled to enforce.

I. DISCHARGE BY FAILURE TO GIVE NOTICE OF DISHONOR

If notice of dishonor is required and not given, the indorser is discharged from his indorsement obligation. Drawers and makers usually are not entitled to notice.

J. DISCHARGE BY ACCEPTANCE OF A DRAFT BY A BANK

If a draft is accepted by a bank after indorsement, the indorser is discharged. If a draft is accepted by a bank, the drawer is discharged.

K. DISCHARGE BY ALTERATION

Fraudulent alterations discharge every party obligated on the instrument unless a party assents or is estopped from asserting the alteration, but HDCs may enforce according to the original terms (or terms as completed in cases of fraudulent completion).

X. STATUS OF BANK IN COLLECTION PROCESS

Article 4 of the U.C.C. covers bank deposits and collections. Unless clearly to the contrary, a bank is an agent for collection, and risk of loss is on the depositor. If the bank advances money, it has a security interest in instruments and is an HDC to that extent. Thus, a bank is an agent when it wants to be and a purchaser when it needs to be (*i.e.,* the bank almost never loses). A bank that has made provisional settlement of a check deposited by a customer may charge back the credit if the deposited check is dishonored before final settlement.

CONFLICT OF LAWS

TABLE OF CONTENTS

CONFLICT OF LAWS

I. WHAT COURT CAN DECIDE THE CASE?

The first step in a conflicts analysis is to establish whether the court deciding the case has proper jurisdiction. This issue is addressed in your civil procedure materials, and is not specifically covered below.

II. RECOGNITION OF FOREIGN JUDGMENTS

A. FULL FAITH AND CREDIT OF STATE JUDGMENTS

Consider three problem areas: (i) Have the full faith and credit *requirements* been met? (ii) Are there any *defenses* to full faith and credit? (iii) What are the *effects* of recognizing a sister state judgment, and who will be bound by it?

1. Full Faith and Credit Requirements

(i) There must have been *proper jurisdiction* in the rendering court. (ii) The judgment must be *on the merits*. (iii) The judgment must be *final*.

CMR **Exam Tip** In determining whether the full faith and credit requirements have been met, remember that this issue is determined according to the law of the state that *rendered* the judgment.

a. Proper Jurisdiction

The judgment sought to be enforced must have been rendered by a court with proper jurisdiction over both the parties and the subject matter. An exception exists where the bootstrap doctrine applies. If the question of jurisdiction was fully and fairly litigated in the original action, that determination itself is res judicata and entitled to full faith and credit even if erroneous.

b. Judgment "On the Merits"

A judgment must be on the merits to be entitled to full faith and credit. A judgment for the defendant is not on the merits if it is based on the lack of jurisdiction over the defendant, the plaintiff's lack of capacity to bring suit, misjoinder of parties or causes of action, improper venue, or time bars such as the statute of limitations.

Default and consent judgments give rise to merger and bar, and are thus deemed to be on the merits for the full faith and credit purposes of recognition of the judgment. They do not give rise to collateral estoppel.

If a demurrer is sustained because of the plaintiff's failure to state a cause of action, the judgment is on the merits only if the plaintiff cannot amend to allege a cause of action.

c. Judgment Must Be Final

Only final judgments are entitled to full faith and credit. Finality refers to whether any further judicial action by the rendering court is necessary to resolve the litigation. Modifiable judgments are usually not considered final.

Note that a judgment that is modifiable as to future installments (*e.g.,* child support payments) might well be final as to past due installments, and the latter can be enforced in a sister state.

FULL FAITH AND CREDIT

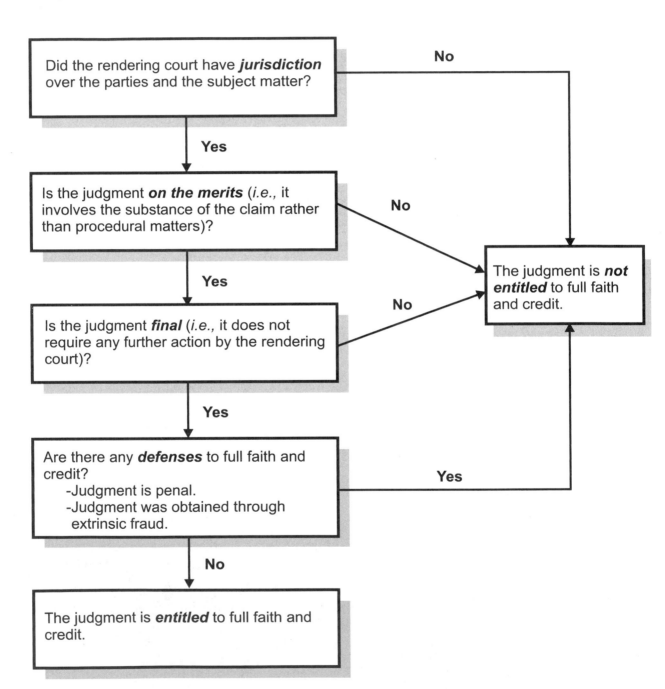

Did the rendering court have *jurisdiction* over the parties and the subject matter?

No

Yes

Is the judgment *on the merits* (*i.e.*, it involves the substance of the claim rather than procedural matters)?

No

Yes

The judgment is *not entitled* to full faith and credit.

Is the judgment *final* (*i.e.*, it does not require any further action by the rendering court)?

No

Yes

Are there any *defenses* to full faith and credit?
- Judgment is penal.
- Judgment was obtained through extrinsic fraud.

Yes

No

The judgment is *entitled* to full faith and credit.

2. **Defenses to Full Faith and Credit**

   a. **Sufficient Defenses**

   The following are defenses to full faith and credit: (i) the judgment is a *penal judgment* (*i.e.,* a judgment punishing an "offense against the public"); and (ii) the judgment is subject to an *equitable defense* in the rendering state (judgment was obtained by extrinsic, but not intrinsic, fraud).

   b. **Insufficient Defenses**

   The following are *not* defenses to full faith and credit: (i) the judgment is a tax judgment; (ii) the judgment is contrary to the public policy of the enforcing state; and (iii) the rendering court made a mistake of law or fact. (*Note:* The inconsistent final judgment fact pattern is resolved by recognizing the last judgment.)

3. **Effect of Recognition of Sister State Judgment**

   a. **Res Judicata Effects**

   1) *Merger* of the plaintiff's cause of action into the judgment.

   2) *Bar* against the plaintiff suing on the same cause of action when the judgment favored the defendant.

   3) *Collateral estoppel* as to an issue resolved in the first litigation (cause of action different in second action, but issue of fact same) as long as the issue is actually litigated in the prior proceeding and is essential to the first suit's outcome.

   CMR **Exam Tip** Default and consent judgments do not give rise to collateral estoppel because no issues have been *actually litigated*. Recall, however, that default and consent judgments are deemed to be on the merits for the full faith and credit purposes of recognition of the judgment.

   b. **Mutuality**

   There is some question as to whether a stranger to the first action can rely upon collateral estoppel (rule of mutuality). The trend is to abandon strict conformity to the mutuality rule—courts decide collateral estoppel questions on a case-by-case basis. Both parties and their privies will be bound by these res judicata effects.

4. **Enforcement of the Judgment**

   If a judgment is entitled to full faith and credit, it must be enforced, even if granted erroneously (assuming that the error does not otherwise qualify as a defense to full faith and credit). The law of the enforcing state governs the method of enforcement (generally bringing an action on a judgment in the second state).

5. **Judgments of Federal Courts and Administrative Tribunals**

   Judgments of administrative tribunals are generally entitled to full faith and credit. The Full Faith and Credit Clause has been made applicable to the federal courts by statute. Recognition of judgments is required between state and federal courts, as well as between two federal courts.

B. **RECOGNITION OF FOREIGN COUNTRY JUDGMENTS**

1. **Comity**
   Foreign country judgments are recognized by application of the comity principle. This is a voluntary recognition, and, as such, is discretionary. Some states impose a reciprocity requirement. In exercising the discretionary remedy, courts look to see if (i) the foreign court had jurisdiction, and (ii) fair procedures were used in adjudicating the case. (The enforcing state's standards are used.)

2. **Uniform Foreign Money-Judgments Recognition Act**
   Foreign country judgments granting or denying recovery of a sum of money are generally subject to this act. The act does not cover a judgment for taxes, penal judgments, or judgments for alimony and child support.

C. RECOGNITION OF DIVORCE JUDGMENTS
Divorce decrees of sister states are entitled to full faith and credit if the jurisdictional requirement is met, *i.e.,* one of the spouses is domiciled in the state granting the divorce.

CMR SUMMARY CHART

BILATERAL DIVORCE VS. EX PARTE DIVORCE		
	Bilateral	**Ex Parte**
Subject Matter Jurisdiction: For the court to have subject matter jurisdiction, must at least one spouse be domiciled in the rendering state?	Yes	Yes
Personal Jurisdiction: Must personal jurisdiction exist over one spouse or both spouses?	Both	One
Full Faith and Credit:		
Must the judgment be given full faith and credit as to the termination of the marriage?	Yes	Yes
Must the judgment be given full faith and credit as to ancillary matters, such as property rights, alimony, and child custody?	Yes (unless modifiable and therefore nonfinal)	No (*exceptions:* (i) court may adjudicate both parties' rights to marital property located within the forum state if that state has sufficient "minimum contacts" with the defendant and the property, and (ii) under the UCCJA and UCCJEA, child custody determination is enforceable if the rendering state is the child's home state)

1. **Ex Parte Divorce**

   a. **Rebuttable Presumption as to Domicile**
   An enforcing court can delve into the domicile question in evaluating whether full faith and credit should be given. However, the judgment is aided by a rebuttable presumption as to the plaintiff's domicile. The person attacking the presumption has the burden of proof.

   Note: The person attacking a divorce judgment may introduce evidence as to relevant facts, including facts occurring after the divorce (such as an immediate return to the prior home state) that tend to cast doubt on the plaintiff's intent to be domiciled in the divorcing state.

   b. **Lack of Jurisdiction**
   If the recognizing state, having jurisdiction over both parties, decides that the ex parte divorce is void for lack of jurisdiction, then that state will not give full faith and credit to the divorce. As a result, any subsequent marriage of either spouse would be bigamous.

2. **Consent Divorce**
   The mere fact that a court has personal jurisdiction over both spouses will not, by itself, be a sufficient jurisdictional basis to satisfy the full faith and credit requirements. This is so even if both spouses have voluntarily made appearances. At least one of the spouses must be domiciled in the forum.

   If the court has personal jurisdiction over both spouses and at least one of the parties is domiciled in the forum state, then the divorce judgment will be entitled to full faith and credit, *i.e.,* bilateral divorce.

3. **Estoppel Against Collateral Attack**
   Generally, any interested person may collaterally attack the validity of another state's divorce decree. Certain persons, however, will be estopped from attacking: (i) parties to prior proceedings, (ii) privies of parties (*e.g.,* daughter in privity with father), and (iii) persons who accept a foreign divorce and remarry in reliance thereon. Note that a divorce judgment cannot be attacked by a stranger if the stranger would have no standing to challenge in the state of its rendition.

   CMR   **Exam Tip**   If a bar exam question requires you to assess the validity of a divorce decree, be sure to also consider whether an estoppel issue is present; *i.e.,* is the person challenging the divorce one who should be estopped from doing so?

4. **Alimony, Property Rights, and Child Custody**
   Bilateral divorce is generally conclusive as to alimony, property rights, and child custody determinations. Ex parte divorce serves to grant only the divorce; it generally will not affect property rights or rights to support. Such rights must be settled by courts having personal jurisdiction over both parties (doctrine of divisible divorce). (Note that in ex parte divorce cases a court may adjudicate both parties' rights to marital property *located within the forum state*, if that state has sufficient "minimum contacts" with the defendant and the property.) Under the UCCJEA, an ex parte child custody determination is enforceable if the rendering state qualifies as the child's "home state."

5. Right to Remarry

According to the majority view, parties validly divorced in one state can remarry despite the existence of a prohibition against remarriage in the state in which the divorce was obtained.

6. Foreign Country Divorce Judgments

The courts will extend comity to a foreign country divorce judgment if the "domicile" requirement is met. As to other aspects of the divorce decree (*e.g.*, alimony), the rules are generally the same as for sister state judgments.

III. DOMICILE

A. DOMICILE OF INDIVIDUALS

An individual may have only one domicile. Domicile may arise (i) by choice or (ii) by operation of law.

1. Domicile of Choice

There are two requirements for domicile of choice: (i) *physical presence* and (ii) *intention to be domiciled*. These are questions of fact. The intention of an individual to be domiciled somewhere will be found to exist if he intends to remain there indefinitely. The courts will not look to the underlying motive. It is necessary, of course, that a person have legal capacity. One can always change a domicile of choice by meeting the two requirements. If there is more than one dwelling, look to see if one is the "principal home."

CMR | **Exam Tip** | A bar exam question might present the following issues related to domicile:

(i) A new domicile may be acquired in *a very short time* if the requisite intent is present.

(ii) Do not confuse *intent* with *motive*. A person may change domicile with the motive of gaining an advantage in litigation, as long as he has a genuine intent to change his domicile and is physically present in the new domicile.

(iii) A person retains her present domicile *until she perfects the two-part test elsewhere* (presence plus intent).

2. Domicile by Operation of Law

Domicile by operation of law arises when a person bears a certain legal "incapacity," *e.g.*, children, married women, and incompetents.

a. Children

A child's domicile follows that of her custodial parent(s). A minor may establish a separate domicile by emancipation or by marriage.

b. Married Women

Historically, the domicile of a married woman was that of her husband, at least as long as she was living with him. Upon separation, she could acquire a domicile of choice. The modern trend is for women to have a domicile of choice even though married.

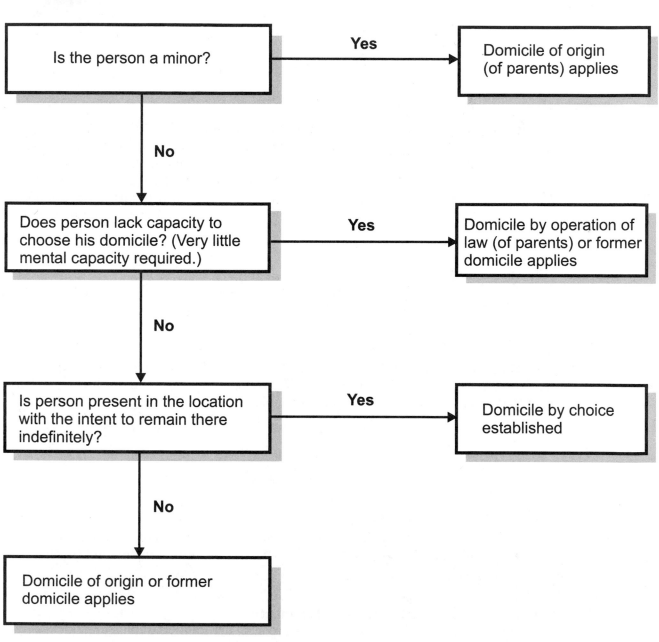

APPROACH TO DETERMINING DOMICILE

| Is the person a minor? | **Yes** → | Domicile of origin (of parents) applies |

No ↓

| Does person lack capacity to choose his domicile? (Very little mental capacity required.) | **Yes** → | Domicile by operation of law (of parents) or former domicile applies |

No ↓

| Is person present in the location with the intent to remain there indefinitely? | **Yes** → | Domicile by choice established |

No ↓

| Domicile of origin or former domicile applies |

c. **Incompetents**
One who lacks the legal capacity to select a domicile will retain the domicile of his parents. If a person previously had capacity and at that time chose his domicile, only later becoming incompetent, he will retain the domicile of his choice.

B. **DOMICILE OF CORPORATIONS**
A corporation is always domiciled in its state of incorporation.

IV. LIMITS ON CHOICE OF LAW

A. **CONSTITUTIONAL LIMITATIONS**
Constitutional limitations arise under the Due Process Clause and the Full Faith and Credit Clause. Generally speaking, if the forum state has any significant contacts with the parties or subject matter of an action whereby it has a legitimate interest in regulating the outcome of litigation, it is *not* constitutionally bound to apply a foreign state's conflicting law by reason of either the Due Process or Full Faith and Credit Clauses. Note that even without any such contact, a state may refuse to apply foreign law without violating the Constitution, *e.g.,* penal laws, tax claims.

 Exam Tip If a bar exam question presents facts indicating that the forum state lacks contacts with the parties or subject matter of the action, the intended issue is probably personal jurisdiction and not constitutional limits on choice of law.

B. **STATUTORY LIMITATIONS**
A state may have its own statutory provisions directing it as to what law must be applied in a given case, *e.g.,* borrowing statutes, U.C.C. choice of law provisions, etc. Federal law may also preempt a state from taking jurisdiction over certain subject matters.

V. CHOICE OF LAW

A. **ANALYTICAL APPROACHES—IN GENERAL**
There are three main analytical approaches: (i) the vested rights approach of the First Restatement, (ii) the most significant relationship approach of the Second Restatement, and (iii) the governmental interest approach.

1. **Vested Rights Approach of the First Restatement**
In the vested rights approach (the traditional approach), the following three analytical steps are taken: (i) characterize the area of substantive law, (ii) determine the particular choice of law rule, and (iii) localize the rule to be applied. *Note:* The forum will generally apply its own law in characterizing an issue, even if the state where the issue arose would apply a different characterization.

CMR APPROACH CHART

PRINCIPAL CHOICE OF LAW ANALYTICAL APPROACHES

Analytical Steps	Vested Rights	Most Significant Relationship	Governmental Interest
	1. Characterize the area of substantive law. 2. Determine the particular choice of law rule. 3. Localize the rule to be applied.	1. Consider the connecting facts: the specific contacts with each jurisdiction. 2. Consider the policy-oriented principles: (i) needs of interstate systems; (ii) relevant policies of forum; (iii) policies and interests of other jurisdictions; (iv) expectations of parties; (v) basic policies underlying substantive law; (vi) predictability and uniformity of result; (vii) ease of determination of foreign law.	1. Assume the forum will apply its own law, unless requested to apply another. 2. If it is requested to apply another state's law, check for false conflict (forum has no interest). 3. If false conflict, apply the law of interested state. 4. If true conflict, the forum reconsiders its policies. 5. If the forum has no great interest in applying its own law, it should dismiss the case if forum non conveniens is available; if not, it may apply interested state's law or law of the state that most closely resembles its own law. 6. If no interested state, most courts apply law of forum.
Does Approach Differ According to Substantive Area of Law?	Yes	Yes	No

(*See* chart for specific areas)

2. **Most Significant Relationship Approach of the Second Restatement**
In the most significant relationship approach, consider the connecting facts in a given case and whether the following policy-oriented principles should be considered: (i) What are the needs of the interstate or international systems? (ii) What are the relevant policies of the forum? (iii) What are the policies and interests of the other interested jurisdictions? (iv) Are the justified expectations of the parties to be protected? (v) What are the basic policies underlying the particular substantive field of law? (vi) Will application of a given law aid certainty, predictability, and uniformity of result? (vii) May the determination and application of a specific law be made with ease?

3. **Governmental Interest Approach**
In the governmental interest approach, start from the assumption that the forum will apply its own law. Then, consider whether the forum has any interest in the litigation; if not, it is a "false conflict" situation and the forum will apply the law of the second state. A problem arises when both the forum and the second state have interests; this is a "true conflict" situation and the forum will "reconsider" its own policies. If it finds it has a legitimate interest, its law will apply. If it is a "disinterested forum" and forum non conveniens is available, the forum should dismiss the case. If forum non conveniens is not available, then the forum may take one of two routes: (i) it may make its own value judgment as to which law of the two or more other states having legitimate competing interests is better, or (ii) it may apply the law of that state that most closely resembles its own law. If it is an "unprovided-for" case (no state has a legitimate interest), the proper approach is unsettled. However, the most widely accepted solution is to apply the law of the forum.

B. **CHOICE OF LAW RULES FOR SPECIFIC AREAS OF SUBSTANTIVE LAW**

1. **Torts**

   a. **In General**

      1) **First Restatement Approach**
      Look to the place of the wrong, *i.e.,* of the injury.

      2) **Second Restatement Approach**
      Look to the place of the injury; the place where the conduct causing the injury occurred; the domicile, residency, nationality, place of incorporation, and place of business of the parties; and the place where the relationship, if any, between the parties is centered. The place of the injury is most important. Also consider whether any policy-oriented principles are involved. *Note:* The seven policy principles are equally applicable to all analyses under this approach irrespective of the substantive area of law involved.

      3) **Governmental Interest Approach**
      Same as with all substantive areas.

   b. **Liability**

      1) **Cause of Action**
      First Restatement: The law of the place of the wrong. ***Second Restatement:*** The

law of the place with the most significant relationship to the occurrence and the parties. *Governmental Interest:* Look to the forum state, assuming it had a legitimate interest in applying its own law.

2) **Defenses**

The courts of states without guest statutes are hesitant to apply another state's statute if it would serve to deprive their residents of a remedy. Hence, this has been one more area for application of the modern approaches. The intrafamily tort defense under modern approaches is governed by the law of the state of common domicile. For the defense of charitable immunity, under the *Second Restatement*, the court will look to both the place of the injury and of the conduct in determining the place with the most significant relationship. (The Second Restatement, however, indicates that there might be an exception if the charity's principal place of business and the plaintiff's domicile are the same.)

CMR **Exam Tip** Although a declining number of states have guest statutes or recognize broad charitable or intrafamily tort immunity, the possible existence of these defenses should be mentioned when a bar exam question presents the appropriate facts and specifies a fictitious state (*e.g.,* State A).

3) **Vicarious Liability**

Under the *First Restatement*, the place of the wrong governs questions of vicarious liability. Some states have characterized the cases as lying in contract rather than in tort; *i.e.,* they could then apply contract choice of law rules, thereby reaching a different result. Under the *Second Restatement*, look to the law of the state having the most significant relationship to the transaction.

c. **Damages**

First Restatement: The law of the place of the wrong. *Second Restatement:* The law of the place having the most significant relationship to the transaction. *Governmental interest:* The state of the plaintiff's domicile has a legitimate interest in having its law of damages applied.

d. **Contribution Among Joint Tortfeasors**

First Restatement: The law of the place of the wrong. *Second Restatement:* The law of the place most significantly related to the case; however, if both tortfeasors are domiciled in the same place, this might be the most significantly related state, particularly if there is a special relationship between them.

e. **Survival and Abatement of Actions**

First Restatement: The law of the place of the wrong. *Second Restatement:* The law of the place with the most significant relationship.

f. **Wrongful Death**

First Restatement: The law of the place where the wrong occurred, *i.e.,* where injuries resulting in death occurred, not the place of death. *Second Restatement:* The law of the place having the most significant relationship. *Governmental interest:* The forum state would generally apply its own wrongful death statute. Note that statutes of limitations,

damages provisions, and who may sue, included in wrongful death statutes, will also be applied as a general rule.

g. Multiple State Torts
If the tort injury occurs in more than one state, under the majority rule the law of the plaintiff's domicile is applied (assuming that the injury also occurred there).

h. Workers' Compensation

1) Which Statute Applies
Generally, states seek to apply their own workers' compensation statute in cases over which they have jurisdiction—so will they take jurisdiction? Look to see if: (i) the employment contract was entered into in the state, (ii) the injury occurred in the state, (iii) the employee resides in the state, or (iv) the employment relationship was performed in the state. Remember, if the parties expressly stated what law is to be applied, this law will govern (as long as the choice was reasonable).

2) Recovery in More than One State
A worker may recover in more than one state. However, any recovery in one state will be credited against an award in a second state.

3) Recovery in Tort or Wrongful Death
May an employee bring a tort or wrongful death action against a defendant from whom she has already been awarded damages in a workers' compensation suit in another state? Courts will not allow such an action if the workers' compensation statute of the first state grants the defendant immunity from tort liability. This recognition of the first state's statutory immunity is generally discretionary with the forum state. Immunity in these cases will usually only be given to an individual who is obligated under the terms of the applicable act. Often only the employer is so obligated; in this case, third parties such as co-contractors or manufacturers of defective equipment will be liable in tort actions.

2. Contracts

a. Express Choice of Law Prevails
First determine if there is an express choice of law provision in the contract. If so, that law will govern unless (i) it is contrary to public policy, (ii) there is no reasonable basis for the parties' choice, or (iii) "true consent" was not given, *e.g.,* fraud, mistake, and adhesion contracts.

b. Analytical Approaches
If there is no valid express choice of law provision that governs, look to the analytical approaches.

1) **First Restatement Approach**
The place where the contract was made controls validity and construction of the contract, and the place where the contract is to be performed governs issues relating to performance (although there is some overlap here).

2) **Second Restatement Approach**
In addition to the seven policy factors previously mentioned, the Second Restatement would look to: the place(s) of contracting, negotiation, and performance; the location of the contract subject matter; and the domicile, residency, nationality, place of incorporation, and place of business of the parties. Note that if the place of negotiation and performance are the same, that law will generally be deemed most significantly related. The Second Restatement also has rules applicable to specific types of contracts; *e.g.,* land contracts are controlled by the law of the situs, personalty contracts are controlled by the law of the place of delivery, life insurance contracts are controlled by the law of the insured's domicile, casualty insurance contracts are controlled by the law of the location of the insured risk, loan contracts are controlled by the law of the place where repayment is required, contracts of suretyship are controlled by the law governing the principal obligation, and transportation contracts are controlled by the law of the place of departure. The validity of a possibly usurious contract will be upheld if the contract is valid under the law of any state that is significantly related.

Note: Rules as to specific kinds of contracts are subject to the exception that if other facts show a more significant relationship with another state, that state's rules may be applied.

CMR **Exam Tip** "Land contracts" controlled by the law of the situs under the Second Restatement are those contracts ***creating or transferring an interest in land***. This does ***not*** include contracts peripherally related to land such as real estate broker listing agreements, which are not necessarily governed by the law of the situs of the relevant land.

3) **Governmental Interest Approach**
The governmental interest approach is equally applicable to choice of law problems involving contracts.

c. **Specific Issues in Contract Cases**

1) **Validity Issues**
Under the *First Restatement*, the existence of capacity is governed by the law of the place of contracting. Under the *Second Restatement*, capacity is governed by the law of the place where the party whose capacity is in question is domiciled. The Second Restatement states that formalities that meet the requirements of the place where the parties executed the contract will usually be applicable. The same rule was generally applied under the traditional view. Legality of the contract is governed by the law of the place where made (although under the Second Restatement if performance is illegal in the state of performance, the contract usually is denied enforcement).

        a)   Rule of Validation
The state's law that serves to uphold the contract and thereby give effect to the "justified expectations" of the parties will apply. (This rule has been incorporated in the Second Restatement.)

    2)   Performance Issues
Performance issues are generally governed by the law of the place of performance under the *First Restatement*. Under the *Second Restatement*, courts look to the state having the most significant relationship.

    3)   Rights and Powers of Third Parties
Under the *First Restatement*, courts look to the law of the place of making the contract to determine rights of third-party beneficiaries and whether the contract can be assigned. Under the *Second Restatement*, courts look to the law of the state having the most significant relationship.

3.   Property

a.   Real Property
Under the *First Restatement* and *Second Restatement* approaches, look to the law of the situs, although under the Second Restatement one could find another state more significantly related. The *governmental interest* approach places less emphasis on situs.

b.   Personal Property
Under both the *First Restatement* and the *Second Restatement* approaches, look to the law of the situs *at the time of the relevant transaction* (although, once again, the Second Restatement could find another state more significantly related). If the property is intangible, the applicable law will generally be that of the "situs of the debt," *i.e.,* the domicile of the debtor. (Note that intangibles represented by documents, *e.g.,* negotiable instruments, stock certificates, etc., are treated as tangible property.) Domicile of a spouse or of a deceased replaces the situs for transfers by operation of law upon marriage or death.

c.   Administration of Trusts
Matters of administration are generally governed by the law of the place where the trust is administered.

4.   Inheritance
Devolution of real property by intestacy or under a will is governed by the lex situs. This may include a variety of questions, *e.g.,* validity of wills, rights of nonmarital or adopted children to inherit land, marital rights in land, etc. The same kinds of questions will be resolved with respect to personal property by the law of the deceased's domicile at the date of death. (Note that if a will directs the executor to sell real property, the doctrine of equitable conversion will apply.)

5. **Family Law**

   a. **Marriage**

   A marriage valid where celebrated is valid everywhere; a marriage void where celebrated is void everywhere. An exception to the general rule of validity exists if the marriage, even though valid at the place of celebration, violates a "prohibitory rule" of the domicile of one of the parties and the parties immediately return to, and become domiciled in, that state. Third states could, of course, recognize the marriage nonetheless.

      1) **Directory Rules vs. Prohibitory Rules**

      A distinction must be made between directory rules, the violation of which will not render the marriage invalid in the place of domicile, and prohibitory rules, which will render it invalid. Directory rules include rules requiring a marriage license, parental consent, and a certificate of a blood test. Prohibitory rules are generally those that express the strong public policy of the state, *e.g.,* rules against incest, polygamy, and marriage under a minimum age.

      2) **Same Sex Marriage**

      Same sex marriages are not afforded full faith and credit.

      3) **Annulment**

      Annulment is governed by the law of the place where the marriage was celebrated (although there is a trend to apply the law of the state with the most significant relationship to the marriage in preference to the state of celebration).

   b. **Divorce**

   Choice of law questions relating to the grounds for divorce are governed by the law of the plaintiff's domicile, *i.e.,* the forum state. The enforceability of premarital agreements is usually governed by the law of the state in which the agreement was executed or the state with the most significant relationship to the parties and the transaction.

   c. **Child's Status**

   Subsequent attempts to legitimate (*i.e.,* change a child's status from nonmarital to marital) are valid if valid under the law of the father's domicile. The recent trend is to uphold validity if sufficient under the law of the child's domicile. Property incidents of status, under the *First Restatement*, are governed by the law governing disposition of the property in question. The *Second Restatement*, however, looks to the law of the state creating the status to decide property incidents unless contrary to strong public policy of the forum.

   d. **Adoption**

   A court applies its own local law to govern adoptions. Property incidents of adoption are the same as those based on a child's status.

6. **Corporations**

   Under the *First Restatement*, choice of law questions regarding matters of internal corporate affairs are governed by the law of the place of incorporation; the *Second Restatement* also refers to the place of incorporation for many conflicts questions. The *governmental interest* approach with regard to corporations issues is the same as with other subject matters.

CHOICE-OF-LAW RULES FOR SPECIFIC AREAS OF SUBSTANTIVE LAW

Substantive Area of Law	"Vested Rights" Approach	"Most Significant Relationship" Approach
Torts	Place of wrong (injury).	Consider the place of: - Injury; - Conduct causing the injury; - Residence and/or business of parties; - Center of parties' relationship
Contracts	*Validity problem*—place of making. *Performance problem*—place of performance.	Consider the place of: - Contracting; - Negotiation; - Performance; - Location of subject matter; - Domicile, residence, nationality, incorporation and business of parties.
Workers' Compensation	Forum.	
Property	*Real property*—situs. *Personal property*— Testamentary and intestate transfer—domicile of owner at time of death. Inter vivos transactions—situs of property at the time of the relevant transaction.	
Family Law	*Marriage*—place of celebration (if marriage can be upheld under that law). *Legitimation after birth*—father's domicile. *Adoption*—forum.	
Corporations	Place of incorporation.	

Note: The "governmental interest" approach does not vary according to the substantive area of law.

C. DO ARGUMENTS AGAINST APPLICATION OF A FOREIGN LAW EXIST?

Three arguments are to be considered: (i) the law to be applied is procedural, (ii) the law is against the forum's public policy, and (iii) the law is a penal or tax law.

1. Substance/Procedure Dichotomy

The law of the forum is usually employed to determine whether a law is substantive or procedural. A forum will always apply ***its own procedural laws***.

CMR SUMMARY CHART

PROCEDURE VS. SUBSTANCE

Procedural	Substantive
✔ Civil practice rules in general	✔ Civil practice rules that would change outcome
✔ Burden of proof in general	
✔ Rebuttable presumptions	✔ Irrebuttable presumptions
✔ Statutes of limitations in general	✔ Statutes of limitations that condition a substantive right or limit a contractual right, and borrowing statutes
✔ Direct action statutes	
✔ Ability to bring counterclaims	✔ Statute of Frauds
✔ Privileges	✔ Parol evidence rule
	✔ Contribution among joint tortfeasors
	✔ Survival of actions
	✔ Adverse possession
	✔ Damages

2. The Foreign Law Is Against Public Policy

If a law is contrary to the public policy of the forum state, the court may refuse to apply the law. Use this defense sparingly. Note, further, that the ***governmental interest*** approach does not incorporate this defense. Rather, the forum will apply public policy affirmatively in reaching a decision as to whether or not its own law should be applied.

3. **Foreign Law Is Penal or Tax Law**
Under the ***First Restatement***, it could be a valid defense that a foreign state's law was a tax or penal law (the latter serves as punishment for an offense against the public). The ***Second Restatement*** seems to prohibit only penal laws. A number of causes of action not considered penal include wrongful death statutes and those based on statutory liability of directors, officers, or shareholders of a corporation for corporate debts. In any event, revenue laws will be enforced by most states.

D. DEPEÇAGE

The ***First Restatement*** approach to choice of law directs the forum to apply the law of a single state to all the issues presented. In contrast, the modern approaches direct the forum to focus on each issue separately. Therefore, under the modern approaches, the laws of different states may govern the resolution of the different issues in a single case, creating the situation known as depeçage.

E. RENVOI

1. **Possible Results**
Remission: The conflicts rules of the second state refer the forum state back to its own law. Reference to only the internal law is "partial," and to the whole law is "total." ***Transmission:*** The conflicts rules of the second state refer the forum state to the law of a third state. Transmission may be partial or total. ***"Never ending circle":*** In this situation, there are constant references to the whole law of each state.

2. **Present Status**
Most states "reject" renvoi. Some "accept" reference back and apply their own law. Renvoi is available today in certain situations, such as: (i) validity of marriages, (ii) status of parents' kinship with child, and (iii) dispositions of interests in land. However, several modern approaches reject any application whatsoever of renvoi.

3. **Federal Tort Claims Act**
A forum will first refer to the place of the act/omission and then apply the conflicts rule of that place, which will ordinarily refer it to the place of the injury.

F. IS STATE OR FEDERAL LAW TO BE APPLIED?

1. **Federal Law in State Courts**
In several areas only federal courts have subject matter jurisdiction, *e.g.,* federal antitrust, bankruptcy, and patent laws. In some areas, state courts are permitted to enforce federal law concurrently with federal courts. Some federal statutes direct state courts to enforce federally created rights, *e.g.,* the Federal Employer's Liability Act. It is unclear whether they must do so. (Apparently, the answer is yes, if they would enforce analogous rights. If so, they may not avoid the enforcement requirement by characterizing it as procedural.)

CMR **Exam Tip** Watch for a factual situation on the bar exam in which a state court is asked to enforce a federal substantive right, but application of a state rule characterized as procedural would result in denial of the federal right (a "converse *Erie*" problem). In this situation, the state might be required to use the federal rule applicable to the situation in order to give effect to federal policy.

2. **State Law in the Federal Courts**

There is no federal general common law. Under *Erie*, federal district courts must apply the substantive law of the state in which the district court sits. This is extended in *Klaxon* to require application of conflict of laws rules as well.

The "outcome determinative test" enunciated in *Guaranty Trust* has been diminished in recent years. In short, the "outcome determinative test" is still used, but it is not the only consideration.

G. PROOF OF FOREIGN LAW

Under the traditional view, the law of a second state is not law at all, but fact. Today, most states take judicial notice of both sister state and federal law. It is treated as law rather than fact. Foreign country law, however, must still be proved as fact. If foreign law is not proved, the court may take several approaches: (i) presume the foreign law is similar to the forum law, (ii) apply the forum law, or (iii) dismiss the action.

CORPORATIONS

TABLE OF CONTENTS

CORPORATIONS

PART ONE—CHARACTERISTICS AND FORMATION OF CORPORATION

I. CORPORATION VS. OTHER BUSINESS ENTITIES

A. GENERAL CHARACTERISTICS OF A CORPORATION

A corporation is a legal entity distinct from its owners and may be created only by filing certain documents with the state.

1. Limited Liability for Owners, Directors, and Officers

The owners of a corporation (called "shareholders") generally are not personally liable for the obligations of the corporation; neither are the corporation's directors or officers. Generally, only the corporation itself can be held liable for corporate obligations. The owners risk only the investment that they make in the business to purchase their ownership interests ("shares").

2. Centralized Management

Generally, the right to manage a corporation is not spread out among the shareholders, but rather is centralized in a board of directors, who usually delegate day-to-day management duties to officers.

3. Free Transferability of Ownership

Generally, ownership of a corporation is freely transferable.

4. Continuity of Life

A corporation may exist perpetually and generally is not affected by changes in ownership (*i.e.*, sale of shares).

5. Taxation

    a. C Corporation

    Generally, a corporation is taxed as an entity distinct from its owners. (Under the tax laws, it is a "C corporation.") The corporate tax rate generally is lower than the personal tax rate, and so this arrangement can be advantageous to persons who want to delay the realization of income. However, this advantage comes at a price—double taxation—because when the corporation does make distributions to shareholders, the distributions are treated as taxable income to the shareholders, even though the corporation has already paid taxes on its profits.

    b. S Corporation

    The tax laws permit certain corporations to elect to be taxed like partnerships and yet retain the other advantages of the corporate form (*see* above). Such corporations are called "S corporations" under the tax laws. Partnerships and S corporations are not subject to double taxation—profits and losses flow through the entity to the owners. There are a number of restrictions on S corporations (*e.g.*, stock can be held by no more than 100 persons, generally shareholders must be individuals, there can be only one class of stock, etc.).

B. COMPARISON WITH SOLE PROPRIETORSHIP

In a sole proprietorship, one person owns all of the assets of the business. There is no business

entity distinct from the owner. The owner is personally liable for the business's obligations, and the business "entity" cannot continue beyond the life of the owner. Ownership is freely transferable, and all profits and losses from the business flow through directly to the owner.

C. COMPARISON WITH PARTNERSHIP

A partnership is similar to a sole proprietorship except that there are at least two owners of a partnership. Little formality is required to form a partnership (just an intention to carry on as co-owners a business for profit). Partnerships generally are not treated as legal entities apart from their owners. Partners are personally liable for obligations of the partnership, and management rights generally are spread among the partners. Ownership interests of partners cannot be transferred without the consent of the other partners. A partnership generally does not continue beyond the lives of its owners. Finally, profits and losses of a partnership flow through directly to the partners.

D. COMPARISON WITH LIMITED PARTNERSHIP

A limited partnership is a partnership that provides for limited liability of some investors (called "limited partners"), but otherwise is similar to other partnerships. A limited partnership can be formed only by compliance with the limited partnership statute. There must be at least one general partner, who has full personal liability for partnership debts and has most management rights.

E. LIMITED LIABILITY COMPANY

The limited liability company ("LLC") is designed to offer the limited liability of a corporation and the flow through tax advantages of a partnership. Like a corporation, it may be formed only by filing appropriate documents with the state, but otherwise it is a very flexible business form: owners may choose between centralized management and owner management, free transferability of ownership or restricted transferability, etc. For more detail, *see* XI., *infra*.

F. CONSTITUTIONAL CHARACTERISTICS OF A CORPORATION

1. "Person"
A corporation is a "person" entitled to due process, equal protection, and attorney-client privilege, but not to the Fifth Amendment privilege against self-incrimination.

2. "Citizen"
A corporation is not a citizen for purposes of the Privileges and Immunities Clause. For federal diversity jurisdiction purposes, a corporation is a citizen of any state of incorporation and the state of its principal place of business.

3. "Resident"
A corporation is a resident of its state of incorporation, where it is doing business, and where it is qualified to do business.

4. "Domicile"
A corporation is a domiciliary of any state in which it is incorporated.

II. FORMATION AND STATUS OF CORPORATION

A. CREATED UNDER STATUTE

Corporations are created by complying with state corporate law, which in a majority of states is based on the Revised Model Business Corporation Act ("RMBCA").

B. FORMATION TERMINOLOGY

A corporation formed in accordance with law is a *de jure* corporation. If all corporate laws have not been followed, a *de facto* corporation might result or a corporation might be recognized through *estoppel*.

C. DE JURE CORPORATION

To create a de jure corporation, the incorporators must comply with all applicable statutory requirements. Basically, the *incorporators* must file *articles of incorporation* with the secretary of state. The articles of incorporation must contain the name of the corporation, the number of shares that the corporation is authorized to issue, the name and address of the corporation's registered agent, and the name and address of each incorporator. The articles may also include any other provision regarding operation of the corporation that is not inconsistent with law.

1. Business Purposes

Traditionally, corporations have included a statement of business purposes in their articles. Absent such a statement, the RMBCA presumes that a corporation is formed to conduct *any lawful business* and is allowed to undertake any act that is necessary or convenient for carrying on their business purpose, including making charitable donations and lending money to employees, officers, and directors.

CMR **Exam Tip** Under modern corporations statutes, a corporation is given the power to do all things necessary or convenient to effect its purposes. Most modern statutes also provide that a corporation may be formed for any lawful purpose. Combined, these provisions provide authority for a corporation to do almost anything that is rationally related to a business purpose. Thus, unless an exam question restricts a corporation's purposes, you should usually find corporate acts to be within the corporation's powers.

a. Ultra Vires Acts

If a corporation includes a narrow business purpose in its articles, it may not undertake activities unrelated to achieving the stated business purpose. Activities beyond the scope of the stated business purposes are said to be "ultra vires." Under common law, ultra vires acts were void and unenforceable. Under the RMBCA, ultra vires acts generally are enforceable, and the ultra vires nature of an act can be raised in only three situations:

1) *A shareholder* may sue the corporation to enjoin a proposed ultra vires act;

2) *The corporation* may sue an officer or director for damages for approving an ultra vires act; and

3) *The state* may bring an action to dissolve a corporation for committing an ultra vires act.

 Exam Tip Keep in mind that under modern statutes, the ultra vires defense is very limited. Therefore, you should not allow a corporation to get out of a contract merely because the contract is outside the scope of the corporation's stated purposes.

2. Corporate Existence Begins on Filing
The articles must be submitted to the state, and if they comply with law, the state will file them. Corporate existence begins upon this filing by the state. The filing is conclusive proof of corporate existence.

3. Additional Procedures—Bylaws
After the articles are filed, the corporation will have an organizational meeting to elect directors, appoint officers, and adopt bylaws. Bylaws may contain any provision for managing the corporation that is not inconsistent with the articles or law. Generally, bylaws are adopted by directors, but they may be modified or repealed by a majority vote of either the directors or the shareholders.

D. RECOGNITION OF CORPORATENESS WHEN FORMATION DEFECTIVE
One of the main reasons to incorporate is to avoid personal liability for obligations that the corporation incurs. Corporate shareholders, directors, and officers generally are veiled with protection from personal liability if a de jure corporation has been formed, but the veil of protection may also be applied where a de jure corporation has not been formed—under the de facto corporation or corporation by estoppel doctrines.

1. De Facto Corporation

a. Characteristics and Requirements
Under the common law, a de facto corporation has all the rights and powers of a de jure corporation but remains subject to direct attack in a quo warranto proceeding by the state. For a de facto corporation to exist, there must have been:

1) A *statute* under which the entity could have validly incorporated;

2) *Colorable compliance* with the statute and a good faith attempt to comply; and

3) The *conduct of business* in the corporate name and the exercise of corporate privileges.

b. Limitation
The RMBCA provides that persons who purport to act on behalf of a corporation *knowing* that there has been no incorporation are liable for all liabilities created in so acting. Thus, the de facto doctrine can be raised as a defense to personal liability only by a person who is unaware that there was no valid incorporation.

2. Corporation by Estoppel
Under the common law doctrine of corporation by estoppel, persons who have dealt with the entity as if it were a corporation will be estopped from denying the corporation's existence. The doctrine applies in contract to prevent the "corporate" entity, and parties who have dealt with the entity as if it were a corporation, from backing out of their contracts. However, it does not apply to tort victims.

3. **Application of Doctrines**
   Generally, if a de facto corporation is found, it is treated like any other corporation for all purposes, except that the state may seek dissolution in a quo warranto proceeding. Estoppel applies only on a case-by-case basis. The de facto doctrine applies equally in contract and tort situations, but estoppel generally is applied only in contract cases (on the rationale that a tort victim does not allow himself to be injured in reliance on the business's status as a corporation). If there is no valid incorporation and the facts do not support a de facto or estoppel argument, generally, the courts will hold only the *active* business members personally liable, and their liability is joint and several.

CMR COMPARISON CHART

	CORPORATE STATUS		
	De Jure	**De Facto**	**Estoppel**
Method of Formation	Follow *all* statutory provisions	Colorable compliance with most statutory provisions and exercise of corporate privileges	Parties act as if there is a corporation; no requirement of following statutory provisions
Effect on Personal Liability	Insulates against personal liability of shareholders	Insulates against personal liability of shareholders, but corporation subject to quo warranto proceeding by state	Insulates against personal liability in contract, but not in tort

E. **DISREGARD OF CORPORATE ENTITY (PIERCING THE CORPORATE VEIL)**
   Under the doctrine of piercing the corporate veil, the courts will disregard a corporate entity and hold individuals liable for corporate obligations.

1. **Elements Justifying Piercing**
   There are three situations in which the corporate veil is often pierced:

   a. **Alter Ego**
      Where the corporation ignores corporate formalities such that it may be considered the "alter ego" of the shareholders or another corporation, the corporate veil may be pierced. These situations may arise where shareholders treat corporate assets as their own, fail to observe corporate formalities, etc., *and* some basic injustice results. *But note:* Sloppy administration alone may not be enough to pierce the corporate veil.

   b. **Inadequate Capitalization at Time of Formation**
      The corporate veil may be pierced where the corporation is inadequately capitalized, so that *at the time of formation* there is not enough unencumbered capital to reasonably cover prospective liabilities.

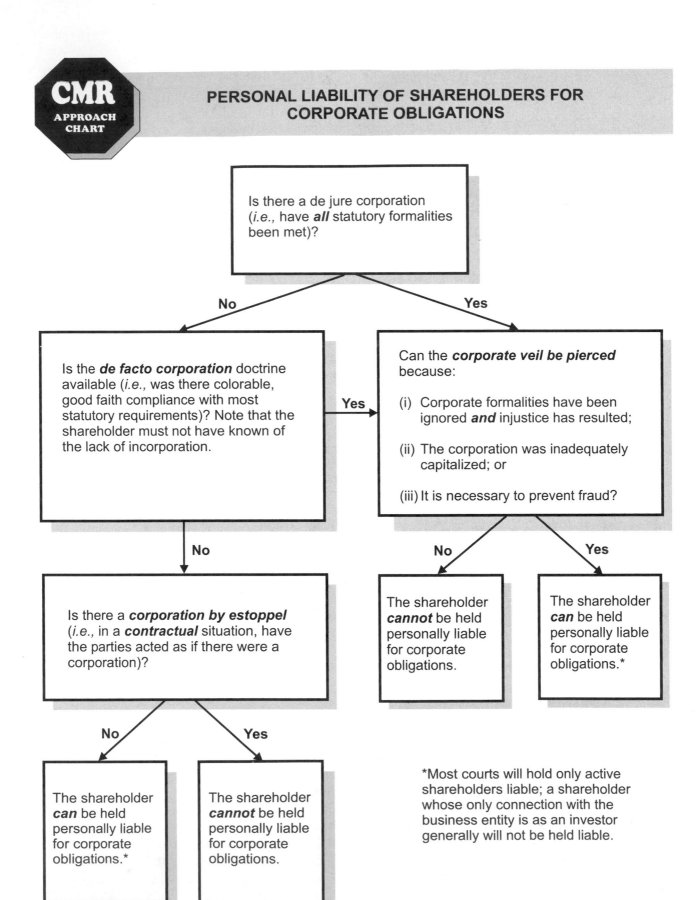

Is there a de jure corporation (*i.e.,* have *all* statutory formalities been met)?

No → **Is the *de facto corporation* doctrine available (*i.e.,* was there colorable, good faith compliance with most statutory requirements)? Note that the shareholder must not have known of the lack of incorporation.**

Yes → **Can the *corporate veil be pierced* because:**

(i) Corporate formalities have been ignored *and* injustice has resulted;

(ii) The corporation was inadequately capitalized; or

(iii) It is necessary to prevent fraud?

From *de facto corporation* box — **No** → **Is there a *corporation by estoppel* (*i.e.,* in a *contractual* situation, have the parties acted as if there were a corporation)?**

From *corporation by estoppel* box:

No → The shareholder *can* be held personally liable for corporate obligations.*

Yes → The shareholder *cannot* be held personally liable for corporate obligations.

From *corporate veil* box:

No → The shareholder *cannot* be held personally liable for corporate obligations.

Yes → The shareholder *can* be held personally liable for corporate obligations.*

*Most courts will hold only active shareholders liable; a shareholder whose only connection with the business entity is as an investor generally will not be held liable.

c. **Avoidance of Existing Obligations, Fraud, or Evasion of Statutory Provisions**
The corporate veil may be pierced where necessary to prevent fraud or to prevent an individual shareholder from using the entity to avoid his *existing* personal obligations. But the mere fact that an individual chooses to adopt the corporate form of business to avoid *future* personal liability is not itself a reason to pierce the corporate veil.

2. **Who Is Liable**
Normally, only shareholders who were active in the operation of the business will be personally liable. Liability is joint and several.

3. **Types of Liability**
The corporate veil is easily pierced in tort cases, but not in contract cases since parties who contracted with the corporation had an opportunity to investigate its stability. Where the corporation is insolvent, claims of shareholder-creditors may be subordinated to outside creditors' claims if equity so requires (*e.g.,* because of fraud).

4. **Who May Pierce**
Generally, creditors may be allowed to pierce the corporate veil. Courts almost never pierce the veil at the request of a shareholder.

III. CAPITAL STOCK STRUCTURE

A. DEBT SECURITIES
Debt securities arise where a corporation has borrowed funds from outside investors and promises to repay them. Holders of debt securities do not have an ownership interest in the corporation. Debt obligations may be secured (a "bond") or unsecured (a "debenture"), and may be payable either to the holder of the bond (a "bearer" or "coupon" bond) or to the owner registered on the corporation's records (a "registered" bond). A debt obligation may also have special features; *e.g.,* it may provide that it is convertible into equity securities at the option of the holder, or it might provide that the corporation may redeem the obligation at a specified price before the obligation matures.

B. EQUITY SECURITIES (SHARES)
Equity securities give their holders an ownership interest in the issuing corporation.

1. **Terminology**
Shares described in the corporation's articles of incorporation are *authorized* shares. Those shares that have been sold are *issued and outstanding.* Those shares that have been reacquired by the corporation through repurchase or redemption are *authorized but unissued*; but if the articles so provide, the number of authorized shares is reduced by the number of shares repurchased. (Formerly, reacquired shares were authorized, issued, but not outstanding *treasury* shares.) Shares may be certificated (*i.e.,* represented by a certificate) or uncertificated.

2. **Classification of Shares**
A corporation may choose to issue only one type of shares, giving each shareholder an equal

ownership right (in which case the shares are generally called "***common shares***"). Alternatively, ownership rights may be varied if the articles provide that the corporation's stock is to be divided into ***classes*** or ***series within a class.***

a. Classes and Series Must Be Described in Articles

If shares are to be divided into classes or series within a class, the articles must (i) prescribe the number of shares of each class; (ii) prescribe a distinguishing designation for each class (*e.g.*, "Class A preferred," "Class B preferred," etc.); and (iii) either describe the rights, preferences, and limitations of each class or series or provide that the rights, preferences, and limitations of any class or series within a class shall be determined by the board of directors prior to issuance.

3. Stock Subscriptions

Stock subscriptions are promises from subscribers to buy stock in the corporation.

a. Preincorporation Subscription

Under the RMBCA, preincorporation subscriptions are ***irrevocable for six months*** unless otherwise provided in the terms of the subscription agreement or unless all subscribers consent to revocation.

b. Payment

Unless otherwise provided, payment is upon demand by the board. Demand may not be made in a discriminatory manner. A subscriber who fails to pay may be penalized by sale of the shares or forfeiture of the subscription and any amounts paid thereon, at the ***corporation's*** option.

4. Consideration

a. Forms of Consideration

Under the RMBCA, shares may be paid for with ***any tangible or intangible property or benefit to the corporation.***

CMR **Exam Tip** The RMBCA greatly expanded what is acceptable consideration for the issuance of shares. Older statutes did not allow shares to be issued for promissory notes or promises of future work. These forms of consideration are acceptable under the RMBCA. Similarly, a promise to convey property in the future would also be acceptable. Watch for exam questions that test on this dramatic change.

b. Amount

Traditionally, stock could not be issued by a corporation for less than the stock's stated par value, and the consideration received for par value stock had to be held in a certain account containing at least the aggregate par value of the outstanding par value shares. The RMBCA generally has eliminated the concept of par and allows corporations to issue shares for whatever consideration the directors deem appropriate. Consideration received for the issuance of stock need not be placed in any special account. If the corporation issues stock in exchange for consideration other than cash, the stock is considered fully paid and nonassessable as soon as the corporation receives the consideration for which the board authorized the issuance. Of course, a shareholder who fails to pay the full amount agreed upon can be held liable for any sums remaining unpaid.

CMR   **Exam Tip**   While the concept of par value is mostly dead under the RMBCA, a last vestige remains—a corporation's articles can specify a par value for stock. In such a circumstance, if the directors authorize a sale of stock for less than the stated par value, the shares will probably be treated as validly issued, but the directors who authorized the issuance can probably be held liable for breach of fiduciary duty. The RMBCA itself provides no clear guidelines on this issue.

PART TWO—INTRACORPORATE PARTIES

IV. PROMOTERS

A. PROMOTERS PROCURE CAPITAL AND OTHER COMMITMENTS

Before a corporation is formed, promoters procure commitments for capital and other instrumentalities that will be used by the corporation after its formation.

B. PROMOTERS' RELATIONSHIP WITH EACH OTHER

Absent an agreement to the contrary, promoters are joint venturers who occupy a fiduciary relationship with each other. They will breach their fiduciary duty if they secretly pursue personal gain at the expense of their fellow promoters.

C. PROMOTERS' RELATIONSHIP WITH CORPORATION

A promoter's fiduciary duty to the corporation is one of fair disclosure and good faith.

1. Breach of Fiduciary Duty Arising from Sales to the Corporation

A promoter who profits by selling property to the corporation may be liable for his profit unless all material facts of the transaction were disclosed. If the transaction is disclosed to an independent board of directors and approved, the promoter has met his duty and will not be liable for his profits. If the board is not completely independent, the promoter still will not be liable for his profits if the subscribers knew of the transaction at the time they subscribed or unanimously ratified the transaction after full disclosure. Disclosure must be to *all who are contemplated* to be part of the initial financing scheme. If the promoters purchase all the stock and subsequently sell their individual shares to outsiders, the promoters cannot be held liable for the profits from the sale of property to the corporation.

2. Fraud

Promoters may always be liable if plaintiffs can show that they were damaged by the promoters' fraudulent misrepresentations or fraudulent failure to disclose all material facts.

3. State or Federal Securities Law

Many states have enacted securities laws (known as "blue sky" laws) similar to the federal securities laws. However, federal law preempts state regulation of securities *except* with regard to: (i) penny stocks (generally, stocks selling for less than $5); (ii) intrastate offerings exempt under the 1933 Act; (iii) actions against brokers for fraud; and (iv) notice filing requirements for stocks sold within the state.

D. PROMOTERS' RELATIONSHIP WITH THIRD PARTIES—PREINCORPORATION AGREEMENTS

    1. Promoter's Liability

    Under the RMBCA, anyone who acts on behalf of a corporation knowing that it is not in existence is jointly and severally liable for the obligations incurred. Thus, if a promoter enters into an agreement with a third party on behalf of a planned but unformed corporation, the ***promoter is personally liable*** on the contract. The promoter's liability ***continues after the corporation is formed***, even if the corporation adopts the contract and benefits from it. The promoter will be released from liability only if there is an express or implied ***novation*** (*i.e.*, agreement among all three parties to release the promoter from liability and substitute the corporation).

        a. Exception—Agreement Expressly Relieves Promoter of Liability

        If the agreement expressly relieves the promoter of liability, there is no contract; such an arrangement may be construed as a revocable offer to the proposed corporation, and the promoter has no rights or liability under the agreement.

    CMR | **Exam Tip** | Questions often require you to discuss whether a promoter will be liable on a preincorporation contract. If you keep in mind that promoters are *forming* a corporation, these questions should be fairly easy to answer. For there to be a valid contract, someone must be bound with the third party. It can't be the corporation since it does not exist; therefore, the promoter is liable even though she was acting on behalf of the corporation to be formed. (If the agreement expressly relieves the promoter of liability, it will be treated as an offer to the corporation.)

    Note that if the promoter is bound, she is not relieved merely by the corporation's creation or its adoption of the contract; only if the third party agrees to substitute the corporation for the promoter (a novation) will the promoter be relieved.

        b. Promoter's Right to Reimbursement

        A promoter who is held personally liable on a preincorporation contract may have a right to reimbursement from the corporation to the extent of any benefits received by the corporation.

    2. Corporation's Liability

    Since the corporate entity does not exist prior to incorporation, it is ***not bound*** on contracts entered into by the promoter in the corporate name prior to incorporation. The corporation may become bound by expressly or impliedly ***adopting*** the promoter's contract.

V. SHAREHOLDERS

A. SHAREHOLDER CONTROL OVER MANAGEMENT

The power to manage the corporation generally is vested in the directors. Generally, the shareholders have no direct control in management of the corporation's business. However, the RMBCA allows the shareholders to enter into agreements to dispense with the board and vest management power in the shareholders. If the articles do not include such a special provision, shareholders exercise only indirect control of the corporation through their voting power, by which they elect and remove directors, adopt and modify bylaws, and approve fundamental changes in the corporate structure.

CMR | **Exam Tip** | If the examiners question you about the power of the shareholders to run the day-to-day affairs of their corporation, unless the corporation's articles or a shareholder agreement provides otherwise, you should generally respond that the shareholders have no such power; that power is vested in the board of directors, and the shareholders have the power to elect the board.

B. SHAREHOLDERS' MEETINGS AND VOTING POWER

1. Convening Meetings

a. Annual Meetings

Corporations must hold annual shareholders' meetings. If the annual meeting is not held within the earlier of six months after the end of the corporation's fiscal year or 15 months after its last annual meeting, a court may order the meeting to be held.

b. Special Meetings

Special meetings may be called by the board of directors, the holders of 1/10 or more of all shares entitled to be cast at the meeting, or other persons so authorized in the articles or bylaws.

2. Place of Meetings

Meetings of shareholders may be held within or outside the state.

3. Notice

Shareholders must be notified of meetings *not less than 10 or more than 60* days before the meeting. Notice must state the place, day, and hour of the meeting and, for *special meetings*, the purpose. Notice may be waived in writing or by attendance.

4. Eligibility to Vote

Shareholders of record on the record date may vote at the meeting. The *record date is fixed by the board* of directors but may not be more than 70 days before the meeting. If directors do not set a record date, the record date is deemed to be the day the notice of the meeting is mailed to the shareholders. Unless the articles provide otherwise, each share is entitled to one vote.

5. Proxies

A shareholder may vote her shares in person or by proxy executed in writing.

a. Duration

Proxies are valid for 11 months unless they provide otherwise. A proxy is generally revocable by the shareholder and may be revoked by the shareholder attending the meeting to vote himself or by subsequent appointment of another proxy. A proxy will be irrevocable only if it states that it is irrevocable and is *coupled with an interest* or *given as security*.

b. Statutory Proxy Control
The rules governing proxy solicitation provide that (i) there must be full and fair disclosure of all material facts with regard to any management-submitted proposal upon which the shareholders are to vote; (ii) material misstatements, omissions, and fraud in connection with the solicitation of proxies are prohibited; and (iii) management must include certain shareholder proposals on issues other than election of directors, and allow proponents to explain their position.

6. Mechanics of Voting

a. Quorum
A quorum is usually a *majority of outstanding shares* entitled to vote, unless the articles or bylaws require a *greater* number. Note also that once a quorum is present, it cannot be broken by withdrawal of shares from the meeting.

b. Voting—In General
Absent a contrary provision in the articles, each share is entitled to one vote. The articles may provide for weighted voting or contingent voting. If a quorum is present, shareholders will be deemed to have approved a matter if the *votes cast in favor of the matter exceed the votes cast against the matter*, unless the articles or bylaws require a greater proportion. Less than a quorum may adjourn the meeting.

c. Director Elections
Unless the articles provide otherwise, directors are elected by a *plurality* of the votes cast.

1) Cumulative Voting Optional
Instead of the normal one share, one vote paradigm, the articles may provide for cumulative voting in the election of directors. Under cumulative voting, each shareholder is entitled to a number of votes equal to the number of his voting shares multiplied by the number of directors to be elected. The total number may be divided among the candidates in any manner that the shareholder desires, including casting all for the same candidate.

d. Class Voting on Article Amendments
Whenever an amendment to the articles of incorporation will affect only a particular class of stock, that class has a right to vote on the action even if the class otherwise does not have voting rights.

7. Shareholders May Act Without Meeting by Unanimous Written Consent
Shareholders may take action without a meeting by the unanimous written consent of all shareholders entitled to vote on the action.

C. SHAREHOLDER AGREEMENTS

1. Voting Trust
A voting trust is a written agreement of shareholders under which all of the shares owned by the parties to the agreement are transferred to a trustee, who votes the shares and distributes the dividends in accordance with the provisions of the voting trust agreement. A copy of the

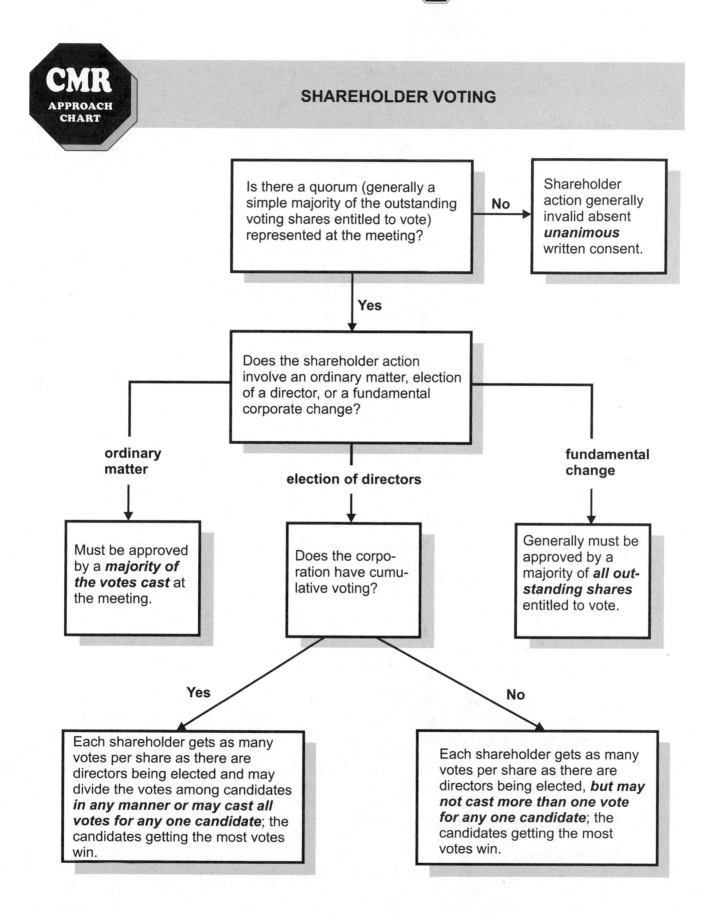

SHAREHOLDER VOTING

Is there a quorum (generally a simple majority of the outstanding voting shares entitled to vote) represented at the meeting?

No → Shareholder action generally invalid absent *unanimous* written consent.

Yes

Does the shareholder action involve an ordinary matter, election of a director, or a fundamental corporate change?

ordinary matter

Must be approved by a *majority of the votes cast* at the meeting.

election of directors

Does the corporation have cumulative voting?

fundamental change

Generally must be approved by a majority of *all outstanding shares* entitled to vote.

Yes

Each shareholder gets as many votes per share as there are directors being elected and may divide the votes among candidates *in any manner or may cast all votes for any one candidate*; the candidates getting the most votes win.

No

Each shareholder gets as many votes per share as there are directors being elected, *but may not cast more than one vote for any one candidate*; the candidates getting the most votes win.

trust agreement and the names and addresses of the beneficial owners of the trust must be given to the corporation. The trust is not valid for more than 10 years unless it is extended by the agreement of the parties.

2. Voting Agreement
Rather than creating a trust, shareholders may enter into a written and signed agreement providing for the manner in which they will vote their shares. Unless the agreement provides otherwise, it will be specifically enforceable. It need not be filed with the corporation and is not subject to any time limit.

CMR
COMPARISON CHART

VOTING TRUST VS. VOTING AGREEMENT

	Voting Trust	Voting Agreement
Purpose	Any proper purpose	Any proper purpose
Duration	10-year maximum but renewable	Can be perpetual
Share Ownership	Legal ownership transferred to trustee; shareholders retain beneficial ownership	Shareholders retain both legal and beneficial ownership

3. Shareholder Management Agreements
The shareholders may enter into agreements among themselves regarding almost any aspect of the exercise of corporate power (*e.g.*, an agreement: eliminating the board and vesting board power in one or more persons, establishing who shall be officers or directors, requiring distributions on certain conditions, etc.). To be valid, the agreement must be set forth in the articles, bylaws, or a written agreement approved by all persons who are shareholders at the time of its adoption. Such agreements are valid for 10 years unless they provide otherwise, but will terminate if the corporation's shares become listed on a national securities exchange or are otherwise regularly traded on a national securities market.

4. Restrictions on Transfer of Stock
Stock transfer restrictions *must be reasonable* (*e.g.,* a right of first refusal). A third-party purchaser is bound by the provisions of an agreement restricting transfer of stock if: (i) the restriction's existence is *conspicuously noted* on the certificate (or is contained in the information statement required for uncertificated shares), or (ii) the third party had knowledge of the restriction at the time of the purchase.

D. SHAREHOLDERS' INSPECTION RIGHTS

1. Qualified Right
Under the RMBCA, a shareholder may inspect the corporation's books, papers, accounting

records, shareholder records, etc., upon *five days' written notice stating a proper purpose* (*i.e.,* a purpose reasonably related to the person's interest as a shareholder) for the inspection. The shareholder need not personally conduct the inspection; he may send an attorney, accountant, or other agent.

2. **Unqualified Right for Certain Records**
   The RMBCA also includes an exception to the general rule. It provides that any shareholder may inspect the following records *regardless of purpose*: (i) the corporation's articles and bylaws, (ii) board resolutions regarding classification of shares, (iii) minutes of shareholders' meetings from the past three years, (iv) communications sent by the corporation to shareholders over the past three years, (v) a list of the names and business addresses of the corporation's current directors and officers, and (vi) a copy of the corporation's most recent annual report.

E. PREEMPTIVE RIGHTS

Under the RMBCA, shareholders do not have a preemptive right to purchase newly issued shares in order to maintain their proportional ownership interest unless the articles of incorporation provide the right. Moreover, even if the articles do provide a preemptive right, shareholders generally have no preemptive right in shares issued: (i) for consideration other than cash (*e.g.*, for services of an employee), (ii) within six months after incorporation, or (iii) without voting rights but having a distribution preference.

F. SHAREHOLDER SUITS

1. **Direct Actions**
   A direct action may be brought for a breach of a fiduciary duty owed to the shareholder by an officer or director. To distinguish breaches of duty owed to the corporation and duties owed to the shareholder, ask: (i) who suffers the most immediate and direct damage, the corporation or the shareholder; and (ii) to whom did the defendant's duty run, the corporation or the shareholder. In a shareholder direct action, any recovery is for the benefit of the individual shareholder.

2. **Derivative Actions**
   In a derivative action, the shareholder is asserting the corporation's rights rather than her own rights. Recovery in a derivative action generally goes to the corporation rather than to the shareholder bringing the action. Nevertheless, the corporation is named as a defendant.

   a. **Standing—Ownership at Time of Wrong**
      To commence and maintain a derivative proceeding, a shareholder must have been a shareholder at the time of the act or omission complained of or must have become a shareholder through transfer by operation of law from one who was a shareholder at that time. Also, the shareholder must fairly and adequately represent the interests of the corporation.

   b. **Demand Requirements**
      The shareholder must make a *written demand* on the corporation to take suitable action. A derivative proceeding may not be commenced until 90 days have elapsed from the date of demand, unless: (i) the shareholder has earlier been notified that the corporation has rejected the demand; or (ii) irreparable injury to the corporation would result by waiting for the 90 days to pass.

c. Will Be Dismissed If Found Not in Corporation's Best Interests
If a majority of the directors (but at least two) who have no personal interest in the controversy find ***in good faith after reasonable inquiry*** that the suit is not in the corporation's best interests, but the shareholder brings the suit anyway, the suit may be dismissed on the corporation's motion.

1) Burden of Proof
To avoid dismissal, in most cases the ***shareholder*** bringing the suit has the burden of proving to the court that the decision was ***not*** made in good faith after reasonable inquiry. However, if a majority of the directors had a personal interest in the controversy, the ***corporation*** will have the burden of showing that the decision was made in good faith after reasonable inquiry.

d. Discontinuance or Settlement Requires Court Approval
A derivative proceeding may be discontinued or settled only with the approval of the court.

e. Court May Order Payment of Expenses
Upon termination of a derivative action, the court may order the corporation to pay the plaintiff's reasonable expenses if it finds that the action has resulted in a substantial benefit to the corporation. If the court finds that the action was commenced or maintained without reasonable cause or for an improper purpose, it may order the plaintiff to pay reasonable expenses of the defendant.

G. DISTRIBUTIONS

1. Types of Distributions
Distributions can take the form of dividends, redemptions of shares, repurchases of shares, distribution of assets upon liquidation, etc.

2. Rights to Distributions
At least one class of stock must have a right to receive the corporation's net assets on dissolution. Beyond this rule, distributions generally are discretionary.

a. Declaration Generally Solely Within Board's Discretion
Even if the articles authorize distributions, the decision whether or not to declare distributions generally is ***solely within the directors' discretion***, subject to solvency limitations (below) and any provisions to the contrary in a shareholders' agreement or the articles. The shareholders generally have no general right to compel a distribution.

1) Limitations

a) Solvency Requirements
A distribution is not permitted if, after giving it effect, either:

(1) The corporation would ***not be able to pay its debts as they become due*** in the usual course of business (*i.e.*, the corporation is insolvent in the bankruptcy sense); or

(2) The corporation's *total assets would be less than the sum of its total liabilities* plus (unless the articles permit otherwise) the amount that would be needed, if the corporation were to be dissolved at the time of the distribution, to satisfy the preferential rights on dissolution of shareholders whose preferential rights are superior to those receiving the distribution (*i.e.,* the corporation is insolvent in the balance sheet sense).

b) Restrictions in the Articles

The articles may restrict the board's right to declare dividends (*e.g.*, a creditor might insist that the corporation include in its articles a provision prohibiting payment of any distributions unless the corporation earns a certain amount of profits).

c) Share Dividends

Distributions of a corporation's own shares (*i.e.,* "share dividends" or "stock dividends") to its shareholders are excluded from the definition of "distribution." Therefore, the above restrictions are inapplicable. However, shares of one class or series may not be issued as a share dividend in respect of shares of another class or series unless one of the following occurs: (i) the articles so authorize; (ii) a majority of the votes entitled to be cast by the class or series to be issued approves the issue; or (iii) there are no outstanding shares of the class or series to be issued.

b. Contractual Rights in Regard to Distributions

1) Limitations and Preferences

Shares may be divided into classes with varying rights (*e.g.*, some classes may be redeemable, others not; some may have no right to receive distributions, others could have preferences; etc.).

a) Common Preference Terms

Preferred shares have a right to receive dividends before common shareholders may receive dividends. The right to the preferred dividend may or may not accumulate if unpaid in a particular year (*i.e.,* "cumulative" vs. "noncumulative" preferred shares), or may accumulate only if there are sufficient current earnings (*i.e.,* "cumulative if earned" preferred shares). Preferred shares have no right to a share of the distributions made on common shares unless the preferred shares provide that they are "participating."

2) Rights After Declaration—Same as a General Creditor

Once a distribution is lawfully declared, the shareholders generally are treated as creditors of the corporation and their claim for the distribution is equal in priority to claims of other unsecured creditors. However, a distribution can be enjoined or revoked if it was declared in violation of the solvency limitations, the articles, or a superior preference right.

c. Who May Receive—Shareholder of Record on Record Date

Dividends are declared payable to persons whom the corporate records show to be shareholders on a specified date—known as the record date. The owner on the record date (not the date of declaration) is entitled to the dividend.

3. Liability for Unlawful Distributions

A director who votes for or assents to a distribution that violates the above rules is personally liable to the corporation for the amount of the distribution that *exceeds what could have been properly distributed*. However, a director is not liable for distributions approved in good faith: (i) based on financial statements prepared according to reasonable accounting practices, or on a fair valuation or other method that is reasonable under the circumstances; or (ii) by relying on information from officers, employees, legal counsel, accountants, etc., or a committee of the board of which the director is not a member. A director who is held liable for an unlawful distribution is entitled to contribution from (i) every other director who could be held liable for the distribution (*i.e.,* those who voted in favor of the distribution) and (ii) each shareholder, for the amount she accepted while knowing that the distribution was improper.

H. SHAREHOLDERS' LIABILITIES

1. General Rule—No Fiduciary Duty

Generally, shareholders may act in their own personal interests and have no fiduciary duty to the corporation or their fellow shareholders. Shareholder liability generally is limited to the liabilities discussed above for unpaid stock, a pierced corporate veil, or absence of de facto corporation.

2. Liability Pursuant to Shareholder Agreement

If the shareholders enter into agreements that vest some or all of the right to manage the corporation in one or more shareholders, the managing shareholder(s) have the liabilities that a director ordinarily would have with respect to that power.

3. Close Corporations

Shareholders in a close corporation (*i.e.,* a corporation with few shareholders) are generally held to owe each other the same duty of loyalty and utmost good faith that is owed by partners to each other.

4. Limitations on Controlling Shareholders

A controlling shareholder must refrain from using his control to cause the corporation to take action that unfairly prejudices minority shareholders (*e.g.,* a controlling shareholder may be liable for selling the corporation to individuals who subsequently loot the company).

VI. BOARD OF DIRECTORS

A. GENERAL POWERS

The directors are responsible for the management of the business and affairs of the corporation.

B. QUALIFICATIONS

In the absence of any requirements by the articles or bylaws, the directors *need not be shareholders* in the corporation or residents of any particular state.

C. NUMBER, ELECTION, AND TERM OF OFFICE

There need be only one director. However, the articles or bylaws may require as many directors as desired, without limitation. The directors are elected at each annual shareholders' meeting, subject

to contrary provisions in the articles. If there are at least nine directors, they may be divided into two or three equal size classes, with terms of office expiring in staggered years from one to three.

1. Vacancies

Vacancies on the board generally may be filled by the shareholders or the directors.

D. REMOVAL OF DIRECTORS

Directors may be removed by the shareholders for cause or ***without cause***. However, a director elected by cumulative voting cannot be removed if the votes cast against removal would be sufficient to elect her if cumulatively voted at an election of directors. Similarly, a director elected by a voting group of shares can be removed only by that class.

E. DIRECTORS' MEETINGS

1. Types of Meetings; Notice

Directors may act in regular or special meetings. Regular meetings may be held without notice; special meetings require two days' written notice of the date, time, and place of the meeting. Attendance constitutes waiver of any required notice unless attendance is for the sole purpose of protesting lack of notice.

CMR COMPARISON CHART

SHAREHOLDERS' AND DIRECTORS' MEETINGS

	Shareholders'		Directors'	
	Annual	**Special**	**Regular**	**Special**
When?	As board of directors directs, but must be within earlier of 6 months after end of fiscal year or 15 months after prior annual meeting	As board of directors directs, or at call of 1/10 of all shares or persons authorized in the articles or bylaws	As bylaws provide	As bylaws provide
Where?	Anywhere	Anywhere	Anywhere	Anywhere
Notice Requirements	Can be by mail between 10 and 60 days before meeting; must include time and place	Can be by mail between 10 and 60 days before meeting; must include time, place, and ***purpose***	None needed	Two days' notice of date, time, and place of the meeting
Proxy Voting Allowed?	Yes	Yes	No	No

2. Quorum

A *majority* of the board of directors constitutes a quorum for the meeting unless a higher or lower number is required by the articles or bylaws, but a quorum can be no fewer than one-third of the board members. Unlike shareholders, a director can break the quorum by withdrawing from a meeting.

3. Approval of Action

If a quorum is present, resolutions will be deemed approved if approved by a majority of directors present.

a. Action by Unanimous Written Consent

Any action required to be taken by the directors at a formal meeting may be taken by *unanimous consent*, in writing, without a meeting.

CMR | **Exam Tip** | The examiners often ask about the formalities of directors' meetings by setting up facts where there is *no meeting*. That is, the facts tell you that a director has entered into an extraordinary contract with another entity on the corporation's behalf, either on his own accord or with the approval of some of the directors, or with the approval of all of the directors, who were called individually. You must recognize that a director does not have the power to bind the corporation in contract unless there is actual authority to act. Actual authority generally can arise only if: (i) proper notice was given for a directors' *meeting*, a *quorum* was present, *and* a *majority* of the directors approved the action, *or* (ii) there was unanimous *written* consent of the directors.

F. DELEGATION OF AUTHORITY

Unless the articles or bylaws provide otherwise, the board may create one or more committees, with two or more members, and appoint members of the board of directors to serve on them. The committees may act for the board, but the board remains responsible for supervision of the committees. The board may also delegate authority to officers.

G. DIRECTORS' RIGHT TO INSPECT

Directors have a right to inspect corporate books.

H. DIRECTORS' DUTIES AND LIABILITIES

1. Personal Liability of Directors May Be Limited

The articles may limit or eliminate directors' personal liability for money damages to the corporation or shareholders for actions taken or for failure to take action. However, the articles may not limit or eliminate liability for financial benefits received by the director to which she is not entitled, an intentionally inflicted harm on the corporation or its shareholders, unlawful corporate distributions, or an intentional violation of criminal law.

2. Duty of Care

Directors have a duty to *manage to the best of their ability.* They must discharge their duties:

(i) In *good faith*;

(ii) *With the care that an ordinarily prudent person in a like position* would exercise under similar circumstances; and

(iii) In a manner the directors *reasonably believe to be in the best interests of the corporation*.

Directors who meet this standard will not be liable for corporate decisions that in hindsight turn out to be poor or erroneous. At common law, this was known as the "*business judgment rule*."

a. **Burden on Challenger**

The person challenging the directors' action has the burden of proving that the statutory standard above was not met.

b. **Director May Rely on Reports or Other Information**

In discharging her duties, a director is entitled to rely on information, opinions, reports, or statements (including financial statements), if prepared or presented by: (i) *corporate officers or employees* whom the director reasonably believes to be reliable and competent; (ii) *legal counsel, accountants, or other persons* as to matters the director reasonably believes are within such person's professional competence; or (iii) a *committee* of the board of which the director is not a member, if the director reasonably believes the committee merits confidence.

3. **Duty to Disclose**

The directors also have a duty to disclose material corporate information to other members of the board.

4. **Duty of Loyalty**

a. **Conflicting Interest Transactions**

1) **What Constitutes a Conflicting Interest Transaction**

A director has a conflicting interest with respect to a transaction if the director knows that she or a related person—such as a spouse, parent, child, grandchild, etc.—either: (i) *is a party to the transaction*; (ii) *has a beneficial financial interest* in, or is so closely linked to, the transaction that the *interest would reasonably be expected to influence the director's judgment* if she were to vote on the transaction; or (iii) is a *director, general partner, agent, or employee* of another entity with whom the corporation is transacting business and the *transaction is of such importance to the corporation that it would in the normal course of business be brought before the board* (the so-called interlocking directorate problem).

2) **Standards for Upholding Conflicting Interest Transaction**

A conflicting interest transaction will not be enjoined or give rise to an award of damages due to the director's interest in the transaction if:

(i) The transaction was approved by a *majority of the directors* (but at least two) *without a conflicting interest* after *all material facts have been disclosed* to the board;

(ii) The transaction was approved by *a majority of the votes entitled to be cast by shareholders without a conflicting interest* in the transaction after *all material facts have been disclosed* to the shareholders (notice of the meeting must describe the conflicting interest transaction); or

(iii) The transaction, judged according to circumstances at the time of commitment, was *fair to the corporation*.

a) Interested Director's Presence at Meeting Irrelevant
The presence of the interested director(s) at the meeting at which the directors or shareholders voted to approve the conflicting interest transaction does not affect the action.

b) Special Quorum Requirements
For purposes of the vote on a conflicting interest transaction (i) *at a directors' meeting*, a majority of the directors without a conflicting interest, but not less than two, constitutes a quorum; and (ii) *at a shareholders' meeting*, a quorum consists of a majority of the votes entitled to be cast, not including shares owned or controlled directly or beneficially by the director with the conflicting interest.

c) Factors to Be Considered in Determining Fairness
In determining whether a transaction is fair, courts look to factors such as adequacy of the consideration, corporate need to enter into the transaction, financial position of the corporation, and available alternatives.

d) Statutory Interpretation
Despite the statute's absolute terms, a transaction approved by the board or shareholders might still be set aside if the party challenging the transaction can prove that it constitutes a waste of corporate assets.

e) Remedies
Possible remedies for an improper conflicting interest transaction include enjoining the transaction, setting the transaction aside, damages, and similar remedies.

CMR **Exam Tip** Interested director transactions probably are the most tested issues in Corporations. Remember, if a director will benefit from a transaction her corporation is about to enter into, the director must disclose this information to the board (or to the shareholders). Disinterested directors (or the shareholders) must then approve the transaction. If there is no disclosure, the transaction can be set aside *unless it is fair* to the corporation. Alternatively, the corporation can recover damages equal to the director's profit.

3) Directors May Set Own Compensation
Despite the apparent conflict of interest, unless the articles or bylaws provide otherwise, the board has authority to fix director compensation. Nevertheless, an unreasonable compensation will breach the directors' fiduciary duties.

b. Corporate Opportunity Doctrine
The directors' fiduciary duties prohibit them from diverting a business opportunity from

their corporation to themselves without first giving their corporation an opportunity to act. This is sometimes known as a "usurpation of a corporate opportunity" problem.

1) Corporation Must Have Interest or Expectancy

A usurpation problem arises only if a director takes advantage of a business opportunity in which the corporation would have an *interest or expectancy*. A corporation's interest does not extend to every conceivable business opportunity, but neither are opportunities limited to those necessary to the corporation's current business. The closer the opportunity is to the corporation's *line of business*, the more likely a court will find it to be a corporate opportunity.

2) Lack of Financial Ability Not a Defense

The corporation's lack of financial ability to take advantage of the opportunity probably is not a defense. The director should still present the opportunity to the corporation and allow it to decide whether it can take advantage of the opportunity.

3) Board Generally Decides

Because the board generally makes decisions concerning management of the corporation, it is the board that must decide whether to accept an opportunity or to reject it.

4) Remedies

If a director does not give the corporation an opportunity to act, but rather usurps the opportunity, the corporation can recover the profits that the director made from the transaction or may force the director to convey the opportunity to the corporation, under a constructive trust theory, for whatever consideration the director purchased the opportunity.

CMR | **Exam Tip** | Usurpation of a corporate opportunity is a very common Corporations exam issue. Whenever the facts of a question mention that a director learns of a business opportunity, be sure to consider whether her corporation would be interested. If so, she must present the opportunity to her corporation, disclosing all material facts, and can take advantage of the opportunity personally only if the corporation decides not to pursue it. If the corporation is not given a chance to take advantage of the opportunity, the director can be forced to turn over the opportunity and/or any profits derived from the opportunity to the corporation.

c. Competing Business

Directors may engage in unrelated businesses, but engaging in a competing business probably creates a conflict of interest.

d. Common Law Insider Trading—Special Circumstances Rule

A director has no common law duty to disclose all facts relevant to a securities transaction between the director and the other party to the transaction. However, courts have found a duty to disclose where a director knows of special circumstances (*e.g.,* an upcoming extraordinary dividend or a planned merger).

VII. OFFICERS

A. IN GENERAL

The RMBCA does not require a corporation to have any specific officers, but rather provides that a corporation shall have the officers described in its bylaws or appointed by the board pursuant to the bylaws. An officer may appoint other officers or assistant officers if so authorized by the bylaws or the board. One person may simultaneously hold more than one office.

B. DUTIES

Officers' duties are determined by the bylaws or, to the extent consistent with the bylaws, by the board or an officer so authorized by the board.

C. POWERS

Ordinary rules of agency determine authority and powers. Authority may be actual or apparent. Unauthorized actions may become binding on the corporation because of ratification, adoption, or estoppel. The corporation is liable for actions by its officers within the scope of their authority, even if the particular act in question was not specifically authorized.

D. STANDARD OF CONDUCT

Officers must carry out their duties in good faith, with the care an ordinarily prudent person in a like position would exercise under similar circumstances, and in a manner they reasonably believe to be in the best interests of the corporation.

E. RESIGNATION AND REMOVAL

Despite any contractual term to the contrary, an officer has the power to resign at any time by delivering notice to the corporation, and the corporation has the power to remove an officer at any time, **with or without cause**. If the resignation or removal is a breach of contract, the nonbreaching party may have a right to damages, but note that mere appointment to office itself does not create any contractual right to remain in office.

VIII. INDEMNIFICATION OF DIRECTORS, OFFICERS, AND EMPLOYEES

A. MANDATORY INDEMNIFICATION

Unless limited by the articles, a corporation **must** indemnify a director or officer who **prevailed** in defending a proceeding against the officer or director for reasonable expenses, including attorneys' fees, incurred in connection with the proceeding.

B. DISCRETIONARY INDEMNIFICATION

A corporation **may** indemnify a director for reasonable expenses incurred in **unsuccessfully defending** a suit brought against the director on account of the director's position if:

(i) The director acted in **good faith**; and

(ii) Believed that her conduct was: (a) in the **best interests of the corporation** (when the conduct at issue was within the director's official capacity); (b) **not opposed to the best interests of the corporation** (when the conduct at issue was not within the director's official capacity); or (c) **not unlawful** (in criminal proceedings).

1. **Exceptions**

   A corporation does not have discretion to indemnify a director who is unsuccessful in defending (i) a direct or derivative action in which the *director is found liable to the corporation* or (ii) an action charging that the director received an *improper benefit*.

2. **Who Makes Determination**

   Generally, the determination whether to indemnify is to be made by a disinterested majority of the board, or if there is not a disinterested quorum, by a majority of a disinterested committee or by legal counsel. The shareholders may also make the determination (the shares of the director seeking indemnification are not counted).

3. **Officers**

   Officers generally may be indemnified to the same extent as a director.

C. COURT-ORDERED INDEMNIFICATION

A court may order indemnification when the court feels this is appropriate.

D. ADVANCES

A corporation may advance expenses to a director defending an action as long as the director furnishes the corporation a statement that the director believes he met the appropriate standard of conduct and that he will repay the advance if he is later found to have not met the appropriate standard.

E. LIABILITY INSURANCE

A corporation may purchase liability insurance to indemnify directors for actions against them even if the directors would not have been entitled to indemnification under the above standards.

F. AGENTS AND EMPLOYEES

The RMBCA does not limit a corporation's power to indemnify, advance expenses to, or maintain insurance on agents and employees.

PART THREE—CHANGES IN STRUCTURE

IX. FUNDAMENTAL CHANGES IN CORPORATE STRUCTURE

A. GENERAL PROCEDURE FOR FUNDAMENTAL CHANGES

The following procedure applies to fundamental changes: (i) the board adopts a resolution; (ii) written notice is given to shareholders; (iii) shareholders approve changes by a majority of the votes entitled to be cast; and (iv) the changes in the form of articles are filed with the state.

CMR **Exam Tip** Note the distinction between shareholder voting on regular issues and shareholder voting on fundamental changes: Regular issues can be approved by a majority of the shares *cast at a meeting*, as long as there is a quorum, whereas a fundamental corporate change must be approved by a majority of *all votes entitled to be cast*—not just those cast at a meeting.

B. AMENDMENTS TO ARTICLES OF INCORPORATION

The corporation can amend its articles with any provision that would be lawful in original articles.

Certain "housekeeping" amendments (*e.g.*, deleting the names of initial directors named in the articles or changing the number of authorized shares after a stock split) can be made without shareholder approval, but most require approval by the shareholders.

C. MERGER, SHARE EXCHANGE, AND CONVERSION

A merger involves the blending of one or more corporations into another corporation, and the latter corporation survives while the merging corporations cease to exist following the merger. A share exchange involves one corporation purchasing all of the outstanding shares of one or more classes or series of another corporation. A conversion involves one business entity changing its form to another business entity, such as a corporation converting itself into an LLC.

1. Not All Shareholders Need Approve

Mergers, share exchanges, and conversions vary a little from the basic fundamental changes procedure in that not all shareholders have a right to approve these procedures under certain circumstances.

a. Merger

1) No Significant Change to Surviving Corporation

Approval of a plan of merger by shareholders of the *surviving* corporation is not required *if all the following conditions exist*: (i) the articles of incorporation of the surviving corporation will not differ from the articles before the merger; (ii) each shareholder of the survivor whose shares were outstanding immediately prior to the effective date of the merger will hold the same number of shares, with identical preferences, limitations, and rights; and (iii) the voting power of the shares issued as a result of the merger will comprise no more than 20% of the voting power of the shares of the surviving corporation that were outstanding immediately prior to the merger.

2) Short Form Merger of Subsidiary

A parent corporation owning at least 90% of the outstanding shares of each class of a subsidiary corporation may merge the subsidiary into itself *without the approval of the shareholders or directors of the subsidiary*. The parent must mail a copy of the plan of merger to each shareholder of the subsidiary.

b. Share Exchange

Only the shareholders of the corporation whose shares will be acquired in the share exchange need approve a share exchange; a share exchange is *not* a fundamental corporate change for the acquiring corporation.

c. Conversion

The procedure for effecting a conversion generally is the same as the procedure for approving a merger in which the converting corporation is not the survivor.

D. DISPOSITION OF PROPERTY OUTSIDE THE USUAL AND REGULAR COURSE OF BUSINESS

A sale, lease, exchange, or other disposition of *all or substantially all* (*e.g.,* more than 75% of a corporation's assets, accounting for at least 75% of its revenues) of a corporation's property outside the usual and regular course of business is a fundamental corporate change *for the corporation*

disposing of the property. Thus, the corporation disposing of the property must follow the fundamental change procedure.

1. Effect on Purchaser

Generally, the purchaser of another corporation's property does not become liable for the seller's obligations; the seller remains solely liable. However, if the disposition of property is really a disguised merger, a court might treat it as a merger under the de facto merger doctrine and hold the purchaser liable for the seller's obligations just as if a merger had occurred.

E. PROTECTION AGAINST AND LIMITATIONS ON FUNDAMENTAL CHANGES

1. Dissenting Shareholders' Appraisal Remedy—Who May Dissent

If a corporation approves a fundamental change, shareholders who dissent from the change may have the right to have the corporation purchase their shares. This right is known as the "right of appraisal" or "dissenters' rights." The following have a right to the appraisal remedy: (i) any shareholder *entitled to vote* on a plan of merger and *shareholders of the subsidiary* in short form merger; (ii) shareholders of the corporation whose shares are being *acquired* in a share exchange; (iii) a shareholder who is *entitled to vote* on a disposition of all or substantially all of the corporation's property; and (iv) a shareholder whose rights will be *materially and adversely affected* by an amendment of the corporation's articles.

2. Procedure

a. Corporation Must Give Shareholders Notice

If a proposed corporate action will create dissenters' rights, the notice of the shareholders' meeting at which a vote on the action will be taken must state that the shareholders will be entitled to exercise their dissenting rights.

b. Shareholder Must Give Notice of Intent to Demand Payment

Before a vote is taken, the shareholder must deliver *written notice of her intent to demand payment* for her shares if the proposed action is taken. She cannot vote in favor of the proposed action.

c. Corporation Must Give Dissenters Notice

If the action is approved, the corporation must notify, *within 10 days* after approval, all shareholders who filed an intent to demand payment. The notice must include the time and place to submit their shares and the other terms of the repurchase.

d. Shareholders Must Demand Payment

A shareholder who is sent a dissenter's notice must then *demand payment* in accordance with the notice given by the corporation.

e. Corporation Must Pay

The corporation must pay the dissenters the *amount the corporation estimates as the fair value* of the shares, plus accrued interest.

f. Notice of Dissatisfaction

If the shareholder is dissatisfied with the corporation's determination of value, the

shareholder has 30 days in which to send the corporation her *own estimate of value* and demand payment of that amount (or the difference between her estimate and the amount sent by the corporation).

g. Court Action

If the corporation does not want to pay what the shareholder demanded, *the corporation* must file an action in court within 60 days of receiving the shareholder's demand, requesting the court to determine the fair value of the shares. Otherwise, the corporation must pay what the shareholder demanded.

3. Tender Offers and Corporate Control Problems

a. Federal Regulation—The Williams Act

The federal Williams Act controls tender offers (*i.e.,* offers by a "bidder" to purchase shares from shareholders of a "target" corporation).

1) Regulation of the Bidder

If a bidder makes a tender offer (a widespread public offering to purchase a substantial percentage of the target's shares), and the offer will result in the bidder obtaining more than **5%** of a class of securities of the target, the bidder must file a schedule 14D containing extensive disclosure regarding:

a) The bidder's *identity, source of funds, past dealings with the target*, and *plans concerning the target*;

b) The *bidder's financial statements* if the bidder is not an individual; and

c) Any *arrangements* made with persons in important positions at the target.

2) Regulation of the Offer

Under the Williams Act:

a) A tender offer must be held open for *at least 20* days and *must* be *open to all members of the class* of securities sought;

b) Shareholders must be *permitted to withdraw* tendered shares while the offer remains open;

c) If the offer is oversubscribed, the bidder *must purchase on a pro rata basis* from among the shares deposited during the first 10 days of the offer; and

d) If the offer price is increased, the *higher price must be paid to all tendering shareholders*.

3) Regulation of the Target

The management of the target must either (i) give its shareholders a recommendation concerning the offer, with a statement of reasons, or (ii) explain why it cannot make a recommendation.

4) **General Anti-Fraud Provision**
The Williams Act also prohibits any false or misleading statements or omissions in connection with the offer. Shareholders can sue for damages for any false statements, and the Securities and Exchange Commission may seek to enjoin any false statements.

b. **State Regulation—Control Share Acquisition Statutes**
State control share acquisition statutes regulate takeovers by providing that if a designated stock ownership threshold is crossed (*e.g.,* a bidder purchases shares that give him more than 20% of a class of shares), the shares so purchased will not have voting rights *unless* the holders of a majority of the disinterested shares vote to grant voting rights in the acquired shares. Note that a state may have more than one threshold (*e.g.,* 20%, 33%, and 50%), and crossing from one level of ownership to the next will trigger the statute.

1) **Limitation on Scope**
To be valid, control share acquisition statutes must be limited to corporations or transactions having a *significant connection to the regulating state* (*e.g.,* limiting application to purchases where 1,000 shareholders or at least 10% of the outstanding shares are located in the state).

X. DISSOLUTION AND LIQUIDATION

A. VOLUNTARY DISSOLUTION

1. **Dissolution by Incorporators or Initial Directors**
If *shares have not yet been issued or business has not yet been commenced*, a majority of the incorporators or initial directors may dissolve the corporation by delivering articles of dissolution to the state. All corporate debts must be paid before dissolution, and if shares have been issued, any assets remaining after winding up must be distributed to the shareholders.

2. **Dissolution by Corporate Act**
The corporation may dissolve by a corporate act approved under the fundamental change procedure.

3. **Effect of Dissolution**
A corporation that has been dissolved continues its corporate existence, but is not allowed to carry on any business except that which is appropriate to winding up and liquidating its affairs.

a. **Barring Claims Against the Corporation**
A claim can be asserted against a dissolved corporation, even if the claim does not arise until after dissolution, to the extent of the corporation's undistributed assets. If the assets have been distributed to the shareholders, a claim can be asserted against each shareholder for his pro rata share of the claim, to the extent of the assets distributed to him. However, a corporation can cut short the time for bringing known claims by notifying claimants in writing of the dissolution and giving them a deadline of not less than 120 days in which to file their claim. The time for filing unknown claims can be

limited to five years by publishing notice of the dissolution in a newspaper in the county where the corporation's known place of business is located.

4. Revocation of Voluntary Dissolution
The corporation may revoke a voluntary dissolution by using the same procedure that was used to approve the dissolution.

B. ADMINISTRATIVE DISSOLUTION
The state may bring an action to administratively dissolve a corporation for reasons such as the failure to pay fees or penalties, failure to file an annual report, and failure to maintain a registered agent in the state. The state must serve the corporation with written notice of the failure. If the corporation does not correct the grounds for dissolution or show that the grounds do not exist within *60* days after service of notice, the state effectuates the dissolution by signing a certificate of dissolution. A corporation that is administratively dissolved may apply for reinstatement within three years after the effective date of dissolution. The application must state that the grounds for dissolution either did not exist or have been eliminated. Reinstatement relates back to the date of dissolution, and the corporation may resume carrying on business as if the dissolution had never occurred.

C. JUDICIAL DISSOLUTION

1. Action by Attorney General
The attorney general may seek judicial dissolution of a corporation on the ground that the corporation *fraudulently obtained its articles* of incorporation or that the corporation is *exceeding or abusing its authority*.

2. Action by Shareholders
Shareholders may seek judicial dissolution on any of the following grounds:

(i) The *directors are deadlocked* in the management of corporate affairs, the shareholders are unable to break the deadlock, and *irreparable injury* to the corporation is threatened, or corporate affairs cannot be conducted to the advantage of the shareholders because of the deadlock;

(ii) The directors have acted or will act in a manner that is *illegal, oppressive, or fraudulent*;

(iii) The shareholders are deadlocked in voting power and have *failed to elect one or more directors* for a period that includes at least two consecutive annual meeting dates; or

(iv) *Corporate assets are being wasted, misapplied, or diverted for noncorporate purposes*.

a. Election to Purchase in Lieu of Dissolution
If the corporation's shares are not listed on a national securities exchange or regularly traded in a market maintained by one or more members of a national or affiliated securities association, the corporation (or one or more shareholders) may elect to purchase the shares owned by the petitioning shareholder at their fair value.

3. Action by Creditors
Creditors may seek judicial dissolution if: (i) the creditor's claim has been reduced to

judgment, execution of the judgment has been returned unsatisfied, and *the corporation is insolvent*; or (ii) the corporation has admitted in writing that the creditor's claim is due and owing and *the corporation is insolvent*.

4. Court Supervision of Voluntary Dissolution
A court may dissolve a corporation in an action by the corporation to have its voluntary dissolution continued under court supervision.

PART FOUR—LIMITED LIABILITY COMPANIES, PROFESSIONAL CORPORATIONS, AND FOREIGN CORPORATIONS

XI. LIMITED LIABILITY COMPANIES

A. INTRODUCTION
A limited liability company ("LLC") is a hybrid business organization that (i) is taxed like a partnership, (ii) offers its owners (called members) the limited liability of shareholders of a corporation, and (iii) can be run like either a corporation or a partnership. There is no limit on the number of owners (members) as there would be in a Subchapter S corporation (a corporation that is taxed like a partnership under the tax code), and no one has to accept full personal liability for the organization's debts, as would be required in a limited partnership.

B. FORMATION
An LLC is formed by filing articles of organization with the secretary of state.

1. Contents of Articles
The articles of an LLC must include the following:

   a. A *statement that the entity is an LLC*;

   b. The *name* of the LLC, which must include an indication that it is an LLC;

   c. The street address of the LLC's *registered office* and name of its *registered agent*; and

   d. The names of all of the *members*.

2. Management
Management of the LLC is presumed to be by all members, but the articles may provide for some other type of management. If management is by the members: (i) a majority vote is required to approve most decisions and (ii) each member is an agent of the LLC (*i.e.*, the LLC may be bound by the acts of any member apparently carrying on the business of the LLC). Managers of an LLC owe the LLC duties of care and loyalty similar to those owed by a director of a corporation.

C. LIABILITY OF MEMBERS
Members are *not* personally liable for the LLC's obligations.

D. SHARING OF PROFITS AND LOSSES
Profits and losses of an LLC are allocated on the basis of contributions.

E. MEMBERS' ACTIONS AGAINST THE LLC

A member who has been injured personally by his LLC can bring a direct action against the LLC to recover. A member may also bring a derivative action on behalf of the LLC under circumstances similar to those in which a shareholder may bring a derivative action against his corporation. (*See* V.F.2., *supra.*)

F. TRANSFERS OF INTEREST

An assignment of a member's interest in an LLC transfers only the member's right to receive profits and losses. Management rights are not transferred. One can become a member (*i.e.,* management rights can be transferred) only with the consent of **all** members.

G. DISSOLUTION

Dissociation (*e.g.,* death, retirement, resignation, bankruptcy, incompetence, etc.) of an LLC member generally causes dissolution.

XII. PROFESSIONAL CORPORATIONS

Most states prohibit professionals from forming corporations under the general corporations statute for the purpose of practicing their professions. This rule was based on the idea that professionals should not be able to avoid personal liability for their own malpractice by hiding behind the corporate veil. However, most states have adopted special statutes permitting professionals to incorporate so that they can take advantage of certain federal tax provisions that are available only to corporations. The statutes generally treat professional corporations like any other corporation but limit share ownership to licensed professionals and make it clear that a professional practicing in the corporation will still be **personally liable** for his own malpractice, despite the corporate form.

XIII. FOREIGN CORPORATIONS

A foreign corporation may not transact business within a state until it has obtained a certificate of authority from the secretary of state. A foreign corporation may not be denied a certificate of authority merely because the laws of its state of incorporation governing its organization and internal affairs differ from the host jurisdiction. If a foreign corporation is doing business in a state and has not obtained a certificate of authority to do business, it generally cannot bring suit in the foreign state, although it can defend suits. However, failure to obtain a certificate does not usually impair the validity of any contract or corporate act.

PART FIVE—SECURITIES REGULATION

XIV. RULE 10b-5, SECTION 16(b), AND SARBANES-OXLEY

A. RULE 10b-5

Rule 10b-5 makes it illegal for any person to use any means or instrumentality of interstate commerce to employ any scheme to defraud, make an untrue statement of material fact (or omit a material fact), or engage in any practice that operates as a fraud in connection with the purchase or sale of any security.

1. **General Elements of Cause of Action**
   A private plaintiff must show the following elements to recover damages under rule 10b-5:

   a. **Fraudulent Conduct**
      The plaintiff must show that the defendant engaged in some fraudulent conduct. This can take a number of forms, *e.g.*, making a material misstatement or making an omission of material fact.

      1) **Materiality**
         A statement or omission will be considered material if there is a ***substantial likelihood that a reasonable investor would consider it important*** in making an investment decision.

      2) **Scienter**
         To be actionable under rule 10b-5, the conduct complained of must have been undertaken with an ***intent to deceive, manipulate, or defraud***. Recklessness as to truth also appears to be sufficient culpability.

   b. **In Connection with the Purchase or Sale of a Security by Plaintiff**
      If the plaintiff is a private person, the fraudulent conduct must be connected to the purchase or sale of a security by the plaintiff. This *excludes* potential purchasers who do not buy and people who already own shares and refrain from selling.

      1) **Nontrading Defendants Can Be Held Liable**
         Note that the defendant need not have purchased or sold any securities; a nontrading defendant, such as a company that intentionally publishes a misleading press release, can be held liable to a person who purchased or sold securities on the market on the basis of the press release.

   c. **In Interstate Commerce**
      The fraudulent conduct must involve the use of some means of interstate commerce; however, something as simple as use of the telephone or the mail will suffice.

   d. **Reliance**
      A private plaintiff must prove that he relied on the defendant's fraudulent statement, omission, or conduct. But note that in cases based on omissions, reliance generally will be presumed if the plaintiff proves that the omission was material.

   e. **Damages**
      A private plaintiff must show that the defendant's fraud caused the plaintiff damages. Damages are limited to the difference between the price paid (or received) and the average share price in the 90-day period after corrective information is disseminated.

2. **Insider Trading**
   Rule 10b-5 also prohibits most instances of trading securities on the basis of inside information (*i.e.*, information not disclosed to the public that an investor would think is important when deciding whether or not to invest in a security). A person violates rule 10b-5 if by trading he breaches a ***duty of trust and confidence*** owed to: (i) the issuer, (ii) shareholders of the issuer, or (iii) in the case of misappropriators (*see* below), another person who is the source of the material nonpublic information.

a. **Who May Be Liable**

1) **Insiders**

Anyone who breaches a duty not to use inside information for personal benefit can be held liable under rule 10b-5 (*e.g.*, directors, officers, controlling shareholders, employees of the issuer, and the issuer's CPAs, attorneys, and bankers).

2) **Tippers and Tippees**

If an insider gives a tip of inside information to someone else who trades on the basis of the inside information, the tipper can be liable under rule 10b-5 if the tip was made for any *improper purpose* (*e.g.*, in exchange for money or a kickback, as a gift, for a reputational benefit, etc.). The tippee can be held liable only if the tipper breached a duty *and* the tippee knew that the tipper was breaching the duty.

3) **Misappropriators**

Under the misappropriation doctrine, *the government* can prosecute a person under rule 10b-5 for trading on market information (*i.e.*, information about the supply of or demand for stock of a particular company) in breach of a duty of trust and confidence *owed to the source of the information*; the duty need not be owed to the issuer or shareholders of the issuer.

B. **SECTION 16(b)**

Section 16(b) requires surrender to the corporation of any profit realized by any director, officer, or shareholder owning more than 10% of a class of the corporation's stock from the purchase and sale, or sale and purchase, of any equity security within a six-month period. The section applies to publicly held corporations (i) with more than $10 million in assets and 500 or more shareholders in any outstanding class *or* (ii) whose shares are traded on a national exchange.

1. **Strict Liability**

The purpose of section 16(b) is to prevent unfair use of inside information and internal manipulation of price. This is accomplished by imposing strict liability for covered transactions.

2. **Elements of Cause of Action**

a. **Purchase and Sale or Sale and Purchase Within Six Months**

The test of whether a transaction is a sale or purchase for purposes of section 16(b) is whether the transaction is one in which abuse of inside information is likely to occur (*e.g.,* forced sales might not be counted).

b. **Equity Security**

An equity security is any security other than a pure debt instrument, including options, warrants, preferred stock, common stock, etc.

c. **Officer, Director, or More than Ten Percent Shareholder**

Officers, directors, and more than 10% shareholders include not only those actual persons, but also anyone who has deputized one of those persons to act for him. Transactions occurring before one becomes an officer or director are excluded from section 16(b), but transactions occurring within six months after ceasing to be an officer or

director can be covered. Share ownership is measured at the time of both the purchase and the sale.

3. **Profit Realized**
    The recoverable profit under section 16(b) is determined by matching the ***highest sales price against the lowest purchase price*** for any six-month period. Thus, the "profit" can be either a gain or an avoided loss.

C. THE SARBANES-OXLEY ACT OF 2002

1. **Public Company Accounting Oversight Board**
    The Sarbanes-Oxley Act of 2002 ("SOA") provides for the creation of a Public Company Accounting Oversight Board to register public accounting firms that prepare audit reports for companies registered under the 1934 Act. The Board will establish rules for auditing, quality control, ethics, and independence relating to preparation of audit reports. Only a public accounting firm registered with the Oversight Board may prepare or issue audit reports with respect to a registered company.

2. **Corporate Responsibility**

    a. **Public Company Audit Committees**
        The SOA requires the board of directors of each 1934 Act company to establish an audit committee comprised of board members. The committee oversees the work performed by the registered public accounting firm and establishes internal procedures for receiving and handling complaints about the company's accounting, internal accounting controls, and auditing procedures. Audit committee members must not receive compensation from the company other than for their position on the board of directors.

    b. **Corporate Responsibility for Financial Reports**
        The SOA directs the SEC to adopt rules requiring companies filing reports under the 1934 Act to have their CEO, CFO, or similar person certify in each report, among other things, that: (i) the officer has reviewed the report; (ii) based on the officer's knowledge, the report is true and does not contain any material omissions; and (iii) the signing officer is responsible for establishing internal controls, has designed such controls to ensure that material information is made known to the officer, and has evaluated the controls within 90 days prior to the report.

    c. **Forfeiture of Bonuses and Profits**
        If a company is required to restate financial reports because of misconduct with respect to the reports, the company's CEO ***and*** CFO must reimburse the company for any bonus or other incentive-based compensation received by them during the 12-month period after the inaccurate reports were filed with the SEC or made public (whichever is earlier). The officers must also turn over to the company any profit that they made from the sale of the company's securities during the same 12-month period.

    d. **Prohibition Against Insider Trades During Pension Blackout Periods**
        Directors and executive officers of 1934 Act companies may not purchase or sell the company's stock during a period when persons participating in the company's pension plan are not allowed to sell company stock.

    e.   Prohibition Against Personal Loans to Executives

A company generally may not make any new personal loans to any director or executive officer of the company, except to the extent that the loans are made in the ordinary course of the company's consumer credit business and on terms no more favorable than the company offers to the general public.

    f.   Disclosure of Audit Committee Financial Expert

The SOA directs the SEC to issue rules requiring companies to disclose, in their annual reports, whether or not (and if not, why not) the audit committee has at least one member who is a financial expert.

3.   Corporate and Criminal Fraud

    a.   Criminal Penalties for Destruction, Alteration, Etc.

The SOA makes it a crime punishable by fine and imprisonment for up to 20 years for anyone to knowingly alter, destroy, mutilate, falsify, etc., a document or record with intent to impede a federal investigation.

    b.   Criminal Penalty for Destruction of Corporate Audit Records

The SOA makes it a crime for an accountant who conducts an audit of a 1934 Act company, punishable by fine and up to 10 years' imprisonment, to willfully fail to keep all workpapers related to the audit for at least five years.

    c.   Statute of Limitations for Fraud

The SOA provides that the statute of limitations for private cases for securities fraud is the later of two years after discovery of the facts giving rise to the cause of action or five years after the action accrued.

    d.   Whistleblower Protection

The SOA creates a statutory cause of action for persons who are discharged because they lawfully provided information to their supervisors or the federal government regarding any conduct that they reasonably believed to be a violation of the securities laws.

    e.   Criminal Penalties for Defrauding Shareholders and the Public

The SOA makes securities frauds punishable by up to 25 years' imprisonment.

EQUITY

TABLE OF CONTENTS

EQUITY

I. NATURE OF EQUITY

Equity, for bar examination purposes, is concerned with the granting of certain types of remedies. These are injunctive relief against tortious conduct, specific performance, rescission, reformation, constructive trust, and equitable liens and mortgages. There is no absolute right to equitable relief (as compared to a legal remedy, which issues as a matter of right), and an equitable remedy generally will not be granted if the harm caused by granting the remedy will greatly outweigh the benefit that the moving party would receive. Usually, there is no right to a jury trial in equity.

CMR   **Exam Tip**   Equity is a very important topic; not only can it be tested on the state portion of the exam, but also equity concepts can appear on the Multistate exam in Contracts or Real Property questions.

II. INJUNCTIVE RELIEF

A. IN GENERAL

Briefly, a plaintiff can obtain injunctive relief against tortious conduct being or about to be committed if the plaintiff can show that (i) the legal remedy is inadequate; (ii) a property right, or at least a protectable interest, is involved; (iii) enforcement of an equitable decree would be feasible, practicable, and effective to vindicate the plaintiff's rights; (iv) the hardship to the defendant, where relevant, does not greatly outweigh the benefit that the plaintiff may get from the relief sought; and (v) no defenses are available.

1. Personal Jurisdiction Required

Personal jurisdiction over the defendant usually is required for injunctive relief because enforcement is through contempt.

2. Enforcement of Injunction by Contempt

Equity courts enforce injunctions by holding a noncomplying party in contempt and imposing a fine or imprisonment. Contempt is considered criminal if the sanction imposed seeks to punish the contemnor and civil if the sanction seeks to coerce the contemnor into obeying a court order. If criminal, normal criminal procedures apply. The only defense is that the court lacked jurisdiction; courts generally will not consider the validity of the merits of the underlying injunction.

3. Classifications

Injunctions can be mandatory (ordering that something be done) or negative (ordering that something not be done), interlocutory (*i.e.,* temporary) or permanent.

4. Who Is Bound

An injunction binds the parties, their agents who receive notice, and anyone else who has notice of the injunction and is acting in concert or collusion with the parties and their agents. *Note:* A person may not be held in contempt for violating an injunction unless she has received some form of notice of the injunction.

5. Duration

An injunction must be followed until it is vacated or modified by the courts, even if it appears to have been erroneously granted, unless the court was without jurisdiction.

AVAILABILITY OF INJUNCTIVE RELIEF

Determine the nature of the wrong (tort) and then ask:

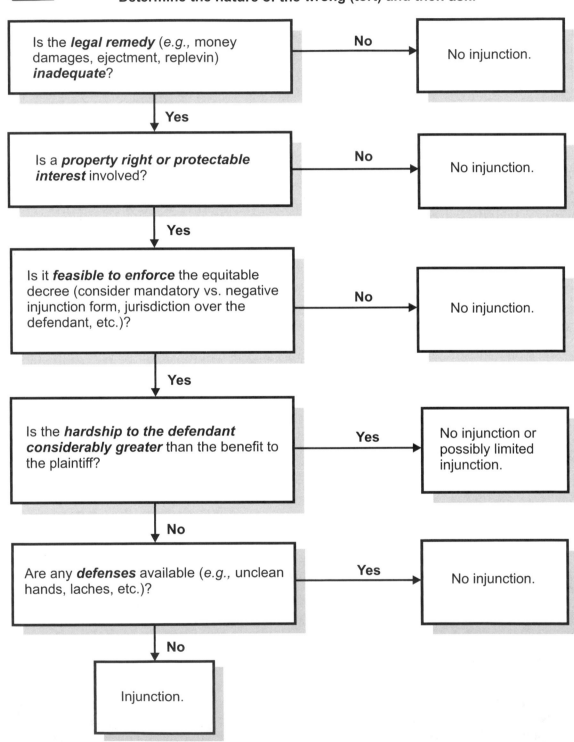

Is the *legal remedy* (*e.g.,* money damages, ejectment, replevin) *inadequate*? → **No** → No injunction.

↓ **Yes**

Is a *property right or protectable interest* involved? → **No** → No injunction.

↓ **Yes**

Is it *feasible to enforce* the equitable decree (consider mandatory vs. negative injunction form, jurisdiction over the defendant, etc.)? → **No** → No injunction.

↓ **Yes**

Is the *hardship to the defendant considerably greater* than the benefit to the plaintiff? → **Yes** → No injunction or possibly limited injunction.

↓ **No**

Are any *defenses* available (*e.g.,* unclean hands, laches, etc.)? → **Yes** → No injunction.

↓ **No**

Injunction.

B. INJUNCTIVE RELIEF AGAINST TORTIOUS CONDUCT

1. What Is the Tort?

CMR **Exam Tip** While an injunction question can involve any tort, the state examiners seem to favor nuisance, trespass to land, and misappropriation of trade secrets (including secret customer lists).

a. Nuisance
Consider the balance of hardships. Injunctive relief against nuisance will generally be granted only against a private nuisance; an individual will not have the right to enjoin a public nuisance unless he can show that he has standing to sue, *e.g.,* a special injury.

b. Trespass to Land
Consider the balance of hardships. Injunctive relief is proper where the trespass is continuous.

c. Waste
If waste exists, is it destructive, permissive, or ameliorative? Generally, equity will not grant injunctive relief in ameliorative waste situations.

d. Conversion of or Trespass to Chattels
These torts involve interference with an owner's interest in a chattel. Injunctive relief is proper where the interference is continuous or the converted chattel is unique.

e. Defamation
Look for the existence of a property right, but remember that equity courts are hesitant to enjoin mere libel or slander because of free speech rights.

f. Invasion of Right of Privacy
Again, be sure there is a property right and consider potential free speech problems if a "publication" is involved.

g. Abuse of Judicial Process
This may be a (i) wrongfully instituted suit or (ii) wrongfully obtained judgment. Regarding the first type of abuse, recall that the court can enjoin the *litigants*, not the other court. As to a wrongfully obtained judgment, only *extrinsic* (not intrinsic) fraud is sufficient for equitable relief against enforcement of the judgment.

h. Unfair Competition

1) Inducing Breach of Contract and/or Refusal to Deal
An injunction is generally proper when a defendant encourages someone to breach a contract with, or refuse to do business with, defendant's competitor.

2) Use of Competitor's Trade Secrets
A trade secret will be protected by the courts.

a) **Is the Property a Trade Secret?**
A trade secret is information not readily available that gives its possessor a competitive advantage.

b) **How Was the Trade Secret Taken?**
Courts are more likely to issue an injunction if the information was *wrongfully obtained* (*e.g.*, secretly photocopied).

c) **What Is the Relationship of Taker to Owner?**
Was there either a fiduciary relationship or a contract relationship? If so, an injunction is more likely. *Express covenants* not to disclose trade secrets are always specifically enforceable. However, an express contractual covenant is *not* required in seeking an injunction against disclosure of trade secrets.

d) **Who May Be Enjoined?**
Both the wrongful taker and/or the person who intends to use the trade secret can be enjoined.

2. Is the Legal Remedy Inadequate?
A legal remedy could be money damages, replevin, or ejectment.

a. Money Damages
If money damages will make the plaintiff whole, equity will not act. Money damages might be *inadequate* if:

1) Damages are speculative;

2) Defendant is insolvent;

3) The injury is irreparable;

4) A multiplicity of actions might be necessary; or

5) Plaintiff has no right to damages (*e.g.*, the tort is only prospective).

b. Replevin and Ejectment
Replevin may be inadequate if defendant could put up a replevin bond for a *unique* chattel or if there has been a change in the chattel (so that the sheriff would not be able to identify it). The legal remedy of ejectment may be inadequate because the sheriff refuses to act.

3. Is a Property Right Involved?

a. Liberal Construction of Facts
Remember that the courts will stretch to find existence of a property right, so consider whether a tort could in any conceivable way cause a money loss (*e.g.*, personal defamation that might get back to a person's boss and cause the person to lose his job).

b. **Modern Trend**

The modern trend is to give relief, even absent a property right, *i.e.,* where there is a "protectable" right (*e.g.,* right of privacy action).

4. **Is Enforcement Feasible?**

a. **Is the Injunction Sought "Negative" or "Mandatory"?**

A negative injunction is easier to get since no supervision is required. The recent trend is to be more liberal in giving "mandatory" injunctions. In these cases, look to the complexity of the act to be performed and whether continuous acts are required. Remember, a court may avoid the problem by couching the decree's terms negatively.

b. **Does Injunction Require an Out-of-State Act?**

The recent trend is to grant such injunctions, but be sure the court has sufficient contacts with the defendant (*e.g.,* defendant is a resident of the court's jurisdiction). The courts are more hesitant to grant a mandatory injunction in these cases, but will still do so under proper circumstances.

5. **Are the Hardships Balanced?**

Weigh the ***benefit to the plaintiff*** if the injunction is granted against the ***hardship to defendant*** that would result from the injunction. If the benefit to the plaintiff is outweighed by the burden on defendant, the court generally will not issue an injunction. Also, consider the defendant's behavior: A willful defendant generally will not profit from this rule.

6. **Does Defendant Have Any Defenses?**

a. **Unclean Hands**

It is a defense that the party seeking the injunction has ***acted improperly in the transaction in question***.

CMR **Exam Tip** Be careful in using the unclean hands defense. It is available only if the unclean hands conduct is related to the case at hand. Unrelated unfair conduct is irrelevant. Thus, for example, the fact that plaintiff has committed fraud in the sale of other parcels of land in a subdivision will not help defendant if there was no fraud in the sale to defendant.

b. **Laches**

Laches may be available if plaintiff has ***unreasonably delayed*** in bringing an action ***and*** the delay is ***prejudicial*** to defendant. Laches commences to run when the plaintiff has knowledge that a right has been infringed. Laches may serve as an earlier time bar than the statute of limitations; however, laches cannot be longer than the statute of limitations.

CMR **Exam Tip** It is important to remember that the statute of limitations is concerned with the mere passage of time, whereas laches is concerned with the ***effect*** of the passage of time.

c. **Defenses of Impossibility, Hardship, and Freedom of Speech**

In appropriate circumstances, impossibility, hardship, or free speech rights may be used as a defense to an action for injunctive relief.

C. INTERLOCUTORY INJUNCTIONS

An interlocutory injunction is used to *preserve the status quo* between the parties until a full trial on the merits can be held. Notice of the hearing for an interlocutory injunction is generally required to be given to a defendant, and a bond is usually required to secure a defendant's losses in case the injunction should not have been issued. To obtain an interlocutory injunction, the plaintiff must show that she is *likely to prevail on the merits* but will suffer *irreparable injury before the trial can be held* unless the interlocutory injunction is granted.

1. Temporary Restraining Order

In drastic circumstances (*i.e.,* where irreparable harm will occur before a hearing on a preliminary injunction can be held), a temporary restraining order ("TRO") may be sought. Less formal notice is required than with a preliminary injunction. Indeed, a TRO may be granted without notice if the moving party can make a strong showing why notice should not be required. Of course, the restrained party cannot be held liable for violating the TRO unless he knew about it when he acted.

CMR Exam Tip If the question does not tell you what type of injunction is sought, assume you are dealing with a permanent injunction. If the question asks about temporary injunctive relief, be sure to note that the purpose of such relief is to *preserve the status quo* to prevent irreparable injury before a trial can be held.

CMR COMPARISON CHART — INJUNCTIONS

	Permanent Injunction	Temporary Injunction	Temporary Restraining Order
Purpose	To grant the relief sought	To preserve the status quo	To preserve the status quo
Duration	As long as necessary	Until completion of the judicial proceeding	Usually 10 days (14 days in federal court)
Requirements for Issuing	Notice and adversarial hearing	Notice and adversarial hearing	Some notice if practicable

D. INJUNCTIVE RELIEF AGAINST CRIMINAL CONDUCT

Injunctive relief generally is not available against criminal conduct on constitutional grounds, as it would deprive defendant of the right to a trial by jury. But consider whether the crime is also a tort, which may be enjoined.

E. **INJUNCTIVE RELIEF INVOLVING POLITICAL RIGHTS**

Injunctive relief involving political rights generally is not available because of the availability of legal remedies; *e.g.,* mandamus usually is sufficient. But consider whether the conduct endangering the political right is also tortious and thus subject to relief.

III. SPECIFIC PERFORMANCE

A. **IN GENERAL**

To obtain specific performance, a plaintiff must show that (i) a contract exists, (ii) all contractual conditions have been fulfilled, (iii) the legal remedy is inadequate, (iv) enforcement is feasible, (v) mutuality of remedy exists, and (vi) there are no defenses available to the defendant.

B. **DOES A CONTRACT EXIST?**

Obviously, there must be a valid contract for specific performance. Remember that equity requires the contract terms to be somewhat ***more certain*** than would a court in an action at law, although parol evidence may be used to make the contract more certain. The contract must be supported by consideration. Generally, equity courts will not examine the sufficiency of consideration unless it is unconscionable. Unconscionable contracts are not entitled to equitable relief.

C. **HAVE PLAINTIFF'S CONDITIONS BEEN FULFILLED?**

There are only two conditions issues that are likely to appear on the bar exam:

1. **Time of the Essence Clause**

A clause requiring performance within a stipulated period of time must be expressly included in the contract; in its absence, a reasonable time to perform will be implied.

a. **Type of Contract**

If the contract is ***wholly executory***, the clause will be ***strictly enforced***. If the contract is ***partially executed***, the court will seek to avoid the effect of the clause so as to ***avoid forfeiture***. The court will be likely to avoid the effect of the clause if (i) loss to the other party is small, (ii) the forfeiting party would suffer undue hardship, (iii) tardiness is "de minimis," or (iv) the seller has performed acts giving rise to a waiver situation. Also look to see if judicial sale might be appropriate.

2. **Deficiencies**

The main concern here is whether the seller can deliver the quantity or quality of land promised. If there is a deficiency, the seller may get specific performance only if the deficiency is ***minor***. A buyer, on the other hand, can generally get specific performance despite ***substantial*** deficiencies but will be unable to get specific performance if the deficiency is ***very large***. In any case, if specific performance is granted, there must be an abatement in price for the deficiency.

CMR | **Exam Tip** | On the Multistate exam, the examiners will often try to trick you with a marketable title question. Remember that the duty to provide marketable title does not arise until closing. Thus, if the closing will result in marketable title (*e.g.,* because closing funds will be used to pay off a mortgage), there is no marketable title problem.

SPECIFIC PERFORMANCE

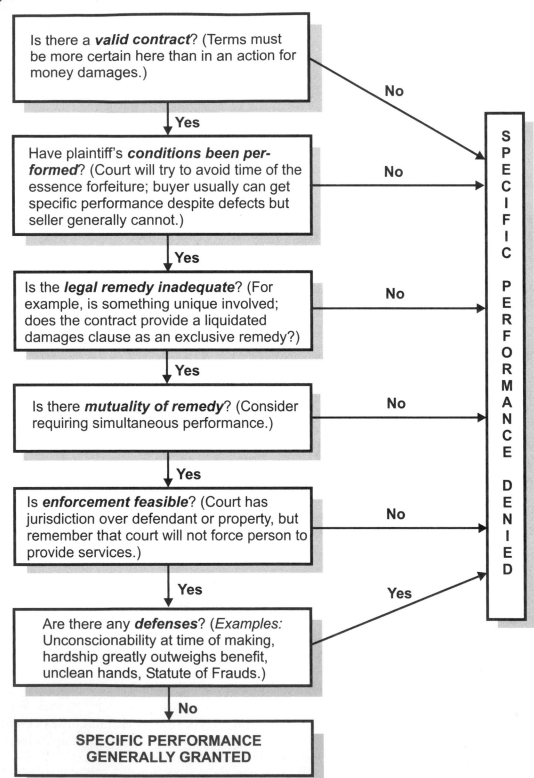

Is there a **valid contract**? (Terms must be more certain here than in an action for money damages.)

— No →

Have plaintiff's **conditions been performed**? (Court will try to avoid time of the essence forfeiture; buyer usually can get specific performance despite defects but seller generally cannot.)

— No →

Is the **legal remedy inadequate**? (For example, is something unique involved; does the contract provide a liquidated damages clause as an exclusive remedy?)

— No →

Is there **mutuality of remedy**? (Consider requiring simultaneous performance.)

— No →

Is **enforcement feasible**? (Court has jurisdiction over defendant or property, but remember that court will not force person to provide services.)

— No →

Are there any **defenses**? (*Examples:* Unconscionability at time of making, hardship greatly outweighs benefit, unclean hands, Statute of Frauds.)

— Yes →

SPECIFIC PERFORMANCE DENIED

↓ No

SPECIFIC PERFORMANCE GENERALLY GRANTED

D. IS THE LEGAL REMEDY INADEQUATE?

1. Thing Bargained for Is Rare or Unique

a. Land

Land is always unique. Thus, both the buyer and seller of land can get specific performance.

CMR | **Exam Tip** | Be wary of questions describing a "generic" parcel of land and telling you that the seller is willing to give the buyer similar or even better land right next door to the parcel. Don't be fooled. All land is considered unique. Therefore, similar or better land is *not* a sufficient remedy. Grant specific performance to the buyer.

b. Personal Property

If personal property is involved, see whether it is (i) unique in kind, (ii) of personal significance to the buyer (using a reasonable person test), or (iii) in short supply. If not, money damages are adequate.

c. Personal Services

If personal services are involved, check to see if they are unique. If not, money damages are adequate. Even if the services are unique, equity will not force a person to perform services because of "involuntary servitude" problems and the difficulty of enforcement. However, the defendant can be prevented from working for someone else.

2. Inadequacy of Money Damages

Money damages may be inadequate when damages are speculative, the defendant is insolvent, or multiple suits would be necessary. Remember, a liquidated damages clause can make the legal remedy adequate if it provides that it is the *exclusive* remedy of the parties.

E. DOES MUTUALITY OF REMEDY EXIST?

There are two types of mutuality problems. Negative mutuality involves the argument that plaintiff should not be allowed to enforce the contract because defendant would not be able to. If, however, both parties are *capable of performing* and *counterperformance may be sufficiently secured*, negative mutuality is not a problem. Affirmative mutuality involves the argument that plaintiff should be allowed to enforce the contract because defendant would have been able to. Its only relevance today is to land sale contracts (*i.e.,* the seller can get specific performance because the buyer could).

F. IS ENFORCEMENT FEASIBLE?

1. Personal Services Contract

A personal services contract will not be enforced, both because it would be tantamount to slavery and because it would be difficult to supervise performance. However, a noncompetition covenant may result in the granting of relief.

2. Land Sale Contract

In land sale contracts, check to see if the parties and/or land are in the jurisdiction.

a. *If both the parties and the res* are before the court, enforcement is feasible.

b. *If the seller and the res* are before the court, enforcement is feasible if the purchaser is bringing the action. If the seller brings the action, it is difficult to grant specific performance

because it requires the buyer to make a payment of money, which is an in personam order.

c. *If the buyer and the res* are before the court, enforcement is feasible since the court will simply act in rem and transfer the property by court order if the seller does not comply.

d. *If both parties* are before the court, but the *res is outside of the jurisdiction*, the recent trend has been for equity courts to decree that the property be conveyed, and the court may hold the seller in contempt if he does not make the required conveyance.

G. ARE THERE ANY DEFENSES AVAILABLE TO DEFENDANT?

1. Standard Contract Defenses
Standard contract defenses, including the Statute of Frauds, inadequate consideration, misrepresentation, impossibility, and mistake, may be raised. The most important here is the Statute of Frauds and the exception to its application, the part performance doctrine.

a. Part Performance Doctrine
The part performance doctrine may operate to take a contract out of the Statute of Frauds (*i.e.,* allow it to be specifically enforced). An oral contract for the *sale of land* may be enforced if there is part performance that *unequivocally indicates* that the parties have contracted for the sale of land.

2. Misrepresentation
To be a defense, the misrepresentation must go to a *material factor*. Concealment of a material fact will prevent specific performance as long as the party concealing this information stands in a confidential relationship to the other contracting party. The level of misrepresentation necessary to qualify as a defense to specific performance is not as high as that necessary to result in a rescission of the contract.

3. Mistake
To be a defense, the mistake must be bilateral, material, and a mistake of fact rather than a mistake of law. Unilateral mistake is a defense to specific performance only if the nonmistaken party either knew or reasonably should have known of the mistake.

4. Equitable Defenses
Equitable defenses include, *e.g.,* unclean hands, laches, unconscionability (*tested at the time of contract formation*), and great hardship.

CMR | **Exam Tip** | It is important to remember that the test for unconscionability is very strict; there must be some gross unfairness at the time the contract was made. The fact that a party merely made a bad deal is not enough.

H. SPECIFIC PERFORMANCE—PARTICULAR PROBLEMS

1. Covenants Not to Compete

a. Covenants in Employment Contract
Although an employment contract will not be specifically enforced, a covenant not to compete may be if: (i) the services are *unique,* (ii) the covenant is *reasonably necessary*

to protect the employer's interests, and (iii) the covenant is *reasonable as to both geographical scope and duration*. Even if these elements are shown, however, most courts will not enforce a covenant that will result in harm to the public.

b. Covenants in Sale of Business

Noncompetition covenants expressly included in contracts for the sale of business will be enforceable if the covenant is *reasonably necessary to protect the buyer* and *reasonable in geographical scope and duration*. Remember, some courts will "blue pencil" down a covenant not to compete in a personal services or sale of business contract to reasonable scope as long as the contract is not patently unreasonable.

c. Covenants Not to Disclose Trade Secrets

Covenants not to disclose trade secrets are specifically enforceable.

2. Specific Enforcement of Contracts to Make Particular Testamentary Dispositions or Execute Mutual Wills

As long as the property involved is unique, equity will specifically enforce a contract to make a particular disposition by imposing a constructive trust on the property in the hands of the personal representative. Equity will also enforce a contract to execute mutual wills by imposing a constructive trust on the personal representative of the party who failed to execute a will in accordance with the contractual terms. Where such contracts relate to real property, they must be in writing to be enforceable. Nonetheless, under proper circumstances (*e.g.,* part performance doctrine), specific performance will be granted.

3. Equitable Conversion

Under the doctrine of equitable conversion, after a contract for the sale of land has been entered into, the seller has a personalty interest and the buyer has a realty interest. For equitable conversion to come into effect, the land sale contract between the parties must be specifically enforceable.

IV. RESCISSION AND REFORMATION

A. RESCISSION

Rescission voids the contract and leaves the parties as though the contract had never been made.

1. Grounds for Rescission

Grounds for rescission must have occurred either *before* or *at the time the contract is entered into*.

a. Mistake

1) Mutual Mistake

Remember the general rule is that only a mutual mistake will suffice for rescission. The mistake must go to a *material fact*. Mutual mistakes as to collateral facts (*e.g.,* quality, desirability, or fitness of the property involved) are not grounds for rescission where there have been no express or implied representations.

2) Unilateral Mistake

Unilateral mistake generally will *not suffice* for rescission. However, exceptions

to the rule exist when the other party knew or should reasonably have known of the mistake or, under the modern trend, when the nonmistaken party has not yet taken steps in reliance on the contract or when the mistaken party would suffer great hardship.

CMR **Exam Tip** Unilateral mistake is often tested both on the state portion of the bar exam and in the Contracts section of the MBE. Questions frequently require you to know the unilateral mistake exception: although rescission generally is not available for a unilateral mistake, it will be available if the nonmistaken party either *knew or should have known* of the mistake. The favorite fact pattern contains a contractor's bid that is substantially lower than the other bids; the bid is so low that the other party should know it is a mistake.

b. Misrepresentation
For the court to rescind the contract, there must be a *material* misrepresentation of fact or law.

c. Other Grounds for Rescission
Rescission may also be granted for duress, undue influence, illegality, lack of capacity, or failure of consideration.

2. Defenses to Action for Rescission
The usual equitable defenses (*e.g.*, unclean hands or laches) are available. Note that under the general rule, negligence of a plaintiff is *not* a defense to a suit for rescission.

B. REFORMATION
Reformation changes the written agreement to make it conform to the original intent of the parties.

CMR **Exam Tip** Be careful not to confuse rescission with reformation. With rescission, you are arguing that there is no contract because there was no true "meeting of the minds." With reformation, you are arguing that there was a "meeting of the minds" but that the agreement is not accurately reflected in the written contract.

1. Is There a Valid Contract?
Remember that to be reformed, a valid contract must exist in the first instance.

2. Grounds for Reformation

a. Mistake
Mutual mistake will always suffice. The recent trend is to allow reformation for unilateral mistake where the writing does not conform to the original agreement and one of the parties is aware of this (unilateral mistake coupled with fraud or inequitable conduct).

b. Misrepresentation
Misrepresentation is sufficient grounds for reformation. It may be innocent or fraudulent. An instrument will be reformed to reflect the *expressed* intent of the parties.

3. Defenses to Reformation
Look for the usual equitable defenses such as unclean hands, laches, etc. Note the following special cases:

a. Bona Fide Purchaser
Equity courts will not allow reformation where the subject matter of the contract sought to be reformed has been sold to a bona fide purchaser for value and without notice.

b. "Nondefenses"
Generally, a plaintiff's negligence (*e.g.,* failure to read the contract) is *not* a bar to reformation. And, as a general rule, the Statute of Frauds and parol evidence rule do *not* apply in reformation cases.

4. Reformation of Gifts

a. Reformation by Donor
A donor may have a gift instrument reformed if it does not express his true intention except where the donee has substantially relied on the gift as conveyed.

b. Reformation by Donee
A donee may *not* have a gift instrument reformed, even if the gift instrument does not conform to the original intent of the donor. Some courts, however, allow reformation where the donee has *detrimentally relied* on the donor's original intent, which was not expressed in the instrument. The majority would allow the donee to have the gift reformed against the donor's heirs.

CMR
COMPARISON
CHART

RESCISSION VS. REFORMATION

	Rescission	Reformation
Purpose	To cancel a contract for lack of true consent	To conform a writing to the oral agreement of the parties
Grounds	Mutual mistake Unilateral mistake if the nonmistaken party either knew or should have known Misrepresentation (coupled with *actual reliance if fraudulent* and *reasonable reliance if innocent*) Duress Undue influence Illegality Lack of capacity Failure of consideration	Mutual mistake Unilateral mistake coupled with fraud or inequitable conduct Misrepresentation (either innocent or fraudulent)
Effect	Releases parties from contract	Parties bound to contract, but terms are the ones originally agreed to

V. MISCELLANEOUS EQUITABLE REMEDIES

A. CONSTRUCTIVE TRUST

A constructive trust is a restitutionary remedy imposed by courts to ***prevent unjust enrichment*** when a wrongdoer has gained title to property through misappropriation of another's money or property. Defendant's title must be ***traceable solely*** to the misappropriated property (most courts also require a showing that the legal remedy is inadequate). If established, the court will force the trustee to convey to the plaintiff title to the misappropriated property or its product. This gives the plaintiff priority over unsecured creditors. The usual equitable defenses are applicable, and transfer to a bona fide purchaser terminates a plaintiff's equitable right to the property.

B. EQUITABLE LIEN

1. Requirements

The requirements for imposition of an equitable lien are similar to those for a constructive trust: An equitable lien can be imposed on property to which the defendant holds title and to which the wrongfully obtained property can be traced. Like a constructive trust, an equitable lien gives the plaintiff priority over other creditors with interests in the property subject to the lien. Unlike a constructive trust, however, an equitable lien can be imposed on property that was merely improved with the plaintiff's property or the proceeds thereof. Most courts require a showing that the legal remedy is inadequate, but the defendant's insolvency usually suffices.

2. Compared with Constructive Trust

An ***equitable lien*** is appropriate when the property in the defendant's hands is worth less than plaintiff's claim, or where misappropriated money is used to improve, not acquire title to, property. (A ***constructive trust*** should be used when defendant holds property worth more than plaintiff's claim, because the plaintiff will receive the more valuable property.) The usual equitable remedies apply and transfer to a BFP prevents imposition of an equitable lien.

C. EQUITABLE MORTGAGE

An equitable mortgage is imposed by a court against a deed absolute when a creditor has received the deed from a debtor ***solely to secure an obligation*** and later refuses to reconvey the property on satisfaction of the debt. Under these circumstances, the courts will treat the deed as a mortgage and force the creditor to foreclose if the mortgage is unpaid or reconvey if the mortgage is paid.

D. SUBROGATION

Subrogation permits a person who is required to pay the loss or obligation of another, or to discharge a lien on another's property, to succeed to the rights of the person paid.

CMR
COMPARISON
CHART

CONSTRUCTIVE TRUST VS. EQUITABLE LIEN

	Constructive Trust	Equitable Lien
Purpose	To prevent unjust enrichment.	To prevent unjust enrichment.
When available	Defendant has acquired property at the expense of another through fraud, undue influence, abuse of confidence, mistake, or the like.	Defendant has acquired property at the expense of another through fraud, undue influence, abuse of confidence, mistake, or the like.
Which to use when both available	Use when property acquired at plaintiff's expense is worth as much as or ***more than his claim*** (*e.g.,* defendant has defrauded plaintiff out of stock that has subsequently increased in value). Cannot be used where defendant has improved other property with plaintiff's property (*e.g.,* where defendant uses embezzled money to build an addition to his house).	Use when property acquired at plaintiff's expense is worth as much as or ***less than his claim*** (*e.g.,* defendant has defrauded plaintiff out of stock that has subsequently decreased in value) or defendant has improved other property with plaintiff's property (*e.g.,* defendant has sold the stock that he fraudulently obtained from plaintiff and has built an addition to his house with the proceeds).
Effect	Defendant must transfer title to plaintiff; no deficiency judgment is available.	Plaintiff obtains a lien on property obtained or improved ***and*** may obtain a deficiency judgment.
Tracing	Required.	Required.
Priority over unsecured creditors	Yes.	Yes.
Lose to BFP	Yes.	Yes.

FAMILY LAW

TABLE OF CONTENTS

FAMILY LAW

I. GETTING MARRIED

A. MARRIAGE IN GENERAL

Marriage is the creation of the status of husband and wife, with the accompanying obligations and liabilities.

B. CONTROVERSIES ARISING IN ANTICIPATION OF MARRIAGE

1. Breach of Promise to Marry

The action for breach of promise to marry (a quasi-tort, quasi-contract action) has been abolished in most states. Where retained, recovery may be allowed for actual damages (money spent in preparation of marriage), as well as for loss of reputation, mental anguish, injury to health, and punitive damages.

2. Gifts in Contemplation of Marriage

If the marriage does not take place, engagement gifts (those made in anticipation of marriage) must be returned.

C. LIMITATIONS ON WHO MAY MARRY

Generally, to get married, the parties must: (i) be a minimum age (usually 18, although frequently younger with parental or judicial approval); (ii) not be too closely related; (iii) be of the opposite sex; (iv) have capacity to consent (the ability to comprehend and voluntarily agree); and (v) not have a prior undissolved marriage to a living spouse.

D. PROCEDURAL REQUIREMENTS

1. License

Most states require that persons intending to marry obtain a license prior to the solemnization (*see* below). To acquire a license, some states require each party to obtain a certificate from a physician stating that the party is free from specified communicable diseases. Many states also provide for a waiting period of up to 72 hours before the license will be issued.

2. Solemnization

Generally, a marriage may be solemnized by a ceremony performed by a judicial officer or member of the clergy.

E. STATE OF MIND REQUIREMENTS

The parties must understand their actions and voluntarily agree to them. Thus, someone under the influence of alcohol or drugs may lack the mental capacity to enter into a valid marriage. Also, because the parties must intend to enter into marriage, if one party is induced to marry because of fraud, duress, coercion, or force, the marriage is subject to attack.

F. COMMON LAW MARRIAGE

A valid common law marriage requires:

(i) An exchange of consents between two people with capacity;

(ii) Cohabitation; and

(iii) A holding out publicly of living together as husband and wife.

No solemnization is required. Common law marriage has been abolished in most states. However, if a valid common law marriage is formed under the laws of one state, it will generally be regarded as valid even in those states that do not recognize common law marriages.

G. PREMARITAL CONTRACTS

Premarital contracts, which usually pertain to the distribution of property upon divorce or death, are valid contracts to which the principles of contract construction apply. The marriage is sufficient consideration to support a premarital contract.

1. Content of Contract

Under the Uniform Premarital Agreement Act ("UPAA"), parties to the agreement may contract with respect to: (i) the parties' rights and obligations in property of either or both of them; (ii) the right to buy, sell, lease, assign, dispose of, or control property; (iii) disposition of property upon separation, dissolution, death, or any other event; (iv) modification or elimination of spousal support; (v) the making of a will or trust; (vi) choice of law governing construction of the agreement; and (vii) any other matter not in violation of public policy or criminal statute.

2. Enforcement by Courts

For a premarital contract to be enforceable, most courts require the following:

(i) The agreement must be *entered into voluntarily*;

(ii) The contract must be *in writing* and signed by the party to be charged;

(iii) Both parties must make a *full and fair disclosure of their financial worth*; and

(iv) The economic provisions must be *fair and reasonable*.

Note: Under the UPAA, a premarital agreement is unenforceable if a party did not act voluntarily or if the agreement was unconscionable when executed and the party was not provided fair disclosure, did not waive in writing such disclosure, and did not have adequate knowledge of the other party's property.

3. Other Enforcement Issues

Although not required, if both parties are represented by independent counsel, it is far less likely that a court will find overreaching and refuse to enforce the contract. Courts may, however, refuse to enforce provisions that would eliminate or severely limit alimony upon divorce, especially if a spouse would be left a pauper in need of public assistance.

Note: If a marriage is found to be void, a premarital agreement is enforceable only to the extent necessary to avoid an inequitable result.

II. THE MARRIAGE RELATIONSHIP

A. RIGHTS AND RESPONSIBILITIES OF SPOUSES

1. Individual Rights

Legal disabilities placed upon married women and their property have, for the most part, been eliminated.

2. Property

Each spouse controls her own property.

a. Tenancy by the Entirety

In many states, if spouses take title to real estate in their joint names, a tenancy by the entirety is presumptively created. A tenancy by the entirety includes a right of survivorship and prohibits the conveyance or encumbrance of the property by one spouse. Upon dissolution, tenants by the entirety become tenants in common.

b. Marital Property

Marital property includes most property acquired during marriage (*see* III.B.5.b., *infra*). Upon dissolution, the court has broad discretion in the equitable distribution of this property.

3. Support

Each spouse has an obligation to support the other during the marriage. In addition, principles of agency may require that one spouse be held liable to a third party for the other spouse's authorized purchases. Even in the absence of agency authority, one spouse is liable for ***necessaries*** (food, clothing, medical care) purchased by the other spouse.

4. Name Change Not Required

A woman need not adopt her husband's surname.

5. Suits Between Spouses

Many states have abolished interspousal immunity, retaining exceptions only for highly private activity (marital privileges and consensual acts) and simple domestic negligence.

6. Marital Rape

Many states have removed the marital exception from their rape laws, but because force and consent may be more difficult to establish in a marital relationship, some states attach more significance to whether the parties are living apart when the offense occurs.

7. Spousal Abuse and Protective Orders

Many states have legislation that criminalizes spousal abuse and increases police involvement. In addition, all 50 states allow battered spouses to seek some form of "stay away" protection orders against violent spouses.

B. FAMILY PRIVACY

Generally, the internal affairs of a family cannot be regulated by the courts. Families have the right to expect privacy for actions within their homes and freedom from governmental interference in their domestic affairs.

1. **Constitutional Privacy**
   The United States Supreme Court has recognized the right of privacy as implicit in the concept of "liberty" within the protection of the Due Process Clause. Privacy is a fundamental right; therefore, any regulation of it (other than in the abortion area) is invalid unless it is found to be *necessary to a compelling government interest*. The following rights are considered to fall within the constitutionally protected right to privacy:

   a. The right to marry;

   b. The right to procreate;

   c. The right to use or sell contraceptives;

   d. Within limits, the right to abortion;

   e. The right of related persons to live together;

   f. The right of parents to educate their children outside the public schools; and

   g. The right of parents to decide issues concerning the care, custody, and control of their children.

2. **Husband-Wife Evidentiary Privilege**
   A married person cannot be compelled to testify against his spouse in any *criminal* proceeding. This "spousal immunity" can be invoked only during a valid marriage. In addition, either spouse, whether or not a party, is privileged to refuse to disclose and to prevent the other from disclosing a confidential communication made between them while they were husband and wife. The communication must have been made in confidence in reliance upon the intimacy of the marital relationship. This privilege for confidential communications survives divorce. Neither of these privileges applies in actions between the spouses or in cases involving crimes against the testifying spouse or the children.

C. TORTIOUS INTERFERENCE WITH THE MARITAL RELATIONSHIP

1. **Alienation of Affections**
   If a third person diverts the affection of one spouse so that the other is deprived of a marital relationship, the deprived spouse has a cause of action for alienation of affections against the third person. These actions have been abolished in most states.

2. **Criminal Conversation**
   When one spouse has sexual relations with a third person, the other spouse has a cause of action against the third person. Only the act need be proved, and the spouses may have been living apart at the time of the act. Criminal conversation actions, too, have been abolished in most states.

3. **Negligent Interference with Consortium or Services**
   In most states, either spouse may maintain an action for loss of the other's consortium due to injuries from a defendant's negligence (*see* VII.E.2., *infra*).

III. TERMINATION OF MARRIAGE

A. ANNULMENT

An annulment is a declaration that a marriage is invalid because there was an impediment at the time of the marriage. Once an annulment decree has been entered, the parties generally are treated as though they were never married.

1. Void/Voidable Distinction

a. Void Marriage

A void marriage is a complete nullity. No subsequent act can ratify a void marriage. Parties may walk away from a void marriage without a court order; an annulment action is usually brought to determine property distribution and child custody. Any interested party may seek annulment of a void marriage, and the marriage is subject to collateral attack (in actions other than annulment actions) even after the death of one of the parties.

CMR **Exam Tip** Watch for a fact pattern where an impediment causing the marriage to be void is removed (*e.g.*, spouse from previous valid marriage dies). When this happens, the marriage becomes merely voidable, and thus subject to ratification.

b. Voidable Marriage

A voidable marriage is deemed valid, but because of an impediment that existed at the time of the marriage, *one of the spouses* may bring an action to have the marriage declared invalid. If the spouse with the cause of action ratifies the marriage by continuing in the relationship after the impediment is removed, or if one spouse dies, the marriage can no longer be invalidated.

2. Grounds

a. Bigamy or Polygamy

If either party has another living spouse, the marriage is *void*.

b. Consanguinity

Marriages between parties who are too closely related (*e.g.*, direct lineal ascendants or descendants, or aunt, uncle, brother, sister, niece, or nephew) are prohibited. Most states consider these marriages *void*.

c. Nonage

A spouse who was under the statutory age and married without getting the required consent can have the marriage invalidated. These marriages are usually *voidable*; thus, the underage spouse may ratify the marriage by continuing in the relationship after reaching the statutory age.

d. Incurable Physical Impotence

The inability to have normal sexual relations with a spouse is a ground for annulment. These marriages are *voidable* and thus subject to ratification.

VOID AND VOIDABLE MARRIAGES—ANNULMENT

	Void Marriage	Voidable Marriage

Grounds	• Bigamy
	
	• Consanguinity
	
	• Nonage (some states)
		• Nonage (most states)
		
		• Incurable physical impotence
		
		• Lack of capacity
		  • Mental incompetence
		  • Duress
		  • Fraud involving the essentials of marriage

Effect	• Cannot be ratified • A complete nullity even without a court order • Any interested party may seek annulment • Subject to collateral attack (*e.g.,* in probate proceedings) • Subject to attack after death of one of the parties	• Can be ratified • Valid until declaration of annulment • Only spouses may seek annulment • Not subject to collateral attack • Not subject to attack after death of one of the parties
Defenses	• Impediment does not exist (If impediment has been removed, marriage becomes voidable and defenses to voidable marriage, such as ratification, apply.)	• Impediment does not exist • Ratification (*i.e.,* continuing in relationship after impediment removed) • Laches • Estoppel • Unclean hands (not valid in most states)

CMR | **Exam Tip** | Keep in mind that the inability to have children is not impotence. But if the ability to have children was misrepresented, the marriage may be annulled on the ground of fraud (*see* below).

e. Lack of Capacity

A lack of capacity sufficient to annul a marriage may be: (i) a lack of understanding due to a mental condition or the influence of drugs or alcohol; (ii) a lack of mutual assent to the marriage; (iii) duress; or (iv) fraud going to the essentials of marriage (*e.g.*, misrepresentation as to ability or willingness to engage in sexual relations or bear children).

3. Defenses

The only way to defend an action to annul a void marriage is to deny the existence of the defect. If the impediment has been removed, the marriage becomes voidable. Ratification is the most common defense in an action to annul a voidable marriage. Other equitable defenses (*e.g.*, laches, estoppel) may also be used, but are usually subsumed in the ratification defense.

4. Children of Annulled Marriage

The children of an annulled marriage are *marital* children. Support and custody issues are handled in the same way as in a divorce action (*see* C., D.; IV., *infra*).

5. Spousal Support

Generally spousal support is not awarded in annulment actions. Also, once spousal support has been terminated by remarriage, it will not be reinstated following an annulment of that marriage.

6. Division of Property

Courts attempt to place the parties in their pre-marriage position, and usually give each party that property to which he has legal or equitable title.

7. Jurisdiction

In states without statutes on the subject, annulment actions are heard by the equity courts. Among states, the state of domicile of either of the parties has jurisdiction to hear the annulment action. Many states also provide that the place of the celebration of the marriage also has jurisdiction. Annulment decrees rendered with proper jurisdiction are entitled to full faith and credit.

B. DIVORCE AND SEPARATION

1. Divorce

A decree of absolute divorce terminates the marriage relationship.

a. "No-Fault" Divorce

Most state divorce statutes provide for divorce without regard to marital fault. This usually requires a showing that: (i) the marriage is irretrievably broken (irreconcilable differences or incompatibility); and/or (ii) the parties have been living apart for a specified time. The only defense to a no-fault divorce is to deny the existence of one of the above grounds.

b. Fault Grounds

The usual fault grounds for divorce are: (i) adultery; (ii) willful desertion for a specified time; (iii) extreme physical or mental cruelty; (iv) voluntary drug addiction or habitual drunkenness; and (v) a spouse's mental illness.

1) Defenses to Fault Grounds

a) Collusion

Collusion is an agreement between the spouses to simulate grounds for divorce or to forgo raising a valid defense. In some jurisdictions, collusion will prevent the granting of a divorce.

b) Connivance

Connivance is the willing consent by one spouse to the other spouse's misconduct. This is usually limited to adultery cases, and has been abolished in many states.

c) Condonation

Condonation is the forgiveness of marital offenses with full knowledge of their commission. Resumption of marital relations after the forgiveness is the key element of this defense.

d) Recrimination

Recrimination is a defense that arises when the party seeking the divorce is also guilty of misconduct for which a divorce may be granted. This defense is no longer recognized. Even where it remains on the books, courts avoid applying it.

2. Legal Separation

An order of legal separation does not terminate the marriage, but the parties may have all of their rights regarding property, spousal support, custody, and child support adjudicated in this proceeding. A legal separation is usually capable of being enlarged into an absolute divorce if the parties so request.

3. Jurisdiction and Recognition of Decrees

a. Residency Requirements

One of the parties must be a bona fide resident of the jurisdiction where the action is brought. Most states set a durational residency requirement (*e.g.*, 90 days) before an action may be filed.

b. In Rem Action

The divorce itself is viewed as an in rem action; thus, certain types of constructive service (*e.g.*, publication) are permitted. To have jurisdiction over spousal support, property rights, etc., however, the court must have personal jurisdiction over the defendant.

c. Recognition of Decree—Full Faith and Credit

As long as one of the parties was domiciled in the state that granted the divorce, the decree is recognized as valid in all other states. Provisions of the decree relating to

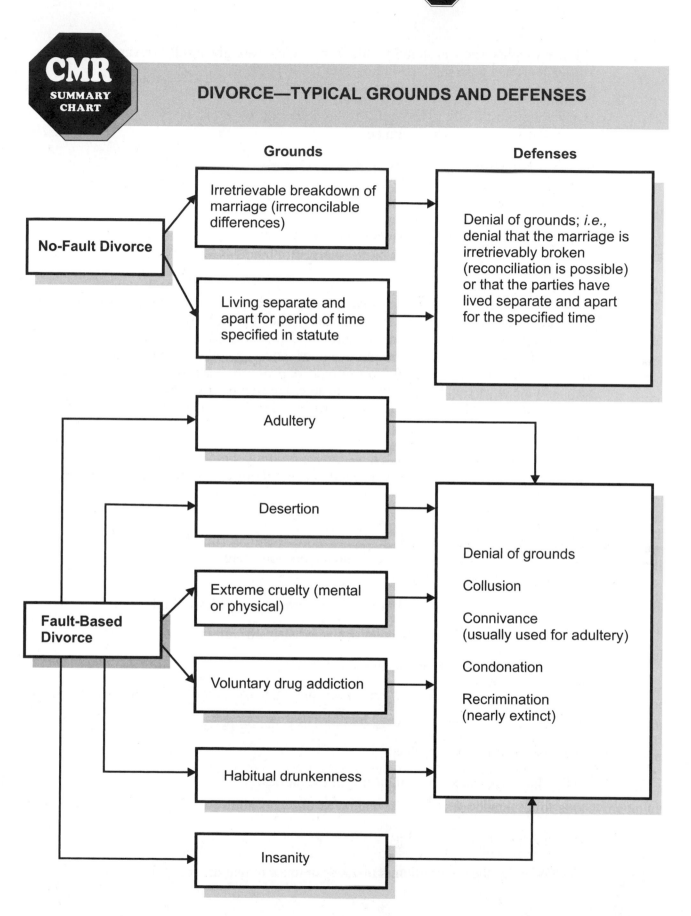

DIVORCE—TYPICAL GROUNDS AND DEFENSES

Grounds

Defenses

No-Fault Divorce

Irretrievable breakdown of marriage (irreconcilable differences)

Living separate and apart for period of time specified in statute

Denial of grounds; *i.e.,* denial that the marriage is irretrievably broken (reconciliation is possible) or that the parties have lived separate and apart for the specified time

Fault-Based Divorce

Adultery

Desertion

Extreme cruelty (mental or physical)

Voluntary drug addiction

Habitual drunkenness

Insanity

Denial of grounds

Collusion

Connivance (usually used for adultery)

Condonation

Recrimination (nearly extinct)

property rights, spousal support, child support, etc., are given full faith and credit only if the court had personal jurisdiction over the defendant.

d. Comity
Courts are most likely to recognize foreign decrees when one party was domiciled in the country rendering the judgment.

4. Preliminary Interlocutory Decrees and Final Orders
Some states provide that divorce decrees are interlocutory when initially granted, and do not become final decrees until after a specified period of time.

CMR **Exam Tip** Watch for a fact pattern that states that a decree was granted but is not yet final. During that time, the parties cannot remarry, and they continue to inherit from one another.

5. Division of Property
The three approaches to division of property upon divorce are: (i) *community property* (all property acquired during the marriage is deemed owned one-half by each spouse, and all property brought into the marriage or acquired by gift or bequest is separate property); (ii) *equitable division of all property* owned by either spouse, whether acquired before or after the marriage; and (iii) *equitable division of marital property* (each spouse takes his separate property and the court divides the property acquired during the marriage). This last approach is the most common and is addressed below. Property distribution decrees are *not modifiable*.

a. Separate Property
Generally, each spouse can take the separate property that she owned prior to the marriage as well as any separate property acquired during the marriage by gift, bequest, or descent.

b. Marital Property
Marital property, which is all other property acquired during the marriage, is subject to equitable distribution by the court. The factors considered in dividing the property usually include:

(i)   The age, education, background, and earning capacities of both parties;

(ii) The duration of the marriage, and whether there were any prior marriages;

(iii) The standard of living during the marriage;

(iv) The present incomes of both parties, and their vocational skills and employability;

(v)   The source of the money used to purchase the property;

(vi) The health of the parties;

(vii) The assets, debts, and liabilities of the parties;

(viii) The needs of the parties;

(ix) The child custody provisions;

(x)   Whether the distribution is in addition to, or in lieu of, spousal support;

(xi) Each party's opportunity to acquire future income and assets;

(xii) Each party's contribution to the acquisition of, or enhancement of the value of, the existing marital assets;

(xiii) Each party's contribution as a homemaker to the family unit; and

(xiv) Whether either party has dissipated marital property.

1) Pensions
The portion of a pension earned during a marriage is marital property subject to distribution.

2) Professional License or Degree
Most jurisdictions that have considered the matter have held that a professional license or educational degree is *not distributable property*. However, to avoid unfair results, some jurisdictions have compensated supporting spouses for their contribution during the other spouse's education or training (*e.g.,* by amending statutes to make the supporting spouse's contribution a factor on which alimony may be based).

3) Damage Awards in Tort Suits
Many states hold that if a cause of action for personal injury accrues between the date of marriage and final separation, the proceeds from the settlement or award are marital assets subject to distribution.

4) Stock Options
The majority rule is that stock options earned during marriage are marital property even if they will not be exercised until after the divorce.

c. Mixed Property
Separate property may become marital property if: (i) the separate property is inextricably mingled with marital property or with the separate property of the other spouse to the extent that it can no longer be traced, or (ii) the separate property is treated in a way that evidences an intention for the property to be marital property (*e.g.,* placing separate property in the names of both spouses). When separate property is improved by the use of marital funds or the effort of the nonowning spouse, courts generally hold that the property remains separate property, but most jurisdictions grant the marital estate or the nonowning spouse reimbursement for the value added to the separate property.

d. Tax Consequences of Property Division
Property division is not considered a taxable event; therefore, any payments made as part of a property settlement are not income to the recipient spouse and may not be used as a deduction by the payor spouse.

6. Spousal Support
Spousal support may be awarded while the parties are still married, during the pendency of a divorce proceeding, and/or as part of the divorce decree. In most states, marital fault is generally not considered in deciding whether to award spousal support.

TYPES OF SPOUSAL SUPPORT

Type	Description	Modifiability	Termination
Permanent	Paid regularly **for the lifetime** of the recipient	Modifiable upon substantial change in circumstances	Terminates upon the death of either spouse or the remarriage of the recipient spouse
Rehabilitative	Paid regularly **for a limited period** of time	Modifiable upon substantial change in circumstances	Terminates upon the death of either spouse or the remarriage of the recipient spouse
Lump Sum	Payable **all at once** or in a **series of payments**	Nonmodifiable	Survives the death of either spouse
Reimbursement	Payable **at once**	Nonmodifiable	Survives the death of either spouse

   a.   **Amount**

The court has great discretion in awarding as much spousal support as necessary for the maintenance of the requesting spouse. Factors considered include: (i) the duration of the marriage and the standard of living established during the marriage; (ii) the age and physical and emotional condition of the parties; (iii) the financial resources of the parties; (iv) the contribution of each party to the marriage; (v) the time needed for the party seeking support to obtain the training necessary to find appropriate employment; and (vi) the ability of the payor spouse to meet his needs while paying spousal support.

   b.   **Types of Spousal Support**

Permanent periodic spousal support is paid regularly (*e.g.*, monthly) to support a spouse who has neither the resources nor the ability to be self-sustaining. *Rehabilitative spousal support* consists of periodic payments for a limited time to enable a spouse to gain skills to become self-supporting. Permanent periodic and rehabilitative spousal support awards are prospectively modifiable for changed circumstances. Alternatively, a court can award a *lump sum* payment (a nonmodifiable, fixed amount payable either all at once or broken down into a series of payments). Also, a growing minority of jurisdictions occasionally award *reimbursement spousal support* to a spouse who supported the other spouse while the latter obtained a professional license or degree. Such support is awarded as a fixed sum, which is neither modifiable nor terminable, and is based on the amount of the supporting spouse's contribution, *not* the value of the professional license or degree.

   c.   **Termination of Spousal Support**

Periodic spousal support terminates upon the death of either spouse or the remarriage of the recipient spouse. Some states would also terminate spousal support if the recipient spouse cohabits with another person of the opposite sex. Lump sum spousal support is not modifiable and survives the death of either spouse.

   d.   **Tax Consequences of Spousal Support**

In general, spousal support payments are includible in the income of the recipient spouse and are deductible by the payor spouse.

C.   CHILD SUPPORT

Both parents share equally a duty to support their children. The amount of the award of support to the custodial parent is usually arrived at by the use of a formula based on the number of children, their ages and special needs, and the parents' incomes. Parties can also be ordered to provide medical insurance for the children.

1.   Independent from Visitation Rights

The child support obligation is independent of the noncustodial parent's visitation rights. Visitation cannot be withheld because of failure to pay child support.

2.   Termination of Duty to Support

The duty to support a child ceases upon the child's emancipation (usually age 18), the child's marriage, the termination of parental rights, or, traditionally, the death of the supporting parent. Child support may be indefinite for a severely disabled child. Some courts require child support payments up to a certain level of education, but others have held that statutes requiring a parent to pay for college are unconstitutional.

3. **Tax Consequences of Child Support**

Child support payments are neither includible in the income of the custodial parent nor deductible by the payor parent.

D. MODIFICATION OF SPOUSAL SUPPORT AND CHILD SUPPORT AWARDS

1. **Spousal Support**

Only periodic spousal support (*i.e.,* permanent or rehabilitative) may be modified. Periodic spousal support may be modified if there is a ***substantial change in circumstances*** regarding the needs of the recipient spouse or the ability of the payor spouse to pay.

CMR **Exam Tip** A self-induced reduction in income by the payor spouse is not sufficient to have spousal support reduced. Be alert to this issue if a fact pattern involves a payor spouse who quits his job.

2. **Child Support**

Child support is modifiable based on a ***substantial change of circumstances*** affecting the needs of the child or the ability of the parent to pay, such as: changes in employment, the growth of the child, inflation, income, retirement, or disabling illness. Under the federal Full Faith and Credit for Child Support Orders Act, full faith and credit must be given to the child support orders of a court in another state.

3. **Overdue Payments Not Modified**

Past due installments of support cannot be retroactively modified.

E. ENFORCEMENT OF AWARDS

Spousal support and child support awards may be enforced by holding the nonpaying party in contempt of court (usually civil contempt, but may be criminal if failure to pay is willful). Other sanctions include: a judgment against the noncomplying party; seizure of his real estate; attachment of his wages; and the order of payment of attorneys' fees. In addition, child support may be enforced through automatic wage withholding once the court has issued a support order; interception of the noncomplying parent's tax return; or nonrenewal or refusal of a professional or driver's license.

1. **Uniform Interstate Family Support Act**

The Uniform Interstate Family Support Act ("UIFSA") provides methods of enforcement and guidelines for modifications of support orders issued in another state.

a. **Enforcing a Support Order**

An income withholding order may be mailed directly to the obligor's out-of-state employer, and this automatically triggers withholding unless there is a timely objection from the obligor. Alternatively, the order may be mailed to the support enforcement agency in the obligor's state to seek administrative enforcement of the order. UIFSA also provides for registration of a support order with a sister state through court action: The issuing state sends the order to the state where the obligor resides, where it is registered and filed as a foreign judgment, and then the order is subject to the same enforcement procedures as if the order had been issued in that state.

SPOUSAL SUPPORT AND CHILD SUPPORT AWARDS

	Spousal Support	**Child Support**
Amount	Court has wide discretion. Considers factors such as prior standard of living; duration of marriage; financial resources of both parties; time and training needed for recipient spouse to become employable; etc.	Based on monetary need and ability to pay, but court generally must follow statutory guidelines based on number of children, their ages and special needs, and the parents' incomes.
Enforcement	Contempt; judgment against noncomplying party; seizure of real estate; attachment of wages; order to pay attorneys' fees; and other methods under UIFSA.	Contempt; judgment against noncomplying party; seizure of real estate; attachment of wages; order to pay attorneys' fees; wage withholding; and other methods under UIFSA.
Modification	A substantial change in circumstances regarding the needs of the recipient spouse or the payor spouse's ability to pay.	A substantial change in circumstances affecting the needs of the children or the ability of the parents to pay.
Termination	Periodic spousal support terminates on the death of either spouse or remarriage of the recipient spouse.	Duty of support usually terminates upon emancipation of child by age or marriage, or by termination of parental rights.
Taxation	Spousal support payments are includible in the income of the recipient and are deductible by the payor.	Child support payments are neither includible in the income of the custodial parent nor deductible by the payor parent.

> b. **Modifying a Support Order**
> The role of the obligor's state is *only to enforce* the original order, *unless*: (i) the parties no longer reside in the issuing state, or (ii) the parties consent in a record to the nonissuing court's assertion of jurisdiction to modify the order.

F. MEDIATION

In some states, the court may refer the parties to a divorce action to a court-approved mediator. A mediator is a neutral party who helps the divorcing parties work through such issues as child support, custody, and visitation. An agreement reached by the parties is to be based on the decision of the parties and not the decisions of the mediator, who may not advocate for either party, or coerce a party to make a decision. Mediator misconduct may result in the court setting aside the agreement. All of the mediation proceedings and records are confidential.

1. Mediator Duties

Mediators must *explain* the mediation process, including the *right to independent counsel,* to the parties; ensure that the parties have enough information for *informed decision making*; be *impartial* and disclose any potential bias; and control for any *power imbalance* between the parties.

G. SEPARATION AGREEMENTS

A separation agreement is an agreement entered into during marriage under which the parties agree to live apart and resolve economic issues (spousal support, property division, child support) and custody rights. To be enforceable, the agreement must be voluntary, and there must have been a full and fair disclosure by both parties. Consideration for the agreement is found in the mutual promises of the parties.

1. Effect of Provisions

Provisions relating to property and spousal support will be enforced by the court. Child custody and support provisions, however, will be enforced by the court only if they are in the child's best interest; *i.e.,* the court is not bound by those provisions.

2. Separation Agreements and Divorce Decrees

If the divorce decree states that the separation agreement is *merged* into the decree, or if the specific provisions of the agreement are repeated in the decree, the whole agreement assumes the *status of a court judgment* and is enforceable as such. If the agreement is *not merged* in this way, it retains its separate character as a contract and is enforceable as such. A statement by the court that it is incorporating the agreement by reference is generally insufficient to constitute merger.

IV. CHILD CUSTODY

A. CUSTODY DEFINED

Custody of a minor can mean *legal custody* (the right to make major decisions affecting the child's life) or *physical custody* (actual possession and control of the child). *Joint custody* can mean either joint legal custody, joint physical custody, or both.

B. THE UNIFORM CHILD CUSTODY JURISDICTION AND ENFORCEMENT ACT

1. **Purposes—To Avoid Jurisdictional Disputes and Strengthen Enforcement Procedures**
   The purposes of the Uniform Child Custody Jurisdiction and Enforcement Act ("UCCJEA") are to avoid jurisdictional disputes with courts of other states in matters of child custody and visitation, to promote interstate cooperation, and to facilitate the interstate enforcement of custody and visitation orders.

2. **Initial Custody Determination**

   a. **Primary Test—Home State Jurisdiction**
      A court has jurisdiction to initially enter or modify a child custody or visitation order if the state (i) is the ***child's home state***, or (ii) was the child's home state within the past six months and the child is absent from the state, but a parent or person acting as a parent (*e.g.*, guardian) continues to live in the state. A child's home state is the state in which the child lived with a parent (or a person acting as a parent) for ***at least six consecutive months*** immediately before the commencement of the proceeding (or the state where the child has lived since birth if younger than six months old), disregarding temporary absences.

   CMR ▊Exam Tip▊ This is the most important jurisdictional test, and it is frequently tested on the bar exam.

   b. **When "Home State" Rule Does Not Apply**
      A court has jurisdiction to enter or modify a child custody or visitation order if ***no other state has or accepts home state jurisdiction*** and (i) the child and at least one parent (or person acting as a parent) have a ***significant connection*** with the state, and (ii) ***substantial evidence*** concerning the child is available in the state. In addition, a court has jurisdiction to enter or modify a child custody or visitation order if no other state has jurisdiction under another test.

3. **Exclusive Continuing Jurisdiction**
   The court that made the initial child custody or visitation determination has exclusive continuing jurisdiction over the matter until the court determines that: (i) neither the child nor the child's parents (or persons acting as parents) continue to reside in the state; ***or*** (ii) the child no longer has a significant connection with the state (*e.g.*, a close relationship with a parent who lives in the state) and substantial evidence relating to the matter is no longer available in the state.

4. **When Court May Decline Jurisdiction**
   A court that has jurisdiction under one of the above tests may decline to exercise its jurisdiction if it determines that it is an ***inconvenient forum*** under the circumstances and that a court in another state is a more appropriate forum. Additionally, a court may decline to exercise jurisdiction if the party seeking to invoke the court's jurisdiction has engaged in ***unjustifiable conduct*** (*e.g.*, wrongfully taking the child from another state).

5. **Temporary Emergency Jurisdiction—Abandonment or Abuse**
   A court has temporary emergency jurisdiction if the child has been abandoned or it is necessary in an emergency to protect the child because the child or her sibling or parent is subjected to or threatened with abuse.

6. **Enforcement of Another State's Order**

A custody or visitation order of one state can be registered in another state and enforced in that state in the same manner as one of its own orders. In addition, the court can order the respondent to appear in person and award immediate physical possession of the child to the petitioner. The court may issue a warrant to take physical possession of the child if the child is imminently likely to suffer serious physical harm or be removed from the state. A prosecutor, law enforcement officer, or other public official may take any lawful action to locate a child, obtain the return of a child, or enforce a custody or visitation order when requested by a court or if there is a reasonable belief that the person holding the child has violated a criminal statute.

C. BEST INTEREST OF THE CHILD STANDARD

The standard applied in awarding custody and visitation is the ***best interest of the child***. Factors considered in making that determination usually include: the wishes of the child and the parents; the child's relationship with the parents, siblings, and others; the child's adjustment to home, school, and community; and the physical and mental health of the individuals involved.

1. **Child's Preference**

Preferences of older children (over age 12) are given great weight, but the preference of a young child (under age eight) may either be disregarded or given very little weight.

2. **Effect of Primary Caregiver Status**

In most states, preference cannot be shown to one parent because of gender or financial ability. If, after considering all of the relevant factors, the court is left to decide between two qualified parents, the award will often go to the parent who has been the primary caregiver (*i.e.,* the one most involved in the child's day-to-day life).

D. COUNSEL FOR CHILD

Most courts may appoint counsel or a guardian ad litem for the child in a custody dispute, but this is done only when counsel can provide substantial assistance in reaching the result in the child's best interest.

E. VISITATION

When an award of sole physical custody is made to one parent, the other parent must be given reasonable visitation rights. As discussed above, this right is independent of the child support obligation and cannot be withheld because of arrearages.

1. **Limitations Imposed for Misconduct**

A court may limit a parent's right to visitation (*e.g.,* by ordering supervised visitation) if that parent engages in conduct that might injure the child, but absolute denial of visitation is rare.

2. **Removal of Child from Jurisdiction by Custodial Parent**

Most courts allow the custodial parent to move out of state as long as it is motivated by benefit to the parent and not merely to frustrate visitation rights.

3. **Remedy—Contempt**

Contempt is the primary remedy for violation of visitation orders. Consistent and willful denial of visitation rights could result in a modification of custody.

4. **Third-Party Visitation**

Nearly all states have statutes entitling certain third parties (*e.g.*, grandparents) to visitation rights in certain circumstances, such as where the child's parents have divorced or died. In many states, the current standard in the award of these rights is the best interest of the child, and the determinative factor is often the prior relationship between the child and the third party. However, this standard *may be unconstitutional*. The United States Supreme Court has stated that a judge may not override a *fit* parent's decision regarding third-party visitation merely because it would be in the best interest of the child.

F. JOINT CUSTODY

In determining whether joint custody is appropriate, courts often consider:

(i) The fitness of both parents;

(ii) Whether the parents agree on joint custody;

(iii) The parents' ability to communicate and cooperate concerning the child's well-being;

(iv) The child's preference;

(v) The level of involvement of both parents in the child's life;

(vi) The geographical proximity of the two homes;

(vii) The similarity or dissimilarity of the homes;

(viii) The effect of the award on the child's psychological development; and

(ix) The parents' ability to physically carry out the joint custody order.

If the parents agree to joint custody the court will usually go along unless it is not in the child's best interest.

G. CUSTODIAL DISPUTES BETWEEN PARENTS AND THIRD PARTIES
See VII.G., *infra*.

H. ENFORCEMENT

Child custody awards may be enforced by contempt proceedings; state habeas corpus proceedings; suits in equity; and the UCCJEA. Under the federal Parental Kidnapping Prevention Act ("PKPA"), full faith and credit must be given to another state's custody or visitation determination if the Act's jurisdictional requirements are met. The jurisdictional standards set forth in the PKPA are substantially the same as those in the UCCJEA, except that emergency-based jurisdiction is not made temporary in the PKPA.

I. MODIFICATION OF CUSTODY DECREES

Although custody orders are always modifiable, most states require a certain amount of time to elapse between the prior custody order and a request for modification, unless the child's physical, mental, moral, or emotional health is endangered. Generally, custody awards will be modified

only if there is a *substantial or material change in circumstances*. However, a court will also consider facts existing at the time of the decree if those facts were not then before the court. The party seeking the modification bears the burden of proof, and as always, the child's best interest is the overriding concern.

V. RIGHTS OF UNMARRIED COHABITANTS

A. SAME-SEX COUPLES
Six states now recognize same-sex marriage: Connecticut, Iowa, Maine, Massachusetts, New Hampshire, and Vermont. In lieu of recognizing same-sex marriage, some states have enacted legislation allowing same-sex couples to enter into domestic partnerships or civil unions, providing a variety of rights that previously were reserved for married couples. However, there is no legal recognition of same-sex couples under federal law.

B. CONTRACTS BETWEEN UNMARRIED COHABITANTS
Express contracts between unmarried cohabitants regarding earnings and property rights will generally be enforced. These contracts are unenforceable only when sexual relations constitute the only consideration provided. Courts are less likely to enforce an implied contract between unmarried cohabitants.

C. DIVISION OF PROPERTY
In the absence of an express contract, courts often grant an equitable distribution of property based on theories of constructive trust, resulting trust, or quantum meruit (quasi-contract recovery for valuable services).

D. GENERAL STATUS OF COHABITANTS' RIGHTS
Unmarried cohabitants do not assume any special status by living together, but they do retain their individual rights.

VI. NONMARITAL CHILDREN

A. NONMARITAL STATUS DEFINED
A nonmarital child (sometimes called an illegitimate child or a child born out of wedlock) is one born to an unmarried woman. (*But see* IX.B.3., *infra*, regarding gestational mother under a gestational agreement.)

B. PRESUMPTION OF MARITAL CHILD
The child of a married woman is presumed to be the child of her husband.

C. CONSTITUTIONAL LIMITS ON DISCRIMINATION
Distinctions made between marital and nonmarital children are subject to the intermediate scrutiny standard, and are stricken unless the action is *substantially related to an important governmental interest*.

1. **No Punitive Purpose**

   The Supreme Court will not uphold discriminatory legislation intended to punish the off-spring of illicit relationships. Thus, it has held that: nonmarital children cannot be precluded from inheriting from their fathers; statutes of limitations on paternity suits are discriminatory; nonmarital children have the same right to child support as marital children; government benefits may not be denied to nonmarital children merely because they are born out of wedlock; and nonmarital children may not be precluded from suing for a parent's wrongful death. Note, however, that because of the plenary power over immigration, the Court upheld a federal law granting immigration preferences to marital children.

2. **Treatment of Unmarried Parents**

   a. **Tort Recovery**

      An unmarried mother may recover in tort for the death of her child, but an unmarried father may be precluded from so doing if he did not previously legally recognize the child.

   b. **Citizenship of Child Born Abroad to Unmarried American Parent**

      When an unmarried American woman gives birth abroad, her child is automatically granted United States citizenship. In contrast, when the child of an unmarried American man is born abroad, the man must take specific steps to establish his paternity in order to make his child a United States citizen.

   c. **Unwed Fathers' Due Process Rights**

      If an unwed father is a part of the family unit that includes the child, the relationship between the father and child will be protected by due process, if the unmarried father has demonstrated a full commitment to the responsibilities of parenthood by participating in the rearing of his child. The court will consider whether the father shouldered any significant responsibility with respect to the daily supervision, education, protection, or care of the child. To have due process rights with respect to a *newborn* infant, the unwed father must be willing to assume custody of the child *himself*—not merely block adoption by others. Other considerations are: public acknowledgment of paternity; payment of pregnancy and birth expenses; steps taken to establish legal responsibility for the child; and other factors showing a commitment to the child.

D. **CHANGE IN STATUS**

Under most state statutes, every child is the lawful child of his mother, but is the lawful child of his father only if: the parents were married after the child's birth; the father holds the child out as his biological child, consents to be named on the birth certificate, or formally acknowledges paternity; or there is a judicial decree establishing paternity.

E. **SUIT TO ESTABLISH PATERNITY**

A paternity suit seeking support may be brought by the child, the mother, or the state (if the child is receiving support from the state). Once paternity is established, the duty of support attaches, and rights to visitation and custody may be asserted by the father.

1. **Statute of Limitations**

   Since the statute is tolled during the child's minority, the limitations period is something more than 18 years at a minimum.

2. **Evidence**
Admissible evidence includes: exhibition of the child to show resemblance to the defendant; statements regarding paternity; medical testimony, and blood or genetic tests. If blood or genetic tests show that the defendant cannot be the father, the case must be dismissed. States vary on the level of proof required to establish paternity. Some require "clear and convincing evidence," but a "preponderance of the evidence" standard has been upheld.

3. **Records Usually Sealed**
Records of paternity actions are usually kept sealed.

VII. PARENT, CHILD, AND THE STATE

A. LEGAL DISABILITIES OF CHILDHOOD
A child may own and convey property, but can disaffirm any conveyance upon reaching the age of majority. Similarly, a child may enter into and enforce contracts, but, with the exception of contracts for necessaries, the child may disaffirm his contracts at any time before reaching majority and for a reasonable time thereafter. Although exceptions are made for minors seeking abortions, birth control, or treatment for sexually transmitted diseases, most children are incapable of consenting to medical care. The state can override the withholding of parental consent if to do otherwise would cause irremediable injury to the child. Children cannot make valid wills. Children can commit torts, but may be judged by a more lenient standard, and children who commit crimes are generally adjudicated under delinquency laws rather than criminal statutes.

B. EMANCIPATION
Emancipation is the removal of the disabilities of minority, and the child is considered an adult. Most states consider married minors to be emancipated.

C. DUTY OF SUPPORT
Parents have a duty to support their children, and in some states, children also have a duty to support their elderly parents.

D. EDUCATION
States can require that children attend school up to a certain age, but parents can decide where their children attend school.

E. TORT SUITS AND THE FAMILY

1. **Intrafamily Tort Immunities**
Either spouse may maintain a tort action against the other. Most states have abolished parent-child immunity, but grant broad discretion to parents in their exercise of parental supervision. The states that retain parent-child immunity do not apply it in cases of intentional tortious conduct and (in some) automobile accident cases. To the extent that these immunities still exist, they apply to personal, not property, injuries.

2. **Interference with the Marital Relationship**
In most states, either spouse may bring an action for the loss of the other spouse's consortium or services due to injuries resulting from a defendant's tortious conduct.

3. **Interference with the Parent-Child Relationship**

   a. **Tortious Injury**

   A child may not recover against one who tortiously injures his parent, but a parent may recover when a child is tortiously injured.

   b. **Interference with Custody**

   A parent whose lawful custody is interfered with may recover tort damages in actions for abduction or enticement. In addition, parties who conspire to conceal information about a newborn child's birth or location may be held liable for their participation in a civil conspiracy.

4. **Nature of Action for Family Relationship Interference**

   Except for claims based on direct interference with relationships (*e.g.*, suit for abduction), actions for interference with family relationships are derivative; thus, recovery depends on the success of the injured family member's own action.

   CMR | **Exam Tip** | Because of the derivative nature of these interference actions, in addition to defenses against the plaintiff, any defense that would prevent recovery by the injured family member (*e.g.*, contributory negligence) will also prevent recovery in the interference action.

F. **PARENTAL AUTONOMY**

   Parents have authority to make decisions on most matters concerning the upbringing of their child, but certain state interests (*e.g.*, prevention of abuse and neglect, compulsory education) take precedence over parental autonomy.

   1. **Children in Need of Supervision**

   Courts have jurisdiction over children whose behavior does not meet certain standards, but is not criminal (*e.g.*, habitual truancy, running away from home), and can pursue different remedies such as: ordering counseling, placing the child under the supervision of a social worker, or placing the child with a state agency.

   2. **Termination of Parental Rights**

   Because the right to raise one's children is a fundamental constitutional right, parents must have due process before their rights can be terminated. This includes the right to counsel (including the right to appointment of counsel if indigent, should fundamental fairness so require). Grounds for termination must be proved by *clear and convincing evidence*.

   a. **Grounds**

   Grounds for termination include: infliction of serious physical harm on the child, including sexual abuse; abandonment; neglect or deprivation (failure to meet minimum standards of care); failure to provide support without justifiable cause; mental illness or retardation so severe as to make the parent incapable of caring for the child; and parental unfitness (conduct by the parent that seriously harms the child physically or psychologically).

G. **CUSTODIAL DISPUTES BETWEEN PARENTS AND THIRD PARTIES**

   In disputes between parents and third parties, the decision does not rest solely on the child's best interest. A natural parent has a right to raise his child, and absent voluntary relinquishment, the

parent is entitled to custody unless it is shown that the parent is unfit. However, a court may find that based on special circumstances (*e.g.*, abandonment of the child), the biological parent has lost the right to rear the child, and the child should remain with a third party.

VIII. ADOPTION

A. DEFINED
Adoption is a legal proceeding terminating the relationship between the child and his biological parents (if necessary) and establishing a new relationship between the child and his adoptive parents. Adoption is purely statutory.

B. JURISDICTION
Most states require that the person seeking to adopt be a resident of the county where the petition is filed. Some states permit filing in the county where the child resides or where the office of the child placement agency is located.

C. PROCEDURAL CONSIDERATIONS

1. Consent of Natural Parents
The consent of the child's natural parents is generally required, but the father's consent may not be necessary if the parents are unmarried.

a. Rights Terminated
Parental consent is not necessary if parental rights have been terminated.

b. Waiver if Unreasonably Withheld
The parental consent requirement may be waived if the court concludes it is being unreasonably withheld against the best interest of the child (*e.g.*, natural parent has deserted the child). A nonconsenting parent is entitled to notice of the hearing and an opportunity to be heard.

c. Rights of Unmarried Fathers
In deciding whether an unwed father can veto a prospective adoption, the court considers the level of the father's involvement with the child, such as: whether he lived with and cared for the child, or visited the child regularly; admitted paternity; or paid child support. As to a newborn infant, a father's right to a continued parental relationship depends on his manifestations of parental responsibility (*see* VI.C.2.c., *supra*). A father of a nonmarital child who has never attempted to establish a legal or personal relationship with that child has no right to notice prior to the adoption of the child by others.

2. Consent of Adoptee
Prospective adoptees over a certain age, usually 12, must also consent to their own adoption.

3. Withdrawal of Consent
Consent cannot be withdrawn after a decree of adoption is entered. Prior to entry of the decree, consent may be withdrawn if the court finds that withdrawal is in the best interest of the adoptee. Notice and a hearing must be given to the person seeking the adoption, the person seeking withdrawal, and the agency placing the child for adoption.

4. **Investigation and Court Approval**
    Most states require that there be an investigation of the suitability of the proposed adoption, and approval of the adoption by the court.

5. **Payment of Money Prohibited**
    Most states prohibit the payment of money to the natural parents other than medical costs related to the pregnancy.

6. **Confidentiality of Adoption Proceedings—Sealed Records**
    Records of adoption cases are sealed, and in most states, information contained in them is not available to the public or the adoptees.

D. **VIOLATION OF ADOPTION STATUTE**
    Violation of adoption statutes is often punishable as a crime.

E. **CONSEQUENCES OF ADOPTION**
    Upon adoption, a new birth certificate is issued, listing the adoptive parents as the child's parents. The adoption cuts off the biological parents' rights and obligations, and creates new rights and obligations in the adoptive parents.

IX. ALTERNATIVES TO ADOPTION

A. **IN GENERAL**
    When only the intended parents are involved in a procedure such as artificial insemination, in vitro fertilization, or embryo transplantation, there is no problem; they are clearly the resulting child's parents. To deal with consequences when third parties are involved, the Uniform Status of Children of Assisted Conception Act was promulgated in 1988 and later incorporated into the Uniform Parentage Act. Many states have not yet adopted the Uniform Acts; therefore it is best to discuss both general legal principles and the uniform law if a question does not specify the law of the particular jurisdiction.

B. **UNIFORM PARENTAGE ACT**
    "Assisted reproduction" means a method of causing pregnancy other than sexual intercourse and includes: (i) intrauterine insemination; (ii) donation of eggs; (iii) donation of embryos; and (iv) in-vitro fertilization and transfer of embryos. Assisted reproduction does *not* apply to the birth of a child conceived as a result of a gestational agreement.

1. **Maternity and Paternity**
    Except as provided with regard to gestational agreements (below), a woman who gives birth to a child is the child's mother. Likewise, except with regard to gestational agreements, the husband of a woman who bears a child through assisted reproduction is the child's father. Maternity and paternity may also be established by adjudication or adoption.

2. **Donors**
    A donor is a person, other than an intended parent, who produces egg or sperm used for assisted reproduction. A donor is *not* a parent of the resulting child.

3. Gestational Agreement

A gestational mother (sometimes called a surrogate mother) is an adult woman who enters into an agreement to bear a child, conceived through assisted reproduction, for intended parents.

a. Agreement

A gestational mother, her husband (if she is married), and the intended parents enter into a written agreement whereby the gestational mother relinquishes her rights and duties as a parent of a child to be conceived, and the intended parents become the legal parents of the child.

b. Required Findings for Court Approval

The court may approve a gestational agreement if: the court has jurisdiction; an appropriate agency has made a home study of the intended parents (unless the court waives this requirement); all parties have voluntarily entered into the agreement with an understanding of its ramifications; adequate provision has been made for health care costs; and if the gestational mother is promised consideration, it is reasonable.

c. Where Agreement Not Approved by Court

If the agreement is not approved by the court before conception, the agreement is unenforceable, the gestational mother is the legal mother of the resulting child, and the gestational mother's husband is the father. If the gestational mother is unmarried, or if her husband is not a party to the agreement, paternity is governed by existing law.

d. Termination of Agreement

After the agreement is approved, but before the prospective gestational mother is pregnant, any party (or the court for cause) may terminate the agreement by giving written notice to the other parties.

e. Parentage Under Approved Agreement

If the agreement has been approved by the court and has not been terminated, upon the child's birth, the intended parents must file notice of the birth within 300 days of the assisted reproduction. The court will then issue an order establishing the intended parents as the parents of the child.

f. Gestational Mother's Discretion to Make Health Decisions

The agreement may not limit the gestational mother's right to make decisions regarding her health care or that of the fetus.

g. Subsequent Marriage of Gestational Mother

The marriage of the gestational mother after the agreement is approved does not affect the validity of the order, and the husband's consent is not required.

h. Presumption as to Child Born Within 300 Days of Assisted Conception

A child born to a gestational mother within 300 days after assisted conception pursuant to an approved agreement is presumed to result from the assisted conception.

i. Gestational Agreements Not Permitted in Some States

Some states do not give effect to gestational agreements. To encourage these states to

adopt the 2000 Uniform Parentage Act, the section of the Act on gestational agreements (Article 8) may be omitted without affecting the rest of the Act.

C. OWNERSHIP OF FERTILIZED OVUM IN VITRO

A cryogenically preserved product of in vitro fertilization (a "frozen embryo") poses many difficult questions, particularly when the couple divorces. Such questions include whether the embryo is property or a person, and who will decide whether any transplantation will take place.

FEDERAL JURISDICTION AND PROCEDURE

TABLE OF CONTENTS

FEDERAL JURISDICTION AND PROCEDURE
I. PERSONAL JURISDICTION

A. OVERVIEW

Personal jurisdiction refers to the ability of the court having subject matter jurisdiction (*i.e.,* jurisdiction over the type of case) to exercise power over a particular defendant or item of property.

1. Limitations on Personal Jurisdiction

An exercise of personal jurisdiction must not exceed the limitations of either state statutes or the United States Constitution. If no state statute grants the court the power over the parties before the court, then the court lacks personal jurisdiction. Under the Due Process Clause, parties directly affected by the court action must receive fair and adequate notice of the action. Furthermore, there must be minimum contacts between the defendant or property and the forum state so that the assumption of jurisdiction is fair and reasonable. Absent some special federal provision, each federal court must analyze personal jurisdiction *as if it were a court of the state in which it is located*.

2. Three Types of Jurisdiction

In personam jurisdiction exists when the forum has power over the *person of a particular defendant*. An in personam judgment is entitled to full faith and credit in all other states. *In rem* jurisdiction exists when the court has power to adjudicate the rights of *all* persons in the world with respect to a particular item of property. *Quasi in rem* jurisdiction exists when the court has power to determine the rights of *particular individuals* with respect to *specific property* within the court's control. Unlike in rem jurisdiction, quasi in rem jurisdiction does not permit the court to determine the rights of all persons in the world. A quasi in rem judgment does not bind the defendant personally and cannot be enforced against any other property belonging to the defendant.

B. STATUTORY LIMITATIONS ON IN PERSONAM JURISDICTION

Most states have statutes granting their courts in personam jurisdiction based on the following five situations:

1. Defendant Is Present in Forum State and Is Personally Served with Process

Service plus even transitory presence may be a sufficient basis for in personam jurisdiction. Service by fraud or force is invalid. Most states grant immunity from personal jurisdiction to nonresidents who are parties or witnesses in a judicial proceeding.

2. Defendant Is Domiciled in Forum State

Domicile refers to the place where a person maintains her permanent home. If a person lacks capacity, domicile is determined by law.

3. Defendant Is a Citizen

A United States citizen, even though domiciled abroad, is subject to personal jurisdiction in the United States. The extent of this jurisdiction is unclear, because no state has ever attempted to enact a law or rule that enables such jurisdiction. The Supreme Court, however, has ruled that a federal court may subpoena a United States citizen domiciled abroad to return to give testimony.

4. **Defendant Consents to Jurisdiction**
   Consent may be express or implied, or through the making of a general appearance. A person can give advance consent by contract or by appointment of an agent to accept service of process. Many states allow "special appearances" through which a defendant can object to the court's exercise of jurisdiction. This special appearance must be made in the defendant's initial pleading to the court.

5. **Defendant Has Committed Acts Bringing Him Within Forum State's Long Arm Statutes**
   The long arm statutes of a few states give their courts power over any person or property over which the state can constitutionally exercise jurisdiction. Most states, however, have long arm statutes that specify in detail the situations in which their courts can exercise jurisdiction, *e.g.,* a "tort" occurs within the state, or a cause of action arises out of the "transaction of business" or ownership of property in the state.

C. CONSTITUTIONAL LIMITATIONS ON IN PERSONAM JURISDICTION

1. **Sufficient Nexus with the Forum**

   a. **Traditional Rule: Physical Power**
   Traditionally, jurisdiction was based on the power to arrest the person (based on presence, residence, or consent) to force compliance with a judgment.

   b. **Modern Due Process Standard: Contact and Fairness**
   The Supreme Court has listed several factors to use to assess the constitutionality of personal jurisdiction. In general, the factors fall under two headings: *contact* and *fairness*.

      1) **Contact**
      In personam jurisdiction requires that the defendant have "such *minimum contacts*" with the forum such that the exercise of jurisdiction would be fair and reasonable. The contacts cannot be accidental; the court must find that, through these contacts, the defendant *purposefully availed* herself "of the privilege of conducting activities in the forum state, thus invoking the benefits and protections of its laws." The defendant also *must know or reasonably anticipate* that her activities in the forum render it *foreseeable* that she may be "haled into court" there.

      2) **Fairness**
      The exercise of jurisdiction also must not offend the "traditional notions of fair play and substantial justice." The court has listed several factors relevant to fairness. One factor is whether the claim arises from the defendant's contacts with the forum. If the claim is *related to the defendant's contacts* with the forum, a court is more likely to find that jurisdiction as to that claim ("specific jurisdiction") is fair and reasonable. If the defendant engages *in systematic and continuous activity* in the forum state, the court could find this activity a sufficient basis for exercising in personam jurisdiction over any cause of action ("general jurisdiction"). *Convenience* to the defendant is another factor. A forum is constitutionally acceptable unless it is "so gravely difficult and inconvenient" that the defendant is put at a severe disadvantage. The forum state may also have a *legitimate interest* in providing redress for its resident. Other factors include the plaintiff's interest in obtaining convenient and effective relief, the interstate judicial system's interest in efficiency, and the shared interest of the states in furthering social policies.

CMR SUMMARY CHART

LIMITS ON IN PERSONAM JURISDICTION

Statutory

States generally require that the defendant:

1. Is **present** in the forum state at the time of service;

2. Is **domiciled** in the forum state;

3. Has given express or implied **consent** to jurisdiction; or

4. Meets the requirements of the forum state's **long arm or other statute**.

Constitutional

There must be sufficient minimum contacts so that the exercise of in personam jurisdiction over the defendant is fair.

1. Contacts

The contacts must show that the defendant:

a. **Purposefully availed** herself of the forum state's laws; and

b. **Knew or reasonably should have anticipated** that her activities in the forum made it **foreseeable** that she may be "haled into court" there.

2. Fairness

a. If the claim is **related to the defendant's contact** with the forum, a court is more likely to find that jurisdiction as to that claim ("specific jurisdiction") is fair and reasonable; or

b. If the defendant engages in **systematic and continuous activity** in the forum state, the court could find this activity a sufficient basis for exercising in personam jurisdiction over any cause of action ("general jurisdiction"); and

c. The court will consider **other factors**:

   * Whether the **forum is "so gravely difficult and inconvenient"** that the defendant is put at a severe disadvantage;

   * The **forum state's legitimate interest** in providing redress for its resident;

   * The **plaintiff's interest** in obtaining convenient and effective relief;

   * The **interstate judicial system's interest in efficiency**; and

   * The shared interest of the states in **furthering social policies**.

3. Notice

Defendant must be **notified** of the lawsuit by a **reasonable method** and given an **opportunity to appear and be heard**.

CMR **Exam Tip** Some authorities discuss the relationship of the contact to the claim as part of the "contact" assessment, while others consider it to be part of the "fairness and reasonableness" assessment. On your exam, the important point is that you address the issue, whether under the contact prong or fairness prong.

2. **Notice**

In addition to the contact and fairness requirement, there is also a due process requirement that a reasonable method be used to notify the defendant of a pending lawsuit so that she may have an opportunity to appear and be heard.

   a. **Requirement that Agent Notify Defendant**

   If the plaintiff appointed the defendant's agent for the service of process under a contractual right for the plaintiff's benefit or the appointment is by operation of law, the agent's failure to notify the defendant will prohibit jurisdiction.

   b. **Requirements for Cases Involving Multiple or Unknown Parties**

   When there are multiple or unknown parties, the best practical means of notice available must be used. However, if certified mail is used, and the mail is returned as unclaimed, the plaintiff cannot proceed in the face of such knowledge when other practicable means to serve the defendant exist.

D. IN REM JURISDICTION

Most states have statutes providing for in rem jurisdiction in actions for condemnation, title registration, distribution of estate assets, grant of divorce when only the complaining spouse is present and subject to personal jurisdiction, etc. The presence of the property in the state is constitutionally sufficient for the exercise of jurisdiction over the property. A court has no in rem power over property outside the state or when property is brought into the state by fraud or force. Persons whose interests are affected and whose addresses are known must at least be notified by ordinary mail.

E. QUASI IN REM ACTIONS

There are two types of quasi in rem jurisdiction. The first type involves disputes between parties over their rights in property within the state. The second type involves disputes unrelated to the property. The minimum contacts standard applies to both cases. In the first type of case, the close connection between the litigation and the contact provides the necessary minimum contacts. In the second type of case, the mere presence of the property within the state is not a sufficient contact; there must be some other basis to exercise jurisdiction (*e.g.*, such contacts exist so that in personam jurisdiction over the defendant would be proper).

II. DIVERSITY OF CITIZENSHIP JURISDICTION

A. DIVERSITY AMONG THE PARTIES

1. **Complete Diversity When Action Commenced**

   Every plaintiff must be of diverse citizenship from every defendant. If one defendant and one plaintiff are co-citizens of the same state, there is no diversity jurisdiction. This is the rule of "complete diversity." The matter in controversy must also exceed the sum or value of $75,000, exclusive of interest and costs.

CMR **Exam Tip**   If the facts of a bar exam question describe in detail the citizenship of the parties and present an elaborate amount in controversy scenario, you should, of course, analyze whether the requirements for diversity jurisdiction are present. Do not be misled, however, into failing to also check for the presence of a federal question. Even if the court does not have diversity jurisdiction, it might have federal question jurisdiction (*see* III., *infra*).

a. Interpleader Exception
There is a federal interpleader statute exception where "minimal diversity" and an amount in controversy of $500 or more are sufficient to confer jurisdiction.

b. Alienage Jurisdiction
A federal court has subject matter jurisdiction over disputes between a citizen of a state and an alien, but not over two aliens.

c. Diversity When Action Commenced
Diversity of citizenship must exist as of the time the suit is instituted. It need not exist at the time the cause of action arose, and it is not defeated if, after commencement of the action, a party later becomes a citizen of the same state as one of his opponents.

2. Questions of Citizenship

a. Individuals
The determination of the state of citizenship of a natural person depends on the permanent home to which he intends to return. The citizenship of a child is that of her parents.

b. Corporations
A corporation is deemed a citizen of every state of its incorporation, and also of its principal place of business. When a corporation has its executive offices in one state and its physical operation wholly or predominantly in another state, the principal place of business is the state where physical operations are conducted. When the corporation performs its operational activities in many states, the courts have applied a "home office" or "nerve center" test and held that the principal place of business is the state where the executive offices are located.

CMR **Exam Tip**   Do not confuse the issue of the citizenship of a corporation for purposes of determining diversity with the issue of where a corporate defendant is deemed to reside for *venue* purposes, *i.e.,* in any judicial district in which it is subject to personal jurisdiction at the time the action is commenced (discussed *infra*).

1) Corporations Chartered in Foreign Countries
A corporation is deemed exclusively a citizen of the foreign country of incorporation and thus is an ***alien for diversity purposes***. If the foreign corporation has its principal place of business in this country, it is ***also a citizen of the state*** in which that place is located.

c. Unincorporated Associations and Limited Liability Companies
For diversity purposes, an unincorporated association, such as a partnership or labor union, is considered a citizen of each state of which any member is a citizen. A limited liability company is treated like an unincorporated association for citizenship purposes.

d. Legal Representatives

The legal representative of the estate of a decedent, an infant, or an incompetent is deemed to have the same citizenship as the decedent, infant, or incompetent.

e. Class Actions

For class actions, diversity is determined on the basis of the citizenship of the named members of the class who are suing.

f. Nonresident United States Citizens and Aliens

A United States citizen domiciled abroad is not a citizen of any state and is also not an alien. (Alienage depends on nationality, not domicile.) A permanent resident alien is deemed to be a citizen of the state in which he is domiciled.

3. Collusion and Devices to Create or Defeat Diversity

If a party attempts to create diversity by a sham transaction, such as assigning a claim for collection purposes only to create diversity, the courts look through the transaction and declare that diversity does not exist.

a. Class Actions and Voluntary Changes of Citizenship

In class action suits, diversity may be created by properly selecting named plaintiffs to bring the action on behalf of others. A plaintiff can also create diversity by changing his state citizenship after the cause of action accrued but before suit is commenced; however, the change must be genuine and not temporary.

b. Defeating Diversity

No rule exists to prevent assignment of a claim to defeat diversity. On the other hand, fraudulent joinder of an in-state defendant to defeat diversity is no bar to removal.

4. Realignment According to Interest

In determining whether diversity exists, the court will look beyond the nominal designation of the parties in the pleadings and realign them according to their true interests in the dispute. Thus, realignment may create diversity or destroy it.

a. Shareholder Derivative Actions

In shareholder derivative actions, the court will realign the corporation as a defendant to determine diversity.

5. Ancillary (Supplemental) Jurisdiction

Under the doctrine of *ancillary jurisdiction* (now codified under the rubric *"supplemental jurisdiction"*), a court may entertain claims that could not, by themselves, invoke federal question jurisdiction or diversity jurisdiction if the claims arise from a *common nucleus of operative fact* as the claim that invoked federal subject matter jurisdiction.

CMR **Exam Tip** On your exam, sometimes how you get to an answer is as important as the answer itself. For example, on an essay question, it would be a huge omission to merely state that "the supplemental jurisdiction statute would allow the claim" without first addressing whether the claim has an independent basis for subject matter jurisdiction (*i.e.,* federal question jurisdiction or diversity of citizenship jurisdiction).

6. **Subsequent Addition of Parties**

A claim by or against an additional party, like any claim in federal court, must satisfy some basis of federal subject matter jurisdiction such as diversity or federal question jurisdiction. If the claim does not satisfy either of these, it might invoke supplemental jurisdiction if the common nucleus test described above can be satisfied. However, for cases based solely on diversity, supplemental jurisdiction may not be used to support claims (i) by plaintiffs against impleaded parties, compulsorily or permissively joined parties, or intervening parties; (ii) by persons who are to be compulsorily joined as plaintiffs; and (iii) by persons seeking to intervene as plaintiffs.

a. **Intervention of Right**

Traditionally, a person seeking to intervene in a case as of right did not have to show an independent basis for jurisdiction as long as the requirements for intervention were met. Under the supplemental jurisdiction statute, however, there is no ancillary jurisdiction for claims by or against intervenors, and such a claim can proceed only if an independent basis for jurisdiction can be shown.

b. **Substitution of Parties**

When a party is substituted, the citizenship of the substituted party is disregarded, and that of the original party controls; thus, diversity jurisdiction is not affected. *Compare:* If a party is replaced (*e.g.,* because plaintiff sued the wrong party) rather than substituted, the citizenship of the replacement party controls, and diversity jurisdiction could be lost.

c. **Third-Party Practice—Impleader**

Generally, no diversity or specific amount in controversy is required in third-party practice between the third-party defendant and the third-party plaintiff or the original plaintiff **unless** the plaintiff asserts a claim against the third-party defendant.

d. **Cross-Claims**

A cross-claim is a claim by one co-party against another, and it may be asserted if the claim arises from the same transaction or occurrence as the underlying dispute. If the cross-claimant does not have an independent subject matter basis (*i.e.,* diversity of citizenship or federal question jurisdiction), the cross-claim may nonetheless be asserted in federal court through the ancillary form of supplemental jurisdiction.

B. **JURISDICTIONAL AMOUNT—IN EXCESS OF $75,000**

Actions brought in federal court under the diversity statute must be in excess of $75,000, exclusive of interest and costs. The amount is determined from the plaintiff's good faith allegation. The complaint can be dismissed only if it appears there is no legal possibility of a recovery exceeding the jurisdictional amount. Jurisdiction is not retroactively defeated by the fact that the amount actually recovered is less than the jurisdictional amount.

1. **What Is "In Controversy"?**

Collateral consequences of the judgment (*e.g.,* rights to payment of future installments on disability policy) may not be considered. Interest and costs are also excluded. However, attorneys' fees that are recoverable by contract or by statute are considered part of the matter in controversy. Interest that constitutes a part of the claim itself, as distinguished from interest payable by virtue of a delay in payment, is also part of the jurisdictional amount. A

punitive damage claim permitted under state substantive law may be used in meeting the dollar amount requirement.

2. **Aggregation of Separate Claims**

For purposes of meeting the jurisdictional amount, a plaintiff may aggregate all her claims against a single defendant. A plaintiff who has an action against several defendants can aggregate her claims against them only if the defendants are jointly liable to the plaintiff. She cannot aggregate liabilities based on separate claims or concurrent liabilities. Several plaintiffs can aggregate their claims only if they are seeking "to enforce a single title or right in which they have a common or undivided interest . . . ."

3. **Supplemental Jurisdiction over Claims Not Exceeding $75,000 in Diversity Cases**

Claims that do not meet the amount in controversy requirement may invoke supplemental jurisdiction if they arise from the same nucleus of operative fact as a claim that invoked diversity of citizenship jurisdiction. *However, supplemental jurisdiction cannot be used to override the complete diversity requirement*.

4. **Counterclaims**

A defendant's counterclaim cannot be combined with the plaintiff's claim to reach the jurisdictional amount. A compulsory counterclaim need not meet the jurisdictional amount requirement, as the court may hear it under its supplemental jurisdiction. However, a permissive counterclaim (one arising out of an *unrelated* transaction) must have an independent jurisdictional basis, and thus must meet the jurisdictional amount requirement.

   a. **Removal from State Courts**

   A plaintiff who claims $75,000 or less in a state court action who is met with a counterclaim for more than $75,000 may not remove the suit to federal court, regardless of whether the counterclaim is compulsory or permissive, because removal is permitted only by defendants. Also, a plaintiff with a small claim can require a defendant with a large claim to litigate it in state court simply by being the first to file. Even though this is the traditional rule, there is a trend allowing removal.

C. ***ERIE* DOCTRINE**

Under the *Erie* doctrine, a federal court in a diversity case will apply its own procedural law, but must apply the substantive law and conflict of laws rules of the state in which it is sitting. When it is unclear whether a state law rule is substantive or procedural, courts use the "outcome determinative" test—a state law rule that substantially determines "outcome" of the litigation must be applied. However, if a federal rule is "arguably procedural," it will be applied. Some state statutes may have both substantive and procedural elements. (*See* chart *infra*.)

D. **EXCEPTIONS TO DIVERSITY OF CITIZENSHIP JURISDICTION**

For historical reasons, federal courts generally will not exercise diversity jurisdiction over domestic relations or probate proceedings. To fall within the probate exception, the claim asserted must involve the actual probate or annulment of a will, or seek to reach property in the custody of a state probate court.

E. **MULTIPARTY, MULTIFORUM TRIAL JURISDICTION ACT OF 2002**

The Multiparty, Multiforum Trial Jurisdiction Act applies to accidents in which at least *75 people have died from a single accident* at a discrete location. Minimal diversity is required; *i.e.*, one

APPROACH TO *ERIE* QUESTIONS

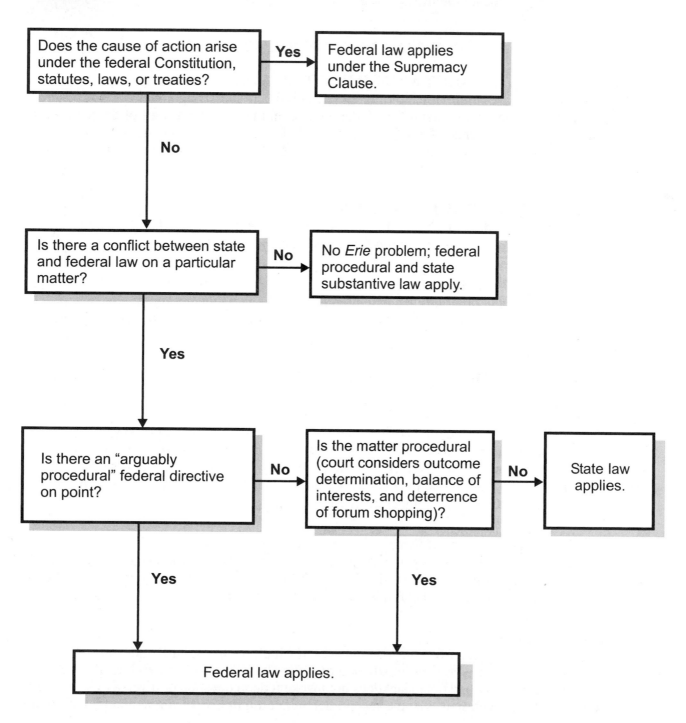

Does the cause of action arise under the federal Constitution, statutes, laws, or treaties? — **Yes** → Federal law applies under the Supremacy Clause.

No ↓

Is there a conflict between state and federal law on a particular matter? — **No** → No *Erie* problem; federal procedural and state substantive law apply.

Yes ↓

Is there an "arguably procedural" federal directive on point? — **No** → Is the matter procedural (court considers outcome determination, balance of interests, and deterrence of forum shopping)? — **No** → State law applies.

Yes ↓ / **Yes** ↓

Federal law applies.

plaintiff must be of diverse citizenship of one defendant. One of three other conditions must be met: (i) one defendant must reside in a different state from the place where a substantial part of the accident took place; (ii) any two defendants must reside in different states; or (iii) substantial parts of the accident must have taken place in different states. Finally, anyone with a claim arising from the accident is permitted to intervene as a plaintiff even if she could not have maintained an action in the district in which the case is pending, and nationwide service of process is allowed.

III. FEDERAL QUESTION JURISDICTION

A. FEDERAL QUESTION MUST APPEAR IN COMPLAINT

The district courts have original jurisdiction over all civil actions arising under the Constitution, laws, or treaties of the United States. The federal question must appear as part of the plaintiff's cause of action. The existence of a defense based on federal law will not create federal question jurisdiction. A complaint does not raise a federal question if it does so only in anticipation of some defense.

B. IMPLIED FEDERAL RIGHT OF ACTION

There can be an implied federal right of action—it is not essential that the federal statute expressly provide for a civil cause of action for a violation.

C. FEDERAL CORPORATIONS

Federal question jurisdiction does not arise merely from the fact that a corporate party was incorporated by an act of Congress unless the United States owns more than one-half of the corporation's capital stock.

D. PENDENT (SUPPLEMENTAL) JURISDICTION

1. Pendent Claims

If a plaintiff has both federal and state claims, the federal court has discretion to exercise pendent jurisdiction over the claim based on state law if the two claims "derive from a common nucleus of operative fact" and are such that a plaintiff "would ordinarily be expected to try them all in one judicial proceeding." Pendent jurisdiction, along with ancillary jurisdiction, is now codified under the name "supplemental jurisdiction."

a. Effect of Dismissal of Federal Claim on Pendent Claim

The court may exercise pendent jurisdiction over the state claim even if the federal claim is dismissed on the merits. However, the state claim should probably also be dismissed if the federal claim is dismissed before trial.

2. Pendent Parties

Pendent parties jurisdiction can arise in cases in which (i) the plaintiff sues more than one defendant, (ii) there is federal jurisdiction over the claim against one defendant, and (iii) the claim against the second defendant does not invoke federal question or diversity of citizenship jurisdiction. The claim against the second defendant might invoke supplemental jurisdiction if it arises from the same nucleus of common fact as the claim against the defendant. Pendent parties jurisdiction can also arise when multiple plaintiffs assert claims against one defendant. Here, assuming again the second plaintiff's claim is derived from the same nucleus of fact, the second plaintiff might invoke supplemental jurisdiction to support a state law claim in a federal question case.

E. SPECIFIC STATUTORY GRANTS

There is no amount in controversy requirement in federal question cases (with the limited exception for cases brought against private parties under the Consumer Product Safety Act). Jurisdiction of the federal courts is exclusive of the state courts in: (i) bankruptcy proceedings; (ii) patent and copyright cases; (iii) many cases where the United States is involved; (iv) cases where consuls and vice-consuls are sued as defendants; (v) antitrust cases; (vi) actions against foreign states removed from state courts to federal court; (vii) postal matters; (viii) Internal Revenue Service cases; (ix) Securities Exchange Act cases; and (x) admiralty cases (only in limitation of liability proceedings and maritime actions in rem).

IV. VENUE

A. SUBJECT MATTER JURISDICTION DISTINGUISHED

Subject matter jurisdiction is the power of the court to adjudicate the matter before it. Venue relates to the proper district in which to bring the action. Subject matter jurisdiction is a question of power or authority; venue is a question of convenience. Subject matter jurisdiction cannot be conferred by agreement; venue can be. A court can have subject matter jurisdiction without having proper venue.

B. GENERAL RULES

Venue in civil actions in the federal courts is proper in:

1. A judicial district where *any defendant resides*, if all defendants reside in the same state;

2. A judicial district in which *a substantial part of the events or omissions* giving rise to the claim occurred, or *a substantial part of property* that is the subject of the action is situated; or

3. If there is no district anywhere in the United States that satisfies 1. or 2.,

   a. For actions based *solely on diversity*, a judicial district in which *any defendant is subject to personal jurisdiction at the time the action is commenced*; or

   b. For actions *not based solely on diversity*, a judicial district in which *any defendant may be found*.

C. RESIDENCE

1. Individuals
An individual's residence for federal venue purposes is determined by the person's domicile.

2. Corporations
For purposes of venue, a defendant corporation is deemed to reside in any jurisdiction in which it is subject to personal jurisdiction.

3. Unincorporated Associations
An unincorporated association is deemed to reside where it does business.

D. VENUE IN "LOCAL ACTIONS"
Local actions must be brought in a district where the property that is the subject matter of the action is located.

E. IMPROPER VENUE MAY BE WAIVED
Unlike jurisdiction over the subject matter, venue may be waived by the parties. Venue is considered to be waived unless timely objection is made to the improper venue.

F. TRANSFER
Even if venue is proper, the court may transfer the case for the convenience of the parties to any court where it could have originally been filed. If original venue is improper, transfer is more appropriate than dismissal except in extraordinary circumstances. The standard for transfer is "the interest of justice." The transferee forum must have subject matter jurisdiction and in personam jurisdiction over the defendant, and venue must be proper.

G. LAW APPLICABLE UPON TRANSFER
If original venue was proper, apply the law of the state in which the *transferor* court sits.
If original venue was improper, apply the law of the state in which the *transferee* court sits.

CMR | **Exam Tip** | Note that the law of the transferor court applies even where the plaintiff, having chosen an inconvenient (but proper) venue in the first place, later seeks a transfer for convenience.

V. REMOVAL JURISDICTION

A. ORIGINAL JURISDICTION NECESSARY
An action originally filed in a state court may be removed to federal court if: (i) the case could have originally been filed in a federal court; and (ii) for cases removed on the basis of diversity, no defendant is a citizen of the state where the action is filed. The prevailing rule is that jurisdiction is tested as of the date of removal, but some courts have held that original jurisdiction must have existed both at the time the suit was instituted in the state court and at the time of removal.

1. Federal Defense Insufficient
A defendant cannot remove on the basis that he has a defense grounded in federal law, since

the existence of a federal defense is insufficient to confer original federal question jurisdiction.

2. State Court Need Not Have Had Jurisdiction
Even when the state court has no jurisdiction because the action is exclusively federal, the federal court may hear and decide the case under its removal jurisdiction.

B. ONLY DEFENDANTS MAY REMOVE
Only defendants can exercise the right of removal. If there is more than one defendant, all defendants must join in the petition for removal.

C. VENUE
Venue lies in the federal district court "embracing the place where such [state] action is pending."

D. DEFENDANT MAY REMOVE SEPARATE AND INDEPENDENT CLAIM
When there are multiple claims or multiple parties, a defendant may remove a whole case if it contains "a separate and independent claim or cause of action" within federal question jurisdiction.

E. DISMISSAL OF NONDIVERSE PARTY ALLOWS REMOVAL
When no federal question is involved and diversity does not exist because a party is a co-citizen of an opposing party, removal will be permitted if the nondiverse parties are thereafter dismissed from the action and there is complete diversity between the remaining parties.

1. Limitations on Removal in Diversity of Citizenship Cases
When jurisdiction of the federal court is based on diversity and one of the defendants is a citizen of the state in which the state action was brought, the action is not removable. Also, a case may not be removed on the basis of diversity jurisdiction more than one year after it was commenced in state court.

F. PROCEDURE FOR REMOVAL
A defendant seeking removal must file a notice of removal in the federal district court in the district and division within which the action is pending. A copy of the notice should be sent to the other parties and to the state court. Once this is done, the state court can no longer deal with the case.

1. Time
The notice of removal must be filed within 30 days after defendant receives notice, through service of a summons, pleading, amended pleading, etc., that the case is or has become removable, but (for diversity cases only) in no event more than one year after the case was commenced.

2. Remand
The plaintiff can file a motion to have the case remanded to the state court. A case will be remanded if there is no federal jurisdiction. The federal court has discretion to remand a case to state court once all federal claims have been resolved, leaving only state claims over which there is no diversity jurisdiction.

REMOVAL ISSUES

The key points to remember are:

☑ A **federal court must have jurisdiction** over the case; **jurisdiction need not have been proper in the state court**.

☑ Removal is to the federal district court **whose territory encompasses the state court**.

☑ **Only defendants can remove**; **all** defendants must join in the removal.

☑ A case **based on diversity** may **not be removed** if **any defendant** is a **citizen of the forum** state.

☑ Notice of removal must be **filed within 30 days** of the date defendant receives a copy of the initial pleading.

☑ If a case later becomes removable (as by dismissal of a nondiverse defendant), the case may be removed **within 30 days of the date it becomes removable, but (for diversity cases) not more than one year after it was brought in state court**.

☑ If the case contains a **separate and independent claim based on a federal question,** defendant may remove the **whole case**.

VI. CONFLICT OF JURISDICTION
BETWEEN STATE AND FEDERAL COURTS

A. INJUNCTIONS AGAINST STATE COURT PROCEEDINGS

1. Pending State Proceedings

A federal court generally is prohibited from enjoining a *pending* state court proceeding unless *expressly* authorized by statute or when necessary in aid of its jurisdiction, or to protect or effectuate its judgments. If a state action is not enjoined, the case coming to a final decision first will have preclusive effect on the other.

2. Threatened State Proceedings

Federal courts may not enjoin a threatened state criminal proceeding unless irreparable harm is clear and imminent (usually limited to a showing of serious interference with First Amendment rights) and the appellate remedy is clearly inadequate to provide relief.

B. ABSTENTION

Unless abstention applies, nothing prohibits a federal court from hearing a case that is pending in state court.

1. **Grounds**

   A federal court will abstain and require a litigant to seek relief in a state court (while retaining jurisdiction):

   a. If the state law is unclear and could be interpreted to avoid the federal constitutional question; or

   b. If there is a state administrative regulatory plan that would be disturbed by the federal court taking the case.

2. **Procedure**

   After the federal court abstains, the litigants must present their issues to the state court in light of their federal contentions. The federal court will ordinarily stay the federal action rather than dismiss it.

3. **Federal Intervention**

   Federal intervention on constitutional grounds may occur if the federal plaintiff can demonstrate: (i) great and immediate irreparable injury; (ii) bad faith in the prosecution of state action; or (iii) harassment or other unusual circumstances calling for federal equitable relief.

VII. FEDERAL RULES OF CIVIL PROCEDURE

A. COMMENCEMENT OF ACTION

An action is commenced by filing a complaint with the court. This filing will satisfy the statute of limitations in federal question cases and in diversity cases where the state rule is similar. If the state rule is that action is commenced, for statute of limitations purposes, only upon service of process, that rule must be applied in a diversity case.

B. SERVICE OF PROCESS

1. **How Service Is Made**

   Any person who is at least 18 years old and not a party to the action may serve process. Personal service, service left at the defendant's usual place of abode, or service upon an authorized agent of the defendant is valid service of process. Alternatively, service may be made as provided by state rules or by mail under the waiver of service provision.

2. **Parties Served Outside State**

   The court will also acquire personal jurisdiction over parties served outside the state: (i) under the state's statutes and rules for extraterritorial service; (ii) if they are third-party defendants or required to be joined for just adjudication, if served within 100 miles from the place where the action is pending; (iii) if out-of-state service is permitted by federal statute (*e.g.,* interpleader); and (iv) for cases that involve a federal question, if a defendant is served with process, provided that he is not subject to general jurisdiction in any state, that he has sufficient contacts with the United States, and that jurisdiction is not prohibited by statute.

3. **Immunity from Process**

   The federal courts recognize immunity from service of process of parties, witnesses, and attorneys who enter a state to appear in another action. In addition, if a party was induced by

the plaintiff's fraud or deceit to enter a state so that he could be served, the service is invalid to confer personal jurisdiction.

C. EXTENSION OF TIME PERIODS
Certain time periods may never be extended: renewed motion for judgment as a matter of law, motion to amend judgment, and motion for new trial, all of which must be filed within 28 days of entry of judgment.

D. INTERLOCUTORY

1. Preliminary Injunctions
A party may seek a preliminary injunction prior to trial to preserve the status quo. The adverse party must be given notice and an opportunity to be heard.

2. Temporary Restraining Orders
If irreparable injury will occur before the hearing on the preliminary injunction can be held, a party may seek a temporary restraining order ("TRO") to preserve the status quo until the hearing. Generally, the adverse party must be given notice, but a TRO may be imposed without notice of the hearing for the issuance of the TRO for a maximum 14-day period if three conditions are met:

(i) The moving party states specific facts in an affidavit or verified complaint of the irreparable injury she will suffer if the TRO is not granted;

(ii) The moving party certifies in writing the efforts she made to notify the adverse party and the reasons why notice should not be required;

(iii) The moving party provides security to pay for any damages incurred by the adverse party if the court later finds he was wrongfully restrained.

Note: Although a TRO may be issued without notice of hearing, a person must have actual notice of the TRO (or any injunction) before he may be held in contempt for violating it.

E. PLEADINGS

1. Notice Pleading
Federal courts follow notice rather than fact pleading. Hence, they generally require less specificity than state pleadings. However, the Supreme Court, in recent years, has required that the plaintiff state facts supporting a plausible, not just possible, claim.

2. Pleading a Cause of Action
A complaint must state: (i) grounds of federal jurisdiction; (ii) a short statement of the claim showing that the pleader is entitled to relief; and (iii) a demand for judgment for relief, which may be in the alternative.

3. Pre-Answer Motion

a. Rule 12(b)
The defendant may file a motion and raise any or all of the following defenses: (i) lack of subject matter jurisdiction; (ii) lack of personal jurisdiction; (iii) improper venue; (iv) insufficiency of process; (v) insufficiency of service of process; (vi) failure

to state a claim upon which relief can be granted; or (vii) failure to join an indispensable party. The defendant must raise defenses (ii) through (v) the first time he files a motion or his answer—whichever is first. If he does not, the defendant waives these defenses. Defenses (vi) and (vii) can be made at any time prior to trial or at trial. Defense (i) can be raised at any time until all appeals have been exhausted.

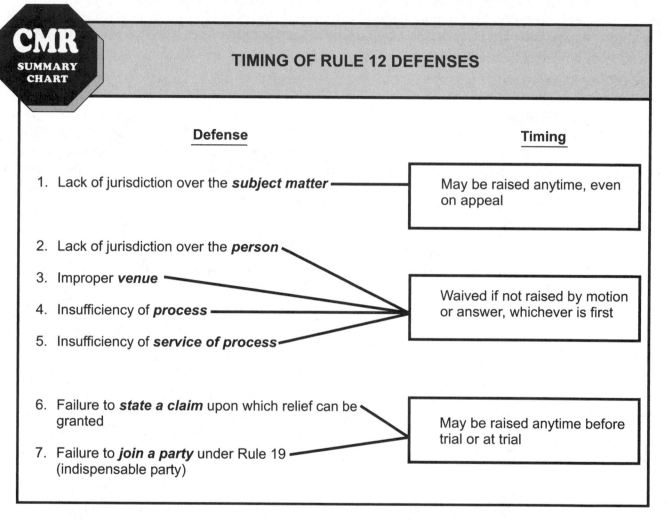

CMR SUMMARY CHART

TIMING OF RULE 12 DEFENSES

Defense | **Timing**

1. Lack of jurisdiction over the **subject matter** — May be raised anytime, even on appeal

2. Lack of jurisdiction over the **person**
3. Improper **venue**
4. Insufficiency of **process** — Waived if not raised by motion or answer, whichever is first
5. Insufficiency of **service of process**

6. Failure to **state a claim** upon which relief can be granted — May be raised anytime before trial or at trial
7. Failure to **join a party** under Rule 19 (indispensable party)

b. **Rule 12(e)**

A party may move for a more definite statement before responding to a pleading that is vague.

c. **Rule 12(f)**

Before responding to a pleading, a party may move to have stricken any insufficient defense or any redundant, immaterial, or scandalous matter.

4. **Answer**

The answer must contain a specific denial or admission of each averment of the complaint, or a general denial with specific admissions of the averments admitted may be made. If the defendant is without knowledge or information sufficient to form a belief, a statement to that effect constitutes a denial. A failure to deny constitutes an admission. The answer must

also state any affirmative defenses the defendant may have. If no Rule 12 motion is made, a defendant who was formally served must present an answer within 21 days after service; a defendant to whom a complaint was mailed and who waives formal service must answer within 60 days after the request for waiver was mailed to her. If a Rule 12 motion is made and the court does not fix another time, the responsive pleading must be served within 14 days after the court's denial or postponement of the motion. The answer is due within 14 days after service of a more definite statement if the court grants a Rule 12(e) motion. After that period expires, a defendant who fails to answer may be defaulted and have a default judgment entered against him.

5. Counterclaims

a. Compulsory
If the claim arises from the same transaction or occurrence as the plaintiff's claim, it must be pleaded as a counterclaim or it will be thereafter barred. *Note:* A federal court has ancillary (supplemental) jurisdiction over a compulsory counterclaim that otherwise does not meet the requirements for diversity of citizenship or federal question jurisdiction.

b. Permissive
Any other claim the defendant has against the plaintiff may be asserted as a permissive counterclaim if it meets the jurisdictional requirements for filing a claim in federal court.

6. Inconsistent Claims or Defenses
A party may set out as many alternative claims or defenses as he may have, regardless of consistency.

7. Reply
A reply by the plaintiff is required only when the defendant's answer contains a counterclaim denominated as such or when the court so orders. The reply must be served within 20 days after service of the answer or, if the reply is ordered by the court, within 20 days after the court order.

8. Amendments and Supplemental Pleadings
A pleading may be amended once within 21 days of its service, or, if the pleading is one to which a responsive pleading is required, 21 days after service of a responsive pleading or pre-answer motion. Thereafter, leave to amend is by consent or by leave of court, which must be freely given. An amendment to a pleading must satisfy due process requirements. Amendments relate back to the date of the original pleading if the same events are involved. An amendment naming a new adverse party relates back if, within the time for service of process, the new party had sufficient notice to avoid prejudice and knew (or should have known) that, but for a mistake, she would have been named originally. Supplemental pleadings, which relate to matters occurring after the original pleading, require permission of the court.

9. Rule 11

a. Certification upon Presenting Paper to Court
In federal civil cases, the attorney (or unrepresented party), by presenting to the court a pleading, written motion, or other paper, certifies that to the best of her knowledge,

information, and belief formed after an inquiry reasonable under the circumstances: (i) the paper is not presented for any improper purpose (harassment, delay, etc.); (ii) the legal contentions therein are warranted by existing law or a nonfrivolous argument for the modification of existing law or the establishment of a new law; (iii) the allegations and factual contentions either have, or upon further investigation or discovery, are likely to have, evidentiary support; and (iv) denials of factual contentions are warranted on the evidence or, if specified, are reasonably based on a lack of information and belief.

b. Sanctions

The court has discretion to impose sanctions against a party who presents a paper to the court in violation of the above requirements. The matter may be raised in either of two ways: (i) the court, on its own initiative, may enter an order describing the matter that appears to violate Rule 11 and direct the proponent to show cause why sanctions should not be imposed, or (ii) the opposing party may serve a motion for sanctions on the proponent, and if the proponent does not withdraw or correct the matter within 21 days, the opposing party may then file the motion for sanctions with the court. The sanctions may consist of either nonmonetary directives or monetary penalties, including payment of expenses or attorneys' fees incurred because of the improper paper.

F. JOINDER

1. Joinder of Parties

a. Compulsory Joinder

A party should be joined if: (i) complete relief cannot be given to existing parties in his absence; (ii) disposition in his absence may impair his ability to protect his interest in the controversy; *or* (iii) his absence would expose existing parties to a substantial risk of double or inconsistent obligations. If such a party is amenable to process *and* her joinder will not destroy diversity or venue, *she must be joined*.

1) When Joinder Not Feasible

When joinder is not feasible, the court must decide whether the action can proceed in the party's absence or must be dismissed. The court must consider the following: (i) whether the judgment in the party's absence would prejudice him or the existing parties; (ii) whether the prejudice can be reduced by shaping the judgment; (iii) whether a judgment in the party's absence would be adequate; and (iv) whether the plaintiff will be deprived of an adequate remedy if the action is dismissed.

b. Permissive Joinder

Parties may join as plaintiffs or be joined as defendants whenever: (i) some claim is made by each plaintiff and against each defendant relating to or arising out of the same series of occurrences or transactions; and (ii) there is a question of fact or law common to all the parties. The rule permitting broad joinder does not alter the requirements of jurisdiction: there must be complete diversity and each claim must satisfy the jurisdictional amount, except that plaintiffs with a common undivided interest in a claim exceeding $75,000 may join in asserting it even if their individual share in the interest is $75,000 or less. However, there may be supplemental jurisdiction over claims by permissively joined plaintiffs. (*See* II.B.3., *supra.*)

2. Joinder of Claims

A plaintiff can join any number and type of claims against a defendant; when multiple plaintiffs or multiple defendants are involved, it is essential only that at least one of the claims arise out of a transaction in which all were involved. A plaintiff may join two claims if success on the first is a prerequisite to the second. When jurisdiction is based on diversity of citizenship between the plaintiff and the defendant, the plaintiff may aggregate all claims that he has against the defendant to satisfy the jurisdictional amount. When jurisdiction is based on a federal question claim, a nonfederal claim can be joined only if it is regarded as part of the same case or controversy as the federal claim.

a. Class Actions

1) Requirements

Under Rule 23, a class action is proper if:

a) The class is so *numerous* that joinder of all members is *impracticable*;

b) There are *questions of law or fact common* to the class;

c) *Named parties' interests are typical* of the class;

d) Named parties will *adequately represent* the interests of the absent members of the class; and

e) *One* of the following three situations is present:

(1) Separate actions would create a *risk of inconsistent results* or *impair the interests of unnamed parties*;

(2) The defendant has acted or refused to act on grounds applicable to the class and *injunctive or declaratory relief is appropriate* for the class as a whole; or

(3) *Common questions of law or fact predominate* over individual issues and a class action is *superior to alternate methods of adjudication*.

2) Considerations in Treating the Case as a Class Action

The court should determine at an early practicable time whether to certify the class, but it can determine that a class action is *not* appropriate at any time. Considerations in determining whether to certify a class include: (i) the interest of individual control; (ii) the extent and nature of litigation elsewhere on the same subject; (iii) the desirability of a joint trial; and (iv) the difficulties in managing a class action. When certifying the class, the court must define the class and the class claims, issues, or defenses. The court must also appoint class counsel, who must fairly and adequately represent the interests of the class.

3) Effect of Judgment

All members of a class will be bound by the judgment rendered in a class action except those in a common question class action who notify the court that they do not wish to be bound. Note that if the substantive claim of the individual representing the class is mooted, this does not render the class action moot.

4) **Notice**

Notice to all members of the class is required only in common question suits so that class members can opt out. Notice to members of the class in other class suits is discretionary with the court. The notice must state: (i) the nature of the action; (ii) the definition of the class; (iii) the class claims, issues, or defenses; and (iv) the binding effect of a class judgment.

5) **Jurisdiction**

In class actions founded on diversity, only the citizenship of the named representatives of the class is taken into account to establish diversity. One class representative's claim generally must exceed $75,000, as the amount in controversy may be aggregated only in the rare situation in which the claims of the parties are "joint" or "common." However, class members with claims not exceeding $75,000 may invoke supplemental jurisdiction as long as complete diversity is not destroyed.

6) **Court Approval**

The court must approve the dismissal or settlement of a class action. The class must satisfy the requirements of certification before a court can approve a settlement. Notice of settlement also must be given. In a "common question" class action, the court *may* provide the parties with a second opportunity to opt out. A fairness hearing also must be held.

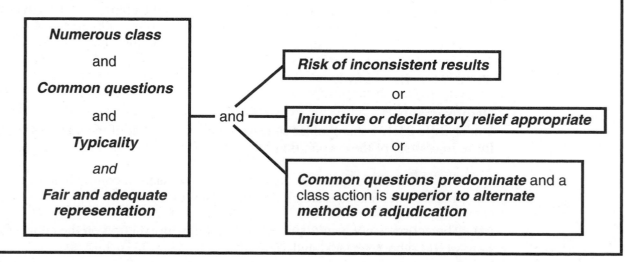

CMR SUMMARY CHART

FEDERAL CLASS ACTION REQUIREMENTS

A federal class action must meet all four requirements on the left side of the chart and one of the requirements on the right. The three alternatives on the right determine the type of federal class action. Only the third type, *i.e.,* the common question type, *requires* notice to all class members and allows opting out.

Numerous class

and

Common questions

and

Typicality

and

Fair and adequate representation

— and —

Risk of inconsistent results

or

Injunctive or declaratory relief appropriate

or

Common questions predominate and a class action is **superior to alternate methods of adjudication**

b. Class Action Fairness Act

Under the Class Action Fairness Act ("CAFA"), subject matter jurisdiction is established if: (i) *any* class member (not just the representative, but anyone in the plaintiff class) is of diverse citizenship from *any* defendant; (ii) the amount in controversy *in the aggregate* (*i.e.*, adding all the class claims together) *exceeds $5 million*; and (iii) there are at least *100 members* in the proposed class or classes. Additionally, *any* defendant, rather than *all* defendants, may remove the case from state to federal court. Moreover, the case may be removed under the CAFA even if a defendant is a citizen of the forum.

1) Excluded Actions

There is no federal court jurisdiction under the CAFA if the *primary defendants are states, state officials, or other governmental entities* against whom the court may be foreclosed from ordering relief, or over a class action that *solely* involves a claim under *federal securities laws* or that relates to the *internal affairs of a corporation and is based on the laws of the state of incorporation*.

2) Local Considerations May Defeat Jurisdiction

The CAFA has some provisions designed to defeat federal jurisdiction in class actions that are relatively local in nature.

a) Mandatory Decline of Jurisdiction

A district court *must* decline jurisdiction provided by the CAFA if: (i) *more than two-thirds* of the members of the proposed plaintiff class *are citizens of the state in which the action was filed*; (ii) *a defendant* from whom *"significant relief"* is sought is *a citizen of that state*; and (iii) the *"principal injuries"* were incurred *in the state in which the action was filed*.

b) Discretionary Decline of Jurisdiction

A district court *may* decline jurisdiction provided by the CAFA if *more than one-third but less than two-thirds* of the proposed plaintiff class are *citizens of the state in which the action was filed* and the *"primary defendants" are also citizens of that state*. In that case, the court considers whether (i) the claims involve matters of national interest; (ii) the claims will be governed by the law of the state in which it was filed; and (iii) the state has a "distinct nexus" with the class members, the alleged harm, or the defendants.

c. Shareholder Derivative Suits

1) Requirements

Under Rule 23.1, a shareholder can sue to enforce a right of the corporation that those in control of the corporation refuse to assert if she can allege and prove that:

(i) She was *a shareholder at the time* of the transaction complained of (or received her shares thereafter by operation of law);

(ii) The action is not a *collusive* effort to confer jurisdiction on the court that it would otherwise lack; and

(iii) She made a ***demand on the directors*** and, if required by state law, on the shareholders; or the reasons why she did not make such demands. For this requirement, facts must be pleaded with particularity.

Rule 23.1, like Rule 23, requires that the class representative be able to fairly and adequately represent the class.

2) Jurisdictional Amount and Venue

A judgment in a derivative action runs to the corporation, and therefore the jurisdictional amount looks to the damages allegedly suffered by the corporation. Venue is proper wherever the corporation could have sued the same defendants (*i.e.,* usually in the state of its incorporation).

CMR **Exam Tip** Remember, when faced with a shareholder derivative suit under the federal court's diversity jurisdiction, the corporation is treated as a plaintiff for purposes of determining jurisdictional amount (*i.e.,* the court will look to the corporation's damages), but generally is treated as a defendant for purposes of determining whether there is diversity among the parties.

d. Interpleader

1) Nature

An interpleader suit is instituted by a person in the position of a stakeholder to require the adverse claimants to determine which has the valid claim to the stake. It applies if separate actions might result in double liability against the stakeholder. Federal law has abolished the common law requirements that the stakeholder must admit liability to the proper claimant and that the claims have a common origin.

2) Grounds

There are two interpleader procedures in the federal courts: Rule 22 interpleader and section 1335 interpleader.

a) Rule 22 interpleader requires (i) complete diversity between the stakeholder and all adverse claimants and in excess of $75,000 in issue, or (ii) a federal question claim. Normal service and venue rules apply.

b) Section 1335 interpleader requires only minimum diversity between the claimants (one claimant must be diverse from one other) and $500 in issue. Service may be nationwide and venue is proper where any claimant resides.

CMR **Exam Tip** *Mnemonic*: **R**ule 22 interpleader must follow the **R**egular **R**ules; **S**tatutory interpleader has **S**pecial, **S**impler **S**tandards.

e. Intervention

Intervention may be granted to a party of right or permissively. Intervention of right is available whenever the applicant claims an interest in the property or transaction that is the subject matter of the action, and the disposition of the action without him may impair his ability to protect that interest. There appears to be no supplemental (ancillary) jurisdiction over claims by or against one seeking to intervene in a diversity action. Permissive intervention is available when the applicant's claim or defense and the main action have a question of fact or law in common; no direct personal or pecuniary interest is required. Permissive intervention must be supported by its own jurisdictional ground.

f. Third-Party Practice

A defending party may implead a nonparty who is or may be liable to him for any part of a judgment that the plaintiff may recover against him (*e.g.,* claims based on indemnity). If federal question or diversity jurisdiction is not available, supplemental (ancillary) jurisdiction probably would be available, because a claim for indemnity will likely arise from the common nucleus of fact as the underlying claim. Additionally, venue need not be proper for the third-party defendant. The defending party may also join any other claims she has against the third-party defendant, and these claims would also need some jurisdictional basis. The third-party defendant may assert defenses to the plaintiff's original claim as well as defenses to the third-party liability asserted against him. The court may sever any third-party claim to be tried separately if that is just.

g. Cross-Claims

Co-parties may assert claims against each other that arise out of the same transaction or occurrence as the main action by filing cross-claims. Since a cross-claim is related to the existing action, it is commonly considered to come within the court's supplemental jurisdiction.

G. DUTY OF DISCLOSURE; DISCOVERY

1. Disclosure Requirements

Rule 26 requires parties to disclose, without being asked, information to other parties about their case.

a. Types of Disclosure Required

Before making her disclosures, a party has an obligation to make a reasonable inquiry into the facts of the case. Rule 26 requires parties to disclose all information "then reasonably available" that is not privileged or protected as work product. A party is not relieved from her obligation of disclosure merely because she has failed to complete her investigation or because another party has not made his disclosures or has made inadequate disclosures. Three types of disclosure are required: *initial* disclosures, disclosure of *expert testimony*, and *pretrial* disclosures.

1) Initial Disclosures

Without waiting for a discovery request, a party must provide to other parties:

(i) The names, addresses, and telephone numbers of individuals likely to have discoverable information that the disclosing party may use to support its claims or defenses, unless solely for impeachment;

(ii) Copies or descriptions of documents, electronically stored information, and tangible things that are in the disclosing party's possession or control that the disclosing party may use to support its claims or defenses, unless solely for impeachment;

(iii) A computation of damages claimed by the disclosing party and copies of materials upon which the computation is based; and

(iv) Copies of insurance agreements under which an insurer might be liable for all or part of any judgment that might be entered.

These disclosures must be made within 14 days after the conference of the parties required by Rule 26(f), (discussed at H.1., *infra*), unless a different time is set by court order or by stipulation.

a) Exemptions from Initial Disclosure Requirement
Initial disclosures are not required in particular types of cases (*e.g.*, actions to review an administrative record, actions to enforce an arbitration award, pro se litigation brought by prisoners, actions to quash or enforce subpoenas, or habeas corpus petitions).

2) Disclosure of Expert Testimony
A party must also disclose to other parties the identities of expert witnesses expected to be used at trial. This disclosure must be accompanied by a report prepared and signed by each expert witness stating her qualifications, the opinions to be expressed, and the basis for those opinions. This disclosure must be made at the time directed by the court or, in the absence of any directions or any stipulations among the parties, at least 90 days before trial. However, if the evidence is intended solely to rebut another party's disclosure of expert testimony, it must be made within 30 days after disclosure of the evidence being rebutted.

3) Pretrial Disclosures
At least 30 days before trial, a party must disclose the witnesses she expects to call at trial, the witnesses she will call if the need arises, the witnesses whose testimony will be presented by means of a deposition and a transcript of pertinent portions of the deposition, and a list of documents or exhibits she expects to offer or might offer if needed. Within 14 days after this disclosure, a party may serve objections to use of the depositions at trial and to the admissibility of disclosed documents and exhibits. Such objections are waived if not made at this point, except for objections that the evidence is irrelevant, prejudicial, or confusing under Federal Rules of Evidence 402 and 403.

2. Scope of Disclosure and Discovery

a. In General
In general, discovery may be had of any nonprivileged matter that is relevant to any party's claim or defense. "Any matter" encompasses both documentary evidence and individuals with knowledge of any discoverable matter. Furthermore, as long as the information sought is reasonably calculated to lead to the discovery of admissible evidence or a claim or defense in the case, it is not required that the information itself be admissible at trial.

b.   Trial Preparation Materials

Work product of lawyers and others in anticipation of litigation is discoverable only upon showing "substantial need" and to avoid "undue hardship" in obtaining materials in an alternative way. If the court orders disclosure, it must take steps to avoid the disclosure of mental impressions, opinions, and conclusions. However, a party may obtain, without a showing of need and hardship or a court order, a copy of any statement previously made by that party.

c.   Experts

A party may depose testifying experts. The opinions of consulting experts may be discovered through depositions or interrogatories only if the party seeking discovery shows that it is impracticable to obtain such facts or opinions by other means.

d.   Protective Orders

Protective orders may be obtained to limit the nature and scope of examination or to terminate examination if discovery is abused.

e.   Privileged Information

When a party withholds information she believes is privileged, the party must make the claim expressly and describe the nature of the documents not disclosed in a manner that will enable other parties to assess the applicability of the privilege.

f.   Supplementation of Disclosures and Discovery Responses

A party must supplement required disclosures and prior responses to interrogatories, requests for production, or requests for admissions if she learns that the information disclosed was materially incomplete or incorrect and the new information has not been made known to the other party in discovery or in writing. The duty to supplement also applies to experts' reports and information from any deposition of an expert.

3.   Types of Discovery

The following types of discovery are available: pre-action depositions (perpetuating one's own or another's testimony); oral deposition of a witness, including a party-witness; depositions of witnesses upon written questions; interrogatories to the parties; production of physical material; physical and mental examinations when the party's physical or mental condition is in controversy; and requests for admission as to the truth or genuineness of any matter or document described in the request.

4.   Enforcing Disclosure and Discovery

a.   Motion to Compel and for Sanctions

If a party fails to provide or provides incomplete disclosures or discovery, the other party may move to compel discovery. If a party fails to comply with an order to provide discovery, the court may: (i) order the matters to be treated as admitted; (ii) prohibit the party from supporting or opposing designated claims or defenses; (iii) strike pleadings, stay or dismiss the action, or render default judgment; or (iv) hold the delinquent party or witness in contempt.

b. **Immediate Sanction**

If a party fails to attend his own deposition or fails to provide *any* answers to interrogatories, a party may move for immediate sanctions. The court may make such orders in regard to the failure as are "just," including (i), (ii), and (iii) above.

c. **Automatic Sanction**

The Rules also provide for automatic sanctions against a party who "without substantial justification" fails to disclose information as required under Rule 26, or who fails to supplement or amend discovery responses under Rule 26(e)(1) or (2). The party who fails to make required disclosures will not be permitted to use the information withheld as evidence at trial, at a hearing, or on a motion, unless such failure was "harmless." Other appropriate sanctions may be imposed including (i), (ii), and (iii) above, as well as informing the jury of the failure to make the disclosure. The court also may assess reasonable expenses incurred, including attorneys' fees.

5. **Use of Depositions at Trial or Hearing**

Subject to the rules of evidence, a deposition may be used: (i) to impeach the testimony of the deponent as a witness; (ii) for any purpose if the court finds that the deponent is dead or at a distance greater than 100 miles from the place of trial, or that the deponent is unable to testify because of age, sickness, etc.; or (iii) for any purpose if the deponent is an adverse party.

H. PRETRIAL CONFERENCES

1. **Rule 26(f) Conference of Parties—Planning for Discovery**

The parties must confer to consider their claims and defenses, the possibility of settlement, initial disclosures, and a discovery plan. The parties must submit to the court a proposed discovery plan addressing the timing and form of required disclosures, the subjects on which discovery may be needed, the timing of and limitations on discovery, and relevant orders that may be required of the court.

2. **Rule 16(b) Scheduling Conference**

The court must hold a scheduling conference among the parties or counsel. The conference may be held by telephone, mail, or other suitable means. The court must enter a scheduling order limiting the time for joinder, motions, and discovery. The order may also include dates for pretrial conferences, a trial date, and any other appropriate matters. This schedule cannot be modified except by leave of court upon a showing of good cause.

3. **Pretrial Conferences**

Additional conferences may be held to expedite trial and foster settlement. A final pretrial conference may be held to formulate a plan for the trial, including a program for the admission of evidence. An order entered pursuant to a final pretrial conference may be modified only for good cause.

4. **Sanctions**

The court may use a broad range of sanctions against parties or counsel who fail to attend conferences, participate in good faith, or obey orders entered pursuant to a conference.

I. ALTERNATIVE DISPUTE RESOLUTION

Alternative dispute resolution ("ADR") is a process in which a neutral person resolves a dispute or helps the parties to resolve their dispute.

1. Contractual Arbitration

A written agreement to arbitrate a dispute is valid and enforceable unless a contractual ground for revocation exists (*e.g.,* illegality). Court proceedings are stayed until the arbitration proceedings are completed. The appointment of the arbitrator usually will be provided for in the arbitration agreement. The arbitrator can subpoena witnesses and require them to bring documentary evidence to the hearing. After the arbitrator renders the award, a party can move to have the court confirm the award, and the opposing party may move to vacate the arbitration award on the grounds of fraud, evident partiality of the arbitrator, a manifest disregard of the law, etc. If the award is confirmed, it is considered to be final and binding, and it is enforceable as a court judgment.

2. Judicial Arbitration

"Judicial arbitration" is a dispute-resolution process conducted by a neutral person under the auspices of the court in an attempt to resolve the action without trial. Judicial arbitration is voluntary.

3. Mediation

Mediation involves the use of a neutral person to help parties to a dispute reach a mutually acceptable agreement. The mediator does not have decisionmaking power; his role is to facilitate the process by which the parties reach their own voluntary agreement. Unless an express statutory exception exists, parties and mediators are prohibited from disclosing any written or oral communications made during mediation. Mediation is accomplished by local district rule.

J. TRIAL

1. Jury Trial Problems

a. Right to Jury Trial

A party who desires a jury trial must file a written demand with the court and serve it on the parties. A jury demand may be withdrawn only with the consent of all parties. Failure to make a demand within 14 days after the filing of the pleading in which the jury-triable issue arose constitutes a waiver by that party of any right to trial by jury. Note the following:

1) If legal and equitable claims are joined in one action involving common fact issues, the *legal claim should be tried first to the jury*, and then the equitable claim to the court.

2) If a procedure formerly available only in equity, such as a class suit or interpleader, is now permitted under the Federal Rules for determining a "legal" claim, a *jury should try the fact issues*.

3) If damages are claimed as part of an action seeking an injunction, the defendant cannot be denied a *jury on the damages* issues on grounds that they are "incidental" to the equitable relief.

b.   **Jury Trials in Diversity Cases**

The federal court must permit a jury trial in any diversity "suit at common law" even though the state court would deny a jury. In addition, a federal court will generally follow the federal practice of submitting issues of fact to the jury even though the state law assigns the issue to the court. State law is disregarded in determining the sufficiency of the evidence to create a jury issue.

c.   **Jury Instructions**

Objections to giving or failing to give instructions must be made before the jury retires to consider the verdict.

d.   **Jury Verdicts**

The court may instruct the jury to decide by general verdict (by which the jury finds for the plaintiff or defendant), by special verdict (by which the jury makes findings of fact and the court applies the law), or by general verdict with special interrogatories (a combination of the first two).

2.   **Consolidation and Separate Trials**

The court may consolidate actions then before it when the actions have a common question of law or fact, or order separate trials of any claim, cross-claim, counterclaim, or other issues when separation will foster judicial economy.

3.   **Voluntary Dismissal by Plaintiff**

A plaintiff may dismiss his action without prejudice as a matter of right only before the defendant files an answer or a summary judgment motion, or by stipulation of all parties. Otherwise, a dismissal without prejudice can be taken only with leave of the court. If there is a counterclaim pending in the action, there can be no dismissal over the defendant's objection unless the counterclaim remains pending.

4.   **Judgment as a Matter of Law (Formerly Directed Verdict)**

A motion for judgment as a matter of law, formerly known as a motion for a directed verdict, allows judgment to be granted for either party if the evidence is such that reasonable persons could not disagree. The evidence must be viewed in the light most favorable to the nonmoving party. A motion for judgment as a matter of law is a prerequisite for the making of a renewed motion for judgment as a matter of law.

5.   **Renewed Motion for Judgment as a Matter of Law (Formerly Judgment Notwithstanding the Verdict)**

A renewed motion for judgment as a matter of law, formerly known as a motion for judgment notwithstanding the verdict ("JNOV"), may be filed no later than 28 days after entry of judgment. A party generally is limited to those issues raised in the judgment as a matter of law.

6.   **Motion for New Trial**

A motion for a new trial must be filed no later than 28 days after judgment. The court may grant a new trial because of an error during the trial, or because the verdict is against the weight of the evidence. If the verdict is excessive, the court may order a new trial or offer the plaintiff remittitur, which allows the plaintiff to choose between a lesser award or a new trial.

PROCEDURAL DEVICES THAT MAY TERMINATE CASE

Method	Circumstances	Timing
Pre-Answer Motion [Rule 12(b)]	Addresses the following preliminary matters: defects in subject matter jurisdiction, personal jurisdiction, venue, process, and service of process; failure to state claim; failure to join needed party.	(*See* summary chart *supra* for timing of Rule 12 defenses.)
Voluntary Dismissal by Plaintiff [Rule 41(a)]	Without prejudice once as a matter of right; also possible by stipulation or court order.	If dismissed as a matter of right without prejudice, must be done before defendant files answer or motion for summary judgment.
Involuntary Dismissal [Rule 41(b)]	Plaintiff fails to prosecute the case or to comply with the Rules or a court order.	Anytime.
Motion for Judgment on the Pleadings [Rule 12(c)]	On the face of the pleadings (without considering matters outside the pleadings), the moving party is entitled to judgment. Treated as motion for summary judgment if accompanied by outside matters.	After pleadings are closed but not so late as to delay trial.
Summary Judgment [Rule 56]	No genuine issue of material fact and moving party is entitled to judgment as a matter of law. May support by pleadings, affidavits, discovery materials.	Anytime, but the judge may delay ruling on the motion.
Judgment on Partial Findings [Rule 52]	In a nonjury trial, the judge may enter a judgment as a matter of law if she makes dispositive partial findings on the claim.	During trial, once the judge has heard sufficient evidence to make dispositive findings and all parties have been fully heard on the issue.
Motion for Judgment as a Matter of Law (Directed Verdict) [Rule 50(a)]	Evidence viewed in light most favorable to motion's opponent leads reasonable person to conclusion in favor of moving party.	After opponent has presented case but before submission of case to jury.
Renewed Motion for Judgment as a Matter of Law ("JNOV") [Rule 50(b)]	The verdict returned could not have been reached by reasonable persons. Moving party must have previously sought judgment as a matter of law sometime during the trial.	Within 28 days after entry of judgment.

a. **With Renewed Motion for Judgment as a Matter of Law**
When a renewed motion for judgment as a matter of law and a motion for a new trial are made in the alternative and the renewed motion is granted, the court must rule hypothetically on the new trial motion so that no remand is required if the judgment on the merits ruling is subsequently reversed on appeal.

7. **Effect of Failure to Move for a Renewed Judgment as a Matter of Law or for a New Trial**
If a party fails to move for either a renewed judgment as a matter of law or for a new trial, that party is precluded from raising the question of evidentiary sufficiency on appeal.

8. **Judgment on Partial Findings**
In a nonjury trial, once there is sufficient evidence to make dispositive findings, the judge may rule on an issue as a matter of law, provided all parties have been fully heard. Alternatively, the judge may wait until all evidence is presented before ruling. The ruling must be supported by findings of fact and conclusions of law.

9. **Summary Judgment**
Summary judgment may be granted if, from the pleadings, affidavits, and discovery materials on file, it appears that no genuine issue of material fact exists and that the moving party is entitled to judgment as a matter of law. A motion for summary judgment may be made at any time, but the judge has discretion to delay ruling on the motion to allow the party opposing the motion to prepare a meaningful response (*e.g.,* to allow an opposing party to conduct discovery). Summary judgment may be partial. Denial of the motion for summary judgment is not appealable. Note that a motion to dismiss a complaint or for judgment on the pleadings (as opposed to a summary judgment motion) addresses only the legal sufficiency of the complaint.

VIII.   ATTACK ON THE JUDGMENT AT THE TRIAL COURT LEVEL

A.   RELIEF FROM JUDGMENT OR ORDER

1. **Clerical Mistakes**
A clerical error may be corrected at any time on motion of the court or any party.

2. **Other Grounds for Relief from Judgment**
On motion and just terms, the court may relieve a party from a final judgment or order on the grounds of (i) mistake, inadvertence, surprise, or excusable neglect; (ii) newly discovered evidence that by due diligence could not have been discovered in time to move for a new trial; (iii) fraud, misrepresentation, or other misconduct of an adverse party; (iv) the judgment being void; (v) the judgment being satisfied, released, or discharged; a prior judgment on which it is based having been reversed or otherwise vacated; or the fact that it is no longer equitable that the judgment should have prospective application; or (vi) any other reason justifying relief from the operation of the judgment. For grounds (i), (ii), and (iii), the motion must be made within one year; for the other grounds, the motion must be made within a reasonable time.

B.   INDEPENDENT ACTION IN EQUITY TO SET ASIDE THE JUDGMENT
A court, in its discretion, may entertain an independent action to relieve a party from a judgment

or order, to grant relief to a defendant not actually personally notified of the action, or to set aside a judgment for fraud on the court. The plaintiff must show that he is likely to win if a new action is allowed. The only advantage of an independent action is that it will not be barred by the specific time limits outlined in A., above. However, the aggrieved party must act promptly once he knows or should know of the ground for relief. An independent action will be rejected if a motion to set aside the judgment has been rejected on the merits.

IX. FINAL JUDGMENT AND APPELLATE REVIEW

A. JUDGMENT

1. Relief that May Be Given
Except in default cases, the court is not limited to the demand for relief in the pleadings and may give any relief that is appropriate based on the evidence.

2. Multiple Claims or Parties
When multiple claims or multiple parties are involved in an action, the court may enter a final judgment as to fewer than all of the claims or parties only upon (i) an express determination that there is no just reason for delay; and (ii) an express direction for the entry of judgment. Unless the trial judge makes such an express determination, the order determining the merits of fewer than all of the claims or dismissing fewer than all of the parties is not a final judgment and is not appealable.

3. Final Decision on Merits May Be Valid Despite Lack of Subject Matter Jurisdiction
Occasionally, lack of subject matter jurisdiction is not raised until the decision is final and all appeals are completed. The question then is whether the decision may be collaterally attacked—*i.e.,* be set aside in an independent proceeding or treated as invalid in a later case. The factors that must be balanced in making this determination are: (i) lack of jurisdiction is clear; (ii) jurisdiction depends on a question of law, not fact; (iii) the court is of limited, not general, jurisdiction; (iv) the question of jurisdiction was not litigated; and (v) strong policy exists against the court acting beyond its jurisdiction.

B. TIME FOR APPEALS
An appeal may be taken by filing a notice of appeal with the district court within 30 days from the entry of the judgment appealed from. However, if a timely renewed motion for judgment as a matter of law, for new trial, or to set aside or amend the judgment is made, the running of the 30 days is terminated. Upon the entry of an order based on such post-trial motions, a new 30-day period begins to run. However, notice of appeal filed during the pendency of a post-trial motion will become effective on final disposition of the motion by the trial court.

C. REVIEWABLE ORDER
Generally, only final orders are reviewable. However, certain interlocutory orders are also reviewable.

1. Interlocutory Orders as of Right
Interlocutory orders reviewable as of right include: injunctions; appointments of receivers; and certain admiralty, patent infringement, and property possession cases.

2. **Interlocutory Appeals Act**

    Under the Interlocutory Appeals Act, review is discretionary when: (i) the trial judge certifies that the interlocutory order involves a controlling question of law, as to which there is substantial ground for difference of opinion, and immediate appeal from the order may materially advance the ultimate termination of the litigation; and (ii) the court of appeals then agrees to allow the appeal. Interlocutory orders with respect to less than all claims or parties may be reviewable.

3. **Collateral Order Rule**

    If the claim or issue is separable from and collateral to the main suit, and is a claim too important to require deferring appellate review, it may be classified as a judgment in a separate proceeding and thus be appealable.

4. **Certification of Class Actions**

    An order granting or denying the certification of a class action may be reviewed at the court's discretion within 14 days after entry of the order.

5. **Orders Made Appealable (or Nonappealable) by Writ**

    In exceptional cases, the final order rule may be circumvented through the appellate writs of mandamus (compelling a judge to act) and prohibition (prohibiting a judge from acting).

D. STAY PENDING APPEAL

No execution on judgments is allowed for 14 days after entry except injunctions or receiverships. Judgments are enforceable during pendency of post-trial motions unless a court otherwise orders in its discretion and on such conditions for the security of the adverse party as are proper. A supersedeas bond is required in sufficient size to satisfy the judgment, costs, interest, and damages for delay, should the appeal be dismissed or affirmed.

E. SUPREME COURT JURISDICTION

The Supreme Court has direct appeal jurisdiction from any order granting or denying an injunction in any proceeding required to be heard by a three-judge court. The Supreme Court may review any case in the court of appeals by certiorari. The Supreme Court may review cases from the highest state court having jurisdiction over the case by certiorari when the validity of federal law is called into question or the validity of state law is called into question on the ground that it violates the Constitution or federal law.

X. EFFECTS OF JUDGMENT ON FUTURE CASES

A. RES JUDICATA (CLAIM PRECLUSION)

Under the doctrine of res judicata, once a final judgment on the merits has been rendered on a particular cause of action, the plaintiff is barred from trying the same cause of action in a later lawsuit. While various tests have been used to define "cause of action," the modern approach is to require assertion of all claims arising out of the same transaction or occurrence that is the subject matter of a claim asserted by the plaintiff.

B. COLLATERAL ESTOPPEL (ISSUE PRECLUSION)

Under the doctrine of collateral estoppel, judgment for the plaintiff or defendant is conclusive in a subsequent action on a different cause of action between them, as to issues actually litigated and essential to the judgment in the first action.

C. WHICH PERSONS ARE BOUND BY A JUDGMENT?

Parties, privies to parties, and persons whose interests are represented are bound by a judgment. Nonparties are normally not bound. In jurisdictions where the mutuality principle has been eroded, four tests are usually applied to determine whether a stranger may rely on a prior judgment: (i) Was the issue decided in the first case identical to that in the second? (ii) Was there a final judgment on the merits? (iii) Did the party against whom the judgment is to be used have a fair opportunity to be heard on the critical issue? and (iv) Is the posture of the case such that it would not be unfair or inequitable to a party to apply collateral estoppel? If *all* these questions are answered affirmatively, collateral estoppel will normally be upheld.

PARTNERSHIP

TABLE OF CONTENTS

PARTNERSHIP

I. NATURE OF A PARTNERSHIP

A. IN GENERAL

A partnership is an association of two or more persons to carry on as co-owners a business for profit. Partnership law is based on the law of contract and agency.

CMR **Exam Tip** Remember that there must be at least *two persons* involved in forming a partnership. A partnership may not exist with only one partner. But also remember that a "person" may be an individual, trust, corporation, partnership, or other entity. Thus, Partnership A and Corporation B can agree to form Partnership C.

B. PARTNERSHIP IS A LEGAL ENTITY

Except with respect to partners' personal liability for partnership obligations, a partnership is a legal entity distinct from its partners. Title to land may be in the partnership name. A partnership may sue or be sued in the partnership name.

C. GOVERNING LAW

Generally, the Revised Uniform Partnership Act ("R.U.P.A.") provides a default set of rules. Partners are free to agree—through a *partnership agreement*—to abide by different rules for governing the relationships among themselves, and the R.U.P.A. will govern only those issues not provided for in the partnership agreement. Note, however, that certain R.U.P.A. provisions cannot be waived (*e.g.*, the duty of loyalty, the right of a court to expel a partner).

II. FORMATION OF A PARTNERSHIP

A. HOW A PARTNERSHIP IS FORMED

A partnership is formed as soon as two or more people associate to carry on as co-owners a business for profit.

1. **Agreement**

No formal agreement is required to form a partnership; the parties' intent may be implied from their conduct.

2. **Writing Generally Not Required**

No writing is required to form a partnership. However, because of the Statute of Frauds, if partners wish to have an enforceable agreement to remain partners for more than one year, they generally must execute a writing reflecting their agreement.

3. **Capacity**

Anyone who is capable of entering into a binding contract may be a partner. A would-be partner who lacks capacity is liable only to the extent of his capital contribution, but the partnership with such person is not void; it will continue to exist until steps are taken to dissolve it.

4. Legality of Purpose

A partnership formed to achieve an illegal purpose is void, and the courts will not compel an accounting or a settlement of a void partnership's affairs.

5. Consent

Unless otherwise agreed, no one can become a partner without the express or implied consent of all partners.

6. Statement of Partnership Authority

A partnership may choose to file a statement of partnership authority with the secretary of state, which can give constructive knowledge of the extent of the partners' authority with regard to the partnership.

B. PROOF OF PARTNERSHIP EXISTENCE

Since no formalities are required to form a partnership, it is sometimes difficult to determine whether the relationship between parties is a partnership or something else. To determine whether a partnership exists, courts generally look to the ***intent of the parties***. If they intended to carry on a business as co-owners, there is a partnership even if they did not subjectively intend to be partners. Where the parties' intent is uncertain, the courts consider the following rules:

1. Sharing of Profits Raises Presumption of Partnership

Sharing of profits raises a presumption of partnership unless the share was received as payment of a debt, for services rendered, as rent payment, as an annuity or other retirement benefit, as interest on a loan, or for the sale of goodwill of a business.

2. Evidence Indicative of Partnership

The following factors may be additional evidence that a partnership has been formed. However, in contrast to the sharing of profits, these factors ***do not*** raise a presumption of partnership:

a. Title to property is ***held in joint tenancy or in common***;

b. The ***parties designate their relationship as a partnership***;

c. The venture undertaken by the parties requires ***extensive activity*** (*e.g.*, if A and B each contribute $100,000 to buy a building of rental apartments that must be managed, it is more likely that they are partners than if they each contributed $100,000 to buy shares in a company that manages real estate); and

d. ***Sharing of gross returns***.

CMR | **Exam Tip** | Sometimes exam questions will merely describe the relationship among parties involved in a business and will ask about the rights of the parties among themselves or about the liabilities of the parties for obligations of the business. In such questions, you must determine whether there is a partnership; do this by considering and discussing the factors above. Remember that the ***sharing of profits*** generally raises a ***presumption of partnership***, but the presumption can be rebutted by other factors indicating that a partnership was not intended.

C. PURPORTED PARTNERS

1. Liability of Person Held Out as Partner

When a person by words or conduct represents himself as a partner or consents to being represented by another as a partner, he will be liable to third parties who extend credit to the actual or apparent partnership in reliance on the representation.

a. No Duty to Deny Partnership
Note that a person held out by another as a partner is not liable as a partner unless he actually consents to the holding out—mere failure to deny a representation of partnership does not give rise to liability as a purported partner.

2. Liability of Person Who Holds Another Out as Partner
When a person holds another out as a partner, he thereby makes that person his agent to bind him to third parties. (If there is a partnership, only those partners who know of or consent to this holding out will be bound.)

III. PARTNERSHIP PROPERTY

A. CLASSIFICATIONS

1. Partnership Capital
Partnership capital is the property or money contributed by each partner for the purpose of carrying on the partnership's business.

2. Partnership Property
Partnership property, in its broadest sense, is everything the partnership owns, including both capital and property subsequently acquired in partnership transactions.

B. WHAT IS INCLUDABLE IN PARTNERSHIP PROPERTY
There is no restriction on what may be partnership property, and sometimes it is not always obvious whether property is partnership property or the individual property of a partner. The R.U.P.A. has a number of provisions concerning ownership of *titled property* (both titled personal property and real property). For property that is not titled, the common law has developed a number of criteria to analyze.

1. Titled Property—R.U.P.A. Provisions

a. Property Deemed to Be Partnership Property
Under the R.U.P.A., titled property is deemed to be partnership property if:

1) It is *titled in the partnership name*; or

2) It is titled in the name of one or more partners and the *instrument transferring title notes the titleholder's capacity as a partner or the existence of a partnership*.

b. Property Presumed to Be Partnership Property
Under the R.U.P.A., property is rebuttably presumed to be partnership property if it was *purchased with partnership funds*, regardless of in whose name title is held. "Partnership funds" includes not only the partnership's cash, but also the partnership's credit.

c. Property Presumed to Be Partner's Separate Property
Under the R.U.P.A., if (i) property is held in the name of one or more partners, (ii) the instrument transferring title *does not indicate the person's capacity as a partner or mention the existence of a partnership,* and (iii) *partnership funds were not used* to acquire the property, the property is rebuttably presumed to be separate property, even if the property is used for partnership purposes.

HOW TO DETERMINE WHETHER PROPERTY IS PARTNERSHIP PROPERTY UNDER THE R.U.P.A.

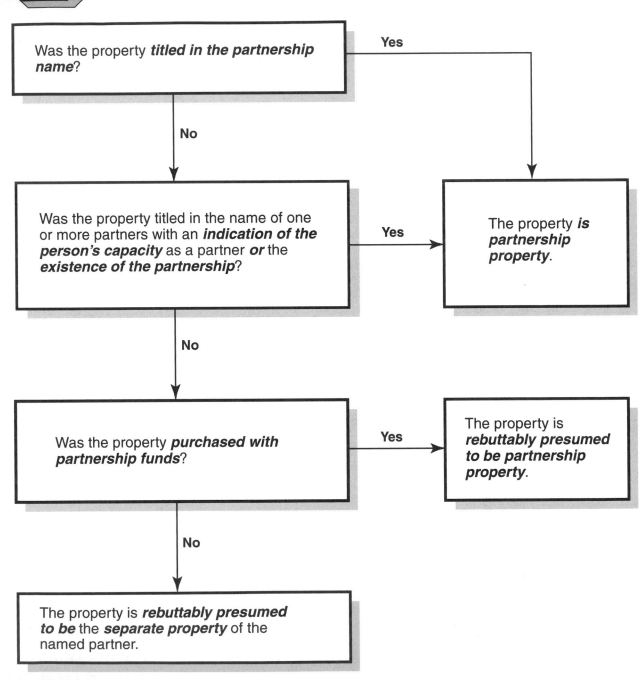

Was the property *titled in the partnership name*?

Yes →

No ↓

Was the property titled in the name of one or more partners with an *indication of the person's capacity* as a partner *or* the *existence of the partnership*?

Yes →

The property *is partnership property*.

No ↓

Was the property *purchased with partnership funds*?

Yes →

The property is *rebuttably presumed to be partnership property*.

No ↓

The property is *rebuttably presumed to be* the *separate property* of the named partner.

2. **Untitled Property—Common Law Criteria**

In cases not governed by the explicit R.U.P.A. provisions (*e.g.*, in cases of property that is not titled), in determining whether property is partnership property or the separate property of a partner, courts will probably continue to look to the following common law criteria which tend to indicate that the property was intended to be partnership property:

a. Acquisition of the property with *partnership funds*;

b. *Use of the property by the partnership* in conducting the partnership's business;

c. Entry of the *property in the partnership books* as a partnership asset;

d. A close *relationship between the property and the business* operations of the partnership;

e. *Improvement of the property with partnership funds*; and

f. *Maintenance of the property with partnership funds*.

C. RIGHTS OF PARTNER IN PARTNERSHIP PROPERTY

A partner is *not a co-owner* of partnership property, and thus has no transferable interest in specific property of the partnership.

CMR | **Exam Tip** | It is important to remember that a partner has no right to use partnership property other than for the benefit of the partnership.

IV. PARTNER'S INTEREST IN THE PARTNERSHIP

A. IN GENERAL

Each partner has a transferable interest in the partnership, which consists of his share of partnership profits, losses, and distributions.

B. INTEREST IS PERSONAL PROPERTY, ASSIGNABLE, AND ATTACHABLE

This interest is:

(i) Treated as *personal property*;

(ii) *Assignable* without dissolving the partnership; and

(iii) *Attachable*.

Note that absent an agreement to the contrary, a partner shares equally in the partnership profits and must contribute to the losses in proportion to his share of the profits. Note also that an assignment of a partner's interest in the partnership gives the assignee no rights with regard to the operation of the partnership. It merely entitles the assignee to receive profits to which the assigning partner would otherwise be entitled. A partner may not sell his partner status (*i.e.*, may not make another a partner) without the unanimous consent of the other partners.

V. RELATIONS BETWEEN PARTNERS

A. RIGHT TO PARTICIPATE IN MANAGEMENT

All partners have **equal rights** in the management of partnership business absent an agreement to the contrary. Decisions involving ordinary business can be controlled by a majority vote of the partners, but matters outside the ordinary course of business require the unanimous consent of the partners.

B. FIDUCIARY DUTIES

Each partner owes two fiduciary duties to the partnership. The duty of **loyalty** requires that the partner (i) account for all profits or other benefits derived by the partner in connection with partnership business; (ii) not deal with the partnership as one with an adverse interest; and (iii) not compete with the partnership. The duty of **care** requires the partner to refrain from engaging in negligent, reckless, or unlawful conduct or intentional misconduct.

C. PARTNERS' ACCOUNTS

Each partner is deemed to have an account that is credited with an amount equal to the partner's contribution plus his share of any profits and debited with the partner's share of any losses and partnership liabilities.

D. REMUNERATION

Absent an agreement to the contrary, a partner has no right to remuneration for services rendered to the partnership except for reasonable compensation for services performed in winding up the partnership business. When a partner has impliedly or expressly promised to devote time to the partnership business and fails to do so, she may be charged in an accounting for damages caused to the partnership.

E. INDEMNIFICATION AND OTHER REPAYMENT

A partnership must indemnify every partner with regard to payments made and obligations reasonably incurred in carrying on the partnership business. If a partner makes a payment or advance on behalf of the partnership beyond the contribution the partner agreed to make, the payment or advance constitutes a loan which must be repaid with interest.

F. RIGHTS UPON DISSOLUTION

Upon dissolution, a partner is entitled to a settlement of her account.

G. BOOKS AND INFORMATION

Books and information must be kept at the partnership's chief executive office. Each partner has a right to inspect and copy the partnership books. Upon demand, each partner must render true and full information of all things affecting the partnership.

H. LEGAL ACTIONS BY AND AGAINST PARTNERS

A partnership may sue or be sued **in its own name**; however, to reach a partner's personal assets, there must be a judgment against the individual partner. A **partnership may sue a partner** for breach of the partnership agreement or of a duty owed to the partnership. A **partner may sue the partnership** or other partners to enforce a right created by partnership act or agreement, or a right otherwise belonging to the partner.

RIGHTS OF PARTNERS

Management— All partners have an *equal right* to participate in the management of the partnership unless the partnership agreement provides otherwise.

Distributions— Partners have whatever rights are granted in the partnership agreement as to distribution of profits. If the agreement is silent, partners share profits (and losses) *equally*.

Remuneration— Partners have *no right* to remuneration for their services to the partnership except for winding up the partnership business.

Indemnification— A partner has a right to be indemnified by fellow partners for expenses incurred on behalf of the partnership.

Contribution— A partner has a right to contribution from fellow partners where the partner has paid more than his share of a partnership liability.

Inspection— A partner has a right to inspect and copy the partnership books.

Lawsuits— Generally, a partner may sue his partnership and the partnership may sue a partner in an action at law or in equity.

VI. RELATIONS OF PARTNERS TO THIRD PARTIES

A. IN GENERAL—APPLICATION OF AGENCY LAW
The R.U.P.A. generally provides that each partner is an agent of the partnership for the purpose of its business. The authority of a partner to bind the partnership when dealing with third parties roughly follows agency law.

B. APPARENT AUTHORITY
The R.U.P.A. provides that:

(i)   The act of *any partner*;

(ii) For apparently carrying on *in the ordinary course* the partnership business *or business of the kind* carried out by the partnership;

(iii) Binds the partnership *unless*:

i.   The partner had *no authority* to act for the partnership in the particular matter; *and*

ii. The person with whom the partner was dealing *knew or had received notification* that the partner lacked authority.

 Exam Tip   It is very important to remember that as agents of the partnership, partners have *apparent authority* to bind the partnership to *any contract within the scope of the partnership business*. If a contract is outside the scope of partnership business, the partnership generally will not be bound unless the partner has *actual authority*.

1. **Business of the Kind**

Note that apparent authority is not limited merely to transactions that are in fact within the ordinary course of business for the partnership in question, but extends also to transactions that would apparently be for carrying on business of the kind run by the partnership.

2. **Limitation—Knowledge or Notification**

A partnership will not be bound by a partner's act if the partner lacked actual authority and the person with whom the partner dealt either *knew* or *received notification of* such fact.

a. **Knowledge**

Under the R.U.P.A., knowledge means *subjective knowledge*—what the person actually knew. What the person should have known based on the circumstances is irrelevant.

b. **Notification**

Under the R.U.P.A., a notification is effective either when it comes to the person's attention or when it is duly delivered. Thus, if a notification limiting a partner's authority is duly delivered to a third party (*e.g.*, at the third party's place of business), the third party cannot rely on apparent authority with regard to the limitation even if the third party has not actually read the notification.

3. **Transfers of Partnership Property**

a. **Partnership Interest Indicated**

Any partner may transfer property held in the name of the partnership. If partnership property is held in the name of one or more partners (who are identified as such) but the partnership is not named, transfer by the titleholders in their own names is effective. In either case, if the transferring partner lacked authority, the partnership may recover the property from the initial transferee but not from a subsequent bona fide purchaser.

b. **Partnership Interest Not Indicated**

If the partnership's interest is not indicated in the instrument transferring the property, the transfer may be made by those in whose names the property is held. If the transferee gives value without notice of lack of authority, she takes free of the partnership interest.

C.   ACTUAL AUTHORITY

A partnership also will be bound by an act of a partner if the partner has actual authority. Actual authority is the authority a partner reasonably believes he has based on the communications between the partnership and the partner. Such actual authority can come from the partnership agreement or a vote of the partners. A majority vote of the partners is required to authorize ordinary business; a unanimous vote of the partners is required to authorize extraordinary acts.

D.   EXPANDING AND LIMITING AUTHORITY—STATEMENT OF AUTHORITY

A statement of authority grants or limits a partner's authority to enter into transactions on behalf of the partnership. The statement must be filed with the secretary of state and, for real property transfers, with the county recorder. Note that a ***grant*** of authority in a properly filed statement of authority is ***conclusive*** in favor of a bona fide purchaser for value. A properly filed ***limitation of authority to transfer real property*** gives purchasers constructive knowledge of a lack of authority, but filing a limitation does not give constructive knowledge of the limitation with regard to any other transaction.

E.   NOTICE

Under the R.U.P.A., a partner has notice of a fact when the partner: (i) has actual knowledge of the fact, (ii) is notified of the fact, or (iii) has reason to know of the fact based on the surrounding circumstances.

1.   When Notification Effective

Notification is effective not only if and when it comes to a partner's attention, but also when it is delivered to a place of business held out by the partner as a place for receiving communications.

2.   Notice Imputed to Partnership

A partner's notice of a fact relating to the partnership is imputed to the partnership ***immediately*** unless the partner having notice is participating in a fraud against the partnership.

F.   LIABILITY OF PARTNERS

1.   Civil Liability

a.   Types of Liability

Partners are liable for ***all contracts*** entered into by a partner in the scope of partnership business or with authority of the partnership. Similarly, partners also are liable for ***all torts*** committed by any partner or employee of the partnership within the ordinary course of partnership business or with authority of the partnership.

b.   Nature of Liability

Liability is joint and several (***one or more*** partners may be sued) for ***all*** obligations of the partnership, whether arising in tort or contract. A judgment is not personally binding on a partner unless she has been served and the creditor has exhausted partnership assets, or exhaustion is excused by agreement or court order or because the partnership is bankrupt.

c.   Extent of Liability

Each partner is personally and ***individually liable for the entire amount of partnership obligations***. A partner who pays more than his fair share of an obligation is entitled to contribution from the other partners, and a partner who pays the whole obligation of the partnership is entitled to indemnification.

d. Liability of Incoming Partner

An incoming partner is not personally liable for obligations incurred by the partnership before the person became a partner.

e. Liability of Outgoing (Dissociated) Partner

An outgoing or dissociated partner remains liable for obligations arising while he was a partner unless there has been payment, release, or novation. An outgoing partner can also be liable for acts done after dissociation. (*See* VII.A.2.b., *infra.*)

CMR Exam Tip Examiners often test the difference in liability between an incoming partner and an outgoing partner. Remember, an outgoing partner generally remains liable for all partnership obligations incurred while he was a partner, whereas an incoming partner generally has no liability for obligations incurred before she became a partner.

2. Criminal Liability

Partners will not be criminally liable for the crimes of other partners committed within the scope of the partnership business, unless the other partners participated in the commission of the crime either as principals or accessories.

VII. DISSOCIATION AND DISSOLUTION OF A PARTNERSHIP

A. DISSOCIATION

Dissociation is a change in the relationship of the partners caused by any partner ceasing to be associated in the carrying on of the business. Dissociation of a partner does not necessarily cause a dissolution and winding up of the partnership business.

1. Events of Dissociation

A partner becomes dissociated from the partnership by: (i) notice of the partner's *express will* to withdraw; (ii) *happening of an agreed event*; (iii) *expulsion* of the partner pursuant to agreement, by unanimous vote if unlawful to continue business with the partner, or by judicial decree; (iv) the partner's *bankruptcy*; (v) the partner's *death or incapacity* to perform partnership duties; (vi) appointment of a *receiver*; or (vii) *termination of a business entity* that is a partner.

2. Consequences of Dissociation

Upon a partner's dissociation, his right to participate in management ceases. The partnership must purchase (buy out) his interest at either liquidation or going-concern value, and must indemnify him against known predissociation liabilities, as well as against postdissociation liabilities not incurred by the dissociating partner's acts. A partner who dissociates in violation of the partnership agreement or before the expiration of a partnership term or completion of a particular partnership undertaking is liable to the partnership for damages caused by the wrongful dissociation. Moreover, a partner who wrongfully dissociates before the expiration of a partnership term or completion of a particular undertaking is not entitled to payment of the buyout price until the term expires or the undertaking is completed, unless he can establish that earlier payment will not cause undue hardship to the partnership business. Interest must be paid on the buyout price from the date of dissociation to the date of payment.

    a.   **Dissociated Partner's Power to Bind Partnership**

A partnership can be bound by an act of a dissociated partner undertaken within *two years* after dissociation if: (i) the *act would have bound the partnership* before dissociation, and (ii) the other party to the transaction (a) *reasonably believed* the dissociated partner was still a partner and (b) *did not have notice* of the dissociation.

    b.   **Dissociated Partner's Liability to Other Parties**

A dissociated partner can be liable for obligations incurred by the partnership within *two years* after the partner dissociates if (i) when entering the transaction the other party *reasonably believed* the dissociated partner was still a partner and (ii) *did not have notice of the partner's dissociation.* Note that a dissociated partner can cut short this period of liability by filing a *notice of dissociation* with the secretary of state; all persons are deemed to have notice of a dissociation 90 days after such a notice is filed.

B. DISSOLUTION

Unlike dissociation, dissolution generally requires the partnership business to be wound up.

1. Events Causing Dissolution

The following events trigger dissolution under the R.U.P.A.:

a.   In a partnership at will, *notification by any partner of an intent to withdraw*;

b.   In a partnership for a definite term or particular undertaking: (i) *expiration of the term* or completion of the undertaking, (ii) *consent of all of the partners* to dissolve, or (iii) within 90 days after a partner's death, bankruptcy, or wrongful dissociation, *at least half of the remaining partners wish to dissolve*;

c.   The *happening of an event agreed to in the partnership agreement* that requires winding up the partnership business;

d.   The *happening of an event that makes it unlawful* for the partnership to continue;

e.   *Issuance of a judicial decree* on application by a *partner* that (i) the economic purpose of the partnership is likely to be *frustrated*, (ii) a partner has engaged in conduct making it *not reasonably practicable* to carry on the business, or (iii) the *business cannot practicably be carried on* in conformity with the partnership agreement; and

f.   *Issuance of a judicial decree* on application by a *transferee* of a partner's interest that it is equitable to wind up the partnership (i) after the term expires or the undertaking is completed in a partnership for a definite term or particular undertaking, or (ii) at any time in a partnership at will.

2. Partner's Power to Bind Partnership After Dissolution

A partnership can be bound after dissolution by any act of a partner appropriate for winding up the partnership's business. The partnership will also be liable for other acts if the party with whom a partner dealt did not have notice of the dissolution. Such liability can be limited by filing a statement of dissolution with the secretary of state; all persons are deemed to have notice of a dissolution 90 days after such a notice is filed.

3. Partnership Continues After Dissolution

The partnership continues to exist after dissolution until the partnership is wound up.

4. Who May Wind Up

As a general rule, **all living partners** have a right to participate in the winding up of the partnership's business except partners who have wrongfully dissolved the partnership and bankrupt partners. If all partners have died, the executor or administrator of the last surviving partner may wind up.

5. Partners May Waive Dissolution and Continue the Business

Any time before the winding up of the partnership business is complete, the partners may decide to waive the dissolution and continue the partnership by unanimous vote of the partners who have not wrongfully dissolved. Such waiver does not affect the rights of persons who have relied on the dissolution before receiving notice of the waiver.

C. DISTRIBUTION OF ASSETS

1. Order of Distribution

Partnership assets are reduced to cash and partnership liabilities are paid in the following order:

a. *Creditors, including partners who are creditors;* and

b. *Partners' accounts.*

2. Partner Who Pays More than His Share Entitled to Contribution

Where a partner is forced to pay more than his share of the partnership's debts, he is entitled to contribution from the other partners to equalize the shares.

VIII. LIMITED LIABILITY PARTNERSHIPS

A. INTRODUCTION

The R.U.P.A. allows the creation of limited liability partnerships ("L.L.P.s"). The major advantage of operating as an L.L.P. is that partners are *not personally liable* for the L.L.P.'s obligations.

B. FORMATION

1. Voting

The terms and conditions on which a partnership becomes an L.L.P. must be approved by whatever vote is necessary *to amend the partnership agreement* or, if specified, the vote necessary to amend the contribution obligations of the partners. If the partnership agreement is silent as to how it may be amended, *all* partners must approve the terms and conditions of the partnership becoming an L.L.P.

2. Filing

To become an L.L.P., a partnership must file a statement of qualification with the secretary of state. The statement must be executed by at least two partners and contain such information as: (i) the name and address of the partnership; (ii) a statement that the partnership elects to become an L.L.P.; and (iii) a deferred effective date, if any. The partnership becomes an L.L.P. at the time of filing the statement or on the date specified in the statement.

C. NAME

The partnership name must **end** with the words "Registered Limited Liability Partnership" or "Limited Liability Partnership" or the abbreviation "R.L.L.P.," "RLLP," "L.L.P.," or "LLP."

D. LIABILITY

A partner in an L.L.P. **is not personally liable** (directly, indirectly, or by way of contribution) for the obligations of the partnership, whether arising in contract, tort, or otherwise. However, a partner remains personally liable for her **own wrongful acts**.

CMR **Exam Tip** If on an exam you have to determine the liability of a partner in an L.L.P. for a tort committed by a co-partner, recall that a partner's liability is usually limited; *i.e.*, she will **not** be personally liable for the co-partner's tort. But be sure to check to see if the partner **engaged in the tort;** if she did, she will not be shielded from liability.

IX. LIMITED PARTNERSHIPS

A. INTRODUCTION

A limited partnership is comprised of one or more general partners and one or more limited partners. The general partner(s) is personally liable for partnership obligations, while the limited partner(s) generally does not have any liability beyond the liability to make agreed-upon contributions. A limited partnership differs from a general partnership in that a limited partnership can be created only by filing a certificate of formation with the state. Like a modern partnership, a limited partnership is an entity distinct from its partners and has a perpetual duration unless otherwise provided.

B. FORMATION

1. Certificate of Limited Partnership

A certificate of limited partnership signed by all general partners and setting forth the name of the partnership, the names and addresses of the agent for service of process and of each **general** partner, and whether the limited partnership is a limited liability limited partnership.

2. Records Office

A limited partnership must maintain in its state of organization an office with records of the certificate, any partnership agreements, the partnership's tax returns for the three most current years, etc. The partnership agreement or some other record must contain the amount and description of each partner's contribution, special rights of partners regarding distributions, etc.

3. Agent for Service of Process

A limited partnership must maintain in the state an agent for the service of process.

CMR **Exam Tip** It is important to remember that a limited partnership is a creature of statute and thus can exist only on compliance with the limited partnership statute. Watch out for exam questions that set up facts where one partner wants limited liability and the other partner tells him that he can be a limited partner, but there is no filing with the secretary of state. Because there is no statutory compliance, a limited partnership is not created and all partners are subject to full liability.

C. NAME OF PARTNERSHIP

The partnership name may contain the name of *any* partner (general or limited) and must contain the words "limited partnership," or the abbreviation "L.P." unless the limited partnership is a limited liability limited partnership, in which case that must be reflected in the name (*e.g.*, "L.L.L.P.")

D. ADMISSION OF ADDITIONAL GENERAL AND LIMITED PARTNERS

A person may be admitted to the limited partnership as a general or limited partner as provided in the partnership agreement, as a result of a merger or conversion, or on the *consent of all partners*.

E. PARTNERS' CONTRIBUTIONS

A partner has no rights to distributions unless the partner makes a contribution to the partnership. A contribution may be in the form of *any benefit* to the partnership (*e.g.*, money, property, services, and promises to make such contributions). A partner's contribution obligation is not excused by death or other disability and may be compromised only on the *consent of all partners*. *Note:* If a partner fails to make an agreed-upon nonmonetary contribution (*e.g.*, the partner fails to provide promised property or services), the limited partnership has the option of seeking cash in lieu of the agreed-upon contribution.

F. LIABILITY OF PARTNERS

1. Liability of General Partner

Except as provided by statute or in the partnership agreement, a general partner of a limited partnership is jointly and severally liable for all obligations of the limited partnership. *Note:* A general partner may also be a limited partner and have the rights of a limited partner, but such a dual capacity does not relieve the general partner of his duties as a general partner.

a. Incoming Partners

A person who becomes a general partner of an existing limited partnership is *not* personally liable for an obligation that the limited partnership incurred before he became a limited partner.

b. Limited Liability Limited Partnership

Any liability incurred while a limited partnership is a limited liability limited partnership belongs to the partnership alone; the general partner(s) is not personally liable on the obligation.

2. Liability of Limited Partner

A limited partner is *not* personally liable for an obligation of the limited partnership solely by reason of being a limited partner. Note that earlier limited partnership acts made limited partners personally liable if their names were used in the partnership name or they participated in the management or control of the partnership. The U.L.P.A. no longer includes such provisions.

G. DUTIES OF PARTNERS

1. General Partner

A general partner owes the limited partnership limited fiduciary duties of care and loyalty, similar to those owed by a partner in a general partnership. A general partner does *not* automatically violate the duty of loyalty merely because the general partner's conduct furthers his own interests.

CMR
APPROACH
CHART

LIABILITY OF A LIMITED PARTNER TO THIRD PARTIES

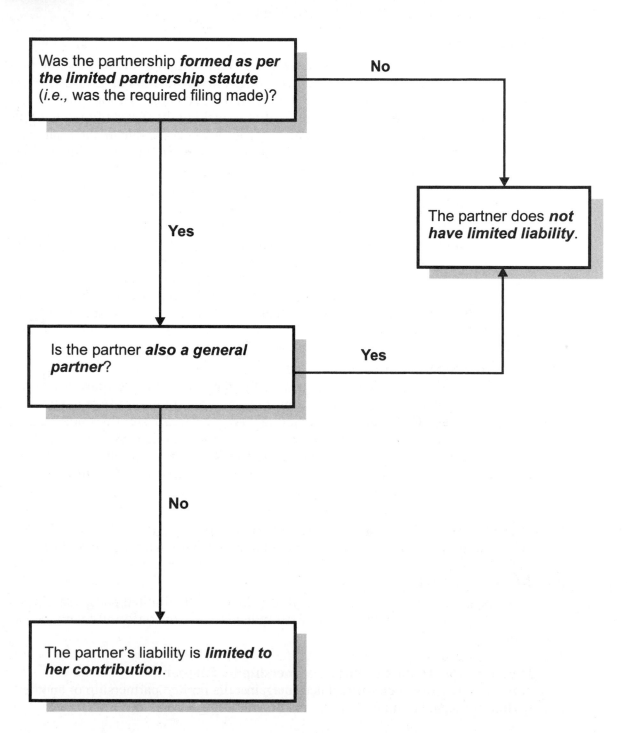

Was the partnership *formed as per the limited partnership statute* (*i.e.,* was the required filing made)?

No → The partner does *not have limited liability*.

Yes ↓

Is the partner *also a general partner*?

Yes → The partner does *not have limited liability*.

No ↓

The partner's liability is *limited to her contribution*.

2. Limited Partner

Generally, a limited partner owes no fiduciary duty to the partnership and, thus, is free to compete with the partnership and have interests adverse to those of the partnership, unless the partnership agreement provides otherwise.

H. RIGHTS OF PARTNERS

1. Rights of Both General and Limited Partners

a. Right to Distributions

The U.L.P.A.'s provisions for distributions are very similar to the distribution provisions for corporations. Distributions must be made on the basis of the partners' contributions (*i.e.,* in proportion to the value of each partner's contribution), and a limited partnership may not make a distribution if after making the distribution the limited partnership would be unable to pay its debts as they become due *or* the limited partnership's total assets would be less than the sum of its total liabilities, including sums needed to satisfy superior preferential rights upon dissolution.

1) Liability for Improper Distributions

A general partner who consents to an improper distribution is personally liable to the limited partnership for the amount that the distribution exceeds what could properly have been distributed. Any partner who receives an improper distribution *knowing* that it is improper may be forced to return the improper amount to the partnership. However, no personal liability for an improper distribution arises if the distribution appeared to have been proper based on reasonably prepared financial statements.

b. Right to Assign Partnership Interest

A partner's right to distributions is personal property that may be transferred, in whole or in part. Such a transfer gives the transferee only the right to receive the transferred distributions and to demand an accounting thereon. The transfer does not make the transferee a partner or give the transferee any rights as a partner. Moreover, the transfering partner remains a partner, and the transfer does not constitute a dissociation or cause a dissolution. However, transfer of a partner's *entire transferable interest* in the partnership is a ground for expulsion.

c. Right to Transact Business with the Partnership

A partner may lend money to and transact other business with the limited partnership.

d. Right to Dissolve

Any partner may apply for a decree of dissolution of the limited partnership whenever it is not reasonably practicable to carry on the business in conformity with the partnership agreement.

e. Direct Action Against Limited Partnership by Partner

A partner may maintain a direct action against the limited partnership or another partner for legal or equitable relief to enforce her rights and interests.

f. Derivative Action

A partner may maintain a derivative action to enforce a right of a limited partnership if: the partner first makes a demand on the general partners to bring an action to enforce the right and the general partners do not bring the action within a reasonable time; or a demand would be futile.

2. Rights Specific to General Partners

a. Management Rights

Each general partner has equal rights in the management and conduct of the limited partnership's activities. Generally, any matter relating to the activities of the limited partnership may be exclusively decided by the general partner or, if there is more than one general partner, by a majority of the general partners. However, the approval of ***all general partners and all limited partners*** is required to: (i) amend the partnership agreement; (ii) convert the partnership to a limited liability limited partnership; (iii) dispose of all or substantially all of the limited partnership's property outside the usual and regular course of the partnership's activities; (iv) admit a new partner; or (v) compromise a partner's obligation to make a contribution or to return an improper distribution.

b. Right to Information

A general partner's right to information is similar to that of a partner in a general partnership.

c. Indemnification

A general partner is not entitled to remuneration for services performed for the partnership. However, the limited partnership must indemnify a general partner for liabilities that she incurs in the ordinary course of the activities of the partnership.

3. Rights Specific to Limited Partners

a. Management Rights

Limited partners may participate in the management and control of the limited partnership. Participation does not cause a limited partner to become personally liable for an obligation of the limited partnership.

b. Right to Information

Each limited partner has the right to inspect and copy any partnership records required to be maintained (*see* B.2., *supra*).

I. DISSOCIATION

The events that will cause dissociation of a partner in a general partnership (*see* VII.A.1., *supra*) will also cause dissociation of a partner (general or limited) in a limited partnership. Note that a limited partner has ***no right*** to dissociate before termination of the limited partnership. A general partner's right to dissociate is similar to the right of a partner to dissociate in a general partnership.

1. Effect on Limited Partner

After dissociation, a limited partner is treated as a transferee of the limited partner's transferable interest.

2. Effect on General Partner

Thc cffects of dissociation of a general partner in a limited partnership are similar to the effects of dissocation of a partner in a general partnership, discussed at VII.A.2., *supra*.

J. DISSOLUTION AND DISTRIBUTION

1. Dissolution in General

A limited partnership may be judicially dissolved upon application of a partner if it is no longer reasonably practicable to carry on the limited partnership in conformity with the limited partnership agreement. A limited partnership may also be administratively dissolved by the secretary of state for failure to pay fees or file an annual report, but the partnership may apply for reinstatement by curing the defect within two years of the dissolution. Otherwise, a limited partnership may be dissolved only upon the occurrence of one of the following:

a. The happening of an *event specified in the partnership agreement*;

b. The *consent* of *all general partners* and *limited partners* holding a *majority* of the right to receive distributions ("majority in interest");

c. After *dissociation of a general partner*, upon consent of partners owning a majority in interest if another general partner remains; if no general partner remains, after 90 days unless the partners admit a new general partner; and

d. *Ninety days after dissociation of the last limited partner*, unless a new limited partner is admitted within the 90 days.

2. Winding Up

A limited partnership continues after dissolution only for the purpose of winding up its activities. In winding up, the partnership *must* discharge liabilities, settle and close partnership activities, and marshal and distribute its assets.

3. Power to Bind Partnership After Dissolution

After dissolution, a partnership will be bound by any acts of a general partner that are *appropriate for winding up* the partnership. The partnership can also be bound by acts of a general partner that are *not* appropriate for winding up if the acts would have bound the partnership before dissolution and the party with whom the general partner dealt did not have notice of the dissolution.

4. Distribution of Assets upon Winding Up

Upon winding up a limited partnership, the assets are distributed in the following order:

(i) First, to *creditors* (including partners who made loans to the limited partnership); and

(ii) Second, any surplus must be paid in cash as a *distribution*.

a. Distribution Where Assets Are Insufficient to Satisfy Debts

If limited partnership assets are insufficient to satisfy all obligations to creditors, each person who was a general partner when the obligation was incurred must contribute to the partnership to satisfy the obligation. The contribution due is in proportion to the right to receive distributions in effect when the obligation was incurred. If a person does not contribute the full amount required, the other persons required to contribute must pay the additional amount necessary to discharge the obligation, in proportion to the right to receive distributions in effect when the obligation was incurred. A person who pays an additional contribution may recover from any person whose failure to contribute necessitated the additional contribution, but may not recover more than the amount additionally contributed.

K. CONVERSION AND MERGER

A limited partnership may convert to or merge with another form of business entity upon the *consent of all partners* and *filing of a certificate* (of conversion or merger) with the secretary of state.

CMR SUMMARY CHART

MAJOR DIFFERENCES BETWEEN A REGULAR PARTNERSHIP AND A LIMITED PARTNERSHIP

Requirements	Regular Partnership	Limited Partnership
Writing required?	No	Yes (certificate of limited partnership)
Records office required?	No	Yes
Special name required?	No	Yes (must include words "limited partnership")
Liability limited?	No	Yes (for limited partners)
Partners have management rights?	Yes	No (for limited partners, but they may if otherwise provided by agreement)
Partners share profits and losses?	Yes (equally)	Yes (according to value of contributions)

PERSONAL PROPERTY

TABLE OF CONTENTS

PERSONAL PROPERTY

I. REAL AND PERSONAL PROPERTY DISTINCTIONS

A. GENERAL DISTINCTIONS

Real property is ***immovable*** property and consists of land, things fixed to land, or things incident or appurtenant to land. Personal property is ***movable,*** which includes anything that is not real property. Real property may be converted into personal property by severance, and personal property may be converted to real property by an annexation intended to be permanent.

B. LEASEHOLDS

Leases of land for a term of years are classified as personal property (chattels).

C. CROPS

1. Fructus Naturales vs. Fructus Industriales

Crops that grow spontaneously on land are ***real property*** (fructus naturales), while crops that are the result of human labor are generally regarded as ***personalty*** (fructus industriales).

2. Conveyance

A conveyance of land includes annual crops.

3. Mortgage

A prior mortgage, whether it be of the land or crops, will prevail over any subsequent mortgage of the land or crops.

4. Doctrine of Emblements

Under the doctrine of emblements, a former tenant can reenter and remove crops planted by him prior to the termination of his estate where: (i) the tenancy was for an uncertain duration, and (ii) the tenancy terminated without the tenant's fault.

D. FIXTURES

Under the concept of fixtures, a chattel annexed to real property is converted from personalty into realty.

CMR | **Exam Tip** | The fact question as to whether something is a fixture is one of ***intent***, either expressly stated or otherwise implied from the facts, as to whether the annexor intended to make the item a permanent part of the premises.

II. ACQUISITION AND LOSS OF RIGHT OR TITLE TO PERSONAL PROPERTY

A. PRINCIPAL MODES

Rights and title to personal property are acquired or lost by occupancy, adverse possession, accession, confusion, judgment, or gift; or when the chattel is lost, mislaid, or abandoned. In general, the owner of personal property cannot be divested of title without his consent. The intent of the parties is controlling in determining when title passes.

B. OWNERSHIP

A thing capable of ownership, but not then owned, belongs to the person who acquires actual or constructive **dominion and control** over it and has the **intent** to assert ownership over it.

1. Wild Animals

a. Possession

Wild animals in their natural state are unowned but become private property upon being reduced to possession. **Dominion** and **control** over the animal is considered possession. Animals caught in a trap or net belong to the one who owns and has set the trap or net (constructive possession). Mere pursuit does not constitute dominion and control, but a vested property right in the animal accrues when it has been mortally wounded.

b. Trespass

Although a landowner is **not** the owner of wild animals on his land, a trespasser who kills game on another's land forfeits his title in favor of the landowner.

c. Escaped Animals

If an owned wild animal escapes, the former owner loses his property right in it, unless the animal is marked and the owner is endeavoring to recapture the animal or if the animal periodically returns to its owner.

2. Literary Property

For one to be entitled to copyright protection, the work must be: (i) in **concrete form**; (ii) **new**; and (iii) **fixed** in a tangible medium of expression for a period of more than transitory duration. Protection is limited to the author's **lifetime plus 70 years**, or if the author was anonymous or working for hire, 95 years from publication or 120 years from creation, whichever expires first. There is no protection for a similar or identical work product **independently** created. Ideas receive no copyright protection but may give rise to a property right if original, concrete, useful, and disclosed where compensation is contemplated. A claim of copyright ownership must be properly registered in order to enforce the author's rights. Until a work is preregistered or registered, an author cannot bring an action for copyright infringement, but once a work is properly registered, an infringement action may be brought even for infringement occurring before registration.

3. Tortious Conversion

Tortious conversion of personal property does not deprive the true owner of title. One who does not have title to goods cannot pass title, even to a bona fide purchaser, except:

a. With regard to transfers of **money and negotiable instruments**;

b. Where a bona fide purchaser has received goods through a wrongdoer to whom the **owner intended to transfer title**; or

c. Where a bona fide purchaser has relied in good faith upon the **true owner's representations** that the possessor is the owner or has authority to sell.

C. LOST, MISLAID, AND ABANDONED PROPERTY

1. Concept

When property is lost or mislaid, there is no divestiture of title, but there is loss of title when property is abandoned.

a. **Lost Property**

To determine whether property is "lost," the key factor is the place *where it is found*. The test is whether a reasonable person would judge that the owner had *accidentally and involuntarily* parted with possession of the property and does not know where to find it.

b. **Mislaid Property**

Property is "mislaid" when, judging from the place found, it can reasonably be determined that the property was *intentionally placed* there and thereafter forgotten.

c. **Abandoned Property**

Property is "abandoned" when the owner has voluntarily relinquished all ownership with the *intent to give up both title and possession*. Title to abandoned property is acquired by actual or constructive dominion and control over the thing with an intent to assert ownership over it. When abandoned property is held by an intermediary with no property interest in the property, the state may assume title to the property through a process called *escheat*.

2. **Finder of Lost Property**

One who reduces lost property to his possession becomes its finder and is entitled to the possession of the lost property against all the world *except the true owner*.

a. **The Trespasser**

A trespasser will not be allowed to secure possessory rights in lost property; thus, the right of possession falls to the owner of the locus in quo (place where the property is found).

b. **Highly Private Locus**

Where a chattel is found in a highly private locus, the owner of the locus in quo and not the finder will acquire possessory rights. (This is also applicable to buried articles.) If the place of discovery is open to the public, then the finder becomes entitled to the right of possession. The mere fact that the place of discovery is privately owned is not sufficient to render it a highly private locus.

c. **Employer-Employee**

If an employee finds an article by virtue of an act specifically directed by the employer, the employer should acquire the rights of possession in the article.

3. **Finder of Mislaid Property**

The finder of mislaid property does *not* acquire the right to possession. The owner of the locus in quo becomes entitled to possess it against all the world except the true owner.

4. **Rights and Duties of Possessor**

One who has acquired the right of possession as against the whole world except the true owner is a *quasi-bailee* with a *duty to find the true owner* if known or reasonably discoverable and a duty of due care. These obligations persist until an abandonment arises or the statute of limitations has run, at which point the possessor is the new owner.

5. **Treasure Trove**

Treasure trove is any gold, silver, or paper representative thereof found concealed, the owner of which is unknown. At common law, treasure trove belonged to the finder, even if

he was a trespasser, against all the world. However, the modern view treats treasure trove as any lost property.

6. **Uniform Unclaimed Property Act**
    Most states have adopted a version of the Uniform Unclaimed Property Act (the "Act"), which provides for the disposition of intangible property and property in safe deposit boxes. Under the Act, such property is *presumed abandoned* if the owner does not claim it or otherwise demonstrate an interest in it for the statutory period (generally five years).

CMR
SUMMARY
CHART

LOST, MISLAID, AND ABANDONED PROPERTY

	Circumstances	Example	Finder's Rights
Lost	Owner accidentally and involuntarily parted with possession and does not know where to find property	O does not notice that his watch has slipped off his wrist and landed on the street	Finder entitled to possession against all the world except the true owner (*exceptions:* if finder is a trespasser or if property is found in a highly private locus or buried, owner of locus gets possessory rights; certain employer-employee situations)
Mislaid	Owner intentionally placed property in the spot where it is found and thereafter forgot it	O lays his watch on the sink in a hotel room and forgets to pick it up	Owner of locus entitled to possession against all the world except the true owner (because the owner might return to the locus looking for the item)
Abandoned	Owner voluntarily relinquished ownership with intent to give up both title and possession	O throws his old watch into a garbage can because a new battery for it would cost too much	Finder obtains both possession and title if she exercises control over the property with intent to assert ownership

D. **ACCESSION**
    Accession is the addition of value to property by the expenditure of labor or the addition of new materials. If the addition cannot be detached from the principal chattel, the issue is who owns the enhanced chattel.

CMR Exam Tip If a bar exam question asks about title to property that has undergone a great increase in value through accession after being taken from its original owner, the conclusion is likely to depend primarily on whether the trespass on the property was *willful* or *innocent*.

1. **Accession by Innocent Trespasser**

   Generally, the original owner retains title, and the trespasser cannot sue for compensation for the value of his labor or materials added to the chattel. The owner may seek damages for conversion or replevin. However, where the species of property has been completely changed or has been enhanced in value to a great extent by an innocent trespasser, the original owner may not recoup the chattel but may only sue for damages.

2. **Accession by Willful Trespasser**

   A willful trespasser cannot gain any rights of ownership by accession. The original owner is entitled to the property in its improved state, regardless of the degree of augmentation in value made by the trespasser. The original owner may elect to sue the trespasser for damages for conversion or for replevin.

E. CONFUSION

Confusion is an *intermixture* of nonidentifiable goods owned by different persons such that the property of each can no longer be distinguished.

1. **Known Contributions**

   Where there are known contributions and the goods are of the same kind and quality, the parties are *tenants in common in proportion* to their respective interests, regardless of how the confusion took place.

2. **Unknown Contributions**

   Where the contributions are unknown and the confusion is *innocent*, the owners are *tenants in common of the mass* and share equally. Where the confusion is *wrongful*, the burden is on the wrongdoer to identify his goods or the entire mass belongs to the innocent party. Most cases say negligent confusion is wrongful.

F. ADVERSE POSSESSION—STATUTE OF LIMITATIONS

Title to personal property by adverse possession results from the running of a statute of limitations, after which the presumption that one in possession has the right to possession cannot be overcome by the former owner.

1. **Requirements**

   The possession relied upon must be actual, open and notorious, hostile and adverse, under a claim of right, and exclusive and continuous.

   CMR Exam Tip In considering the adverse possession requirement that possession must have been continuous, be sure to make the following distinction: Several brief *interrupted* periods of possession cannot be added together to meet the time requirement, even if all possession was by the same person. *Tacking*, by contrast, is permitted. Tacking involves continuous possession by a sequence of persons in privity with each other.

2. **Statute of Limitations**

   Title passes when the statutory limitation period has run.

a. Tacking

Tacking is permissible where there is privity.

b. Tolling the Statute

The statute is tolled where the plaintiff suffers from a disability (*e.g.,* plaintiff is a minor, mentally incompetent, or imprisoned), and where the defendant is out of the jurisdiction or has fraudulently concealed himself to avoid service.

G. TITLE BY JUDGMENT

1. Election of Remedies

The remedies of one who is wrongfully deprived of possessory rights in chattel include:

a. Replevin

Replevin is an action to recover ***the chattel itself***.

b. Trespass

An action in trespass is to recover ***money damages*** incurred by reason of the dispossession.

c. Trover

An action in trover is to recover the ***value of the chattel plus damages*** for dispossession.

2. Conversion

An owner may allege conversion and sue the wrongdoer in trover. This is a forced sale based on the value of the chattel as of the date of conversion, and title becomes vested in the converter by operation of law. Title relates back to the date of conversion. Anyone in actual possession or with right to possession may maintain an action for trover. The tortfeasor or subsequent transferee, even if a bona fide purchaser, is liable for conversion.

H. GIFT

A gift is a present voluntary transfer of property without any consideration or compensation.

CMR **Exam Tip** Do not confuse a gift and a promise to make a gift. A gratuitous promise to make a gift in the future is not binding under contract law because it lacks consideration, but a gift, once made, is binding and cannot be withdrawn by the donor.

1. Gifts Inter Vivos

Gifts inter vivos require donative intent, delivery, and acceptance.

a. Donative Intent

A donor must have present mental capacity and an intent to make an effective gift of property. While an intent to have title pass at some future date is ineffective as a gift, a donor may reserve the right of possession until some future date, provided there is an intent to immediately vest title in the donee.

b. Delivery

1) Actual Physical Delivery

There is actual physical delivery where the donee has acquired dominion and control over the subject matter of the gift.

2) Constructive Delivery

Where it would be impossible or impracticable to deliver an item, substitute delivery is proper where the donor surrenders as much control over the subject matter of the gift as he presently possesses.

3) Delivery by Written Instrument

Delivery by written instrument is effectual if the writing manifests donative intent, describes the subject matter, is signed by the donor, and is delivered.

4) Symbolic Delivery

When manual delivery is impossible or impracticable, the donor may hand over some object that is symbolic of the actual item.

5) Donee Already in Possession

If the donee is already in possession of the article, the donor need not repossess and then return the article to the donee.

6) Gift Through Agent

If the donee has an agent, the gift is effective when the donor delivers to the agent. If the donor has an agent, the gift is effective when the agent delivers to the donee.

CMR **Exam Tip** The time of effectiveness of a gift through an agent can best be remembered by considering who controls the agent. A donor who has sent a gift via her own agent can theoretically recall the agent at the last minute; but a donor who delivers a gift to the donee's agent has no power to instruct the agent to return the gift.

7) Special Problems in Delivery

a) Checks and Promissory Notes

The mere manual delivery of a check executed by the donor (as maker) does not fulfill the delivery requirement until and unless the check is cashed. If, however, the check of another is physically delivered, the delivery requirement is satisfied. The same rules apply to delivery of a promissory note.

b) Stock Certificates and Life Insurance Policies

Physical delivery of shares of stock (*i.e.,* stock certificates) with the requisite donative intent is sufficient to satisfy the delivery requirement even though the stocks are not endorsed and even though the donor continues to receive the dividends thereon up to the time of his death. The same rule applies to a life insurance policy.

c) Bank Savings Deposits

Delivering a bank book to the donee with the intent to make a gift is a sufficient symbolic delivery.

d) Joint Checking Account

In some jurisdictions, when one party puts in all or most of the money in a joint checking account, there is a rebuttable presumption that this is done for the convenience of that party and not as a gift, particularly where the person whose money is involved is unable to get to the bank easily. In other jurisdictions, the survivor becomes the owner absent fraud, undue influence, mental incapacity, or mistake.

DELIVERY OF GIFT

	Circumstances	Example
Actual Physical Delivery	Donor physically vests donee with possession of the item such that donee has dominion and control over it	X hands a pearl necklace to Y
Constructive Delivery	Item's size or location makes physical delivery impractical, but donor surrenders as much control as he possesses	X, intending to give Y a two-ton safe and its contents, gives Y a slip of paper with the combination written on it
Delivery by Written Instrument	Donor executes and delivers to donee a written document evidencing a gift; document must show donative intent, describe the item, and be signed by donor	X executes a document stating that he is giving to Y a certain painting currently on loan to an art museum
Symbolic Delivery	Donor delivers to donee some object (usually a written instrument) that is symbolic of the actual gift that he is conveying	X gives Y a document conveying 500 shares of stock in X's company
Donee Already in Possession	Intended donee is already in possession of an item donor now wishes to give her (*e.g.,* she has it on loan); donee need not return item for redelivery but donor must make donative intent objectively clear	X, who has lent a painting to an art museum, writes to the curator stating that the museum may keep the painting as a gift
Gift Through Agent	Donor instructs his agent to deliver a gift to donee	X tells jewelry store (X's agent) to deliver a pearl necklace to Y
	Donor delivers gift to agent of donee	X personally delivers a pearl necklace for Y to Y's butler

c. **Acceptance of Donee**

When the gift is beneficial to the donee, acceptance is presumed. However, the donee may refuse to accept a gift by an affirmative act.

d. **Gifts in Contemplation of Marriage**

Most jurisdictions hold that engagement gifts are made in contemplation of marriage and are conditioned on the subsequent ceremonial marriage taking place. If the marriage does not occur, engagement gifts must be returned. While an engagement ring by definition is given in contemplation of marriage, this may not be the case with other gifts given during the engagement period. Courts consider factors such as the type of property given, fraud, conditions attached to the gift, and the intent of the donor to determine whether the gift will be deemed to be given in contemplation of marriage (and thus recoverable by the donor if the marriage does not occur).

2. **Gifts Causa Mortis**

A gift causa mortis is one given in contemplation of death.

CMR **Exam Tip** A bar exam question might require you to distinguish between a gift inter vivos, a gift causa mortis, and an improper testamentary transfer without the formalities of a will. If what otherwise appears to be a gift causa mortis lacks the element of delivery, it may be an invalid attempted testamentary transfer (*e.g.,* O on her deathbed tells daughter, "If I die, I want you to have this diamond bracelet," but does not deliver the bracelet to daughter). Also, note that it is possible to be near death and still make an ordinary inter vivos gift (*e.g.,* "I'm dying, so I'm going to give you your birthday present early"). In other words, the circumstances must be analyzed carefully.

a. **Requirements**

1) **Present Mental Capacity, Delivery, and Acceptance**

As with gifts inter vivos, present mental capacity, intent to make the gift, delivery, and acceptance are required. However, there are a number of states holding that the donor may not accomplish a gift causa mortis by symbolic delivery.

2) **Gift Must Be Personal Property**

Real property cannot be conveyed as a gift causa mortis.

3) **Anticipation of Death**

The donor must be suffering from an actual illness that threatens his life. A mere abstract fear of death from some future cause is not sufficient. Some courts still require the donor to die as anticipated, although the recent trend is to liberally construe "as anticipated." Note that generally the gift is valid as long as the donor fails to recover, even though the precise cause of death is different. If the donor recovers, the gift is revoked by operation of law. Finally, because only personal property can be conveyed as a gift causa mortis, there is no revocation by recovery where the gift is realty.

4) **Absence of Revocation**

In addition to failure of donor to recover, there must be no other revocation (*i.e.,* by donor's affirmative act or by donee's failure to survive donor).

b. **Creditors' Claim**

A gift causa mortis is always subject to the claims of creditors of the donor's estate.

I. UNIFORM TRANSFERS TO MINORS ACT

1. Subject Matter of Gift and Title

The Uniform Transfers to Minors Act ("UTMA") covers an irrevocable gift of any type of property that conveys to the minor indefeasibly vested legal title, subject only to the rights, powers, duties, and authority of the custodian. Each gift may be to only one minor.

2. Possession of Gift

Neither failure of the donor to put the gift in possession and control, nor designation of an ineligible person as custodian, nor renunciation by the custodian affects the consummation of the gift.

3. Creation of Custodial Property

Custodial property is created when, as appropriate, a security is registered in the name of the custodian, money is delivered for credit to a broker or financial institution account, a life insurance policy or annuity is registered and delivered, an interest in real property is recorded, or a certificate of title to a vehicle is issued.

4. Custodian

a. Duties

The custodian must collect, hold, manage, invest, and reinvest custodial property as would a prudent person of discretion and intelligence who is seeking a reasonable income and preservation of capital. He shall pay the minor amounts for support, maintenance, education, and benefit of the minor.

b. Compensation

The custodian is entitled to reasonable compensation and expenses, but may act without compensation.

c. Successors

If a custodian resigns, he may designate a successor or one may be appointed by the court.

d. Removal

The custodian may be removed by court order.

5. Final Distribution

Final distribution should be made to the minor when she reaches the age of majority, or to the minor's estate if she dies before reaching majority.

6. Uniform Gifts to Minors Act

A few states continue to use this older act, which is similar to the UTMA but applies only to lifetime outright gifts of securities, money, or life insurance or annuity contracts.

III. LIENS

A. IN GENERAL

1. **Concept**

A lien is the right of one (lienor) to possess and retain personal property that she has improved or enhanced in value or otherwise serviced as security for the payment by the person claiming the property (lienee) of all charges for the improvement or service.

2. **Classes of Liens**

a. **General Lien**

A general lien is a right to retain all of the property of another as security for a general balance due. A general lien arises only out of contract, statute, or well-established usage or custom of a particular trade.

b. **Special Lien**

A special lien is the right to retain specific property as security for charges due for services concerning that specific property. The lienor must have possession and (generally) have added value to the chattel.

c. **Consequences of Classification**

When the lien is general and some of the chattels are released, the lienor may hold the unreleased chattels until the entire lien charge is paid. When the lien is a special lien and there is a release of chattels, the lien is waived to the extent of the chattels released. In case of doubt, a lien is treated as a special lien.

B. **WAIVER OF LIEN**

1. **By Contract**

A lien may be waived by a contract inconsistent with the existence of a lien, as when one agrees to deliver goods before payment for services.

2. **By Acceptance of Other Security**

Where a lienor accepts security for payment, the security eliminates the common law lien.

3. **By Demand for Excess Charges**

When the lienor, in good faith, includes amounts in excess of the original charges in her valid lien, the lien is not waived. If, however, the lienee has already tendered the original amount of the lien, the lien must be discharged; if it is not, the lienor becomes liable in an action for replevin or trover or for statutory penalties.

4. **Reservation of Lien or Temporary Use by Bailor**

There is no waiver if the lienholder surrenders the goods, specially reserving her lien, or where temporary use of the property is permitted.

C. **MECHANIC'S LIEN VS. PERFECTED SECURITY INTEREST**

In many states, a mechanic who performs labor at the request of the mortgagor has priority as against the holder of a perfected security interest.

D. **ENFORCEMENT OF LIEN**

At common law, a lien was only a possessory lien, but now statutes give the lienor power to enforce the lien by sale, either by notice or judicial foreclosure.

IV. BAILMENTS

A. CONCEPT

A bailment is the relationship created by the transfer of personal property by one called the bailor to another called the bailee for the accomplishment of a certain purpose. There is no transfer of title to the bailee; she possesses the property and is obligated to return or dispose of the property only in accord with the terms of the bailment. An express contract is not necessary.

B. ELEMENTS

1. Possession of the Property
Bailee must possess the property, which entails physical custody over the property coupled with intent to exercise control.

2. Consent Required
Possession cannot be thrust upon the bailee without her consent. Mere custody of a chattel is not sufficient to constitute possession.

3. Knowledge of Presence
The bailee must have actual or constructive knowledge of the article's presence. If a bailment does exist with respect to an article, it does not follow that a bailment exists with respect to something that is concealed within that article.

C. DISTINGUISHED FROM OTHER TRANSACTIONS

1. Renting
A lease is characterized by the owner's retention of control over the chattel, as where an individual retains her keys upon parking her car in a parking lot, as opposed to a bank safe deposit box where the bank retains almost absolute control over the box and its contents.

2. Employer-Employee
Ordinary possession by an employee of an employer's goods does not amount to a bailment, since control of the goods remains with the employer because the employee is subject to the orders and control of his employer.

3. Consignment
A consignee is authorized to sell the goods in the ordinary course of trade; therefore, a consignment may be described as a special bailment for the purpose of sale.

4. Sale

a. Risk of Loss
A sale involves the transfer of title to the vendee, while a bailment only involves the transfer of possession to the bailee. This is important because he who has title has assumed the risk of loss.

b. Test for Bailment vs. Sale
The general rule is that when the identical thing delivered is to be returned in the same or altered form, the contract is one of bailment; but when there is no obligation to restore the specific article, and the receiver is at liberty to return another thing of equal value or the money value, and the title to the property is changed—it is a sale.

c. **Sale on Approval and Sale or Return**
Sale on approval is a bailment with the bailee having an option to purchase. A "sale or return" is a sale with the vendee having a privilege to reinvest title in the vendor, and upon notice the vendee becomes a bailee.

5. **Pledge**
A pledge is a particular type of bailment by which the bailor delivers property to the bailee to secure an obligation owed by the bailor to the bailee.

6. *Intra Hospitum*
A hotel or innkeeper is an insurer of the goods of a guest that are taken into custody and control of the hotel, and is liable unless the loss or damage was caused by an act of God, a public enemy, or fault of the guest.

D. BAILEE'S RIGHTS IN BAILED CHATTEL

1. **Possession**
The bailee has the exclusive right of possession, against even the true owner, as long as the bailee is exercising possession according to the terms and conditions of the bailment. A creditor of the bailor has no greater rights than the bailor himself and no right to take the bailed goods by attachment.

2. **Use**
Ordinarily the bailee has no right to use the subject matter of the bailment unless there is an express provision in the contract or there are circumstances where such an intent is presumed. Any intentional unauthorized use of the goods which results in loss or damage renders the bailee absolutely liable to the bailor, irrespective of the question of care or negligence.

E. BAILOR'S RIGHTS IN BAILED CHATTEL

1. **Actions Against Bailee**
Where the bailed goods have been lost or damaged due to the wrongful acts of the bailee, the bailor can maintain an action for damages in tort or contract, replevy the goods, or sue for conversion.

2. **Actions Against Third Parties**

   a. **Bailment of Definite Duration**
   Where the bailment is for a definite time, the bailor cannot maintain actions for trover or replevin during the life of the bailment, since these are predicated upon the immediate right to possession.

   b. **Terminable Bailment**
   Where the bailment is terminable, the bailor may treat the bailment as ended and maintain actions for conversion or replevin.

   c. **Actions for Damage to Future Right of Possession**
   The bailor may sue for injuries to his reversionary interest, and any negligence by the bailee is not imputed to the bailor. The sole issue is whether the third party was negligent.

F. BAILEE'S DUTIES WITH RESPECT TO BAILED GOODS

1. Duty of Care

A bailee owes a duty of due care, but she is not an insurer of the safety of the goods. If the goods are damaged or lost through no fault of the bailee, the loss falls on the bailor. The specific degree of negligence upon which liability will rest varies with the type of bailment. When the bailment is solely for the bailor's benefit, only slight diligence is required and liability rests on gross negligence. When the bailment is solely for the benefit of the bailee, great diligence is required and liability will result from slight negligence. Bailments for hire and pledges are for the mutual benefit of bailee and bailor and ordinary due care is required.

CMR SUMMARY CHART

BAILEE'S DUTY OF CARE

Standard of Care	When Applied	Example
Slight Diligence	Bailment is *solely for the benefit of the bailor*	X leaves his car at a gas station operated by his friend Y for a free car wash
Ordinary Care	Bailment is for the *mutual benefit* of bailor and bailee, as in bailments for hire	X leaves his car with a mechanic for service
Great Diligence	Bailment is *solely for the benefit of bailee*	X gratuitously lends his sports car to his friend Y to drive to Y's class reunion
Absolute Liability	Bailee *departs from terms* of bailment or *fails to redeliver item* (*exception:* delivery to impostor holding "indispensable instrument")	X has turned the keys to his sports car over to Y's parking garage; Y's employee drives X's car to her class reunion. (But probably no absolute liability if X loses the claim check and Y's employee, without notice, turns X's car over to dishonest finder of the claim check)

Note: There is a modern trend away from the above classifications and toward a rule requiring *ordinary care under all circumstances*.

2. **Burden of Proof as to Bailee's Negligence**

Where the loss is during the bailment, the burden is on the bailee to prove that the loss was caused despite her due care. When bailor shows delivery to the bailee and the latter fails to return the goods on proper demand or returns them in a damaged state, the bailor has shown a prima facie case for recovery.

3. **Contractual Limits on Liability**

a. **Waiver**

An ordinary bailee may exempt herself from liability for her own negligence. On the other hand, a waiver of liability for negligence by a *professional bailee* is not permitted. However, a professional bailee may *limit* that liability, provided the bailor knows, or should know, of the limitation and assents.

b. **Posted Sign**

Where the limitation is posted on a sign, it is not binding in the absence of proof that the bailor read the notice or under the circumstances should have read the notice.

c. **Claim Check**

The mere fact that the limitation is contained on a claim check is not sufficient proof that the bailor actually knew of this term.

d. **Hotels**

Hotels may limit liability for articles placed in their care by providing notice thereof. If they provide a safe for storing valuables and such notice, they may also limit liability for goods lost from hotel rooms.

4. **Absolute Liability**

The bailee is absolutely liable for loss or damage without regard to her care where she has departed from the terms of the bailment by using the goods in a manner not agreed upon, removing the goods from the agreed place of storage, or breaching an agreement to insure the goods.

5. **Duty to Redeliver**

Upon termination of the bailment, the bailee owes a duty to redeliver or account for the bailed items. Delivery must be made to the bailor or one claiming under him.

a. **Absolute Liability**

Failure to redeliver or improper delivery is a breach of the contract giving rise to absolute liability. Some courts make an exception to the rule of absolute liability when the bailee delivers the chattel to one holding an indispensable instrument as long as the bailee had no notice or knowledge that the one presenting the instrument was not the original bailor.

b. **Adverse Claimants**

When the bailee knows, or should know, of an adverse claim to the property, she will be absolutely liable to the true owner for delivery to the original bailor if the original bailor is not the true owner. Thus, the bailee should interplead all claimants of the property.

c. **Excuses for Nondelivery**
The bailee is excused from delivery where the bailor has sold the property and notified the bailee, a third-party claimant has paramount title, or the property is taken from the bailee by judicial process.

6. **Bailee Estopped to Deny Bailor's Title**
The bailee cannot excuse failure to return property by asserting a claim to it herself or on behalf of another.

7. **Conversion by Bailee**
Use of chattel in an unauthorized way is a conversion for which the bailor may maintain trover. A conversion makes a bailee an insurer and thus liable without reference to the question of negligence.

8. **Liability to Third Parties**
The bailee—and not the bailor—is liable for damages to others caused by the bailee's use of the bailed property.

G. COMPENSATION AND REIMBURSEMENT

In a bailment for mutual benefit, the bailee is entitled to the agreed-upon or reasonable compensation. If the bailment is for the sole benefit of either party, there is no compensation. Ordinary expenses must be borne by the bailee and extraordinary expenses by the bailor. The bailee has a special lien over the bailed property.

H. BAILEE'S RIGHTS OF ACTION

1. **Against Bailor**
The bailee can maintain an action against the bailor for wrongfully taking and converting the subject of the bailment.

2. **Against Third Parties**
Any recovery by the bailee beyond her interest in the bailed goods in actions against third parties regarding the bailed goods is for the benefit of the bailor.

I. DEFECTS IN SUBJECT OF BAILMENT

Where the bailment is gratuitous, the bailor must inform the bailee of known defects. Where the bailment is for hire, the bailor is bound to inform the bailee of all known defects and those which, by the exercise of reasonable diligence, should have been known.

J. TERMINATION OF BAILMENT

A bailment may be terminated by agreement, upon lapse of time, by accomplishment of specified purpose, or by specific conduct of the parties.

V. COMMON CARRIERS

A. CONCEPT

A common carrier is one who undertakes to transport persons or goods from place to place.

There must be a holding out to perform services for all who apply, the carriage must be for hire, and the service must be one for carriage.

B. LIABILITY FOR LOSS OR DAMAGE OF GOODS SHIPPED

A common carrier is an insurer of goods given to it by a shipper and is liable for loss or damage under any circumstances, except where loss is due to an act of God, state, or a public enemy, an act of the shipper, or the inherent nature of the goods.

1. Commencement of Liability

Liability begins when the goods are delivered and accepted by the carrier for immediate transportation.

2. Limitation of Liability

The common carrier may contract to limit its liability. This limitation of liability is binding even though the shipper has not read the contract, but the carrier must offer some additional consideration for the limitation. A contract that relieves the carrier from all liability due to its own negligence is void. No limitation is permitted for liability arising out of the Interstate Commerce Act.

3. Baggage

A common carrier is liable for baggage delivered to it and for nonbaggage knowingly accepted. A carrier is not liable as an insurer for goods retained in the possession or control of the passenger, but it may be liable in a negligence action for failure to properly protect its passengers.

SECURED TRANSACTIONS

TABLE OF CONTENTS

SECURED TRANSACTIONS

I. INTRODUCTION

A. OVERVIEW OF STATUTORY SCHEME

Secured transactions involve credit transactions. Typically one party (the ***debtor***) buys something on credit from another party (the ***creditor*** or ***secured party***) but does not pay immediately. To ensure payment, the creditor takes a security interest in specific personal property (the ***collateral***) of the debtor, which allows the creditor to take the property if the debtor fails to fulfill the credit obligation. For the security interest to be effective between the parties, certain steps known as ***attachment*** must be taken. After attachment, if the debtor defaults, the creditor has a right to take the property to satisfy the obligation. However, attachment generally does not provide the creditor with any rights against other parties who might also have an interest in the same collateral. To gain rights against such parties, the creditor must take additional steps to ***perfect*** the security interest. When more than one creditor has an interest in the same collateral, rules of ***priority*** determine whose interest is superior.

B. SCOPE OF ARTICLE 9

Article 9 applies to the following transactions:

1. ***Contractual security interests*** (interests in personal property or fixtures that secure payment or performance of an obligation);

2. ***Sales of accounts, chattel paper, payment intangibles, and promissory notes*** (*see* E.2., *infra*, for definitions of terms);

3. ***Commercial consignments*** of goods worth a total of $1,000 or more to persons who (i) deal in goods of that kind under a name other than the consignor's, (ii) are not auctioneers, and (iii) are not generally known by their creditors to be substantially engaged in selling the goods of others;

4. ***Agricultural liens,*** *i.e.,* nonpossessory liens on farm products that are created by state statute in favor of persons providing goods, services, or rental land to farmers (only the ***perfection and priority*** of agricultural liens are governed by Article 9; creation and enforcement of the liens are governed by state statutes); and

5. ***Leases*** that are ***intended to serve as security arrangements*** (but not true leases).

C. EXCEPTIONS

The most notable exception to Article 9 coverage is that it does not apply to most transfers of interests in ***land*** (except for interests in fixtures).

D. SECURITY INTERESTS—PMSIs

A purchase money security interest ("PMSI") is a special type of security interest in goods. A person who holds a PMSI has priority over other security interests in the same goods if certain requirements are met (*see* IV.B.3.c., *infra*). A PMSI can arise in two ways: (i) the creditor ***sells the goods*** to the debtor on credit, retaining a security interest in the goods for the purchase price (*e.g.,* a debtor buys a stereo from a store on credit and the store retains a security interest in the

A TYPICAL SECURED TRANSACTION SCENARIO

CMR EXAMPLE CHART

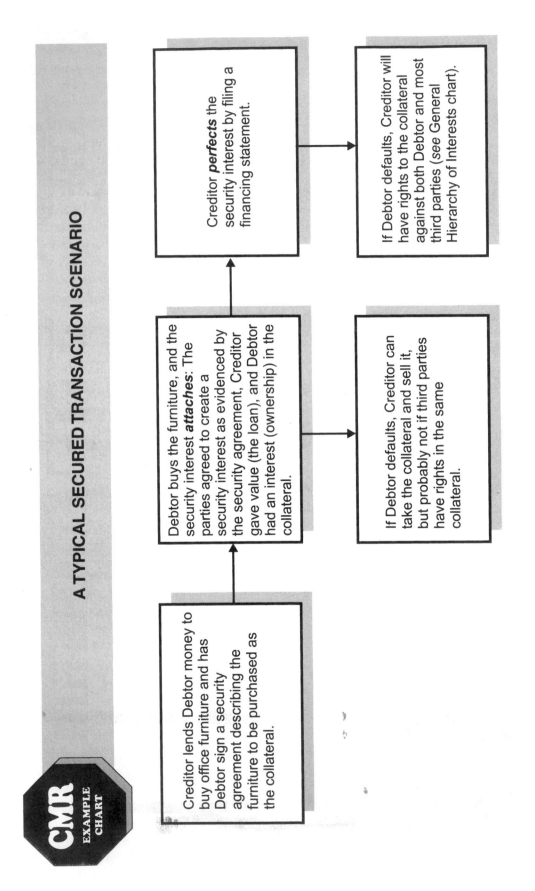

Creditor lends Debtor money to buy office furniture and has Debtor sign a security agreement describing the furniture to be purchased as the collateral.

Debtor buys the furniture, and the security interest *attaches*: The parties agreed to create a security interest as evidenced by the security agreement, Creditor gave value (the loan), and Debtor had an interest (ownership) in the collateral.

Creditor *perfects* the security interest by filing a financing statement.

If Debtor defaults, Creditor can take the collateral and sell it, but probably not if third parties have rights in the same collateral.

If Debtor defaults, Creditor will have rights to the collateral against both Debtor and most third parties (*see* General Hierarchy of Interests chart).

stereo), or (ii) the creditor *advances the debtor the funds* used to buy the goods, and the creditor takes a security interest in the goods (*e.g.,* a debtor borrows money from a bank to buy a stereo and the bank takes a security interest in the stereo for the purchase price).

1. **Dual Status Rule**

A security interest in *nonconsumer goods* (*i.e.,* goods that were not bought or used for personal, family, or household purposes) *does not lose its status as a PMSI* if: (i) the security interest also is secured by property that was not purchased with the loan money or credit (*e.g.,* if the security interest also is secured by after-acquired property), (ii) the collateral also secures advances that were not made for the purchase of the collateral (*e.g.,* if the collateral also secures future advances), or (iii) the PMSI has been refinanced, consolidated, etc. If the goods are *consumer goods* (*i.e.,* goods bought or used for personal, family, or household purposes), the *courts* must determine appropriate rules for such PMSIs.

E. **COLLATERAL**

While almost any type of personal property may serve as collateral, certain Article 9 rules (*e.g.,* how to perfect) vary depending on the type of collateral. There are various types of collateral that may be divided into three broad classifications: tangible collateral or goods; intangible or semi-intangible collateral; and proceeds.

1. **Tangible Collateral or Goods**

There are four types of tangible collateral (also known as goods). The category into which tangible collateral is placed depends on *the primary use to which the debtor puts the property:*

   a. *Consumer goods*—goods bought or used for personal, family, or household purposes (*e.g.,* a home stereo system);

   b. *Inventory*—goods held for sale or lease and goods consumed by a business (*e.g.,* fuel used to run a factory);

   c. *Farm products*—goods (including crops and animals) used or produced in farming that are in the possession of or used by a farmer; and

   d. *Equipment*—goods that are not consumer goods, inventory, or farm products (*e.g.,* durable goods used by a business, such as machinery used in a factory).

CMR **Exam Tip** Secured transactions questions often involve perfection issues that hinge on the type of tangible collateral involved. Thus, it is very important for you to understand the difference between the above categories.

2. **Intangible or Semi-Intangible Collateral**

There are eight types of intangible or semi-intangible collateral. The category into which intangible or semi-intangible collateral is placed depends on *the nature of the collateral* (rather than its use):

   a. *Instruments*—notes, drafts, and certificates of deposit;

   b. *Documents*—bills of lading and warehouse receipts;

   c.   *Chattel paper*—records (*i.e.,* written or electronically stored information) evidencing both a monetary obligation and a security interest in or lease of goods, such as a promissory note and written security agreement;

   d.   *Accounts*—rights to payment for goods, services, etc., such as accounts receivable;

   e.   *Deposit accounts*—savings accounts, passbook accounts, etc. (note that Article 9 only applies to *nonconsumer* deposit accounts and consumer deposit accounts that are claimed as *proceeds* of other collateral);

   f.   *Investment property*—stocks, bonds, mutual funds, brokerage accounts, etc.;

   g.   *Commercial tort claims*—tort claims filed by organizations and tort claims filed by individuals that arose out of the individuals' business and do not involve personal injury (note that Article 9 only applies to *commercial* tort claims and noncommercial tort claims that are claimed as *proceeds* of other collateral); and

   h.   *General intangibles*—intangibles not fitting the definitions of other types of intangibles, such as copyrights and goodwill (note that a general intangible in which the principal obligation of one of the parties is the payment of money is a *payment intangible*).

3. Proceeds

Proceeds include whatever is received upon the sale, exchange, collection, or other disposition of collateral or proceeds. Proceeds include second generation proceeds. Insurance payable by reason of loss or damage to the collateral is a proceed, unless it is payable to someone other than the debtor or secured party. Claims arising out of the loss of, defects in, or damage to collateral also are proceeds.

II. CREATION (ATTACHMENT) OF SECURITY INTEREST

A. INTRODUCTION

Article 9 concerns the secured party's rights against both the debtor and third parties. Rights against the debtor are established by attachment; rights against third parties are established by perfection.

B. REQUISITES FOR ATTACHMENT

A security interest is not enforceable unless it has attached. There are three requirements for attachment, which *must coexist:*

   (i)   The parties must *agree to create* the security interest, as evidenced by (i) the creditor taking *possession* of the collateral, (ii) the debtor's *authentication* of (*i.e.,* signing or electronically marking) a security agreement describing the collateral (and the land concerned if the collateral is timber to be cut), or (iii) the creditor taking *control* of certain types of collateral (*see* 2., *infra*); *and*

(ii) **Value** must be given by the secured party (a preexisting debt is deemed value if the security interest is intended as security for the preexisting debt); **and**

(iii) The debtor must have **rights** (*e.g.,* ownership) **in the collateral**.

1. **Description of Collateral in Authenticated Security Agreement**

   In an authenticated security agreement, collateral can be described broadly by category or type (*e.g.,* "equipment") or specifically (*e.g.,* by serial number). However, a supergeneric description of collateral such as "all of the debtor's assets" is not a sufficient description. *Exception:* Consumer goods, consumer securities accounts, and commercial tort claims cannot be described by type alone; a more specific description is needed.

2. **Methods of Obtaining Control**

   A creditor can obtain control over the following types of collateral: ***nonconsumer deposit accounts, electronic chattel paper***, and ***investment property***.

   a. **Nonconsumer Deposit Accounts**

      The **bank** in which a nonconsumer deposit account is maintained **automatically** has control over the deposit account. If the secured party is **not** such a bank, it may obtain control over a nonconsumer deposit account by either: (i) putting the deposit account in the secured party's name, or (ii) agreeing in an authenticated record with the debtor and the bank in which the deposit account is maintained that the **bank will comply with the secured party's orders** regarding the deposit account without requiring the debtor's consent.

   b. **Electronic Chattel Paper**

      Chattel paper that is stored in an electronic medium (*e.g.,* stored on computer) is called "***electronic chattel paper***" and chattel paper that is stored in a tangible medium (*e.g.,* written on paper) is called "***tangible chattel paper***." Control of electronic chattel paper is the functional equivalent of possession of tangible chattel paper. To obtain control over electronic chattel paper, the secured party must have the ***authoritative copy*** of the records constituting the electronic chattel paper (*e.g.,* computer files) that identifies the secured party as the assignee of record of the chattel paper. Any other copy of the records that is not the authoritative copy must be marked as such.

   c. **Investment Property**

      1) **Certificated Securities**

         A secured party obtains control over a certificated security (*i.e.,* a stock or bond represented by a certificate) by taking possession of the certificate if it is in ***bearer*** form. If the certificate is in registered form, the secured party must take possession ***and*** the certificate must either be indorsed to the secured party or registered by the issuer in the name of the secured party.

      2) **Securities Accounts**

         A secured party obtains control over a securities account if the owner of the account instructs the securities intermediary that:

a) The secured party has the same rights in the account as the owner; or

b) The intermediary may comply with the secured party's orders without the consent of the owner.

3. **Rights and Duties of Secured Party in Possession or Control**
The secured party in *possession* must use reasonable care in storing and preserving the collateral, but is entitled to reimbursement for reasonable expenses in caring for the collateral. Risk of loss of property in the secured party's possession is on the debtor to the extent of any insurance deficiency. The secured party in *possession or control* may hold any increase in value of, or profits from, the collateral (except money) as additional security, but money so received must be given to the debtor or applied against the secured obligation. The secured party in possession or control may also pledge the collateral.

CMR **Exam Tip** The most important things to remember about attachment are: (i) *all three requirements* for attachment must be present—they can occur in any order, but there is no attachment until the last of the three occurs; and (ii) there must be an *authenticated security agreement or* the creditor must *take possession or control* of the collateral. Note that a *financing statement* (*see* III.B.1., *infra*) is not necessary for attachment; it relates to perfection.

C. **PROPERTY THAT DEBTOR ACQUIRES IN FUTURE—AFTER-ACQUIRED PROPERTY AND FUTURE ADVANCES**

1. **After-Acquired Property**
A security agreement may create a security interest in property to be acquired in the future. The security interest will attach to the property as soon as the debtor acquires an interest in the collateral. Generally, such an interest may be created only by including an after-acquired property clause in the security agreement. *Exception:* A security interest will attach automatically to proceeds from the disposition of collateral and to accounts and new items of inventory collateral, even without an after-acquired property clause.

Note: An after-acquired property clause does not apply to *consumer goods* unless the debtor acquires rights in the goods within 10 days after the creditor gives value. In addition, an after-acquired property clause does not apply to any *commercial tort claims*.

2. **Future Advances**
A security agreement may provide that the collateral will serve as security not only for the present obligation, but also for advances the creditor makes to the debtor in the future.

III. PERFECTION OF SECURITY INTEREST

A. **IN GENERAL**
As discussed *supra,* attachment establishes the secured party's rights to the collateral as against the *debtor*. However, other parties may also have rights in the collateral (*e.g.,* subsequent purchasers, unsecured creditors, other priority creditors). To acquire maximum priority in the collateral over most such *third parties*, the secured party must "perfect." There are five methods of perfection: (i) filing; (ii) taking possession of the collateral; (iii) control; (iv) automatic perfection; and (v) temporary perfection.

1. **Time of Perfection**

A security interest is not enforceable against anyone until it has attached to the collateral. If all of the steps for perfection are taken before the security interest has attached, perfection will occur upon attachment.

CMR **Exam Tip**   A key point to remember about perfection is that a security interest cannot be perfected before it attaches to the collateral. For example, if a creditor has filed a financing statement but has not yet given value to the debtor, perfection is not complete until attachment is complete (*i.e.,* when the value is given). Thus, attachment and perfection can occur simultaneously.

CMR
SUMMARY CHART

	ATTACHMENT VS. PERFECTION	
	Attachment	**Perfection**
Purpose	Establishes secured party's rights in the collateral as *against the debtor*.	Establishes secured party's rights in the collateral as *against third parties*.
Requirements	(i) An *agreement* to create a security interest evidenced by possession, by the debtor's authentication of the security agreement, or by control; (ii) *Value* given by the secured party; and (iii) *Debtor has rights in the collateral*.	(i) Attachment; and (ii) One of the following: • *Filing* (in the proper place) of a *financing statement* describing the collateral, • *Taking possession* of the collateral, • *Taking control* of the collateral, • *Automatic* perfection (*e.g.,* of a PMSI in consumer goods), or • *Temporary* perfection (*e.g.,* of a security interest in proceeds received from the sale of collateral).

B. PERFECTION BY FILING

1. **Records to Be Filed**

A secured party may obtain perfection by filing (either in writing or electronically) a *financing statement*. The financing statement must contain:

(i) The *debtor's name and mailing address*;

(ii)   The *secured party's name and mailing address*;

(iii) An *indication of the collateral* covered by the financing statement; and

(iv)   If the financing statement covers real property-related collateral (*i.e.,* minerals, timber to be cut, and fixtures), a *description of the real property* to which the collateral is related.

Note that a security interest may be perfected by filing as to all kinds of collateral except deposit accounts and money.

a.   Effect of Error in Debtor's Name

Financing statements are indexed under the debtor's name. *Minor errors* in the debtor's name—those that would not prevent a reasonably prudent subsequent creditor from discovering the prior filing—will not invalidate a financing statement, but seriously misleading errors will.

1)   Debtor Name Change

If the debtor makes a "seriously misleading" name change after a financing statement is filed, the financing statement is only effective against collateral acquired by the debtor *before* the name change and within *four months* after the change. For collateral acquired after the four-month period, the secured party must refile using the debtor's new name.

b.   Effect of Missing Address

If a financing statement that does not contain the debtor's and/or secured party's mailing address is *accepted by the filing office*, the financing statement is *effective* despite the lack of the address(es).

c.   Indication of Collateral

As is the case with an authenticated security agreement, an indication of collateral in a financing statement is sufficient if it indicates the collateral broadly by category or type (*e.g.,* "equipment") or specifically (*e.g.,* by serial number). However, unlike the requirements for an authenticated security agreement, a financing statement may contain a supergeneric indication of the collateral, such as "all assets."

d.   Debtor Must "Authorize" Filing of Financing Statement

For a financing statement to be effective, the debtor must *authorize it in an authenticated record* (*i.e.,* the authorization cannot be oral) either before or after it is filed. The debtor authorizes the financing statement if she *authenticates the financing statement* or *a security agreement* covering the same collateral as the financing statement.

e.   After-Acquired Property

The financing statement need *not* mention after-acquired property to perfect a security interest in such property if the description in the financing statement is broad enough to cover the after-acquired property (*e.g.,* in the *financing statement*, a description of "equipment" is sufficient to perfect an interest in new pieces of equipment if the *security agreement* includes an after-acquired property clause).

2. **Place of Filing**

   a. **General Rule—File Centrally**
   Generally, filing must be done *"centrally"* in the office of the secretary of state.

   b. **Exception—Timber to Be Cut, Minerals, and Fixtures**
   Filing for security interests in timber to be cut, minerals, and fixtures is *"local,"* in the county where a mortgage on real estate is filed. In the case of fixture filing, it is safest to file both in real estate records and at the place that would be proper if the goods were not fixtures.

3. **Period for Which Filing Is Effective**
   Filing is valid for *five years.* A continuation statement may be filed, good for an additional five years. The continuation statement can only be filed within six months before the lapse of the filed statement. The authorization of the debtor is *not* required for a continuation statement; the secured party may authorize it.

4. **Certificate of Title Law**
   Security interests in motor vehicles required to be titled (except those created by dealers) are perfected by *notation on the certificate of title* (no Article 9 filing). Security interests created by dealers in vehicles held for sale or lease are perfected by ordinary filing under the U.C.C., even if a certificate of title covering the vehicle is outstanding.

C. **PERFECTION BY TAKING POSSESSION (PLEDGE)**

1. **Collateral that Cannot Be Pledged**
   Security interests in most types of collateral can be perfected by possession, but security interests in general intangibles, nonconsumer deposit accounts, nonnegotiable documents, electronic chattel paper, certificate of title goods, and accounts *cannot* be perfected by possession.

2. **Time of Perfection**
   Where the secured party takes actual possession of the collateral, the security interest is perfected from the moment of possession and continues as long as possession is retained. Where the collateral (other than certificated securities and goods covered by a document) is in the hands of a bailee, the secured party is deemed to be in possession from the moment the bailee authenticates a record acknowledging that it is holding the collateral for the secured party's benefit.

CMR **Exam Tip** Note that taking possession can simultaneously satisfy the requirements for attachment and perfection; *i.e.,* possession may be the last thing needed for attachment, and attachment plus possession results in perfection.

D. **PERFECTION BY CONTROL**
   Security interests in investment property, nonconsumer deposit accounts, and electronic chattel paper may be perfected by "control." (*See* II.B.2., *supra,* regarding methods of obtaining control.)

E. AUTOMATIC PERFECTION—PMSI IN CONSUMER GOODS

A PMSI in consumer goods is perfected as soon as it attaches; neither filing nor possession by the creditor is necessary. Recall that a seller has a PMSI when the security interest was retained to secure at least part of the purchase price.

1. Limitations

A security interest in motor vehicles can be perfected only by notation on the vehicle's certificate of title, and a PMSI in fixtures will have priority over an encumbrancer of the real estate only if the PMSI holder files.

CMR | **Exam Tip** | Note well that the only type of PMSI that is automatically perfected is a ***PMSI in consumer goods***. A PMSI in inventory or equipment must be filed to be valid.

F. TEMPORARY PERFECTION

1. Twenty-Day Period for Proceeds

A security interest in proceeds from original collateral is continuously perfected for 20 days from the debtor's receipt of the proceeds. This security interest becomes unperfected after 20 days unless the statutory requirements are complied with (*see* G., *infra*); however, in many cases the requirements are automatically met.

2. Twenty-Day Period for Instruments, Negotiable Documents, and Certificated Securities

a. New Value

Where new value is given under an authenticated security agreement for instruments, negotiable documents, or certificated securities, perfection is valid for ***20 days after attachment;*** neither filing nor possession is necessary.

b. Delivery of Collateral to Debtor for Disposition

Where the creditor who has perfected her security interest by possession delivers instruments, negotiable documents, certificated securities, or goods in the possession of a bailee to the debtor for disposition (*e.g.,* where the creditor gives the debtor a promissory note, which is serving as collateral, so that the debtor can present the note to its maker for payment), perfection is valid for ***20 days,*** after which the creditor must reperfect (by filing or taking possession) or lose his perfection.

3. Interstate Shipments

When the debtor moves from one state to another, and the location of the debtor determines which state's law governs perfection, a security interest in the collateral that was perfected in the original state will remain temporarily perfected in the new state. (*See* VI., *infra*, for a detailed explanation.)

G. CONTINUATION OF PERFECTION OF INTEREST IN PROCEEDS

As stated above, a secured party has a temporarily (20-day) perfected security interest in proceeds of collateral. The security interest in proceeds will continue to be perfected ***beyond*** the 20 days if:

1. The security interest in the original collateral was *perfected by filing* a financing statement, a security interest in the type of collateral constituting the proceeds would be *filed in the same place* as the financing statement for the original collateral, and the proceeds were not purchased with cash proceeds of the collateral (this is sometimes called the "same office" rule);

2. The *proceeds are identifiable cash proceeds* (this is sometimes called the "cash proceeds" rule); or

3. The security interest in the proceeds is *perfected within the 20-day period*.

CMR SUMMARY CHART — **METHODS OF PERFECTION**

Filing— Effective for *all classes* of collateral *except* deposit accounts and money.

Possession— Effective for *all classes* of collateral *except* general intangibles, accounts, nonconsumer deposit accounts, nonnegotiable documents, and electronic chattel paper, although it is impractical for some classes of collateral (*e.g.,* if secured party takes debtor's equipment or inventory, it will be difficult for debtor to run his business).

Automatic— Effective *only* as to PMSIs in *consumer goods*, small-scale assignments of accounts, sales of payment intangibles and promissory notes, beneficial interests in a decedent's estate, and certain investment property transactions.

Temporary— Effective for *20 days* (and possibly longer) for proceeds; *20 days* when a secured party gives new value under a security agreement where collateral is a negotiable document, instrument, or certificated security; *20 days* where a secured party makes available a negotiable document, instrument, certificated security, or goods in possession of a bailee on a temporary basis (*e.g.,* for debtor to present for payment or to sell); *four months* where debtor moves from one state to another if debtor's location governs perfection.

Control— Effective *only* for nonconsumer deposit accounts, electronic chattel paper, and investment property.

IV. PRIORITIES

A. INTRODUCTION

The heart of Article 9 is its allocation of priority among conflicting interests in the same collateral. For example, one creditor has a PMSI in collateral and another creditor has a prior perfected

security interest in the same collateral by virtue of an after-acquired property clause; if the debtor defaults on the obligations owed to both creditors, which creditor has priority in the collateral?

B.   SECURED PARTY VS. SECURED PARTY

1.   Priority Between Unperfected Secured Parties
When two unperfected security interests conflict, the first to attach has priority.

2.   Priority Between Unperfected and Perfected Secured Parties
A perfected security interest generally prevails over an unperfected security interest.

3.   Priority Between Perfected Secured Parties
Conflicting perfected security interests rank in priority *according to time of filing or perfection.* Priority dates from the time a filing is first made covering the collateral, or the time the security interest is first perfected—whichever is earlier—provided there is no period thereafter when there is neither filing nor perfection.

CMR **Exam Tip**   Remember that it is the date of filing or perfection that determines priority—not the date of attachment.

a.   Special Priority Rules for Conflicting Security Interests in Investment Property
The first to file or perfect rule generally governs priority questions regarding investment property. However, a security interest *perfected by control has priority* over a security interest perfected by any other method (*i.e.*, by filing or automatic perfection).

b.   Purchase Money Security Interests
PMSIs enjoy a *superpriority*—they are superior to prior perfected security interests in the same collateral if certain conditions (discussed below) are met. Recall that a PMSI arises only where the seller sells the collateral to the debtor on credit and reserves a security interest in the collateral, or where the creditor advances funds to allow the debtor to purchase the collateral and takes a security interest in the collateral.

1)   Inventory PMSI
A PMSI in inventory collateral has priority over a conflicting security interest in the same inventory or proceeds of the inventory that are chattel paper, instruments, or cash if:

(i)   It is *perfected at the time the debtor gets possession* of the inventory (filing must take place before the inventory is delivered to the debtor); and

(ii)   Any secured party who has perfected his security interest in the same inventory receives *written notification* of the PMSI before the debtor receives possession of the inventory, and the notification states that the purchase money party has or expects to take a PMSI in inventory of the debtor described by kind or type.

Note: A similar rule applies to PMSIs in livestock.

PRIORITY BETWEEN PERFECTED SECURITY INTERESTS

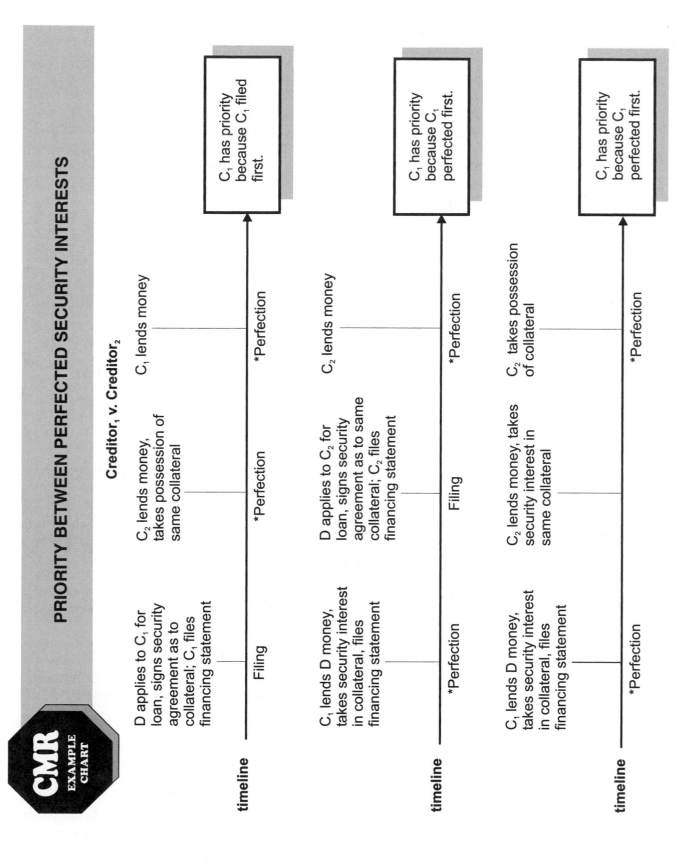

Creditor₁ v. Creditor₂

D applies to C_1 for loan, signs security agreement as to collateral; C_1 files financing statement

Filing

C_2 lends money, takes possession of same collateral

*Perfection

C_1 lends money

*Perfection

C_1 has priority because C_1 filed first.

timeline

C_1 lends D money, takes security interest in collateral, files financing statement

*Perfection

D applies to C_2 for loan, signs security agreement as to same collateral; C_2 files financing statement

Filing

C_2 lends money

*Perfection

C_1 has priority because C_1 perfected first.

timeline

C_1 lends D money, takes security interest in collateral, files financing statement

*Perfection

C_2 lends money, takes security interest in same collateral

C_2 takes possession of collateral

*Perfection

C_1 has priority because C_1 perfected first.

timeline

a) Consignor Has PMSI in Inventory

Under Article 9, a consignor's interest in the consigned goods is considered to be a PMSI in inventory. Therefore, a consignor can acquire PMSI superpriority in consigned goods if she complies with the above requirements for gaining PMSI superpriority in inventory.

2) PMSI in Goods Other than Inventory and Livestock

A PMSI in goods other than inventory and livestock (*e.g.*, equipment) has priority over conflicting security interests in the same goods *or their proceeds* if the interest is perfected before or within *20 days* after the debtor receives possession of the goods.

3) Conflicting PMSIs

If more than one party has PMSI superpriority in collateral, the following rules apply:

a) A secured party who has a PMSI in collateral *as a seller* has priority over a secured party who has a PMSI in the same collateral as a lender.

b) Otherwise, the *first* secured party to file or perfect prevails.

CMR **Exam Tip** It is very important to determine the class of collateral when a PMSI is involved because what is necessary for perfection varies. Remember:

- A PMSI in *consumer goods* is automatically perfected;

- A PMSI in *equipment* can be perfected (usually by filing) anytime within 20 days after the debtor gets possession of the collateral; and

- A PMSI in *inventory* must be perfected (usually by filing) by the time the debtor gets possession of the collateral—there is no 20-day grace period—and others with a security interest in the inventory must be given written notice.

c. "Purchasers" of Chattel Paper and Instruments

Article 9 contains special rules for *"purchasers"* of (who include parties taking a *security interest* in) chattel paper and instruments.

1) Chattel Paper Purchasers

If a purchaser of chattel paper in *good faith* gives *new value* and takes *possession* of the chattel paper in the ordinary course of business (or takes *control* of electronic chattel paper), the purchaser will have priority over:

(i) A security interest in chattel paper that arises merely as *proceeds of inventory,* as long as the chattel paper does not indicate that it has been assigned to anyone other than the purchaser; and

(ii) *Any other security interest* in the chattel paper, as long as the chattel paper purchaser acquired its interest *without knowledge that its purchase violated the rights of the secured party.*

PMSI SUPERPRIORITY—AN EXAMPLE

Creditor$_1$ v. Creditor$_2$

Timeline 1:

C_1 lends D money, takes a security interest in D's equipment (present and after-acquired), files a financing statement	C_2 sells D a piece of equipment (the collateral) on credit, retaining a security interest (PMSI)	C_2 files a financing statement within 20 days after the sale	D defaults on payments to C_1 and C_2
*Perfection		*Perfection	Default

C_2 has priority in the equipment it sold to D because C_2's PMSI was perfected within the statutory period, but C_1 has priority as to D's other equipment.

Timeline 2:

C_1 lends D money, takes a security interest in D's inventory (present and after-acquired), files a financing statement	C_2 notifies C_1 that it is selling D more inventory (the collateral), files a financing statement, sells D the inventory on credit, and retains a security interest (PMSI)	D defaults on payments to C_1 and C_2
*Perfection	*Perfection	Default

C_2 has priority in the collateral because C_2 gave C_1 notice and properly filed its security interest.

Timeline 3:

C_1 lends D money, takes a security interest in D's consumer goods (present and after-acquired), files a financing statement	Two days later, C_2 sells D a home stereo unit (the collateral) on credit and retains a security interest (PMSI)	D defaults on payments to C_1 and C_2
*Perfection	*Automatic Perfection	Default

C_2 has priority in the stereo over C_1 because C_2's PMSI was automatically perfected upon attachment.

Note: A chattel paper purchaser also has priority in the *proceeds* of the chattel paper if either (i) she would have had priority under the *general priority rules* (*i.e.,* the purchaser was the first party to file or perfect), or (ii) the proceeds are the *specific goods covered by the chattel paper or cash proceeds of the specific goods.*

2) Instrument Purchasers

A purchaser of an instrument has priority over a perfected security interest in the instrument if the purchaser gives *value* and takes *possession* of the instrument in *good faith* and *without knowledge that the purchase violates the rights of the secured party.*

d. Priority in Proceeds

For purposes of determining the priority of security interests in proceeds, the Code divides collateral into "filing collateral" and "non-filing collateral." *Filing collateral* is collateral in which a secured party would normally achieve priority by filing a financing statement (*i.e.,* goods, accounts, commercial tort claims, general intangibles, and nonnegotiable documents); *non-filing collateral* is collateral in which a secured party would normally achieve priority by possession or control, rather than filing (*e.g.,* cash, chattel paper, nonconsumer deposit accounts, negotiable documents, instruments, and investment property).

1) General Rule

Generally, a perfected security interest in proceeds will have the *same date of priority* as the perfected security interest in the original collateral (*e.g.,* under the "first to file or perfect" rule), as long as the perfection of the security interest in the proceeds extends beyond the 20-day temporary perfection period (*see* III.F.1., *supra*). Recall that there are also special superpriority rules for certain proceeds of collateral subject to PMSIs (*see* b., *supra*).

2) Special Rule for Certain Proceeds of Non-Filing Collateral

Because the rules governing priority in non-filing collateral contain many exceptions to the "first to file or perfect" rule (*e.g.,* a party with control over a deposit account has priority over a party without control, regardless of when control was obtained), the Code contains a special priority rule for certain proceeds of that collateral. A secured party has priority in the proceeds of non-filing collateral if: (i) she has *priority* in the original collateral, (ii) her security interest in the proceeds is *perfected*, and (iii) the proceeds are *cash proceeds or proceeds of the same type as the original collateral.* If the proceeds are proceeds of proceeds, all *intervening proceeds* must either be cash proceeds, proceeds of the same type as the original collateral, or accounts relating to the collateral.

a) Exception—Filing Collateral as Proceeds of Non-Filing Collateral

If a security interest in *original collateral* that is *non-filing collateral* is perfected by a method other than filing, and the *proceeds* of the original collateral are *filing collateral*, the first secured party to *file* a financing statement covering the proceeds has priority in the proceeds.

e. **Security Interests in Fixtures, Accessions, and Crops**

Fixtures are goods that become so attached to real property that an interest in them arises under real property law (*e.g.,* a built-in oven). Accessions are goods that are physically united with other goods in such a manner that the identity of the original goods is not lost (*e.g.,* new pedals on a bike).

1) **Fixtures**

Generally, in a contest between a holder of a security interest in a fixture and a holder of an interest in the real property to which the fixture is attached, the *first party to file a fixture filing* (*i.e.,* a filing in the local real estate records describing the real property to which the fixture is attached) *or record its real property interest prevails. Exception:* A PMSI secured party who makes a fixture filing within *20 days* after affixation will prevail over any real property interest in the same fixture that was recorded prior to affixation (except a construction mortgage if the goods became fixtures before the completion of construction).

2) **Accessions**

Usually, the general rules for priority (*e.g.,* first to file or perfect, PMSI super-priority) apply to accessions. *Exception:* If the accession (*e.g.,* a new motor) becomes part of a whole that is subject to a security interest perfected by notation on a certificate of title (*e.g.,* a car), the security interest in the whole (the car) has priority over the security interest in the accession (the new motor).

3) **Effect of Fixture or Accession Interest with Priority**

When the security interest in the fixture/accession has priority over all interests in the real property or goods, the holder of the security interest in the fixture/accession may, upon default, remove the fixture/accession from the real property or goods, but she must reimburse any owner of the real property or goods *who is not the debtor* for the cost of any repairs of physical injury to the real property or goods caused by removal (but not for any other diminution in value).

4) **Crops**

A perfected security interest in crops has priority over a conflicting interest in the real property on which the crops are growing, regardless of the time of filing or perfection.

C. SECURED PARTY VS. BUYER OR OTHER TRANSFEREE

1. **Unperfected Secured Party vs. Buyer or Lessee**

A person who buys or leases the collateral from the debtor generally has an interest in the collateral superior to a person who has an unperfected security interest in the collateral if the buyer or lessee, *without knowledge of the security interest*, gives value and receives delivery of the collateral. *Note:* If the collateral is an account, electronic chattel paper, a general intangible, or investment property other than a certificated security, there is *no delivery requirement* because there is nothing tangible to deliver.

a. **PMSI Grace Period Exception**

If a secured party *attaches a PMSI* in the debtor's collateral *before* the buyer or lessee without knowledge pays value and receives delivery (if required), the secured party

will have *priority* over the buyer or lessee if she *files within 20 days* after the *debtor* receives the collateral.

2. **Perfected Secured Party vs. Buyer or Lessee**
Generally, a holder of a perfected security interest in goods has rights in the goods superior to those of a subsequent buyer or lessee. *Exceptions:*

a. If the *secured party consents* to a disposition of the collateral free of the security interest, the transferee takes free of the perfected security interest.

b. A *buyer or lessee in the ordinary course of business* takes free of a nonpossessory perfected security interest in the goods unless the buyer or lessee knows that the sale or lease is in *violation* of the security interest.

c. A *consumer purchaser from a consumer* has priority over PMSIs in consumer goods unless the purchaser knows of the security interest or a financing statement has been filed.

d. A *buyer or lessee not in the ordinary course of business* has priority over future advances or commitments to make future advances made by a secured party either after the secured party learns of the purchase or lease or more than 45 days after the purchase or lease.

3. **Secured Party vs. Holder in Due Course or the Like**
A holder in due course of a negotiable instrument (and similar holders of negotiable documents of title or securities) has *priority* over a security interest in the negotiable instrument.

4. **Secured Party vs. Transferee of Money or Deposit Account Funds**
If a debtor transfers money or deposit account funds (*e.g.,* by writing a check or making an electronic funds transfer) to a person, that person *takes free of any security interest in the money or funds,* unless the transferee acts in collusion with the debtor in violating the rights of the secured party.

D. **SECURED PARTY vs. JUDICIAL LIEN CREDITOR OR HOLDER OF POSSESSORY LIEN**

1. **Unperfected Secured Party vs. Judicial Lien Creditor**
A judicial lien creditor (*i.e.,* a person who has acquired a lien on the collateral through judicial attachment, levy, or the like, or a bankruptcy trustee) prevails over the holder of a security interest in collateral if the lien creditor becomes such *before* the security interest is *perfected*.

a. **PMSI Grace Period Exception**
A secured party who *attaches a PMSI* in the debtor's collateral *before* a judicial lien creditor acquires an interest in the collateral will have *priority* over the judicial lien creditor if she *files within 20 days* after the debtor receives the collateral.

2. **Perfected Secured Party vs. Judicial Lien Creditor**
Generally, a *prior* perfected security interest has priority over a lien.

a. **Exception—Future Advances**
A judicial lien will have priority over a future advance (*i.e.,* an advance of value under an earlier security agreement; *see* II.C.2., *supra*) that was *perfected before* the lien arose but made *more than 45 days after* the lien arose, *unless* the future advance was

made (i) *without knowledge* of the lien, or (ii) *pursuant to a commitment made without knowledge* of the lien.

3. **Secured Party vs. Possessory Lien Holder**

   A possessory lien imposed by other (*i.e.,* non-U.C.C.) state law in favor of those who supply goods or services (*e.g.,* an artisan's lien or a materialman's lien) has priority over a security interest as long as the goods or services were provided in the ordinary course of business and the collateral remains in the lien holder's possession.

E. SECURED PARTY VS. ARTICLE 2 CLAIMANT

If Article 2 grants a buyer or seller a possessory security interest in goods (*e.g.,* if the buyer rightfully revokes acceptance of goods), the Article 2 claimant has priority over an Article 9 secured party as long as the Article 2 claimant retains *possession* of the goods.

F. PRIORITIES IN A NUTSHELL

When a debtor defaults and a number of persons have an interest in the same item of collateral, remember the following hierarchy—the person with the highest priority has first rights in the collateral; if any part of the collateral or its proceeds is left, the next person can recover, etc. Excluding investment property and nonconsumer deposit accounts, in which the party with *control* generally has priority, the ranking is as follows:

1. *Buyer in the ordinary course* of business who does not know the sale is in violation of the security interest.

2. *Holder in due course* and the like of a negotiable instrument.

3. *Transferee of money or funds from deposit accounts*.

4. Certain *purchasers of chattel paper or instruments* who have possession or control.

5. *Possessory lien holder*.

6. *Article 2 claimant with possession* of goods.

7. *PMSI* (except a consumer purchaser from a consumer—such as a neighbor buying from a neighbor—has priority over an *automatically perfected* PMSI in the consumer goods).

8. *Perfected security interests* and *judicial liens that have attached* to the collateral (including *trustees in bankruptcy* as of the date the bankruptcy petition is filed).

   a. As between perfected security interests in the same collateral, the *first to file or perfect* has priority.

   b. As between a perfected security interest and an attached lien, the attached lien generally has priority if it attached before the security interest was perfected. Otherwise, the security interest has priority.

9. *Purchaser* of collateral who *buys for value and receives delivery without notice* of any unperfected security interest.

10. *Unperfected security interests* (rank in priority according to order of attachment).

11. *Debtor*.

barbri

GENERAL HIERARCHY OF INTERESTS IN COLLATERAL

Buyers in Ordinary Course of Business, HDCs, and the Like

prevail over

PMSI Holders with Superpriority

prevail over

Perfected Secured Creditors
Perfected Secured Creditor vs. Perfected Secured Creditor: First to file or perfect wins

Lien Creditors
Perfected Secured Creditor vs. Lien Creditor: First to perfect (security interest) or attach (lien) wins

prevail over

Unperfected Secured Creditors
Unperfected Secured Creditor vs. Unperfected Secured Creditor: First to attach wins

prevail over

Debtor

V. RIGHTS ON DEFAULT

A. DETERMINING WHEN DEFAULT HAS OCCURRED

Article 9 does not define the events that will trigger a default, but the security agreement usually will define default to include events such as failure to pay or maintain insurance. Default on an agricultural lien is determined by the lien statute.

B. RIGHT TO TAKE POSSESSION AND SELL COLLATERAL

1. Taking Possession and Sale

The secured party has the right either: (i) to sue on the debt itself; or (ii) to take possession of the collateral (even without judicial process, if this can be done *without breach of the peace*), sell it by *public or private sale*, and then sue to collect the deficiency. All aspects of the sale must be *commercially reasonable*, and the debtor, any sureties on the debt, and, in nonconsumer goods cases, other secured parties generally are entitled to *notice*. The notice must be sent within a reasonable time before the sale (notice sent 10 days before the sale is deemed reasonable in nonconsumer transactions), and it must contain details about the parties, the collateral, the time and method of sale, etc. The sale gives the buyer whatever rights the debtor had in the collateral and discharges the security interest under which the sale was made and all subordinate security interests.

CMR **Exam Tip** If an exam question raises the issue of the reasonableness of the sale, keep in mind that the secured party must show that he made an effort to obtain the best price for the collateral. The courts will consider, and your answer should discuss, factors such as the following:

(i) The *sufficiency of the advertising*;

(ii) If the collateral had a limited market, whether *people in that market were contacted*;

(iii) Whether the collateral needed *cleaning or repair*; and

(iv) If the sale was by public auction, the *convenience of the time and place*.

Remember, low price alone is not enough to make the sale not commercially reasonable, but if the price is very low, courts will give extra scrutiny to the other circumstances of the sale.

2. Retention of Collateral in Satisfaction of Debt

If the debtor has paid 60% of the cash price on a PMSI in consumer goods, or 60% of the loan on a non-PMSI in consumer goods, the secured party *must* dispose of the collateral within 90 days after repossession, or the debtor may recover it in conversion. With respect to any other collateral, the secured party may propose to retain the collateral in *full satisfaction of the obligation*, but (i) the debtor must consent to the retention in an authenticated record after default or, in cases where the debt is being fully satisfied, not object to the retention within 20 days after notice is sent by the secured party, and (ii) the secured party must send written notice of such proposal to the debtor (and to other secured parties), and if a person entitled to notice objects in writing within 20 days of sending of such notification, the secured party *must* dispose of the collateral and properly disburse the proceeds. *Note:* If the collateral is *nonconsumer goods*, the secured party may retain the goods in *partial satisfaction of the obligation* and seek a *deficiency judgment* for the remainder of the debt if the above requirements are met.

3. **Debtor's Right of Redemption**

Until the secured party has sold the collateral or has discharged the debt by retention of the collateral, the debtor, surety, or any other secured party or lienholder may redeem the collateral by paying all obligations secured by the collateral plus additional reasonable expenses.

4. **Failure to Comply with Code Requirements**

A secured party is liable for actual damages caused by his failure to follow the rules of Article 9. If a secured party violates a Code default requirement and the collateral is consumer goods, the debtor may recover, at a minimum, 10% of the cash price of the goods plus an amount equal to all the interest charges to be paid over the life of the loan. In addition, a secured party who violates the default rules may lose her right to a deficiency judgment. In **nonconsumer transactions,** the *"rebuttable presumption rule"* applies—*i.e.,* unless the secured party proves otherwise, the value of the collateral is presumed to equal the amount of the debt, and a proper sale would have generated enough money to pay off the debt entirely. ***The Code does not provide a rule for consumer transactions,*** and leaves the determination of a rule to the courts. Courts have generally taken three approaches. They either:

a. Follow the above ***rebuttable presumption rule;***

b. Deny the secured party a deficiency regardless of whether the secured party can prove that the collateral is worth less than the debt (the ***"absolute bar rule"***); or

c. Allow the secured party to recover the deficiency minus any actual damages that the debtor can prove (the *"setoff rule"*).

C. OTHER RIGHTS OF SECURED PARTY ON DEFAULT

Instead of taking possession and selling the collateral under Article 9, the secured party on default may bring an ordinary judicial action for the amount due and levy on the collateral after judgment.

D. REMEDIES ARE CUMULATIVE

A secured party's remedies under Article 9 (*i.e.,* sale, strict foreclosure, and judgment) are cumulative. However, the secured party is entitled to only one satisfaction.

VI. JURISDICTIONAL RULES

A. WHICH STATE'S LAW GOVERNS PERFECTION?

The question of which state's law governs the perfection of a security interest is especially important when a security interest is perfected by filing, because filing must occur in the proper state.

1. **General Rule—Law of State Where Debtor Is Located Governs Perfection**

The law of the ***state where the debtor is located*** generally governs perfection of the security interest.

a. **Location of Debtor**

If the debtor is an ***individual,*** she is located in the state of her ***principal residence.*** If the debtor is a *registered organization* (*e.g.,* a corporation, limited liability company, or limited partnership), the debtor is located in the state under whose laws it is *organized* (*i.e.,* where its articles of incorporation are filed). If the debtor is an *unregistered organization* (*e.g.,* a general partnership), it is located at its *place of business* if it only has one place of business or at its *chief executive office* if it has more than one place of business.

2. Exceptions

a. Possessory Security Interests and Security Interests in Fixtures and Timber to Be Cut

The perfection of possessory security interests, as well as security interests in fixtures and timber to be cut, is governed by the law of the *state in which the collateral is located.*

b. Goods Covered by Certificate of Title

If goods are covered by a certificate of title, the law of the *state issuing the most recent certificate of title* governs perfection.

c. Deposit Accounts

If the collateral is a deposit account, unless the debtor's agreements with the bank provide *otherwise,* the law of the *state in which the bank has its chief executive office* governs perfection.

d. Investment Property

If the collateral is a *certificated security,* the law of the *state where the certificated security is located* governs perfection. If the collateral is an *uncertificated security,* unless the debtor's agreements with the issuer provide otherwise, the law of the *state where the issuer was organized* governs perfection. If the collateral is a *securities account,* unless the debtor's agreements with the securities intermediary provide otherwise, the law of the *state where the securities intermediary's chief executive office is located* governs perfection.

1) Exception—Perfection by Filing or Automatic Perfection

If a security interest in investment property *is perfected by filing,* or if it is *automatically perfected* by a securities intermediary, the law of the *state where the debtor is located* governs perfection.

e. Agricultural Liens

The perfection of an agricultural lien is governed by the law of the *state in which the farm product covered by the lien is located.*

B. MOVEMENT OF DEBTOR OR COLLATERAL FROM ONE STATE TO ANOTHER

1. Collateral in Which Perfection Is Governed by Debtor's Location

If the perfection of a security interest is governed by the law of the state in which the *debtor is located,* and the debtor moves from one state to another, the security interest generally will remain perfected without any further action until *four months* after the debtor moves or until perfection in the first state *lapses*, whichever occurs earlier. If the collateral is *transferred*

to a new debtor located in a different state, the security interest will remain perfected without any further action until *one year* after the sale of the collateral or until perfection in the first state *lapses,* whichever occurs earlier.

2. Other Collateral

a. Collateral in Which Security Interest Is Perfected by Possession

If a perfected security interest in collateral is a *possessory* security interest (which is governed by the law of the state in which the *collateral is located*), and the collateral is moved from one state to another, the security interest will remain perfected without any further action as long as the security interest is also perfected by possession under the laws of the *new* state.

b. Certificate of Title Property (Automobiles and Other Vehicles)

If a vehicle is moved from one state to another, and is covered by a certificate of title issued by the new state, a security interest in the vehicle that was properly perfected in the original state *lasts as long as it would have if the vehicle had not been covered by the new certificate of title*.

1) Exception—Purchasers for Value

If a vehicle subject to a perfected security interest in one state is moved to a new state and is covered by a certificate of title issued by the new state, the security interest in the original state is perfected as against a *purchaser for value* of the vehicle only until the *earlier* of:

a) The time when the security interest would have become *unperfected* in the original state if the vehicle had not been covered by the new certificate of title (same rule as the general rule); *or*

b) *Four months* after the vehicle is covered by the new certificate of title.

2) Exception—Clean Certificate of Title Issued in New State

If the certificate of title issued in the new state *does not note the secured party's interest* in the vehicle, the following parties have priority over the secured party:

a) A *buyer* of the vehicle who is not in the business of selling vehicles who purchases for *value* and receives *delivery* of the vehicle *without knowledge* of the security interest; and

b) A *secured party* who *perfects* a security interest in the vehicle *without knowledge* of the other security interest *after* the clean certificate of title is issued in the new state.

c. Deposit Accounts, Uncertificated Securities, and Securities Accounts

If the bank, issuer, or securities intermediary moves to a new state, perfection of an interest in the deposit account, uncertificated security, or securities account *continues until the earlier of:*

1) The time when the security interest would have become **unperfected** in the original state if the bank, issuer, or securities intermediary had not moved to the new state; **or**

2) **Four months** after the bank, issuer, or securities intermediary moves to the new state.

TRUSTS

TABLE OF CONTENTS

TRUSTS

I. INTRODUCTION

For purposes of the bar exam, you will need to be familiar with the common law of trusts, on which this outline is based. However, references to the Uniform Trust Code ("UTC"), enacted in nearly half the states, will be made throughout the outline to highlight some of the reforms contained therein.

II. EXPRESS PRIVATE TRUSTS

A. CHARACTERISTICS OF AN EXPRESS TRUST

A trust is a fiduciary relationship with respect to specific property (*res*) wherein the *trustee* holds legal title to the property subject to enforceable equitable rights of the *beneficiary*. The creator of the trust is the *settlor*, who must have had the *intent* to create the trust. The trust must have a valid *trust purpose*. No consideration is required.

1. Intention to Create a Trust

The settlor's intention to create a trust is essential to the existence of an express trust. Intent may be manifested by written or spoken words or by the conduct of the settlor—unless the Statute of Wills or the Statute of Frauds applies. An oral trust of *personal* property is valid. Communication of intent to the beneficiaries is not necessary; delivery of the deed to the trustee is sufficient—unless the settlor is also the trustee, in which case he must segregate trust assets or otherwise show trust intent.

a. Must Be Manifested While Settlor Owns Property and Prior to Conveyance

An intention to create a present trust must have been externally manifested by the settlor *at the time he owned property* and prior to its conveyance to another. (However, the conduct of the parties subsequent to the conveyance may be evidence of an earlier intent.)

1) Must Intend Trust Take Effect Immediately

The settlor's intent must be that the trust take effect immediately, not at some future time—although a future interest can be trust property.

b. Precatory Expressions

A settlor's expression of a hope, wish, or mere suggestion that the property be used in a certain way is called precatory language. The usual inference is that precatory expressions *do not create a trust*. This inference can be overcome by:

1) *Definite and precise* directions;

2) Directions addressed to a *fiduciary* (*e.g.*, executor under a will);

3) A resulting *"unnatural" disposition* of property (*e.g.*, close relative will otherwise take nothing) if no trust imposed; or

4) Extrinsic evidence showing that the settlor *previously supported* the intended beneficiary.

2. **Trustee**
Once established, a trust will not fail because the trustee dies, refuses to accept appointment, or resigns. The court will appoint a successor trustee unless it is clear that the settlor intended the trust to continue only so long as a particular trustee served. The absence of a trustee may cause an attempted inter vivos trust to fail for lack of delivery.

a. **Trustee Must Have Duties**
A "passive trust" (where trustee has no duties) is void, and the beneficiaries take legal title. In many jurisdictions, the duty to convey title to the beneficiaries is enough to make the trust "active."

b. **Qualifications of Trustee**
Anyone who has capacity to acquire and hold property for his own benefit and has capacity to administer the trust may be a trustee. (Minors and insane persons can hold property, but cannot administer.) State statutes limit the right of some persons or corporations to serve as trustee (*e.g.*, foreign corporations).

c. **Removal of Trustee**
A court can remove a trustee or refuse to confirm an appointment. Grounds for removal include: serious breach of trust, old age, habitual drunkenness, conflict of interest, etc. The basic factor considered is whether continuation in office would be detrimental to the trust. If the settlor knew of the grounds for removal at the time she created the trust, the court may choose not to remove the trustee.

1) **Beneficiaries Must Have Grounds to Remove**
Absent grounds, beneficiaries cannot remove the trustee *unless* the power is specifically granted to them by the trust instrument.

d. **Disclaimer or Resignation by Trustee**
Before acceptance, a trustee can disclaim or refuse appointment for any reason. However, a trustee cannot accept a trust in part and disclaim it in part.

1) **Relation Back of Acceptance**
A testamentary trust is treated as in existence as of the settlor's death, and the trustee's acceptance "relates back" to that date. It is thus possible for a trustee, by accepting, to become liable (in his fiduciary capacity) on tort claims arising prior to the time he accepted.

2) **Resignation**
Once an appointment has been accepted, the trustee cannot resign without court permission, *unless* all beneficiaries consent or the trust provides otherwise.

e. **Merger of Title Where Sole Trustee Is Also Sole Beneficiary**
If the sole trustee and sole beneficiary are the same individual and hold precisely the same interests, titles merge and the trust terminates.

3. **Trust Property**

a. **No Res—No Trust**
Where there is no trust property, the trust fails because the trustee has no property to manage.

b. **Trust Property Must Be Existing Interest in Existing Property**
A future interest may be held in trust, but an interest not yet in legal existence (*i.e.*, a mere expectancy) cannot be held in trust. Future profits from an existing contract can be a trust res.

c. **Property that Settlor Has Power to Convey Can Be Subject of Trust**
The trust res must be existing property that the settlor has the power to convey, including intangibles (*e.g.*, promissory notes) in which the settlor has an assignable interest.

d. **Trust Res Must Be Segregated from Other Property**
The res must be identifiable and segregated, but the res may be a fractional or undivided interest in specific property.

e. **Debtor Cannot Hold Own Debt in Trust**
A debtor cannot hold his own debt in trust, but the debtor can declare himself trustee of particular property from which the debt is to be paid; and the debt can be held in trust by another person.

f. **Unenforceable Gratuitous Promise Cannot Be Trust Res**
An unenforceable gratuitous promise cannot be the subject of a trust.

4. **Beneficiaries**
A trust cannot exist without someone to enforce it. Thus, a beneficiary is necessary to the validity of every trust except charitable and honorary trusts (*see* III.C., G., *infra*).

a. **Capacity**
Any person, natural or artificial, capable of taking and holding title to property can be a beneficiary of a private trust.

b. **Incidental and Indirect Beneficiaries**
Not everyone who benefits from a trust is considered to be a beneficiary. The trust must operate **directly** to benefit the person (*e.g.*, attorney designated by trust instrument is not beneficiary).

c. **Notice to and Acceptance by Beneficiary**
Notice to a beneficiary is not essential to the validity of a trust. Lack of such notice may indicate, however, that no trust was intended. Acceptance by the beneficiary is required, but can take place after a valid trust is created. Acceptance may be express or implied and is generally presumed. However, the trust will not be forced on a beneficiary, and he may within a reasonable time renounce his rights thereunder.

d. **Definiteness of Beneficiaries Under Private Trust**
There must be definite beneficiaries in order to have a private trust (not required in charitable trusts).

1) **Unascertained Beneficiaries**
Beneficiaries may be "definite" even though not yet ascertained (*e.g.*, unborn beneficiaries). Beneficiaries must be **ascertainable** by the time their interests are to come into enjoyment. Acts of independent legal significance and incorporation by reference may be relied upon to ascertain beneficiaries.

2) Class Gifts

If a private trust exists for the benefit of a class, the class must be ***reasonably definite***. As long as the class is reasonably definite, the trust may authorize the trustee to exercise his discretion in selecting members to be benefited, or may provide that only those who meet certain requirements will benefit. Broad power to choose beneficiaries, however, may constitute a gift or a power of appointment rather than a trust.

e. Resulting Trust Remedy

If a trust fails for lack of a beneficiary, a resulting trust in favor of the settlor or his successors is presumed.

5. Trust Purposes

A trust purpose is invalid if: (i) it is illegal, (ii) its performance requires a criminal or tortious act, or (iii) it is otherwise contrary to public policy (*e.g.*, encourages immorality). If a ***condition*** attached to an interest is against public policy:

a. The ***settlor's alternative*** desire controls if expressed.

b. If the illegal condition is a condition ***subsequent***, the condition is invalidated but the trust is valid.

c. If the illegal condition is a condition ***precedent***, the preferred view is to hold the interest valid unless there is evidence that the settlor's wish would be to void the beneficiary's interest altogether if the condition is unenforceable.

ELEMENTS OF VALID PRIVATE TRUST

To determine whether a valid private trust has been created, look for the following characteristics:

☑ ***Intent*** to create a trust (manifested by settlor's words, writing, or conduct)

☑ ***Trustee*** (inter vivos trusts only; a testamentary trust will not fail for lack of a trustee)

☑ ***Trust property*** (res)

☑ ***Definite beneficiary(ies)*** (*Note:* Same person cannot be ***sole*** trustee and ***sole*** beneficiary)

☑ ***Valid trust purpose*** (one that is not illegal, tortious, or against public policy)

B. CREATION OF EXPRESS TRUSTS

A trust can be created by inter vivos transfer, by inter vivos declaration of trust, or by will (testamentary trust).

1. **Inter Vivos Trusts**

   a. **Present Declaration or Transfer of Trust Required**
   A trust can be created either by a person declaring himself trustee for another or by the transfer of property to another as trustee. The present intent required must be manifested by conduct (delivery) or words (declaring oneself trustee). Delivery means placing the trust property out of the settlor's control (unless the settlor serves as trustee).

   CMR **Exam Tip**   Failure to name a trustee, or a promise to name a trustee in the future, may evidence a lack of present intent and prevent delivery of the res.

   1) **Must Manifest Intent When Trust Res Exists**
   If a present trust is not established because there is no trust res, the trust arises when the settlor subsequently acquires the res and remanifests trust intent.

   b. **Formal Requirements—Statute of Frauds**

   1) **Writing Required for Trusts of Land**
   Most states do not require a writing for a trust of *personal property*. For a trust of *land*, however, a written instrument signed by the person entitled to impress the trust upon the property is commonly required under the Statute of Frauds. Note that an otherwise invalid oral trust of land may be enforced by imposing a *constructive trust* (*see* VIII.C.5., *infra*).

   2) **Parol Evidence Rule**
   Most states allow extrinsic evidence where an ambiguity appears on the face of the writing.

2. **Testamentary Trusts**

   a. **Formalities**
   Trust intent and the essential terms of the trust (trust res, beneficiaries, and trust purpose) must be ascertained from the will itself, from a writing incorporated by reference into the will, from facts having independent legal significance, or from the exercise of a power of appointment created by the will.

   b. **"Secret" and "Semi-Secret" Trusts**

   1) **"Secret Trust"—Constructive Trust Imposed**
   Where a will makes a gift that is absolute on its face, but was in fact made in reliance on the beneficiary's promise to hold the property in trust for another, the intended trust beneficiary may present extrinsic evidence of the promise. If the promise can be proven by *clear and convincing evidence*, a constructive trust will be imposed on the property in favor of the intended trust beneficiary.

   CMR **Exam Tip**   Keep in mind that a constructive trust will be imposed in the above case even if the will beneficiary did not make the promise until *after* the will was executed. Furthermore, it does not matter whether the will beneficiary *intended* to perform the promise when he made it; all that matters is that the testator *relied* on the promise.

2) **"Semi-Secret Trust"—Resulting Trust Implied**
In a semi-secret trust, the will makes a gift in trust but fails to name the beneficiary. The gift fails, and the named trustee holds the property on a resulting trust for the testator's heirs.

SECRET VS. SEMI-SECRET TESTAMENTARY TRUST

Secret Trust	Semi-Secret Trust
Absolute gift in will made in reliance on beneficiary's promise to hold the property in trust for another	Gift in will to a person "in trust," but does not name trust beneficiary
Extrinsic evidence admitted	Extrinsic evidence not allowed
Constructive trust imposed in favor of intended beneficiary	"Trustee" holds on resulting trust for testator's legatees or heirs

III. CHARITABLE AND HONORARY TRUSTS

A. DISTINCTIVE RULES APPLY TO CHARITABLE TRUSTS
The rules governing charitable trusts differ from those applicable to private trusts in three important ways: a charitable trust must have *indefinite beneficiaries*, it may be *perpetual*, and the *cy pres doctrine* applies.

B. TRUST MUST BE FOR CHARITABLE PURPOSES
A charitable trust must have a purpose considered to benefit the public. Charitable purposes include the relief of poverty; the advancement of knowledge, education, or religion; the promotion of health; and the accomplishment of governmental purposes (*e.g.,* parks and museums). The class to be benefited may be limited, but may not be so narrow as to only benefit a few individuals whom the settlor wishes to aid personally.

C. BENEFICIARIES MUST BE INDEFINITE
Beneficiaries of a charitable trust must be indefinite.

D. ENFORCING CHARITABLE TRUSTS
In many states, the settlor and potential beneficiaries have no standing to enforce the terms of a charitable trust. The duty of enforcement is placed upon the state *attorney general*. Under the UTC, however, the settlor and qualified beneficiaries (*i.e.,* current beneficiaries and first-line remaindermen) *have standing* to enforce the trust.

E. RULE AGAINST PERPETUITIES

A charitable trust may be perpetual. Also, the Rule Against Perpetuities does not apply to the shifting of the beneficial interest in a trust from one charity to another on the happening of a condition. The Rule *does* apply, however, to shifts between private and charitable uses.

F. CY PRES

When a charitable purpose selected by the settlor is impracticable, the court will select an alternative under the doctrine of cy pres, which means *"as near as possible."* The court must find a general charitable intent on the part of the settlor and ascertain her primary purpose.

G. HONORARY TRUSTS

Honorary trusts are commonly established for the benefit of pets or for the maintenance of burial places. Because there is no human beneficiary to enforce an honorary trust, the trustee is "on her honor" to carry out its terms. Courts uphold honorary trusts as long as the named trustee is *willing* to perform her duties; failing this, a resulting trust is imposed. Absent special statutes, many jurisdictions will void an honorary trust on the basis of the Rule Against Perpetuities if its duration may be more than a (human) life in being plus 21 years. Under the UTC, honorary trusts *are enforceable* up to 21 years by someone named in the trust instrument or appointed by the court. The UTC also recognizes trusts for the care of an animal alive during the settlor's lifetime, which terminate when the animal dies.

1. Constructional Outs

To avoid the perpetuities problem, some courts use constructional outs to save the gift, such as by holding that: (i) the trust is personal to the named trustee; and/or (ii) because the fund will be exhausted within the perpetuities period, it cannot last beyond the period and does not violate the Rule.

IV. TRANSFER OF THE BENEFICIARY'S INTEREST

A. ALIENABILITY IN GENERAL

1. Voluntary Alienation

Absent restrictions by statute or by the trust instrument, a beneficiary may freely transfer his interest in the trust. The assigned interest remains subject to all previous conditions and limitations.

2. Involuntary Alienation

Absent restrictions by statute or by the trust instrument, an insolvent trust beneficiary's creditors may levy on his beneficial interest. The interest is subject to judicial sale. To avoid this, a court may order the trustee to pay the beneficiary's income to the creditors until the debt is satisfied.

B. RESTRAINTS ON ALIENATION—SPENDTHRIFT TRUSTS

A spendthrift trust precludes the beneficiary from voluntarily or involuntarily transferring his interest in the trust, and his creditors are precluded from reaching it to satisfy their claims. The purpose is to protect the beneficiary from his own improvidence. Although a spendthrift trust is a restraint on alienation, most courts uphold spendthrift restrictions.

1. **Rights of Creditors**
   A beneficiary's creditors cannot reach his interest until income has been paid to him.

2. **Restraint on Involuntary Alienation Only—Invalid**
   A restriction permitting the beneficiary to voluntarily alienate his interest, but purporting to deny creditors the right to reach the beneficiary's interest, is probably invalid.

3. **Attempted Assignment in Violation of Spendthrift Provision**
   A beneficiary's assignees cannot force the trustee to pay them (although the trustee can do so if the beneficiary has not repudiated the trustee's authorization to pay assignees).

4. **Exception—Settlor as Beneficiary**
   A spendthrift provision is invalid if the settlor is the beneficiary (the settlor cannot protect his own retained interests from his creditors).

   CMR **Exam Tip** When it is unclear whether a beneficiary is the settlor, determine who *furnished the consideration* for the creation of the trust. If a person furnishes the consideration, he is the settlor even though the trust is created by another person.

5. **Exceptions for Special Classes of Creditors**
   Many states allow certain classes of creditors (*e.g.,* dependents, furnishers of necessities) to reach a beneficiary's assets notwithstanding a spendthrift restraint.

C. DISCRETIONARY TRUSTS

Where a trustee is given discretion whether to apply or withhold payments to the beneficiary, the beneficiary's creditors or assignees have the same rights as the beneficiary. They take only if the trustee exercises his discretion to pay, unless the beneficiary's interest is also protected by a spendthrift restriction. (But where the settlor is the discretionary beneficiary, his creditors *can* compel payments.) A court will intervene where a trustee abuses his discretion.

D. SUPPORT TRUSTS

A support trust directs the trustee to pay only so much of the income or principal (or both) as is necessary for the beneficiary's support. The interest of the beneficiary cannot be assigned or reached by creditors. It is a question of the settlor's *intent* as to whether the beneficiary's other resources should be considered in determining the amount payable to him out of the trust fund.

V. MODIFICATION AND TERMINATION OF TRUSTS

A. TERMINATION OF TRUST BY ITS OWN TERMS

A trust terminates automatically upon the expiration of the term specified in the instrument or when all of the purposes of the trust have been accomplished.

B. POWER OF SETTLOR TO REVOKE OR MODIFY

The power to revoke generally also includes the power to amend. In many states, the settlor may not revoke or amend a trust unless he expressly reserved that right. Under the UTC and by statute in several non-UTC states, a trust is *presumed revocable* unless the trust instrument expressly provides that it is irrevocable.

C. MODIFICATION OR TERMINATION BY AGREEMENT OF BENEFICIARIES

Beneficiaries may compel modification or termination only when *all consent*, and the modification or termination will *not frustrate any material trust purpose*, such as protecting a beneficiary from lack of ability to manage property.

1. Liability of Trustee

Where *all* beneficiaries consent to termination, the trustee is not liable if he accommodates them by distributing the trust assets.

2. Role of Settlor in Terminating Inter Vivos Trust

As long as the beneficiaries have a right to terminate, the settlor's objections are not a bar (but may be evidence as to whether termination would defeat trust purposes). However, joinder of the settlor may be deemed a waiver of a material purpose that would otherwise block termination.

D. JUDICIAL POWER TO TERMINATE OR MODIFY TRUST

1. Premature Termination

A court may prematurely terminate the trust where the trust's purpose has become *impossible or illegal* or has been *completed*.

2. Doctrine of Changed Circumstances

A court may also, upon a change of circumstances unanticipated by the settlor, authorize a deviation from the *administrative terms* where necessary to achieve the trust purpose. Such changes may not deprive the beneficiaries of their interests in the income or corpus; however, where the primary purpose of the trust was to support the income beneficiary, modern statutes have given the court power to invade the corpus. In addition, a court can accelerate vested rights.

VI. TRUST ADMINISTRATION

A. POWERS OF THE TRUSTEE

1. Sources of Trustee's Power

A trustee has those powers *expressly* conferred by the trust instrument, state law, and court decree plus all powers *implied* as are necessary or appropriate to accomplish the trust purposes. The UTC confers even broader powers on the trustee. Powers normally attach to the office and pass to successor trustees, *i.e.*, they are not personal.

2. Joint Powers

Under the traditional view, joint trustees must exercise their power by *unanimous* agreement. Today, in nearly half the states, any power vested in three or more trustees may be exercised by a *majority* of them.

3. Imperative and Discretionary Powers

A power is "imperative" if the trust instrument requires its exercise. "Discretionary" powers are ones that the trustee may or may not perform. Both are subject to judicial review for

abuse of discretion. A trustee is not immune from review even if given "uncontrolled" discretion, and the court will intervene if the trustee fails to exercise any judgment at all.

4. Implied Powers
Implied powers include such things as are necessary to operate the trust (*e.g.,* power of sale, to invest, to meet expenses, to lease land). Normally, a trustee has *no* implied power to borrow money, or to mortgage or otherwise encumber trust property. However, such powers are expressly conferred by the UTC.

B. DUTIES OF THE TRUSTEE

1. Standard of Care Required of Trustee
The trustee must exercise that degree of care, skill, and caution that would be exercised by a *reasonably prudent person* in managing her own property. And, if the trustee has greater or special skill, she will be held to a higher standard.

2. Duty of Loyalty
Absent court approval or express waiver in the trust instrument, a trustee cannot enter into any transaction in which she is dealing with the trust in her individual capacity. A trustee owes a *duty of undivided loyalty* to the trust and its beneficiaries.

(i) A trustee *cannot buy or sell trust assets* even if the price is a fair one.

(ii) A trustee *may not sell property of one trust to another trust* of which she is also trustee.

(iii) A trustee *may not borrow trust funds nor loan her personal funds* to the trust, and any interest paid on such a loan must be returned to the trust.

(iv) A trustee *cannot use trust assets to secure a personal loan*.

(v) A trustee *cannot personally gain* through her position as trustee.

(vi) A corporate trustee *cannot invest in its own stock* as a trust investment. But it can *retain* its own stock if such stock was a part of the original trust res when the trust was established, provided that retention of the stock meets the prudent investor standard.

(vii) *Self-employment* can constitute a form of prohibited dealing. However, if the trustee renders extraordinary services to the trust, she may be entitled to additional compensation.

CMR | **Exam Tip** | When faced with a question involving a self-dealing trustee, remember that a trustee's good faith or actual benefit to the trust is irrelevant.

a. Indirect Self-Dealing
The above self-dealing rules also apply to sales or loans to a trustee's relatives and business associates, and to corporations of which the trustee is a director, officer, or principal shareholder.

b. Duty to Account
The duty to keep and render accounts ensures that the trustee is meeting her obligation of loyalty.

DUTIES OF THE TRUSTEE

CMR
SUMMARY
CHART

Duties	Definition	Examples of Breach	Remedy
Loyalty	Trustee cannot represent both her personal interest and the interest of the trust; *i.e.,* **no self-dealing**	Buying or selling trust assets for self or another trust; borrowing from or making loans to trust; personal gain through position as trustee; etc.	Beneficiary may recover any profit from trustee, affirm the transaction, or set aside the transaction
Separate and Earmark Property	Trust assets must be kept physically separate from trustee's personal assets and assets of other trusts; *i.e.,* **no commingling**	Placing personal and trust funds in same account	Trustee is liable for any resulting loss; property lost or destroyed is presumed trustee's, and any increase in value in commingled property belongs to trust
Perform Personally	Trustee must personally perform functions that a reasonably prudent person would **not** delegate	Delegation of entire administration of trust	Trustee is liable for the amount of actual loss to trust
Preserve and Make Trust Property Productive	Trustee must use reasonable care to invest the property (**prudent investor rule**), collect claims due, lease or manage land, record documents, pay taxes, and secure insurance	Failure to diversify in making investments; failure to obtain reasonable yield on investments; failure to promptly review investments; failure to insure property; etc.	Trustee is liable for losses resulting from breach and for any profit that would have accrued to the trust but for the breach, plus interest

    c.   **Duty Extends to All Beneficiaries**
The duty of loyalty extends equally to all beneficiaries, unless the trust instrument specifies otherwise.

    d.   **Beneficiary's Rights in Case of Prohibited Transaction**
If a prohibited transaction takes place, the beneficiary may: (i) *set aside* the transaction, (ii) *recover any profit* made by the trustee, or (iii) *affirm* the transaction.

3.   **Duty to Separate and Earmark Trust Property—No Commingling**
A trustee must keep trust assets physically separate from other assets. Trust property must be titled in the trustee as trustee for a specific trust. If the trustee commingles trust assets with her own and some of the property is lost or destroyed, it is presumed that the property lost was the *trustee's*, and the property still on hand belongs to the *trust*. Also, if a portion of commingled assets increases in value and a portion of the commingled assets decreases in value, it is presumed that it was the *trustee's* assets that decreased in value and the *trust's* assets that increased in value.

4.   **Duty to Perform Personally (Prohibition on Delegation of Duties)**
A trustee may only delegate acts that would be *unreasonable* to require her to perform personally; she may never delegate the entire administration of a trust.

    a.   **Investment and Management Decisions**
Traditionally, investment decisions could not be delegated, but under the Uniform Prudent Investor Act ("UPIA"), a trustee may delegate investment and management functions that a prudent trustee of comparable skills could properly delegate under the circumstances.

    b.   **Remedy**
If a trustee improperly limits or surrenders her control, she becomes a *guarantor* of the fund and is responsible for actual losses, no matter what the cause of the loss.

5.   **Duty to Defend Trust from Attack**
A trustee owes a duty to defend the trust from legal attack unless examination reveals that the challenge is well-founded.

6.   **Duty to Preserve Trust Property and Make It Productive**
The power to invest is normally implied from the duty to make trust property productive. The trustee is expected to take actions to, *e.g.,* lease land, collect claims, and invest money. The measure of damages for breach of this duty is the amount of income that would normally accrue from proper investments.

C.   **INVESTMENTS**
A trustee's investment responsibilities are governed by either the UPIA or statutory "legal lists." Regardless of the approach used by a state, the trust terms can expand or limit the trustee's powers—UPIA or legal list provisions apply only if there is no contrary provision in the trust instrument. If the trust instrument provides that investments may be made in the trustee's discretion, it is a question of interpretation whether the trustee's power is expanded beyond the UPIA

or legal list. Although the investment power may be broadened, such language will be strictly construed.

CMR **Exam Tip** In a *"prudent investor"* jurisdiction, only prudent investments are permissible regardless of the trust's terms. In a *"legal list"* jurisdiction, however, trust language giving the trustee broad discretion is likely to free the trustee from the list and permit investment similar to that under the prudent investor rule.

1. Uniform Prudent Investor Act

a. Standard of Care
A trustee must exercise *reasonable care, skill, and caution* when investing and managing trust assets. A trustee with special skills or expertise, or who has represented herself as having such knowledge, has a duty to use such skills or expertise.

b. Loyalty and Impartiality
A trustee must act exclusively for the beneficiary when investing and managing trust assets. If there is more than one beneficiary, she must act impartially in investing and managing the trust assets.

c. Prudence Evaluated as to Overall Investment Strategy
Investment decisions must be evaluated in the context of the *entire trust portfolio* (corpus) and as part of an *overall investment strategy* that has risk and return objectives reasonably suited to the particular trust.

d. Any Type of Investment Permitted
The UPIA permits a trustee to invest in *any kind of property or any type of investment* provided she acts prudently; no particular type of investment is inherently imprudent.

e. Factors Considered in Making Investment Decisions
The following circumstances are relevant and must be considered by the trustee in making investment decisions: (i) general economic conditions; (ii) the possible effect of inflation or deflation; (iii) the expected tax consequences of investment decisions or strategies; (iv) the role that each investment plays within the overall trust portfolio; (v) the expected total return from income and the appreciation of capital; (vi) other resources of the beneficiaries; (vii) needs for liquidity, regularity of income, and preservation or appreciation of capital; and (viii) an asset's special relationship or value to the purposes of the trust or to one or more of the beneficiaries.

f. Diversification of Investments
A trustee must diversify the investments of the trust unless she reasonably determines that the purposes of the trust are better served without diversification.

g. Reviewing Compliance with Act
Compliance with the UPIA is determined in light of the facts and circumstances existing *at the time of the trustee's decision or action*. A trustee who acts in substantial compliance with the Act will not be held liable.

h. Delegation of Investment and Management Functions Permitted
A trustee may delegate investment and management functions but must act prudently in

(i) *selecting* an agent; (ii) *establishing the scope and terms* of the delegation; and (iii) *periodically reviewing* the agent's actions.

2. **Statutory Legal Lists**

Statutory "legal lists" set forth approved investments for trust assets. If the list is "permissive," the trustee can invest in securities outside the list. If the list is "mandatory," the trustee probably commits a breach of trust if he invests in properties outside the list. Under either type of statutory list, the trustee cannot blindly follow the list; he must exercise reasonable care, skill, and caution in investing while taking into account all relevant circumstances. Proper investments include government securities, first mortgages on land with adequate security, and high grade corporate bonds.

a. **Unsecured Loans and Second Mortgages**

Unsecured loans and second mortgages are generally improper investments.

b. **Corporate Stocks**

Most statutory lists exclude common and preferred stocks.

c. **Land**

Courts are divided on whether investment in land is proper. Unproductive land is not a proper investment.

d. **Investment Arrangements**

Mortgage participations, common trust funds, and mutual funds are increasingly permitted by statute.

e. **Testator's Business**

A trustee cannot carry on the testator's business unless expressly authorized by the trust.

D. **SUMMARY—THE FIDUCIARY OBLIGATION**

Standards imposed on the trustee are harsh and designed to deter wrongful conduct and to ease the burden of proving a breach of duty. Ask yourself:

1. Was the act one that the trustee was authorized to perform by the instrument, by state law, or by implication?

2. If the act was proper to perform, did the trustee do so with the appropriate care, skill, and caution?

E. **LIABILITIES OF TRUSTEE**

1. **Enforcement by Beneficiaries**

Beneficiaries may seek damages or removal of the trustee for breach of duty. The settlor may sue if he is also a beneficiary, but outsiders cannot enforce the trust. The trustee is liable for losses resulting from breach, lost profits to the trust, and interest on her liability from the time of breach. Prior to actual breach, a court of equity will compel the trustee to perform her duties and enjoin her from committing breach.

a. **Defenses**

Equity will not enforce the trust if the beneficiaries consented to or joined in the breach

of trust. The beneficiary must sue within a reasonable time or he will be estopped by the doctrine of laches. Mere failure to object at time of breach, however, does not constitute consent.

2. **More than One Breach of Trust—Losses Cannot Be Offset**
A trustee is not permitted to offset loss from one breach by gain that resulted from another breach.

3. **Trustee's Liability for the Acts of Others**

   a. **Agents**
   A trustee will be liable for the acts of her agents if she: (i) directs, permits, or acquiesces in the act, conceals the act, or fails to compel the agent to redress his wrong; (ii) improperly selects or improperly delegates; or (iii) fails to exercise reasonable supervision over the agent.

   b. **Co-Trustees**
   A trustee will be liable for acts of a co-trustee if she: (i) approved, acquiesced, or participated in the breach or negligently disregarded her own duties; (ii) concealed the breach or failed to take steps to compel redress; or (iii) improperly delegated authority to the co-trustee.

   c. **Predecessor Trustees**
   A trustee will be liable for a predecessor trustee's breach if she: (i) knew or should have known of the breach and failed to compel redress, or (ii) was negligent in determining what property should have been delivered to her.

   d. **Successor Trustees**
   Successor trustees can maintain the same actions as the original trustee.

4. **Effect of Exculpatory Clauses**
Clauses attempting to relieve a trustee of liability for breach of trust generally are strictly construed, but are enforceable where (i) no bad faith, intentional breach, or recklessness is involved; or (ii) they were not inserted in the trust as a result of the trustee's abuse of a confidential relationship with the settlor. Clauses absolving the trustee from *all* liability, however, are void.

5. **Trustee's Liability to Third Parties**

   a. **Contract Liability**
   Unless the contract specifically provides otherwise, a trustee is personally liable to third parties on contracts made in the course of trust administration. A trustee is entitled to reimbursement (*indemnification*) from the trust, however, if the contract was within her powers and she acted with reasonable prudence.

   b. **Tort Liability**
   A trustee is personally liable for torts committed in the course of the trust administration, including those committed by the trustee's agents. There is indemnification only if the trustee was not personally at fault or the tort occurred as a normal incident to activity in which the trustee was properly engaged. If the trustee is entitled to indemnification, creditors to whom she is liable can reach trust assets to satisfy claims.

F. LIABILITY OF THIRD PARTIES TO THE TRUST

1. Property Improperly Transferred to Party Who Is Not Bona Fide Purchaser
A beneficiary or successor trustee can set aside transactions that are breaches of trust if the property is not in the hands of a bona fide purchaser ("BFP").

2. Transfer to BFP Cuts Off Beneficiaries' Interests
A BFP "cuts off" the beneficiaries' equitable interests. A third party is a BFP if he acquires the property for value and without notice of the trust. A person who knows of facts requiring an inquiry, which if pursued would have revealed the existence of a trust, is not a BFP. An innocent donee of trust property is not liable for damages but must restore the property, its value, or its substitute to the trust.

3. Participation in Breach of Trust
A knowing participant in a breach of trust is liable for the resulting loss to the trust estate.

4. Direct Suit by Beneficiaries
Direct suits by beneficiaries are not permitted against third parties who damage trust property; the trustee alone can sue. The beneficiaries' remedy is to bring suit in equity to compel the trustee to sue the third party.

a. Exceptions
Direct actions by beneficiaries against third parties are permitted where the trustee: (i) participated in the breach, (ii) has left the jurisdiction and no successor trustee is appointed, or (iii) fails to sue a third person liable in tort or contract.

G. ALLOCATION OF RECEIPTS AND EXPENSES BETWEEN INCOME AND PRINCIPAL ACCOUNTS

1. Uniform Principal and Income Act
A majority of states have enacted the Uniform Principal and Income Act ("UPAIA"). This Act, which applies to *all trusts and estates* unless the governing instrument provides otherwise, gives the trustee or personal representative an *adjustment power* to reallocate investment portfolio return. This adjustment power authorizes the trustee to characterize items such as capital gains, stock dividends, etc., as income if the trustee deems it appropriate or necessary to carry out the trust purposes.

a. Duty of Fairness to All Beneficiaries
The trustee is under a *duty to administer the trust impartially*, except to the extent that the trust or the will manifests an intent that one or more of the beneficiaries is to be favored over the others.

b. Adjustment Power
If the trust calls for distribution of trust income to a beneficiary, the trustee must follow traditional trust accounting rules by distributing interest and dividend income, etc., to the beneficiary. If the resulting distribution effectuates the settlor's intent and the purposes of the trust, then nothing further needs to be done. If, however, the trustee determines that by distributing only the trust's income she is unable to comply with the requirement that all beneficiaries be treated fairly, the trustee may adjust between principal and income to the extent necessary.

borbri

c. **Factors to Be Considered**
In deciding whether and to what extent to exercise the adjustment power, the trustee must consider the following factors: (i) the nature, purpose, and expected duration of the trust; (ii) the intent of the settlor; (iii) the identity and circumstances of the beneficiaries; (iv) the needs for liquidity, regularity of income, and preservation and appreciation of capital; (v) the nature of the trust's assets; (vi) the net amount allocated to income under the other sections of the Act and the increase or decrease in the value of the principal assets; (vii) whether and to what extent the trust gives or denies the trustee the power to invade principal or accumulate income; (viii) the actual and anticipated effect of economic conditions on principal and income and effects of inflation and deflation; and (ix) the anticipated tax consequences of an adjustment.

d. **Adjustment Not Permitted If Result Would Be Adverse Tax Consequences**
The trustee may not make an adjustment if the trustee is a beneficiary of the trust, as this would give the beneficiary a general power of appointment for estate tax purposes, and the trust assets would be taxed in the beneficiary's estate. Also, an adjustment cannot be made if the adjustment power would disqualify the trust for a federal estate tax marital or charitable deduction.

2. **Allocation of Receipts**
In general, the allocation rules follow traditional accounting rules; *e.g.*, net rental income is income and the proceeds of sale of a trust asset are principal.

a. **Receipts from Entity**
Money received from an entity such as a corporation (*e.g.*, cash dividends) is characterized as income unless the money is characterized as a capital gain for federal income tax purposes, or is received in partial or total liquidation of the entity. *All property other than money* received from an entity (*e.g.*, stock dividends) is characterized as principal.

b. **Insurance Policies and Other Contracts**
Proceeds from a life insurance policy or other contract in which the trust or trustee is named beneficiary are allocated to principal. If a contract insures the trustee against a type of loss, the proceeds are allocated to income. Dividends on an insurance policy are allocated to the account from which the premiums are paid.

c. **Deferred Compensation—Ten Percent Default Rule**
For periodic receipts from a deferred compensation plan (*e.g.*, pension plan), the receipt is income to the extent that the payment is characterized by the payor as income, and the balance is principal. If no part of the payment is characterized as income or as a dividend, 10% of the payment is characterized as income and the balance is principal.

d. **Liquidating Assets Such as Patents, Copyrights—Ten Percent Rule**
A "liquidating asset" is an asset whose value will diminish over time because the asset is expected to produce receipts over a limited period. Proceeds from such liquidating assets (*e.g.*, patents, copyrights) are allocated 10% to income and 90% to principal.

e. **Mineral Interests—Ten Percent Rule**
For most oil, gas, mineral lease, and water right payments, receipts are allocated 10% to income and 90% to principal.

ALLOCATING RECEIPTS AND EXPENSES UNDER THE UPAIA

INCOME	PRINCIPAL
Receipts	**Receipts**
Ordinary receipts from use or investment of trust property (*e.g.,* rents, interest)	Extraordinary receipts (*e.g.,* proceeds from sale of trust assets)
Cash dividends	Stock dividends
Proceeds from contract insuring trustee against loss	Proceeds from life insurance policy naming trust or trustee as beneficiary
10% of payment from a deferred compensation plan (*e.g.,* pension plan), unless otherwise characterized	90% of payment from a deferred compensation plan (*e.g.,* pension plan), unless otherwise characterized
10% of proceeds received from a liquidating asset (*e.g.,* patents, copyrights)	90% of proceeds received from a liquidating asset (*e.g.,* patents, copyrights)
10% of proceeds received from a working interest (*e.g.,* oil and gas interests)	90% of proceeds received from a working interest (*e.g.,* oil and gas interests)
Expenses	**Expenses**
50% of regular compensation of the trustee and any person providing investment services	50% of regular compensation of the trustee and any person providing investment services
50% of all expenses for accountings, judicial proceedings, and other matters affecting income and remainder interests	50% of all expenses for accountings, judicial proceedings, and other matters affecting income and remainder interests
Ordinary expenses	Expenses of a proceeding that concerns a principal interest
Insurance premiums covering loss of a principal asset	Payments on the principal of a trust debt
	Estate taxes
	Disbursements related to environmental matters

f. Unproductive Property

Under the former law, if a particular trust asset produced little or no income, on the asset's sale, the income beneficiary was entitled to a portion of the sale proceeds under the principle of "delayed income." Because the UPIA looks to the ***total return from the overall portfolio***, the unproductive property rule was repealed except for certain trusts that are intended to qualify for the estate tax marital deduction.

3. Allocation of Expenses

a. Expenses Charged to Income

The following expenses are charged against income: one-half of the regular compensation of the trustee and of any person providing investment advisory or custodial services to the trustee; one-half of all expenses for accountings, judicial proceedings, and other matters affecting both income and remainder interests; the entire cost of ordinary expenses; and insurance premiums covering the loss of a principal asset.

b. Expenses Charged to Principal

The following expenses are charged against principal: the remaining one-half of the compensation of the trustee and any person providing investment advisory or custodial services to the trustee; the remaining one-half of all expenses for accountings, judicial proceedings, and other matters affecting both income and remainder interests; payments on the principal of a trust debt; expenses of a proceeding that concerns primarily an interest in principal; estate taxes; and disbursements related to environmental matters.

VII. WILL SUBSTITUTES

A. IN GENERAL

If a person wants to transfer property at the moment of death, he must comply with formal requirements for making a will. However, a settlor may make certain inter vivos (lifetime) transfers without the formalities of a will.

B. REVOCABLE INTER VIVOS TRUSTS

The test for distinguishing a trust from a will is whether the transfer creates some ***present*** gift, even if that gift is of a future interest subject to divestment (*i.e.*, revocable trust is valid because interest passes to the beneficiary during the settlor's lifetime; it merely becomes possessory on the settlor's death).

1. Determining Whether an Interest Passes

a. Settlor May Retain Powers Over Trust Property

The tendency is to uphold trusts even where the settlor has retained great rights and powers over the trust property. If the settlor retains a life estate and the power to revoke, the trust is generally upheld.

b. Where Settlor Is Trustee

Even if the settlor is the trustee, as well as the life tenant with power to revoke, most

courts uphold the trust where the settlor notified third parties or took some action that made his intention to establish a trust clear.

2. Advantages of Revocable Trust

A revocable trust may be used for convenient management of assets, to plan for the possibility of incapacity, to avoid probate costs and delays, to permit secrecy as to beneficiaries and assets, and to allow the settlor to choose the applicable state law. In some states, a revocable trust can defeat the spouse's forced share. But many states deem a revocable trust to be illusory, so that a surviving spouse can reach the trust's assets and set aside the transfer to the extent of her forced share.

3. Pour-Over Gift from Will to Revocable Trust

Under the Uniform Testamentary Additions to Trusts Act, a settlor can make gifts by will to a trust—even an amendable and revocable trust—established during his lifetime. The trust must have been established before or at the same time as the will, and may remain unfunded during the settlor's lifetime. The trust must be clearly identified from language in the will.

C. LIFE INSURANCE TRUSTS

Despite the absence of a significant res prior to the settlor's death, inter vivos life insurance trusts are upheld.

D. TOTTEN TRUST BANK ACCOUNTS

In a Totten trust, a bank account depositor declares himself trustee of the account for a person who is to receive the money in the account at the time of the depositor's death. The depositor retains full control of the money in the account during his lifetime. These accounts are not really trusts because they do not separate legal and equitable title, nor do they meet the formal requirements of wills. A Totten trust is revocable by: (i) the *withdrawal* of funds; (ii) any *lifetime act* manifesting the intent to revoke; and (iii) unlike joint accounts, a specific contradictory provision *in a will*. It does not protect funds in the account from creditors' claims, and it terminates if the beneficiary predeceases the depositor.

E. UNIFORM TRANSFERS TO MINORS ACT

The Uniform Transfers to Minors Act ("UTMA") provides a convenient procedure for making gifts to minors who have no legal capacity to manage or sell property, under which property may be transferred to a person as custodian for a minor. A custodianship is not a trust. The custodian does not hold legal title to the custodial property; legal title is in the minor, subject to the custodian's statutory power. The custodian is a fiduciary subject to the standard of care of a prudent person dealing with property of another. A custodial gift made pursuant to the UTMA qualifies for the $13,000 per donee annual federal gift tax exclusion.

VIII. TRUSTS ARISING AS A MATTER OF LAW— RESULTING AND CONSTRUCTIVE TRUSTS

A. IN GENERAL

Resulting and constructive trusts are implied by law or imposed by courts. Resulting trusts involve *reversionary interests* and are based on the presumed intent of the settlor. Constructive trusts are used to prevent *unjust enrichment*. They arise either where there is no valid express

declaration of trust or, frequently, when no trust was even intended. The Statute of Frauds is inapplicable.

B. RESULTING TRUSTS—WHEN WILL THEY BE IMPLIED?

Resulting trusts are of three types: (i) purchase money resulting trusts, (ii) resulting trusts arising on failure of an express trust, and (iii) resulting trusts arising from an incomplete disposition of trust assets (*i.e.,* excess corpus).

1. Purchase Money Resulting Trusts

A purchase money resulting trust is ***presumed*** whenever X (the "beneficiary") furnishes the consideration (usually money, but any other valuable consideration suffices) for the acquisition of real or personal property but, with X's consent, title is taken in the name of Y (the "trustee").

a. Form of Consideration Immaterial

The consideration paid by X must be for ***purchase*** of the property. Sums paid by X to make improvements on the property or to pay taxes on it do not give rise to a trust.

b. Time When Consideration Furnished

The consideration (or obligation to pay) must be supplied ***at or before*** the time Y takes title.

c. Burden of Proof on One Claiming as Beneficiary

The burden is on X, the party claiming to be the beneficiary of a resulting trust, to prove by ***clear and convincing evidence*** that he supplied the consideration.

d. Rebuttable Presumption of Resulting Trust

Once X proves that he supplied the consideration, a resulting trust is presumed; but Y can rebut by showing that no trust was intended (*e.g.,* payment was a ***gift*** or ***loan*** to Y or ***satisfaction of a debt*** owing to Y). Recitals as to who paid consideration are not conclusive.

e. Exceptions

1) No Trust Presumption Where Parties Closely Related

Where there is a ***close personal relationship*** between the parties (*e.g.,* X, the party paying consideration, is the parent, grandparent, or spouse of Y), a ***gift*** is presumed rather than a trust. This presumption is also rebuttable. The normal presumption of a trust applies where the person furnishing consideration is the uncle, aunt, brother, sister, child, or grandchild of the person receiving title.

2) Unlawful Purpose

If X and Y take title for an illegal purpose, a trust cannot be implied, although modern cases suggest that the implied trust is still proper where X's misconduct is slight compared to the unjust enrichment Y will enjoy if permitted to keep the property.

3) Transferee Obtained Title Wrongfully

No resulting trust arises when the transferee obtained title wrongfully (*e.g.,* by fraud), although a ***constructive*** trust may be imposed.

f. Pro Rata Resulting Trusts
Where X supplies only *part* of the consideration, the resulting trust in his favor is only for a pro rata portion of the property.

2. Resulting Trust on Failure of Express Trust

a. Circumstances Giving Rise to Resulting Trust
A resulting trust arises where a settlor has conveyed property to a trustee under an express trust and (i) the trust is *void or unenforceable*, or (ii) the beneficiary is *dead or cannot be located*. A resulting trust may also apply on failure of a charitable trust where *cy pres is inapplicable*. In such event, the express trust terminates and the settlor becomes the beneficiary of the resulting trust.

b. Circumstances Where Resulting Trust Not Implied
A resulting trust will *not* be implied where: (i) the trust instrument *specifically or implicitly provides for disposition* of trust property when the trust has failed or been completed; (ii) the settlor was given *consideration* for his original transfer in trust; (iii) the settlor created the trust for an *illegal purpose*; or (iv) *cy pres is applicable* in cases of charitable trusts.

3. Resulting Trust Implied from Excess Corpus
A resulting trust in favor of the settlor also arises when the trust purpose is fully satisfied and some trust property remains. There could be a resulting trust of part of the corpus even before the trust is terminated if it is clear that there is excess trust corpus.

C. CONSTRUCTIVE TRUSTS—WHEN WILL THEY BE IMPLIED?
A constructive trust is not really a trust but rather is a *flexible equitable remedy* to prevent unjust enrichment resulting from *wrongful conduct*, such as fraud, undue influence, or breach of a fiduciary duty. The constructive trustee's only duty is to convey the property to the person who would have owned it but for the wrongful conduct. Proof of the facts necessary to establish a constructive trust must be made by *clear and convincing evidence*.

1. Constructive Trust Arising from Theft or Conversion
If Y steals property from X, title remains in X; there is no need to imply a trust. But if Y uses the property to acquire other items, he takes title to the items and holds them in constructive trust for X.

2. Constructive Trust Arising from Fraud, Duress, Etc.
Where Y acquires property from X by fraud, duress, mistake of fact, or by breach of a fiduciary duty owed to X, Y holds the property in constructive trust for X's benefit. If property is conveyed to a third party who is not a BFP, the third party can be declared a constructive trustee. If Y takes property under a forged or fraudulent will, he holds it in constructive trust for its rightful inheritor. This is true even if Y is innocent.

3. Constructive Trust Arising from Breach of Fiduciary Duty
The fiduciary's duty forbids him from taking title to property belonging to a beneficiary and from seizing for himself an opportunity to acquire property that comes to him in his capacity as fiduciary. If he violates this duty, courts may impose a constructive trust in favor of the person to whom he owes the duty.

4. **Constructive Trust Arising from Homicide**
If Y kills X and is convicted of murder or manslaughter, he holds any property acquired from X by will or intestacy as constructive trustee in favor of whomever would have taken the property had Y predeceased X.

   a. **Where Victim and Killer Held Property in Joint Tenancy**
   Where X and Y were joint tenants, the killer Y may be trustee of only a one-half interest and own the balance free of trust, or he may hold the whole interest in constructive trust less his life estate in one-half (depending on the jurisdiction).

5. **Constructive Trust Arising from Breach of Promise**

   a. **General Rule—No Constructive Trust**
   The general rule is that a mere breach of a promise will *not* raise a constructive trust. Thus, where A transfers real property to B on B's oral promise to hold it for C, some jurisdictions consider the Statute of Frauds a bar. But the trend is to impose a constructive trust for C.

   b. **Exceptions to General Rule**
   A constructive trust will be imposed in the following cases:

      1) *Fraudulent* promise (promisor never intended to keep it);

      2) Breach of promise by one in a *confidential relationship*;

      3) Breach of promise by the decedent's *devisee or heir* to hold property for the benefit of a third person;

      4) Breach of promise by the *decedent* to devise property to one rendering services in reliance thereon (but no constructive trust here if damages adequate); or

      5) Breach of promise to the debtor by the *buyer at the foreclosure sale* to hold the property for the debtor, causing the debtor to forgo bidding at the sale (but in many jurisdictions no constructive trust if *damages* adequate).

   c. **Standard of Proof**
   The burden of proof is on the party seeking the constructive trust to establish facts relied upon by clear and convincing evidence.

D. **OBLIGATIONS OF TRUSTEE OF CONSTRUCTIVE OR RESULTING TRUST**
Constructive and resulting trusts are passive trusts. Once the court has declared such a trust to exist, the trustee's *sole duty* is to convey legal title to the beneficiary. The trustee must also account for profits taken from the property or fair rental value of his use of it from the time of the occurrences raising the implied trust. There is no duty on the trustee to invest trust property.

E. **APPLICATION OF EQUITABLE PRINCIPLES**
Actions to impress constructive or resulting trusts are in equity, and most equitable principles are fully applicable (*e.g.*, the "unclean hands" doctrine, and the rule that one seeking equity must "do equity"—such as requiring the beneficiary to reimburse the trustee for sums expended in good

faith to improve the property, pay taxes on it, etc.). However, the rule that an "adequate remedy at law" bars equitable relief is **not** applicable—except to the breach of an **oral** promise to make a will, or to hold property purchased at a foreclosure sale for the benefit of the promisee.

WILLS—ILLINOIS

TABLE OF CONTENTS

WILLS—ILLINOIS

I. INTESTATE SUCCESSION

A. WHEN INTESTATE SUCCESSION RULES APPLY

Property may pass by intestate succession when:

1. A decedent dies *without having made a will*;

2. A decedent's will is *denied probate*;

3. A decedent's will *does not dispose of all of his property* either because a gift has failed or because the will contains no residuary clause; or

4. A decedent's will *specifies* that his property should pass according to laws of intestate succession.

B. INTESTATE SHARE OF SURVIVING SPOUSE

If the decedent is survived by a spouse and descendants, the surviving spouse takes *one-half* of the estate; the other half passes to the descendants. If the decedent is survived by a spouse but not descendants, the spouse takes the *entire* estate.

C. INTESTATE SHARES OF OTHER HEIRS

1. Descendants Take Per Stirpes

The portion of the estate that does not pass to the surviving spouse, or the entire estate if there is no surviving spouse, passes to the decedent's descendants per stirpes. Under the *strict per stirpes* method used in Illinois, the property is divided into equal shares at the first generational level (*i.e.*, the child level) regardless of whether there are any living takers at that level. Each living person at that level takes a share, and the share of each deceased person at that level passes to his issue by right of representation. Any child who predeceased the decedent leaving no surviving descendants is disregarded in determining the number of stirpital shares.

CMR | **Exam Tip** | Remember that parents and collateral kin (*e.g.*, brothers, sisters, aunts, uncles) never inherit if the intestate is survived by children or more remote descendants.

2. Not Survived by Spouse or Descendants

If the decedent is not survived by a spouse or descendants, the estate is distributed to other heirs in the order below, proceeding down the list until takers are found:

(i) Parents and siblings take equal shares (sole surviving parent takes double portion);

(ii) One-half to paternal grandparents and one-half to maternal grandparents and their descendants (both halves to one side if no takers on the other side);

(iii) One-half to paternal great-grandparents and one-half to maternal great-grandparents and their descendants (both halves to one side if no takers on the other side); and

(iv) The entire estate to the nearest kindred in equal degree in equal shares and without representation.

Failing all of the above, the estate escheats to the county.

INTESTATE DECEDENT'S ESTATE

passes to

Spouse	and/or	Descendants or Their Issue

if none to

Parents (Sole survivor takes double portion)	and/or	Siblings or Their Issue

if none to

Maternal Grandparents or Their Descendants	and/or	Paternal Grandparents or Their Descendants

if none to

Maternal Great-Grandparents or Their Descendants	and/or	Paternal Great-Grandparents or Their Descendants

if none to

Nearest Kindred in Equal Degree in Equal Shares

if none to

The County

D. SPECIAL CASES

1. Adopted Children

a. When Adopted Child Inherits From and Through Adopting Parents
Children adopted *under age 18* inherit from and through adoptive parents the same as a natural child. The same rule also applies for children adopted *over the age of 18* for purposes of distributing the *adopting parent's estate*. However, for purposes of distributing anyone else's estate, a person adopted as an adult is *not* treated as a descendant of the adopting parent *unless* the adopted person resided with the parent before attaining age 18.

b. When Adopted Child Inherits From and Through Natural Parents
An adopted child is not treated as a child of the natural parents for inheritance purposes or for purposes of determining property rights *unless*: (i) the child's natural parents died before the child was adopted, (ii) the child was adopted by a relative, or (iii) a contrary intent is established by the terms of the instrument by clear and convincing evidence.

c. Child Adopted by Relative—Only One Share
An adopted child who is related to a decedent through more than one line of relationship is entitled only to the share based on the relationship that gives the largest share.

2. Stepchild or Foster Child Has No Inheritance Rights
In Illinois, a stepchild or foster child has no inheritance rights from her stepparent or foster parent. Some states allow a stepchild or foster child to inherit if the stepparent or foster parent obtained custody through an agreement with the natural parent to adopt the child but never carried out the agreement (this is known as *adoption by estoppel*). However, Illinois does not expressly recognize this doctrine.

3. Inheritance By and From Nonmarital Children
A nonmarital child has full inheritance rights from the child's mother and her kin (and vice versa). The child may inherit from the father and his kin if: (i) the father *married* the mother after the child's birth and acknowledged the child as his own, (ii) the father *acknowledged* paternity of the child during his lifetime, (iii) the decedent was *adjudged* to be the father of the child in a paternity suit during his lifetime, or (iv) after his death, the decedent was *proven* to be the father of the child by clear and convincing evidence. A parent of a nonmarital child may inherit from the child if, during the child's lifetime, he acknowledged the child as his own, established a parental relationship with the child, and did not breach his duty to support the child.

4. Posthumous Heirs *born after parent died*
Generally, one claiming as the heir of a decedent must be alive at the decedent's death; however, a posthumous *child of the decedent* takes as though he had been born during his father's lifetime.

5. Collateral Kin of Half Blood
Collaterals of the half blood (*e.g.*, brothers and sisters with only one common parent) have the same inheritance rights as collaterals of the whole blood.

6. Attempt to Disinherit by Will Ineffective

To disinherit an intestate heir, a decedent *must make a complete disposition* of his property by his will. Any property not disposed of by will passes under the intestacy statute, regardless of any expression of intent that the decedent did not wish the property to pass in that way. For example, a will provision stating, "I do not wish my children to take any part of my estate," would be ineffective to prevent the testator's children from taking their portion of intestate property.

II. SUCCESSION PROBLEMS COMMON TO INTESTACY AND WILLS

A. SIMULTANEOUS DEATH

Illinois has adopted the Uniform Simultaneous Death Act ("USDA"), which provides that when disposition of property (by will, intestacy, joint tenancy, etc.) depends on the order of death and the order cannot be established, the property of each decedent is distributed as if he had survived the other. In the case of a joint tenancy with right of survivorship, the property is distributed as though it were held as a tenancy in common. The USDA applies unless there are specific contrary provisions in the will (or other instrument). Illinois has not adopted the Uniform Probate Code ("UPC") rule requiring a person to survive a decedent by 120 hours in order to take property as an intestate heir, will or life insurance beneficiary, or surviving joint tenant.

B. DISCLAIMERS

1. Disclaimed Interest Passes as Though Disclaimant Predeceased Decedent

A beneficiary or heir may disclaim any interest that otherwise would pass to the person from the decedent, with the consequence that the interest passes as though the disclaiming party predeceased the decedent.

a. Creditors' Claims

A disclaimer can be used to defeat creditors' claims; the disclaimant has no interest that can be reached by creditors. However, a disclaimer cannot be used to defeat a federal tax lien.

2. Requirements for Effective Disclaimer

The disclaimer must: (i) be *signed* by the heir or beneficiary, (ii) *describe* the interest disclaimed, and (iii) be *delivered* to the testator's personal representative, the trustee, or the person having possession of the property. A copy of the disclaimer must be filed with the clerk of the court in which the estate is being administered. If real property is disclaimed, an executed copy of the disclaimer must be recorded in the county where the land is located. A disclaimer filed under the statute is irrevocable and is effective on the date it is filed. A spendthrift clause does not prevent a disclaimer.

3. Disclaimer May Be Made on Behalf of Infant, Incompetent, or Decedent

A disclaimer may be made on behalf of an infant, incompetent, or decedent, but the court must first find that it is in the *best interests* of those interested in the estate and is not detrimental to the best interests of the beneficiary.

4. No Time Limit on Making Disclaimer

Unlike most states, Illinois does not set a time limit on when a disclaimer must be made, but the right to disclaim is barred if the beneficiary or heir has accepted the property or any of its benefits or has assigned or mortgaged the interest.

a. **Nine-Month Limit for Gift Tax Purposes**
To be effective for federal gift tax purposes, the disclaimer must be made within nine months after the decedent's death. A beneficiary under the age of 21 has until nine months after her 21st birthday to make the disclaimer.

b. **Disclaiming Future Interests and Life Estates**
The Illinois statute allows the holder of a future interest to disclaim that interest after the future interest *vests in possession*. However, to be effective for tax purposes, the future interest must be disclaimed within nine months after the interest was *created*. Disclaimer of a life estate accelerates the remainder.

C. DECEDENT'S DEATH CAUSED BY HEIR OR BENEFICIARY

A person who *intentionally and unjustifiably* causes the death of another forfeits any property or other interest that passes by reason of that death, whether as an heir, legatee, beneficiary, or in any other capacity. The property, benefit, or other interest passes as if the person causing the death predeceased the decedent. A final judgment of conviction of murder in any degree is conclusive for purposes of the statute. A person who is convicted of (i) criminal abuse or neglect of an elderly or disabled person, (ii) abuse or neglect of a long-term care facility resident, or (iii) financial exploitation of an elderly or disabled person likewise forfeits any property or other interest that passes by reason of the person's death.

D. ADVANCEMENT OF INTESTATE SHARE

An advancement is a lifetime gift by an intestate decedent to a next of kin, intended by him to be a prepayment of the recipient's share. In Illinois, a gift is *not* an advancement *unless*: (i) expressed in writing by the donor, or (ii) so acknowledged in writing by the donee.

1. Procedure If Advancement Found

If found to be an advancement, the gift's value when given is added back into the estate for purposes of calculating shares, and then subtracted from the donee's share. The heir need not return the amount of an advancement in excess of the value of her intestate share.

2. Advancee Predeceases Intestate

If the donee fails to survive the decedent, the advancement is applied to the share of the donee's descendants.

E. SATISFACTION OF LEGACIES

Illinois has no statute on satisfaction of legacies. A lifetime gift to a *child* is presumptively in satisfaction of the prior legacy. By contrast, a lifetime gift to a beneficiary *other than a child* (*e.g.,* a niece) is presumptively not in satisfaction of the prior legacy. Satisfaction of legacies applies to cash legacies and bequests of the residuary estate, while ademption applies to specific bequests of property.

III. FORMAL REQUISITES AND EXECUTION OF WILLS

A. WHAT CONSTITUTES A WILL

A will is an instrument executed with certain formalities that usually directs the disposition of a person's property at death, although an instrument that merely appoints a personal representative or revokes an earlier will can be a will. A will is revocable during the testator's lifetime and operative at the testator's death. A *codicil* is a supplement to a will that modifies it.

 CMR | **Exam Tip** | Because a will is not operative until the testator's death, a beneficiary has merely an *expectancy* (not a property interest) until that time.

B. FORMAL REQUISITES

1. Testamentary Capacity

The testator must be *age 18 or older and of sound mind* at the time he makes a will.

CMR | **Exam Tip** | Beware of a fact pattern where a testator executes a will before age 18, feels satisfied with it, never executes another, and dies at a ripe old age. Any will executed while under age 18 is invalid.

2. Testamentary Intent

The testator must have present intent that the instrument operate as his will. Promises to make a will in the future and ineffective deeds are not given effect as wills.

3. Conditional Wills

A conditional will is one that provides that it is to be operative only if a stated condition is satisfied (*e.g.,* "if I do not return from this trip . . ."). Parol evidence may not be admitted to show conditions. Note that a court might interpret what appears to be a condition as merely ~~expressing the~~ *as* *motive* for making the will, and might give the will effect even if the condition does not occur.

4. Holographic and Oral Wills

Holographic wills (handwritten by the testator and signed but not properly witnessed) and oral wills are *not recognized in Illinois*. However, a holographic will validly written in another state could be admitted to probate in Illinois.

CMR | **Exam Tip** | Remember that most states that do recognize holographic wills give effect to handwritten changes made by the testator *after* the holographic will is completed. However, interlineations made after the execution of an *attested* will are usually not given effect, unless the changes are sufficient to constitute a valid holographic codicil.

C. EXECUTION OF WILLS

An Illinois will *must* be: (i) *in writing*, (ii) *signed by the testator* (or by another person in his presence and at his direction), and (iii) *witnessed by two credible witnesses*, who must sign *in the testator's presence*.

1. Testator's Signature

Any mark affixed by the testator with the intent that it operate as his signature satisfies the signature requirement. A testator may be assisted in signing his will, and a proxy signature is even permissible if done in the testator's presence and at his direction. The exact order of signing among the testator and witnesses is not material, as long as all of the signings occurred as a part of a single, continuous transaction.

order irrelevant

2. Witnesses Must Sign in Testator's Presence

The witnesses do not have to attest the will in the presence of each other, but each witness must attest the will in the testator's presence, *i.e.,* either within the uninterrupted range of the testator's vision (*scope of vision test*—Illinois rule), or in such a manner that the testator comprehends that they are signing through sight, hearing, or otherwise (*conscious presence test*—UPC rule). But the testator does not actually have to see the witnesses sign. The testator must acknowledge the instrument as his own and acknowledge its execution, but the witnesses need not see the testator sign or the testator's signature.

3. Witnesses Must Be "Credible"

Competency is determined *at the time the will is executed*. A person is considered an attesting witness only if he signs the will with that intention and not for some other purpose (*e.g.* as a notary).

4. Attestation Clause

An attestation clause recites the requirements for execution of the will. It is useful because it is *prima facie evidence* of due execution in probate proceedings (in lieu of the witnesses' testimony).

CMR | **Exam Tip** | The presumption of validity raised by an attestation clause is not overcome by the testimony of the attesting witnesses that they cannot now remember whether execution was proper or even that they deny a fact necessary to establish the will's validity.

5. Requirements in Other States that Are Not Required in Illinois

In Illinois, the testator's signature can appear anywhere on the will; there is no "publication" requirement, so the witnesses need not know they are attesting a will; and it is not necessary that a will bear the date of its execution.

D. INTERESTED WITNESSES

In Illinois, the fact that the will makes a gift to an attesting witness never results in denial of probate of the will. However, if a will makes a bequest to an attesting witness *or to the witness's spouse*, the bequest is void. The bequest is not void if the will was also witnessed by two disinterested witnesses because, in that case, the beneficiary is a "supernumerary" witness.

If the beneficiary would have been entitled to a share of the estate if the will were not probated (*i.e.,* as an heir, or as a beneficiary under an earlier will), he is entitled to the lesser of: (i) the bequest in the will, or (ii) the share of the estate he would have taken if the will were not established. The interested witness statute does not apply to creditors or attorneys. Executors and testamentary trustees who sign as witnesses are not entitled to compensation as fiduciaries.

E. ATTORNEY LIABILITY FOR NEGLIGENCE

An attorney's duty extends to beneficiaries, and they can sue the attorney for a negligently prepared will.

IV. REVOCATION OF WILLS

A. IN GENERAL

A person who has testamentary capacity may revoke her will at any time prior to her death. Even one who has validly contracted not to revoke her will may do so.

B. REVOCATION BY OPERATION OF LAW

1. Subsequent Marriage Does Not Affect Will

Marriage following execution of a will has no effect on the will or any of its provisions.

2. **Divorce Revokes All Provisions and Appointments in Favor of Former Spouse**

If the testator is divorced or the marriage is annulled after making a will, all gifts to the former spouse and all appointments of the spouse as executor or trustee under the will are revoked. Revocation occurs regardless of whether the will was executed before or after the marriage. The statute applies only to a divorce by the testator (not by others) and does not apply to life insurance policies or to revocable trusts that make a gift to the former spouse.

3. **Pretermitted Children**

Under Illinois's pretermitted child statute (*see* VIII.B., *infra*), if the testator fails to provide in his will for any children born or adopted after the execution of the will, the child takes an *intestate share*. In making up the child's share, all legacies abate proportionately and the will is revoked to that extent.

C. REVOCATION BY WRITTEN INSTRUMENT

An instrument executed with the formal requirements of a will that declares the prior will re- voked is effective as a revocation. A later will or codicil that is inconsistent with a prior will revokes the prior will to the extent of the inconsistency. Both wills are entitled to probate.

D. REVOCATION BY PHYSICAL ACT

A will or codicil can be revoked by burning, tearing, canceling, or obliterating it with the intent to revoke. The intent must be concurrent with the act. The physical act may be performed by another if done at the testator's direction and in his presence.

CMR **Exam Tip** Remember that the *accidental* destruction of a will does not revoke it—even if the testator later decides he wanted to revoke it—because the intent to revoke must be present at the time of the physical act of destruction.

1. **Presumptions as to Revocation**

If a will last seen in the testator's possession or control cannot be found after his death or is found in a mutilated condition, a rebuttable presumption arises that the testator revoked it.

2. **Partial Revocation**

Most states, but not Illinois, permit an executed will to be partially revoked by physical act, *e.g.,* by striking out a clause. In Illinois, the stricken clause is given effect as if nothing had been done to it.

3. **Effect of Revocation on Other Testamentary Instruments**

When a will has been executed in duplicate, an act of revocation done to either copy revokes the will. The revocation of a will revokes all codicils, but revocation of a codicil does not revoke the will. Note that there is no revival of revoked wills in Illinois; once a will is revoked by language in a later will, it cannot be revived unless it is *reexecuted* or *republished*.

4. **Lost or Destroyed Wills**

If a will is lost or destroyed (and the presumption that the testator revoked it is overcome), the contents of the will may be proved by a photocopy or carbon copy, or by the testimony of someone who had read the will and recalls its contents.

E. DEPENDENT RELATIVE REVOCATION

Under the doctrine of dependent relative revocation ("DRR"), a court may disregard a revocation

REVOCATION OF WILLS

	Method	Full or Partial	Result
Operation of Law	Divorce	Partial only (unless will left everything to former spouse)	All provisions in favor of former spouse revoked
	Birth or adoption of children	Partial	Gifts abated (and therefore revoked) to extent necessary to make up share for pretermitted child
Subsequent Instrument	Express revocation in instrument	Either	Will revoked to extent stated in subsequent instrument
	Inconsistent provisions	Either	If no express revocation, prior will revoked only to extent inconsistent with provisions in subsequent instrument
Physical Act	Burning, tearing, obliterating, or canceling a material portion of will with intent to revoke	Full	Absent valid subsequent will, estate will pass by intestacy. Because partial revocation is not permitted, a stricken clause is given effect

if it was premised on a mistake of law or fact and would not have occurred but for the testator's mistaken belief that another disposition of his property was valid. If the other disposition fails, the revocation also fails and the will remains in force. DRR is applied only if it comes closer to what the testator tried (but failed) to do than would an intestate distribution.

V. DOCTRINES RELATING TO THE COMPONENTS OF A WILL

A. INTEGRATION

A will consists of all papers present at the execution that were intended by the testator to be part of the will. Physical attachment and internal coherence of pages raise a presumption that they were present and intended to be part of the will when it was executed. Proof of integration can also be provided by testimony or other extrinsic evidence.

B. INCORPORATION BY REFERENCE

An extrinsic document, not present at the time the will was executed, may be incorporated into the will provided that: (i) the document is *in existence* when the will is executed; (ii) the will *refers* to the paper incorporated as being in existence at the time of execution of the will; and (iii) the document is *identifiable* by language in the will.

C. ACTS OF INDEPENDENT SIGNIFICANCE

A will may dispose of property by reference to acts and events, even though they are in the future and unattested, if they have significance apart from their effect on dispositions made by the will. For example, a bequest to "each person in my employ at the time of my death" is valid because a testator would not make employment decisions solely for the purpose of disposing of her property.

D. ALTERATIONS ON FACE OF WILL

Any addition, alteration, interlineation, or deletion made after the will has been signed and attested is ineffective to change the will, unless the will is reexecuted with proper formalities.

E. REPUBLICATION BY CODICIL

The doctrine of republication by codicil operates to: (i) *redate* the will, (ii) *validate* the terms of a defective will, and (iii) *revive* a prior revoked will if there is sufficient incorporation by reference.

F. NONPROBATE ASSETS CANNOT BE DISPOSED OF BY WILL

A will cannot make a gift of "nonprobate assets"—*i.e.,* interests that pass at death other than by will or intestacy. There are three categories of nonprobate assets: (i) property passing by contract (*e.g.,* life insurance proceeds and employee benefits), (ii) property passing by right of survivorship, and (iii) property held in trust.

VI. CONTRACTS RELATING TO WILLS

A. DEFINITIONS

A *joint will* is a will of two or more persons executed on the same piece of paper. *Mutual wills* are two separate wills containing reciprocal provisions. A *joint and mutual* will is a joint will containing reciprocal provisions; it is synonymous with "contractual will."

EFFECT OF CONTRACT NOT TO REVOKE WILL

A and B enter into a contract not to revoke their wills, which provide for the disposition of a particular item of property.

Status of Parties		Action	Result	Rationale
A	B	A revokes will; notifies B. B sues.	No relief granted.	B has not been damaged; B still has an opportunity to change his will.
~~A~~	B	A revokes will without notifying B, and then dies. B sues.	No relief granted.	B has not been damaged; B still has an opportunity to change his will.
~~A~~	B	A dies in compliance (no revocation); then B revokes his will, but does nothing more. The beneficiary of the contractual will sues.	No relief granted.	B is not in breach of the contract until his death.
~~A~~	B	A dies in compliance (no revocation); B attempts to dispose of the property covered by the agreement (*i.e.*, the particular item of property obtained from A's estate). The beneficiary of the contractual will sues.	Constructive trust imposed on the property in favor of the beneficiary of the contractual will.	A died with an estate plan made in reliance on B's promise, and unjust enrichment would result if B were allowed to dispose of the property.
~~A~~	~~B~~	A dies in compliance (no revocation); B then revokes, makes a new will, and dies.	New will probated, but a constructive trust imposed in favor of the beneficiary of the contractual will.	A died with an estate plan made in reliance on B's promise, and unjust enrichment would result from allowing B to make an alternate disposition of his estate.

B. IS THE WILL CONTRACTUAL?

If the will is contractual, the contract is that the survivor cannot revoke the will after the death of the first to die. During the joint lifetimes of the testators, either party may rescind the contract after giving notice to the other.

1. Factors in Determining Whether Joint Will Is Contractual

Courts look to the terminology of the will to determine whether a contract exists. Factors include: (i) labeling of the will as "joint and mutual," (ii) reciprocal provisions, (iii) unitary disposition of all of the testators' pooled property, (iv) a uniform dispositive scheme upon the death of the survivor (rather than "to the survivor in fee simple"), and (v) the use of plural possessive pronouns. If most of these factors are present, the will is considered contractual.

2. When Constructive Trust Is Imposed

If a will is found to be contractual, and the survivor revokes the will and executes another in breach of contract, the second will is probated, but a *constructive trust* is imposed against the beneficiaries of the second will in favor of the beneficiaries of the contractual will.

3. Lifetime Gifts Cannot Defeat Agreed-Upon Disposition

The surviving party under a contractual will cannot defeat the intended testamentary plan by making inter vivos gifts.

C. CONTRACT TO MAKE A WILL

A contract to make a will or a particular devise is enforceable only if proven by *clear and convincing evidence*. A contract may be implied where: (i) no family relationship exists, (ii) housekeeping and caregiving services were rendered at the decedent's request, and (iii) the decedent had no reason to suppose that the services were gratuitous.

VII. CHANGES IN BENEFICIARIES AND PROPERTY AFTER THE WILL'S EXECUTION

A. LAPSED GIFTS AND THE ANTI-LAPSE STATUTE

If a will beneficiary predeceases the testator, his gift lapses (*i.e.,* it fails) and passes as part of the residue.

1. Illinois Anti-Lapse Statute

By statute in Illinois, a gift by will to a *descendant of the testator* who predeceases the testator generally does not lapse, but rather goes to the descendants of the predeceased descendant, per stirpes.

2. Lapse in the Residuary Estate

Where a residuary gift to several persons lapses as to fewer than all of them, and the anti-lapse statute does not apply, the remaining persons share the lapsed portion; it does not pass intestate.

3. Class Gifts

Where a member of the class predeceases the testator, absent a contrary will provision, the other members of the class succeed to his share. But if the deceased member of the class was a descendant of the testator, the anti-lapse statute applies and descendants of that beneficiary take his share of the class gift.

4. **Void Gifts**

If the beneficiary is dead when the will is executed, the gift is generally void. In Illinois, however, void gifts are treated the same as lapsed gifts, and the anti-lapse statute may apply.

5. **Future Interests**

also

The Illinois anti-lapse statute also covers a bequest of a future interest when the beneficiary dies *before or after* the testator, but before the beneficiary's interest becomes possessory (*e.g.,* beneficiary survives testator but not life tenant). The statute does not apply to a future interest that is indefeasibly vested at the testator's death or at any time thereafter before it takes effect in possession or enjoyment.

B. ADEMPTION

If specifically bequeathed property is not owned by the testator at his death, the gift is adeemed; *i.e.,* it fails. Ademption applies only to *specific legacies*, which are gifts of specifically described property that can be satisfied only with that property. Note that a gift may be partially adeemed if a portion of it is disposed of prior to the testator's death. Ademption does not apply to general legacies (*i.e.,* gifts of dollar amounts to be paid out of general assets) or to demonstrative legacies (*i.e.,* gifts of dollar amounts indicating a particular asset as a source of payment). Ademption also may not apply to gifts of sale proceeds or the testator's interest.

1. **Bequest of Securities**

Courts usually construe bequests of securities as *general legacies*. If, however, the bequest is of "*my* 100 shares," it will be considered a specific bequest.

2. **Executory Contract for Sale**

If the testator contracts to sell specifically bequeathed property, and the contract is still executory at his death, the beneficiary takes the testator's rights under the contract. The doctrine of equitable conversion (*see* Multistate Real Property outline) does *not* apply in this situation.

3. **Ademption Requires Act of Testator Indicating Intent to Revoke**

Illinois courts, in applying the ademption doctrine, require an act by the testator indicating an intent to revoke the gift. Thus, the sale of property by the testator's guardian or conservator or the accidental destruction of the property with no opportunity to change the will does not result in ademption of the gift. Instead, the beneficiary is entitled to any remaining sale proceeds or insurance proceeds.

C. STOCK SPLITS AND STOCK DIVIDENDS

A specific bequest includes any additional shares produced by a stock split, but does not include shares produced by a stock dividend.

VIII. RESTRICTIONS ON THE POWER OF DISPOSITION— PROTECTION OF THE FAMILY

A. SURVIVING SPOUSE'S RIGHT OF RENUNCIATION

A spouse may renounce the will and take instead the share of the estate she is entitled to by statute. If a spouse so elects, she is entitled to *one-third* of the estate (after payment of claims) if the testator was survived by descendants or *one-half* of the estate if he was not. For this purpose,

the estate does not include nonprobate assets (including real property located outside Illinois) or any lifetime transfers. The same-sex partner of a decedent is not eligible to apply for an elective share.

1. **Who May Exercise Right**

A guardian of an incapacitated spouse can make the election to renounce only if he can show that it is necessary for the spouse's support. If the spouse dies within the time allowed to renounce (*i.e., **seven months** after admission to probate*), the right dies with her; a personal representative cannot file a renunciation.

2. **Elective Share Charged Against Residuary Estate**

The elective share is charged against the residuary estate, and other legacies and bequests abate only if the residuary estate is insufficient.

3. **Remainders Accelerated**

The will is read as though the renouncing spouse predeceased the testator; thus, remainders following a life estate that had been devised to the spouse are accelerated.

B. **PRETERMITTED CHILD TAKES INTESTATE SHARE**

A child born or adopted after the will is executed is entitled to the portion of the estate to which he would have been entitled if the testator had died intestate unless: (i) provision is made for the child in the will, or (ii) it appears *from the will* (and not extrinsic evidence) that it was the intention of the testator to disinherit the child. The Illinois statute applies only to afterborn and after-adopted children. It applies only to the testator's children; grandchildren are not included.

CMR **Exam Tip** Remember that *republication* of a will by codicil can result in a change in a child's status with respect to pretermission. A child born before the republication is not considered pretermitted and is not entitled to the protection of the statute.

C. **SURVIVING SPOUSE'S AND CHILD'S AWARD**

A surviving spouse is entitled to an award of at least $10,000 plus $5,000 for each dependent child to support the family during the probate of the estate. If there is no surviving spouse, the decedent's minor and adult dependent children are entitled to an award of at least $10,000 plus $5,000 for each dependent child. The award is divided equally.

D. **MISCELLANEOUS LIMITATIONS**

The right of testation is limited by certain rules, such as the Rule Against Perpetuities, the rule against accumulations, and the rules against transfers for illegal purposes or purposes contrary to public policy. Provisions requiring or encouraging the beneficiary to do an illegal, immoral, or grossly improper act (*e.g.,* gifts conditioned on divorce or unreasonable total restraints on marriage) are not enforced by Illinois courts. Unlike some states, Illinois places no limitations on gifts to charitable organizations.

IX. PROBATE AND ESTATE ADMINISTRATION

A. **PROBATE PROCESS**

"Probate" refers to the proceeding in which an instrument is judicially established as the duly executed last will of the decedent. After the will is admitted to probate (or the heirs are determined), the court issues "letters" to the personal representative who administers the estate. Venue lies in the county of the decedent's residence or, if a nonresident, in the county in which the greatest part of her real property is located. Any person who has a will in his possession must file it with the court in the proper county upon the testator's death. In Illinois, there is **no time limit** on when a will may be offered for probate.

B. PROOF OF WILLS

1. Testimony of Attesting Witnesses
Unless due execution of the will is proved by the will's attestation clause or by affidavit, two attesting witnesses must testify as to the testator's signature and competency and the witness's own signature. If the witness resides outside the county or is unable to attend court, her testimony may be by deposition or interrogatory. If a witness is unavailable or outside the state, the court may admit proof of the witness's signature.

2. Notice to Interested Parties
Within 14 days after entry of an order admitting or denying admission of a will to probate or appointing a personal representative, interested parties (*i.e.,* legatees named in the will and testator's heirs) must be given notice of the court order.

C. PERSONAL REPRESENTATIVE

1. Persons Qualified to Act
Any person who is at least 18 years old can serve as personal representative unless she is "of unsound mind," has been adjudged a disabled person, or is a convicted felon. Both administrators and executors can be nonresidents.

2. Order of Preference for Selection
Unless disqualified, the person designated in the will as executor must be appointed as executor and issued letters testamentary. If no executor is appointed, the order of preference is: (i) surviving spouse, (ii) legatee or devisee, (iii) child, (iv) grandchild, (v) parent, etc.

3. Fiduciary Bond
A corporate fiduciary is not required to give bond, but (unless the will waives the requirement of a bond) an individual appointed as personal representative must post a surety bond.

4. Resignation and Removal
Upon petition of a personal representative, a court may permit her to resign. The court may remove a personal representative if not qualified to act or for other good cause.

D. MECHANICS OF ADMINISTRATION

1. Inventory and Appraisal
Within 60 days of the issuance of letters, the personal representative must file in court a verified inventory of the estate's real and personal property and any cause of action on which she has a right to sue.

2. Citation to Recover Property

The personal representative or any interested person may petition the court to order a citation issued to any person believed to have property or information about property that belongs to the estate.

3. Property Management

Specifically bequeathed personal or real property or property selected by the surviving spouse or child may not be sold, mortgaged, or pledged unless necessary for the proper administration of the estate. The personal representative may operate the decedent's unincorporated business for one month following issuance of her letters unless the court directs otherwise. After that month, prior court approval must be obtained. Estate assets may be invested only in "legal investments." However, with court approval, investments can be made in "common trust funds."

4. Approval of Accounts

Within 60 days after the close of the claim period, the personal representative must file an account showing all receipts and disbursements. Upon approval of the account, absent fraud, accident, or mistake, the account is binding on all who were given notice and the personal representative will be discharged.

5. Distribution on Presumption of Death

Where administration is based on a presumption of death, the distributee must post a bond for double the amount to be distributed, so as to refund the sum if the "decedent" is alive. A surety need only be provided for 10 years, but the distributees' duty to make a refund to the "decedent" continues.

E. CREDITORS' CLAIMS

1. Notice

The personal representative must publish notice of administration once a week for three weeks in the county where the estate is being administered. In addition, the personal representative must mail or deliver notice to creditors whose names and addresses are known or ascertainable by the representative. If personal notice is not given, the claim is not barred by the six-month nonclaim statute (*see* below). However, creditors who have actual notice of the administration will be held to the six-month period regardless of whether they received personal notice.

2. Statute of Limitations

The claim of a creditor to whom notice was mailed or delivered will be barred unless he files his claim within the *later of*: (i) six months after the first publication of notice, or (ii) three months after the delivery of the notice. Unknown and unascertainable creditors must file their claims within six months of the first publication of notice. Even if no notice is published, creditors' claims must be filed within two years of the decedent's death.

3. Statutory Custodial Claim

A spouse, parent, brother, sister, or a child of a disabled person who lives with the disabled person and dedicates himself to that disabled person's care for at least three years is entitled to a claim against the disabled person's estate. The amount is based on the nature and extent of the disability, and may be reduced to the extent the living arrangements physically or financially benefited the claimant.

4. **Priority for Payment**

When an estate is not sufficient to pay all claims, the claims are classified and paid in the following order:

Class 1: Funeral and administration expenses and statutory custodial claims.

Class 2: The surviving spouse's or child's award.

Class 3: Debts due the United States government.

Class 4: Money due the decedent's employees, and expenses of the decedent's last illness.

Class 5: Money received or held in trust by the decedent that cannot be identified.

Class 6: Debts due the state, county, township, city, town, or school district.

Class 7: All other claims.

If the estate is insufficient to pay all the claims in any class, the claims in that class are paid pro rata.

5. **Abatement of Legacies**

Generally, claims are paid out of the residuary estate. If that is insufficient, the general legacies are applied, and if that is still insufficient, the specific legacies are used. Within the categories, the gifts abate pro rata.

CMR [**Exam Tip**] To the extent they can be satisfied from the designated source, demonstrative legacies are treated as specific legacies for abatement purposes. To the extent the fund is insufficient, demonstrative legacies are treated as general legacies for abatement purposes.

6. **Estate Taxes**

Under the doctrine of equitable apportionment, each person interested in the estate (including beneficiaries of nonprobate transfers) bears a pro rata portion of the tax burden. Note that a gift that qualifies for the marital or charitable tax deduction does not bear any portion of the tax.

7. **No Exoneration of Liens**

Unless directed in the will, liens on specifically bequeathed property are not paid off by the estate.

F. **SPECIAL PROCEDURE FOR SMALL ESTATES**

Where decedent's personal estate ***does not exceed $100,000***, a special small estates procedure provides that persons holding personal property of, or owing money to, the decedent may satisfy their obligations ***without probate*** by paying in accord with an affidavit made by an heir or legatee of the decedent. The debtor is protected just as if he had paid a duly appointed personal representative.

G. **INDEPENDENT ADMINISTRATION**

Any testate or intestate estate may be administered by an independent administrator without court involvement if the will does not forbid independent administration and no interested party objects. If an interested party objects, the court will determine whether a supervised administration is necessary to protect the objector's interest.

X. WILL CONTESTS

A. IN GENERAL

1. Grounds for Contesting a Will
Grounds include defective execution of the will, lack of testamentary capacity, insane delusion, undue influence, fraud, mistake, and the testator's lack of knowledge of the contents of his will.

2. Contest Must Be Filed Within Six Months After Will's Admission to Probate
A will can be contested at the time the will is offered for probate, or within six months after the will has been formally admitted to probate. The right to file a will contest is not waived by failure to raise the issues on which the contest is based at the hearing on admission of the will to probate. Only an interested party (*i.e.,* one who would take under an earlier will or by intestate succession) may file a petition contesting admission of the will to probate.

CMR **Exam Tip** Be careful to distinguish between a will contest and the offer of a more recent will. The six-month limitation does not apply to a petition to probate a later will, even if it revokes an earlier will that has been admitted to probate.

B. LACK OF TESTAMENTARY CAPACITY
There is a presumption that every person is of sound mind. Thus, the burden is on the will contestant to show that, at the time of executing the will, the testator did not have sufficient capacity to: (i) understand that he was writing a will; (ii) know the nature and character of his property; (iii) know the objects of his bounty; or (iv) make a disposition of his property according to a plan formed in his own mind. Capacity to make a will may exist where capacity to make a contract does not. The testator need only have capacity *at the time the will is executed*.

C. INSANE DELUSION
The insane delusion must be overpowering and much more than mere eccentricity. One may have "sound mind and memory" and still suffer from an insane delusion that affects to whom he leaves his property. Unless the terms of the will have been affected by the insane delusion, it will have no effect on the validity of the will. If any part of the will was affected by an insane delusion, the entire will is invalidated.

D. UNDUE INFLUENCE
To prove undue influence sufficient to invalidate a will, the contestant must show that: (i) specific acts of influence were exerted; (ii) the effect of the influence was to overpower the mind and free will of the testator; and (iii) the will or gift therein would not have been made "but for" the influence. The burden of proving undue influence is initially on the contestant.

CMR **Exam Tip** For exam purposes, keep in mind that mere pleading, begging, nagging, cajoling, or even threatening do not constitute undue influence. The free will of the testator must be destroyed.

1. Presumption of Undue Influence
A rebuttable presumption of undue influence arises when the will gives a substantial benefit to a party who stood in a *confidential relationship* with the testator and the party was instrumental in preparing or procuring the will. This presumption shifts the burden of proof

to the beneficiary. Because it is expected that spouses have a confidential relationship, the presumption of undue influence does *not* apply to spousal relationships.

2. Remedy

The part of a will that is affected by undue influence is stricken, and the remainder of the will is allowed to stand if doing so will not defeat the testator's intent or destroy the testamentary scheme.

E. FRAUD IN PROCUREMENT

To show fraud sufficient to invalidate a will, the contestant must show that: (i) someone made a false representation of material fact, knowing or believing it to be false; (ii) the representation was made for the purpose of inducing the testator to write or not write a will, or make a particular gift; and (iii) the testator reasonably believed in and relied on the statement in making the will.

F. MISTAKE

1. Mistake in Execution

Extrinsic evidence is admissible to show that a testator did not know that the instrument he was signing was a will, because the existence of testamentary intent is at issue. If the testator mistakenly signs the wrong will (*e.g.,* H and W sign each other's will), some courts will deny relief, but the better view is that the court will grant relief where the nature of the mistake is obvious.

2. Mistake in Inducement—No Relief

If the mistake involves the reasons that led a testator to make his will or a particular gift therein, the court will not normally grant relief. Relief might be granted, however, if the mistaken inducement appears on the face of the will.

3. Mistake as to Contents of Will—Extrinsic Evidence Not Admissible

Extrinsic evidence is not admissible to show that a provision was omitted or is incorrect. Under the *plain meaning rule*, evidence is not admissible to contradict the plain, unambiguous language of a will.

4. Ambiguity—Extrinsic Evidence Admissible

A *latent* ambiguity arises if a will's language is clear on its face but results in a misdescription as applied; a *patent* ambiguity exists if the uncertainty appears on the face of the will. Extrinsic evidence is admissible to cure latent ambiguities because it does not have the effect of rewriting the will. Under the traditional view, extrinsic evidence would not be admissible to cure patent ambiguities, but the modern, better view (followed in Illinois) would admit it.

a. Types of Extrinsic Evidence Admissible

The types of extrinsic evidence admissible include: (i) testimony as to the circumstances surrounding the will's execution, the testator's relationship and association with the persons who may have been intended as beneficiaries, and any motives that may have actuated the testator; and (ii) statements made by the testator to the attorney who prepared the will. The testator's statements to other persons are not admissible.

GROUNDS FOR WILL CONTEST

Defective Execution	One or more of the requirements for execution is missing (*e.g.,* signature missing, witnesses did not sign in testator's presence).
Valid Revocation	The will has been validly revoked by operation of law, subsequent instrument, or physical act.
Lack of Testamentary Capacity	The testator was under the age of 18 or lacked the mental capacity required at the time of execution. To have capacity, the testator must: understand that she is writing a will, know the nature and character of her property, know the natural objects of her bounty, and make a disposition of property according to a plan formed in her own mind.
Undue Influence	Influence was exerted on the testator that overpowered the mind and free will of the testator, and resulted in a will or gift that would not have been made but for the influence. The burden is shifted to the will proponent if the beneficiary was in a confidential relationship with the testator and was active in procuring the will.
Fraud	Either (i) a misrepresentation is made as to the nature or contents of the instrument (fraud in the factum), or (ii) the testator is induced into making a will or gift by misrepresentations of fact that influence her motivation (fradulent inducement).
Mistake	Either (i) the testator was mistaken as to the nature of the instrument (*e.g.,* thought it was a power of attorney) or in some cases, (ii) the testator's mistake in inducement appears on the face of the will.
Lack of Knowledge of Will Contents	The testator must be aware of and approve the contents of her will.

G. TESTATOR LACKED KNOWLEDGE OF CONTENTS OF WILL

For the required testamentary intent to be present, the testator must know and approve of the words contained in her will. The mere execution of a will with the testator's signature raises a presumption, in the absence of fraud or imposition, that the testator was aware of the contents and understandingly executed the will. If it can be proven that the testator had no opportunity to read a will prepared for her or that she cannot read, and the contents of the will were not explained to her, the executed will is invalid.

H. NO-CONTEST CLAUSES

A clause in a will providing that a beneficiary will forfeit her interest in the estate if she contests the will is valid and enforceable in Illinois, but will be strictly construed. However, a suit to construe a will is not a "contest" for purposes of such a clause.

I. TORTIOUS INTERFERENCE WITH EXPECTANCY TO INHERIT

To effectively plead a cause of action for tortious interference with expectancy to inherit, the plaintiff must allege: (i) an expectancy; (ii) the defendant's intentional interference with the expectancy; (iii) the interference involved tortious conduct (*e.g.,* fraud, duress, undue influence); (iv) a reasonable certainty that the devise to the plaintiff would have been received but for the interference; and (v) damages.

XI. POWERS OF APPOINTMENT

A. TERMINOLOGY OF POWERS

A power of appointment is the authority created in a person (***donee***) to designate, within the limits prescribed by the creator of the power (***donor***), the persons who will take the property and the manner in which they will take it. The ***objects*** of the power are those in whose favor a power is exercisable. ***Takers in default of appointment*** are the persons designated to take the property if the donee fails to effectively exercise his power.

1. General Power vs. Special Power

A general power of appointment is one exercisable in favor of the donee herself, her estate, her creditors, or the creditors of her estate. A special power is one exercisable in favor of a specified class of persons that does ***not*** include the donee, her estate, her creditors, or the creditors of her estate.

2. Presently Exercisable Power vs. Testamentary Power

A presently exercisable power is one exercisable by the donee during her lifetime. A testamentary power is exercisable only by the donee's will. Unless expressly limited to the donee's lifetime, a presently exercisable power is also exercisable by the donee's will.

B. GENERAL POWERS OF APPOINTMENT

1. Donee Acts as Donor's Agent

The donee is acting as the donor's agent in appointing the property; thus, when the donee exercises the power, the appointee takes title directly from the donor. If the donee dies without exercising the power, it terminates. Appointive property is not subject to the elective share statute.

2. Failure to Exercise General Power

If a donee fails to exercise a general power and there is no gift in default, the property passes to the ***donor's*** heirs or residuary legatees.

3. Donee's Creditors

A donee's creditors can reach property subject to a presently exercisable general power. They cannot reach property subject to a postponed or testamentary general power unless the donee is also the donor.

C. SPECIAL POWERS OF APPOINTMENT

1. Exclusive vs. Nonexclusive Special Powers

A special power is *exclusive* if it may be exercised in favor of some objects of the power to the exclusion of others; *i.e.*, the donee may appoint to some objects and not others, or may appoint unequal shares. A special power is ***nonexclusive*** if it ***must*** be exercised in favor of ***all*** of the appointees. Special powers are presumed to be exclusive unless the donor expressly provides otherwise.

2. Implied Gift in Default of Appointment

If the donee of a special power fails to exercise it and there is no gift in default of appointment, a gift to the objects of the power is implied.

3. Donee's Creditors

The donee's creditors ***cannot*** reach property subject to a special power. This is true even if the donee of the special power is also the donor, unless the transfer was in ***fraud*** of the donor-donee's creditors.

D. EXERCISE OF POWERS OF APPOINTMENT

1. Any Instrument Can Exercise Power

Unless the donor directs otherwise, a power of appointment can be exercised by any instrument effective to transfer title to property.

2. Residuary Clause Does Not, By Itself, Exercise Testamentary Power

A residuary clause, by itself, does not exercise any power of appointment. If, however, a donee's will devises "all the rest, residue, and remainder of my property, ***including any property over which I may have a power of appointment***," this blanket exercise will be given effect unless the donor called for an appointment specifically referring to the power.

3. Exercise by Implication

If a donee purports to dispose of appointive property as if it were her own, or if a disposition cannot be given meaning unless the donee is treated as having exercised the power, the power will be deemed exercised by implication.

4. Interests that Can Be Created by Power's Exercise

Absent a contrary provision in the instrument creating the power, the donee can: appoint the property outright or in trust, create life estates and future interests, impose conditions and limitations on the interests created, and create additional powers of appointment.

5. **Trustee Can Rely on Apparently Valid Exercise of Power**
In distributing trust property subject to a testamentary power of appointment, a trustee acting in good faith is not liable to any appointee or taker in default of appointment for relying on an apparently valid exercise of a power. The party to whom the distribution should have been made can recover the distributed property from the persons who received the distribution.

CMR
COMPARISON CHART

GENERAL VS. SPECIAL POWERS OF APPOINTMENT		
	Exercisable in Favor of Donee, Her Creditors, or Her Estate	Exercisable Inter Vivos	Exercisable by Will
Presently Exercisable General Power	✓	✓	✓
General Testamentary Power	✓		✓
Presently Exercisable Special Power		✓	✓
Special Testamentary Power			✓

E. APPLICATION OF RULE AGAINST PERPETUITIES
A power of appointment raises the following perpetuities issues: (i) the validity of the power itself, (ii) the validity of its exercise, and (iii) the validity of the gift in default of appointment.

1. **Presently Exercisable General Powers**
If it is certain that the power will become *exercisable* or fail within the perpetuities period, it is valid. When a presently exercisable general power is exercised, the perpetuities period begins to run from the date of exercise; therefore, the interests created must vest or fail within 21 years after the death of a life in being on the date of exercise. Gifts in default of a presently exercisable general power are rarely invalid under the Rule. The perpetuities period begins to run only when the power ceases.

2. **Special and Testamentary Powers**
If a special or testamentary power *may* be exercised beyond the perpetuities period, which begins to run from the creation of the power, it is void. Thus, unless expressly limited to the perpetuities period, any special or testamentary power given to an unborn person is invalid.

   a. **Relation-Back Doctrine**
   Interests created by the exercise of a special or testamentary power are read back into

the original instrument creating the power, and the perpetuities period begins on the date that power was created.

    b.   Second Look Doctrine
    Even though the exercise of the power is read back into the donor's instrument, facts and circumstances existing on the date of exercise are taken into account in determining the validity of the interests created by the exercise.

    c.   Gifts in Default of Appointment
    Gifts in default of appointment are subject to the Rule Against Perpetuities, but the second look doctrine also applies to them.

3.   Effect of Invalid Appointment
If a donee makes an invalid appointment, the property passes to the taker in default of appointment, if any. If none, the property reverts back to the donor's estate. However, if the donee of a *general power* manifests an intent to take the property out of the creating instrument and "capture" it for the donee's estate, the property will pass to the donee's estate.

F.   CONTRACTS TO APPOINT

1.   Testamentary Powers—Contract to Appoint Invalid
The donee of a testamentary power cannot contract to make an appointment. To allow this would defeat the intention of the donor by, in effect, transforming a testamentary power into a presently exercisable power.

2.   Presently Exercisable Powers—Contract to Appoint Valid
The donee of a presently exercisable power can contract to make an appointment, but cannot contract to confer a benefit on a nonobject of a special power.

XII. ADVANCE HEALTHCARE DIRECTIVES: LIVING WILLS AND DURABLE HEALTHCARE POWERS

A.   INTRODUCTION
A living will states an individual's desires regarding whether to: (i) administer, withhold, or withdraw *life-sustaining procedures*; (ii) provide, withhold, or withdraw *artificial nutrition or hydration*; and (iii) provide treatment to *alleviate pain*. A durable healthcare power appoints an agent to make healthcare decisions on behalf of the principal, but is not effective *until the principal becomes incapacitated*, and it remains effective despite the incapacity. Generally, a durable healthcare power is broader in scope than a living will.

B.   CREATION AND EXECUTION
Living wills and durable healthcare powers must be: (i) in *writing*, (ii) *signed* by the testator or another at his direction, and (iii) *witnessed* by two adults. The testator must be an adult or an emancipated minor and of sound mind. Capacity is normally presumed, but if challenged, the burden of proof is on the challenger to show that the testator or principal lacked capacity or was unduly influenced.

C. REVOCATION

Living wills and durable healthcare powers can be revoked *at any time* by: (i) obliterating, burning, tearing, or destroying the document; (ii) a properly executed written revocation; or (iii) an oral or other expression of intent to revoke, provided it is made in the presence of an adult who signs and dates a written confirmation that the expression was made.

1. Revocation of Prior Powers

Generally, the execution of a valid durable healthcare power revokes any prior durable healthcare powers. Also, the designation of a principal's spouse as his agent is *automatically revoked* if the marriage is annulled or dissolved.

D. INDIVIDUALS ELIGIBLE TO ACT AS AGENT UNDER DURABLE HEALTHCARE POWER

A principal can appoint as agent anyone *except* his attending physician or other healthcare provider unless that healthcare provider is not administering care to the principal.

E. AUTHORITY OF AGENT UNDER DURABLE HEALTHCARE POWER

The agent has the authority to make any healthcare decisions on the principal's behalf that the principal could have made for himself while having capacity. The authority of the agent is within the discretion of the principal and must be stated in the instrument creating the durable healthcare power. The agent is not required to exercise powers granted in the instrument, but if she does she must act with due care and in the principal's *best interest*. The agent is not subject to liability or discipline for conduct relating to healthcare decisions provided she acted in *good faith*.

barbri®

The Conviser
Mini Review

Table of Contents

To be used in conjunction with the Summer 2010 and Winter 2011 BAR/BRI Bar Review Courses

CMR

CONSTITUTIONAL LAW

TABLE OF CONTENTS

CONSTITUTIONAL LAW

PART 1: POWERS OF THE FEDERAL GOVERNMENT

I. THE JUDICIAL POWER

A. ARTICLE III

Federal judicial power extends to cases involving:

1. *Interpretation* of the Constitution, federal laws, treaties, and admiralty and maritime laws; and

2. *Disputes* between states, states and foreign citizens, and citizens of diverse citizenship.

B. POWER OF JUDICIAL REVIEW

The Supreme Court may review the constitutionality of acts of other branches of the federal government. It may also review state acts pursuant to the Supremacy Clause.

C. FEDERAL COURTS

Only Article III courts (*i.e.,* courts established by Congress pursuant to Article III) are the subject of this outline. Congress has plenary power to delineate the original and appellate jurisdiction of these courts but is bound by the standards set forth in Article III as to subject matter and party jurisdiction and the requirement of a "case or controversy." Congress can also create courts under Article I (*e.g.,* tax courts). Judges in those courts do not have life tenure as do Article III judges, and Congress may not assign to Article I courts jurisdiction over cases that have traditionally been tried in Article III courts.

D. JURISDICTION OF THE SUPREME COURT

1. Original Jurisdiction

The Supreme Court has original jurisdiction in all cases affecting ambassadors, public ministers, consuls, and those in which a state is a party, but Congress has given concurrent jurisdiction to lower federal courts in all cases except those between states.

2. Appellate Jurisdiction

The Supreme Court has appellate jurisdiction in all cases to which federal power extends, subject to congressional exceptions and regulation. Cases can come to the Court by one of two ways:

a. Writ of Certiorari—Most Cases

The Supreme Court has complete *discretion* to hear cases that come to it by certiorari. The cases that come by certiorari are:

1) Cases from *state courts* where (i) the constitutionality of a federal statute, federal treaty, or state statute is in issue, or (ii) a state statute allegedly violates federal law.

2) All cases from *federal courts* of appeals.

b. Appeal—Rare Cases

The Supreme Court *must* hear cases that come to it by appeal. These cases are confined to decisions by three-judge federal district court panels that grant or deny injunctive relief.

E. CONSTITUTIONAL AND SELF-IMPOSED LIMITATIONS ON EXERCISE OF FEDERAL JURISDICTION—"STRICT NECESSITY"

Whether a case is "justiciable" (*i.e.*, a federal court may address it) depends on whether there is a "case or controversy." In addition to the "case or controversy" requirement, there are other limitations on federal court jurisdiction.

1. No Advisory Opinions

There must be specific ***present harm*** or threat of specific future harm. Federal courts can hear actions for declaratory relief if there is an actual dispute between parties having adverse legal interests. Complainants must show that they have engaged in (or wish to engage in) specific conduct and that the challenged action poses a ***real and immediate danger*** to their interests. However, the federal courts will not determine the constitutionality of a statute if it has never been enforced and there is no real fear that it ever will be.

2. Ripeness—Immediate Threat of Harm

A plaintiff is not entitled to review of a statute or regulation before its enforcement (*i.e.*, may not obtain a declaratory judgment) unless the plaintiff will suffer some harm or immediate threat of harm.

3. Mootness

A real controversy must exist at all stages of review. If the matter has already been resolved, the case will be dismissed as moot.

a. Exception

Controversies capable of repetition, but evading review are not moot. *Examples:* Issues concerning events of short duration (*e.g.*, abortion) or a defendant who voluntarily stops the offending practice but is free to resume.

b. Class Actions

A class representative may continue to pursue a class action after the representative's controversy has become moot if claims of other class members are still viable.

CMR **Exam Tip** Ripeness bars consideration of claims ***before*** they have been developed; mootness bars their consideration ***after*** they have been resolved.

4. Standing

A person must have a concrete stake in the outcome of a case.

a. Components

1) Injury

Plaintiff must show that she has been or will be ***directly*** and ***personally*** injured by the allegedly unlawful government action, which affects her rights under the Constitution or federal law. The injury ***need not be economic***.

2) Causation

There must be a causal connection between the injury and the conduct complained of.

3) Redressability

A decision in the litigant's favor must be capable of eliminating her grievance.

CMR **Exam Tip** Remember that standing just allows the plaintiff to get into court. Thus, a successful ruling on the standing issue does not mean that the plaintiff wins his suit; it merely means that he gets an opportunity to try it.

b.   **Common Standing Issues**

1)   **Congressional Conferral of Standing**
Congress has no power to eliminate the case or controversy requirement and, thus, cannot grant standing to someone not having an injury. However, a federal statute may create new interests, injury to which may be sufficient for standing.

2)   **Standing to Enforce Government Statutes**
A plaintiff may have standing to enforce a federal statute if she is within the "*zone of interests*" Congress meant to protect.

3)   **Standing to Assert Rights of Others**
Generally, one cannot assert the constitutional rights of others to obtain standing, but a *claimant with standing* in her own right may also assert the rights of a third party *if*:

a)   It is difficult for the third party to assert her own rights (*e.g.*, an association may attack a law requiring disclosure of membership lists, because members cannot attack the law without disclosing their identities); or

b)   A special relationship exists between the claimant and the third party (*e.g.*, a doctor can assert a patient's rights in challenging an abortion restriction).

4)   **Standing of Organizations**
An organization has standing if (i) there is an injury in fact to members that gives them a right to sue on their own behalf, (ii) the injury is related to the organization's purpose, *and* (iii) individual member participation in the lawsuit is not required.

5)   **No Citizenship Standing**
People have no standing merely as "citizens" to claim that government action violates federal law or the Constitution. The injury is too generalized.

6)   **Taxpayer Standing Requisites**
A taxpayer has standing to litigate her tax bill, but a taxpayer generally has no standing to *challenge government expenditures*, because the taxpayer's interest is too remote. *Exception:* Suits attacking *congressional* taxing and spending measures on First Amendment *Establishment Clause* grounds (*e.g.*, congressionally approved federal expenditures to aid parochial schools).

CMR **Exam Tip** For a taxpayer to have standing, *Congress's spending power* must be involved. Thus, for example, there is no standing to challenge federal government grants of surplus property to religious groups or expenditures of general executive branch funds.

5. **Adequate and Independent State Grounds**

   The Supreme Court will not exercise jurisdiction if the state court judgment is based on adequate and independent state law grounds—even if federal issues are involved. State law grounds are adequate if they are fully dispositive of the case. They are independent if the decision is not based on federal case interpretations of identical federal provisions. When the state court has not clearly indicated that its decision rests on state law, the Supreme Court may hear the case.

6. **Abstention**

   a. **Unsettled Question of State Law**

      A federal court will temporarily abstain from resolving a constitutional claim when the disposition rests on an unsettled question of state law.

   b. **Pending State Proceedings**

      Federal courts will not enjoin pending state ***criminal*** proceedings (and in some cases pending state administrative or civil proceedings involving an important state interest), except in cases of proven harassment or prosecutions taken in bad faith.

7. **Political Questions**

   Political questions will not be decided. These are issues (i) constitutionally committed to another branch of government or (ii) inherently incapable of judicial resolution.

   a. **Examples of Political Questions**

      Challenges based on the "Republican Form of Government" Clause of Article IV; challenges to congressional procedures for ratifying constitutional amendments; whether a person elected to Congress meets the age, residency, or vote requirements; and the President's conduct of foreign policy are political questions.

   b. **Compare—Nonpolitical Questions**

      Legislative apportionment, arbitrary exclusion of a congressional delegate, and production of presidential papers and communications are not political questions.

8. **Eleventh Amendment Limits on Federal Courts**

   The Eleventh Amendment prohibits ***federal courts*** from hearing a private party's or foreign government's claims against a state government.

   a. **What Is Barred?**

      The prohibition extends to actions in which the state is named as a party or in which the state will have to pay retroactive damages. Similarly, the Supreme Court has held that the ***doctrine of sovereign immunity bars*** suits against a state government in state court, even on federal claims, unless the defendant state consents.

   b. **What Is Not Barred?**

      The prohibition does not extend to actions against local governments, actions by the United States or other states, or proceedings in federal bankruptcy courts.

   c. **Exceptions**

1) Certain Actions Against State Officers
The following actions can be brought against state officers in federal court despite the Eleventh Amendment: (i) actions to enjoin an officer from future conduct that violates the Constitution or federal law, even if this will require prospective payment from the state; and (ii) actions for damage against an officer personally.

2) Congress Removes the Immunity
Congress can remove Eleventh Amendment immunity *as to actions created under the Fourteenth Amendment*, but it must be unmistakably clear that Congress intended to remove the immunity.

II. LEGISLATIVE POWER

The federal government has limited powers. Every exercise of federal power must be traced to the Constitution.

A. ENUMERATED AND IMPLIED POWERS

Congress can exercise those powers *enumerated* in the Constitution plus all auxiliary powers *necessary and proper* to carry out all powers vested in the federal government.

1. Necessary and Proper "Power"
Congress has the power to make all laws necessary and proper (appropriate) for executing *any* power granted to *any* branch of the federal government.

CMR **Exam Tip** The Necessary and Proper Clause standing alone cannot support federal law. It must work in conjunction with another federal power. Thus, an answer choice that states that a law is supported by the Necessary and Proper Clause (or is valid under Congress's power to enact legislation necessary and proper) will be incorrect unless another federal power is linked to it in the question.

2. Taxing Power
Congress has the power to tax, and most taxes will be upheld if they bear some *reasonable relationship to revenue production* or if Congress has the *power to regulate* the activity taxed. However, neither Congress nor the states may tax exports to foreign countries.

3. Spending Power
Congress may spend to "provide for the common defense and general welfare." Spending may be for *any public purpose*.

CMR **Exam Tip** The federal government can tax and *spend* for the general welfare; it cannot directly legislate for it. Thus, nonspending regulations cannot be supported by the General Welfare Clause.

Also recall that although the power to spend for the general welfare is broad (any public purpose), it is still limited by the Bill of Rights and other constitutional provisions.

4. Commerce Power

Congress has the *exclusive* power to regulate all foreign and interstate commerce. To be within Congress's power under the Commerce Clause, a federal law regulating interstate commerce must either:

(i) *Regulate the channels* of interstate commerce;

(ii) *Regulate the instrumentalities* of interstate commerce and persons and things in interstate commerce; or

(iii) *Regulate activities that have a substantial effect* on interstate commerce.

a. Intrastate Activity

When Congress attempts to regulate *intrastate* activity under the third prong, above, the Court will uphold the regulation if it is of *economic or commercial activity* (*e.g.,* growing wheat or medicinal marijuana even for personal consumption) and the court can conceive of a *rational basis* on which Congress could conclude that the activity *in aggregate* substantially affects interstate commerce. However, if the regulated intrastate activity is noncommercial and noneconomic (*e.g.,* possessing a gun in a school zone or gender-motivated violence), it cannot be regulated under the Commerce Clause unless Congress can factually show a substantial economic effect on interstate commerce.

5. War and Related Powers

The Constitution gives Congress power to declare war, raise and support armies, and provide for and maintain a navy.

a. Economic Regulation

Economic regulation during war and in the postwar period to remedy wartime disruptions has been upheld.

b. Military Courts and Tribunals

Congress is authorized to make rules for the government and regulation of armed forces.

1) Judicial Review

Regular federal (or state) courts have no general power to review court-martial proceedings.

2) Enemy Civilians and Soldiers

Enemy civilians and soldiers may be tried by military courts. However, Congress has no power to deny habeas corpus review to all aliens detained as enemy combatants absent a meaningful substitute for habeas corpus review.

3) American Soldiers

Military courts have jurisdiction over *all offenses* committed by persons who are members of the armed services both at the time of the offense *and* when charged.

4) American Civilians

American civilians may be tried by military courts under martial law only if actual warfare forces the federal courts to shut down.

5) Detention of Citizen Enemy Combatants
Due process requires that a ***citizen held in the United States*** as an "enemy combatant" have a meaningful opportunity to contest the factual basis for his detention before a neutral decisionmaker.

6. Investigatory Power
The power of Congress to investigate is implied. Investigation must be expressly or impliedly authorized by the appropriate congressional house.

7. Property Power
Congress has the power to dispose of and make rules for territories and other properties of the United States. While there is no express limitation on Congress's power to ***dispose*** of property, federal ***takings*** (eminent domain) must be for the purpose of effectuating an enumerated power under some other provision of the Constitution.

8. No Federal Police Power
Congress has no general police power. However, Congress has police power type powers over the District of Columbia, federal lands, military bases, and Indian reservations (based on its power over the capital and its property power).

CMR Exam Tip If an answer choice attempts to support federal action on the basis of the police power (*e.g.,* "Congress can constitutionally act under the police power" or "the action is valid under the federal police power"), see whether the facts state that the action pertains to the District of Columbia or other federal possessions. If not, it is a wrong choice.

9. Bankruptcy Power
Congress's power to establish uniform rules for bankruptcy is nonexclusive; states may legislate in the field as long as their laws do not conflict with federal law.

10. Postal Power
The postal power is exclusive. Under the postal power, Congress may validly classify and place reasonable restrictions on use of the mails, but may not deprive any citizen or group of citizens of the general mail "privilege."

11. Power Over Citizenship
Congress may establish uniform rules of naturalization. This gives Congress plenary power over aliens.

a. Exclusion of Aliens
Aliens have no right to enter the United States and can be refused entry summarily because of their political beliefs. However, ***resident aliens*** are entitled to ***notice and a hearing*** before they can be deported.

b. Naturalization and Denaturalization
Congress has ***exclusive*** power over naturalization and denaturalization. However, Congress may not take away the citizenship of any citizen—native born or naturalized—without his consent.

12. **Admiralty Power**

Congress's admiralty power is plenary and exclusive unless Congress leaves maritime matters to state jurisdiction.

13. **Power to Coin Money and Fix Weights and Measures**

Congress has the power to coin money and fix standards for weights and measures.

14. **Patent/Copyright Power**

Congress has the power to control the issuance of patents and copyrights.

SOURCES OF CONGRESSIONAL POWER

Government Action	Source of Power
1. Congress enacts divorce laws for the District of Columbia.	General federal police power for D.C. (as well as military bases and federal lands).
2. Congress pays for highways.	Spending Power and Commerce Clause.
3. Federal income tax.	Taxing Power.
4. Congress conditions aid to states for medical programs on state funding of AIDS research.	Spending Power.
5. Congress adopts a tax to regulate banknotes rather than to raise revenue.	Power to coin money.
6. Congress prohibits hunting on federal lands.	Property Power.
7. Congress bars racial discrimination at places of public accommodation.	Commerce Clause.
8. Congress requires all employers, including state governments, to comply with federal minimum wage and overtime provisions.	Commerce Clause.

Note: The Amendments to the Constitution may also be a source of power (*e.g.,* the Thirteenth Amendment gives Congress power to outlaw badges of slavery; thus Congress may require a private seller to sell land to blacks as well as whites). (*See infra.*)

B. **DELEGATION OF LEGISLATIVE POWER**

Legislative power may generally be delegated to the executive or judicial branch as long as intelligible standards are set and the power is not uniquely confined to Congress (*e.g.*, powers to declare war, impeach).

Note: Congress may not appoint members of a body with administrative or enforcement powers (*see* III.A.1.a., *infra*).

CMR **Exam Tip** Although you should know that a valid delegation of legislative power requires "intelligible standards" for the delegate to follow (*see* above), in applying that rule almost anything will pass for an intelligible standard, and thus no legislative delegation has been invalidated since 1936.

C. SPEECH AND DEBATE CLAUSE—IMMUNITY FOR FEDERAL LEGISLATORS

Conduct that occurs in the regular course of the federal legislative process and the motivation behind that conduct are immune from prosecution.

Note: Immunity does not cover bribes, speeches outside Congress, or the republication in a press release or newsletter of a defamatory statement originally made in Congress.

D. CONGRESSIONAL "VETO" OF EXECUTIVE ACTIONS INVALID

A legislative veto is an attempt by Congress to overturn an executive agency action *without* bicameralism (*i.e.,* passage by both houses of Congress) or presentment (*i.e.,* giving the bill to the President for his signature or veto). Legislative vetoes of executive actions are invalid.

III. THE EXECUTIVE POWER

A. DOMESTIC POWERS

1. Appointment and Removal

a. Appointment Powers

The executive appoints "all ambassadors, other public ministers and consuls, justices of the Supreme Court, and all other officers of the United States whose appointments are not otherwise provided for," with advice and consent of the Senate. Congress, however, may vest the appointment of *inferior officers* in the President alone, the courts, or the heads of departments. Congress itself may *not* appoint members of a body with administrative or enforcement powers.

b. Removal of Appointees

1) By President

The President can remove high level, purely executive officers (*e.g.,* cabinet members) at will, without any interference by Congress. However, Congress may provide statutory limitations (*e.g.,* removal only for good cause) on the President's power to remove all other executive appointees.

2) By Congress

Congress may remove executive officers *only* through the impeachment process.

2. Pardons

The President may grant pardons for all federal offenses but not for impeachment or civil contempt. The pardon power cannot be limited by Congress.

3. **Veto Power**
   If the President disapproves (vetoes) an act of Congress, the act may still become law if the veto is overridden by a ***two-thirds*** vote of ***each*** house.

   a. **Pocket Veto**
      The President has 10 days to exercise the veto power. If he fails to act within that time, the bill is automatically vetoed if Congress is not in session. If Congress is in session, the bill becomes law.

   b. **Line Item Veto Unconstitutional**
      The veto power allows the President only to approve or reject a bill *in toto*; he cannot cancel part (through a line item veto) and approve other parts.

4. **Power as Chief Executive**
   The President's powers over internal affairs are unsettled. Clearly the President has some power to direct subordinate executive officers, and there is a long history of Presidents issuing executive orders. Perhaps the best guide is as follows:

   a. If the President acts with the express or implied authority of Congress, his authority is at its maximum and his actions likely are valid;

   b. If the President acts where Congress is silent, his action will be upheld unless it usurps the power of another governmental branch or prevents another branch from carrying out its tasks; and

   c. If the President acts against the express will of Congress, he has little authority, and his action likely is invalid (*e.g.*, the President has no power to refuse to spend appropriated funds when Congress has expressly mandated that they be spent).

B. **POWER OVER EXTERNAL AFFAIRS**

1. **War**
   The President has ***no power*** to declare war but may act militarily in actual hostilities against the United States without a congressional declaration of war. However, Congress, under its power to enact a military appropriation every two years, may limit the President.

2. **Foreign Relations**
   The President has paramount power to represent the United States in day-to-day foreign relations.

3. **Treaty Power**
   The President has the power to enter into treaties with the consent of two-thirds of the Senate.

   a. **Supreme Law**
      Like other federal law, treaties are the "supreme law of the land" if they are self-executing (*i.e.*, effective without any implementation by Congress). ***State*** laws that conflict with a self-executing treaty are invalid. Note that the President generally does not have any independent power to issue a memorandum ordering compliance with a treaty that is not self-executing.

b. **Conflict with Federal Laws**

A conflict between a congressional act and a valid treaty is resolved by order of adoption: *the last in time prevails*.

c. **Conflict with Constitution**

Treaties are *not* co-equal with the Constitution; a treaty may not be inconsistent with the Constitution.

 **Exam Tip**   Treaties are subject to constitutional limits. Thus, no treaty (or executive agreement) can confer on Congress authority to act in a manner inconsistent with any specific provision of the Constitution.

4. **Executive Agreements**

Executive agreements are signed by the President and the head of a foreign country. They can be used for any purpose that treaties can be used for. They do *not* require the consent of the Senate.

a. **Conflict with State Laws**

If a state law conflicts with an executive agreement, the agreement prevails.

b. **Conflict with Federal Laws**

If an executive agreement conflicts with a federal law, the federal law prevails over the agreement.

CMR SUMMARY CHART

HIERARCHY OF U.S. LAW

United States Constitution

prevails over

Treaties and Federal Statutes
(in a conflict between these
two, the last in time prevails)

prevail over

Executive Agreements

prevail over

State Law

C. EXECUTIVE PRIVILEGE/IMMUNITY

1. Executive Privilege
The President has a privilege to keep certain communications secret. National security secrets are given great deference by the courts.

a. Exception
In criminal proceedings, presidential communiques will be available to the prosecution where a need for such information is demonstrated.

2. Executive Immunity
The President has *absolute immunity* from civil damages based on any action he took within his official responsibilities, but there is no immunity for acts that allegedly occurred before taking office. If presidential aides have exercised discretionary authority in a sensitive area, they may share in the immunity for suits brought concerning that area.

D. IMPEACHMENT
The President, Vice President, and all civil officers of the United States are subject to impeachment (the bringing of charges). Grounds include treason, bribery, high crimes, and misdemeanors. A *majority* vote in the House is necessary to invoke the charges of impeachment, and a *two-thirds* vote in the Senate is necessary to convict and remove from office.

PART 2:   THE FEDERAL SYSTEM

IV.   RELATIVE SPHERES OF FEDERAL AND STATE POWERS

A.   EXCLUSIVE FEDERAL POWERS

1.   Power of States Expressly Limited
Some powers are exclusively federal because the Constitution limits or prohibits the use of the power by states (*e.g.,* treaty power, coinage of money).

2.   Inherent Federal Powers
Other powers are exclusively federal because the nature of the power itself is such that it can be exercised only by the federal government (*e.g.,* declaration of war, federal citizenship).

B.   EXCLUSIVE STATE POWERS
All powers not delegated to the federal government are reserved to the states. Note, however, that federal powers are given an expansive interpretation, and thus little state power is exclusive.

C.   CONCURRENT FEDERAL AND STATE POWER—EFFECT OF SUPREMACY CLAUSE
Because of the Supremacy Clause, a federal law may supersede or preempt local laws.

1.   Conflict Between State and Federal Laws
If a state law conflicts with federal law, the state law will be invalidated.

2. **State Prevents Achievement of Federal Objective**

If a state or local law prevents achievement of a federal objective, it will be invalidated. This is true even if the state law was enacted for some valid purpose and not to frustrate the federal law (*e.g.,* state law providing for suspension of driver's license of persons who fail to pay off an auto accident case judgment, regardless of the person's discharge in bankruptcy, is invalid).

3. **Preemption**

A valid federal statute or regulation may expressly or impliedly "occupy" the entire field, thus precluding any state or local regulation *even if the state or local regulation is nonconflicting*. Express preemption clauses will be narrowly construed. When a federal law does not expressly preempt state law, the courts will try to deduce Congress's intent, but especially in cases involving a field traditionally within the power of the states (*e.g,* regulations involving health, safety, or welfare), courts will start with the *presumption* that the historic state police powers are *not* to be superseded unless that was the *clear and manifest purpose of Congress.*

D. **ABSENCE OF FEDERAL AND STATE POWERS**

Some powers are denied to both Congress and the states. For example, the qualifications for serving in Congress are set by the Constitution and cannot be altered by Congress or the states.

E. **INTERSTATE COMPACT CLAUSE**

The Interstate Compact Clause concerns agreements between states. If the agreement increases the states' power at the expense of federal power, congressional approval is required.

F. **FULL FAITH AND CREDIT CLAUSE**

By virtue of the Full Faith and Credit Clause, if a judgment is entitled to full faith and credit, it must be recognized in sister states (*i.e.,* a party who loses a case in New York generally may not relitigate it in New Jersey; the New Jersey courts are bound by the New York ruling). This Clause applies only if: (i) the court that rendered the judgment had *jurisdiction* over the parties and the subject matter; (ii) the judgment was *on the merits*; and (iii) the judgment is *final*.

V. INTERSOVEREIGN LITIGATION

A. **SUITS BY UNITED STATES AGAINST A STATE**

The United States may sue a state without its consent.

B. **SUITS BY A STATE AGAINST UNITED STATES**

Public policy forbids a state from suing the United States without its consent. Congress can pass legislation that permits the United States to be sued by a state in given situations.

C. **FEDERAL OFFICER AS DEFENDANT**

1. **Limitation**

A suit against a federal officer is deemed to be brought against the United States itself if the judgment sought would be satisfied out of the public treasury or would interfere with public administration and therefore is not permitted.

2. Specific Relief Against Officer
Specific relief against an officer as an individual will be granted if the officer acted ultra vires (beyond his authority).

D. SUITS BY ONE STATE AGAINST ANOTHER
One state may sue another state without the latter's consent. The Supreme Court has exclusive original jurisdiction.

VI. INTERGOVERNMENTAL TAX AND REGULATION IMMUNITIES

A. FEDERAL TAXATION AND REGULATION OF STATE OR LOCAL GOVERNMENTS

1. Tax or Regulation Applying to Both State and Private Entities—Valid
Congress may subject state and local government activities to regulation or taxation if the law or tax applies to *both* the public sector and the private sector (*e.g.,* minimum wage laws).

2. Tax or Regulation Applying Only to States
A federal tax or regulation that is not applicable to private businesses and that merely taxes or regulates a purely state or local governmental activity may be limited by the Tenth Amendment (*e.g.,* requiring states to either regulate radioactive waste or take title to it is beyond Congress's power).

a. Exception—Civil Rights
Congress may restrict state activities that violate civil liberties.

b. Exception—Spending Power Conditions
Congress may "indirectly" regulate states through the spending power by imposing conditions on the grant of money (*e.g.,* federal highway funds will be given only to states with a 21-year minimum age for drinking of alcohol).

CMR **Exam Tip** As a practical matter, the Court almost never strikes down on Tenth Amendment grounds a federal regulation or tax that impacts on state or local government entities. Thus, a choice on an MBE question that suggests that the Tenth Amendment will invalidate a federal action is almost always wrong.

3. Commandeering State Officials
While not specifically resting on the Tenth Amendment, the Supreme Court has held that Congress may not require state executive officials (*e.g.,* the police) to enforce federal laws because such a requirement would upset the Constitution's "dual sovereignty" structure (*i.e.,* both the states and the federal government are sovereigns).

B. STATE TAXATION AND REGULATION OF FEDERAL GOVERNMENT
A state may not directly tax federal instrumentalities without the consent of Congress. However, *nondiscriminatory, indirect* taxes are permissible if they do not unreasonably burden the federal government (*e.g.,* state income tax on federal employees). States may not regulate the federal government or its agents while performing their federal functions.

VII. PRIVILEGES AND IMMUNITIES CLAUSES

A. ARTICLE IV—PRIVILEGES OF STATE CITIZENSHIP

The Interstate Privileges and Immunities Clause prohibits discrimination by a state *against nonresidents*.

Note: Corporations and aliens are *not* protected by this clause. (In contrast, corporations and aliens are protected by the Equal Protection and Due Process Clauses of the Fourteenth Amendment, as well as the Dormant Commerce Clause, discussed *infra.*)

1. Only "Fundamental Rights" Protected

Only "fundamental rights"—those involving important *commercial activities* (*e.g.,* the pursuit of livelihood) and *civil liberties*—are protected.

2. Substantial Justification Exception

The state law may be valid if the state has a substantial justification for the different treatment. In effect, the state must show that nonresidents either cause or are part of the problem that the state is attempting to solve and that there are *no less restrictive means* to solve the problem.

3. Note—Relationship to Commerce Clause

Although the Article IV Privileges and Immunities Clause and the Dormant Commerce Clause may apply different standards and produce different results, they tend to mutually reinforce each other. Consequently, they both have to be considered in analyzing bar exam questions.

CMR EXAMPLE CHART

ARTICLE IV PRIVILEGES AND IMMUNITIES CLAUSE

Invalid Discrimination

1. Statute requiring $2,500 license fee from nonresident *commercial fishermen*, while residents paid $25.

2. Statute giving resident creditors priority over nonresident creditors to assets of foreign corporations in receivership proceedings.

3. Statute imposing a residency requirement for abortion.

4. Rule limiting bar admission to state residents.

5. Statute requiring *private sector* employers to give hiring preference to residents.

Discrimination Upheld

Statute requiring nonresidents to pay $225 license fee, as opposed to $30 residents' fee, for *recreational* hunting.

B. FOURTEENTH AMENDMENT—PRIVILEGES OF NATIONAL CITIZENSHIP

States may not deny their citizens the privileges or immunities of *national* citizenship (*e.g.,* the right to petition Congress for redress of grievances, the right to vote for federal officers, and the right to interstate travel). Corporations are not protected by this Clause.

PART 3: STATE REGULATION OR TAXATION OF COMMERCE

VIII. REGULATION OF FOREIGN COMMERCE

With a few minor exceptions, the power to regulate foreign commerce lies exclusively with Congress.

IX. REGULATION OF INTERSTATE COMMERCE

A. REGULATION OF COMMERCE BY CONGRESS

1. **Power of Congress to Supersede or Preempt State Regulation**
   When Congress regulates interstate commerce, conflicting state laws are *superseded* and even nonconflicting state or local laws in the same field may be *preempted*. (*See* IV.C.3., *supra.*)

2. **Power of Congress to Permit or Prohibit State Regulation**
   Congress may permit state regulations that would otherwise violate the Commerce Clause. Likewise, Congress may prohibit state regulations that could otherwise be upheld under the Commerce Clause. Congress may *not*, however, permit states to violate civil liberties.

B. STATE REGULATION OF COMMERCE IN THE ABSENCE OF CONGRESSIONAL ACTION

If Congress has not enacted laws regarding the subject, a state or local government may regulate local aspects of interstate commerce. To do so, however, it must *not discriminate against* or *unduly burden* interstate commerce. If it does, the state or local regulation will violate the Commerce Clause.

CMR **Exam Tip** The examiners sometimes use the terms "Dormant Commerce Clause" and "Negative Commerce Clause." These are merely descriptive terms that reflect the above idea: even where Congress has not acted, the Commerce Clause restricts state regulation of interstate commerce; states may not favor local economic interests or unduly burden interstate commerce.

1. **Discriminatory Regulations**
   State or local regulations that discriminate against interstate commerce to protect local economic interests *are almost always invalid* (*e.g.,* New York cannot ban California wines or tax them at a higher rate than local wines).

   a. **Exception—Important State Interest**
      A discriminatory state or local law may be valid if it furthers an important, noneconomic state interest and there are *no reasonable nondiscriminatory alternatives*

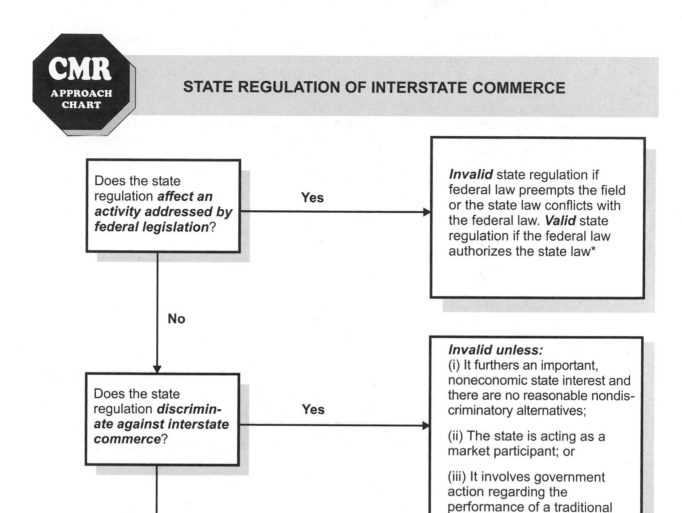

CMR
APPROACH
CHART

STATE REGULATION OF INTERSTATE COMMERCE

Does the state regulation *affect an activity addressed by federal legislation*?

Yes → *Invalid* state regulation if federal law preempts the field or the state law conflicts with the federal law. *Valid* state regulation if the federal law authorizes the state law*

No ↓

Does the state regulation *discriminate against interstate commerce*?

Yes → *Invalid unless:*
(i) It furthers an important, noneconomic state interest and there are no reasonable nondiscriminatory alternatives;

(ii) The state is acting as a market participant; or

(iii) It involves government action regarding the performance of a traditional government function

No ↓

Does the state regulation *burden interstate commerce*?

Yes → *Invalid unless* the state's interest in the regulation outweighs the burden on interstate commerce

No ↓

Valid state regulation

*Of course, Congress has no power to authorize legislation that would violate other constitutional provisions, such as the Privileges and Immunities Clause of Article IV.

available. *Example:* A state could prohibit *importation* of live bait fish because parasites could have a detrimental effect on its own fish population. However, a state could not prohibit *export* of live bait fish when no major state interest was involved.

b. **Exception—State as "Market Participant"**
A state may prefer its own citizens when acting as a market participant (*e.g.,* when buying or selling, hiring labor, or giving subsidies).

c. **Favoring Government Performing Traditional Government Functions**
The Supreme Court applies a more lenient standard when a law favors government action that involves the performance of a traditional government function (such as waste disposal). Discrimination against interstate commerce in such a case is permissible because it is likely motivated by legitimate objectives rather than by economic protectionism.

CMR **Exam Tip** Remember that discriminatory laws may also violate the Privileges and Immunities Clause of Article IV (*see* chart *infra*) or the Equal Protection Clause.

2. **Nondiscriminatory Laws—Balancing Test**
If a nondiscriminatory state law (*i.e.,* a law that treats local and out-of-state interests alike) burdens interstate commerce, it will be valid *unless* the burden outweighs the promotion of a legitimate local interest. The court will consider whether less restrictive alternatives are available. *Example:* An Iowa statute banning trucks over 60 feet was invalid because the state showed no significant evidence of increased safety and the burden on commerce was substantial.

a. **State Control of Corporations**
A different standard may apply to statutes *adopted by the state of incorporation* regulating the *internal governance of a corporation.* Because of the states' long history of regulating the internal governance of corporations that they create, and because of their strong interest in doing so, even a statute that heavily impacts interstate commerce may be upheld (*e.g.,* a state may deny voting rights to persons who acquire a controlling interest in a state corporation without approval from other shareholders, despite the impact that this may have on interstate commerce).

CMR **Exam Tip** When a bar exam question involves a state regulation that affects the free flow of interstate commerce, you should ask:

- Does the question refer to any *federal legislation* that might (i) *supersede* the state regulation or *preempt* the field or (ii) *authorize* state regulation otherwise impermissible?

- If neither of these possibilities is dispositive, does the state regulation either *discriminate* against interstate or out-of-state commerce or place an *undue burden* on the free flow of interstate commerce? If the regulation is discriminatory, it will be invalid unless (i) it furthers an important, noneconomic state interest *and* there are no reasonable nondiscriminatory alternatives, or (ii) the state is a market participant. If the regulation does not discriminate but burdens interstate commerce, it will be invalid if the burden on commerce outweighs the state's interest.

CMR
COMPARISON
CHART

COMMERCE CLAUSE VS. ARTICLE IV
PRIVILEGES AND IMMUNITIES

	Commerce Clause	**Privileges and Immunities Clause of Article IV**
State/local action _discrim-inates_ against out-of-state entities	If the discrimination burdens interstate commerce and there is no applicable federal legislation, the action is **_invalid unless:_** (i) It furthers an **_important, noneconomic state interest_** and there are no reasonable nondiscriminatory alternatives; (ii) The state is a **_market participant_** (_i.e.,_ purchaser, seller, subsidizer); or (iii) It involves government action regarding the performance of a traditional governmental function	If the action denies the out-of-state person important economic interests (_e.g.,_ livelihood) or civil liberties, the law is **_invalid unless_** the state has a **_substantial_** justification and there are no less restrictive means.
State/local action does _not_ _discriminate_	If the law burdens interstate commerce and the burden outweighs the state's interest in the action, the law is **_invalid_**.	Privileges and Immunities Clause does not apply where there is no discrimination.
May an alien or a corporation be a plaintiff?	Yes	No
Is there a market participant exception?	Yes	No

Note: The Article IV Privileges and Immunities Clause is stronger than the Commerce Clause (no market participant exception), but it is much narrower in scope (applies only to discrimination against economic interest; does not protect corporations or aliens).

C. TWENTY-FIRST AMENDMENT—STATE CONTROL OVER INTOXICATING LIQUOR

1. Intrastate Regulation
State governments have wide latitude over the *importation* of liquor and the conditions under which it is *sold or used* within the state. However, regulations that constitute only an economic preference for local liquor manufacturers may violate the Commerce Clause.

2. Interstate Regulation
Liquor in interstate commerce is subject to the Commerce Clause.

3. Federal Power
Congress may regulate economic transactions involving liquor (*e.g.*, sales of alcoholic beverages) through the federal commerce power (*e.g.*, antitrust laws) or by conditioning grants of money (*e.g.*, highway funds given only to states with minimum drinking age of 21).

X. POWER OF STATES TO TAX INTERSTATE COMMERCE

The same general considerations that apply to state regulation of commerce (*see supra*) apply to state taxation of commerce.

A. GENERAL CONSIDERATIONS
Congress has complete power to authorize or forbid state taxation that affects interstate commerce.

1. Discriminatory Taxes
Unless authorized by Congress, state taxes that discriminate against interstate commerce (*e.g.*, tax on out-of-state businesses higher than tax on in-state businesses) violate the Commerce Clause. Note that these taxes may also violate other constitutional provisions (*e.g.*, the Privileges and Immunities Clause of Article IV or the Equal Protection Clause).

2. Nondiscriminatory Taxes
A nondiscriminatory tax will be valid *if* the following requirements are met:

a. Substantial Nexus
To be valid, the tax must apply to an activity having a substantial nexus to the taxing state; *i.e.*, there must be significant or substantial activity within the taxing state. (Lack of a substantial nexus might also violate the due process requirement of minimum contacts, but substantial nexus requires more in-state connections.)

b. Fair Apportionment
To be valid, the tax must be fairly apportioned according to a rational formula. However, the taxpayer has the burden of proving unfair apportionment. (An unfairly apportioned tax may also violate equal protection.)

c. Fair Relationship
To be valid, the tax must be fairly related to the services or benefits provided by the state.

B. USE TAXES

1. Permissible in Buyer's State
Use taxes are imposed on goods purchased outside the state but used within it. They are valid.

STATE TAXATION OF INTERSTATE COMMERCE

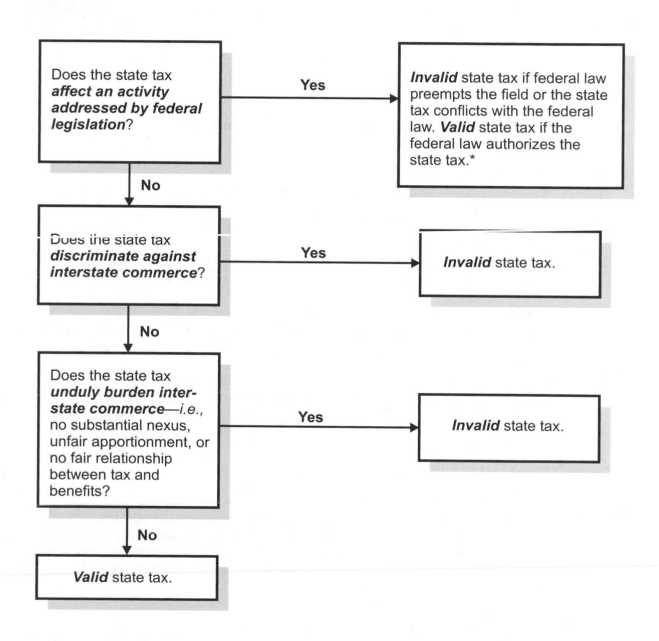

Does the state tax **affect an activity addressed by federal legislation**?

Yes → **Invalid** state tax if federal law preempts the field or the state tax conflicts with the federal law. **Valid** state tax if the federal law authorizes the state tax.*

No ↓

Does the state tax **discriminate against interstate commerce**?

Yes → **Invalid** state tax.

No ↓

Does the state tax **unduly burden inter-state commerce**—*i.e.,* no substantial nexus, unfair apportionment, or no fair relationship between tax and benefits?

Yes → **Invalid** state tax.

No ↓

Valid state tax.

*Of course, Congress has no power to authorize taxes that would violate the Constitution (*i.e.,* go beyond Congress's taxing power).

2. State May Force Seller to Collect Use Tax

An interstate seller may be required to collect a use tax *if* the seller has a ***sufficient nexus*** with the taxing state (*e.g.,* maintains offices in the taxing state). Merely soliciting orders by mail and shipping orders into the state is not sufficient.

C. SALES TAXES

Sales taxes are taxes imposed on the seller of goods for sales consummated within the state. They generally do not discriminate against interstate commerce; rather, the issue usually involves whether there is a substantial nexus between the taxpayer and the taxing state or whether the tax is properly apportioned.

D. AD VALOREM PROPERTY TAXES

Ad valorem property taxes are based on the assessed value of the property in question.

1. No Tax on Commodities in Course of Interstate Commerce

Commodities in interstate transit are entirely *exempt* from state taxation.

a. When Does Interstate Transportation Begin?

Interstate transportation begins when the cargo (i) is delivered to an interstate carrier *or* (ii) actually starts its interstate journey.

b. Effect of "Break" in Transit

A break in the continuity of transit does not destroy the interstate character of the shipment unless the break was intended to end or suspend the shipment.

c. When Does Interstate Shipment End?

The interstate shipment usually ends when the cargo reaches its destination; thereafter the goods are subject to local tax.

2. Tax on Instrumentalities Used to Transport Goods Interstate

The validity of ad valorem property taxes on instrumentalities of commerce (*e.g.,* trucks or airplanes) depends on (i) whether the instrumentality has acquired a ***"taxable situs"*** in the taxing state (*i.e.,* whether there are sufficient "contacts" with the taxing state to justify the tax) and (ii) whether the value of the instrumentality has been ***properly apportioned*** according to the amount of the "contacts" with each taxing state.

a. Taxable Situs

An instrumentality has a taxable situs in a state if it receives benefits or protection from the state. (There may be more than one taxable situs). *Example:* An airplane was held to have a taxable situs in a state—even though the airline owned no other property in the state—because the airline made 18 regularly scheduled flights daily from a rented depot in the state.

b. Apportionment Requirement

A tax apportioned on the value of the instrumentality will be upheld if it fairly approximates the average physical presence of the instrumentality in the taxing state. The taxpayer's domiciliary state can tax the full value of instrumentalities used in interstate commerce unless the taxpayer can prove that a defined part thereof has acquired a "taxable situs" elsewhere.

E.　PRIVILEGE, LICENSE, FRANCHISE, OR OCCUPATIONAL TAXES

These so-called "doing business" taxes are generally permitted. Such taxes may be measured by a flat amount or by a proportional rate based on contact with the taxing state. In either case, the basic requirements must be met: (i) the activity taxed must have a **substantial nexus** to the taxing state; (ii) the tax must be **fairly apportioned**; (iii) the tax must **not discriminate** against interstate commerce; and (iv) the tax must **fairly relate to services provided** by the state.

CMR **Exam Tip**　When a question involves state taxation that affects interstate commerce, you should ask:

1.　Does the question refer to any federal legislation that might (i) **forbid** the state tax or **pre-empt** the field, or (ii) **authorize** state taxation?

2.　If neither of these possibilities is dispositive, does the state tax **discriminate** against or **unduly burden** the free flow of interstate commerce? If the state tax discriminates or is unduly burdensome (no substantial nexus, unfair apportionment, or no fair relationship), it is invalid.

CMR
SUMMARY CHART

STATE TAXATION OF INTERSTATE COMMERCE— SPECIFIC TYPES OF TAXES

Type	Definition	Validity Under Commerce Clause
Use Tax	Tax on goods purchased outside of the state, but used within it	Valid unless higher than sales tax.
Sales Tax	Tax on the sale of goods consummated within the state	Generally valid if there is a substantial nexus to the taxing state and the tax is properly apportioned (if more than one state can tax the sale).
Ad Valorem Tax	Tax on the assessed value of some property	*Commodities:* Valid only if property is no longer in interstate commerce. *Instrumentalities:* Valid if instrumentality has "taxable situs" in state and tax is fairly apportioned. Full tax by domiciliary state valid unless taxpayer can prove a defined part has acquired taxable situs elsewhere.
Privilege, License, Franchise, and Occupational Tax	Tax placed on some activity ("doing business" tax)	Valid if (i) substantial nexus to taxing state, (ii) fairly apportioned, (iii) does not discriminate against interstate commerce, and (iv) fairly relates to services provided by the state.

XI. POWER OF STATES TO TAX FOREIGN COMMERCE

The Import-Export Clause and the Commerce Clause greatly limit the states' power to tax foreign commerce.

PART 4: INDIVIDUAL GUARANTEES AGAINST GOVERNMENTAL OR PRIVATE ACTION

XII. LIMITATIONS ON POWER AND STATE ACTION REQUIREMENT

A. CONSTITUTIONAL RESTRICTIONS ON POWER OVER INDIVIDUALS

Note: The Constitution sets the minimum threshold of rights. States generally are free to grant broader rights than those granted by the United States Constitution.

1. **Bill of Rights**

   By its terms, the Bill of Rights (the first 10 Amendments to the United States Constitution) limits *federal* power. However, the Fourteenth Amendment Due Process Clause applies almost all provisions of the Bill of Rights to the states. *Exceptions:* The most notable exceptions to incorporation are: (i) the Fifth Amendment's prohibition of criminal trials without a grand jury indictment and (ii) the Seventh Amendment's right to a jury trial in civil cases.

2. **Thirteenth Amendment**

   The Thirteenth Amendment prohibits slavery and involuntary servitude. Under the Thirteenth Amendment's Enabling Clause, Congress can prohibit racially discriminatory action by *anyone* (the government or a private citizen).

3. **Fourteenth and Fifteenth Amendments**

   The Fourteenth Amendment prevents *states* from depriving any person of life, liberty, or property without due process and equal protection of law. The Fifteenth Amendment prevents both the *federal and state governments* from denying a citizen the right to vote on account of race or color. Generally, private conduct is not prohibited by these amendments—only where some *state action* is involved. (Purely private conduct may be prohibited, however, on a separate constitutional basis, such as the Commerce Clause.)

   a. **Scope of Congressional Power Under Fourteenth Amendment**

      Section 5 of the Fourteenth Amendment gives Congress the power to adopt *appropriate legislation* to enforce the rights and guarantees provided by the Fourteenth Amendment. Under Section 5, Congress may *not* expand existing constitutional rights or create new ones—it may only enact laws to prevent or remedy violations of rights already recognized by the courts. To adopt a valid law, Congress must point to a history or pattern of state violation of such rights and adopt legislation that is *congruent and proportional* (*i.e.,* narrowly tailored) to solving the identified violation.

4. **Commerce Clause**

   Under the broadly construed commerce power, Congress may prohibit *private* racial discrimination in activities that might have a substantial effect on interstate commerce.

CMR **Exam Tip**   Because almost any activity taken cumulatively might have a substantial effect on interstate commerce, the Commerce Clause is an important basis for civil rights laws.

5. Rights of National Citizenship

Congress has inherent power to protect rights of citizenship (*e.g.,* rights to interstate travel, assemble, and petition Congress for redress).

B. STATE ACTION REQUIREMENT

Because the Constitution generally applies only to governmental action, to show a constitutional violation "state action" must be involved. *Note:* This concept applies to government and government officers at all levels—local, state, or federal. Note, however, that state action can be found in actions of seemingly private individuals who (i) perform exclusive public functions or (ii) have significant state involvement.

1. Exclusive Public Functions

Activities that are so ***traditionally*** the ***exclusive*** prerogative of the state are state action no matter who performs them.

2. Significant State Involvement—Facilitating Private Action

State action also exists wherever a state ***affirmatively*** facilitates, encourages, or authorizes acts of discrimination by its citizens.

CMR EXAMPLE CHART

STATE ACTION VS. NO STATE ACTION

State Action	No State Action
Public Function	
Running a town	Running a shopping mall (does not have all the attributes of a town)
Conducting an election	Holding a warehouseman's lien sale
Significant State Involvement	
Enforcing restrictive covenants prohibiting sale or lease of property through use of state courts	Granting a license and providing essential services to a private club
Leasing premises to a discriminatory lessee where state derives extra benefit from the discrimination (*i.e.,* symbiotic relationship exists)	Granting a monopoly to a utility
	Heavily regulating an industry
Allowing state official to act in discriminatory manner under "color of state law"	Granting a corporation its charter and exclusive name
Administering a private discriminatory trust by public officials	

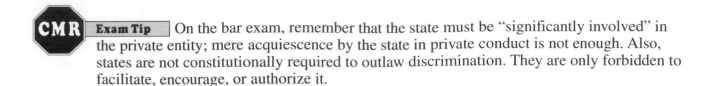 **Exam Tip** On the bar exam, remember that the state must be "significantly involved" in the private entity; mere acquiescence by the state in private conduct is not enough. Also, states are not constitutionally required to outlaw discrimination. They are only forbidden to facilitate, encourage, or authorize it.

XIII. RETROACTIVE LEGISLATION

A. CONTRACT CLAUSE—IMPAIRMENT OF CONTRACT

The Contract Clause prohibits *states* from enacting any law that *retroactively* impairs contract rights. It does not affect contracts not yet entered into.

1. Not Applicable to Federal Government

There is no comparable clause applicable to the federal government, but flagrant contract impairment would violate the Fifth Amendment Due Process Clause.

2. Basic Impairment Rules

a. Private Contracts—Intermediate Scrutiny

State legislation that *substantially impairs* an existing *private* contract is invalid unless the legislation (i) serves an important and legitimate public interest and (ii) is a reasonable and narrowly tailored means of promoting that interest. *Example:* Imposing a moratorium on mortgage foreclosures during a severe depression did not violate the Contract Clause.

b. Public Contracts—Stricter Scrutiny

Legislation that impairs a contract to which the state is a party is tested by the same basic test, but the contract will likely receive stricter scrutiny, especially if the legislation reduces the contractual burdens on the state.

B. EX POST FACTO LAWS

The state or federal government may not pass an ex post facto law (*i.e.,* a law that *retroactively* alters *criminal* offenses or punishments in a substantially prejudicial manner for the purpose of punishing a person for some past activity). A statute retroactively alters a law in a substantially prejudicial manner if it: (i) makes criminal an act that was *innocent when done*; (ii) prescribes *greater punishment* for an act than was prescribed for the act when it was done; or (iii) *reduces the evidence* required to convict a person of a crime from what was required when the act was committed. Note that the Due Process Clauses of the Fifth and Fourteenth Amendments similarly prohibit *courts* from retroactively interpreting criminal laws in an unexpected and indefensible way.

CMR **Exam Tip** The Ex Post Facto Clauses apply only to *criminal* cases. Thus, an answer choice that attempts to apply these prohibitions in a civil case (*e.g.,* regarding a denial of a professional license) is *wrong.*

C. BILLS OF ATTAINDER

Bills of attainder are legislative acts that inflict punishment on individuals without a judicial trial. Both federal and state governments are prohibited from passing bills of attainder.

D. DUE PROCESS CONSIDERATIONS

If a retroactive law does not violate the Contracts, Ex Post Facto, or Bill of Attainder Clauses, it still must pass muster under the Due Process Clause. If the retroactive law does not relate to a fundamental right, it need only be rationally related to a legitimate government interest.

XIV. PROCEDURAL DUE PROCESS

A. BASIC PRINCIPLE

A *fair process* (*e.g.,* notice and a hearing) is required for a government agency to individually take a person's "life, liberty, or property." Only intentional—not negligent—deprivation of these rights violates the Due Process Clause.

B. IS LIFE, LIBERTY, OR PROPERTY BEING TAKEN?

1. **Liberty** ; *significant freedom secured by constitution or statute*

   The term "liberty" is not specifically defined. It includes more than just freedom from bodily restraints (*e.g.,* it includes the right to contract and to engage in gainful employment). A deprivation of liberty occurs if a person:

   a. Loses significant freedom of action; *or*

   b. Is denied a freedom provided by the Constitution or a statute.

2. **Property** ; *an entitlement to a continued receipt of a benefit*

   "Property" includes more than personal belongings and realty, but an abstract need or desire for (or a unilateral expectation of) a benefit is not enough. There must be a *legitimate claim* or *"entitlement"* to the benefit under state or federal law. Examples of property interests include continued attendance at public school, welfare benefits, and (in some cases) government employment.

   CMR | **Exam Tip** | At one time, due process protected a "right" but not a "privilege." This distinction has been rejected by the Court. Thus, an answer that uses that terminology (right versus privilege) should be discarded as a red herring. The proper terminology is "entitlement."

C. WHAT TYPE OF PROCESS IS REQUIRED?

The type and extent of required procedures are determined by a three-part balancing test that weighs:

(i) The *importance of the interest* to the individual; and

(ii) The value of specific *procedural safeguards* to that interest; against

(iii) The *government interest* in fiscal and administrative efficiency.

Presumably, fair procedures and an unbiased decisionmaker will always be required. Notice and chance to respond before termination of the liberty or property interest are usually required.

D. DUE PROCESS RIGHTS ARE SUBJECT TO WAIVER

As a general rule, due process rights are, presumably, subject to waiver if the waiver is *voluntary and made knowingly*.

E. ACCESS TO COURTS—INDIGENT PLAINTIFFS

Government fees (*e.g.,* court filing fees) must be waived when imposition of a fee would deny a fundamental right to the indigent (*see infra,* for discussion of fundamental rights). Thus, for example, a marriage license or divorce court filing fee (privacy rights) or filing fee for candidates for electoral office (voting rights) must be waived. However, fees can be imposed when nonfundamental rights are involved (*e.g.,* fees for a bankruptcy discharge or review of welfare termination).

TYPE OF PROCESS REQUIRED

Interest Involved	Process Required
1. Commitment to Mental Institution	*Adults:* Prior notice and *prior* evidentiary hearing (except in emergency). *Children:* Prior screening by *"neutral factfinder."* (Parental consent alone insufficient.)
2. Welfare Benefits	Prior notice and *prior* evidentiary hearing.
3. Disability Benefits	Prior notice and opportunity to respond, and *subsequent* evidentiary hearing.
4. Public Employment (tenured or termination only "for cause")	Generally, prior notice and opportunity to respond, and *subsequent* evidentiary hearing.
5. Public Education (disciplinary suspension or academic dismissal)	Prior notice and opportunity to respond; *no* formal evidentiary hearing required.
6. Driver's License Suspension	Prior evidentiary hearing. *Exception:* Breathalyzer test suspension statutes.
7. Termination of Parent's Custody Rights	Prior notice and *prior* evidentiary hearing.
8. Civil Forfeitures	*Prior* notice and evidentiary hearing for *real property; subsequent* notice and hearing for *personal property.*
9. Detention of Citizen Enemy Combatants	*Subsequent* notice and a meaningful opportunity to contest the factual basis for detention before a neutral decisionmaker

XV.   THE "TAKING" CLAUSE

A.   IN GENERAL
The Fifth Amendment provides that private property may not be taken for *public use* without *just compensation*. This rule is applicable to the states via the Fourteenth Amendment. The Taking Clause is not a source of power for taking, but rather is a limitation. "Taking" includes not only physical appropriations but also *some* government action that damages property or impairs its use.

B.   "PUBLIC USE" LIMITATION LIBERALLY CONSTRUED
If the government's action is *rationally related* to a *legitimate* public purpose (*e.g.,* for health, welfare, safety, economic, or aesthetic reasons), the public use requirement is satisfied. Authorized takings by private enterprises are included if they redound to the public advantage (*e.g.,* railroads and public utilities).

C.   "TAKING" VS. "REGULATION"
The crucial issue is whether governmental action is a *taking* (requiring payment of just compensation) or merely a *regulation* (not requiring compensation). There is no clear-cut formula for making this determination, but the following general guidelines apply:

1.   Actual Appropriation or Physical Invasion
An actual or physical appropriation of property will almost always amount to a taking. *Exception:* Emergency situations.

2.   Use Restrictions

a.   Denial of *All* Economic Value of Land—Taking
If a government regulation denies a landowner of *all* economic use of his land (*e.g.,* a regulation prohibiting any building on the land), the regulation amounts to a taking unless principles of nuisance or property law make the use prohibitable.

1)   Temporary Denials of All Economic Use
Temporarily denying an owner of all economic use of property does not constitute a per se taking. Instead, the Court will carefully examine and weigh all the relevant circumstances—the planners' good faith, the reasonable expectations of the owners, the length of the delay, the delay's actual effect on the value of the property, etc.—in order to determine whether "fairness and justice" require just compensation.

b.   Decreasing Economic Value—Balancing Test
Regulations that merely decrease the value of property (*e.g.,* prohibit the most beneficial use) do not amount to a taking if they leave an *economically viable use for the property*. The Court will consider the economic impact of the regulation on the claimant and whether the regulation substantially interferes with distinct, investment-backed expectations of the claimant.

CMR EXAMPLE CHART

"TAKING" VS. "REGULATION"

Government Action	Characterization
1. Condemnation of land to build highway	Taking
2. Creating public access easement on private property	Taking
3. Abolishing inheritance rights	Taking
4. Zoning ordinances that merely prohibit the most beneficial use of property	Regulation
5. Ordering destruction of diseased trees	Regulation
6. Landmark ordinances	Regulation

3. Remedy—"Just Compensation"
If the regulation amounts to a taking, the government must:

(i) ***Pay*** the property owner just compensation for the property (*i.e.,* fair market value); ***or***

(ii) ***Terminate the regulation and pay*** the owner for damages that occurred while the regulation was in effect (*i.e.,* temporary taking damages).

a. "Worthless" Property
Just compensation is measured by the ***loss to the owner***, not by the gain to the taker. Thus, while property that is worthless to the owner can be the subject of a taking, no compensation need be paid when it is taken.

XVI. INTRODUCTION TO SUBSTANTIVE DUE PROCESS AND EQUAL PROTECTION

A. RELATIONSHIP BETWEEN SUBSTANTIVE DUE PROCESS AND EQUAL PROTECTION
Both substantive due process and equal protection guarantees require the Court to review the substance of a law rather than the procedures employed.

1. Substantive Due Process
If a law limits liberty of ***all*** persons to engage in some activity, on the MBE it usually is a due process question.

2. **Equal Protection**

   If a law treats a ***person or class of persons*** differently from others, on the MBE it usually is an equal protection problem.

   a. **Class of One**

      The Supreme Court has recognized—at least in relation to property regulation—that an equal protection claim may be brought not only for discrimination against a group, but also for arbitrary treatment against an individual—a class of one. However, the Court has held that an at-will government employee who claims to be a victim of arbitrary discrimination cannot use the class of one theory to make an equal protection claim.

B. **WHAT STANDARD OF REVIEW WILL THE COURT APPLY?**

   Under either guarantee, the Court is reviewing the legitimacy of governmental acts. Three standards of review are used:

   1. **Strict Scrutiny (Maximum Scrutiny)**

      Regulations affecting ***fundamental rights*** (*i.e.,* interstate travel, privacy, voting, and First Amendment rights) or involving ***suspect classifications*** (*i.e.,* race, national origin, and alienage) are reviewed under the strict scrutiny standard: The law is upheld if it is ***necessary*** to achieve a ***compelling*** government purpose. This is a difficult test to meet, and so a law examined under a strict scrutiny standard will often be invalidated—especially if there is a ***less burdensome*** alternative to achieve the government's goal.

      a. **Burden of Proof**

         The government has the burden of proof.

   2. **Intermediate Scrutiny**

      Regulations involving ***quasi-suspect classifications*** (*i.e.,* gender and legitimacy) are reviewed under the intermediate scrutiny standard: The law is upheld if it is ***substantially related*** to an ***important*** government purpose.

      a. **Burden of Proof**

         It is unclear who has the burden of proof. It is probably the government.

   3. **Rational Basis (Minimal Scrutiny)**

      Regulations that do ***not*** affect fundamental rights or involve suspect or quasi-suspect classifications (most laws) are reviewed under the rational basis standard: The law is upheld if it is ***rationally related*** to a ***legitimate*** government purpose. This is a very easy standard to meet; therefore the law is usually valid—unless it is ***arbitrary*** or ***irrational***.

      a. **Burden of Proof**

         The person challenging the law has the burden of proof.

      b. **Classifications that Are Not Suspect or Quasi-Suspect**

         The rational basis standard is used to review regulations involving classifications that are ***not*** suspect or quasi-suspect, such as age, disability, and poverty.

 Exam Tip Many exam questions ask you about the standard that the Court will use to review governmental regulation. Therefore, you need to know which standard will apply in a particular

case (*e.g.,* if a fundamental right is involved, strict scrutiny is applied). However, the choices may not **name** the standard ("strict scrutiny") but merely state it ("upheld if necessary to a compelling government interest"). Be prepared to recognize the standard by name **or** definition.

CMR **Exam Tip** Due process or equal protection questions also commonly test your knowledge of which party bears the burden of proof. Know the standards and their respective burdens.

XVII. SUBSTANTIVE DUE PROCESS

A. CONSTITUTIONAL SOURCE—TWO CLAUSES
The Due Process Clause of the Fifth Amendment applies to the federal government. The Due Process Clause of the Fourteenth Amendment applies to state and local governments. The same tests are applied under each clause.

B. APPLICABLE STANDARDS
When a *fundamental right* is limited, the law or action is evaluated under the *strict scrutiny* standard. In *all other cases*, the *rational basis* standard is applied.

C. A FEW IRREBUTTABLE PRESUMPTIONS MAY BE INVALID
If facts are presumed against a person so that she cannot demonstrate that she is qualified for some important benefit or right, the "irrebuttable presumption" may be unconstitutional.

CMR **Exam Tip** The Supreme Court no longer treats irrebuttable presumptions differently from other regulations or classifications. Thus, if an answer choice says "invalid because it is an irrebuttable presumption," it is probably wrong. You must consider whether it concerns a *fundamental right* or *suspect or quasi-suspect class*, and judge it accordingly.

XVIII. EQUAL PROTECTION

A. CONSTITUTIONAL SOURCE
The Equal Protection Clause of the Fourteenth Amendment is limited to state action. However, grossly unreasonable discrimination by the federal government violates the Due Process Clause of the Fifth Amendment. The Court applies the same tests under either constitutional provision.

B. APPLICABLE STANDARDS
If a *fundamental right* or *suspect classification* is involved, the *strict scrutiny* standard is used to evaluate the regulation. If a *quasi-suspect classification* is involved, *intermediate scrutiny* is the applicable standard. If the classification does not affect a fundamental right or involve a suspect or quasi-suspect classification, the *rational basis* standard applies.

C. PROVING DISCRIMINATORY CLASSIFICATION
For strict or intermediate scrutiny to be applied, there must be *intent* on the part of the government to discriminate. Intent may be shown by:

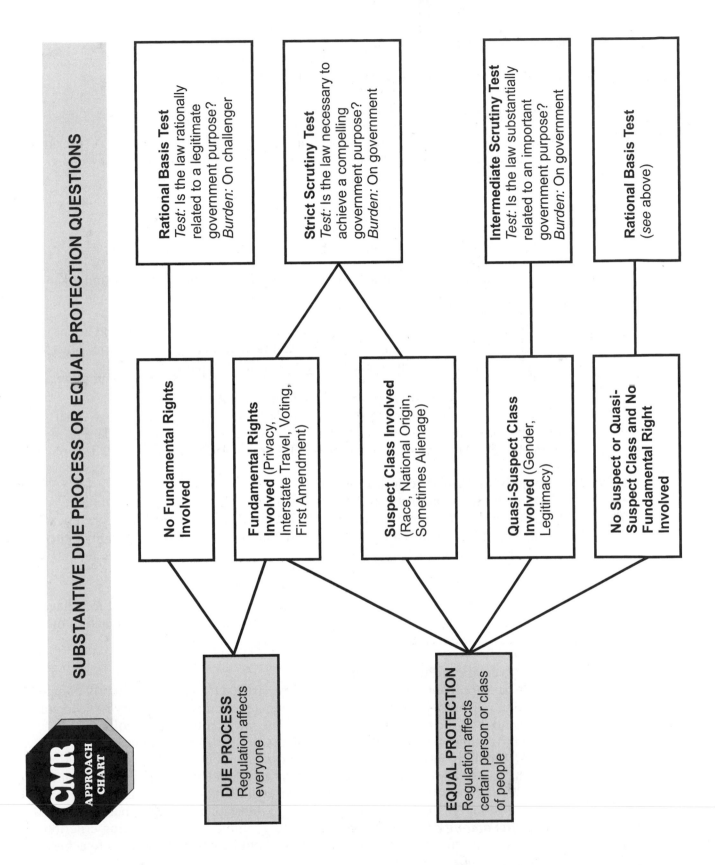

SUBSTANTIVE DUE PROCESS OR EQUAL PROTECTION QUESTIONS

CMR APPROACH CHART

DUE PROCESS
Regulation affects everyone

No Fundamental Rights Involved

Fundamental Rights Involved (Privacy, Interstate Travel, Voting, First Amendment)

Rational Basis Test
Test: Is the law rationally related to a legitimate government purpose?
Burden: On challenger

Strict Scrutiny Test
Test: Is the law necessary to achieve a compelling government purpose?
Burden: On government

EQUAL PROTECTION
Regulation affects certain person or class of people

Suspect Class Involved (Race, National Origin, Sometimes Alienage)

Quasi-Suspect Class Involved (Gender, Legitimacy)

Intermediate Scrutiny Test
Test: Is the law substantially related to an important government purpose?
Burden: On government

No Suspect or Quasi-Suspect Class and No Fundamental Right Involved

Rational Basis Test
(see above)

(i) A law that is *discriminatory on its face*;

(ii) A *discriminatory application* of a facially neutral law; or

(iii) A *discriminatory motive* behind the law.

Note: The third way to show intentional discrimination is the most difficult to prove. A discriminatory effect alone is *not* enough. The legislature's discriminatory motive must be shown (*e.g.,* by evidence of a history of discrimination).

D. SUSPECT CLASSIFICATIONS
Classifications are suspect if they are based on race, national origin, or alienage.

1. Race and National Origin
Classifications based on race or national origin are judged by a strict scrutiny standard.

a. School Integration
Only intentional segregation violates the Constitution. If school systems and attendance zones are established in a racially neutral manner, there is no violation. Thus, there is no violation if housing patterns result in racial imbalance in schools.

b. "Benign" Government Discrimination—Affirmative Action
Government action—whether by federal, state, or local governmental bodies—that *favors* racial or ethnic minorities is subject to the same strict scrutiny standard as is government action discriminating *against* racial or ethnic minorities.

1) Remedying Past Discrimination
The government has a compelling interest in remedying past discrimination against a racial or ethnic minority. The past discrimination must have been persistent and readily identifiable. A race-based plan *cannot* be used to remedy *general* past "societal discrimination."

2) Where There Was No Past Discrimination
Even where the government has not engaged in past discrimination, it may have a compelling interest in affirmative action. However, the governmental action must be *narrowly tailored* to that interest.

a) Diversity in Public Education
The Supreme Court has not found diversity itself to be a sufficiently compelling reason to justify placing students in a particular elementary or secondary school on the basis of race. However, the law is different for colleges and universities. Public colleges and universities have claimed that they have a compelling interest in having a diverse student body, and the Supreme Court has deferred to that claim. But the Court has also held that each applicant to such schools must be considered as an individual. Admissions officers may consider an applicant's race in making admissions decisions, but only as a *plus among a range of factors*. If race or ethnicity is the defining criterion for admission, the admission policy will not be narrowly tailored to achieving the compelling interest of ensuring a diverse student body.

c. **Discriminatory Legislative Apportionment**
Race can be considered in drawing up new voting districts, but it ***cannot be the predominant factor***. If a plaintiff can show that a redistricting plan was drawn up predominately on the basis of racial considerations, the plan will violate the Equal Protection Clause unless the government can show that the plan is narrowly tailored to serve a compelling state interest.

2. **Alienage Classifications**

a. **Federal Classifications**
Because of Congress's plenary power over aliens, federal alienage classifications are ***not*** subject to strict scrutiny. Such classifications are valid if they are not arbitrary and unreasonable.

b. **State and Local Classifications**
Generally, state/local laws on alienage are suspect classifications subject to strict scrutiny. *Examples:* It is unconstitutional for United States citizenship to be required for welfare, civil service jobs, or to become a lawyer.

1) **Exception—Participation in Self-Government Process**
If a law discriminates against alien participation in state government (*e.g.,* voting, jury service, elective office), the ***rational basis*** standard is applied. Also, the rational basis standard is used for state and local laws limiting certain non-elective offices involving important public policy (*e.g.,* police officers, probation officers, and primary and secondary school teachers).

c. **Undocumented Aliens**
Undocumented ("illegal") aliens are ***not*** a suspect classification. Thus, state laws regarding them are subject to a "rational basis" standard. (However, denial of free public education to undocumented alien children is invalid, and more than a simple rational basis standard was used by the Court.)

E. **QUASI-SUSPECT CLASSIFICATIONS**
Classifications based on legitimacy and gender are "quasi-suspect."

1. **Gender Classifications**
Gender classifications are reviewed under the intermediate scrutiny standard: They must be ***substantially related*** to an ***important*** government purpose. The government bears the burden of showing an "exceedingly persuasive justification" for the discrimination.

a. **Women**
Intentional discrimination ***against*** women generally is invalid. Classifications ***benefiting*** women that are designed to ***remedy past discrimination*** generally are valid.

b. **Intentional Discrimination Against Men**
Intentional discrimination against men is generally invalid. However, certain laws have been found to be substantially related to an important government interest (*e.g.,* statutory rape laws, all-male draft).

 Exam Tip The following chart spells out the most likely exam question topics. In any event, remember that most gender classifications are struck down. This is particularly true if they perpetuate stereotypes of economically dependent women.

GENDER CLASSIFICATION	
Classification	**Status**
Gender-based death benefits	Invalid
Gender-based peremptory strikes	Invalid
Alimony for women only	Invalid
State supported all-male or all-female schools	Invalid
Discriminatory minimum drinking age (women at 18, men at 21)	Invalid
Discriminatory statutory rape laws	Valid
All-male draft	Valid
Requiring American fathers (but not mothers) to prove their parentage of nonmarital children born abroad in order to obtain U.S. citizenship for them	Valid

2. Legitimacy Classifications

Legitimacy classifications are also reviewed under the intermediate scrutiny standard: They must be **substantially related** to an **important** government interest. Discriminatory regulations intended to punish illegitimate children (*e.g.,* law providing a benefit to legitimate children but not to illegitimate children) are invalid. *Example:* A law allowing only legitimate children to recover from their father's estate is invalid. *But note:* A law allowing illegitimate children to recover from their father's estate only if parenthood is established before the father's death is **valid**.

F. OTHER CLASSIFICATIONS

All other classifications are evaluated under the **rational basis** standard. These include age, disability, and wealth classifications. For example, mandatory retirement ages may be established; and because education is not a fundamental right, there is no denial of equal protection when wealthier children can afford to pay for access to the best state-operated schools.

Exam Tip For the MBE, you must memorize the suspect classifications (race, national origin, and sometimes alienage), quasi-suspect classifications (gender and legitimacy), and the fundamental rights (right to interstate travel, privacy, voting, and First Amendment rights). Any other classification or any other right is **not** entitled to more than the rational basis test, and thus the government regulation will usually be valid. Do not let your personal feelings lead you to apply the wrong standard (and pick the wrong answer) because you think the right is important or the group is worthy.

XIX. FUNDAMENTAL RIGHTS

A. INTRODUCTION

Certain fundamental rights are protected under the Constitution. If they are denied to everyone, it is a substantive due process problem. If they are denied to some individuals but not others, it is an equal protection problem. The applicable standard in either case is strict scrutiny. Thus, government action must be *necessary* to protect a *compelling* governmental interest. (Remember that there must be no less restrictive means to achieve this goal.)

B. RIGHT OF PRIVACY

Various privacy rights including marriage, sexual relations, abortion, and childrearing are fundamental rights. Regulations affecting these rights are reviewed under the *strict scrutiny* standard.

1. Marriage

The right of a male and female to enter into (and, probably, to dissolve) the marriage relationship is a fundamental right. However, a statute restricting the rights of prison inmates to marry will be upheld if reasonably related to legitimate penological interests.

2. Use of Contraceptives

A state cannot prohibit distribution of nonmedical contraceptives to adults.

3. Abortion

The right of privacy includes the right of a woman to have an abortion without interference from the state under certain circumstances. However, normal strict scrutiny analysis cannot be applied because the state has two compelling interests here that often compete: protecting the woman's health and protecting the fetus that may become a child. In its latest abortion rights approach, the Supreme Court has adopted two basic rules: a pre-viability rule and a post-viability rule.

a. Pre-Viability Rule—No Undue Burdens

Before viability (a realistic possibility that the fetus could survive outside the womb), a state may adopt a regulation protecting the mother's health and the life of the fetus if the regulation does not place an "undue burden" on or substantial obstacle to the woman's right to obtain an abortion.

CMR EXAMPLE CHART

PRE-VIABILITY ABORTION REGULATION	
No Undue Burden	**Undue Burden**
Requiring doctor to give woman relevant information to make *informed consent*.	Requiring woman to *notify spouse* about abortion.
Requiring *24-hour waiting period*.	
Requiring *parental consent* or *parental notice* in order for minors to obtain an abortion, if there is a judicial bypass option.	
Requiring that abortions be performed only *by licensed physicians*.	
Barring a *well-defined partial-birth abortion procedure* when other abortion methods are available.	

    b. Post-Viability Rule—May Prohibit Abortion Unless Woman's Health Threatened
Once the fetus is viable, the state's interest in the fetus's life can override the woman's right to obtain an abortion, but the state cannot prohibit the woman from obtaining an abortion if it is necessary to protect the woman's health or safety.

    c. Remedy
When a court is faced with a statute restricting access to abortions that may be applied in an unconstitutional manner so as to harm the mother's health, it should ***not*** invalidate the statute in its entirety if the statute has valid applications. Instead, the court should attempt to fashion narrower declaratory and injunctive relief against the unconstitutional application.

    d. Financing Abortions
The government has no obligation to pay for abortions.

4. Obscene Reading Material
The right to privacy includes freedom to read obscene material in one's home (except for child pornography), but not the right to sell, purchase, or transport such material.

5. Keeping Extended Family Together
Zoning regulations that prevent family members—even extended ones—from living together are invalid. However, this right does ***not*** extend to unrelated people.

6. Rights of Parents
Parents have a fundamental right to make decisions concerning the care, custody, and control of their children (*e.g.,* a parent has a fundamental right to send a child to private school or to forbid visitation with grandparents).

7. Intimate Sexual Conduct
The state has no legitimate interest in making it a crime for fully consenting adults to engage in private intimate sexual conduct (*e.g.,* sodomy) that is not commercial in nature.

8. Collection and Distribution of Personal Data—No Privacy Right
The state may reasonably gather and distribute information about its citizens. Thus, there is no privacy right to prohibit the accumulation of names and addresses of patients for whom dangerous drugs are prescribed.

C. RIGHT TO VOTE
The right to vote is a fundamental right. Thus, restrictions on that right, other than on the basis of residence, age, and citizenship, are ***invalid*** unless they can pass ***strict scrutiny***.

1. Restrictions on Right to Vote

    a. Residency Requirements
Reasonable time periods for residency (*e.g.,* 30 days) are valid. Note that Congress may override state residency requirements in ***presidential*** elections and substitute its own.

    b. Property Ownership
Conditioning the right to vote or hold office on ownership of property is usually invalid. *Exception:* Special purpose elections (*e.g.,* water storage districts); *see infra.*

c. **Poll Taxes**
Poll taxes are unconstitutional.

d. **Primary Elections**
States may require early registration to vote in primaries. However, states cannot prohibit political parties from opening their primary elections to anyone, whether or not registered with the party.

2. **Dilution of Right to Vote**

a. **One Person, One Vote Principle**
The "one person, one vote" principle applies whenever any level of government, state or local, decides to select representatives to a governmental body by popular election from *individual districts*.

1) **Congressional Elections**
States must use *almost exact mathematical equality* when creating congressional districts within the state. This is not true of Congress, however, when it apportions representatives among the states; Congress's good faith method for apportioning representatives commands more deference and is *not* subject to a precise mathematical formula, as are state plans.

2) **State and Local Elections**
For state and local elections, the variance in the number of persons included within districts must not be more than a few percentage points.

3) **Exception—Appointed Officials and Officials Elected "At Large"**
The apportionment requirement is inapplicable to officials who are appointed or elected at large.

4) **Exception—Special Purpose Election**
The one person, one vote principle does not apply to elections of officials who do not exercise "normal governmental authority" but rather deal with matters of special interest in the community (*e.g.,* water storage districts).

b. **Gerrymandering**
Race (and presumably other suspect classifications) cannot be the predominant factor in drawing the boundaries of voting districts unless the district plan can pass muster under strict scrutiny.

3. **Candidates and Campaigns**

a. **Candidate Qualifications**

1) **Fee Must Not Preclude Indigents**
States may not charge candidates a fee that results in making it impossible for indigents to run for office.

2) Restrictions on Ability to Be a Candidate

A ballot access regulation must be a reasonable, nondiscriminatory means of promoting important state interests. A state may require candidates to show reasonable support to have their names placed on the ballot.

b. Campaign Funding

The government may allocate more public funds to the two "major" parties than to "minor" parties for political campaigns.

D. RIGHT TO TRAVEL

1. Interstate Travel

An individual has a fundamental right to migrate from state to state and to be treated equally after moving into a new state. However, not every restriction on the right to cross state lines is an impairment of the right to travel (*e.g.,* increased penalties for a father abandoning his children and leaving the state are valid). A problem arises when a state imposes a minimum durational residency requirement for receiving its benefits or otherwise dispenses state benefits based on the length of time a person has resided in the state. It is not clear whether the Court always reviews these regulations under the strict scrutiny standard. It may be best to just recall the following examples:

CMR EXAMPLE CHART

DURATIONAL RESIDENCY REQUIREMENT

Residency Requirement	Status
One-year residency to receive full welfare benefits	Invalid
One-year residency to receive state subsidized medical care	Invalid
One-year residency to vote in state	Invalid
Thirty-day residency to vote in state	Valid
One-year residency to get divorced	Valid

2. Right to International Travel

International travel is ***not a fundamental right***. It is, however, protected from arbitrary federal interference by the Fifth Amendment Due Process Clause; the rational basis standard applies.

PART 5: FIRST AMENDMENT FREEDOMS

The First Amendment prohibits Congress from establishing a religion or interfering with the free exercise of religion, abridging the freedoms of speech and press, or interfering with the right of assembly. These prohibitions are applicable to the states through the Fourteenth Amendment.

XX. FREEDOM OF SPEECH AND ASSEMBLY

A. GENERAL PRINCIPLES

Whenever the government seeks to regulate the freedoms of speech or assembly, the Court will weigh the great importance of speech and assembly rights against the interests or policies sought to be served by the regulation. Keep the following guidelines in mind:

1. Government Speech

The Free Speech Clause restricts government *regulation of private speech*; it does not require the government to aid private speech nor restrict the government from expressing its views. The government generally is free to voice its opinions and to fund private speech that furthers its views while refusing to fund other private speech, absent some other constitutional limitation, such as the Establishment Clause or Equal Protection Clause. Because government speech does not implicate the First Amendment, it is not subject to the various levels of scrutiny that apply to government regulation of private speech (*see infra*). Generally, government speech and government funding of speech will be upheld if it is *rationally related to a legitimate state interest.*

a. Public Monuments

A city's placement of a *permanent* monument in a public park is government speech and thus is not subject to Free Speech Clause scrutiny, even if the monument is privately donated.

b. Compare—Government Funding of Private Speech

When the government chooses to fund private messages (*e.g.,* college group newsletters), it generally must do so on a viewpoint neutral basis.

1) Exception—Funding of the Arts

From a financial standpoint, the government cannot fund all artists, and choosing among those it will fund and those it will not inevitably must be based on the content of the art.

2. Content vs. Conduct

Speech and assembly regulations can generally be categorized as either *content* regulations (regulations forbidding communication of specific ideas) or *conduct* regulations (regulations of the conduct associated with speaking, such as the time of the speech, sound level, etc.). Different standards are used to assess the validity of a regulation within each category.

a. Content

It is presumptively unconstitutional to place burdens on speech because of its content except for certain categories of speech (obscenity, defamation, etc.). Content-neutral

speech regulations generally are subject to *intermediate scrutiny*; *i.e.*, they must advance *important* interests unrelated to the suppression of speech and *must not burden substantially more speech than necessary* to further those interests.

b. **Conduct**
Conduct related to speech can be regulated by content-neutral time, place, and manner restrictions. (These rules will be discussed at B., *infra*.) Additionally, all regulations of speech are subject to the following restrictions.

3. **Reasonableness of Regulation**

a. **Overbroad Regulation Invalid**
If a regulation of speech or speech-related conduct punishes a *substantial amount of protected speech* in relation to its plainly legitimate sweep (*e.g.*, a regulation outlawing *all* First Amendment activity in an airport terminal; a regulation prohibiting all canvassers from going onto private residential property to promote *any* cause without first obtaining a permit), the regulation is *facially invalid* (*i.e.*, it may not be enforced against anyone—not even a person engaging in activity that is not constitutionally protected) unless a court has limited construction of the regulation so as to remove the threat to constitutionally protected expression. If the regulation is *not substantially overbroad*, it can be enforced against persons engaging in activities that are not constitutionally protected.

b. **Void for Vagueness Doctrine**
If a criminal law or regulation fails to give persons reasonable notice of what is prohibited (*e.g.*, a prohibition of "lewd" speech), it may violate the Due Process Clause. This principle is applied somewhat strictly when First Amendment activity is involved.

c. **Cannot Give Officials Unfettered Discretion**
A regulation cannot give officials broad discretion over speech issues; there must be *defined standards* for applying the law. If a statute gives licensing officials *unbridled discretion*, it is *void on its face* and speakers need not even apply for a permit. If the licensing statute includes standards, a speaker may not ignore the statute; he must seek a permit and if it is denied, he can challenge the denial on First Amendment grounds.

4. **Scope of Speech**
The freedom to speak includes the freedom *not to speak*. Thus, the government generally cannot require people to salute the flag or display other messages with which they disagree (*e.g.*, a person need not display the state motto "live free or die" on a license plate). The freedom can extend to *symbolic acts* undertaken to communicate an idea (*e.g.*, wearing a black armband to protest the war), although the government may regulate such conduct if it has an *important* interest in the regulation *independent* of the speech aspects of the conduct and the incidental burden on speech is no greater than necessary (*e.g.*, to facilitate a smooth draft, the government can prohibit the burning of draft cards).

a. **Mandatory Financial Support**
Although the government may not compel a person to express a message, it may tax

people and use the revenue to express a message with which they disagree (*e.g.,* a beef producer can be required to pay an assessment to support government sponsored generic advertising of beef even if the producer thinks generic advertising is a waste of money). However, it appears that people *cannot* be compelled to subsidize private messages with which they disagree (*e.g.,* while lawyers may be compelled to pay bar dues and government teachers can be compelled to pay union dues, they cannot be compelled to pay sums to such private associations that will be used to support political views that, or candidates whom, they do not endorse).

1) Exception—University Activity Fees
The government can require public university students to pay a student activity fee even if the fee is used to support political and ideological speech by student groups whose beliefs are offensive to the student, as long as the program is viewpoint neutral.

B. TIME, PLACE, AND MANNER RESTRICTIONS—REGULATION OF CONDUCT
The government has power to regulate the *conduct* associated with speech and assembly, although the breadth of this power depends on whether the forum involved is a public forum, a designated public forum (sometimes called a limited public forum), or a nonpublic forum.

1. Public Forums and Designated Public Forums
Public property that has historically been open to speech-related activities (*e.g.,* **streets, sidewalks, and public parks**) is called a public forum. Public property that has not historically been open to speech-related activities, but which the government has thrown open for such activities on a permanent or limited basis, by practice or policy (*e.g.,* schoolrooms that are open for after-school use by social, civic, or recreation groups), is called a designated or limited public forum. The government may regulate speech in public forums and designated public forums with reasonable time, place, and manner regulations that:

(i) Are *content neutral*;

(ii) Are *narrowly tailored* to serve an *important* government interest; and

(iii) Leave open *alternative channels* of communication.

Note: Almost every legitimate governmental interest satisfies the significant/important standard.

CMR   **Exam Tip**   Remember that even if a regulation meets the time, place, and manner requirements above, it could still be invalid if it is overbroad, vague, or gives unfettered discretion.

a. Injunctions
Injunctions against speech in public forums are treated differently from generally applicable laws. If the injunction is content based, it must be necessary to achieve a compelling interest. If the injunction is content neutral, it must burden no more speech than is necessary to achieve an important government interest.

2. Nonpublic Forums
Speech and assembly can be more broadly regulated in nonpublic forums (*i.e.,* government-owned forums not historically linked with speech and assembly and not held open for

speech activities, such as military bases, schools while classes are in session, government workplaces, etc.). In such locations, regulations are valid if they are:

a. *Viewpoint neutral*; and

b. *Reasonably related to a legitimate* government purpose.

C. UNPROTECTED SPEECH—REGULATION BASED ON CONTENT

To be valid, restrictions on the content of speech must be *narrowly tailored* to achieve a *compelling* government interest. The government has a compelling interest in the following categories of speech, which are deemed "unprotected" speech under the First Amendment:

1. Inciting Imminent Lawless Action

Speech can be burdened if it creates a clear and present danger of imminent lawless action. It must be shown that imminent illegal conduct is *likely* and that the speaker intended to cause it.

2. Fighting Words

True threats (*e.g.,* cross-burning carried out with an intent to intimidate) are not protected by the First Amendment. Speech also can be burdened if it constitutes fighting words (personally abusive words that are likely to incite immediate physical retaliation in an average person). Words that are merely annoying are not sufficient. Note also that the Supreme Court will not tolerate fighting words statutes that are designed to punish only certain viewpoints (*e.g.,* proscribing only fighting words that insult on the basis of race, religion, or gender).

CMR **Exam Tip** While this classification of punishable speech exists in theory, as a practical matter, statutes that attempt to punish fighting words are usually vague or overbroad. Thus, on the examination, they generally should be regarded as *invalid*.

3. Obscenity

Obscene speech is not protected.

a. Elements

Speech is obscene if it describes or depicts sexual conduct that, taken as a whole, by the average person:

1) *Appeals to the prurient interest* in sex, using a *community standard*;

2) Is *patently offensive* and an affront to contemporary *community standards*; and

3) *Lacks serious value* (literary, artistic, political, or scientific), using a *national reasonable person standard*.

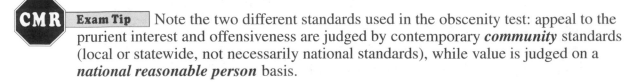

CMR **Exam Tip** Note the two different standards used in the obscenity test: appeal to the prurient interest and offensiveness are judged by contemporary *community* standards (local or statewide, not necessarily national standards), while value is judged on a *national reasonable person* basis.

b. **Standard May Be Different for Minors**
The state can adopt a specific definition of obscenity applying to materials sold to minors, even though the material might not be obscene in terms of an adult audience. However, government may not prohibit the sale or distribution of material to adults merely because it is inappropriate for children.

1) **Pictures of Minors**
To protect minors from exploitation, the government may prohibit the sale or distribution of *visual* depictions of sexual conduct involving minors, even if the material would not be found obscene if it did not involve children.

2) **Compare—Simulated Pictures of Minors**
The government may not bar visual material that only appears to depict minors engaged in sexually explicit conduct, but that in fact uses young-looking adults or computer generated images.

c. **Land Use Regulations**
A land use (or zoning) regulation may limit the location or size of adult entertainment establishments if the regulation is designed to reduce the secondary effects of such businesses (*e.g.*, rise in crime rates, drop in property values, etc.). However, regulations may not ban such establishments altogether.

d. **Liquor Regulation**
Under the Twenty-First Amendment, states have broad power to regulate intoxicating beverages. Laws relating to this power that affect free speech rights generally will not be set aside unless they are irrational.

e. **Private Possession of Obscene Material**
Private possession of obscene material *in the home* cannot be punished (except for possession of child pornography). However, the protection does not extend outside the home.

4. **Defamatory Speech**
Defamatory statements can be burdened. If the defamatory statement is about a *public official* or *public figure* or involves a *public concern*, the First Amendment requires the plaintiff to prove all the elements of defamation *plus falsity* and some degree of *fault*. (*See* Torts outline for detailed discussion.)

CMR **Exam Tip** The First Amendment may also play a role in certain privacy actions. (*See* Torts outline.)

5. **Some Commercial Speech**
As a general rule, commercial speech is afforded First Amendment protection if it is truthful. However, commercial speech that proposes *unlawful activity* or that is *misleading or fraudulent* may be burdened. Any other regulation of commercial speech will be upheld only if it:

a. Serves a *substantial government interest*;

b. *Directly advances* that interest; and

c. Is *narrowly tailored* to serve that interest.

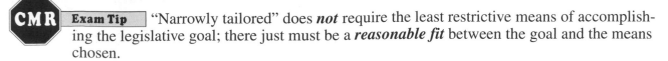 **CMR Exam Tip** "Narrowly tailored" does *not* require the least restrictive means of accomplishing the legislative goal; there just must be a *reasonable fit* between the goal and the means chosen.

D. PRIOR RESTRAINTS

Prior restraints prevent speech before it occurs, rather than punish it afterwards. They are rarely allowed. The government has a heavy burden in justifying a prior restraint; it must show that some *special societal harm* will otherwise result.

1. Procedural Safeguards

To be valid, a system for prior restraint must provide the following safeguards:

(i) The standards must be *narrowly drawn*, *reasonable*, *and definite*;

(ii) Injunction must *promptly* be sought; and

(iii) There must be *prompt and final determination* of the validity of the restraint.

A number of other cases, especially in the area of movie censorship, require that the *government bear the burden* of proving that the speech involved is unprotected.

CMR EXAMPLE CHART	VALID AND INVALID PRIOR RESTRAINTS	
	Valid	**Invalid**
	Prohibiting publishing of troop movements *in times of war*.	Prohibiting publication of *The Pentagon Papers* because it *might* have an effect on the Vietnam War.
	Enforcing *contractual prepublication review* of CIA agent's writings.	Prohibiting grand jury witness from *ever* disclosing testimony.

2. Obscenity Cases

a. Seizures of Books and Films

Seizures of a single book or film may be made with a *warrant* based on probable cause, although if the item is available for sale to the public, a police officer may purchase a book or film to use as evidence without a warrant. Large-scale seizures must be *preceded by a full scale adversary hearing* and a judicial determination of obscenity.

b. Movie Censorship

The Court has found that time delays incident to censorship are less burdensome on movies than on other forms of expression. Thus, the Court allows the government to establish censorship boards to screen movies before they are released, as long as the procedural safeguards discussed above are followed.

c. Burden of Government

When the government adopts a content-based, prior restraint of speech, the government has the burden of proving that the restriction is *narrowly tailored* to accomplish its goal.

E. FREEDOM OF THE PRESS

Generally, the press has *no greater First Amendment freedom* than does a private citizen. Thus, the concepts discussed above apply.

1. Publication of Truthful Information

Generally the press has a right to publish truthful information regarding a matter of public concern, and this right can be restricted only by a sanction that is narrowly tailored to further an interest of the highest order.

2. Access to Trials

The First Amendment guarantees the public and press a right to attend criminal (and probably civil) trials. However, the right may be *outweighed* by an overriding interest stated in the trial judge's findings (*e.g.,* to protect children who are victims of sex offenses). The right includes the right to be present at voir dire and at other pretrial proceedings, unless the judge makes specific findings that closure was narrowly tailored to preserve a higher value.

3. Requiring Press to Testify Before Grand Jury

Members of the press may be required to testify before grand juries.

4. Interviewing Prisoners

The First Amendment does not give journalists a right to interview specified prisoners of their choice or to inspect prison grounds.

5. Business Regulation or Tax

The press and broadcasting companies can be subjected to *general* business regulations or taxes but cannot be targeted for special regulation or taxes. A tax or regulation impacting on the press or a subpart of the press cannot be based on the content of a publication (*e.g.,* a tax exemption cannot be given to "medical journals") absent a compelling justification.

6. Broadcasting Regulations

Radio and television broadcasting may be more closely regulated than the press. The paramount right is the right of *viewers and listeners* to receive information of public concern rather than the right of broadcasters to broadcast what they please. This paramount right allows government to forbid newspaper ownership of radio stations and to prohibit indecent speech over the airwaves.

a. Fairness Doctrine

The First Amendment does not require broadcasters to accept political advertisements. However, a radio station may constitutionally be required to offer free broadcasting

time to certain individuals (*e.g.,* opponents of political candidates or views endorsed by the station, or persons who have been personally attacked in a broadcast).

7. Cable Television Regulation
While generally regulations of newspapers are subject to strict scrutiny, and regulations of the broadcast media are subject to less critical review, regulations of cable television transmissions generally are subject to review by a standard somewhere between these two (*e.g.,* a law requiring cable operators to carry local stations is subject to "intermediate scrutiny"—because it is content-neutral (*see* A.1.a., *supra*)—and is constitutional because it serves the important interest of preserving economic viability of local broadcasters). However, content-based restrictions (*e.g.,* a law forbidding sexually oriented cable programs before 10 p.m.) are subject to strict scrutiny.

8. Internet Regulation
The strict standard of First Amendment scrutiny, rather than the more relaxed standard applicable to broadcast regulation, applies to regulation of the Internet.

XXI. FREEDOM OF ASSOCIATION AND BELIEF

A. NATURE OF THE RIGHT
Although the freedom of association is not mentioned explicitly in the Constitution, it is clearly implied from the rights that are explicitly noted. Pursuant to this freedom, the government may neither prohibit politically unpopular groups nor unduly burden a person's right to belong to such groups. *But note:* This right is not absolute. Infringements of the right may be justified by a **compelling** state interest, unrelated to the suppression of ideas, if the infringements are the **least restrictive means** of protecting the government interest involved.

B. ELECTORAL PROCESS
Laws regulating elections might impact on the First Amendment freedoms of speech, assembly, and association. The Court uses a balancing test to determine whether a regulation of the electoral process is valid: If the restriction on First Amendment activity is severe, strict scrutiny is applied, but if the restriction is reasonable and nondiscriminatory, it generally will be upheld.

1. Limits on Contributions
A statute limiting election campaign contributions is subject to **intermediate scrutiny**—it must be closely drawn to match a "sufficiently important interest." To prevent corruption or the appearance thereof, laws may limit the amount of money that a person, group, or corporation can contribute to a **political candidate**. However, the government may **not** limit the amount of money that may be spent to support or oppose a **ballot referendum**, and there is an exception for groups or corporations formed specifically to participate in the political debate.

2. Limits on Expenditures
Laws may not limit the amount that a candidate or group spends on a political campaign.

3. Compare—Regulations of Core Political Speech
Regulation of "core political speech" (*e.g.,* electioneering, distributing campaign literature), rather than regulation of the process surrounding an election, will be upheld only if it passes

ELECTORAL REGULATIONS

Valid

1. Requiring reasonable number of signatures to get on the ballot.

2. Enforcing a party rule requiring a voter to be registered with a political party to vote in the party's primary.

3. Requiring a voter to be registered in a political party or as an independent to vote in the party's primary (*i.e.*, prohibiting persons registered in one major political party from voting in the other party's primary).

4. Allowing political parties to choose nominees for state judgeships at state conventions.

5. Prohibiting campaign activity within 100 feet of a polling place (involves core political speech but is narrowly tailored) on election day.

6. Prohibiting individuals from appearing on the ballot as the candidate of more than one party.

Invalid

1. Prohibiting party from endorsing or opposing candidates in a primary.

2. Regulating party selection of delegates to national convention.

3. Prohibiting *any* campaigning on election day (involves core political speech and is overbroad).

4. Requiring political parties to allow nonparty members to vote in the parties' primary elections.

5. Increasing contribution limits for a candidate whose wealthy opponent achieves an advantage by spending a lot of his own money on his campaign.

6. Prohibiting judicial candidates from announcing their views on disputed legal and political issues.

muster under strict scrutiny. An ad concerning a political issue will be considered protected core political speech unless it is susceptible of no reasonable interpretation other than one as an appeal to vote for or against a particular candidate.

C. BAR MEMBERSHIPS AND PUBLIC EMPLOYMENT

1. Restraints on Conduct

If a government employer seeks to fire an employee (or to terminate a relationship with an independent contractor) for speech-related conduct, one of two tests will apply, depending on whether the speech involved a matter of public concern. If a matter of public concern is involved, courts must carefully balance the employee's rights as a citizen to comment on a matter of public concern against the government's interest as an employer in efficient performance of public service. If the speech did not involve a matter of public concern, the courts should give a wide degree of deference to the government employer's judgment concerning whether the speech was disruptive.

a. Official Duty Exception

A government employer may punish a public employee's speech whenever the speech is made pursuant to the employee's official duties, even if the speech touches on a matter of public concern.

b. Participation in Political Campaigns

The federal government *may* prohibit federal executive branch employees from taking an active part in political campaigns.

c. Bans on Receiving Honoraria

A provision banning government employees from accepting an honorarium for making speeches, writing articles, or making appearances was held to violate the First Amendment when applied to "rank and file" employees. Such a rule deters speech within a broad category of expression by a massive number of potential speakers and, thus, can be justified only if the government can show that the employees' and their potential audiences' rights are outweighed by the necessary impact the speech would have on actual operation of the government.

d. Patronage

A public employee may not be hired, fired, promoted, transferred, etc., based on party affiliation except as to policymaking positions, where party affiliation is relevant.

e. Must Not Be Vague

A standard for conduct must not be vague (*e.g.,* a prohibition against "treasonable or seditious" utterings is vague).

2. Loyalty Oaths

The government may require employees to take loyalty oaths, as long as the oaths are not overbroad or vague.

a. Overbreadth

An oath cannot prohibit membership in the Communist Party or require abstention from advocating overthrow of the government *as an abstract doctrine*.

b. **Vagueness**

An oath requiring employees to support the Constitution and to oppose the ***unlawful*** overthrow of the government is valid; but an oath requiring public employees to support the flag is invalid (because refusal to salute the flag on religious grounds might conflict with the oath).

3. **Disclosure of Associations**

The government may not force disclosure of every organizational membership in exchange for a government employment or other benefit; it may only inquire into those activities that are relevant to the employment or benefit sought. Even here, however, a person can exercise his Fifth Amendment right to remain silent if the disclosure would be incriminating.

XXII. FREEDOM OF RELIGION

A. CONSTITUTIONAL PROVISION

The First Amendment prohibition on establishment of religion and its protection of the free exercise of religion is applicable to the states through the Fourteenth Amendment.

B. FREE EXERCISE CLAUSE

1. **No Punishment of Beliefs**

The Free Exercise Clause prohibits government from punishing someone on the basis of her religious beliefs. For example, the Clause forbids:

(i) State governments from requiring office holders or employees to take a ***religious oath*** (the federal government is similarly restricted by Article VI);

(ii) States from ***excluding clerics*** from holding public office; and

(iii) Courts from ***declaring a religious belief to be false***.

The Supreme Court has not defined what constitutes religious belief, but it is clear that religious belief need not come from an organized religion or involve a supreme being. The Court has never held an asserted religious belief to be not religious for First Amendment purposes.

CMR **Exam Tip** Technically, the government may deny benefits to or impose a burden on someone based on her religious beliefs ***if there is a compelling interest***. However, the Supreme Court has ***never*** found an interest so compelling that it justifies such action.

2. **General Conduct Regulation—No Religious Exemptions Required**

The Free Exercise Clause cannot be used to challenge government regulation unless the regulation was ***specifically designed*** to interfere with religion (*e.g.,* a law that prohibits the precise type of animal slaughter used in a ritual by a particular religious sect is unconstitutional). Moreover, the Free Exercise Clause does ***not require religious exemptions*** from generally applicable governmental regulations that happen to burden religious conduct; *i.e.,*

a law that regulates the conduct of **all** people can be applied to prohibit the conduct of a person despite the fact that his religious beliefs prevent him from complying with the law.

a. Exception—Unemployment Compensation Cases
A state cannot refuse to grant unemployment benefits to persons who quit their jobs for religious reasons (*i.e.,* the work or conditions of work conflict with tenets of the worker's religion). The worker need not even belong to a formal religious organization in such a situation, as long as the belief is sincere.

b. Exception—Right of Amish Not to Educate Children
The Supreme Court has granted the Amish an exemption from a law requiring compulsory school attendance until age 16, based on the Free Exercise Clause **and** the fundamental right to educate one's children.

CMR **Exam Tip** To summarize, the Free Exercise Clause prohibits government interference with religious **beliefs**, but it generally does **not** prohibit regulation of **conduct**. If the governmental action regulates **general conduct**—including religious conduct—it is **valid** (*e.g.,* banning any use of peyote is valid even though a group's religious beliefs require its use during its ceremonies). The only exceptions to this rule are those pertaining to unemployment compensation and the education of Amish children.

C. ESTABLISHMENT CLAUSE
The Establishment Clause prohibits laws respecting the establishment of religion.

1. Sect Preference
If a government regulation or action includes a preference for one religious sect over another, it is invalid unless it is **narrowly tailored** to promote a **compelling** interest.

CMR **Exam Tip** Although you should know the standard (narrowly tailored to promote a compelling interest) for government preference of a religious sect (or sects), it is unlikely that the government could ever have a compelling interest in preferring one religious group.

2. No Sect Preference—*Lemon* Test
If a government regulation or action contains no sect preference, it is **valid** under the Establishment Clause **if** it:

(i) Has a **secular purpose**;

(ii) Has a **primary effect that neither advances nor inhibits religion**; and

(iii) Does not produce **excessive government entanglement** with religion.

This is known as the *Lemon* test.

a. Cases Unconnected to Financial Aid or Education
A good rule of thumb here is that a law favoring or burdening religion or a specific religious group will be invalid (*e.g.,* exempting certain religious groups—traditional religions—from state registration requirements), but a law favoring or burdening a large segment of society that happens to include religious groups will be upheld (*e.g.,* a Sunday closing law).

CMR
EXAMPLE
CHART

ESTABLISHMENT CLAUSE CASES

Valid	Invalid

Nonfinancial Aid and Education Cases

Valid	Invalid
Legislature's employment of a chaplain.	Delegation of zoning power to religious organization.
Granting religious organizations exemptions from employment discrimination laws where contrary to the organization's beliefs.	Requirement that all employers grant all workers their Sabbath day off.
Christmastime display that includes religious symbols and nonreligious symbols (*e.g.,* nativity scene along with a Christmas tree or Santa).	Christmastime display of *only* religious symbols (*e.g.,* nativity scene or menorah only).
Displaying Ten Commandments when purpose is not predominantly religious.	Displaying Ten Commandments when purpose is predominantly religious.

Recipient-Based Aid

Valid	Invalid
Tax credits for parents of *all* students for educational expenses.	Tax credits only to parents of *private school* students for educational expenses.
Tuition vouchers for poor students that can be used at participating *public and private schools*.	

Aid to Religious Grade and High Schools

Valid	Invalid
Reimbursement to private schools for *compiling* state-required data or *administering* standardized achievement tests.	Reimbursement to private schools for *writing* achievement tests.
Providing government employees to *provide* on-site auxiliary services, such as remedial education, guidance, or job counseling.	Providing private schools with *teachers*, or money to pay teachers, of secular classes.
Exemption from property tax for religious, charitable, *and* educational property.	Tax exemption *only* for religious associations or activities.
Transportation *to and from school* for all students.	
Providing all students with state-approved *textbooks* or lending religiously neutral instructional material (*e.g.,* computers) to private as well as public schools.	

Religious Activities in Public Schools

Valid	Invalid
Ending classes early to allow students to attend *off-school* religious classes.	Ending classes early to give voluntary *in-school* religious classes.
Allowing religious student groups to meet in unused classrooms *as any other* student group.	*Prayer, Bible reading, or posting Ten Commandments* in classrooms or at school football games.
	Requiring that "*creation science*" be taught.

b. **Cases Involving Financial Benefits to Religious Institutions**

The Supreme Court applies the three-part test above with greater strictness when government financial aid is going to a religiously affiliated *grade or high school* than it does when the aid is going to another type of religious institution.

1) **Recipient-Based Aid**

The government may give aid in the form of financial assistance to a defined class of persons as long as the class is defined without reference to religion or religious criteria. Such a program is valid even if most of the people receiving the aid use it to attend a religiously affiliated school.

2) **Aid to Colleges and Hospitals**

Aid to colleges or hospitals will be upheld as long as the government program requires the aid to be used *for nonreligious purposes* and the recipient so agrees.

3) **Aid to Grade Schools and High Schools**

Aid to religious grade schools and high schools is usually found to have a secular purpose, but may fail the other parts of the test. For example, if the program has detailed administrative regulations to prevent the effect of advancement of religion, the law will be stricken for excessive government entanglement.

c. **Religious Activities in Public Schools**

School *sponsored* religious activity is *invalid*, but school *accommodation* of religion is *valid*. Moreover, if a public school allows members of the public and private organizations to use school property when classes are not in session, it cannot deny a religious organization permission to use the property for meetings merely because religious topics will be discussed.

CONTRACTS AND SALES

TABLE OF CONTENTS

I. WHAT IS A CONTRACT?

A. GENERAL DEFINITION

A contract is a promise or set of promises for the breach of which the law gives a remedy or the performance of which the law, in some way, recognizes as a duty.

B. COMMON LAW VS. ARTICLE 2 SALE OF GOODS

Generally, the common law governs contracts. However, special rules have been developed for contracts involving the sale of *goods*, and those rules are contained in Article 2 of the Uniform Commercial Code ("U.C.C."). Article 2 has adopted much of the common law of contracts, but when the common law and Article 2 differ, Article 2 prevails in a contract for the sale of goods.

1. "Goods" Defined

Article 2 defines "goods" as all *things movable* at the time they are identified as the goods to be sold under the contract. Thus, Article 2 applies to sales of most tangible things (*e.g.,* cars, horses, hamburgers), but does not apply to the sale of real estate, services (*e.g.,* a health club membership), or intangibles (*e.g.,* a patent), or to construction contracts.

2. Merchants vs. Nonmerchants

A number of the rules in Article 2 depend on whether the seller and/or buyer are merchants. Article 2 generally defines "merchant" as one who regularly deals in goods of the kind sold or who otherwise by his profession holds himself out as having special knowledge or skills as to the practices or goods involved. For many of the Article 2 provisions dealing with general business practices (*e.g.,* Statute of Frauds, confirmatory memos, firm offers, modification), almost anyone in business is deemed a merchant. However, a few Article 2 provisions (*e.g.,* the implied warranty of merchantability) are narrower and require a person to be a merchant with respect to goods of the kind being sold.

 Exam Tip   For Article 2 provisions dealing with *general business practices*, almost anyone in business can be deemed a merchant. But remember that some Article 2 provisions are narrower and require a person to be a merchant *with respect to goods of the kind involved in the subject transaction* (*e.g.,* the implied warranty of merchantability).

C. TYPES OF CONTRACTS

1. As to Formation

Contracts are frequently described as express, implied, or quasi. Only the first two are actually contracts, and they differ only in the manner in which they are formed.

a. Express Contract

Express contracts are formed *by language*, oral or written.

b. Implied in Fact Contract

Implied contracts are formed by manifestations of assent other than oral or written language, *i.e., by conduct*.

c. Quasi-Contract or Implied in Law Contract

Quasi-contracts are *not contracts* at all. They are constructed by courts to *avoid unjust enrichment* by permitting the plaintiff to bring an action in restitution to recover the amount of the benefit conferred on the defendant.

CMR EXAMPLE CHART

THEORIES OF CONTRACT LIABILITY

Theory	Description	Example
Express Contract	Promises are communicated by **language**.	X promises to paint Y's car in return for Y's promise to pay X $100.
Implied Contract	Parties' **conduct** indicates that they assented to be bound.	(i) X fills her car with gas at Y's gas station. There is a contract for purchase and sale of the gas. (ii) X watches Y paint X's house, knowing that Y mistakenly thought they had an agreement for Y to be paid for it.
Quasi-Contract (Not a contract at all)	One party is **unjustly enriched** at the expense of the other party, so that the enriched party must pay restitution to the other party equal to the unjust enrichment.	X contracts with Y to build a house for Y. X becomes ill and is unable to continue after completing a third of the work. X cannot sue on the contract, but may recover the benefit conferred on Y.

2.   **As to Acceptance**

a.   **Bilateral Contracts—Exchange of Mutual Promises**
The traditional bilateral contract is one consisting of the exchange of mutual promises, *i.e.,* a promise for a promise, in which each party is both a promisor and a promisee.

b.   **Unilateral Contracts—Acceptance by Performance**
The traditional unilateral contract is one in which the offeror requests performance rather than a promise. Here, the offeror-promisor promises to pay upon the *completion of the requested act* by the promisee. Once the act is completed, a contract is formed. In such contracts, there is one promisor and one promisee.

c.   **Modern View—Most Contracts Are Bilateral**
Under Article 2 and Second Restatement, a traditional unilateral contract (*i.e.,* a contract that can be formed only by full performance) occurs in only two situations: (i) when the offeror clearly (unambiguously) indicates that *completion of performance is the only manner of acceptance*; and (ii) where there is an *offer to the public*, such as a reward offer.

3. **As to Validity**

  a. **Void Contract**
      A void contract is one that is totally *without any legal effect* from the beginning (*e.g.,* an agreement to commit a crime). *It cannot be enforced by either party*.

  b. **Voidable Contract**
      A voidable contract is one that one or both parties may *elect to avoid* (*e.g.,* by raising a defense that makes it voidable, such as infancy or mental illness).

  c. **Unenforceable Contract**
      An unenforceable contract is an agreement that is otherwise valid but which may not be enforceable due to a defense extraneous to contract formation, such as the statute of limitations or Statute of Frauds.

  CMR Exam Tip The distinction between void and voidable contracts is sometimes important to an exam question. The key thing to remember is that *void* contracts cannot be enforced, but an aggrieved party may *elect* to enforce a *voidable* contract.

D. **CREATION OF A CONTRACT**
    When a suit is brought in which one party seeks to enforce a contract or to obtain damages for breach of contract, a court must first decide whether there was in fact a contract. In making this determination, a court will ask the following three basic questions:

1. Was there *mutual assent*?

2. Was there *consideration* or some substitute for consideration?

3. Are there any *defenses* to creation of the contract?

CMR Exam Tip Contract formation is a major topic on the exam. For any contract question, be sure that there really is an enforceable contract; *i.e., all three* of the above elements must be present. Fact patterns sometimes greatly emphasize some elements (*e.g.,* offer and acceptance) to try to fool you into thinking that a contract has been formed, but on closer examination, you might find that another element (*e.g.,* consideration) is missing. Remember to check carefully for all three elements. (Of course, if the *facts state* that one or more of the elements is present—or that a valid contract has been formed—don't waste your time analyzing elements already given to you.)

II. MUTUAL ASSENT—OFFER AND ACCEPTANCE

A. **IN GENERAL**
    For an agreement to be enforced as a contract, there must be mutual assent. In other words, one party must accept the other's offer. Whether mutual assent is present will be determined by an objective standard; *i.e.,* did words or conduct manifest a present intention to enter into a contract?

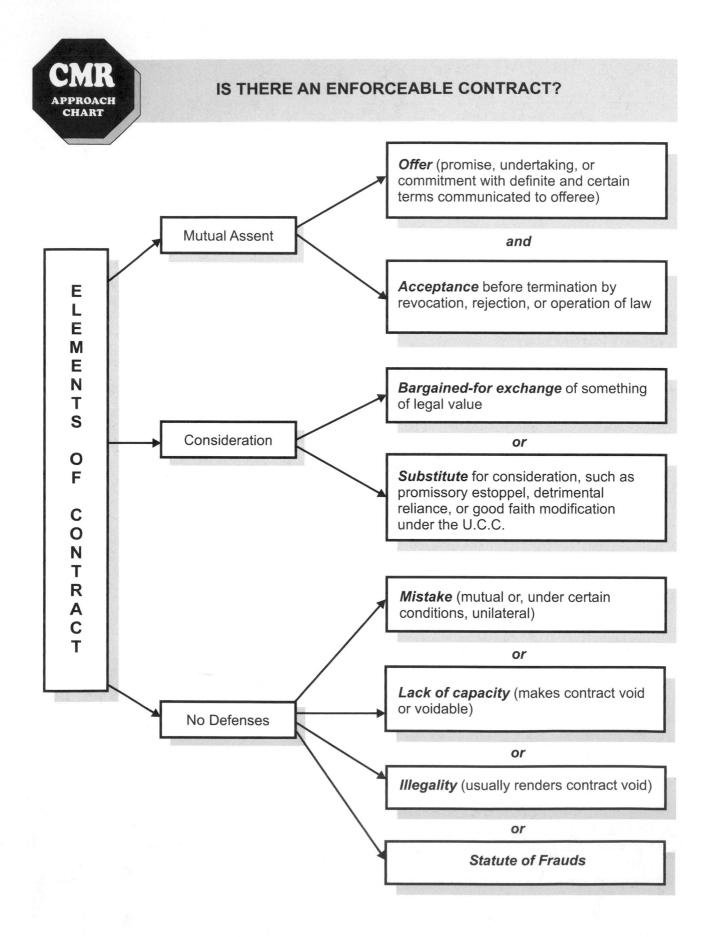

CMR APPROACH CHART

IS THERE AN ENFORCEABLE CONTRACT?

ELEMENTS OF CONTRACT

Mutual Assent

> *Offer* (promise, undertaking, or commitment with definite and certain terms communicated to offeree)

and

> *Acceptance* before termination by revocation, rejection, or operation of law

Consideration

> *Bargained-for exchange* of something of legal value

or

> *Substitute* for consideration, such as promissory estoppel, detrimental reliance, or good faith modification under the U.C.C.

No Defenses

> *Mistake* (mutual or, under certain conditions, unilateral)

or

> *Lack of capacity* (makes contract void or voidable)

or

> *Illegality* (usually renders contract void)

or

> *Statute of Frauds*

B.   THE OFFER

An offer creates a power of acceptance in the offeree and a corresponding liability on the part of the offeror. For a communication to be an offer, it must create a *reasonable expectation* in the offeree that the offeror is willing to enter into a contract on the basis of the offered terms. In deciding whether a communication creates this reasonable expectation, you should ask the following three questions:

(i)   Was there an expression of a *promise*, *undertaking*, *or commitment* to enter into a contract?

(ii)   Were there *certainty and definiteness* in the essential terms?

(iii)   Was there *communication* of the above to the offeree?

1.   Promise, Undertaking, or Commitment

For a communication to be an offer, it must contain a promise, undertaking, or commitment to enter into a contract, rather than a mere invitation to begin preliminary negotiations; *i.e.,* there must be an *intent* to enter into a contract.

a.   Language

The language used may show that an offer was or was not intended. Technical language such as "I offer" or "I promise" is useful, but it is not necessary. Phrases such as "I quote," "I am asking $30 for," and "I would consider selling for" tend to be construed merely as invitations to deal rather than offers.

b.   Surrounding Circumstances

The circumstances surrounding the language will be considered by courts in determining whether an offer exists. For example, if a statement is made in jest, anger, or by way of bragging, and it is reasonably understood in this context, it will have no legal effect.

c.   Prior Practice and Relationship of the Parties

In determining whether certain remarks constitute an offer rather than preliminary negotiations, a court will look to the prior relationship and practice of the parties involved.

d.   Method of Communication

1)   Use of Broad Communications Media

The broader the communicating media (*e.g.,* publications), the more likely it is that the courts will view the communication as merely the *solicitation of an offer*.

2)   Advertisements, Etc.

Advertisements, catalogs, circular letters, and the like containing price quotations are *usually* construed as mere *invitations for offers*.

CMR **Exam Tip**   Most offers are fairly easy to spot, but watch out for language that sounds like an offer but really is an invitation to deal. For example, advertisements often sound like offers but usually are just invitations for people to come in and deal. The more definite the language (*e.g.,* "I'll sell for . . ." or "I'll pay you $10 for . . ."), the more likely the statement

is an offer. However, you need to examine the other factors (surrounding circumstances, prior relationship of parties, etc.). Don't be too hasty in your determination.

CMR **Exam Tip** If there has been a series of communications between the parties, pay attention to the legal significance, if any, of each statement. For example, if you determine that A's first statement to B is not an offer but rather is merely an invitation to deal, then B's response cannot be an acceptance (because there was nothing to accept). You must then consider whether B's response is another invitation to deal or a counteroffer. Keep checking until you find an offer and an acceptance.

2. Definite and Certain Terms

An offer must be definite and certain in its terms. The basic inquiry is whether enough of the essential terms have been provided so that a contract including them would be *capable of being enforced*.

a. Identification of the Offeree

To be considered an offer, a statement must sufficiently identify the offeree or a class to which she belongs to justify the inference that the offeror intended to create a power of acceptance.

b. Definiteness of Subject Matter

The subject matter of the deal must be certain, because a court can enforce a promise only if it can tell with reasonable accuracy what the promise is.

1) Requirements for Specific Types of Contracts

a) Real Estate Transactions

An offer involving realty must identify the *land* and the *price* terms. The land must be identified with some particularity but a deed description is not required (*e.g.*, "my house in Erewhon" is sufficient if the seller has only one house in Erewhon). Most courts will *not* supply a missing price term for realty.

b) Sale of Goods

In a contract for the sale of goods, the *quantity* being offered must be certain or capable of being made certain.

(1) "Requirements" and "Output" Contracts

In a requirements contract, a buyer promises to buy from a certain seller all of the goods the buyer requires, and the seller agrees to sell that amount to the buyer. In an output contract, a seller promises to sell to a certain buyer all of the goods that the seller produces, and the buyer agrees to buy that amount from the seller. It is assumed that the parties will act in good faith; hence, there may not be a tender of or a demand for a quantity *unreasonably disproportionate* to (i) any stated estimate, or (ii) (in the absence of a stated estimate) any normal or otherwise comparable prior output or requirements.

      c)   **Services**
         The nature of the work to be performed is required in an offer for services.

  2) **Missing Terms**
      The fact that one or more terms are left open does ***not prevent the formation*** of a contract if it appears that the parties ***intended to make a contract*** and there is a ***reasonably certain basis*** for giving a remedy. In such a case, the majority of jurisdictions and Article 2 hold that the ***court can supply reasonable terms*** for those that are missing.

      a) **Price**
         Except in contracts for real property, the failure to state the price does not prevent the formation of a contract if the parties intended to form a contract without the price being settled. Note that if a contract for the sale of goods is missing a price term, Article 2 provides that the price will be a ***reasonable price at the time of delivery***.

  3) **Vague Terms**
      The presumption that the parties' intent was to include a reasonable term goes to supplying ***missing*** terms. The presumption ***cannot*** be made if the parties have ***included*** a term that makes the contract too vague to be enforced (*e.g.*, an agreement to split profits on a "liberal basis"). However, uncertainty can be cured by part performance that clarifies the vague term or by acceptance of full performance.

  4) **Terms to Be Agreed on Later**
      Often, an offer will state that some term is to be agreed on at a future date. If the term is a ***material*** term, the offer is ***too uncertain***.

  3. **Communication to Offeree**
    To have the power to accept, the offeree must have ***knowledge*** of the offer. Therefore, the proposal must be communicated to her.

C. TERMINATION OF OFFER
An offer cannot be accepted after it has been terminated. An offer may be terminated by an act of either party or by operation of law.

  1. **Termination by Acts of Parties**

    a. **Termination by Offeror—Revocation**
      A revocation is the retraction of an offer by the offeror. An offeror may revoke by directly communicating the revocation to the offeree (*e.g.*, "I revoke my offer of May 25"). An offer made by publication can be directly revoked only by publication through comparable means (*e.g.*, an offer placed in the *Wall Street Journal* cannot be revoked by publishing in *Better Homes and Gardens*). An offer may also be revoked ***indirectly*** if the offeree receives: (i) correct information, (ii) from a reliable source, (iii) of acts of the offeror that would indicate to a reasonable person that the offeror no longer wishes to make the offer (*e.g.*, after offeror offers to sell his car to offeree, offeree is told by a reliable third party that offeror just sold his car to someone else).

1) **Effective When Received**
A revocation is generally effective when *received* by the offeree. Where revocation is by publication, it is effective when *published.*

2) **Limitations on Offeror's Power to Revoke**
Offers can be revoked at will by the offeror, even if he has promised not to revoke for a certain period, except in the following circumstances:

a) **Options**
An option is a distinct contract in which the *offeree gives consideration* for a promise by the offeror not to revoke an outstanding offer (*e.g.,* an offeror offers to sell her farm to an offeree for $1 million and promises to keep the offer open for 90 days if the offeree pays the offeror $1,000 to keep the offer open).

b) **Merchant's Firm Offer Under Article 2**
Under Article 2: (i) if a *merchant*; (ii) offers to sell goods in a *signed writing*; and (iii) the writing *gives assurances that it will be held open* (*e.g.,* "this offer will be held open for 10 days," "this offer is firm for 10 days," "I shall not revoke this offer for 10 days"); the offer *is not revocable* for lack of consideration during the time stated, or if no time is stated, for a reasonable time (but in no event may such period exceed *three months*).

c) **Detrimental Reliance**
When the offeror could reasonably expect that the offeree would rely to her detriment on the offer, and the offeree does so rely, the offer will be held *irrevocable as an option contract for a reasonable length of time*. At the very least, the offeree would be entitled to relief measured by the extent of any detrimental reliance.

d) **Part Performance—True Unilateral Contract Offers**

(1) **Implied Contract for Reasonable Time**
Under the First and Second Restatements, as well as Article 2, an offer for a true unilateral contract becomes *irrevocable once performance has begun*. The offeror must give the offeree a *reasonable time to complete performance*. Note that the offeree is *not bound* to complete performance—she may withdraw at any time prior to completion of performance and there is no acceptance until performance is complete.

(2) **Distinguish—Preparations to Perform**
Substantial preparations to perform (as opposed to the beginning of performance) do not make the offer irrevocable but *may constitute detrimental reliance* sufficient to make the offeror's promise binding to the extent of the detrimental reliance.

e) **Part Performance—Offer Indifferent as to Manner of Acceptance**
As noted above, most offers are indifferent as to the manner of acceptance, and thus, a bilateral contract may be formed *upon the start of performance*

by the offeree. Therefore, once the offeree *begins performance,* the contract is complete and *revocation* becomes *impossible. But note:* Notification of the start of performance may be necessary. (*See* D.3.b., *infra.*)

b. Termination by Offeree

1) Rejection

a) Express Rejection
An express rejection is a statement by the offeree that she does not intend to accept the offer. Such a rejection will terminate the offer.

b) Counteroffer as Rejection
A counteroffer is an offer made by the *offeree* to the offeror that contains the same subject matter as the original offer, but differs in its terms (*e.g.,* "I'll take the house at that price, but only if you paint it first").

> **CMR** | **Exam Tip** | Remember that a counteroffer is *both* a rejection and a new offer. It terminates the original offer and reverses the roles of the parties: The offeree giving a counteroffer becomes the offeror of a new offer, which the other party may accept or reject. Thus, if A offers to sell his property, Blackacre, to B for $100,000, and B says, "I'll buy it for $90,000," what has happened? A's offer has been rejected and B has made an offer for $90,000, which A may accept or reject. B cannot later say to A, "All right, I'll take Blackacre for $100,000," and accept A's offer. It no longer exists because it was rejected. (Of course, A could accept B's new offer to buy it for $100,000.)

(1) Distinguish—Mere Inquiry
Distinguish between a counteroffer (which constitutes a rejection) and a mere inquiry. An inquiry will not terminate the offer when it is consistent with the idea that the offeree is still keeping the original proposal under consideration (*e.g.,* "Would you consider lowering your price by $5,000?"). The test is whether a *reasonable person* would believe that the original offer had been rejected.

c) Effective When Received
A rejection is effective when *received* by the offeror.

d) Rejection of Option
Because an option is a contract to keep an offer open, a rejection of or a counteroffer to an option does *not* constitute a termination of the offer. The offeree is still free to accept the original offer within the option period unless the offeror has *detrimentally relied* on the offeree's rejection.

2) Lapse of Time
An offer may be terminated by the offeree's failure to accept within the time specified by the offer or, if no deadline was specified, within a reasonable period.

2. Termination by Operation of Law
The following events will terminate an offer by operation of law:

a. ***Death or insanity of either party*** (unless the offer is of a kind the offeror could not terminate, *e.g.*, an option supported by consideration). Death or insanity need ***not*** be communicated to the other party;

b. ***Destruction*** of the proposed contract's ***subject matter***; or

c. ***Supervening illegality***.

CMR
SUMMARY CHART

TERMINATION OF OFFER

	Revocation by Offeror	Rejection by Offeree	Termination by Operation of Law
When Effective	Effective when received	Effective when received	Effective when the death or insanity of either party, the destruction of the subject matter, or the supervening illegality occurs
Methods	Express revocation or implied (*e.g.*, offeree discovers offeror sold subject matter to someone else)	Express rejection, counteroffer, or lapse of reasonable time	Death or insanity of either party, destruction of subject matter, or supervening illegality
Limitations on Power to Terminate	Option contract, merchant's firm offer, detrimental reliance, beginning performance on unilateral contract	Generally cannot reject if already accepted	

D. THE ACCEPTANCE
An acceptance is a manifestation of assent to the terms of an offer.

1. Who May Accept
Generally, only the person to whom an offer is addressed has the power of acceptance. One

may also have the power of acceptance if she is a member of a class to which an offer has been directed. Generally, an offeree's power of acceptance **cannot be assigned**. However, if the offeree has paid consideration to keep the offer open (*i.e.*, an option contract was created), the right to accept **is** transferable.

2. Offeree Must Know of Offer

The offeree must know of the offer in order to accept it, and this is true whether the offer is for a bilateral or unilateral contract. Thus, if A sends B an offer and B sends A an offer unaware of A's offer (*i.e.*, a crossing offer situation), no contract is formed, even if the offers contain the same terms.

3. Acceptance of Offer for Unilateral Contract

If an offer provides that it may be accepted only by performance (*i.e.*, an offer for a unilateral contract), note the following particular rules.

a. Completion of Performance

Most courts hold that an offer to form a unilateral contract is not accepted until performance is completed. The beginning of performance may create an option so that the offer is irrevocable. (*See* C.1.a.2)d), *supra*.) However, the offeree is not obligated to complete performance merely because he has begun performance, as only complete performance constitutes an acceptance of the offer.

CMR **Exam Tip** Keep in mind that like all offerees, the offeree of a unilateral contract **must know of the offer** to accept it. If the "offeree" acts without knowledge and learns of the offer later, his acts were not an acceptance. Thus, if A finds O's watch and returns it to O without knowledge of O's reward offer, A has no contractual right to the reward.

b. Notice

Generally, the offeree is **not** required to give the offeror notice that he has begun the requested performance, but is required to notify the offeror within a reasonable time after performance has been completed. However, no notice is required if: (i) the offeror **waived notice**; or (ii) the offeree's **performance would normally come to the offeree's attention** within a reasonable time.

4. Acceptance of Offer for Bilateral Contract

Recall that unless an offer specifically provides that it may be accepted only through performance, it will be construed as an offer to enter into a bilateral contract and may be accepted either by a promise to perform or by the **beginning of performance** (compare offers for true unilateral contracts, which may be accepted only by full performance).

a. Generally, Acceptance Must Be Communicated

Generally, acceptance of an offer to enter into a bilateral contract must be communicated to the offeree, unless the offer provides that acceptance need not be communicated.

b. Method of Acceptance

Unless otherwise provided, an offer is construed as inviting acceptance in **any reasonable**

manner and by any medium reasonable under the circumstances. Any objective manifestation of the offeree's counterpromise is usually sufficient.

1) Offers to Buy Goods for Current or Prompt Shipment

Under Article 2, an offer to buy goods for current or prompt shipment is construed as inviting acceptance either by a ***promise to ship*** or by ***current or prompt shipment*** of conforming or nonconforming goods.

a) Shipment of Nonconforming Goods

The shipment of nonconforming goods is an acceptance creating a bilateral contract as well as a ***breach*** of the contract unless the seller seasonably notifies the buyer that a shipment of nonconforming goods is offered only as an ***accommodation***. The buyer is not required to accept accommodation goods and may reject them. If he does, the shipper is not in breach and may reclaim the accommodation goods, because her tender does not constitute an acceptance of the buyer's original offer.

c. Acceptance Must Be Unequivocal

Traditional contract law insists on an absolute and unequivocal acceptance of each and every term of the offer (the "mirror image rule").

1) Common Law Rule

At common law, any different or additional terms in the acceptance make the response a ***rejection and counteroffer***.

2) Article 2 Rule—Battle of the Forms Provision

Article 2 has abandoned the mirror image rule, providing instead that the proposal of additional or different terms by the offeree in a definite and timely acceptance does ***not*** constitute a rejection and counteroffer, but rather is ***effective as an acceptance***, unless the acceptance is ***expressly*** made conditional on assent to the additional or different terms. Whether the additional or different terms become part of the contract depends on whether or not both parties are merchants. (*See* V.D.1., *infra*, for a discussion of what terms are included.)

CMR **Exam Tip** Recall that the Article 2 changes the common law rule. Thus, for an offer for the purchase or sale of ***goods***, an acceptance with additional terms is still an acceptance and a contract is formed (with or without the new terms). If the offer is for something ***other than the sale of goods*** (*e.g.,* land), an acceptance proposing additional or different terms is a rejection and a counteroffer; no contract is formed.

3) Bilateral Contracts Formed By Performance

If a contract is not formed by the parties' communications, but they begin to perform as if they formed a contract, a contract is formed.

d. When Effective—The Mailbox Rule

Acceptance by mail or similar means creates a contract at the ***moment of dispatch***, provided that the mail is properly addressed and stamped, ***unless:***

EFFECT OF REJECTION OR REVOCATION ON OFFER

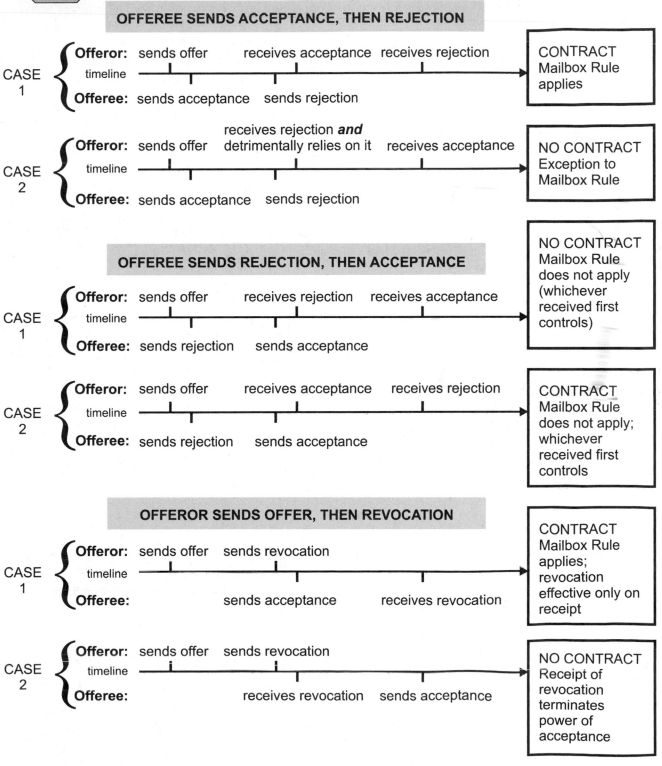

1) The *offer stipulates* that acceptance is not effective until received; or

2) An *option contract* is involved (an acceptance under an option contract is effective only upon *receipt*).

3) If the offeree sends a *rejection and then sends an acceptance*, whichever arrives first is effective.

4) If the offeree sends an acceptance and then a rejection, the acceptance is effective (*i.e.,* the mailbox rule applies) *unless the rejection arrives first and* the offeror *detrimentally relies* on it.

 Exam Tip Remember that the mailbox rule ("effective upon dispatch") applies *only to acceptance*. It does not apply to other events in the contract setting, such as rejection or revocation.

1) Acceptance by Unauthorized Means
An acceptance transmitted by unauthorized means or improperly transmitted by authorized means may still be *effective if it is actually received* by the offeror while the offer is still in existence.

E. AUCTION CONTRACTS
The U.C.C. contains some special rules regulating auction sales. A sale by auction is complete when the auctioneer so announces by the *fall of the hammer* or in another customary manner. An auction sale is with reserve unless the goods are explicitly put up without reserve. "*With reserve*" means the *auctioneer may withdraw the goods* at any time until he announces completion of the sale.

III. CONSIDERATION

A. INTRODUCTION
Courts will enforce a promise as a contract only if it is supported by consideration or a substitute for consideration.

B. ELEMENTS OF CONSIDERATION
Basically, two elements are necessary to constitute consideration: (i) there must be a *bargained-for exchange* between the parties; and (ii) that which is bargained for must be considered of *legal value* or, as it is traditionally stated, it must constitute a benefit to the promisor *or* a detriment to the promisee.

1. Bargained-For Exchange
This element of consideration requires that the promise induce the detriment *and* the detriment induce the promise.

a. Gift
There is no bargain involved (*i.e.,* no consideration) when one party gives a gift to another.

1) **Act or Forbearance by Promisee Must Be of Benefit to Promisor**
An act or forbearance by the promisee (or a promise to act or forbear) is sufficient consideration to form a contract if it benefits the promisor. The benefit, however, need not be economic (*e.g.,* the gratification of influencing the mind of another is sufficient).

b. **"Past" or "Moral" Consideration**
A promise given in exchange for something already done does not satisfy the bargain requirement.

CMR **Exam Tip** Beware of questions that use the word "consideration" to refer to something already done, as in "In consideration of your having done X, I promise you $1,000." Under the general rule, this promise is *not enforceable* because the promise is given in exchange for past acts.

1) **Exceptions**
Where a past obligation is unenforceable because of a technical defense (*e.g.,* statute of limitations), that obligation will be enforceable *if a new promise* is made *in writing* or is *partially performed*. Also, under the modern trend, if a past act benefited the promisor and was performed by the promisee at the promisor's *request* or in response to an *emergency*, a *subsequent promise* to pay for that act will be enforceable.

2. **Legal Value Element**

a. **Adequacy of Consideration**
In general, courts do *not* inquire into the adequacy or fairness of consideration. However, if something is entirely devoid of value (token consideration), it is insufficient. Sham consideration (recited in the contract, but not actually paid) may also be insufficient. But note that if there is a possibility of value in the thing bargained for, consideration will be found even if the value never comes into existence.

b. **Legal Benefit and Legal Detriment Theories**
The majority of courts require that a party incur *detriment* (by doing something he is not legally obligated to do or by refraining from doing something he has a legal right to do) to satisfy the legal value element. Under the minority rule, conferring a benefit on the other party is also sufficient.

c. **Specific Situations**

1) **Preexisting Legal Duty**
Traditionally, performing or promising to perform an existing legal duty is *insufficient* consideration.

a) **Exceptions**
The preexisting legal duty rule is riddled with exceptions; there is consideration if:

(i) *New or different* consideration is promised;

(ii) The promise is to **ratify a voidable obligation** (*e.g.,* a promise to ratify a minor's contract after reaching majority, a promise to go through with a contract despite the other party's fraud);

(iii) The preexisting duty is **owed to a third person** rather than to the promisor;

(iv) There is an **honest dispute** as to the duty; or

(v) There are **unforeseen circumstances** sufficient to discharge a party.

Also, a **good faith** agreement modifying a contract subject to the **U.C.C.** needs **no consideration** to be binding.

 Exam Tip Although payment of a smaller sum than due on an existing debt is generally **not** sufficient consideration for a promise by the creditor to discharge the debt, courts will attempt to avoid this result by applying the above exceptions. Thus, see if there is new or different consideration given in the facts (*e.g.,* payment **earlier** than required or payment in **stock** instead of cash); this change in performance could make the payment of a smaller amount sufficient consideration.

2) Forbearance to Sue
A promise to refrain from suing on a claim may constitute consideration if the claim is valid or the claimant **in good faith** believed the claim was valid.

C. MUTUAL AND ILLUSORY PROMISES—REQUIREMENT OF MUTUALITY
Consideration must exist on both sides of a contract (although the benefit of the consideration generally need not flow to all parties). If only one party is bound to perform, the promise is illusory and will not be enforced. Courts often supply implied promises (*e.g.,* a party must use her best efforts) to infer mutuality.

1. Examples
The following are common examples of contracts that satisfy the mutuality requirement:

a. Requirements and output contracts;

b. Conditional promises, unless the condition is entirely within the promisor's control;

c. Contracts where a party has the right to cancel, if that right is somehow restricted (*e.g.,* a party must give 60 days' notice);

d. Voidable promises (*e.g.,* one made by an infant);

e. Unilateral and option contracts; and

f. Gratuitous suretyship promises made before or at the same time that consideration flows to the principal debtor.

 Exam Tip Closely analyze the wording of contract terms; language can make a big difference here. For example, a valid requirements or output contract term will say, "all the widgets I *require*" or "all that you *produce*," but a term such as "all the widgets I *want*" or "all you *want to sell* me" is illusory.

2. **Right to Choose Alternative Courses**

   A promise to choose one of several alternative means of performance is illusory *unless every alternative* involves legal detriment to the promisor. The promise will not be found illusory if: (i) at least one alternative involves legal detriment and the power to choose rests with the promisee or a third party, or (ii) a valuable alternative (*i.e.,* one involving legal detriment) is actually selected.

D. **PROMISSORY ESTOPPEL OR DETRIMENTAL RELIANCE**

   Consideration is not necessary if the facts indicate that the promisor should be estopped from not performing. Under section 90 of the First Restatement, a promise is enforceable if necessary to prevent injustice if:

   (i) The promisor should reasonably *expect to induce action or forbearance*;

   (ii) *Of a definite and substantial character*;

   (iii) And *such action or forbearance is in fact induced*.

   In the Second Restatement, section 90 no longer requires that the action or forbearance be "of a definite and substantial character." It also provides that the remedy "*may be limited as justice requires*." Typically, if the elements for promissory estoppel are present, a jurisdiction following the First Restatement approach will award expectation damages (*i.e.,* what was promised under the contract), while a jurisdiction following the Second Restatement might award reliance damages (*i.e.,* whatever the promisee spent in reliance on the promise), which usually is something less than expectation damages, but theoretically can exceed them.

 Exam Tip A valid contract is better than an agreement that can be enforced only by promissory estoppel because some states limit recovery under promissory estoppel to that which "justice requires." Thus, in a question asking whether a party can prevail based on an agreement, always check first to see if there is a *valid contract*. Only if there is not should you consider promissory estoppel as a proper choice.

IV. REQUIREMENT THAT NO DEFENSES EXIST

A. **INTRODUCTION**

   Even if an agreement is supported by valuable consideration or a recognized substitute, contract rights may still be unenforceable because there is a defense to formation of the contract, because there is a defect in capacity (making the obligations voidable by one of the parties), or because a defense to enforcement of certain terms exists.

B. **DEFENSES TO FORMATION**

1. **Absence of Mutual Assent**

    a. **Mutual Mistake**
        If both parties entering into a contract are mistaken about facts relating to the agreement, the contract may be voidable by the adversely affected party if:

        (i) The mistake concerns a **basic assumption** on which the contract is made (*e.g.,* the parties think they are contracting for the sale of a diamond but in reality the stone is a cubic zirconia);

        (ii) The mistake has a **material effect** on the agreed-upon exchange (*e.g.,* the cubic zirconia is worth only a hundredth of what a diamond is worth); and

        (iii) The party seeking avoidance **did not assume the risk** of the mistake.

        1) **Assumption of Risk**
            Mutual mistake is not a defense if the adversely affected party bore the risk that the assumption was mistaken. This commonly occurs when one party is in a position to better know the risks than the other party (*e.g.,* contractor vs. homeowner) or where the parties knew that their assumption was doubtful (*i.e.,* when the parties were consciously aware of their ignorance).

            a) **Mistake in Value Generally Not a Defense**
                If the parties to a contract make assumptions as to the value of the subject matter, mistakes in those assumptions will generally not be remedied—even though the value of the subject matter is generally a basic assumption and the mistake creates a material imbalance—because both parties usually assume the risk that their assumption as to value is wrong.

    b. **Compare—Unilateral Mistake**
        If only one of the parties is mistaken about facts relating to the agreement, the mistake will **not** prevent formation of a contract. However, if the nonmistaken party **knew or had reason to know of the mistake** made by the other party, the contract is voidable by the nonmistaken party.

    c. **Mistake by the Intermediary (Transmission)**
        When there is a mistake in the transmission of an offer or acceptance by an intermediary, the prevailing view is that the message **as transmitted** is operative unless the other party knew or should have known of the mistake.

    d. **Latent Ambiguity Mistakes—Mutual Misunderstanding**
        If the contract includes an ambiguous term, the result depends on the parties' awareness of the ambiguity:

        (i) **Neither party aware**—no contract unless both parties intended the same meaning;

        (ii) **Both parties aware**—no contract unless both parties intended the same meaning;

        (iii) **One party aware**—binding contract based on what the ignorant party reasonably believed to be the meaning of ambiguous words.

        Ambiguity is one area where subjective intent is taken into account.

e. **Misrepresentation**

1) **Fraudulent Misrepresentation (Fraud in the Inducement)—Contract Voidable**
If a party induces another to enter into a contract by using *fraudulent misrepresentation* (*e.g.*, by asserting information she knows is untrue), the contract is *voidable* by the innocent party if she *justifiably relied* on the fraudulent misrepresentation. This is a type of *fraud in the inducement.*

2) **Nonfraudulent Misrepresentation—Contract Voidable If Material**
Even if a misrepresentation is *not* fraudulent, the contract is *voidable* by the innocent party if the innocent party *justifiably relied* on the misrepresentation and the misrepresentation was *material.* A misrepresentation is material if either: (i) the information asserted would induce a reasonable person to agree; or (ii) the maker of the misrepresentation knew the information asserted would cause a particular person to agree.

3) **Innocent Party May Rescind Agreement**
Note that the innocent party need not wait until she is sued on the contract, but may take affirmative action in equity to *rescind* the agreement.

2. **Absence of Consideration**
If the promises exchanged at the formation stage lack the elements of bargain or legal detriment, *no contract* exists. In this situation, one of the promises is always illusory.

3. **Public Policy Defenses to Contract Formation—Illegality**
If the *consideration or subject matter* of a contract is illegal (*e.g.*, a contract to commit a murder), the contract is void. *Exceptions:* (i) the plaintiff is unaware of the illegality while the defendant knows of the illegality; (ii) the parties are not in pari delicto (*i.e.*, one party is not as culpable as the other); or (iii) the illegality is the failure to obtain a license when the license is for revenue-raising purposes rather than for protection of the public. If only the *purpose* behind the contract is illegal, the contract is *voidable* by a party who was (i) unaware of the purpose; or (ii) aware but did not facilitate the purpose *and* the purpose does not involve serious moral turpitude.

C. **DEFENSES BASED ON LACK OF CAPACITY**

1. **Legal Incapacity to Contract**

a. **Contracts of Infants (Minors)**
Infants (in most jurisdictions, persons under the age of 18) generally lack capacity to enter into a contract binding on themselves. However, contractual promises of an adult made to an infant are binding on the adult.

1) **Disaffirmance**
An infant may choose to disaffirm a contract any time before (or shortly after) reaching the age of majority. If an infant chooses to disaffirm, she must return anything that she received under the contract *that still remains* at the time of disaffirmance. However, there is no obligation to return any part of the consideration that has been squandered, wasted, or negligently destroyed.

2) Affirmance upon Attaining Majority

An infant may affirm, *i.e.,* choose to be bound by his contract, upon reaching majority. He affirms either expressly or by conduct (*e.g.,* by *failing to disaffirm* the contract *within a reasonable time after reaching majority*).

3) Exceptions

An infant is bound to pay the reasonable value of necessities. What a necessity is depends on the infant's station in life. Some states have additional statutory exceptions (*e.g.,* insurance contracts, student loan contracts).

b. Mental Incapacity

One whose mental capacity is so deficient that he is incapable of understanding the nature and significance of a contract may disaffirm when lucid or by his legal representative. He may likewise affirm during a lucid interval or upon complete recovery, even without formal restoration by judicial action. In other words, the contract is *voidable*. As in the case of infants, mentally incompetent persons are liable in quasi-contract for necessities furnished to them.

c. Intoxicated Persons

One who is so intoxicated that he does not understand the nature and significance of his promise may be held to have made only a *voidable* promise if the other party had reason to know of the intoxication. The intoxicated person may affirm the contract upon recovery. Once again, there may be quasi-contractual recovery for necessities furnished during the period of incapacity.

2. Duress and Coercion

Contracts induced by duress (*e.g.,* "sign the contract or I'll break your legs") or coercion are *voidable* and may be rescinded as long as not affirmed. Generally, taking advantage of another person's economic needs is not a defense. However, withholding something someone wants or needs will constitute economic duress if: (i) the party threatens to commit a wrongful act that would seriously threaten the other contracting party's property or finances; and (ii) there are no adequate means available to prevent the threatened loss.

D. DEFENSES TO ENFORCEMENT

1. Statute of Frauds

In most instances, an oral contract is valid. However, certain agreements, by statute, must be evidenced by a *writing signed by the parties sought to be bound.*

a. Writing Requirement

The Statute of Frauds does not require that the contract be in writing; it requires only that there be one or more writings signed by the person sought to be held liable on the contract that reflect the *material terms* of the contract. Thus, a letter (even to a non-party) or receipt, or even a check indicating a quantity of goods on the memo line could be sufficient.

CMR **Exam Tip** Remember, to be sufficient under the Statute of Frauds, the writing need not be a full-fledged contract, nor need it even be one piece of paper. Thus, several pieces of correspondence between the parties could be sufficient memoranda of the

agreement; a fax or a memo written on a napkin also could suffice. The key is that there be *something in writing* evidencing the *material terms*.

b.   Signature Requirement
The signature requirement is liberally construed by most courts. It need not be hand-written; it can be printed or typed. A party's initials or letterhead may also be sufficient.

CMR **Exam Tip** Note that the memorandum does *not* need to be signed by both parties to the contract. Only the *party to be charged* (*i.e.,* the person to be sued) must sign. Thus, if a fact situation has an otherwise sufficient writing that is signed by the seller but not the buyer, if the buyer is suing the seller, the writing is enough for the Statute of Frauds. However, if the seller sued the buyer, there would not be a sufficient memorandum. (Although there is an exception in contracts for the sale of goods in the case of a merchant's confirmatory memo; *see* c.6)b), *infra*.)

c.   Agreements Covered

1)   Executor or Administrator Promises Personally to Pay Estate Debts
A promise by an executor or administrator to pay the estate's debts out of his own funds must be evidenced by a writing.

2)   Promises to Pay Debt of Another (Suretyship Promises)
A promise to answer for the debt or default of another must be evidenced by a writing. The promise may arise as a result of a tort or contract, but it must be collateral to another person's promise to pay, and not a primary promise to pay. However, if the main purpose or leading object of the promisor is to serve a pecuniary interest of his own, the contract is *not within the Statute of Frauds* even though the effect is still to pay the debt of another (*e.g.,* homeowner promises to pay contractor's debt to building supplier if contractor does not pay, so contractor can obtain supplies to work on homeowner's house).

3)   Promises in Consideration of Marriage
A promise the consideration for which is marriage must be evidenced by a writ-ing. This applies to promises that induce marriage by offering something of value (other than a return promise to marry—*e.g.,* " if you marry my son, I will give the two of you a house").

4)   Interest in Land
A promise creating an interest in land must be evidenced by a writing. This includes not only agreements for the sale of real property, but also:

(i)   *Leases for more than one year;*

(ii)   *Easements of more than one year;*

(iii)   *Fixtures;*

(iv)   *Minerals (or the like) or structures* if they are to be severed by the *buyer*; and

(v)   *Mortgages* and most other security liens.

a) **Items Not Within the Statute**
Contracts to build a building or to find a buyer for a seller (*e.g.,* a broker's contract) do not come within the Statute.

b) **Effect of Performance on Contracts**
If the seller conveys to the purchaser (*i.e.,* fully performs), the seller can enforce the buyer's oral promise to pay. Similarly, the purchaser may be able to specifically enforce a land contract if the "*part performance doctrine*" is applicable. Under the doctrine, conduct (*i.e.,* part performance) that *unequivocally indicates* that the parties have contracted for the sale of the land will take the contract out of the Statute of Frauds. What constitutes sufficient part performance varies among the jurisdictions. Most require *at least two* of the following: payment (in whole or in part), possession, and/or valuable improvements.

5) **Performance Not Within One Year**
A promise that *by its terms cannot be performed within one year* is subject to the Statute of Frauds. Part performance does not satisfy the Statute of Frauds in this case.

a) **Effective Date**
The date runs from the *date of the agreement* and not from the date of performance.

b) **Lifetime Contracts**
A contract measured by a lifetime (*e.g.,* a promise to "employ until I die" or "work until I die") is not within the Statute because it is capable of performance within a year since a person can die at any time.

6) **Goods Priced at $500 or More**
A contract for the sale of goods for a price of $500 or more is within the Statute of Frauds and generally must be evidenced by a signed writing to be enforceable. Note that a writing is sufficient even though it omits or incorrectly states a term, but the contract is *not enforceable beyond the quantity of goods shown in the writing*.

a) **When Writing Not Required**
There are three situations in which contracts are enforceable without the writing described above:

(1) **Specially Manufactured Goods**
If goods are to be specially manufactured for the buyer and are not suitable for sale to others by the seller in the ordinary course of his business, the contract is enforceable if the seller has, under circumstances that reasonably indicate that the goods are for the buyer, made *substantial beginning* in their manufacture or *commitments* for their purchase before notice of repudiation is received.

(2) **Admissions in Pleadings or Court**
If the party against whom enforcement is sought admits in pleadings,

testimony, or otherwise in court that the contract for sale was made, the contract is enforceable without a writing (but in such a case the contract is not enforced beyond the quantity of goods admitted).

(3) Payment or Delivery of Goods

If goods are either received and accepted or paid for, the contract is enforceable. However, the contract is not enforceable beyond the quantity of goods accepted or paid for. Thus, if only some of the goods called for in the oral contract are accepted or paid for, the contract is only partially enforceable. If an indivisible item is partially paid for, most courts hold that the Statute of Frauds is satisfied for the whole item.

b) Merchants—Confirmatory Memo Rule

In contracts between merchants, if one party, within a reasonable time after an oral agreement has been made, sends to the other party a *written* confirmation of the understanding that is sufficient under the Statute of Frauds to bind the sender, it will also bind the recipient if: (i) he has reason to know of the confirmation's contents; and (ii) he does not object to it in writing within 10 days of receipt.

CMR Exam Tip For the Statute of Frauds to be satisfied (and the contract to be enforceable), you need to look carefully for a writing signed *by the party to be charged* (*i.e.,* sued). Often the facts of a question will show that only one party signed the memo. Check first to see if the signature is of the party you need to hold liable. If not, consider the merchants' confirmatory memo rule—it may provide the answer. Be sure, however, that the contract is between *merchants*; if not, the rule does not apply and the signature of one party cannot bind the other.

CMR Exam Tip An acronym for remembering when a writing signed by the party to be charged is *not required* for a sale of goods, even if for $500 or more, is SWAP: *Specially* made goods, *Written confirmation* by a merchant, *Admission* in court, or *Performance*. These things take the contract out of the Statute of Frauds.

c) Requirement of $500 or More—Applied as Modified

In determining whether a contract is for $500 or more, Article 2 gives effect to any modification—if the contract *as modified* is for $500 or more, it must be evidenced by a writing; if the contract *as modified* is for less than $500, no writing is necessary.

CMR Exam Tip Statute of Frauds issues are often raised in MBE questions. Remember that the Statute does not apply to all contracts. You must check the facts to see whether the contract falls within any of the covered areas (above). An easy way to remember agreements covered by the Statute of Frauds is by using the acronym *MY LEGS*:

Marriage,

(Within one) Year,

Land,

Executor (or Administrator),

Goods (for $500 or more),

Surety.

d. Effect of Noncompliance with the Statute
Under the majority rule, noncompliance with the Statute of Frauds renders the contract *unenforceable at the option of the party to be charged* (*i.e.,* the party being charged may raise the lack of a sufficient writing as an affirmative defense). If the Statute is not raised as a defense, it is waived.

e. Remedies If Contract Is Within Statute
If a contract is within the Statute of Frauds because there is noncompliance with the Statute and no applicable exception, in almost all cases a party can sue for the *reasonable value* of the services or part performance rendered, *or* the *restitution* of any other benefit that has been conferred. (*See* VIII.C., *infra,* for a detailed discussion.)

1) Part Performance
If the part performance rendered takes the contract out of the Statute of Frauds, the performing party has the option of suing *on the contract* for expectation damages, rather than merely in restitution for the value of the benefit conferred.

2. Unconscionability
The concept of unconscionability allows a court to *refuse to enforce a provision or an entire contract* (or to modify the contract) to avoid "unfair" terms, usually due to some unfairness in the bargaining process (*i.e.,* procedural unconscionability). Unfair price alone is not a ground for unconscionability.

a. Common Instances of Procedural Unconscionability

1) Inconspicuous Risk-Shifting Provisions
Standardized printed form contracts often contain a material provision that seeks to shift a risk normally borne by one party to the other. Typically, such clauses are found in the fine print ("boilerplate") in printed form contracts. Courts have invalidated these provisions because they are *inconspicuous* or *incomprehensible* to the average person, even if brought to his actual attention.

2) Contracts of Adhesion—"Take It or Leave It"
Courts will deem a clause unconscionable and unenforceable if the signer is unable to procure necessary goods, such as an automobile, from any seller without agreeing to a similar provision.

3) Exculpatory Clauses
An exculpatory clause releasing a contracting party from liability for his own *intentional* wrongful acts is usually found to be unconscionable because such a clause is against public policy in most states. Exculpatory clauses for *negligent* acts may be found to be unconscionable if they are inconspicuous (as discussed above), but commonly are upheld if they are in contracts for activities that are known to be hazardous (*e.g.,* a contract releasing a ski hill operator for liability for negligence often will be upheld).

4) **Limitations on Remedies**

A contractual clause limiting liability for damages to property generally will *not* be found to be unconscionable unless it is inconspicuous. However, if a contract limits a party to a certain remedy and that remedy *fails of its essential purpose* (*e.g.,* the contract limits remedies to repair and the item cannot be repaired), a court may find the limitation unconscionable and ignore it.

b. **Timing**

Unconscionability is determined by the circumstances as they existed *at the time the contract was formed*.

c. **Effect If Court Finds Unconscionable Clause**

If a court finds as a matter of law that a contract or any clause of the contract was unconscionable *when made*, the court may: (i) refuse to enforce the contract; (ii) enforce the remainder of the contract *without* the unconscionable clause; or (iii) *limit the application of any clause* so as to avoid an unconscionable result.

CMR **Exam Tip** Unconscionability is seldom a good defense on the MBE. That a contract turned out badly for one party is insufficient in itself to give rise to unconscionability. Look for great differences in bargaining power (*e.g.,* big company vs. average consumer) before finding a contract or clause is unconscionable.

V. DETERMINING THE TERMS OF THE CONTRACT

A. INTRODUCTION

Once you have determined that a contract exists, the next thing you must do is determine what are its terms.

B. GENERAL RULES OF CONTRACT CONSTRUCTION

There are a number of general rules of construction applied by the courts when interpreting contracts. The following are among the more frequently invoked:

1. *Contracts will be construed as a "whole"*; specific clauses will be subordinated to the contract's general intent;

2. The courts will *construe words according to their "ordinary" meaning* unless it is clearly shown that they were meant to be used in a technical sense;

3. If provisions appear to be inconsistent, *written or typed provisions will prevail over printed provisions*;

4. The courts will generally look to see what *custom and usage* is in the particular business and in the particular locale where the contract is either made or to be performed;

5. It is important to note that the courts generally will *try to reach a determination that a contract is valid and enforceable*;

6. *Ambiguities in a contract are construed against the party preparing the contract*, absent evidence of the intention of the parties.

C. PAROL EVIDENCE RULE—SUPPLEMENTING, EXPLAINING, OR CONTRADICTING TERMS

When the parties to a contract express their agreement in a *writing* with the *intent* that it embody the full and final expression of their bargain (*i.e.,* the writing is an *"integration"*), any other expressions—written or oral—made *prior to* the writing, as well as any oral expressions *contemporaneous with* the writing, are *inadmissible to vary* the terms of the writing under the parol evidence rule.

1. Is the Writing an "Integration"?

The question of whether a writing is an "integration" of all agreements between the parties can be broken down into two further subquestions:

(i) Is the writing intended as a *final* expression? The *more complete* the agreement appears to be on its face, the more likely it is that it was intended as an *integration*.

(ii) Is the writing a *complete* or *partial* integration? If the agreement contains a *merger clause* reciting that the agreement is complete on its face, this clause strengthens the *presumption* that all negotiations were merged into the written document.

a. Who Makes Decision?

The *majority view* is that the question as to whether an agreement is an integration is one of fact to be decided by the *judge*, not the jury.

b. How Determination Is Made

There are two competing tests for determining whether the parties intended the writing to be a complete and final integration: the Corbin test and the Williston test. The Corbin test is followed by most courts. It takes into account the *specific circumstances of the transaction involved* (*e.g.,* are the parties related or strangers, was it a large transaction, etc.) and asks whether parties like these, situated as they are, would naturally and normally include in their writing the extrinsic matter that is sought to be introduced. If people like these under circumstances like this would normally include the extrinsic matter in their writing, it will be excluded under the parol evidence rule. Otherwise, the evidence will be admissible.

2. Extrinsic Evidence Outside Scope of Rule

Because the rule prohibits admissibility only of extrinsic evidence that seeks to vary, contradict, or add to an "integration," other forms of extrinsic evidence may be admitted if they will not bring about this result, *i.e.,* they will fall outside the scope of the parol evidence rule.

a. Attacking Validity

A party to a written contract can attack the agreement's validity. The party acknowledges (concedes) that the writing reflects the agreement but asserts, most frequently, that the *agreement never came into being* because of any of the following:

1) Formation Defects

Formation defects (*e.g.,* fraud, duress, mistake, and illegality) may be shown by extrinsic evidence.

2) **Conditions Precedent**

If a party asserts that there was an oral agreement that the written contract would not become *effective* until a condition occurred, all evidence of the understanding may be offered and received. This would be a condition precedent to effectiveness.

b. **Interpretation**

If there is uncertainty or ambiguity in the written agreement's terms or a dispute as to the *meaning* of those terms, parol evidence can be received to aid the fact-finder in reaching a correct interpretation of the agreement. However, if the meaning of the agreement is plain, parol evidence is inadmissible.

c. **Showing of "True Consideration"**

The parol evidence rule will not bar extrinsic evidence showing the "true consideration" paid (*e.g.,* evidence that the consideration stated in the contract was never paid).

d. **Reformation**

If a party to a written agreement alleges facts (*e.g.,* mistake) entitling him to reformation of the agreement, the parol evidence rule is inapplicable.

3. **Collateral Agreements and Naturally Omitted Terms**

Parol evidence is often said to be admissible if the alleged parol agreement is collateral to the written obligation (*i.e.,* related to the subject matter but not part of the primary promise) and does not conflict with it. The Restatements of Contracts include a similar concept with a more definitive approach: the naturally omitted terms doctrine. The doctrine allows evidence of terms that would naturally be omitted from the written agreement. A term would naturally be omitted if: (i) it *does not conflict* with the written integration; and (ii) it concerns a subject that similarly situated parties *would not ordinarily be expected to include* in the written instrument.

4. **Parol Evidence Rule Not Applicable to Subsequent Modifications**

Parol evidence can be offered to show subsequent modifications of a written contract.

5. **Article 2 Rule**

Article 2 generally follows the rules discussed above (including the Corbin test), providing that a party cannot contradict a written contract but he may add *consistent additional terms* unless: (i) there is a merger clause, or (ii) the courts find from all of the circumstances that the writing was intended as a complete and exclusive statement of the terms of the agreement. Article 2 also provides that a written contract's terms may be *explained* or *supplemented* by the following, whether or not the writing appears to be ambiguous:

a. The parties' *course of dealing* (*i.e.,* the sequence of conduct concerning *previous transactions* between the parties to a particular transaction that may be regarded as establishing a common basis of their understanding);

b. A *usage of trade* (*i.e.,* a *practice or method of dealing*, regularly observed in a particular business setting so as to justify an expectation that it will be followed in the transaction in question);

c. The parties' *course of performance* (*i.e.,* if a contract involves *repeated occasions for performance* by either party and the other party has the opportunity to object to such performance, any course of performance accepted or acquiesced to is relevant in determining the meaning of the contract).

D. OTHER ARTICLE 2 PROVISIONS ON INTERPRETING CONTRACTS

1. Battle of the Forms

Recall that under Article 2, a contract can be formed even though the terms of the acceptance do not match the terms of the offer. (*See* II.D.4.c.2), *supra.*) Article 2 also has specific rules for determining what terms are included in the contract in such a case, and these rules are dependent on whether both parties to the transaction are merchants.

a. Contracts Involving a Nonmerchant—Terms of Offer Govern

If any party to the contract is not a merchant, the additional or different terms are considered to be mere proposals to modify the contract that do ***not*** become part of the contract unless the offeror expressly agrees.

b. Contracts Between Merchants—Additional Terms in Acceptance Usually Included

If *both* parties to the contract are merchants, *additional* terms in the acceptance will be included in the contract unless:

1) They *materially alter* the original terms of the offer (*e.g.,* they change a party's risk or the remedies available);

2) The offer *expressly limits acceptance* to the terms of the offer; or

3) The *offeror has already objected* to the particular terms, or *objects within a reasonable time* after notice of them is received.

c. Contracts Between Merchants—Different Terms in Acceptance May or May Not Be Included

There is a split of authority over whether terms in the acceptance that are *different* from (as opposed to in addition to) the terms in the offer will become part of the contract. Some courts treat different terms like additional terms, and follow the test set out above in determining whether the terms should be part of the contract. Other courts follow the *"knockout rule,"* which states that conflicting terms in the offer and acceptance are knocked out of the contract, because each party is assumed to object to the inclusion of such terms in the contract. Under the knockout rule, gaps left by knocked out terms are filled by the U.C.C. (*see* below).

2. Supplemental ("Gap-Filler") Terms

Recall that the key to forming a contract for the sale of goods is the quantity term (*see* II.B.2.b.1)b), *supra*). If other terms are missing from the agreement, Article 2 has gap-filler provisions to fill in the missing term(s).

a. *If: (i) nothing has been said as to price*; (ii) the price is *left open to be agreed upon* by the parties and they fail to agree; or (iii) the price is to be *fixed in terms of some standard* that is set by a third person or agency and it is not set, then the price is a *reasonable price at the time for delivery*.

ACCEPTANCE WITH ADDITIONAL TERMS

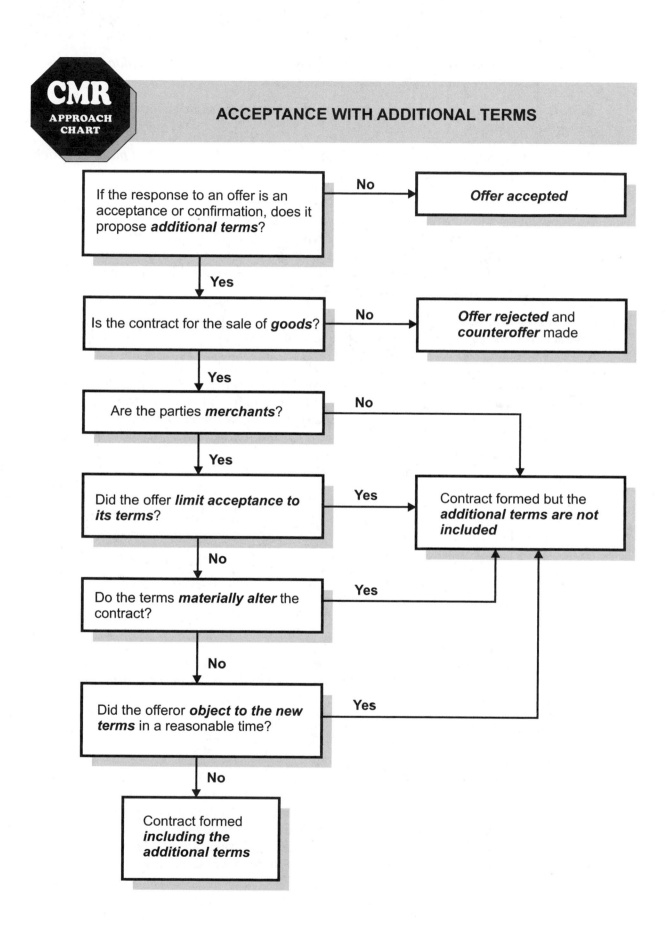

b. *If the place of delivery* is not specified, the place usually is the *seller's place of business*, if he has one; otherwise, it is the seller's home.

c. *If the time for shipment or delivery is not specified*, shipment/delivery is due in a *reasonable time*.

d. *If the time for payment is not specified*, payment is due at the *time and place at which the buyer is to receive the goods*.

e. *If a contract provides that an assortment of goods* is to be delivered (*e.g.,* blouses in various colors and sizes) and does not specify which party is to choose, the assortment is to be *at the buyer's option*. If the party who has the right to specify the assortment does not do so seasonally, the other party is excused from any resulting delay and may either proceed in any reasonable manner (*e.g.,* choose a reasonable assortment) or treat the failure as a breach.

3. Delivery Terms and Risk of Loss
All contracts for the sale of goods require delivery of the goods.

a. Noncarrier Case
A noncarrier case is a sale in which it appears that the parties did not intend that the goods would be moved by a common carrier (*e.g.,* when you buy groceries). In such a case, if the *seller is a merchant*, risk of loss passes to the buyer only when she *takes physical possession* of the goods. If the *seller is not a merchant*, risk of loss passes to the buyer upon *tender of delivery*.

b. Carrier Case
A carrier case is a sale in which it appears that the parties intended the goods to be moved by a carrier (*e.g.,* when you order a book from an Internet website). There are two types of carrier cases: shipment contracts and destination contracts.

1) Shipment Contract
If the contract authorizes or requires the seller to ship the goods by carrier but does not require him to deliver them at a particular destination, it is a shipment contract and risk of loss passes to the buyer when the goods are *delivered to the carrier*.

2) Destination Contracts
If the contract requires the seller to deliver the goods at a particular destination, the risk of loss passes to the buyer when the goods are *tendered to the buyer at the destination*.

3) Common Delivery Terms

a) C.I.F. and C. & F.
C.I.F. stands for "cost, insurance, and freight;" and C. & F. stands for "cost and freight." These terms mean that the price in the contract includes the price of the goods, the cost of shipping them to the buyer, and (in C.I.F. contracts) the cost of purchasing insurance for the benefit of the buyer in case the goods are destroyed in transit. These contracts are *always shipment contracts* (*i.e.,* the risk of loss passes to the buyer as soon as the goods are turned over to the carrier).

b) F.A.S.

F.A.S. stands for "free alongside." The term is generally used only when goods are to be shipped by boat. It is a type of destination contract—risk of loss passes to the buyer once the goods are delivered to the dock.

c) F.O.B.

F.O.B. stands for "free on board." The letters F.O.B. are always followed by a location, and the risk of loss passes to the buyer at the named location. The seller bears the risk and expense of getting the goods to the named location. These contracts can be either shipment contracts or destination contracts, depending on the location named.

CMR
COMPARISON CHART

NONCARRIER VS. CARRIER CONTRACTS

	Noncarrier Contract	Carrier Contract
Place of Delivery	Seller's place of business	***Shipment contract:*** seller must deliver to the shipper ***Destination contract:*** seller must tender delivery of goods to the buyer at the destination
Time for Payment	Upon tender of delivery	When buyer receives the goods
When does the risk of loss shift from the seller to the buyer?	***If seller is a merchant:*** when buyer takes possession ***If seller is not a merchant:*** when seller tenders delivery	***Shipment contract:*** when goods are delivered to the shipper ***Destination contract:*** when seller tenders delivery of goods to the buyer at the destination

c. Effect of Breach on Risk of Loss

1) Defective Goods

If goods are so defective that the buyer has a right to reject them, the risk of loss does not pass to the buyer until the defects are ***cured*** or she ***accepts*** the goods in spite of their defects. Note that a buyer generally has the right to reject for any defect. (*See* VII.C., *infra*.)

2) Revocation of Acceptance

If the buyer rightfully revokes acceptance, the *risk of loss* is treated as having rested *on the seller from the beginning* to the extent of any deficiency in the buyer's insurance coverage.

d. Risk in Sale or Return and Sale on Approval Contracts

1) Sale or Return

For the purpose of determining the risk of loss, a sale or return contract (*e.g.*, the buyer takes goods for resale but may return them if she is unable to resell them) is treated as an ordinary sale and the above rules apply. If the goods are returned to the seller, the *risk remains on the buyer* while the goods are in transit.

2) Sale on Approval

In a sale on approval (*i.e.*, the buyer takes goods for use but may return them even if they conform to the contract), the risk of loss does not pass to the buyer until she *accepts*.

CMR COMPARISON CHART

SALE OR RETURN VS. SALE ON APPROVAL

	Sale or Return	Sale on Approval
Defined	Buyer takes goods for resale but may return them if unable to resell.	Buyer takes goods for trial period and may return them even though they conform to the contract.
Risk of Loss	Rules for ordinary sale apply, but if goods are returned to seller, risk remains on buyer while goods are in transit.	Risk does not pass until buyer accepts goods (by failing to return them or to notify seller of intention within the required time). If buyer decides to return the goods, return is at seller's risk.

4. Insurable Interest and Identification

As noted above, a buyer often bears the risk of loss before receiving the goods purchased. In order to aid buyers in this situation (and a few others), Article 2 gives buyers a special property interest in goods as soon as they are identified as the ones that will be used to satisfy the contract (*e.g.*, as soon as the seller sets them aside for the buyer). This special property interest is insurable.

5. Bilateral Contracts Formed by Performance

Recall that a contract may be formed by the parties' performance where the mirror image

rule is not satisfied and under certain circumstances under Article 2's "battle of the forms" provision. (*See* II.D.4.c.2), *supra*.) In such cases, under Article 2, the contract includes all of the terms on which the writings of both parties agree. Any necessary missing terms are filled in by the supplemental terms provided for in Article 2.

a. Compare—Common Law Last Shot Rule
The rule is different in common law contracts. At common law, the contract will include the terms of the last communication sent to the party who performed.

6. Warranties
Contracts for the sale of goods automatically include a warranty of title (in most cases). They also may include certain implied warranties and express warranties.

a. Warranty of Title and Against Infringement

1) Warranty of Title
Any seller of goods warrants that the title transferred is good, that the transfer is rightful, and that there are no liens or encumbrances against the title of which the buyer is unaware at the time of contracting. This warranty arises automatically and need not be mentioned in the contract.

2) Warranty Against Infringement
A *merchant seller* regularly dealing in goods of the kind sold also automatically warrants that the goods are delivered free of any patent, trademark, copyright, or similar claims. But a *buyer who furnishes specifications* for the goods to the seller must hold the seller harmless against such claims.

b. Implied Warranty of Merchantability

1) When Given
Implied in every contract for *sale by a merchant* who deals in goods of the kind sold, there is a warranty that the goods are merchantable. Note that the serving of food or drink for consumption on the premises is a sale of goods subject to the warranty of merchantability.

2) Elements of the Warranty of Merchantability
To be merchantable, goods must at least be "*fit for the ordinary purposes for which such goods are used.*"

3) Seller's Knowledge of Defect Not Relevant
As in all implied warranty cases, it makes no difference that the seller himself did not know of the defect or that he could not have discovered it. Implied warranties are not based on negligence but rather on *absolute liability* that is imposed on certain sellers.

c. Implied Warranty of Fitness for a Particular Purpose
A warranty will also be implied in a contract for the sale of goods whenever (i) *any*

seller, merchant or not, ***has reason to know the particular purpose*** for which the goods are to be used and that the ***buyer is relying*** on the seller's skill and judgment to select suitable goods; and (ii) the ***buyer in fact relies*** on the seller's skill or judgment.

d. **Express Warranties**
Any affirmation of fact or promise made by the seller to the buyer, any description of the goods, and any sample or model creates an express warranty if the statement, description, sample, or model is part of the ***basis of the bargain***. For the statement, description, sample, or model to be a part of the basis of the bargain, it need only come at such a time that the ***buyer could have relied*** on it when she entered into the contract. The buyer does not need to prove that she actually did rely, although the seller may negate the warranty by proving that the buyer as a matter of fact did not rely. It is not necessary that the seller intended the affirmation of fact, description, model, or sample to create a warranty.

1) **Distinguish—Statements of Value or Opinion**
A statement relating merely to the value of the goods, or a statement purporting to be only the seller's opinion or commendation of the goods, does not create an express warranty.

e. **Disclaimer of Warranties**

1) **Warranty of Title**
The title warranty can be disclaimed or modified only by specific language or by circumstances that give the buyer notice that the seller does not claim title or that he is selling only such rights as he or a third party may have (*e.g.,* a sheriff's sale).

2) **Implied Warranties**
The implied warranties of merchantability and fitness for a particular purpose can be disclaimed by either specific disclaimers or general methods of disclaimer.

a) **Specific Disclaimers**

(1) **Disclaimer of Warranty of Merchantability**
The warranty of merchantability can be specifically disclaimed or modified only by ***mentioning merchantability***. If the sales contract is in writing, the disclaimer must be ***conspicuous***.

(2) **Disclaimer of Warranty of Fitness for a Particular Purpose**
The warranty of fitness for a particular purpose can be specifically disclaimed only by a ***conspicuous writing***. A written disclaimer, according to the statute, is sufficient if it says, for example, "[t]here are no warranties which extend beyond the description on the face hereof."

(3) **"Conspicuous" Defined**
A term is conspicuous when it is "so written, displayed, or presented

that a reasonable person against whom it is to operate ought to have noticed it." Language in the body of a writing is conspicuous if: (i) it is in larger type than surrounding text; (ii) it is in a contrasting type, font, or color; or (iii) it is set off from the text by marks that call attention to it. The court, not the jury, decides any fact question as to conspicuousness.

b)   General Disclaimer Methods
The U.C.C. also provides several general methods for disclaiming implied warranties.

(1)   By General Disclaimer Language
Unless the circumstances indicate otherwise, the implied warranties of merchantability and fitness can be disclaimed by expressions such as "*as is*," "with all faults," or other expressions that in common understanding call the buyer's attention to the fact that there are no implied warranties.

(2)   By Inspection or Refusal to Inspect
If the buyer, before entering into the contract, has examined the goods or a sample or model as fully as she desires or has refused to examine, there is no warranty as to defects that a reasonable examination would have revealed to her.

(3)   By Course of Dealing, Etc.
Implied warranties may also be disclaimed by the course of dealing, course of performance, or usage of trade.

CMR **Exam Tip**   It may seem odd that there are specific disclaimer methods, with detailed requirements, and general disclaimer methods, requiring little formality. In actual practice, it is better to use the specific disclaimers because general disclaimers may be limited by the circumstances. However, on the MBE, an "as is" or "with all faults" disclaimer will generally be as effective as a specific disclaimer.

3)   Express Warranties
The U.C.C. provides that words or conduct relevant to the creation of express warranties and words or conduct tending to negate such warranties shall wherever possible be construed as consistent with each other, but "*negation or limitation is inoperative to the extent that such construction is unreasonable*." In other words, once an express warranty is made, it is very difficult to disclaim.

4)   Limitations on Damages
Parties may include in their contract a clause limiting the damages available in the case of breach of warranty (*e.g.,* "remedy for breach of warranty is limited to repair or replacement of the defective goods"). Such a limitation generally will be upheld unless the limitation is unconscionable (*e.g.,* causes the remedy to fail of its essential purpose; *see* IV.D.2.a.4), *supra*).

WARRANTIES

Type	How Arise	By Whom	Disclaimer
Implied			
Warranty of Title (title is good, transfer rightful, no liens or encumbrances)	By sale of goods	Any seller	By specific language or circumstances showing seller does not claim title
Warranty of Merchantability (fit for ordinary purposes)	By sale of goods of the kind regularly sold by the merchant	Merchant only	By disclaimer mentioning "merchantability" (if written disclaimer, it must be conspicuous)*
Warranty of Fitness for Particular Purpose (fit for buyer's particular purpose)	By sale of goods where seller has reason to know of particular purpose and of buyer's reliance on seller to choose suitable goods	Any seller	By conspicuous **written** disclaimer*
Express	By affirmation of fact, promise, description, model, or sample	Any seller	Extremely difficult to disclaim

*These may also be disclaimed by language such as "as is"; by inspection (or refusal to inspect); or by course of dealing, course of performance, or usage of trade.

5) Timing—Disclaimers and Limitations in the Box

To be effective, a disclaimer of warranty or limitation on remedies must be agreed to during the bargaining process. Thus, although a few courts hold otherwise, most hold that a warranty disclaimer or limitation on remedy included inside the packaging of goods is not effective against the buyer.

a) Compare—"Clickwrap"

Computer software often comes with terms that appear on the user's computer screen during the installation process, and the purchaser must click to agree to the terms before installing. Such limitations and disclaimers typically

are upheld on the rationale that the purchaser can return the software if he disagrees with the conditions.

6) Unconscionability and Warranty Disclaimers

Some courts will, in addition to determining whether disclaimers have met the formal requirements discussed above, test warranty disclaimers by the unconscionability standards. (*See* IV.D.2., *supra*.) Moreover, warranty disclaimers that limit damages for personal injury caused by a breach of warranty on consumer goods are prima facie unconscionable.

f. To Whom Do Warranties Extend?

U.C.C. section 2-318 provides alternative provisions for determining to whom warranty liability extends. Most states have adopted the narrowest provision, ***Alternative A***, which provides that the seller's warranty liability extends to any natural person who is in the ***family*** or ***household*** of the buyer or who is a ***guest*** in the buyer's home if it is reasonable to expect that the person may use, consume, or be affected by the goods and that person suffers ***personal injury*** because of a breach of warranty.

VI. PERFORMANCE AND EXCUSE OF NONPERFORMANCE

A. INTRODUCTION

Having established that there is a contract and having determined what are the terms of the contract, the next issue to consider is what performance is due and whether any nonperformance is excused.

B. PERFORMANCE AT COMMON LAW

A party's basic duty at common law is to substantially perform all that is called for in the contract.

C. PERFORMANCE UNDER ARTICLE 2

Article 2 generally requires a ***perfect tender***—the delivery and condition of the goods must be exactly as promised in the contract. Note the following:

1. Obligation of Good Faith

Article 2 requires all parties to act in good faith, which is defined as "honesty in fact and the observance of reasonable commercial standards of fair dealing."

2. Seller's Obligation of Tender and Delivery

a. Noncarrier Cases

Recall that a noncarrier case is a sale in which it appears that the parties did not intend that the goods be moved by carrier. (*See* V.D.3.a., *supra*.)

1) Tender of Delivery

In a proper tender of delivery, the seller must put and hold conforming goods at the buyer's disposition for a time sufficient for the buyer to take possession. The seller must ***give the buyer notice*** reasonably necessary to enable her to take possession of the goods. The ***tender must be at a reasonable hour***.

2) **Place of Delivery**
In the absence of an agreement otherwise, the place of delivery generally is the *seller's place of business*, or if he has none, his residence.

b. **Carrier Cases**
Recall that a carrier case is a sale in which, due either to the circumstances or to the express terms of the agreement, it appears that the parties intended that a carrier be used to move the goods. (*See* V.D.3.b., *supra*.)

1) **Shipment Contracts—Where Seller Has Not Agreed to Tender at Particular Destination**
In the absence of an agreement otherwise, the seller need not see that the goods reach the buyer, but need only:

a) Put the goods into the hands of a reasonable carrier and make a reasonable contract for their transportation to the buyer;

b) Obtain and promptly tender any documents required by the contract or usage of trade or otherwise necessary to enable the buyer to take possession; and

c) Promptly notify the buyer of the shipment.

2) **Destination Contracts—Where Seller Has Agreed to Tender at Particular Destination**
If the contract requires the seller to tender delivery of the goods at a particular destination (*e.g.,* F.O.B. buyer's warehouse), the seller must, at the destination, put and hold conforming goods at the buyer's disposition.

3. **Buyer's Obligation to Pay—Right to Inspect**

a. **Delivery and Payment Concurrent Conditions**
In *noncarrier cases*, unless the contract provides otherwise, a sale is for cash and the price is due concurrently with tender of delivery. However, unless otherwise agreed, when goods are shipped *by carrier*, the price is due only at the time and place at which the buyer receives the goods. Therefore, in a shipment case the price is due when the goods are put in the hands of the carrier, and in a destination contract the price is due when the goods reach the named destination.

b. **Payment by Check**
Tender of payment by check is sufficient unless the seller demands cash and gives the buyer time to get it. If a check is given, the buyer's duty to pay is suspended until the check is either paid or dishonored. If the check is paid, the buyer's duty to pay is discharged. If the check is dishonored, the seller may sue for the price or recover the goods.

c. **Installment Contracts**
In an installment contract (*i.e.,* one that requires or authorizes delivery in separate installments), the seller may demand payment for each installment if the price can be so apportioned, unless a contrary intent appears.

d. **Buyer's Right of Inspection**
Unless the contract provides otherwise, the buyer has a right to inspect the goods before she pays unless the contract provides for payment C.O.D. or otherwise indicates that the buyer has promised to pay without inspecting the goods.

D. **WHEN HAS A CONTRACTING PARTY'S DUTY TO PERFORM BECOME ABSOLUTE?**
It is important to understand that there is a difference between whether a party is bound under a contract and whether a party who is bound has come under a duty to perform. A person is bound if there has been an offer, an acceptance, and an exchange of consideration. However, the contract may provide (impliedly or explicitly) that a party who is bound does not come under a duty to perform unless or until some specified condition occurs.

1. **Distinction Between Promise and Condition**
In looking at the terms of a contract, a distinction has to be drawn between an absolute promise on the one hand and a condition on the other.

a. **Definitions**

1) **Promise**
A promise is a commitment to do or refrain from doing something. The promise in the contract may be unconditional or conditional. An unconditional promise is absolute; a conditional promise may become absolute by the occurrence of the condition. If the promise is unconditional, the failure to perform according to its terms is a breach of contract.

2) **Condition**
A condition is an event, other than the passage of time, the occurrence or non-occurrence of which will create, limit, or extinguish the other contracting party's absolute duty to perform. A condition is a *"promise modifier."* There can be no breach of promise until the promisor is under an immediate duty to perform.

a) **Distinguish—Failure of Condition vs. Breach of Contract**
The failure of a contractual provision that is only a condition is *not a breach of contract*, but it discharges the liability of the promisor whose obligations on the conditional promise never mature.

CMR **Exam Tip** The distinction between a promise and a condition is important, because the failure of a *promise* gives rise to a *breach*, whereas the failure of a *condition* *relieves* a party of the obligation to perform.

b. **Interpretation of Provision as Promise or Condition**
What determines whether a contract provision is a promise or a condition is the *"intent of the parties."* In determining intent, courts will look at the words and phrases used by the parties, their prior practices, the custom in the business community with respect to the provision, and whether performance is needed from a third party (if performance is to be rendered by a third party, it is more likely to be a condition than an absolute promise). In doubtful situations, most courts will hold that the provision in question is a *promise*.

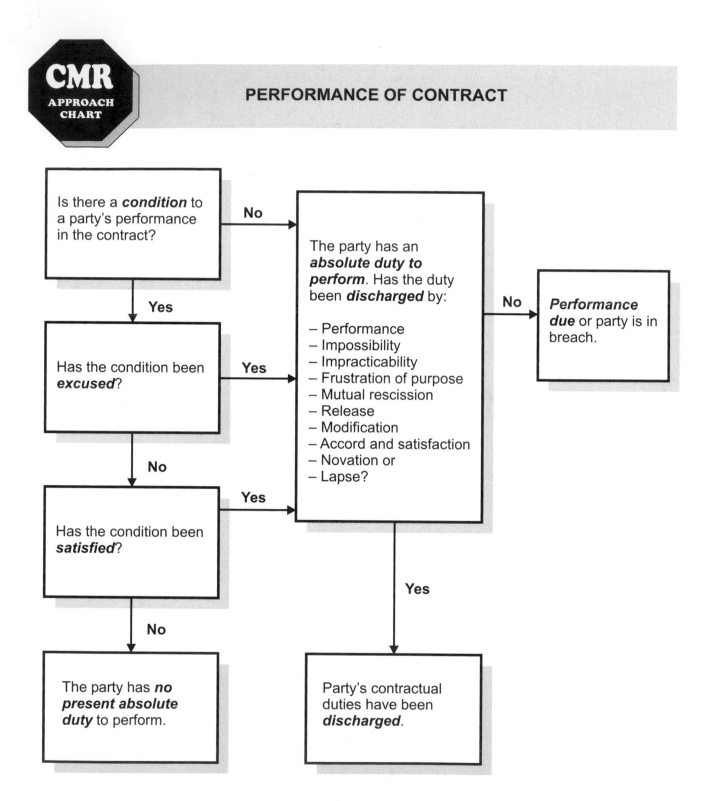

CMR
APPROACH
CHART

Is there a **condition** to a party's performance in the contract?

No →

Yes ↓

Has the condition been **excused**?

Yes →

No ↓

Has the condition been **satisfied**?

Yes →

No ↓

The party has **no present absolute duty** to perform.

The party has an **absolute duty to perform**. Has the duty been **discharged** by:

– Performance
– Impossibility
– Impracticability
– Frustration of purpose
– Mutual rescission
– Release
– Modification
– Accord and satisfaction
– Novation or
– Lapse?

No → **Performance due** or party is in breach.

Yes ↓

Party's contractual duties have been **discharged**.

2. **Classification of Conditions**

    a. **According to Time of Occurrence**

        1) **Condition Precedent**
        A condition precedent is one that must occur *before* an absolute duty of immediate performance arises in the other party.

        2) **Conditions Concurrent**
        Conditions concurrent are those that are capable of occurring *together*, and that the parties are bound to perform at the same time (*e.g.*, tender of deed for cash). Thus, in effect, each is a condition "precedent" to the other.

        3) **Condition Subsequent**
        A condition subsequent is one the occurrence of which *cuts off* an already existing absolute duty of performance.

CMR SUMMARY CHART — CONDITIONS—TIME OF OCCURRENCE

Type	Definition	Effect of Occurrence of Condition	Example
Condition Precedent	Condition must occur before performance is due.	Performance due.	Agreement to pay $10,000 "if my house is sold by April 1." No payment unless house is sold by April 1.
Conditions Concurrent	Conditions to occur at the same time.	If one condition has occurred, performance of the other is due.	Agreement to pay $100,000 for Blackacre. Money and deed exchanged in same transaction.
Condition Subsequent	Condition cuts off already existing duty.	Duty to perform is excused.	Agreement to buy Blackacre for $100,000 unless zoning is changed. If zoning is changed, no duty to pay $100,000 or transfer deed.

    b. **Express, Implied, and Constructive Conditions**

        1) **Express Conditions**
        Express conditions are those expressed in the contract.

2) Implied Conditions

Implied conditions are those fairly to be inferred from evidence of the parties' intention; *i.e.,* their existence is determined by the process of contract interpretation. These are usually referred to as "implied in fact" conditions.

3) Constructive Conditions

a) In General

Constructive conditions are conditions ***read into*** a contract by the court without regard to, or even despite, the parties' intention. This is done in the interest of fairness to ensure that both parties receive the performance for which they bargained. These are usually referred to as "implied in law" conditions.

b) The "Time Test"

The courts will sometimes imply constructive conditions relating to the time for performing under the contract.

(1) Constructive Conditions Concurrent

If both performances can be rendered at the same time, they are constructively concurrent; thus, each is a condition "precedent" to the other. Hence, absent excuse, each party must first tender his own performance if he wishes to put the other under a duty of immediate performance resulting in breach if he fails to perform.

(2) Constructive Conditions Precedent

If one performance will take a period of time to complete while the other can be rendered in an instant, completion of the longer performance is a constructive condition precedent to execution of the shorter performance.

4) Effect of Condition—Equitable Remedy

If a contract is not enforceable due to the failure or occurrence of a condition, and one of the parties has fully or partially performed, he can usually recover under unjust enrichment theories (*see* VIII.C., *infra*), although the measure of damages in that case may be less advantageous than the contract price.

3. Have the Conditions Been Excused?

A duty of immediate performance with respect to a conditional promise does not become ***absolute*** until the conditions (i) have been ***performed***, or (ii) have been ***legally excused***. Thus, in analyzing a question, if the facts do not reveal performance of the applicable condition precedent or concurrent, look to see whether the condition has been excused. Excuse of conditions can arise in a variety of ways.

a. Excuse of Condition by Hindrance or Failure to Cooperate

If a party having a duty of performance that is subject to a condition (*i.e.,* she is the party protected by the condition) prevents the condition from occurring, the condition will be excused if the prevention is ***wrongful*** (*i.e.,* the other party would not have reasonably contemplated or assumed the risk of this type of conduct).

b. **Excuse of Condition by Actual Breach**

An actual breach of the contract when performance is due will excuse the duty of counterperformance. Note, however, that counterperformance will be excused at common law *only* if the *breach is material*. A minor breach may suspend this duty, but it will not excuse it.

c. **Excuse of Condition by Anticipatory Repudiation**

Anticipatory repudiation occurs if a promisor, prior to the time set for performance of his promise, indicates that he will not perform when the time comes. If the requirements set forth below are met, this anticipatory repudiation will serve to excuse conditions.

1) **Executory Bilateral Contract Requirement**

Anticipatory repudiation applies only if there is a bilateral contract with *executory (unperformed) duties on both sides*.

2) **Requirement that Anticipatory Repudiation Be Unequivocal**

An anticipatory repudiation stems from the words or conduct of the promisor *unequivocally* indicating that he cannot or will not perform when the time comes.

3) **Effect of Anticipatory Repudiation**

In the case of an anticipatory repudiation, the nonrepudiating party has four alternatives:

a) Treat the anticipatory repudiation as a total repudiation and *sue immediately*;

b) Suspend his own performance and *wait to sue* until the performance date;

c) Treat the repudiation as an offer to rescind and *treat the contract as discharged*; or

d) Ignore the repudiation and *urge the promisor to perform* (but note that by urging the promisor to perform, the nonrepudiating party is not waiving the repudiation—she can still sue for breach and is excused from performing unless the promisor retracts the repudiation).

4) **Retraction of Repudiation**

A repudiating party may at any time before his next performance is due withdraw his repudiation unless the other party has *canceled, materially changed* her *position* in reliance on the repudiation, or otherwise indicated that she considers the *repudiation final.* Withdrawal of the repudiation may be in any manner that clearly indicates the intention to perform, but must include any assurances justifiably demanded.

d. **Excuse of Condition by Prospective Inability or Unwillingness to Perform**

Prospective failure of condition occurs when a party has reasonable grounds to believe that the other party will be unable or unwilling to perform when performance is due.

1) **Distinguish from Actual and Anticipatory Repudiation**

Prospective inability or unwillingness to perform is not an anticipatory repudiation because such a repudiation must be *unequivocal*, whereas prospective failure

to perform involves conduct or words that merely raise doubts that the party will perform.

2) Effect of Prospective Failure
The effect of prospective failure is to allow the innocent party to suspend further performance on her side until she receives *adequate assurances* that performance will be forthcoming. If the other party fails to provide adequate assurances, the innocent party may be excused from her own performance and may treat the failure to provide assurances as a repudiation.

3) Retraction of Repudiation
As with anticipatory repudiation, retraction is possible if the defaulting party regains his ability or willingness to perform. However, this fact must be communicated to the innocent party in order to be effective.

e. Excuse of Condition by Substantial Performance
Generally, the condition of complete performance may be excused if the party has rendered substantial performance. In this case, the other party's duty of counterperformance becomes absolute. It should be noted, however, that courts generally apply this doctrine only if a *constructive* (implied in law) condition is involved. They will not apply it when there is an *express* condition for fear this would defeat the express intent of the parties.

1) Substantial Performance Arises If Breach Is Minor
The rules for determining substantiality of performance are the same as those for determining materiality of breach. (*See* VII.B.2., *infra.*)

2) Inapplicable Where Breach "Willful"
Most courts will not apply the substantial performance doctrine if the breach has been "willful."

3) Damages Offset
Even though the party who has substantially performed is able to enforce the contract, the other party will be able to mitigate by deducting damages suffered due to the first party's incomplete performance.

4) Generally Inapplicable to Contracts for the Sale of Goods
The doctrine of substantial performance generally is not applicable in contracts for the sale of goods. (*See* VII.C., *infra.*)

f. Excuse of Condition by "Divisibility" of Contract
If a contract is divisible (*see* below) and a party performs one of the units of the contract, he is entitled to the agreed-on equivalent for that unit even if he fails to perform the other units. It is not a condition precedent to the other party's liability that the whole contract be performed. However, the other party has a cause of action for failure to perform the other units and may withhold his counterperformance for those units.

1) What Is a "Divisible" Contract?
Three tests must be *concurrently* satisfied to make a contract divisible:

a) The *performance of each party is divided into two or more parts* under the contract;

b) The *number of parts due from each party is the same*; and

c) The *performance of each part by one party is agreed on as the equivalent of the corresponding part* from the other party, *i.e.,* each performance is the quid pro quo of the other.

2) Sales of Goods—Installment Contracts

Like the common law, Article 2 assumes that a contract is not divisible unless it authorizes deliveries in several lots, in which case the contract is called an installment contract. In installment contracts, the price, if it can be apportioned, may be demanded for *each lot* unless a contrary intent appears.

g. Excuse of Condition by Waiver or Estoppel

One having the benefit of a condition under a contract may indicate by *words or conduct* that she will not insist on that condition's being met. Consideration is not required for a valid waiver of condition.

1) Estoppel Waiver

Whenever a party indicates that she is "waiving" a condition before it is to happen, or she is "waiving" some performance before it is to be rendered, and the person addressed *detrimentally relies* on the waiver, the courts will hold this to be a binding (estoppel) waiver. Note, however, that the promise to waive a condition may be retracted at any time *before* the other party has changed his position to his detriment.

2) Election Waiver

When a condition or a duty of performance is broken, the beneficiary of the condition or duty must make an election; she may: (i) terminate her liability, *or* (ii) continue under the contract. If she chooses to continue, she will be deemed to have waived the condition or duty. This election waiver requires neither consideration nor estoppel (although estoppel elements are often present).

3) Conditions that May Be Waived

If *no consideration* is given for the waiver, the condition must be *ancillary or collateral* to the main subject and purpose of the contract for the waiver to be effective. In other words, one cannot "waive" entitlement to the entire or substantially entire return performance.

4) Waiver in Installment Contracts

In an *installment contract*, if a waiver is not supported by consideration, the beneficiary of the waived condition can insist on strict compliance with the terms of the contract for future installments (so long as there has been no detrimental reliance on the waiver) by giving notice that he is revoking the waiver.

5) Right to Damages for Failure of Condition

It is important to note that a waiver severs only the right to treat the failure of the

condition as a total breach excusing counterperformance. However, the waiving party does **not** thereby waive her right to damages.

h. Excuse of Condition by Impossibility, Impracticability, or Frustration
Conditions may be excused by impossibility, impracticability, or frustration of purpose. (*See* E.5., *infra.*)

E. HAS THE ABSOLUTE DUTY TO PERFORM BEEN DISCHARGED?
Once it is determined that a party is under an immediate duty to perform, the duty to perform must be discharged.

1. Discharge by Performance
The most obvious way to discharge a contractual duty is, of course, by full and complete performance.

2. Discharge by Tender of Performance
Good faith tender of performance made in accordance with contractual terms will also discharge contractual duties.

3. Discharge by Occurrence of Condition Subsequent
The occurrence of a condition subsequent will serve to discharge contractual duties.

4. Discharge by Illegality
If the subject matter of the contract has become illegal due to a subsequently enacted law or other governmental act, performance will be discharged. This is often referred to as "supervening illegality."

Note: If the illegality existed at the time the agreement was made, no contract was formed because of the illegality. (*See* IV.B.3., *supra.*)

5. Discharge by Impossibility, Impracticability, or Frustration
The occurrence of an unanticipated or extraordinary event may make contractual duties impossible or impracticable to perform or may frustrate the purpose of the contract. Where the nonoccurrence of the event was a **basic assumption** of the parties in making the contract and **neither** party has expressly or impliedly **assumed the risk** of the event occurring, contractual duties may be discharged.

a. Discharge by Impossibility
Contractual duties will be discharged if it has become impossible to perform them.

1) Impossibility Must Be "Objective"
For this rule to operate, the impossibility must be "objective"; *i.e.,* the duties could not be performed by anyone. "Subjective" impossibility will not suffice, *i.e.,* where the duties could be performed by someone but not the promisor.

2) Timing of Impossibility
The impossibility must arise **after** the contract has been entered into. If the facts giving rise to impossibility already existed when the contract was formed, the question is not really one of "discharge of contractual duties." Rather, it is a

"contract formation" problem, namely, whether the contract is voidable because of mistake.

3) Effect of Impossibility

If a contract is discharged because of impossibility, each party is excused from duties arising under the contract that are yet to be fulfilled. Either party may sue for rescission and receive restitution of any goods delivered, payments made, etc.

4) Partial Impossibility

If the performance to be rendered under the contract becomes only partially impossible, the duty may be discharged *only to that extent*. The remainder of the performance may be required according to the contractual terms. This is so even though this remaining performance might involve added expense or difficulty.

5) Temporary Impossibility

Temporary impossibility *suspends* contractual duties; it does not discharge them. When performance once more becomes possible, the duty "springs back" into existence unless the burden on either party to the contract would be substantially increased or different from that originally contemplated.

6) Part Performance Prior to Impossibility—Quasi-Contractual Recovery

If a party partially performed before the impossibility arose, that party will have a right to recover in quasi-contract at the contract rate or for the reasonable value of his performance if that is a more convenient mode of valuation.

7) Specific Situations

a) Death or Physical Incapacity

Death or the physical incapacity of a person *necessary* to effectuate the contract serves to discharge it.

Note: Most fact situations on this point involve personal service contracts. Check to see whether the services involved are *"unique."* If the services are the kind that could be delegated (*see* IX.C.2.a., *infra*), the contract is *not* discharged by the incapacity of the person who was to perform them.

CMR | **Exam Tip** | A contract is *not* discharged by the death or incapacity of the person who was to perform the services if the services are of a kind that can be delegated. Thus, if the contract was for personal services of a *unique* kind (*e.g.,* the painting of a portrait by a famous artist), the death or incapacity of that person could make performance impossible, but if the services are not unique (*e.g.,* the painting of a farmer's barn), the death or incapacity of that person would *not* make performance impossible.

b) Supervening Illegality

Supervening illegality may serve to discharge a contract. Many courts treat such supervening illegality as a form of impossibility.

c) **Subsequent Destruction of Contract's Subject Matter or Means of Performance**
If the contract's subject matter is destroyed or the designated means for performing the contract are destroyed, contractual duties will be discharged.

(1) **Compare—Contracts to Build**
A contractor's duty to **construct** a building is **not** discharged by destruction of the work in progress. *Rationale:* Construction is not rendered impossible; the contractor can still rebuild. However, if the destruction was not caused by the contractor, most courts will excuse the contractor from meeting the original deadline.

CMR Exam Tip Be sure to distinguish destruction of the subject matter of a contract to build from destruction of the subject matter of a contract to repair. When a **contract to build's** subject matter is accidentally destroyed (*e.g.*, a house that is almost finished being built is destroyed by accidental fire), the builder's performance is **not** discharged by impossibility because the builder is still capable of starting over and rebuilding. However, when a **contract to repair's** subject matter is accidentally destroyed (*e.g.*, a house getting a new roof is destroyed by accidental fire), the repairer's performance is discharged by impossibility, because there is nothing left to repair.

(2) **Specificity Required**

(a) **Subject Matter**
Note that destruction of the subject matter will render a contract impossible only if the very thing destroyed is necessary to fulfill the contract. If the thing destroyed is not actually necessary, impossibility is not a defense.

(b) **Specificity of Source**
As with the destruction of the subject matter, destruction of a source for fulfilling the contract will render the contract impossible only if the source is the one source specified by the parties.

(3) **If Risk of Loss Has Already Passed to Buyer**
The rules relating to discharge because of destruction of the subject matter *will not apply* if the risk of loss has already passed to the buyer.

b. **Discharge by Impracticability**
Modern courts will also discharge contractual duties where performance has become impracticable.

1) **Test for Impracticability**
The test for a finding of impracticability is that the party to perform has encountered:

a) *Extreme and unreasonable* difficulty and/or expense; and

b) Its nonoccurrence was a ***basic assumption*** of the parties.

2) Contracts for the Sale of Goods

Article 2 generally follows the above rules for impossibility and impracticability. If performance has become impossible or commercially impracticable, the seller will be ***discharged to the extent of the impossibility or impracticability***.

a) Allocation of Risk

Generally, the seller assumes the risk of the occurrence of such unforeseen events and must continue to perform. However, if it is fair to say that the parties would not have placed on the seller the risk of the extraordinary occurrence, the seller will be discharged.

b) Events Sufficient for Discharge

Events sufficient to excuse performance include a ***shortage of raw materials*** or the inability to convert them into the seller's product because of contingencies such as war, strike, embargo, or unforeseen shutdown of a major supplier. Catastrophic local crop failure (as opposed to a mere shortage) also is sufficient for discharge. However, mere increases in costs are rarely sufficient for discharge unless they change the nature of the contract.

Note: There is no bright line test for determining when a rise in price changes the nature of the contract, but an increase in costs of more than 50% has been held to be ***insufficient***.

c) Seller's Partial Inability to Perform

If the seller's inability to perform as a result of the unforeseen circumstance is only partial, he ***must allocate deliveries*** among his customers and, at his option, may include in the allocation regular customers not then under contract.

c. Discharge by Frustration

Frustration will exist if the purpose of the contract has become valueless by virtue of some supervening event not the fault of the party seeking discharge. If the purpose has been frustrated, a number of courts will discharge contractual duties even though performance of these duties is still possible. The elements necessary to establish frustration are as follows:

1) There is some ***supervening act*** or event leading to the frustration;

2) At the time of entering into the contract, the parties ***did not reasonably foresee*** the act or event occurring;

3) The ***purpose*** of the contract has been completely or almost completely ***destroyed*** by this act or event; and

4) The purpose of the contract was realized by ***both parties*** at the time of making the contract.

CMR **Exam Tip** You will likely encounter the doctrine of frustration on your exam. It began when people rented rooms at high rates in advance along the planned route for the coronation procession of the King of England. When the soon to be King's plans changed, the renters sought to cancel their contracts. Because the parties knew that the only reason the rooms were being rented was to view the procession, the court discharged the contracts for frustration of purpose. On an exam, watch for facts showing that a person has rented a venue f*or a specific purpose known to the owner* and a subsequent event (*e.g.,* a storm, a death) that was not reasonably foreseeable and that renders the purpose for renting the place moot.

6. **Discharge by Rescission**
Rescission will serve to discharge contractual duties. Rescission may be either mutual or unilateral.

a. **Mutual Rescission**
The contract may be discharged by an ***express agreement*** between the parties to rescind. The agreement to rescind is itself a binding contract supported by consideration, namely, the giving up by each party of her right to counterperformance from the other.

CMR **Exam Tip** Although mutual rescission generally discharges the parties to a contract, watch out for a third-party beneficiary case. If the rights of a third-party beneficiary have **already vested**, the contract **cannot** be discharged by mutual rescission by the promisor and promisee. (*See* IX.B.2.a., *infra.*)

1) **Contract Must Be Executory**
For a contract to be effectively discharged by rescission, the duties must be executory on **both** sides.

a) **Unilateral Contracts**
If the contract is unilateral (*i.e.,* only one party owes an absolute duty), a contract to mutually rescind where one party still has a duty to perform will be ineffective. For an effective rescission in a unilateral contract situation where the offeree has already performed, the rescission promise must be supported by one of the following:

(1) An offer of ***new consideration*** by the nonperforming party;

(2) Elements of ***promissory estoppel***, *i.e.,* detrimental reliance; or

(3) Manifestation of an ***intent*** by the original offeree to make a ***gift*** of the obligation owed her.

b) **Partially Performed Bilateral Contracts**
A mutual agreement to rescind will usually be enforced when a bilateral contract has been partially performed. Whether the party who has partially performed will be entitled to compensation depends on the terms of the rescission agreement.

2) **Formalities**
Mutual rescission may be made ***orally***. This is so even though the contract to be

rescinded expressly states that it can be rescinded only by a written document, unless the subject matter of the contract to be rescinded falls within the Statute of Frauds (*e.g.,* transfer of land) or the contract is for the sale of goods (Article 2 requires a written rescission or modification if the original contract to be rescinded or modified expressly requires a written rescission).

3) Contracts Involving Third-Party Beneficiary Rights
If the rights of third-party beneficiaries have already **vested** (*see* IX.B.2., *infra*), the contract may **not** be discharged by mutual rescission.

b. Unilateral Rescission
Unilateral rescission results when one of the parties to the contract desires to rescind it but the other party desires that the contract be performed according to its terms. For unilateral rescission to be granted, the party desiring rescission must have adequate legal grounds. Most common among these are mistake, misrepresentation, duress, and failure of consideration. If the nonassenting party refuses to voluntarily grant rescission, the other party may file an action in equity to obtain it.

7. Partial Discharge by Modification of Contract
If a contract is subsequently modified by the parties, this will serve to discharge those terms of the original contract that are the subject of the modification. It will **not** serve to discharge the **entire contract**. To have such a partial discharge, the following requirements must usually be met.

a. Mutual Assent
The modifying agreement must have been mutually assented to. Note, however, that under the doctrine of **reformation,** either of the parties to the contract may bring an equity action to have a contract's terms modified if the writing, through mistake or misrepresentation, does not incorporate the terms orally agreed on.

b. Consideration
Generally, consideration is necessary to modify a contract. However, the courts usually find consideration to be present because each party has limited his right to enforce the original contract as is.

1) Requirement Where Modification Is Only "Correction"
No consideration is necessary if the effect of the modification is merely to correct an error in the original contract.

2) Contracts for the Sale of Goods
No consideration is needed for the modification of a contract for the sale of goods under Article 2, as long as the modification is sought in good faith.

8. Discharge by Novation
A novation occurs when a new contract substitutes a new party to receive benefits and assume duties that had originally belonged to one of the original parties under the terms of the old contract. A novation will serve to discharge the old contract. The elements for a valid novation are: (i) a **previous** valid contract; (ii) an **agreement** among all parties, including the new party (or parties) to the new contract; (iii) the **immediate extinguishment** of contractual duties as between the original contracting parties; and (iv) a valid and enforceable **new** contract.

9. **Discharge by Cancellation**

The destruction or surrender of a written contract will not usually, by itself, discharge the contract. If, however, the parties manifest their *intent* to have these acts serve as a discharge, it will usually have this effect if consideration or one of its alternatives is present.

10. **Discharge by Release**

A release and/or contract not to sue will serve to discharge contractual duties. The release or contract not to sue usually must be in *writing* and supported by *new consideration* or *promissory estoppel* elements.

11. **Discharge by Substituted Contract**

A contract may be discharged by a substituted contract. This occurs when the parties to a contract enter into a second contract that *immediately revokes* the first contract expressly or impliedly.

   a. **Intent Governs**

   Whether a second contract will constitute a substituted contract depends on whether the parties intend an immediate discharge or a discharge only after performance of the second contract. If an immediate discharge is intended, there is a substituted contract. If the parties intend the first contract to be discharged only after performance of the second contract, there is an executory accord (*see* 12.a., *infra*) rather than a substituted contract.

12. **Discharge by Accord and Satisfaction**

A contract may be discharged by an accord and satisfaction.

   a. **Accord**

   An accord is an agreement in which one party to an existing contract agrees to accept, in lieu of the performance that she is supposed to receive from the other party to the existing contract, some other, different performance.

      1) **Requirement of Consideration**

      In general, an accord must be supported by consideration. When the consideration is of a lesser value than the originally bargained-for consideration in the prior contract, it will be sufficient if the new consideration is of a *different type* or if the claim is to be paid to a *third party*.

         a) **Partial Payment of Original Debt**

         One often-encountered problem involves the offer of a smaller amount than the amount due under an existing obligation in satisfaction of the claim, *i.e.,* partial payment of an original debt. The *majority view* is that this will suffice for an *accord and satisfaction* if there is a *"bona fide dispute"* as to the claim or there is otherwise some alteration, even if slight, in the debtor's consideration. (*See* discussion of the preexisting legal duty rule, III.B.2.c.1), *supra*.)

      2) **Effect of Accord**

      The accord, taken alone, will not discharge the prior contract. It merely *suspends* the right to enforce it in accordance with the terms of the accord contract.

   b. **Satisfaction**

   Satisfaction is the performance of the accord agreement. Its effect is to discharge not only the original contract, but also the accord contract as well.

    c.   **Effect of Breach of Accord Agreement Before Satisfaction**

        1)   **Breach by Debtor**
            If the debtor breaches an accord agreement, the creditor may sue either on the original undischarged contract *or* for breach of the accord agreement.

        2)   **Breach by Creditor**
            If a creditor breaches an accord agreement (*i.e.,* he sues on the *original* contract), the debtor has two courses of action available: (i) raise the accord agreement as an equitable defense and ask that the contract action be dismissed; or (ii) *wait until she is damaged* (*i.e.,* the creditor is successful in his action on the original contract) and then bring an action at law for damages for breach of the accord contract.

    d.   **Checks Tendered as "Payment in Full"**
        If a monetary claim is *uncertain* or is subject to a *bona fide dispute*, an accord and satisfaction may be accomplished by a *good faith* tender and acceptance of a check when that check (or an accompanying document) *conspicuously states* that the check is tendered in *full satisfaction* of the debt.

13. Discharge by Account Stated

An account stated is a contract between parties whereby they agree to an amount as a *final balance due* from one to the other. This final balance encompasses a number of transactions between the parties and serves to merge all of these transactions by discharging all claims owed.

14. Discharge by Lapse

If the duty of each party is a condition concurrent to the other's duty, it is possible that on the day set for performance, neither party is in breach and their contractual obligations lapse. If the contract states that time is "of the essence," the lapse will occur immediately; otherwise the contract will lapse after a reasonable time.

15. Effect of Running of Statute of Limitations

If the statute of limitations on an action has run, it is generally held that an action for breach of contract may be barred. Note, however, that only *judicial remedies* are barred; the running of the statute *does not discharge the duties*. (Hence, if the party who has the advantage of the statute of limitations subsequently agrees to perform, new consideration will not be required.)

CMR **Exam Tip** Note the difference between a discharge by lapse and the effect of a statute of limitations. Although both have to do with time and the end result may be similar, technically, lapse *discharges* a contract while the statute of limitations merely *makes it unenforceable* in court.

VII. BREACH

A. WHEN DOES A BREACH OCCUR?

If it is found that (i) the promisor is under an absolute duty to perform, and (ii) this absolute duty of performance has not been discharged, then this failure to perform in accordance with contractual

terms will amount to a breach of the contract. The nonbreaching party who sues for breach of contract must show that she is **willing and able** to perform but for the breaching party's failure to perform.

B. MATERIAL OR MINOR BREACH—COMMON LAW CONTRACTS
Once you have determined that there is a breach of contract, the next determination to be made in a common law contract situation is whether that breach is material or minor.

1. Effect of Breaches

a. Minor Breach
A breach of contract is minor if the obligee gains the **substantial benefit of her bargain** despite the obligor's defective performance. A minor breach does **not relieve** the aggrieved party of her duty of performance under the contract; it merely gives her a right to damages (setoff) for the minor breach.

b. Material Breach
If the obligee does not receive the **substantial benefit of her bargain**, the breach is considered material. If the breach is material, the nonbreaching party (i) may treat the contract as at an end, *i.e.,* any duty of counterperformance owed by her will be discharged, and (ii) will have an **immediate right** to all remedies for breach of the entire contract, including total damages.

c. Minor Breach Coupled with Anticipatory Repudiation
If a minor breach is coupled with an anticipatory repudiation (*see* VI.D.3.c., *supra*), the nonbreaching party may treat it as a material breach; *i.e.,* she may sue immediately for total damages and is permanently discharged from any duty of further performance. Indeed, the courts hold that the aggrieved party must not continue on, because to do so would be a failure to mitigate damages. The U.C.C. modifies this to permit a party to complete the manufacture of goods to avoid having to sell unfinished goods at the lower salvage value. (*See infra.*)

d. Material Breach of Divisible Contract
In a divisible contract, recovery is available for substantial performance of a divisible part even though there has been a material breach of the entire contract.

CMR **Exam Tip** The distinction between a material and a minor breach is important. A minor breach may allow the aggrieved party to recover damages, **but she still must perform** under the contract. If the breach is a material one, the aggrieved party need not perform.

2. Determining Materiality of Breach
In determining whether a breach is material or minor, courts look at:

(i) *The amount of benefit received* by the nonbreaching party;

(ii) *The adequacy of compensation* for damages to the injured party;

(iii) *The extent of part performance* by the breaching party;

(iv) *Hardship* to the breaching party;

(v) *Negligent or willful behavior* of the breaching party; and

(vi) *The likelihood that the breaching party will perform* the remainder of the contract.

The nonbreaching party must show that he was both willing and able to perform.

3. Timeliness of Performance

Failure to perform by the time stated in the contract is generally not a material breach if performance is rendered within a reasonable time. However, if the nature of the contract makes timely performance essential, or if the contract expressly provides that time is of the essence, then failure to perform on time is a material breach.

C. PERFECT TENDER RULE—SALE OF GOODS

Article 2 generally does not follow the common law substantial performance doctrine. Instead, it follows the perfect tender rule—if *goods or their delivery fail to conform to the contract in any way*, the buyer generally may reject all, accept all, or accept any commercial units and reject the rest.

1. Right to Reject Cut Off by Acceptance

A buyer's right to reject under the perfect tender doctrine generally is cut off by acceptance. Under Article 2, a buyer accepts when:

a. After a reasonable opportunity to inspect the goods, she *indicates to the seller that they conform* to requirements or that she will keep them even though they fail to conform;

b. She *fails to reject* within a reasonable time after tender or delivery of the goods or fails to seasonably notify the seller of her rejection; or

c. She does any *act inconsistent with the seller's ownership*.

2. Buyer's Responsibility for Goods After Rejection

After rejecting goods in her physical possession, the buyer has an obligation to hold them with reasonable care at the seller's disposition and to obey any reasonable instructions as to the rejected goods (*e.g.,* arrange to reship the goods). If the seller gives no instructions within a reasonable time, the buyer may *reship* the goods to the seller, *store* them for the seller's account, or *resell* them for the seller's account. If the buyer resells, she is entitled to recover her expenses and a reasonable commission.

3. Buyer's Right to Revoke Acceptance

Once goods are accepted, the buyer's power to reject the goods generally is terminated and the buyer is obligated to pay the price less any damages resulting from the seller's breach. However, under limited situations, a buyer may revoke an acceptance already made. A proper revocation of acceptance has the effect of a rejection.

a. When Acceptance May Be Revoked

The buyer may revoke her acceptance if the goods have a defect that *substantially impairs* their *value* to her *and*:

(i) She accepted them on the *reasonable belief that the defect would be cured* and it has not been; or

(ii) She accepted them because of the *difficulty of discovering defects* or because of the *seller's assurance that the goods conformed* to the contract.

Revocation of acceptance must occur: (i) *within a reasonable time* after the buyer discovers or should have discovered the defects; and (ii) *before any substantial change in the goods occurs* that is not caused by a defect present at the time the seller relinquished possession.

4. Exceptions to the Perfect Tender Rule

a. Installment Contracts

The right to reject when a contract is an installment contract (*i.e.,* when there is to be more than one delivery) is much more limited than in a single delivery contract situation. Installment contracts follow a rule akin to the common law substantial performance doctrine. In an installment contract situation, an installment can be rejected only if the nonconformity *substantially impairs* the value of that installment *and cannot be cured* (*see* below). In addition, the whole contract is breached only if the nonconformity *substantially impairs* the value of the *entire contract*.

b. Seller's Right to Cure

1) Single Delivery Contracts

a) Seller Can Cure by Notice and New Tender Within Time for Performance

If the buyer has rejected goods because of defects, the seller may within the time originally provided for performance "cure" by giving *reasonable notice* of her intention to do so and making a *new tender of conforming goods* that the buyer must then accept.

b) Seller's Right to Cure Beyond Original Contract Time

Ordinarily, the seller has no right to cure beyond the original contract time. However, if the buyer rejects a tender of nonconforming goods that the seller *reasonably* believed would be acceptable "with or without money allowance," the seller, upon a reasonable notification to the buyer, has a *further reasonable time* beyond the original contract time within which to make a conforming tender. A seller will probably be found to have had reasonable cause to believe that the tender would be acceptable if the seller can show that (i) trade practices or prior dealings with the buyer led the seller to believe that the goods would be acceptable, or (ii) the seller could not have known of the defect despite proper business conduct (*e.g.,* packaged goods purchased from a supplier).

2) Installment Contracts

Article 2 provides that a defective shipment in an installment contract cannot be rejected *if the defect can be cured*.

D. ANTICIPATORY REPUDIATION

Recall that an anticipatory repudiation (*see* VI.D.3.c., *supra*) can be treated as an immediate breach of contract.

E. BREACH OF WARRANTY

Sellers give warranties as to the condition of the goods that apply even after acceptance. Failure to live up to these warranties constitutes a breach of warranty, for which a remedy is available.

VIII. REMEDIES

A. NONMONETARY REMEDIES

There are two broad branches of remedies available in breach of contract situations: nonmonetary and monetary. The primary nonmonetary remedy for exam purposes is specific performance, but Article 2 has a number of other specific nonmonetary remedies for certain situations involving contracts for the sale of goods.

1. Specific Performance

If the *legal remedy is inadequate*, the nonbreaching party may seek specific performance, which is an order from the court to the breaching party to perform or face contempt of court charges.

a. Available for Land and Rare or Unique Goods

Specific performance is always available for land sale contracts. It is also available for goods that are rare or unique at the time performance is due (*e.g.*, rare paintings, gasoline in short supply because of oil embargoes, etc.). It is *not* available for breach of a contract to provide *services*, even if the services are rare or unique. This is because of problems of enforcement (it would be difficult for the court to supervise the performance) and because the courts feel it is tantamount to involuntary servitude, which is prohibited by the Constitution.

1) Injunction as Alternate Remedy

In contrast, a court may *enjoin* a breaching employee from working for a competitor throughout the duration of the contract if the services contracted for are rare or unique.

b. Covenant Not to Compete

Most courts will grant an order of specific performance to enforce a contract not to compete if: (i) the services to be performed are *unique* (thus rendering money damages inadequate); and (ii) the covenant is *reasonable*. To be reasonable:

1) The covenant must be reasonably necessary to protect a *legitimate interest* of the person benefited by the covenant (*i.e.*, an employer or the purchaser of the covenantor's business);

2) The covenant must be reasonable as to its *geographic scope and duration* (*i.e.,* it cannot be broader than the benefited person's customer base and typically cannot be longer than one or two years); and

3) The covenant *must not harm the public*.

c. **Equitable Defenses Available**
In addition to standard contract defenses, an action for specific performance is subject to the equitable defenses of:

1) *Laches*—a claim that the plaintiff has delayed bringing the action and that *the delay has prejudiced the defendant*;

2) *Unclean hands*—a claim that the party seeking specific performance is guilty of *wrongdoing in the transaction being sued upon*; and

3) *Sale to a bona fide purchaser*—a claim that the subject matter has been *sold to a person who purchased for value and in good faith*.

2. **Nonmonetary Remedies Under Article 2**

a. **Buyer's Nonmonetary Remedies**

1) **Cancellation**
If a buyer rightfully rejects goods because they do not conform to the contract, one of her options is simply to cancel the contract.

2) **Buyer's Right to Replevy Identified Goods**

a) **On Buyer's Prepayment**
If a buyer has made at least *part payment* of the purchase price of goods that have been identified under a contract and the seller *has not delivered* the goods, the buyer may *replevy* the goods from the seller in two circumstances:

(i) The seller becomes *insolvent* within 10 days after receiving the buyer's first payment; or

(ii) The goods were purchased for *personal, family, or household purposes.*

In either case, the buyer must *tender* any unpaid portion of the purchase price to the seller.

b) **On Buyer's Inability to Cover**
In addition, the buyer may replevy undelivered, identified goods from the seller if the buyer, after reasonable effort, is *unable to secure adequate substitute goods* (*i.e.,* cover).

3) Buyer's Right to Specific Performance
A right closely related to the buyer's right to replevy is her right to specific performance "where the goods are unique or in other proper circumstances." The court may order specific performance *even where the goods have not yet been identified* to the contract by the seller.

b. Seller's Nonmonetary Remedies

1) Seller's Right to Withhold Goods
If the buyer fails to make a payment due on or before delivery, the seller may withhold delivery of the goods. The seller may also withhold goods when the goods are sold on credit and, before the goods are delivered, the seller discovers that the buyer is insolvent. However, in such a case, the seller must deliver the goods if the buyer tenders cash for their payment.

2) Seller's Right to Recover Goods

a) Right to Recover from Buyer on Buyer's Insolvency
If a seller learns that a buyer has received delivery of goods on credit while insolvent, the seller may reclaim the goods upon demand made within 10 days after the buyer's receipt of the goods. However, the 10-day limitation does not apply if a misrepresentation of solvency has been *made in writing* to the particular seller *within three months* before delivery.

b) Right to Recover Shipped or Stored Goods from Bailee

(1) On Buyer's Insolvency
The seller may stop delivery of goods in the possession of a carrier or other bailee if he discovers that the buyer is insolvent. Of course, the seller must deliver the goods if the buyer tenders cash for their payment.

(2) On Buyer's Breach
The seller may stop delivery of carload, truckload, planeload, or larger shipments of goods if the buyer breaches the contract or the seller has a right to withhold performance pending receipt of assurances. (*See* c., *infra,* on the right to demand assurances.)

c. Right to Demand Assurances
Under Article 2, actions or circumstances that increase the risk of nonperformance by the other party to the contract, but that do not clearly indicate that performance will not be forthcoming, may *not* be treated immediately as an anticipatory repudiation (*see* VI.D.3.c., *supra*). Instead, if the party *reasonably* fears that the other party will not perform, he may demand assurances that the performance will be forthcoming at the proper time. Until he receives adequate assurances, he may suspend his own performance. If the proper assurances are not given within a reasonable time (*i.e.,* within 30 days after a justified demand for assurances), he may then treat the contract as repudiated. What constitutes an adequate assurance depends on the facts of the case.

CMR **Exam Tip** Be sure that you understand the difference between circumstances giving rise to a right to demand assurances and those constituting anticipatory repudiation. The right to demand assurances arises when there are *reasonable grounds for insecurity*—something makes a party nervous that the other will not perform. Anticipatory repudiation requires much more than nervousness; there must be a *clear indication* that the other party is unwilling or unable to perform. Thus, for example, "I'm not going to perform" is an anticipatory repudiation, but "I'm not sure if I can perform" most likely is only a reason to demand assurances.

B. MONETARY REMEDY—DAMAGES

1. Types of Damages

a. Compensatory Damages
The usual goal of damages for breach of contract is to *put the nonbreaching party where she would have been had the promise been performed*, so far as money can do this.

1) "Standard Measure" of Damages—Expectation Damages
In most cases, the plaintiff's standard measure of damages will be based on an "expectation" measure, *i.e.,* sufficient damages for her to buy a *substitute performance*. This is also known as *"benefit of the bargain"* damages.

2) Reliance Damage Measure
If the plaintiff's expectation damages are too speculative to measure (*e.g.,* the plaintiff cannot show with sufficient certainty the profits she would have made if the defendant had performed the contract), the plaintiff may elect to recover damages based on a "reliance" measure, rather than an expectation measure. Reliance damages award the plaintiff the cost of her performance; *i.e.,* they are designed to *put the plaintiff in the position she would have been in had the contract never been formed*.

3) Consequential Damages
Consequential damages consist of losses resulting from the breach that any *reasonable person* would have *foreseen* would occur from a breach at the time of entry into the contract. For the plaintiff to prevail, she must show that both parties were aware of the special circumstances that existed at the time of contract formation, which would involve a substantial amount of risk and resulting damage if the contract were to be breached. Note that in contracts for the sale of goods, *only a buyer* may recover consequential damages.

4) Incidental Damages—Contracts for the Sale of Goods
In contracts for the sale of goods, compensatory damages may also include incidental damages. Incidental damages include expenses reasonably incurred by the buyer in inspection, receipt, transportation, care, and custody of goods rightfully rejected and other expenses reasonably incident to the seller's breach, and by the seller in storing, shipping, returning, and reselling the goods as a result of the buyer's breach.

b. Punitive Damages
Punitive damages are generally *not* awarded in contract cases.

c. Nominal Damages
Nominal (token) damages (*e.g.,* $1) may be awarded when a breach is shown but no actual loss is proven.

d. Liquidated Damages
The parties to a contract may stipulate what damages are to be paid in the event of a breach. These liquidated damages must be in an amount that is reasonable in view of the actual or anticipated harm caused by the breach.

1) Requirements for Enforcement
Liquidated damage clauses will be enforceable if the following two requirements are met:

a) Damages for contractual breach must have been *difficult to estimate or ascertain at the time the contract was formed*; and

b) The amount agreed on must have been a *reasonable forecast* of compensatory damages in the case of breach. The test for reasonableness is a comparison between the amount of damages prospectively probable at the time of contract formation and the liquidated damages figure. If the liquidated damages amount is unreasonable, the courts will construe this as a *penalty* and will not enforce the provision.

2) Recoverable Even If No Actual Damages
If the above requirements are met, the plaintiff will receive the liquidated damages amount. Most courts hold this is so even if no actual money or pecuniary damages have been suffered.

2. "Standard Measure"—Specific Situations

a. Contracts for Sale of Goods

1) Buyer's Damages

a) **Seller Does Not Deliver or Buyer Rejects Goods or Revokes Acceptance**
The buyer's basic damages where the seller does not deliver, or the buyer properly rejects or revokes her acceptance of tendered goods, consist of the difference between the contract price and either: (i) the market price (*i.e., benefit of the bargain* damages) or (ii) the cost of buying replacement goods (*i.e., cover*), *plus* incidental and consequential damages (*see* above), if any, *less* expenses saved as a result of the seller's breach.

(1) **Difference Between Contract Price and Market Price**
If the buyer measures damages by the difference between contract price and market price, market price usually is determined as of the time the buyer learns of the breach and at the place of tender.

CMR | **Exam Tip** | Note that the **buyer's damages** are measured as of the **time she learns of the breach**, while the **seller's damages** are measured as of the **time for delivery**. (*See* 2), *infra.*)

(2) Difference Between Contract Price and Cost of Replacement Goods—"Cover"

If the buyer chooses the cover measure (*i.e.*, difference between contract price and cost of buying replacement goods), the buyer must make a **reasonable contract** for substitute goods **in good faith** and **without unreasonable delay**.

b) Seller Delivers Nonconforming Goods that Buyer Accepts

(1) Warranty Damages

If the buyer accepts goods that breach one of the seller's warranties, the buyer may recover as damages "loss resulting in the normal course of events from the breach." The basic measure of damages in such a case is the difference between the **value of the goods as delivered** and the **value they would have had if they had been according to contract**, plus incidental and consequential damages.

(2) Notice Requirement

To recover damages for any defect as to accepted goods, the buyer must, **within a reasonable time after she discovers or should have discovered the defect**, notify the seller of the defect. If she does not notify the seller within a reasonable time, she loses her right to sue. "Reasonable time" is, of course, a flexible standard.

c) Seller Anticipatorily Breaches Contract

The measure of damages when the seller anticipatorily breaches the contract is the difference between the **market price at the time the buyer learned of the breach** and the **contract price**.

2) Seller's Damages

a) Where Buyer Repudiates or Refuses to Accept Conforming Goods

The Code provides three measures for damages for when the buyer wrongfully repudiates or refuses to accept conforming goods. The seller can:

(i) Recover the difference between the **market price** (measured as of the time and at the place of delivery) **and the contract price**;

(ii) Resell the goods and recover the difference between the **contract price and the resale price**; or

(iii) If applicable, recover under a "**lost profits**" measure the difference between the contract price and the cost to the seller. (Note that if the seller is a dealer, his costs would be the costs incurred in obtaining the goods from the manufacturer or another dealer, whereas if the seller is a manufacturer, his costs would be the costs of manufacturing the goods.)

ARTICLE 2 DAMAGE MEASURES FOR TOTAL BREACH
(Buyer Does Not Accept or Seller Does Not Deliver)

BUYER'S MEASURES

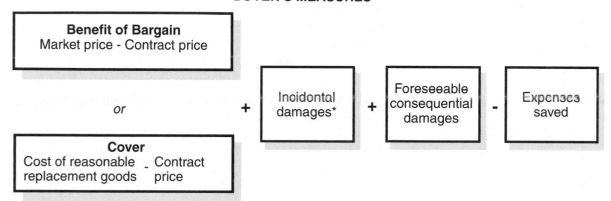

Benefit of Bargain
Market price - Contract price

or

Cover
Cost of reasonable - Contract
replacement goods price

+ Incidental damages* + Foreseeable consequential damages - Expenses saved

SELLER'S MEASURES

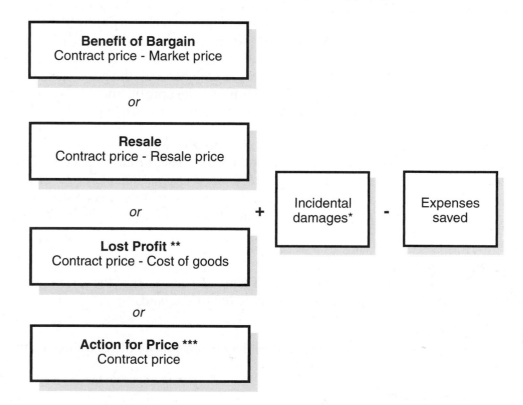

Benefit of Bargain
Contract price - Market price

or

Resale
Contract price - Resale price

or

Lost Profit *
Contract price - Cost of goods

or

Action for Price **
Contract price

+ Incidental damages* - Expenses saved

---

* **Incidental damages** include costs of storing, shipping, etc., due to breach.
** The **lost profit** measure may be used **only if seller has lost sales volume** as a result of the breach
(*e.g.*, seller may obtain or manufacture as many of the goods in question as it can sell).
*** An **action for the price** may be maintained **only if the goods cannot be sold to others at a reasonable
price** (or if the buyer has accepted the goods and not paid for them).

The seller may also recover incidental damages, such as costs of storing, shipping, and reselling the goods as a result of the buyer's breach.

Note: The Code provides that the lost profits measure may be used only when the other measures will not put the seller in as good a position as he would have been in if the buyer had not breached.

Example: Sara contracts to sell an original oil painting to Bob. Bob breaches. Sara sells the painting to Tom. If Sara uses one of the first two damages measures above, she should be fully compensated for Bob's breach; *i.e.,* she will recover what she would have made on the sale to Bob. However, if Sara is a retailer with an unlimited inventory and the contract was for a 50" TV, the result would be different. If Bob refuses to take the TV—even if Sara sells it to Tom—Sara will not be in as good a position as she would have been if Bob had performed, because if Bob had performed, Sara would have sold *two* TV sets. Thus, in this case, the lost profits measure is appropriate to compensate Sara for the breach.

CMR **Exam Tip** Although the Code provides that the lost profits measure is used only if the other two measures do not adequately compensate the seller, this is quite often the case in commercial sales contracts. To determine whether the lost profits measure is appropriate, look at the seller's *supply*. If the seller's supply of goods is *unlimited* (*i.e.,* he can obtain all the goods he can sell), then he is a *lost volume seller*, and the lost profits measure can be used. If the seller's supply is limited (*i.e.,* he cannot obtain all the goods he can sell, as when the sale is for a unique item), the lost profits measure cannot be used, and one of the other two measures must be used instead.

b) **Where Buyer Accepted Goods—Action for Price**
If the buyer has accepted the goods and has not paid, or has not accepted the goods and the seller is *unable to resell* them at any reasonable price, or if the goods have been lost or damaged at a time the risk of loss was on the buyer (*see* V.D.3., *supra*), the seller may maintain an action against the buyer for the full contract price.

b. **Contracts for Sale of Land**
The standard measure of damages for breach of land sale contracts is the difference between the *contract price and the fair market value* of the land.

c. **Employment Contracts**
In employment contracts, check to see whether the breach was by the employer or the employee.

1) **Breach by Employer**
Irrespective of when the breach occurs—*i.e.,* before performance, after part performance, or after full performance, the standard measure of the employee's damages is the *full contract price* (although such damages may be reduced if the employee fails to mitigate—*see* 4.a., *infra*).

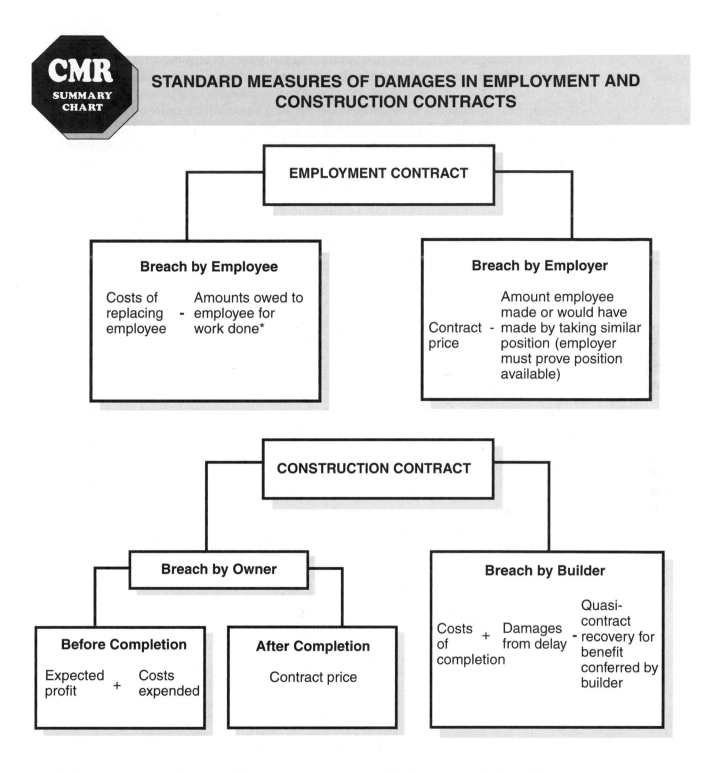

CMR SUMMARY CHART

STANDARD MEASURES OF DAMAGES IN EMPLOYMENT AND CONSTRUCTION CONTRACTS

EMPLOYMENT CONTRACT

Breach by Employee

Costs of replacing employee - Amounts owed to employee for work done*

Breach by Employer

Contract price - Amount employee made or would have made by taking similar position (employer must prove position available)

CONSTRUCTION CONTRACT

Breach by Owner

Before Completion

Expected profit + Costs expended

After Completion

Contract price

Breach by Builder

Costs of completion + Damages from delay - Quasi-contract recovery for benefit conferred by builder

* Some courts allow offset only if the breach was unintended; others allow offset in all cases.

2) Breach by Employee

If the employee is the breaching party, the employer is entitled to a standard measure of damages computed according to what it **costs to replace** the employee, *i.e.,* the difference between the cost incurred to get a second employee to do the work and the cost to the employer had the first breaching employee done the work. If the breach was unintentional (*e.g.,* due to the employee's illness), the employee may have the right to quasi-contractual recovery for the work done to date. The modern view allows employees to offset such amount whether the breach was intentional or unintentional.

d. Construction Contracts

If a construction contract is breached by the **owner**, the builder will be entitled to profits that would have resulted from the contract plus any costs expended. (If the contract is breached after construction is completed, the measure is the full contract price plus interest.) If the contract is breached by the **builder**, the owner is entitled to the cost of completion plus reasonable compensation for the delay. Most courts allow the builder to offset or recover for work performed to date to avoid unjust enrichment of the owner. (If the breach is only late performance, the owner is entitled to damages incurred because of late performance.)

e. Contracts Calling for Installment Payments

If a contract calls for payments in installments and a payment is not made, there is only a partial breach. The aggrieved party is limited to recovering only the missed payment, not the entire contract price. However, the contract may include an **acceleration clause** making the entire amount due on any late payment, in which case the aggrieved party may recover the entire amount.

3. Certainty Rule

The plaintiff must prove that the losses suffered were certain in their nature and **not speculative**. Traditionally, if the breaching party prevented the nonbreaching party from setting up a new business, courts would not award lost profits from the prospective business as damages, because they were too speculative. However, modern courts may allow lost profits as damages if they can be made more certain by observing similar businesses in the area or other businesses previously owned by the same party.

4. Duty to Mitigate Damages

The nonbreaching party has a duty to mitigate damages. Thus, she must refrain from piling up losses after she receives notice of the breach; she must not incur further expenditures or costs, and she must make reasonable efforts to cut down her losses by procuring a substitute performance at a fair price. Should she not do so, she will not be allowed to recover those damages that might have been avoided by such mitigation after the breach. Generally, a party may **recover the expenses of mitigation**. Note the following specific contract situations:

a. Employment Contracts

If the employer breaches, the employee is under a duty to use **reasonable care** in finding a position of the same kind, rank, and grade in the same locale (although it does not necessarily have to be at the same exact pay level). However, note that the burden is on the employer to show that such jobs were available.

b.   Contracts for Sale of Goods
If the buyer is in breach, recall that the seller generally cannot bring an action against the buyer for the full contract price unless the goods cannot be resold at a reasonable price or were damaged or lost when the risk of loss was on the buyer. (*See* 2.a.2)b), *supra.*)

c.   Manufacturing Contracts
Generally, in a contract to manufacture goods, if the person for whom the goods are being manufactured breaches, the manufacturer is under a duty to mitigate by ***not continuing work*** after the breach. However, if the facts are such that completion of the manufacturing project will decrease rather than increase damages, the manufacturer has a right to continue.

d.   Construction Contracts
A builder does not owe a duty to avoid the consequences of an owner's breach, *e.g.,* by securing other work, but does have a duty to mitigate by ***not continuing work*** after the breach. Again, however, if completion will decrease damages, it will be allowed.

 Exam Tip   Keep in mind that the duty to mitigate only ***reduces*** a recovery; it does not prohibit recovery. Thus, if a fact pattern shows a clear breach and the plaintiff does not attempt to mitigate damages, she can recover for the breach, but the recovery will be reduced by the damages that would have been avoided by mitigation.

C.   RESTITUTION

As an alternative to the contract damages discussed above, restitution may be available in a contract-type situation. Restitution is not really part of contract law, but rather is a distinct concept. Restitution is based on preventing ***unjust enrichment*** when one has conferred a benefit on another without gratuitous intent. Restitution can provide a remedy not only when a contract exists and has been breached, but also when a contract is unenforceable, and in some cases when no contractual relationship exists at all between the parties.

1.   Terminology
When a contract is unenforceable or no contract between the parties exists, an action to recover restitutionary damages often is referred to as an action for an ***implied in law*** contract or an action in ***quasi-contract***.

2.   Measure of Damages
Generally, the measure of restitution is the ***value of the benefit conferred***. Although this is usually based on the benefit received by the defendant (*e.g.,* the increase in value of the defendant's property or the value of the goods received), recovery may also be measured by the "detriment" suffered by the plaintiff (*e.g.,* the reasonable value of the work performed or the services rendered) if the benefits are difficult to measure or the "benefit" measure would achieve an unfair result.

3. Specific Applications

a. When Contract Breached

When a contract has been breached and the nonbreaching party has not fully performed, he may choose to rescind the contract and sue for restitution to prevent unjust enrichment. Note that if the plaintiff has fully performed, he is *limited to his damages under the contract.* This may be less than he would have received in a restitutionary action, because a restitutionary remedy is not limited to the contract price.

1) "Losing" Contracts

A restitutionary remedy often is desirable in the case of a "losing" contract (*i.e.*, a contract in which the actual value of the services or goods to be provided under the contract is higher than the contract price), because normal contract expectation damages or reliance damages would be for a lesser amount.

2) Breach by Plaintiff

Under some circumstances, a plaintiff may seek restitution even though the plaintiff is the party who breached. If the breach was intentional, some courts will not grant the breaching party restitution; modern courts, however, will permit restitutionary recovery but limit it to the contract price less damages incurred as a result of the breach.

b. When Contract Unenforceable—Quasi-Contract Remedy

Restitution may be available in a *quasi-contract* action when a contract was made but is unenforceable and unjust enrichment otherwise would result (*e.g.*, celebrity is hired to sign autographs and is paid, but dies before he performs; the other party has a restitutionary action to recover the payment).

c. When No Contract Involved—Quasi-Contract Remedy

Restitution may also be available in a *quasi-contract* action when there is no contractual relationship between the parties if:

1) The plaintiff has *conferred a benefit* on the defendant by rendering services or expending properties;

2) The plaintiff conferred the benefit with the *reasonable expectation of being compensated* for its value;

3) The defendant *knew or had reason to know* of the plaintiff's expectation; and

4) The defendant would be *unjustly enriched* if he were allowed to retain the benefit without compensating the plaintiff.

 Exam Tip Always keep the quasi-contract remedy in the back of your mind. *Look first for a valid contract* allowing the plaintiff relief. But if there is no valid contract, a quasi-contract will provide a remedy if the plaintiff has suffered a loss or rendered services.

IX. RIGHTS AND DUTIES OF THIRD PARTIES TO THE CONTRACT

A. INTRODUCTION
Nonparties to a contract may have rights or duties in connection with the contract.

B. THIRD-PARTY BENEFICIARIES
In the typical third-party beneficiary situation, A (the promisee) contracts with B (the promisor) that B will render some performance to C (the third-party beneficiary).

1. Who Is Third-Party Beneficiary?

a. Intended vs. Incidental Beneficiary
Only intended beneficiaries have contractual rights, not incidental beneficiaries. In determining if a beneficiary is intended, consider whether the beneficiary (i) is *identified* in the contract, (ii) *receives performance directly* from the promisor, or (iii) has some *relationship with the promisee* to indicate intent to benefit.

b. Creditor vs. Donee Beneficiary
There are two types of intended beneficiaries: (i) a creditor beneficiary—a person to whom a debt is owed by the promisee, and (ii) a donee beneficiary—a person whom the promisee intends to benefit gratuitously.

2. When Do the Rights of the Beneficiary Vest?
A third party can enforce a contract only if his rights have vested. This occurs when he (i) *manifests assent* to a promise in the manner requested by the parties; (ii) brings a *suit to enforce* the promise; or (iii) *materially changes position* in justifiable reliance on the promise. Prior to vesting, the promisee and promisor are free to modify or rescind the beneficiary's rights under the contract.

a. Significance of Vesting
Before the intended third-party beneficiary's rights vest, the promisor and promisee are free to modify their contract—including removing the third-party beneficiary altogether—without consulting the third party. Once the third party's rights vest, the promisor and promisee cannot vary his rights without his consent.

3. What Are the Rights of the Third-Party Beneficiary and the Promisee?

a. Third-Party Beneficiary vs. Promisor
A beneficiary may sue the promisor on the contract. The promisor may raise against the third-party beneficiary any defense that the promisor has against the promisee. Whether the promisor may use the defenses the promisee would have against the third-party beneficiary depends on whether the promisor made an absolute promise to pay or only a promise to pay what the promisee owes the beneficiary. If the promise is absolute, the promisor cannot assert the promisee's defenses; if the promise is not absolute, the promisor can assert the promisee's defenses.

DETERMINING INTENDED THIRD-PARTY BENEFICIARY STATUS AND CONTRACTUAL RIGHTS

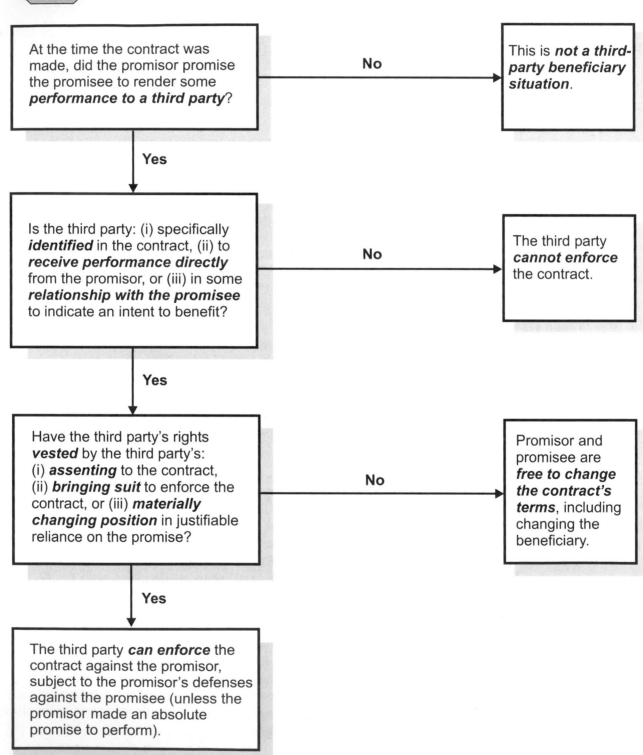

At the time the contract was made, did the promisor promise the promisee to render some **performance to a third party**?

No → This is **not a third-party beneficiary situation**.

Yes ↓

Is the third party: (i) specifically **identified** in the contract, (ii) to **receive performance directly** from the promisor, or (iii) in some **relationship with the promisee** to indicate an intent to benefit?

No → The third party **cannot enforce** the contract.

Yes ↓

Have the third party's rights **vested** by the third party's: (i) **assenting** to the contract, (ii) **bringing suit** to enforce the contract, or (iii) **materially changing position** in justifiable reliance on the promise?

No → Promisor and promisee are **free to change the contract's terms**, including changing the beneficiary.

Yes ↓

The third party **can enforce** the contract against the promisor, subject to the promisor's defenses against the promisee (unless the promisor made an absolute promise to perform).

    b.   **Third-Party Beneficiary vs. Promisee**

A *creditor* beneficiary can sue the promisee on the existing obligation between them. She may also sue the promisor, but may obtain only one satisfaction. A donee beneficiary has no right to sue the promisee unless grounds for a detrimental reliance remedy exist (*see* III.D., *supra*).

    c.   **Promisee vs. Promisor**

A promisee may sue the promisor both at law and in equity for specific performance if the promisor is not performing for the third person.

C.   ASSIGNMENT OF RIGHTS AND DELEGATION OF DUTIES

1.   Assignment

In the typical assignment situation, X (the obligor) contracts with Y (the assignor). Y assigns his right to X's performance to Z (the assignee).

    a.   **What Rights May Be Assigned?**

Generally, all contractual rights may be assigned. *Exceptions:* (i) an assignment that would **substantially change** the obligor's duty or risk (*e.g.*, personal service contracts where the service is unique, requirements and output contracts where the assignee will substantially vary the quantity); (ii) an assignment of future rights to **arise from future contracts** (not future rights in already existing contracts); and (iii) an assignment **prohibited by law** (*e.g.*, wage assignments).

        1)   **Express Contractual Provision Against Assignment**

A clause prohibiting assignment of *"the contract"* will be construed as barring only delegation of the assignor's duties. A clause prohibiting assignment of **contractual rights** generally does not bar assignment, but rather merely gives the obligor the right to sue for damages. However, if the contract provides that attempts to assign **will be void**, the parties can bar assignment. Also, if the assignee has notice of the nonassignment clause, an assignment will be ineffective.

    b.   **What Is Necessary for an Effective Assignment?**

For an assignment to be effective, the assignor must manifest an intent to immediately and completely transfer her rights. A writing is usually not required to have an effective assignment. The right being assigned must be adequately described. It is not necessary to use the word "assign"; any accepted words of transfer will suffice. A gratuitous assignment is effective; consideration is not required.

    c.   **Is Assignment Revocable or Irrevocable?**

An assignment for **consideration** is irrevocable. An assignment not for consideration (*i.e., a gratuitous assignment*) generally is revocable. However, a gratuitous assignment is irrevocable if: (i) the obligor has already performed; (ii) a token chose (*i.e.,* a tangible claim, such as a stock certificate) is delivered; (iii) an assignment of a simple chose (*i.e.,* an intangible claim, such as a contract right) is put in writing; or (iv) the assignee can show detrimental reliance on the gratuitous assignment (*i.e.,* estoppel). A revocable gratuitous assignment may be terminated by: (i) the death or bankruptcy of the assignor; (ii) notice of revocation by the assignor to the assignee or the obligor; (iii) the

assignor taking performance directly from the obligor; or (iv) subsequent assignment of the same right by the assignor to another.

1) Effect of Assignment
The effect of an assignment is to establish privity of contract between the obligor and the assignee while extinguishing privity between the obligor and the assignor.

d. What Are the Rights and Liabilities of the Various Parties?

1) Assignee vs. Obligor
The assignee can sue the obligor, as the assignee is the real party in interest; *i.e.,* the assignee—not the assignor—is entitled to performance under the contract. (The obligor has as a defense against the assignee any defense inherent in the contract, *e.g.,* failure of consideration and other defenses that came into existence before the obligor had knowledge of the assignment.) The obligor cannot raise by way of defense any defenses the assignor might have against the assignee.

2) Assignee vs. Assignor
The assignee can sue the assignor for wrongfully exercising the power to revoke in an irrevocable assignment situation. An action by the assignee against the assignor may also lie where the obligor successfully asserts a defense against the assignor in an action brought by the assignee against the obligor to enforce the obligation. The assignor will not be liable to the assignee if the obligor is incapable of performing.

e. What Problems Exist If There Have Been Successive Assignments of Same Rights?
If the first assignment is revocable, a subsequent assignment revokes it. If it is irrevocable, *the first assignment will usually prevail* over a subsequent assignment. Several exceptions exist (*if* the second assignee has *paid value and taken without notice* of the first assignment): (i) the subsequent assignee gets the first judgment against the obligor; (ii) the subsequent assignee gets the first payment of a claim from the obligor; (iii) the subsequent assignee gets delivery of a token chose; (iv) the subsequent assignee is the party to a novation releasing the assignor; or (v) the subsequent assignee can proceed against the first assignee on an estoppel theory (estoppel could, of course, operate against the subsequent assignee as well).

2. Delegation
In the typical delegation situation, Y (the obligor/delegator) promises to perform for X (the obligee). Y delegates her duty to Z (the delegate).

a. What Duties May Be Delegated?
Generally, all duties may be delegated. *Exceptions:* (i) the duties involve *personal judgment and skill*; (ii) delegation would *change the obligee's expectancy* (*e.g.,* requirements and output contracts); (iii) a *special trust* was reposed in the delegator by the other party to the contract; and (iv) there is a *contractual restriction* on delegation.

b. What Is Necessary for Effective Delegation?
The delegator must manifest a present intention to make a delegation. There are no special formalities to be complied with to have a valid delegation. It may be written or oral.

Exam Tip Although "assignment" and "delegation" have precise meanings (rights are assigned and duties are delegated), on the MBE the terms are often used loosely. Thus, a question might state initially that "Y assigned his rights in the contract to X," but the facts later show that duties were also delegated.

c. What Are the Rights and Liabilities of the Parties?

The obligee must accept performance from the delegate of all duties that may be delegated. The delegator remains liable on the contract; thus, the obligee may sue the delegator for nonperformance by the delegate. The obligee may sue the delegate for nonperformance, but can require the delegate to perform *only if* there has been an *assumption* (*i.e.*, the delegate promises he will perform the duty delegated and this promise is supported by consideration or its equivalent). This promise creates a contract between the delegator and the delegate in which the obligee is a third-party beneficiary.

d. Terminology

Today, words assigning "the contract" or "all my rights under the contract" are usually construed as including an assumption of the duties by the assignee, unless a contrary intention appears.

D. NOVATION DISTINGUISHED

Novation substitutes a new party for an original party to the contract. It requires assent of all parties and completely releases the original party. (*See* VI.E.8., *supra.*)

E. POWER OF PERSON OTHER THAN OWNER TO TRANSFER GOOD TITLE TO A PURCHASER

1. Entrusting

Entrusting goods to a merchant *who deals in goods of that kind* gives him the power (but not the right) to transfer all rights of the entruster to a *buyer in the ordinary course of business*. Entrusting includes both delivering goods to the merchant and leaving purchased goods with the merchant for later pick-up or delivery. Buying in the ordinary course means buying in good faith from a person who deals in goods of the kind without knowledge that the sale is in violation of the ownership rights of third parties.

Example: Amy leaves her watch with Jeweler for repairs. Jeweler sells the watch to Zoe, who does not know that Jeweler has no right to sell. Zoe gets good title as against Amy. Amy's only remedy is to sue Jeweler for damages.

 Exam Tip Note that the requirements for entrustment are very specific: The merchant must be one *who ordinarily deals in goods of the kind* (*e.g.*, a television repair shop that only repairs televisions does not qualify). The sale must be *in the ordinary course of business* (*e.g.*, seizure by a creditor to satisfy a lien does not qualify). Entrustment passes only the rights of the entruster (*i.e.*, if the entruster is not the owner, ownership cannot pass).

2. Voidable Title Concept

Generally, if a sale is induced by fraud, the seller can rescind the sale and recover the goods from the fraudulent buyer (*i.e.*, it is a voidable title). However, the defrauded seller may not recover the goods from a *good faith purchaser for value* who bought from the fraudulent buyer. The rights of a defrauded seller are cut off both by a buyer and by a person who takes a *security interest* in the goods.

3. Thief Generally Cannot Pass Title

If a thief steals goods from the true owner and then sells them to a buyer, the thief is **unable** to pass title to the buyer (because his title is **void**). *Rationale:* A seller can transfer only the title he has or has power to transfer. Therefore, even a good faith purchaser for value generally cannot cut off the rights of the true owner if the seller's title was void. An exception to this rule may apply, however, if the buyer has made **accessions** (*i.e.,* valuable improvements) to the goods or the true owner is **estopped** from asserting title (*e.g.,* if the true owner expressly or impliedly represented that the thief had title).

CRIMINAL LAW

TABLE OF CONTENTS

CRIMINAL LAW

INTRODUCTION: GENERAL APPROACH

The Multistate Examination directs examinees to answer questions according to "the generally accepted view" unless otherwise noted. In Criminal Law, the examiners may tell you the law to apply if there is no prevailing view. For example:

(i)   The call of a question might tell you that the common law applies or that the state follows the Model Penal Code ("M.P.C.") approach;

(ii)   A fact pattern may also include a statute that you are to apply to the facts;

(iii)   Finally, a question might reference a well-known legal doctrine (*e.g.,* the Wharton rule or the *M'Naghten* test).

Note that if the examiners do not tell you whether the common law or a statutory version of the crime applies, it likely means that specific elements of the crime are not relevant to the question—for example, the question may concern whether voluntary intoxication is a defense to a crime, in which case the relevant factor is what type of mental state the crime requires, not other elements of the crime that may vary from jurisdiction to jurisdiction.

I. JURISDICTION AND GENERAL MATTERS

A. JURISDICTION
Generally, a state has jurisdiction over a crime if: any act constituting an element of the offense was committed in the state, an act outside the state caused a result in the state, the crime involved the neglect of a duty imposed by the law of the state, there was an attempt or conspiracy outside the state plus an act inside the state, or there was an attempt or conspiracy inside the state to commit an offense outside the state.

B. SOURCES OF CRIMINAL LAW
There is no federal common law of crimes; all federal crimes are statutory. A majority of the states retain common law crimes. The modern trend is to abolish common law crimes either expressly by statute or impliedly by the enactment of comprehensive criminal codes.

C. THEORIES OF PUNISHMENT
Theories justifying criminal punishment include incapacitation of the criminal, special deterrence of the criminal, general deterrence of others, retribution, rehabilitation, and education of the public.

D. CLASSIFICATION OF CRIMES
There are two classes of crimes: felonies and misdemeanors. Felonies are generally punishable by ***death or imprisonment for more than one year***; other crimes are misdemeanors.

E. VAGUENESS AND OTHER CONSTITUTIONAL LIMITATIONS

Due process requires that a criminal statute not be vague. There must be (i) *fair warning* (*i.e.,* a person of ordinary intelligence must be able to discern what is prohibited), and (ii) *no arbitrary and discriminatory enforcement*. The Constitution places two substantive limitations on both federal and state legislatures—no ex post facto laws and no bills of attainder.

F. INTERPRETATIONS OF CRIMINAL STATUTES

Criminal statutes are construed strictly in favor of defendants. If two statutes address the same subject matter but dictate different conclusions, the more specific statute will be applied rather than the more general. The more recently enacted statute will control an older statute. Under new comprehensive codes, crimes committed prior to the effective date of the new code are subject to prosecution and punishment under the law as it existed at the time the offense was committed.

G. MERGER

1. Common Law

At common law, if a person engaged in conduct constituting both a felony and a misdemeanor, she could be *convicted* only of the felony. The misdemeanor merged into the felony.

2. Modern Law—No Merger

There is no longer any merger *except* that one who solicits another to commit a crime may not be convicted of *both the solicitation and the completed crime* (if the person solicited does complete it). Similarly, a person who completes a crime after attempting it may not be convicted of *both the attempt and the completed crime*. Conspiracy, however, does not merge with the completed offense (*e.g.,* one can be convicted of both robbery and conspiracy to commit robbery).

3. Rules Against Multiple Convictions for Same Transaction

Double jeopardy prohibits trial or conviction of a person for a lesser included offense if he has been put in jeopardy for the greater offense. However, a court can impose multiple punishments at a single trial where the punishments are for two or more statutorily defined offenses specifically intended by the legislature to carry *separate punishments*, even though the offenses arise from the same transaction and constitute the same crime.

II. ESSENTIAL ELEMENTS OF A CRIME

A. ELEMENTS OF A CRIME

A crime almost always requires proof of a physical act (actus reus) and a mental state (mens rea), and concurrence of the act and mental state. It may also require proof of a result and causation (*i.e.,* that the act caused the harmful result).

B. PHYSICAL ACT

Defendant must have either performed a *voluntary* physical act or failed to act under circumstances imposing a legal duty to act. An act is a *bodily movement*.

 Exam Tip Remember that the act must be *voluntary*. In the past, the bar examiners have set up very unlikely scenarios to test this point—*e.g.,* they have an unconscious person shoot a victim.

Don't be fooled by these odd facts; if the facts tell you that the defendant was unconscious, the act was not voluntary, and thus defendant cannot be convicted of a crime based on this act. (The only exception to this rule would be if the defendant knew he was likely to become unconscious and commit the act, but this situation would have to be presented in the facts.)

1. **Omission as an "Act"**
   Failure to act gives rise to liability only if:

   (i) There is a *specific duty to act* imposed by law;

   (ii) The *defendant has knowledge* of the facts giving rise to the duty to act; and

   (iii) It is *reasonably possible to perform* the duty.

   A legal duty to act can arise from a statute, contract, relationship between the defendant and the victim (*e.g.,* a parent has a duty to protect child from harm), voluntary assumption of care by the defendant for the victim, or the creation of peril for the victim by the defendant.

   CMR **Exam Tip** For an omission to be a criminal act, there must be a *duty* to act. There is no general Good Samaritan law requiring people to help others in trouble. Thus, a defendant is not liable for the failure to help or rescue another person unless he has a duty to do so—no matter how easy it would have been to render help. Your moral outrage is not enough for a criminal conviction.

2. **Possession as an "Act"**
   Criminal statutes that penalize the possession of contraband generally require only that the defendant have control of the item for a long enough period to have an opportunity to terminate the possession. Possession need not be exclusive to one person, and possession also may be "constructive," meaning that actual physical control need not be proved when the contraband is located in an area within the defendant's "dominion and control."

   a. **State of Mind Requirement**
      Absent a state of mind requirement in the statute, the defendant must be aware of his possession of the contraband, but he need not be aware of its illegality. However, many statutes add a state of mind element (*e.g.,* "knowingly") to possession crimes. Under such statutes, the defendant ordinarily must know the identity or nature of the item possessed. On the other hand, a defendant may not consciously avoid learning the true nature of the item possessed; knowledge or intent may be inferred from a combination of suspicion and indifference to the truth.

C. **MENTAL STATE**

1. **Specific Intent**
   A crime may require not only the doing of an act, but also the doing of it with a specific intent or objective. The existence of a specific intent cannot be conclusively imputed from the mere *doing* of the act, but the *manner* in which the crime was committed may provide circumstantial evidence of intent. The major specific intent crimes and the intents they require are as follows:

   a. *Solicitation*: Intent to have the person solicited commit the crime.

b. *Attempt*: Intent to complete the crime.

c. *Conspiracy*: Intent to have the crime completed.

d. *First degree premeditated murder*: Premeditation.

e. *Assault*: Intent to commit a battery.

f. *Larceny and robbery*: Intent to permanently deprive the other of his interest in the property taken.

g. *Burglary*: Intent to commit a felony in the dwelling.

h. *Forgery*: Intent to defraud.

i. *False pretenses*: Intent to defraud.

j. *Embezzlement*: Intent to defraud.

CMR **Exam Tip** Never forget that attempt is a *specific intent* crime—even when the crime attempted is not. Thus, although murder does not require a specific intent to kill (*i.e.*, recklessly disregarding a high risk to human life would be enough), attempted murder requires the specific *intent to kill*. Without that intent, a defendant is not guilty of attempted murder.

Examples: 1) D intends to kill V but only wounds him. D had the requisite specific intent (*i.e.*, the intent to kill) and is guilty of attempted murder.

2) D intends to scare V by shooting V's hat off his head. If D's shot kills V, D is guilty of murder; but if V is merely wounded, D is not guilty of attempted murder. (D may, of course, be guilty of battery.)

2. **Malice—Common Law Murder and Arson**
The intent necessary for malice crimes (common law murder and arson) sounds like specific intent, but it is not as restrictive; it requires only a reckless disregard of an obvious or high risk that the particular harmful result will occur. Defenses to specific intent crimes (*e.g.*, voluntary intoxication) do not apply to malice crimes.

3. **General Intent—Awareness of Factors Constituting Crime**
Almost all crimes require at least "general intent," which is an awareness of all factors constituting the crime; *i.e.*, defendant must be aware that she is acting in the proscribed way and that any required attendant circumstances exist. The defendant need not be certain that all the circumstances exist; it is sufficient that she is aware of a high likelihood that they will occur.

a. **Inference of Intent from Act**
A jury may infer the required general intent merely from the doing of the act.

b. **Transferred Intent**
The defendant can be liable under the doctrine of transferred intent where she intends

the harm that is actually caused, but to a different victim or object. Defenses and mitigating circumstances may also usually be transferred. The doctrine of transferred intent applies to homicide, battery, and arson. It does not apply to attempt.

CMR **Exam Tip** A person found guilty of a crime on the basis of transferred intent is usually guilty of two crimes: the completed crime against the actual victim and attempt against the intended victim. Thus, if D intends to shoot and kill X, but instead shoots and kills V, D can be guilty of the murder of V (under the transferred intent doctrine) and the attempted murder of X.

c. Motive Distinguished

Motive is the reason or explanation for the crime; it is different from intent to commit the crime. Motive is immaterial to substantive criminal law.

4. Strict Liability Offenses

A strict liability or public welfare offense is one that does not require awareness of all of the factors constituting the crime; *i.e.,* the defendant can be found guilty from the mere fact that she committed the act. Common strict liability offenses are selling liquor to minors and statutory rape. Certain defenses, such as mistake of fact, are not available.

CMR SUMMARY CHART

REQUISITE INTENT FOR MAJOR CRIMES

Specific Intent	General Intent	Malice	Strict Liability
1. Solicitation	1. Battery	1. Common Law Murder	1. Statutory Rape
2. Attempt	2. Rape	2. Arson	2. Selling Liquor to Minors
3. Conspiracy	3. Kidnapping		3. Bigamy (some jurisdictions)
4. First Degree Premeditated Murder	4. False Imprisonment		
5. Assault (Attempted Battery)			
6. Larceny, Robbery			
7. Burglary			
8. Forgery			
9. False Pretenses			
10. Embezzlement			

5.   **Model Penal Code Analysis of Fault**
     The M.P.C. eliminates the common law distinctions between general and specific intent and adopts the following categories of intent:

a.   **Purposely, Knowingly, or Recklessly**
     When a statute requires that the defendant act purposely, knowingly, or recklessly, a *subjective standard* is used.

     1)   **Purposely**
          A person acts purposely when his ***conscious object*** is to engage in certain conduct or cause a certain result.

     2)   **Knowingly**
          A person acts knowingly when he is ***aware*** that his conduct is of a particular nature or ***knows*** that his conduct will necessarily or very likely cause a particular result. Knowing conduct satisfies a statute requiring willful conduct.

     3)   **Recklessly**
          A person acts recklessly when he ***knows*** of a ***substantial and unjustifiable risk*** and ***consciously disregards*** it. Mere realization of the risk is not enough. Thus, recklessness involves both objective ("unjustifiable risk") and subjective ("awareness") elements. Unless the statute specifies a different degree of fault or is a strict liability offense, the defendant must have acted at least recklessly to be criminally liable.

          CMR **Exam Tip**   A criminal law question often asks you to interpret a statute. Check the language of the statute carefully for the mental state required for each material element of the crime, because whether a defendant is guilty often turns on that mental state. For example, if the statute requires that a defendant act "knowingly" (such as "knowingly selling guns to a felon"), the defendant will not be guilty if she did not have that knowledge (*e.g.,* did not know the purchaser was a felon). In interpreting a statute, also keep in mind that "willfully" is equivalent to "knowingly."

b.   **Negligence**
     A person acts negligently when he ***fails to be aware of a substantial and unjustifiable risk***, where such failure is a substantial deviation from the standard of care. To determine whether a person acted negligently, an ***objective standard*** is used. However, it is not just the reasonable person standard that is used in torts. The defendant must have taken a very unreasonable risk.

6.   **Vicarious Liability Offenses**
     A vicarious liability offense is one in which a person without personal fault may nevertheless be held liable for the criminal conduct of another (usually an employee). The trend is to limit vicarious liability to regulatory crimes and to limit punishment to fines.

CMR SUMMARY CHART

STATE OF MIND

Mens Rea	State of Mind Required	Objective or Subjective Test?
	Common Law	
Specific Intent	Intent to engage in proscribed conduct	Subjective
General Intent	Awareness of acting in proscribed manner	Subjective
Malice	Reckless disregard of a known risk	Subjective
Strict Liability	Conscious commission of proscribed act	Objective
	M.P.C. Fault Standards	
Purposely	Conscious object to engage in proscribed conduct	Subjective
Knowingly	Awareness that conduct is of a particular nature or will cause a particular result	Subjective
Recklessly	Consciously disregarding a substantial known risk	Subjective
Negligently	Failure to be aware of a substantial risk	Objective

7. Enterprise Liability—Liability of Corporations and Associations
At common law, a corporation does not have capacity to commit crimes. Under modern statutes, corporations may be held liable for an act performed by: (i) an agent of the corporation acting within the scope of his office or employment; or (ii) a corporate agent high enough in hierarchy to presume his acts reflect corporate policy.

D. CONCURRENCE OF MENTAL FAULT WITH PHYSICAL ACT
The defendant must have had the intent necessary for the crime at the time he committed the act constituting the crime, and the intent must have actuated the act. For example, if D is driving to V's house to kill him, he will lack the necessary concurrence for murder if he *accidentally* runs V over before reaching the house.

E. CAUSATION
Some crimes (*e.g.,* homicide) require result and causation (*see* VII.C.4., *infra*).

III. ACCOMPLICE LIABILITY

A. PARTIES TO A CRIME

1. Common Law
At common law, parties to a crime included the ***principal in the first degree*** (person who actually engaged in the act or omission that constitutes the offense or who caused an innocent agent to do so), ***principal in the second degree*** (person who aided, commanded, or encouraged the principal and was present at the crime), ***accessory before the fact*** (person who assisted or encouraged but was ***not present***), and ***accessory after the fact*** (person who, with knowledge that the other committed a felony, assisted him to escape arrest or punishment). At common law, conviction of the principal was required for conviction of an accessory and the charge must have indicated the correct theory of liability (*i.e.,* as principal or accessory).

2. Modern Statutes
Most jurisdictions have abolished the distinctions between principals in the first degree and principals in the second degree or accessories before the fact. All such "parties to the crime" can be found guilty of the principal offense. For convenience, however, think of the one who actually engages in the act (either personally or through an innocent agent) or omission as the principal and the other parties as accomplices.

Note: An accessory after the fact (one who assists another knowing that he has committed a felony in order to help him escape) is still treated separately. Punishment for this crime usually bears no relationship to the principal offense.

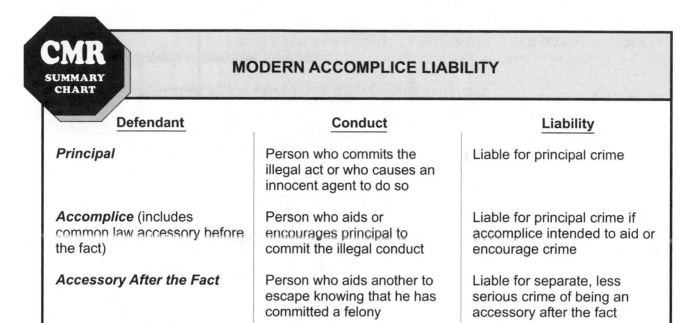

CMR
SUMMARY
CHART

MODERN ACCOMPLICE LIABILITY

Defendant	Conduct	Liability
Principal	Person who commits the illegal act or who causes an innocent agent to do so	Liable for principal crime
Accomplice (includes common law accessory before the fact)	Person who aids or encourages principal to commit the illegal conduct	Liable for principal crime if accomplice intended to aid or encourage crime
Accessory After the Fact	Person who aids another to escape knowing that he has committed a felony	Liable for separate, less serious crime of being an accessory after the fact

B. MENTAL STATE—INTENT REQUIRED

To be guilty as an accomplice, most jurisdictions require that the person give aid, counsel, or encouragement to the principal with the ***intent*** to encourage the crime. In the absence of a statute, most courts would hold that ***mere knowledge*** that a crime will result is not enough, at least where the aid given is in the form of the sale of ordinary goods at ordinary prices (*e.g.,* a gas station attendant will not be liable for arson for knowingly selling a gallon of gasoline to an arsonist). However, procuring an illegal item or selling at a higher price because of the buyer's purpose (*e.g.,* charging the arsonist $100 for the gallon of gas) may constitute a sufficient "stake in the venture" to constitute intent.

C. SCOPE OF LIABILITY

An accomplice is responsible for the crimes he did or counseled ***and*** for any other crimes committed in the course of committing the crime contemplated to the same extent as the principal, as long as the other crimes were ***probable or foreseeable***.

1. Inability to Be Principal No Bar to Accomplice Liability

One who may not be convicted of being a principal may be convicted of being an accomplice. *Example:* At common law a woman cannot be convicted of being the principal in a rape but can be found guilty as an accomplice if she aids the principal.

2. Exclusions from Liability

a. Members of the Protected Class

Members of the class protected by a statute are excluded from accomplice liability. *Example:* A woman transported across state lines cannot be an accomplice to the crime of transporting women across state lines for immoral purposes, since she is within the class protected.

b. Necessary Parties Not Provided For

A party necessary to the commission of a crime, by statutory definition, who is not

CLASSIFICATION OF CRIMES

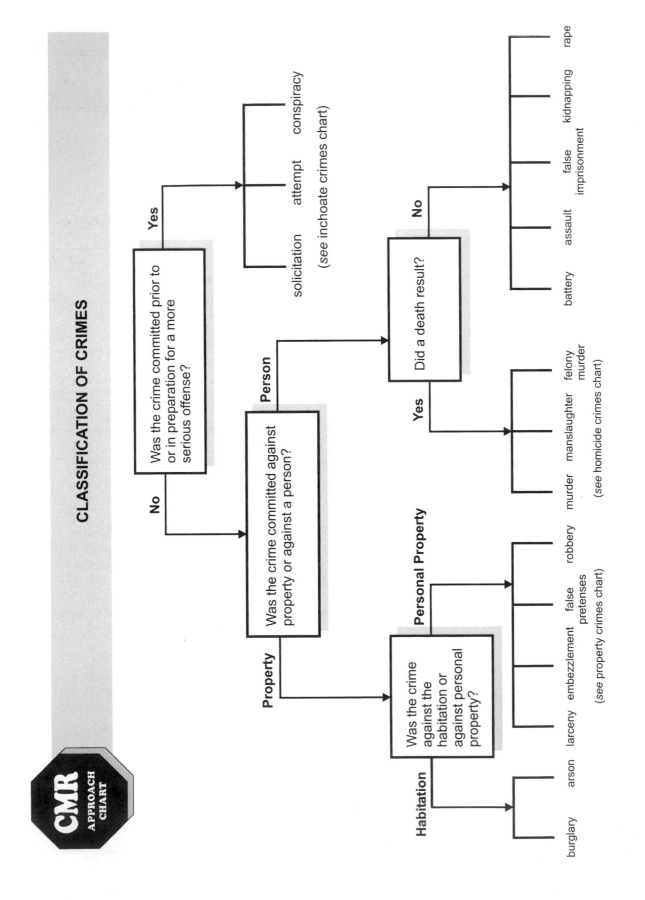

CMR APPROACH CHART

Was the crime committed prior to or in preparation for a more serious offense?

Yes

solicitation   attempt   conspiracy

(see inchoate crimes chart)

No

Was the crime committed against property or against a person?

Person

Did a death result?

No

battery   assault   false imprisonment   kidnapping   rape

Yes

murder   manslaughter   felony murder

(see homicide crimes chart)

Property

Was the crime against the habitation or against personal property?

Personal Property

larceny   embezzlement   false pretenses   robbery

(see property crimes chart)

Habitation

burglary   arson

provided for in the statute is excluded from accomplice liability. *Example:* If a statute makes the sale of heroin illegal, but does not provide for punishment of the purchaser, he cannot be found guilty under the statute as an accomplice to the seller.

   c.   **Withdrawal**
       A person who effectively withdraws from a crime before it is committed cannot be held guilty as an accomplice. Withdrawal must occur *before* the crime becomes unstoppable.

       (i)   *Repudiation* is sufficient withdrawal for mere encouragement.

       (ii) *Attempt to neutralize* assistance is required if participation went beyond mere encouragement.

       Notifying the police or taking other action to prevent the crime is also sufficient.

IV. INCHOATE OFFENSES

CMR COMPARISON CHART

INCHOATE CRIMES

	Solicitation	Conspiracy	Attempt
Culpable Conduct	Solicitation of another to commit a felony	Agreement between two or more people to commit a crime	Performance of an act that would be a crime if successful
Mental State	Specific intent that person solicited commit the crime	Specific intent to: (i) enter into agreement; and (ii) achieve objective	Specific intent to commit the particular crime attempted
Overt Act	No act (other than the solicitation)	Act in furtherance of the conspiracy	Act dangerously close to success (M.P.C.—substantial step test)
Merger into Completed Crime?	Yes	No	Yes
Withdrawal a Defense?	Generally no	No, except for further crimes of co-conspirators	Generally no

A. SOLICITATION

1. Elements
Solicitation consists of *inciting*, *counseling*, *advising*, *urging*, *or commanding* another to commit a crime, with the *intent that the person solicited commit the crime*. It is not necessary that the person solicited respond affirmatively.

2. Defenses
It is not a defense that the person solicited is not convicted, nor that the offense solicited could not in fact have been successful. In most jurisdictions, it is not a defense that the solicitor renounces or withdraws the solicitation. The M.P.C. recognizes renunciation as a defense if the defendant prevents the commission of the crime, such as by persuading the person solicited not to commit the crime. However, it *is a defense* that the solicitor could not be found guilty of the completed crime because of a legislative intent to exempt her (*e.g.,* a woman cannot be found guilty of soliciting a man to transport her across state lines for immoral purposes).

3. Merger
If the person solicited commits the crime solicited, both that person and the solicitor can be held liable for that crime. If the person solicited commits acts sufficient to be liable for attempt, both parties can be liable for attempt. If the person solicited agrees to commit the crime, but does not even commit acts sufficient for attempt, both parties can be held liable for conspiracy. However, under the doctrine of merger, the solicitor *cannot be punished for both* the solicitation and these other offenses.

B. CONSPIRACY
A conspiracy is an agreement between two or more parties to commit a crime.

1. Elements
A conspiracy requires (i) an *agreement* between two or more persons; (ii) an *intent to enter into the agreement*; and (iii) an *intent* by at least two persons *to achieve the objective of the agreement*. A majority of states now also require an *overt act*, but an act of mere preparation will suffice.

CMR | **Exam Tip** | Conspiracy is probably the most tested inchoate crime. One important thing for you to remember is that it takes two to conspire at common law. Make sure that the facts of a question show at least two "guilty minds"—two people who intend to agree *and* intend that the crime be committed. Thus, if the defendant and an undercover police officer "agree" to commit a crime, there is no conspiracy at common law because only the defendant intended that the crime be committed. Similarly, if the defendant and another person "agree" but the facts show that the other person merely pretended to go along and really meant to warn the police, there is no conspiracy.

a. Agreement Requirement
The parties must agree to accomplish the same objective by mutual action. However, the agreement need not be express; it may be inferred from joint activity.

1) Implications of Requirement of Two or More Parties
A conspiracy at common law must involve a "meeting of minds" between at least two independent persons. This requirement presents the following issues:

a) **Husband and Wife**

At common law, a husband and wife could not conspire together, but this distinction has been abandoned in most states.

b) **Corporation and Agent**

There can be no conspiracy between a corporation and a single agent acting on its behalf. There is a split of authority as to whether the agents of a corporation can be deemed co-conspirators with the corporation.

c) **Wharton Rule**

Under the Wharton Rule, where two or more people are necessary for the commission of the substantive offense (*e.g.,* adultery, dueling), there is no crime of conspiracy unless *more parties participate* in the agreement than are necessary for the crime (*e.g.,* because it takes two people to commit adultery, it takes three people to conspire to commit adultery). *Exception:* The Wharton Rule does not apply to agreements with "necessary parties not provided for" by the substantive offense; both parties may be guilty of conspiracy even though both are necessary for commission of the substantive offense.

d) **Agreement with Person in "Protected Class"**

If members of a conspiracy agree to commit a crime designed to protect persons within a given class, persons within that class cannot be guilty of the crime itself or of conspiracy to commit that crime. Likewise, the nonprotected person cannot be guilty of conspiracy if the agreement was with the protected person only.

e) **Effect of Acquittal of Some Conspirators**

Under the traditional view, the *acquittal* of all persons with whom a defendant is alleged to have conspired precludes conviction of the remaining defendant. In some jurisdictions following the traditional view, a conviction for conspiracy against one defendant is allowed to stand when the alleged co-conspirator is acquitted in a *separate trial*.

CMR | **Exam Tip** | Acquittal is the key here. If the defendant and others allegedly conspired and only the defendant is charged and tried (*e.g.,* the other parties are not apprehended or not prosecuted), the defendant can be convicted. But if the defendant is charged and tried and *all the others have been acquitted*, the defendant cannot be convicted. (The acquittals show that there was no one with whom the defendant could conspire.)

f) **Model Penal Code Unilateral Approach**

Under the M.P.C. "unilateral" approach, the defendant can be convicted of conspiracy regardless of whether the other parties have all been acquitted or were only feigning agreement.

b. **Mental State—Specific Intent**

Conspiracy is a specific intent crime. Parties must have: (i) the intent to *agree* and (ii) the intent to *achieve the objective* of the conspiracy.

c. **Overt Act**

Most states require that an act in furtherance of the conspiracy be performed. An act of mere preparation is usually sufficient.

2. **Liability for Co-Conspirators' Crimes**

A conspirator may be held liable for crimes committed by other conspirators if the crimes (i) were committed *in furtherance* of the objectives of the conspiracy and (ii) were *foreseeable.*

3. **Termination of Conspiracy**

The point at which a conspiracy terminates is important because acts and statements of co-conspirators are admissible against a conspirator only if they were done or made in furtherance of the conspiracy. A conspiracy usually terminates *upon completion of the wrongful objective*. Unless agreed to in advance, acts of concealment are *not* part of the conspiracy. Note also that the government's defeat of the conspiracy's objective does not automatically terminate the conspiracy.

4. **Defenses**

a. **Factual Impossibility**

Factual impossibility is *not* a defense to conspiracy.

b. **Withdrawal**

Generally, withdrawal from the conspiracy is *not* a defense *to the conspiracy*, because the conspiracy is complete as soon as the agreement is made and an act in furtherance is performed. Withdrawal *may* be a defense to *crimes committed in furtherance* of the conspiracy, including the substantive target crime of the conspiracy.

1) **When Withdrawal Effective**

To withdraw, a conspirator must perform an affirmative act that notifies all members of the conspiracy of her withdrawal. Notice must be given in time for the members to abandon their plans. If she has also provided assistance as an accomplice, she must try to neutralize the assistance.

CMR | **Exam Tip** | Withdrawal from a conspiracy is another important test issue. You must be careful here not to let your feelings get in the way of a correct answer. Remember that a conspiracy is complete upon the agreement with the requisite intent and an overt act. Since the overt act can be a preparatory act, the conspiracy is usually complete very soon after the agreement. If the crime is complete, the defendant is *guilty of conspiracy*—even if the facts show that she had second thoughts, told her co-conspirators that she was backing out, warned the police, hid the weapons, etc. These actions come too late; defendant is guilty of conspiracy. (Such actions may relieve defendant of criminal liability for her co-conspirators' acts after this withdrawal, but they have no effect on the crime of conspiracy.)

5. **Punishment—No Merger**

Conspiracy and the completed crime are distinct offenses; *i.e.*, there is no merger. A defendant may be convicted of and punished for both.

6. **Number of Conspiracies in Multiple Party Situations**

In complex situations, there may be a large conspiracy with a number of subconspiracies. In such situations, it is important to determine whether members of one subconspiracy are liable for the acts of another subconspiracy. The two most common situations are:

a. Chain Relationship
A chain relationship is a single, large conspiracy in which all parties to subagreements are interested in the single large scheme. In this case, all members are liable for the acts of the others in furtherance of the conspiracy.

b. Hub-and-Spoke Relationship
In a hub-and-spoke relationship a number of independent conspiracies are linked by a common member. Although the common member will be liable for all of the conspiracies, members of the individual conspiracies are not liable for the acts of the other conspirators.

C. ATTEMPT

1. Elements
Attempt is an act, done with *intent to commit a crime*, that *falls short of completing* the crime.

a. Mental State
To be guilty of attempt, the defendant must intend to perform an act and obtain a result that, if achieved, would constitute a crime. Regardless of the intent necessary for the completed offense, an attempt *always requires a specific intent* (*i.e.*, the intent to commit the crime). *Example:* To be guilty of attempt to commit murder, defendant must have had the specific *intent to kill* another person, even though the mens rea for murder itself does not necessarily require a specific intent to kill.

CMR **Exam Tip** Attempt to commit a crime defined as the negligent production of a result (*e.g.*, negligent homicide) is logically impossible because a person docs not intend to be negligent. Thus, there can be no attempted negligent homicide, etc.

b. Overt Act
Defendant must commit an act *beyond mere preparation* for the offense. Traditionally, most courts followed the "*proximity" test*, which requires that the act be "dangerously close" to successful completion of the crime (*e.g.*, pointing a loaded gun at an intended victim and pulling the trigger, only to have the gun not fire or the bullet miss its mark is sufficient). However, today most state criminal codes (and the Model Penal Code) require that the act or omission constitute a "*substantial step* in a course of conduct planned to culminate in the commission of the crime" that strongly corroborates the actor's criminal purpose.

CMR **Exam Tip** Note that the overt act required for attempt is much more substantial than the overt act required for conspiracy.

2. Defenses

a. Impossibility of Success
Legal impossibility arises only when the defendant did, or intended to do, acts that

would not constitute a crime under any circumstances. So defined, *all* states (and the M.P.C.) will recognize this as a defense. *Factual impossibility*—that it would be factually impossible for the defendant to complete his plan (*e.g.,* a robbery victim who has no property)—is not a defense.

CMR Exam Tip If you get stumped on a question that asks you to decide whether impossibility is a defense, ask yourself: "If the defendant were able to complete all of the acts that he intended to do, and if all of the attendant circumstances actually were as the defendant believed them to be, would the defendant have committed a crime?" The answer usually will be yes, in which case the impossibility is factual and not a defense. In the unusual case where the answer is no, the defendant most likely has a legal impossibility defense.

b. Abandonment

Abandonment is *not* a defense at common law. If defendant had the intent and committed an overt act, she is guilty of attempt despite the fact that she changed her mind and abandoned the plan before the intended crime was completed. The M.P.C. provides that a *fully voluntary* and *complete* abandonment is a defense.

3. Prosecution for Attempt—Merger

Attempt merges with the completed crime. Thus, a defendant *cannot be found guilty of both* attempt and the completed crime. Also, a defendant charged only with a completed crime may be found guilty of attempt, but a defendant charged only with attempt may not be convicted of the completed crime.

V. RESPONSIBILITY AND CRIMINAL CAPACITY

A. INSANITY

There are several formulations of the test to be applied to determine whether, at the time of the crime, the defendant was so mentally ill as to be entitled to acquittal.

1. *M'Naghten* Rule

Under this rule, a defendant is entitled to acquittal only if he had a mental disease or defect that caused him to either: (i) *not know that his act would be wrong*; or (ii) *not understand the nature and quality of his actions*. Loss of control because of mental illness is no defense.

2. Irresistible Impulse Test

Under this test, a defendant is entitled to acquittal only if, because of a mental illness, he was *unable to control his actions or conform his conduct to the law*.

3. *Durham* (or New Hampshire) Test

Under this test, a defendant is entitled to acquittal if the *crime was the product of his mental illness* (*i.e.,* crime would not have been committed but for the disease). The *Durham* test is broader than either the *M'Naghten* test or the irresistible impulse test.

4. A.L.I. or Model Penal Code Test

Under the M.P.C. test (which represents the "modern trend"), a defendant is entitled to acquittal if he had a mental disease or defect, and, as a result, he *lacked the substantial capacity* to either:

(i)   *Appreciate the criminality* of his conduct; or

(ii)   *Conform his conduct* to the requirements of law.

CMR   **Exam Tip**   It is important to know these separate insanity tests because questions may ask you about a specific test (*e.g.,* "If the jurisdiction has adopted the M.P.C. test for determining insanity, what is defendant's best argument for acquittal on this ground?"). To answer this type of question, you must know the requirements for that particular test. A shorthand way to remember the test is:

M'Naghten—defendant does *not know right from wrong*;

Irresistible Impulse—(as the name says) an *impulse* that defendant *cannot resist*;

Durham—*but for the mental illness*, defendant would not have done the act;

A.L.I. or M.P.C.—*combination* of *M'Naghten* and irresistible impulse.

5. **Procedural Issues**

    a.   **Burdens of Proof**
       All defendants are presumed sane; the defendant must raise the insanity issue. There is a split among the jurisdictions as to whether the defendant raising the issue bears the burden of proof.

    b.   **When Defense May Be Raised**
       Although the insanity defense may be raised at the arraignment when the plea is taken, the defendant need not raise it then. A simple "not guilty" at that time does not waive the right to raise the defense at some future time.

    c.   **Pretrial Psychiatric Examination**
       If the defendant does *not* raise the insanity issue, he *may* refuse a court-ordered psychiatric examination to determine his competency to stand trial. If the defendant *raises* the insanity issue, he may *not* refuse to be examined by a psychiatrist appointed to aid the court in the resolution of his insanity plea.

6. **Post-Acquittal Commitment to Mental Institution**
In most jurisdictions, a defendant acquitted by reason of insanity may be committed to a mental institution until cured. Confinement may exceed the maximum period of incarceration for the offense charged.

7. **Mental Condition During Criminal Proceedings**
Under the Due Process Clause of the United States Constitution, a defendant may not be tried, convicted, or sentenced if, as a result of a mental disease or defect, he is unable (i) to understand the nature of the proceedings being brought against him; or (ii) to assist his lawyer in the preparation of his defense. A defendant may not be executed if he is incapable of understanding the nature and purpose of the punishment.

8. Diminished Capacity

Some states recognize the defense of "diminished capacity" under which defendant may assert that as a result of a mental defect short of insanity, he did not have the mental state required for the crime charged. Most states allowing the diminished capacity defense limit it to specific intent crimes, but a few states allow it for general intent crimes as well.

B. INTOXICATION

Intoxication may be caused by any substance (*e.g.,* drugs, alcohol, medicine). It may be raised whenever intoxication negates one of the elements of the crime. The law usually distinguishes between voluntary and involuntary intoxication.

1. Voluntary Intoxication

Intoxication is voluntary if it is the result of the intentional taking without duress of a substance known to be intoxicating.

a. Defense to Specific Intent Crimes

Evidence of "voluntary" intoxication may be offered by defendant only if the crime requires ***purpose*** (***intent***) ***or knowledge***, and the intoxication prevented the defendant from formulating the purpose or obtaining the knowledge. Thus, it is often a good defense to ***specific intent*** crimes. The defense is not available if the defendant purposely becomes intoxicated in order to establish the defense.

b. No Defense to Other Crimes

Voluntary intoxication is no defense to crimes involving malice, recklessness, negligence, or strict liability. For this reason, voluntary intoxication will not reduce second degree murder (requiring criminal recklessness) to manslaughter.

2. Involuntary Intoxication

Intoxication is involuntary only if it results from the taking of an intoxicating substance ***without knowledge*** of its nature, ***under direct duress*** imposed by another, or ***pursuant to medical advice*** while unaware of the substance's intoxicating effect. Involuntary intoxication may be treated as a mental illness, and the defendant is entitled to acquittal if she meets the jurisdiction's insanity test.

3. Relationship to Insanity

Continuous, excessive drinking or drug use may bring on actual insanity and thus a defendant may be able to claim both an intoxication defense and an insanity defense.

C. INFANCY

At common law, there could be no liability for an act committed by a child under age seven. For acts committed by a child between ages seven and 14, there was a rebuttable presumption that the child was unable to understand the wrongfulness of his acts. Children age 14 or older were treated as adults. Modern statutes often modify this and provide that no child can be convicted of a crime until a stated age is reached, usually 13 or 14. However, children can be found to be delinquent in special juvenile or family courts.

CMR SUMMARY CHART

DEFENSES NEGATING CRIMINAL CAPACITY

Defense	Elements	Applicable Crimes
Insanity	Meet applicable *insanity test* (*M'Naghten*, irresistible impulse, *Durham*, or M.P.C.)	Defense to *all* crimes
Intoxication -voluntary	*Voluntary, intentional taking* of a substance *known to be* intoxicating	Defense to *specific intent* crime if intoxication prevents formation of required intent
-involuntary	Taking intoxicating substance *without knowledge* of its nature, *under duress*, or pursuant to *medical advice*	Treated as mental illness (*i.e.,* apply appropriate insanity test); may be a defense to *all* crimes
Infancy	Defendant under age 14 *at common law*; under *modern statutes*, defendant under age 13 or 14	*Common law:* Under age seven, absolute defense to *all* crimes; under 14, rebuttable presumption of defense. *Modern statutes:* Defense to adult crimes but may still be delinquent
Diminished Capacity (some states)	As a result of mental defect *short of insanity*, defendant did not have the required mental state to commit the crime	Most states with this defense limit it to *specific intent* crimes

VI. PRINCIPLES OF EXCULPATION

A. JUSTIFICATION

The justification defenses arise when society has deemed that although the defendant committed a proscribed act, she should not be punished because the circumstances justify the action.

CMR **Exam Tip** The right to self-defense or other justification defenses depends on the immediacy of the threat; a threat of future harm is not sufficient. Thus, if someone threatens the defendant by saying, "Tomorrow I'm going to kill you," the defendant is *not justified* in killing the person to "protect" himself.

CMR **Exam Tip** It is crucial to determine the level of force that the defendant used in committing the proscribed act. As a rule of thumb, *nondeadly force* is justified where it appears necessary to

avoid imminent injury or to retain property; ***deadly force*** is justified only to prevent death or serious bodily injury.

1. **Self-Defense**

   a. **Nondeadly Force**
      A person without fault may use such force as ***reasonably appears necessary*** to protect herself from the imminent use of unlawful force upon herself. There is no duty to retreat.

   b. **Deadly Force**
      A person may use deadly force in self-defense if (i) she is without fault; (ii) she is confronted with "unlawful force"; and (iii) she is threatened with imminent death or great bodily harm.

   CMR **Exam Tip** If the defendant kills in self-defense but not all three of the requirements for the use of deadly force are met, some states would find the defendant guilty of manslaughter rather than murder under the "imperfect self-defense" doctrine.

      1) **Retreat**
         Generally, there is no duty to retreat before using deadly force. The minority view requires retreat before using deadly force if the victim can safely do so, ***unless***: (i) the attack occurs in the victim's home, (ii) the attack occurs while the victim is making a lawful arrest, or (iii) the assailant is in the process of robbing the victim.

   c. **Right of Aggressor to Use Self-Defense**
      If one is the aggressor in the altercation, she may use force in defense of herself only if (i) she ***effectively withdraws*** from the altercation and ***communicates*** to the other her desire to do so, ***or*** (ii) the victim of the initial aggression ***suddenly escalates*** the minor fight into a deadly altercation and the initial aggressor has no chance to withdraw.

2. **Defense of Others**
   A defendant has the right to defend others if she reasonably believes that the person assisted has the legal right to use force in his own defense. All that is necessary is the ***reasonable appearance*** of the right to use force. Generally, there need be no special relationship between the defendant and the person in whose defense she acted.

3. **Defense of a Dwelling**
   Nondeadly force may be used to prevent or terminate what is reasonably regarded as an unlawful entry into or attack on the defender's dwelling. ***Deadly force*** may be used only to prevent a violent entry made with the intent to commit a personal attack on an inhabitant, or to prevent an entry to commit a felony in the dwelling.

   CMR **Exam Tip** As a practical matter, deadly force usually is justified in repelling a home invader but the basis for the right to use such force is ***not*** to protect the dwelling, but to protect the safety of the inhabitants of the dwelling.

4. **Defense of Other Property**

a. **Defending Possession**
Deadly force may never be used in defense of property. *Nondeadly force* may be used to defend property in one's possession from unlawful interference, but may not be used if a request to desist or refrain from the activity would suffice.

b. **Regaining Possession**
Force *cannot* be used to regain possession of property wrongfully taken unless the person using force is in immediate pursuit of the taker.

5. **Crime Prevention**
Nondeadly force may be used to the extent that it reasonably appears necessary to prevent a felony or serious breach of the peace. *Deadly force* may be used only to terminate or prevent a dangerous felony involving risk to human life.

6. **Use of Force to Effectuate Arrest**
Nondeadly force may be used by police officers if it reasonably appears necessary to effectuate an arrest. *Deadly force* is reasonable only if it is necessary to prevent a felon's escape *and* the felon threatens death or serious bodily harm.

a. **Private Persons**
A private person has a privilege to use *nondeadly force* to make an arrest if a *crime was in fact committed* and the private person has *reasonable grounds to believe* the person arrested has in fact committed the crime. A private person may use *deadly force only if* the person harmed was *actually guilty* of the offense for which the arrest was made.

7. **Resisting Arrest**
Nondeadly force may be used to resist an improper arrest even if a known officer is making that arrest. *Deadly force* may be used, however, only if the person does not know that the person arresting him is a police officer.

8. **Necessity**
It is a defense to a crime that the person *reasonably believed* that commission of the crime was necessary to avoid an imminent and greater injury to society than that involved in the crime. The test is objective; a good faith belief is not sufficient.

a. **Limitation—Death**
Causing the death of another person to protect property is *never justified*.

b. **Limitation—Fault**
The defense of necessity is not available if the defendant is at fault in creating the situation requiring that he choose between two evils.

c. **Duress Distinguished**
Necessity involves pressure from natural or physical forces; duress involves a human threat (*see* B., *infra*).

9. **Public Policy**
A police officer (or one assisting him) is justified in using reasonable force against another, or in taking property, provided the officer acts pursuant to a law, court order, or process requiring or authorizing him to so act.

10. Domestic Authority

The parents of a minor child, or any person "in loco parentis" with respect to that child, may lawfully use reasonable force upon the child for the purpose of promoting the child's welfare.

CMR SUMMARY CHART

JUSTIFICATION DEFENSES

Defense	Amount of Force Allowed	
	Nondeadly Force	**Deadly Force**
Self-Defense	If reasonably necessary to protect self	Only if threatened with death or great bodily harm
Defense of Others	If reasonably necessary to protect person	Only if threatened with death or great bodily harm
Defense of Dwelling	If reasonably necessary to prevent or end unlawful entry	Only if person inside is threatened or to prevent felony inside
Defense of Other Property	If reasonably necessary to defend property in one's possession (but if request to desist would suffice, force *not* allowed)	Never
Crime Prevention	If reasonably necessary to prevent felony or serious breach of peace	Only to prevent or end felony risking human life
Effectuate Arrest		
– Police	If reasonably necessary to arrest	Only to prevent escape of felon who threatens human life
– Private Person	If crime in fact committed and reasonable belief that this person committed it	Only to prevent escape of person who actually committed felony and who threatens human life
Resisting Arrest	If improper arrest	Only if improper arrest and defendant does not know arrester is a police officer
Necessity	If reasonably necessary to avoid greater harm	Never

B. EXCUSE OF DURESS

It is a defense to a crime *other than homicide* that the defendant reasonably believed that another person would imminently inflict death or great bodily harm upon him or a member of his family if he did not commit the crime.

C. OTHER DEFENSES

1. Mistake or Ignorance of Fact

Mistake or ignorance of fact is relevant to criminal liability only if it shows that the defendant *lacked the state of mind required* for the crime; thus, it is irrelevant if the crime imposes "strict" liability.

a. Reasonableness

If mistake is offered to "disprove" a *specific intent*, the mistake *need not be reasonable*; however, if it is offered to disprove any other state of mind, it *must have been reasonable* mistake or ignorance.

> **CMR** | **Exam Tip** | Don't confuse the defense of mistake of fact with the issue of factual impossibility, discussed earlier. Even though in both situations defendant is mistaken about certain facts, the results are different. *Mistake* is usually raised as a defense to a crime that has been completed; mistake of fact may negate the intent required for the crime. *Impossibility* arises only when defendant has *failed* to complete the crime because of his mistaken belief about the facts, and is being charged with an *attempt* to commit the crime; factual impossibility is *not* a defense to attempt.

2. Mistake or Ignorance of Law—No Defense

Generally, it is not a defense that the defendant believed that her activity would not be a crime, even if that belief was reasonable and based on the advice of an attorney. However, if the reliance on the attorney negates a necessary mental state element, such reliance can demonstrate that the government has not proved its case beyond a reasonable doubt.

a. Exceptions

The defendant has a defense if: (i) the statute proscribing her conduct was not published or made reasonably available prior to the conduct; (ii) there was reasonable reliance on a statute or judicial decision; or (iii) in some jurisdictions, there was reasonable reliance on official interpretation or advice.

b. Ignorance of Law May Negate Intent

If the defendant's mistake or ignorance as to a collateral legal matter proves that she lacked the state of mind required for the crime, she is entitled to acquittal. The ignorance or mistake must involve the *elements* of the crime, *not the existence* of a statute making the act criminal. For example, a defendant cannot be found guilty of selling a gun to a known felon if she thought that the crime the buyer had been found guilty of was only a misdemeanor.

3. Consent

Unless the crime requires the lack of consent of the victim (*e.g.,* rape), consent is usually *not* a defense. Consent is a defense to minor assaults or batteries if there is no danger of serious bodily injury. Whenever consent may be a defense, it must be established that: (i) the consent was *voluntarily and freely given*; (ii) the party was *legally capable* of consenting; and (iii) *no fraud* was involved in obtaining the consent.

EXCULPATORY DEFENSES

Defense	Applicable To	When Available
Justification (self-defense, defense of others, defense of property, necessity, etc.)	Usually crimes of force (*e.g.,* battery, homicide)	**Nondeadly force** may usually be used if reasonably necessary to avoid imminent injury or to retain property; **deadly force** may be used only to prevent serious bodily harm
Duress	All crimes **except** homicide	Defendant reasonably believed that another would **imminently** harm him or a family member if he did not commit the crime
Mistake of Fact	Crimes with a mental state element (*i.e.,* all crimes **except** strict liability)	For **specific intent** crimes, any mistake that negates intent; for other crimes, **only reasonable mistakes**
Mistake of Law	Crimes with a mental state element and statutory crimes	Mistake must **negate awareness of some aspect of law regarding the elements of the crime requires or must be due to**: statute not being reasonably available, reasonable reliance on statute or judicial interpretation, or (in some states) reasonable reliance on official advice
Consent	Crimes requiring lack of consent (*e.g.,* rape) and minor assaults and batteries	Applicable **only** if: consent is freely given, the party is capable of consenting, and no fraud was used to obtain consent
Entrapment	Most crimes, but **not** available if the police merely provide the opportunity to commit the crime	Criminal design **originated with the police** and the defendant was **not predisposed** to commit the crime before contact with police

4. **Condonation or Criminality of Victim—No Defense**
Forgiveness by the victim is no defense. Likewise, the nearly universal rule is that illegal conduct by the victim of a crime is no defense.

5. **Entrapment**
Entrapment exists only if (i) the ***criminal design originated with law enforcement officers*** and (ii) the defendant was ***not predisposed*** to commit the crime prior to contact by the government. Merely providing the opportunity for a predisposed person to commit a crime is not entrapment.

   a. **Unavailable—If Private Inducement or If Material for Crime Provided by Government Agent**
   A person cannot be entrapped by a private citizen. Under federal law, an entrapment defense cannot be based on the fact that a government agent provided an ingredient for commission of the crime (*e.g.,* ingredients for drugs), even if the material provided was contraband.

 Exam Tip   Entrapment is a difficult defense to establish in court and so too on the MBE. In fact, on the exam, the defendant is usually predisposed to commit the crime and thus entrapment usually is a wrong choice.

VII.   OFFENSES AGAINST THE PERSON

A. **ASSAULT AND BATTERY**

1. **Battery**
Battery is an ***unlawful application of force*** to the person of another resulting in either ***bodily injury or an offensive touching***. Simple battery is a misdemeanor. A battery need not be intentional, and the force need not be applied directly (*e.g.,* causing a dog to attack the victim is a battery). Some jurisdictions recognize consent as a defense to simple battery and/or certain specified batteries.

   a. **Aggravated Battery**
   Most jurisdictions treat the following as aggravated batteries and punish them as felonies: (i) battery with a deadly weapon; (ii) battery resulting in serious bodily harm; and (iii) battery of a child, woman, or police officer.

2. **Assault**
Assault is ***either*** (i) an ***attempt to commit a battery*** or (ii) the ***intentional creation***—other than by mere words—***of a reasonable apprehension*** in the mind of the victim of ***imminent bodily harm***. If there has been an actual touching of the victim, the crime can only be battery, not assault.

   a. **Aggravated Assault**
   Aggravated assault (*e.g.,* with a deadly weapon or with intent to rape or maim) is treated more severely than simple assault.

 Exam Tip Think of assault as two separate crimes: (i) attempted battery assault—a *specific intent* crime (*i.e.,* defendant must intend to commit a battery), and (ii) creation of reasonable apprehension assault. Be sure to consider both types of assault in answering a question, because one may apply even though the other does not. For example, if D stops V at knifepoint and demands V's money, D has committed creation of reasonable apprehension assault but *not* attempted battery assault. You would not want to decide that D is not guilty of assault because you thought only about attempted battery assault.

B. MAYHEM

At common law, the felony of mayhem required either dismemberment or disablement of a bodily part. The trend is to abolish mayhem as a separate offense and to treat it instead as a form of aggravated battery.

C. HOMICIDE

1. Common Law Criminal Homicides

At common law, criminal homicide is divided into three categories:

a. Murder

Murder is the unlawful killing of a human being with ***malice aforethought***. Malice aforethought exists if there are no facts reducing the killing to voluntary manslaughter or excusing it (*i.e.,* giving rise to a defense) and it was committed with one of the following states of mind:

(i) Intent ***to kill***;

(ii) Intent ***to inflict great bodily injury***;

(iii) ***Reckless indifference to an unjustifiably high risk to human life*** ("abandoned and malignant heart"); or

(iv) Intent ***to commit a felony*** (felony murder).

Intentional use of a deadly weapon authorizes a permissive inference of intent to kill.

 Exam Tip Homicides are emotionally charged crimes, so you must be careful not to let your emotions lead you to an incorrect answer. If a defendant killed with one of the states of mind above, he is guilty of murder; if he did not, he is not guilty of murder (although he could be guilty of other crimes). Thus, even where the facts go out of their way to paint the defendant as a completely despicable human being (*e.g.,* a mass murderer), you cannot convict him of murder when he drives into a schoolyard, killing three children, if the incident was due to defendant's fiddling with a cigarette lighter. More troublesome is the mercy killing case. If defendant intends to kill, even as an act of love, he *is* guilty of murder. Society does not accept compassion as a sufficient justification for the killing of a human being.

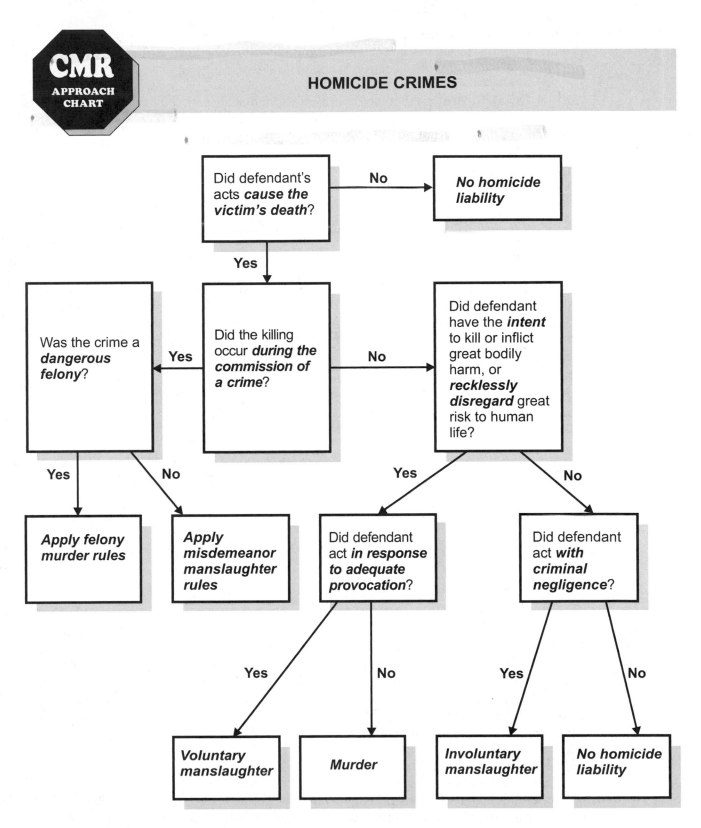

CMR
APPROACH
CHART

HOMICIDE CRIMES

Did defendant's acts **cause the victim's death**? — **No** → **No homicide liability**

↓ **Yes**

Did the killing occur **during the commission of a crime**?

— **Yes** → Was the crime a **dangerous felony**?
- **Yes** → **Apply felony murder rules**
- **No** → **Apply misdemeanor manslaughter rules**

— **No** → Did defendant have the **intent** to kill or inflict great bodily harm, or **recklessly disregard** great risk to human life?

- **Yes** → Did defendant act **in response to adequate provocation**?
  - **Yes** → **Voluntary manslaughter**
  - **No** → **Murder**

- **No** → Did defendant act **with criminal negligence**?
  - **Yes** → **Involuntary manslaughter**
  - **No** → **No homicide liability**

Note: This chart will lead you to the prima facie homicide that defendant committed. You must then decide whether any defenses apply.

b. **Voluntary Manslaughter**

Voluntary manslaughter is a killing that would be *murder but for the existence of adequate provocation*. Provocation is adequate *only if*:

(i) It was a provocation that would arouse *sudden and intense passion* in the mind of an ordinary person, causing him to lose self-control (*e.g.,* exposure to a *threat of deadly force* or finding your *spouse in bed with another* is adequate);

(ii) The defendant was *in fact provoked*;

(iii) There was *not sufficient time* between provocation (or provocations) and killing for passions of a reasonable person to cool; and

(iv) The defendant *in fact did not cool off* between the provocation and the killing.

CMR **Exam Tip** The adequacy of provocation is a key issue in homicide questions. Be sure to consider carefully the four factors for adequate provocation and not just jump to the conclusion that there was adequate provocation because you see some signs of provocation in the fact pattern. Also note the interplay between the reasonable person standard and what actually happened to defendant. Consider:

(i) *Sudden and intense passion* that would cause a *reasonable person to* lose control—passion must be reasonable under the circumstances; defendant cannot have been set off by something that would not bother most others.

(ii) *Defendant lost control*—even if a reasonable person would have been provoked, if defendant was not, there is no reduction to manslaughter.

(iii) *Not enough time* for *reasonable person* to cool off—this is tricky because it is hard to say how much time is needed to cool off; a lot depends on the situation, but the more time that has passed, the more likely it is that a reasonable person would have cooled off.

(iv) *Defendant did not cool off*—this is a little easier to judge; if the facts show that defendant calmed down, there is no reduction to manslaughter.

CMR **Exam Tip** Remember that "heat of passion" is no defense to a killing, although it may *reduce* the killing from murder to manslaughter. Often a question will set up facts showing sufficient provocation and then ask about defendant's criminal liability. Don't be fooled by a choice "Not guilty because defendant acted in the heat of passion." The correct choice will be something like "Guilty of manslaughter, but not murder, because defendant acted in the heat of passion."

1) **Imperfect Self-Defense**

Some states recognize an "imperfect self-defense" doctrine under which murder may be reduced to manslaughter even though (i) the defendant was at fault in starting the altercation; or (ii) the defendant *unreasonably* but honestly believed in the necessity of responding with deadly force (*i.e.,* defendant's actions do not qualify for self-defense).

c. **Involuntary Manslaughter**

A killing is involuntary manslaughter if it was committed *with criminal negligence* (defendant was grossly negligent) or, in some states, *during the commission of an unlawful act* (misdemeanor or felony not included within felony murder rule). Foreseeability of death is also a requirement.

CMR | **Exam Tip** | Some questions refer specifically to the type of manslaughter (voluntary or involuntary), while others just say "manslaughter." If the question does not specify the type, be sure to consider both, although on the MBE, voluntary manslaughter is more often involved.

2. **Statutory Modification of Common Law Classification**

In some jurisdictions, murder is divided into degrees by statute. A murder will be second degree murder unless it comes under the following circumstances, which would make it first degree murder:

a. **Deliberate and Premeditated**

If defendant made the decision to kill in a cool and dispassionate manner and actually reflected on the idea of killing, even if only for a very brief period, it is first degree murder.

CMR | **Exam Tip** | First degree murder based on premeditation requires a specific intent, which may be negated by the defense of *voluntary intoxication*. If the defendant was so intoxicated that he was unable to premeditate, he can be convicted only of second degree or common law murder, which requires only reckless indifference to human life (and for which voluntary intoxication is *not* a defense).

b. **First Degree Felony Murder**

In many states, a killing committed during the commission of *an enumerated* felony is felony murder and called first degree murder. The felonies most commonly listed are burglary, arson, rape, robbery, and kidnapping, but other felonies that are inherently dangerous to human life are often specifically added. Another statute (or case) may provide that a killing during *any* felony is felony murder, but the killing will typically be classified as second degree murder. Some other states do not list the felonies that may be used for felony murder *at all*, and the first degree murder classification is most often attached. Some states require that the felony be inherently dangerous to human life or the felony be dangerous to human life as committed when it provides for felony murder liability based on the commission of a felony that is not enumerated.

c. **Others**

Some statutes make killings performed in certain ways (*e.g.*, by torture) first degree murder.

3. **Felony Murder**

Any death caused in the *commission of*, *or in an attempt to commit*, *a felony* is murder. Malice is implied from the intent to commit the underlying felony.

a. **Felonies Included**

At common law, there are only a handful of felonies (*e.g.*, burglary, arson, rape, sodomy, etc.). Statutes today have created many more felonies.

b. **Limitations on Liability**

There are several limitations on this rule:

(i) The ***defendant must have committed*** the underlying felony; a defense that negates an element of the underlying offense will also be a defense to felony murder.

(ii) The ***felony must be distinct*** from the killing itself (*e.g.*, commission of aggravated battery that causes a victim's death does not qualify as an underlying felony for felony murder liability).

(iii) ***Death must have been a foreseeable result*** of the felony (a minority of courts require only that the felony be malum in se).

(iv) The ***death must have been caused before the defendant's "immediate flight"*** from the felony ended; once the felon has reached a place of "temporary safety," subsequent deaths are not felony murder.

(v) In most jurisdictions, the defendant is ***not*** liable for felony murder when a ***co-felon*** is killed as a result of resistance from the felony victim or the police.

(vi) Under the "agency theory," the defendant is not liable for felony murder when an ***innocent party*** is killed ***unless*** the death is caused by the defendant or his "agent" (*i.e.*, an accomplice). (Under the "proximate cause" theory, the defendant may be liable when an innocent party is killed by the victim or police.)

1) **Misdemeanor Manslaughter**

Note that there are similar limitations on misdemeanor manslaughter. Generally, the misdemeanor must be "malum in se," or, if the misdemeanor involved is not malum in se, the death must have been a foreseeable result of the commission of the misdemeanor.

4. **Causation**

The defendant's conduct must be both the cause-in-fact and the proximate cause of the victim's death.

a. **Cause-in-Fact**

A defendant's conduct is the cause-in-fact of the result if the result would not have occurred "***but for***" the defendant's conduct.

b. **Proximate Causation**

A defendant's conduct is the proximate cause of the result if the result is ***a natural and probable consequence*** of the conduct, even if the defendant did not anticipate the precise manner in which the result occurred. Superseding factors break the chain of proximate causation.

c. **Rules of Causation**

An act that ***hastens an inevitable result*** is still the legal cause of that result. Also, *simultaneous acts* of two or more persons may be independently sufficient causes of a single result. A victim's preexisting weakness or fragility, even if unforeseeable, does not break the chain of causation.

    d.   **Limitations**

        1)   **Year and a Day Rule**
Traditionally, for a defendant to be liable for homicide, the death of the victim must occur within one year and one day from infliction of the injury or wound. Most states that have recently reviewed this rule have abolished it.

        2)   **Intervening Acts**
Generally, an intervening act shields the defendant from liability if the act is a coincidence or is outside the foreseeable sphere of risk created by the defendant. Note that a third party's negligent medical care and the victim's refusal of medical treatment for religious reasons are both foreseeable risks, so the defendant would be liable.

D.   FALSE IMPRISONMENT

False imprisonment consists of the *unlawful confinement* of a person *without his valid consent*. The M.P.C. requires that the confinement must *"interfere substantially"* with the victim's liberty. It is not confinement to simply prevent a person from going where she desires to go, as long as alternative routes are available to her. Note also that consent is invalidated by coercion, threats, deception, or incapacity due to mental illness, retardation, or youth.

E.   KIDNAPPING

Modern statutes often define kidnapping as unlawful confinement of a person that involves either (i) some *movement* of the victim, or (ii) *concealment* of the victim in a "secret" place.

    1.   **Aggravated Kidnapping**
Aggravated kidnapping includes kidnapping for ransom, kidnapping for the purpose of committing other crimes, kidnapping for offensive purposes, and child stealing (the consent of a child to her detention or movement is not of importance because a child is incapable of giving valid consent).

VIII. SEX OFFENSES

A.   RAPE

Rape is the unlawful carnal knowledge of a woman by a man, not her husband, without her effective consent. The slightest penetration is sufficient.

    1.   **Absence of Marital Relationship**
Under the traditional rule and the M.P.C., a husband cannot rape his wife, but most states today either reject this rule entirely or reject it where the parties are estranged or separated.

    2.   **Lack of Effective Consent**
To be rape, the intercourse must be without effective consent. Lack of effective consent exists where:

    (i)   Intercourse is accomplished by *actual force*;

    (ii)   Intercourse is accomplished by *threats of great and immediate bodily harm*;

    (iii) The victim is *incapable of consenting* due to unconsciousness, intoxication, or mental condition; or

    (iv) The victim is *fraudulently caused to believe that the act is not intercourse*.

    Note that consent due to other types of fraud (*e.g.*, perpetrator persuading victim that he is her husband or that he will marry her) *is* effective.

B. STATUTORY RAPE

This is carnal knowledge of a female under the age of consent; it is not necessary to show lack of consent. A showing of reasonable mistake as to age or a showing of voluntary consent is irrelevant since statutory rape is a *strict liability crime*.

C. ADULTERY AND FORNICATION

Adultery is committed by both parties to sexual intercourse if either is validly married to someone else. It is often required that the behavior be open and notorious. Fornication is sexual intercourse or open and notorious cohabitation by unmarried persons.

D. INCEST

Incest consists of marriage or a sexual act between closely related persons.

E. SEDUCTION

Seduction consists of inducing, by promise of marriage, an unmarried woman to engage in intercourse. The M.P.C. does not require chastity or that the female be unmarried.

F. BIGAMY

Bigamy is the common law strict liability offense of marrying someone while having another living spouse.

IX. PROPERTY OFFENSES

A. LARCENY

Larceny consists of:

    (i)   *A taking* (obtaining control);

    (ii)   *And carrying away* (asportation);

    (iii) *Of tangible personal property* (excluding realty, services, and intangibles, but including written instruments embodying intangible rights such as stock certificates);

    (iv) *Of another* with possession;

    (v) *By trespass* (without consent or by consent induced by fraud);

    (vi) *With intent to permanently deprive* that person of her interest in the property.

1. **Possession**

   The property must be taken from the possession of another. If the *defendant* had possession of the property at the time of the taking, the crime is not larceny, but may be embezzlement.

   a. **Custody vs. Possession**

      Possession involves a greater scope of authority to deal with the property than does custody. Ordinarily, low level employees have only custody of an employer's property and so are guilty of larceny for taking it. A bailee, on the other hand, has a greater scope of authority over an owner's property and so is not guilty of larceny for taking it, but may be guilty of embezzlement.

2. **Intent to Permanently Deprive**

   Generally, larceny requires that *at the time of the taking* defendant intended to permanently deprive a person of her property.

   a. **Sufficient Intent**

      An intent to create a substantial risk of loss, or an intent to sell or pledge the goods to the owner, is sufficient for larceny.

   b. **Insufficient Intent**

      Where the defendant believes that the property she is taking is hers or where she intends only to borrow the property or to keep it as repayment of a debt, there is no larceny.

   c. **Possibly Sufficient Intent**

      There *may be* larceny where the defendant intends to pay for the goods (*if* the goods were not for sale) or intends to collect a reward from the owner (*if* there is no intent to return the goods absent a reward).

   CMR | **Exam Tip** | For a larceny question, be sure that the defendant had the intent to permanently deprive *when she took the property*. If not, there is no larceny (unless it is a continuing trespass situation (*see* 4., *infra*)). Many questions turn on this one small point.

3. **Abandoned, Lost, or Mislaid Property**

   Larceny can be committed with lost or mislaid property or property that has been delivered by mistake, but not with abandoned property.

4. **"Continuing Trespass" Situation**

   If the defendant *wrongfully* takes property *without* the intent to permanently deprive (*e.g.,* without permission borrows an umbrella), and later decides to keep the property, she is guilty of larceny when she decides to keep it. However, if the original taking was *not wrongful* (*e.g.,* she took the umbrella thinking it was hers) and she later decides to keep it, it is not larceny.

B. **EMBEZZLEMENT**

   Embezzlement is:

(i)   The *fraudulent*;

(ii) *Conversion* (*i.e.,* dealing with the property in a manner inconsistent with the arrangement by which defendant has possession);

(iii) Of *personal property*;

(iv) Of *another*;

(v)   By a person *in lawful possession* of that property.

1. Distinguish from Larceny
Embezzlement differs from larceny because in embezzlement the defendant misappropriates property while it is in his rightful possession, while in larceny the defendant misappropriates property not in his possession.

2. Fraudulent Intent
Defendant must intend to defraud.

a. Intent to Restore
If the defendant intends to restore the *exact* property taken, it is *not* embezzlement. However, if the defendant intends to restore similar or substantially identical property, it is embezzlement, even if it was money that was initially taken and other money—of identical value—that he intended to return.

b. Claim of Right
As in larceny, embezzlement is not committed if the conversion is pursuant to a claim of right to the property. Whether defendant took the property openly is an important factor.

C. FALSE PRETENSES
The offense of false pretenses is:

(i)   Obtaining *title*;

(ii) To *personal property of another*;

(iii) By an *intentional false statement* of past or existing *fact*;

(iv) With *intent to defraud* the other.

1. "Larceny by Trick" Distinguished
If the victim is tricked—by a misrepresentation of fact—into giving up mere *possession* of property, the crime is larceny by trick. If the victim is tricked into giving up *title* to property, the crime is false pretenses.

2. The Misrepresentation Required
The victim must actually be deceived by, or act in reliance on, the misrepresentation, and this must be a major factor (or the sole cause) of the victim passing title to the defendant. A misrepresentation as to what will occur in the future is not sufficient. A false promise, even if made without the present intent to perform, is also not sufficient.

D. ROBBERY

Robbery consists of:

(i)   A *taking*;

(ii) Of *personal property of another*;

(iii) *From the other's person or presence* (including anywhere in his vicinity);

(iv) *By force or threats of immediate death or physical injury* to the victim, a member of his family, or some person in the victim's presence;

(v)   With the *intent to permanently deprive* him of it.

CMR **Exam Tip**   For a defendant to be guilty of robbery, the victim must give up her property because she feels threatened. If she gives up her property for another reason (*e.g.*, she feels sorry for the defendant, or she wants the defendant to go away), the defendant will not be guilty of robbery. He may, however, be guilty of attempted robbery.

1. Distinguish Larceny

Robbery differs from larceny because robbery requires that the defendant use *force or threats* to obtain or retain the victim's property. Thus, pickpocketing generally would be larceny, but if the victim notices the attempt and resists, the taking would be robbery.

CMR COMPARISON CHART

PROPERTY CRIMES

Crime	Activity	Method	Intent	Title
Larceny	Taking and asportation of property from possession of another person	Without consent or with consent obtained by fraud *Larceny by trick*	With intent to steal	Title does not pass
Embezzlement	Conversion of property held pursuant to a trust agreement	Use of property in a way inconsistent with terms of trust	With intent to defraud	Title does not pass
False Pretenses	Obtaining title to property	By consent induced by fraudulent misrepresentation	With intent to defraud	Title passes
Robbery	Taking of property from another's presence	By force or threat of force	With intent to steal	Title does not pass

E. EXTORTION

Common law extortion consists of the corrupt collection of an unlawful fee by an officer under color of office. Under modern statutes, extortion (blackmail) often consists of obtaining property *by means of threats* to do harm or to expose information. Under some statutes, the crime is complete when threats are made with the intent to obtain property; *i.e.,* the property need not be obtained.

1. Distinguish Robbery

Extortion differs from robbery because in extortion the threats may be of future harm and the taking does not have to be in the presence of the victim.

F. RECEIPT OF STOLEN PROPERTY

Receipt of stolen property consists of:

(i)   Receiving *possession and control*;

(ii) Of *"stolen" personal property*;

(iii) *Known* to have been obtained in a manner constituting a criminal offense;

(iv) *By another person*;

(v)   With the *intent to permanently deprive* the owner of his interest in it.

1. "Possession"

Manual possession is not necessary. The defendant possesses the property when it is put in a location designated by her or she arranges a sale for the thief to a third person (*i.e.,* "fencing").

2. "Stolen" Property

The property must be stolen property *at the time the defendant receives it*.

CMR **Exam Tip** In analyzing receipt of stolen property questions, carefully check the property's status at the time defendant receives it. If the police have already recovered the property and use it *with the owner's permission*, it is no longer stolen, and the defendant cannot be convicted of receipt of stolen property. Note, however, that the defendant *can* be convicted of *attempted* receipt of stolen property if she intended to receive the property believing it to be stolen.

G. THEFT

Under many modern statutes and the M.P.C., some or all of the above property offenses are combined and defined as the crime of "theft."

H. FORGERY

Forgery consists of the following:

(i)   *Making or altering* (by drafting, adding, or deleting);

(ii) A *writing* with apparent legal significance (*e.g.,* a contract, not a painting);

(iii) So that it is *false*; *i.e.,* representing that it is something that it is not, not merely containing a misrepresentation (*e.g.,* a *fake* warehouse receipt, but not an *inaccurate* real warehouse receipt);

(iv) With *intent to defraud* (although no one need actually have been defrauded).

1. Fraudulently Obtaining Signature of Another
If the defendant fraudulently causes a third person to sign a document that the third person does not realize he is signing, forgery has been committed. But if the third person realizes he is signing the document, forgery has not been committed even if the third person was induced by fraud to sign it.

2. Uttering a Forged Instrument
Uttering a forged instrument consists of: (i) *offering as genuine*; (ii) an *instrument* that may be the subject of forgery and is *false*; (iii) with *intent to defraud*.

I. MALICIOUS MISCHIEF
Malicious mischief consists of:

(i) The *malicious*;

(ii) *Destruction* of or damage to;

(iii) The *property of another*.

Malice requires no ill will or hatred. It does, however, require that the damage or destruction have been *intended or contemplated* by the defendant.

X. OFFENSES AGAINST THE HABITATION

A. BURGLARY
Common law burglary consists of:

(i) A *breaking* (creating or enlarging an opening by at least minimal force, fraud, or intimidation; if defendant had the resident's consent to enter, the entry is not a breaking);

(ii) And *entry* (placing any portion of the body or any instrument used to commit the crime into the structure);

(iii) *Of a dwelling* (a structure used with regularity for sleeping purposes, even if used for other purposes such as conducting a business);

(iv) *Of another* (ownership is irrelevant; occupancy by someone other than defendant is all that is required);

(v) *At nighttime*;

(vi) *With the intent to commit a felony in the structure* (felony need not be carried out to constitute burglary).

Modern statutes often eliminate many of the "technicalities" of common law burglary, including the requirements of a breaking, that the structure be a dwelling, that the act occur at nighttime, and that the intent be to commit a felony (*i.e.,* intent to commit misdemeanor theft is often enough).

 Exam Tip The intent to commit a felony within must be present *at the time of entry*; a later-acquired intent is not sufficient. This technicality is tested; remember it.

B. ARSON
Arson at common law consists of:

(i) The *malicious* (*i.e.*, intentional or with reckless disregard of an obvious risk);

(ii) *Burning* (requiring some damage to the structure caused by fire);

(iii) *Of the dwelling*;

(iv) *Of another.*

Like statutory changes for burglary, modern arson statutes (including the M.P.C.) have modified the common law rules, usually to expand potential criminal liability. Most states have expanded the definition of arson to include damage caused by explosion, and expanded the types of property that may be destroyed to include commercial structures, cars, trains, etc.

 Exam Tip Although common law arson requires a burning of a *dwelling*, MBE questions testing on other arson issues often assume, without specifically stating, that arson extends to structures other than dwellings. Many statutes so provide.

1. Damage Required
Destruction of the structure, or even significant damage to it, is not required to complete the crime of arson. Mere blackening by smoke or discoloration by heat (scorching) is not sufficient, but mere *charring is sufficient*.

2. Related Offense—Houseburning
The common law misdemeanor of houseburning consisted of: (i) a malicious; (ii) burning; (iii) of one's own dwelling; (iv) if the structure is situated either in a city or town, or so near to other houses as to create a danger to them.

XI. OFFENSES INVOLVING JUDICIAL PROCEDURE

A. PERJURY
Perjury is the *intentional* taking of a false oath (lying) in regard to a *material matter* (*i.e.,* one that might affect the outcome of the proceeding) in a judicial proceeding.

B. SUBORNATION OF PERJURY
Subornation of perjury consists of *procuring or inducing* another to commit perjury.

C. BRIBERY
Bribery at common law was the corrupt payment or receipt of anything of value for official action. Under modern statutes, it may be extended to nonpublic officials, and either the offering of a bribe or the taking of a bribe may constitute the crime.

D. COMPOUNDING A CRIME

Compounding consists of agreeing, for valuable consideration, not to prosecute another for a felony or to conceal the commission of a felony or the whereabouts of a felon. Under modern statutes, the definition refers to any crime.

E. MISPRISION OF A FELONY

At common law, misprision of a felony consisted of the failure to disclose knowledge of the commission of a felony or to prevent the commission of a felony. Under modern statutes, misprision is no longer a crime, or if it remains a crime, it requires some affirmative action in aid of the felon.

CRIMINAL PROCEDURE

TABLE OF CONTENTS

CRIMINAL PROCEDURE

I. CONSTITUTIONAL RESTRAINTS ON CRIMINAL PROCEDURE

A. CONSTITUTIONAL REQUIREMENTS BINDING ON STATES

The first eight amendments to the U.S. Constitution apply to the federal government. Most of these rights are applicable to the states through the Due Process Clause of the Fourteenth Amendment. The following rights are binding on the states (as well as the federal government):

1. The Fourth Amendment *prohibition against unreasonable searches and seizures*, and the *exclusionary rule*;

2. The Fifth Amendment *privilege against compulsory self-incrimination*;

3. The Fifth Amendment *prohibition against double jeopardy*;

4. The Sixth Amendment right to *speedy trial*;

5. The Sixth Amendment right to a *public trial*;

6. The Sixth Amendment right to *trial by jury*;

7. The Sixth Amendment right to *confront witnesses*;

8. The Sixth Amendment right to *compulsory process* for obtaining witnesses;

9. The Sixth Amendment right to *assistance of counsel* in felony cases and in misdemeanor cases in which imprisonment is imposed; and

10. The Eighth Amendment *prohibition against cruel and unusual punishment*.

B. CONSTITUTIONAL RIGHTS NOT BINDING ON STATES

The right to indictment by a grand jury for capital and infamous crimes has been held not to be binding on the states. It has not yet been determined whether the Eighth Amendment prohibition against excessive bail creates a right to bail. However, most state constitutions create a right to bail and prohibit excessive bail.

II. EXCLUSIONARY RULE

A. IN GENERAL—SCOPE OF RULE

The exclusionary rule is a judge-made doctrine that prohibits introduction of evidence obtained in *violation of a defendant's Fourth, Fifth, and Sixth Amendment rights*. Under the rule, unconstitutionally obtained evidence is inadmissible at trial, and all "fruit of the poisonous tree" (*i.e.*, evidence obtained from exploitation of the unconstitutionally obtained evidence) must also be excluded. *Exceptions to fruit of the poisonous tree doctrine:*

(i) The fruits derived from statements obtained *in violation of Miranda* (*see, e.g.*, IV.D.4.c., *infra*);

(ii) Evidence obtained from a *source independent* of the original illegality;

(iii) An *intervening act of free will* by the defendant (*e.g.*, defendant is illegally arrested but is released and later returns to the station to confess);

(iv) *Inevitable discovery*—*i.e.*, the prosecution can show that the police would have discovered the evidence whether or not the police acted unconstitutionally; and

(v) *Violations of the knock and announce rule* (*see* III.C.3.e., *infra*).

Note: It is difficult to have live witness testimony excluded on exclusionary rule grounds. Also, a defendant may not exclude a witness's in-court identification on the ground that it is the fruit of an unlawful detention.

B. LIMITATIONS ON THE RULE

1. Inapplicable to Grand Juries, Civil Proceedings, Violations of State Law, Internal Agency Rules, and Parole Revocation Proceedings

The exclusionary rule is inapplicable to grand juries unless evidence was obtained in violation of the federal wiretapping statute. The rule is also inapplicable at parole revocation proceedings, in civil proceedings, or where evidence was obtained contrary only to state law or agency rules.

2. Good Faith Reliance on Law, Defective Search Warrant, or Clerical Error

The exclusionary rule does not apply when the police arrest someone erroneously but in good faith thinking that they are acting pursuant to a valid arrest warrant, search warrant, or law.

3. Use of Excluded Evidence for Impeachment Purposes

Some illegally obtained evidence may still be used to impeach defendant's credibility if he takes the stand at trial. Specifically, an otherwise *voluntary confession* taken in violation of the *Miranda* requirements is admissible for impeachment purposes, and *evidence obtained from an illegal search* may be used by the prosecution to impeach defendant's, but not others', statements.

4. Knock and Announce Rule Violations

Exclusion is not an available remedy for violations of the knock and announce rule pertaining to the execution of a warrant.

C. HARMLESS ERROR TEST

If illegal evidence is admitted, a resulting conviction should be overturned *on appeal* unless the government can show beyond reasonable doubt that the error was *harmless*. In a habeas proceeding where the petitioner claims constitutional error, he should be released if he can show that the error had a *substantial and injurious effect or influence* in determining the jury's verdict; if the judge is in grave doubt as to the harm, the petition must be granted.

CMR | **Exam Tip** | The harmless error standard never applies to the denial of the right to counsel *at trial*; *i.e.,* this error is never harmless.

D. ENFORCING THE EXCLUSIONARY RULE

A defendant is entitled to have the admissibility of evidence or a confession decided as a matter of law by a judge out of the hearing of the jury. The government bears the burden of establishing the admissibility by a preponderance of the evidence. The defendant has the right to testify at a suppression hearing without his testimony being admitted against him at trial on the issue of guilt.

III. FOURTH AMENDMENT

A. IN GENERAL
The Fourth Amendment provides that people should be free from unreasonable searches and seizures.

B. ARRESTS AND OTHER DETENTIONS
Governmental seizures of persons, including arrests, are seizures within the scope of the Fourth Amendment and so must be reasonable.

1. What Constitutes a Seizure?
A seizure occurs when a reasonable person would believe that she is not free to leave or terminate an encounter with the government.

2. Arrests
An arrest occurs when the police take a person into custody against her will for purposes of criminal prosecution or interrogation.

a. Probable Cause Requirement
An arrest must be based on probable cause—*i.e.,* trustworthy facts or knowledge sufficient for a reasonable person to believe that the suspect has committed or is committing a crime.

b. Warrant Generally Not Required Except for Home Arrests
A warrant generally is not required before arresting a person *in a public place*. However, police generally must have a warrant to effect a nonemergency arrest of a person in his home.

3. Other Detentions

a. Investigatory Detentions (Stop and Frisk)
If the police have a *reasonable suspicion* of criminal activity or involvement in a completed crime, supported by *articulable facts* (*i.e.,* not merely a hunch), they may detain a person for investigative purposes. If the police also have reasonable suspicion that the detainee is armed and dangerous, they may frisk the detainee for weapons.

1) Duration and Scope
The detention must be no longer than necessary to conduct a limited investigation to verify the suspicion. The police may ask the detained person to identify himself (*i.e.,* state his name) and generally may arrest the detainee for failure to comply with such a request. The detention will also turn into an arrest if during the detention other probable cause for arrest arises.

2) Property Seizures
Brief property seizures are similarly valid if based on reasonable suspicion.

b. Automobile Stops
Generally, police may not stop a car unless they have at least reasonable suspicion to believe that a law has been violated. However, if *special law enforcement needs* are involved, the Supreme Court allows police to set up roadblocks to stop cars without individualized suspicion that the driver violated some law. To be valid, the roadblock must: (i) stop cars on the basis of some neutral, articulable standard (*e.g.,* every car); and (ii) be designed to serve purposes closely related to a particular problem pertaining to automobiles and their mobility (*e.g.,* a roadblock to test for drunk drivers is valid because of the pervasiveness of the drunk driving problem, but a roadblock to search

cars for illegal drugs is not valid because the purpose of such a checkpoint is only to detect evidence of ordinary criminal wrongdoing).

1) Seizure of All Occupants
An automobile stop constitutes a seizure not only of the automobile's driver, but also of any passengers as well. Thus, passengers have standing to raise a wrongful stop as a reason to exclude evidence found during the stop.

2) Police May Order Occupants Out
After lawfully stopping a vehicle, in the interest of officer safety, the officer may order the occupants of the vehicle to get out. Moreover, if the officer reasonably believes the detainees to be armed, he may frisk the occupants and search the passenger compartment for weapons, even after hc has ordered the occupants out.

3) Pretextual Stops
If the police reasonably believe a driver violated a traffic law, they may stop the car, even if their ulterior motive is to investigate whether some other law—for which the police lack reasonable suspicion—has been violated.

c. Detention to Obtain a Warrant
If the police have probable cause to believe that a suspect has hidden drugs in his home, they may, for a reasonable time, prevent him from going into the home unaccompanied so that they can prevent him from destroying the drugs while they obtain a search warrant.

d. Occupants of the Premises
A valid warrant to search for contraband allows the police to detain occupants of the premises during a proper search.

e. Station House Detentions
Police must have full probable cause for arrest to bring a suspect to the station for questioning or fingerprinting.

4. Grand Jury Appearance
Seizure of a person (by subpoena) for a grand jury appearance is not within the Fourth Amendment's protection.

5. Deadly Force
There is a Fourth Amendment "seizure" when a police officer uses deadly force to apprehend a suspect. An officer may not use deadly force unless it is *reasonable to do so under the circumstances* (*e.g.,* where the suspect poses a danger to his own life or the lives of others).

C. EVIDENTIARY SEARCH AND SEIZURE
Like arrests, evidentiary searches and seizures must be reasonable to be valid under the Fourth Amendment, but here reasonableness requires a warrant except in six circumstances (*see* 4., *infra*). Evidentiary search and seizure issues should be approached using the following analytical model:

(i) Does defendant have a *Fourth Amendment right* (seizure by the *government* concerning a place or thing in which defendant had a *reasonable expectation of privacy*)?

(ii) Did the government have a *valid warrant* (issued by a neutral and detached magistrate on a showing of *probable cause* and *reasonably precise* as to the place to be searched and items to be seized)?

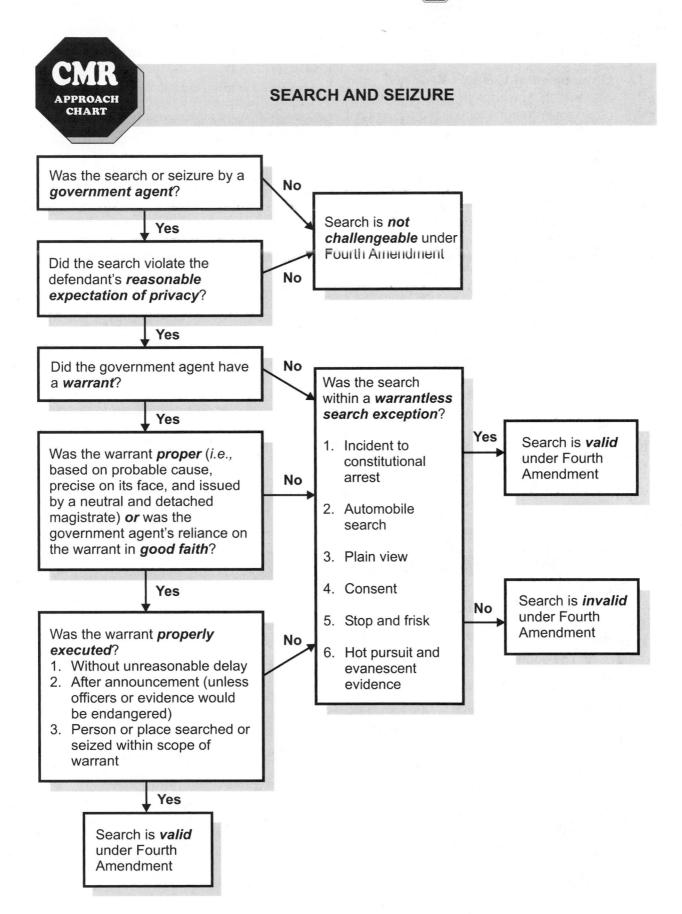

CMR APPROACH CHART

SEARCH AND SEIZURE

Was the search or seizure by a **government agent**?

— No → Search is **not challengeable** under Fourth Amendment

↓ Yes

Did the search violate the defendant's **reasonable expectation of privacy**?

— No → Search is **not challengeable** under Fourth Amendment

↓ Yes

Did the government agent have a **warrant**?

— No → Was the search within a **warrantless search exception**?

↓ Yes

Was the warrant **proper** (*i.e.*, based on probable cause, precise on its face, and issued by a neutral and detached magistrate) **or** was the government agent's reliance on the warrant in **good faith**?

— No → Was the search within a **warrantless search exception**?

↓ Yes

Was the warrant **properly executed**?
1. Without unreasonable delay
2. After announcement (unless officers or evidence would be endangered)
3. Person or place searched or seized within scope of warrant

— No → Was the search within a **warrantless search exception**?

↓ Yes

Search is **valid** under Fourth Amendment

Was the search within a **warrantless search exception**?

1. Incident to constitutional arrest
2. Automobile search
3. Plain view
4. Consent
5. Stop and frisk
6. Hot pursuit and evanescent evidence

— Yes → Search is **valid** under Fourth Amendment

— No → Search is **invalid** under Fourth Amendment

(iii) If the police did not have a valid warrant, did they make a *valid warrantless search and seizure*?

1. Governmental Conduct Required

The Fourth Amendment generally protects only against governmental conduct (*i.e.,* police or other government agents), and not against searches by private persons—including private security guards—unless deputized as officers of the public police.

2. Reasonable Expectation of Privacy

a. Standing

To have a Fourth Amendment right, a person must have his own reasonable expectation of privacy with respect to the place searched or the item seized. The determination is made on the totality of the circumstances, but a person has a legitimate expectation of privacy any time:

1) He owned or had a *right to possession* of the place searched;

2) The place searched was in fact *his home*, whether or not he owned or had a right to possession of it; or

3) He was an *overnight guest* of the owner of the place searched.

b. Things Held Out to the Public

One does not have a reasonable expectation of privacy in objects held out to the public.

Note: Use of sense-enhancing technology that is not in general public use (*e.g.,* a thermal imager as opposed to a telephoto camera lens) to obtain information from inside a suspect's home that could not otherwise be obtained without physical intrusion violates the suspect's reasonable expectation of privacy.

CMR EXAMPLE CHART

NO REASONABLE EXPECTATION OF PRIVACY

One has *no reasonable expectation of privacy in:*

1. The sound of one's voice

2. One's handwriting

3. Paint on the outside of one's vehicle

4. Account records held by a bank

5. The location of one's vehicle on public roads or its arrival at a private residence

6. Areas outside the home and related buildings ("curtilage"), such as a barn

7. Garbage left for collection

8. Land visible from a public place, even from a plane or helicopter

9. The smell of one's car or luggage ("sniff-test")

3. **Searches Conducted Pursuant to a Warrant**

Generally, the police must have a warrant to conduct a search unless it falls within one of the six exceptions to the warrant requirement (*see* 4., *infra*).

a. **Showing of Probable Cause**

A warrant will be issued only if there is probable cause to believe that seizable evidence will be found on the person or premises at the time the warrant is executed. Officers must submit to a magistrate an affidavit setting forth circumstances enabling the magistrate to make a determination of probable cause independent of the officers' conclusions.

1) **Use of Informers**

An affidavit based on an informer's tip must meet the "totality of the circumstances" test. Under this test, the affidavit may be sufficient even though the reliability and credibility of the informer or his basis for knowledge are not established. Note that the informer's identity generally need not be revealed.

2) **Going "Behind the Face" of the Affidavit**

A search warrant issued on the basis of an affidavit will be held invalid if the defendant establishes *all three* of the following:

(i) A *false statement* was included in the affidavit by the affiant (the officer applying for the warrant);

(ii) The affiant *intentionally or recklessly* included the false statement; *and*

(iii) The false statement was *material to the finding of probable cause*.

CMR | **Exam Tip** | This test for invalidating the affidavit is very restrictive—all three requirements for invalidity (falsehood, intentionally or recklessly included, and material to probable cause) must be met. Thus, if the affiant believed the lie, or if he intentionally included the lie but it was not material to the finding of probable cause (because there was sufficient other evidence), the affidavit is valid. Therefore, a defendant is rarely successful in challenging the affidavit.

a) **Police May Reasonably Rely on Validity of Warrant**

Evidence obtained by the police in reasonable reliance on a facially valid warrant may be used by the prosecution, despite an ultimate finding that the warrant was not supported by probable cause. (*See* II.B.2., *supra*.)

CMR | **Exam Tip** | This good faith exception applies *only if the police obtained a warrant* and it is invalid. The exception does not apply if the police failed to obtain a warrant.

b. **Warrant Must Be Precise on Its Face**

A warrant must describe with reasonable precision the place to be searched and items to be seized. If it does not, the warrant is unconstitutional, even if the underlying affidavit gives such detail.

c. Search of Third-Party Premises Permissible

A warrant may be obtained to search premises belonging to nonsuspects, as long as there is probable cause to believe that evidence will be found there.

d. Neutral and Detached Magistrate Requirement

The magistrate who issues the warrant must be neutral and detached (*e.g.*, state attorney general is not neutral).

e. Execution of Warrant

Only the police (and not private citizens) may execute a warrant, and it must be executed without unreasonable delay. Police must knock, announce their purpose, and wait a reasonable time for admittance (unless the officer has reasonable suspicion, based on facts, that announcing would be dangerous or futile or would inhibit the investigation). Police may seize any contraband or fruits or instrumentalities of crime that they discover, whether or not specified in the warrant. In any case, remember that violations of the knock and announce rule *will not* result in the suppression of evidence otherwise properly obtained—the exclusionary rule does not apply here.

1) Search of Persons Found on Searched Premises

A warrant founded on probable cause to search for contraband authorizes the police to *detain* occupants of the premises during a proper search, but a search warrant does *not* authorize the police to *search* persons found on the premises who were not named in the warrant.

4. Exceptions to Warrant Requirement

All warrantless searches are unconstitutional unless they fit into one of six recognized exceptions to the warrant requirement.

a. Search Incident to Constitutional Arrest

Incident to a *constitutional* arrest (*i.e.*, one based on probable cause to believe a law has been violated and that meets other constitutional requirements), the police may search the person and areas into which he might reach to obtain weapons or destroy evidence. The police may also make a protective sweep of the area if they believe accomplices may be present. The search must be *contemporaneous* in time and place with the arrest, but, at least with respect to searches of automobiles, the term "contemporaneous" does not necessarily mean "simultaneous." Thus, *e.g.*, the police may search the interior of an automobile *after* securing a recent occupant of the automobile in a squad car if they have reason to believe that the vehicle contains evidence of the crime for which the recent occupant was arrested. (*See* below.)

1) Constitutional Arrest Requirement

If an arrest is unconstitutional, any search incident to that arrest is also unconstitutional.

2) Automobiles

The police may conduct a search of the passenger compartment of an automobile *incident to arrest* only if at the time of the search:

      a)   The *arrestee is unsecured and still may gain access* to the interior of the vehicle; or

      b)   The police reasonably believe that *evidence of the offense for which the person was arrested* may be found in the vehicle.

3) Search Incident to Incarceration or Impoundment

At the police station, the police may make an inventory search of the arrestee's belongings pursuant to established department procedure. Similarly, the police may make an inventory search of an impounded vehicle.

b. "Automobile" Exception

If the police have probable cause to believe that a vehicle contains fruits, instrumentalities, or evidence of a crime, they may search the whole vehicle and any container that might reasonably contain the item for which they had probable cause to search. If a warrantless search of a vehicle is valid, the police may tow the vehicle to the station and search it later.

Note: If the police have probable cause to believe that an automobile itself is contraband, they may seize it from a public place without a warrant.

CMR **Exam Tip**   Note that the police have fairly broad authority to search a vehicle depending on what they are looking for. If there is probable cause to search the vehicle, the police can search the entire car and anything in it that *might contain the evidence*. Thus, if they are looking for evidence of illegal drugs, they can look in almost anything in the car, but if they are looking for undocumented aliens, they cannot look inside a small suitcase.

1) Passenger's Belongings

The search may extend to packages belonging to a passenger; it is not limited to the driver's belongings.

2) Containers Placed in Vehicle

If the police have probable cause only to search a container in a vehicle (*e.g.,* luggage recently placed in the trunk), they may search only the container, not other parts of the vehicle.

c. Plain View

The police may make a warrantless seizure when they:

(i)   Are *legitimately on the premises*;

(ii)   Discover *evidence, fruits or instrumentalities* of crime, or *contraband*;

(iii)   See such evidence in *plain view*; and

(iv)   *Have probable cause* to believe (*i.e.,* it must be immediately apparent) that the item is evidence, contraband, or a fruit or instrumentality of crime.

CMR **Exam Tip**   For this exception, be sure the police officer is legitimately on the premises (*i.e.,* where she has a lawful right to be), such as on a public sidewalk or in a

VALID WARRANTLESS SEARCHES

Type of Search	Need Probable Cause?	Contemporaneous-ness Requirement?	Other Limitations?
Search Incident to Constitutional Arrest	Yes (for arrest)	Yes	Constitutional arrest
Search Incident to Incarceration (Inventory Search)	No	No	Established routine
"Automobile" Exception	Yes	No	Containers—limited to those that could contain evidence sought
Plain View	Yes (to believe item is evidence, contraband, etc.)	Yes	Lawfully on premises; evidence in plain view
Consent	No	Yes	Voluntary and intelligent consent; apparent authority to consent; cannot be against wishes of a co-occupant who is present and objecting to the search
Stop and Frisk			
Stop	No	Yes	Reasonable and articulable suspicion of criminal activity
Frisk	No	Yes	Reasonable belief that person is armed; limited to patdown of outer clothing
Hot Pursuit, Emergencies	No	Yes	Emergency situation—No time to get warrant

home executing a warrant. If she is, anything the officer sees (or smells, hears, etc.) in plain view is admissible. Thus, if while executing a search warrant for a handgun, the officer opens a small drawer where the gun could be and sees heroin, the heroin is admissible since it was in plain view of an officer who had a right to look there.

d. **Consent**

A warrantless search is valid if the police have a ***voluntary and intelligent*** consent. Knowledge of the right to withhold consent is ***not*** a prerequisite to establishing a voluntary and intelligent consent. The scope of the search may be limited by the scope of the consent, but generally extends to all areas to which a reasonable person under the circumstances would believe it extends.

1) **Authority to Consent**

Any person with an apparent equal right to use or occupy the property may consent to a search, and any evidence found may be used against the other owners or occupants. However, an occupant cannot give valid consent to a search when a co-occupant is present and objects to the search and the search is directed against the co-occupant.

CMR | **Exam Tip** | Exam questions on the validity of warrantless searches often suggest consent as a choice, especially the consent of someone other than the defendant. Be careful to check whether the person has reasonably apparent authority to consent. For example, a homeowner parent can certainly consent to a search of the home's kitchen, and probably to a search of her son's room ***unless*** the facts strongly indicate that the parent does not have a right to go in the room (*e.g.,* always locked, only defendant has key, etc.). *Note:* The Supreme Court has not yet decided whether a parent may consent over the objection of his child.

e. **Stop and Frisk**

1) **Standards**

As noted above, a police officer may stop a person without probable cause for arrest if she has an ***articulable and reasonable suspicion*** of criminal activity. The officer may require the detainee to state his name, and if the officer also reasonably believes that the person may be armed and presently dangerous, she may conduct a protective frisk.

CMR | **Exam Tip** | Remember that a *stop* is not an arrest, and thus an officer need not have probable cause. However, he must have a reason to believe that criminal activity is afoot. Thus, seeing a person pace in front of a jewelry store might justify a stop. A *frisk* will be justified only if the officer reasonably thinks that the suspect has a weapon.

2) **Scope of Intrusion**

The scope of the frisk is generally limited to a patdown of outer clothing, unless the officer has specific information that a weapon is hidden in a particular area of the suspect's clothing. An officer may also order occupants out of a stopped vehicle and frisk them and search the passenger compartment of the vehicle if the officer has a reasonable belief that an occupant is dangerous.

3) Admissibility of Evidence
During a patdown, an officer may reach into the suspect's clothing and seize any item that the officer reasonably believes, based on its "plain feel," is a *weapon or contraband*, and such items are admissible as evidence.

f. Hot Pursuit, Evanescent Evidence, and Other Emergencies
There is no general "emergency" exception (*e.g.*, no need to investigate a fire after it has been extinguished and its cause determined). However, (i) police in hot pursuit of a fleeing felon may make a warrantless search and seizure and may even pursue the suspect into a private dwelling; (ii) police may seize without a warrant evidence likely to disappear before a warrant can be obtained; and (iii) contaminated food or drugs, persons injured or threatened with injury, and burning fires justify warrantless searches and seizures.

5. Administrative Inspections and Searches
Inspectors must have a warrant for searches of private residences and commercial buildings, but the probable cause required to obtain a warrant is more lenient than for other searches: A showing of a general and neutral enforcement plan will justify issuance of a warrant.

a. Exceptions Permitting Warrantless Searches
The following warrantless searches have been upheld:

(i) Administrative searches to *seize spoiled or contaminated food*;

(ii) Administrative searches of a *business within a highly regulated industry*;

(iii) *Inventory searches of arrestees* or their vehicles pursuant to established department procedure;

(iv) Searches of *airline passengers* prior to boarding;

(v) Searches of *parolees and their homes*—even without reasonable grounds for the search, at least as long as there is a statute authorizing such searches;

(vi) Searches of *government employees' desks and file cabinets* where the scope is reasonable and there is a work-related need or reasonable suspicion of work-related misconduct;

(vii) *Drug tests of railroad employees involved in an accident*;

(viii) *Drug tests of persons seeking customs employment in positions connected to drug interdiction*; and

(ix) *Drug tests of public school students who participate in extracurricular activities*.

1) Public School Searches
A warrant or probable cause is not required for public school officials to search public school students or their possessions; only *reasonable grounds* for the search are necessary. A school search will be held to be reasonable only if: (i)

CMR SUMMARY CHART

AUTOMOBILE SEARCHES

TRIGGERING EVENT	JUSTIFICATION NEEDED TO CONDUCT SEARCH	SCOPE OF SEARCH
INVESTIGATORY STOP	Belief detainee is *armed and dangerous* (*i.e.,* stop and frisk exception) **OR** Probable cause to believe that automobile contains contraband or fruits, instrumentalities, or evidence of crime (*i.e.,* automobile exception)	Anywhere in *passenger compartment* from which detainee may obtain weapon Anywhere *in automobile* in which items for which probable cause exists may be hidden
INCIDENT TO CONSTITUTIONAL ARREST	"Unsecured" arrestee may gain access to a weapon or evidence in vehicle **OR** Reason to believe vehicle may have evidence relating to offense for which arrest was made	Anywhere in *passenger compartment* from which arrestee may obtain weapon or have hidden evidence, including closed containers
INVENTORY/ IMPOUNDMENT	Pursuant to law and established department procedure	May search *entire vehicle* as per procedure

it offers a *moderate chance of finding evidence* of wrongdoing; (ii) the measures adopted to carry out the search are *reasonably related to the objectives of the search;* and (iii) the search is *not excessively intrusive* in light of the age and sex of the student and nature of the infraction.

6. Searches in Foreign Countries and at the Border

a. Searches in Foreign Countries
The Fourth Amendment does not apply to searches and seizures by United States officials in foreign countries and involving an alien, at least where the alien does not have a substantial connection to the United States. Thus, for example, the Fourth Amendment was held not to bar the use of evidence obtained in a warrantless search of an alien's home in Mexico.

b. Searches at the Border or Its Equivalent
No warrant is necessary for border searches. Neither citizens nor noncitizens have any Fourth Amendment rights at the border. Roving patrols inside the U.S. border may stop a vehicle for questioning of occupants if an officer *reasonably suspects* that the vehicle contains illegal aliens. Border officials may stop a vehicle at a fixed checkpoint inside the border for questioning of occupants and may disassemble the vehicle, even without reasonable suspicion.

c. Opening International Mail
Permissible border searches include opening of international mail when postal authorities have reasonable cause to suspect that the mail contains contraband.

d. Immigration Enforcement Actions
The Immigration Services Division may do a "factory survey" of the work force in a factory to determine citizenship of each employee. Moreover, even illegally obtained evidence (*i.e.*, evidence obtained in violation of the Fourth Amendment) may be used in a *civil* deportation hearing.

e. Detentions
Officials with "reasonable suspicion" that a traveler is smuggling contraband in her stomach may detain the traveler.

7. Wiretapping and Eavesdropping
Wiretapping (and other forms of electronic surveillance violating a reasonable expectation of privacy) constitutes a search under the Fourth Amendment. A valid warrant authorizing a wiretap may be issued if (i) there is showing of probable cause, (ii) the suspected persons involved in the conversations to be overheard are named, (iii) the warrant describes with particularity the conversations that can be overheard, (iv) the wiretap is limited to a short period of time, (v) the wiretap is terminated when the desired information has been obtained, and (vi) return is made to the court, showing what conversations have been intercepted.

a. Exceptions
A speaker assumes the risk that the person to whom he is talking is an informer wired for sound or taping the conversation. A speaker has no Fourth Amendment claim if he makes no attempt to keep a conversation private.

b.   **Pen Registers**
Although pen registers (devices that record only phone numbers that are dialed from a phone) are not controlled by the Fourth Amendment, by statute judicial approval is required before a pen register may be used.

D.   METHOD OF OBTAINING EVIDENCE THAT SHOCKS THE CONSCIENCE
Evidence obtained in a manner offending a "sense of justice" is inadmissible under the Due Process Clause. The reasonableness of searches within a person's body is determined by balancing society's need against the magnitude of the intrusion. Taking of a blood sample is usually upheld, but surgery (*e.g.*, to remove a bullet) requires great need.

IV.   CONFESSIONS

A.   INTRODUCTION
The admissibility of a defendant's confession (or other incriminating admission) involves analysis under the Fourth, Fifth, Sixth, and Fourteenth Amendments.

B.   FOURTEENTH AMENDMENT—VOLUNTARINESS
For a self-incriminating statement to be admissible under the Due Process Clause, it must be voluntary, as determined by the totality of the circumstances. A statement will be involuntary only if there is some official compulsion (*e.g.*, a confession is not involuntary merely because it is a product of mental illness).

1.   Harmless Error Test Applies
If an involuntary confession is admitted into evidence, the harmless error test applies; *i.e.*, the conviction need not be overturned if there is other overwhelming evidence of guilt.

C.   SIXTH AMENDMENT RIGHT TO COUNSEL
The Sixth Amendment guarantees the right to the assistance of counsel in all criminal proceedings, which include all critical stages of a prosecution *after judicial proceedings have begun* (*e.g.*, formal charges have been filed). It prohibits the police from deliberately eliciting an incriminating statement from a defendant outside the presence of counsel *after the defendant has been charged* unless he has waived his right to counsel.

CMR | **Exam Tip** | Note that there can be no violation of the Sixth Amendment right to counsel before formal proceedings have begun. Thus, a defendant who is arrested but not yet charged does not have a Sixth Amendment right to counsel but does have a Fifth Amendment right to counsel (*see* below) under *Miranda*.

1.   Stages at Which Applicable
A defendant has a right to be represented by privately retained counsel, or to have counsel appointed for him by the state if he is indigent, at the following stages: (i) custodial police interrogation; (ii) post-indictment interrogation, whether or not custodial; (iii) preliminary hearings to determine probable cause to prosecute; (iv) arraignment; (v) post-charge lineups; (vi) guilty plea and sentencing; (vii) felony trials; (viii) misdemeanor trials when imprisonment is actually imposed or when a suspended jail sentence is imposed; (ix) overnight recesses during trial; (x) appeals as a matter of right; and (xi) appeals of guilty pleas.

barbri

RIGHT TO COUNSEL

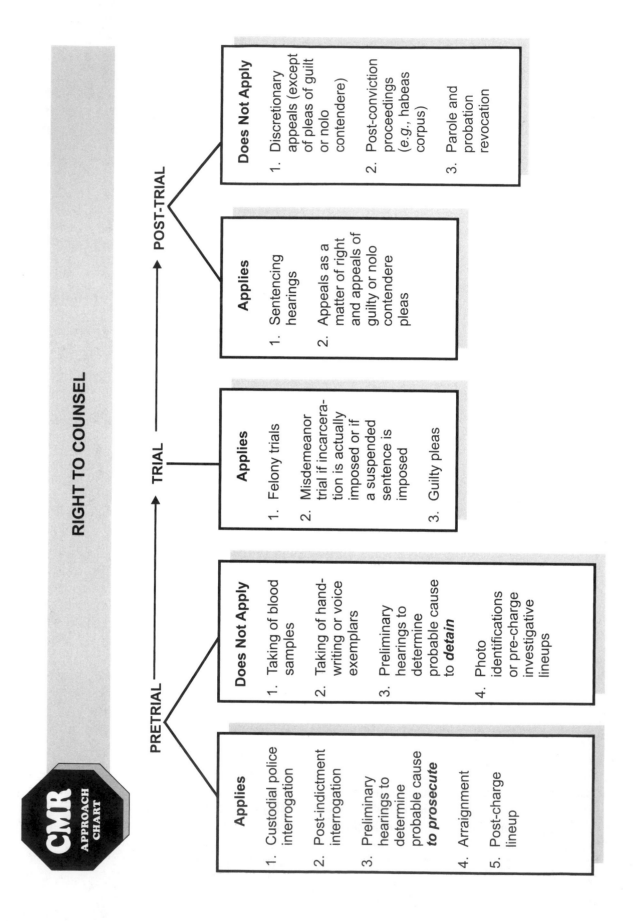

PRETRIAL

Applies

1. Custodial police interrogation
2. Post-indictment interrogation
3. Preliminary hearings to determine probable cause *to prosecute*
4. Arraignment
5. Post-charge lineup

Does Not Apply

1. Taking of blood samples
2. Taking of handwriting or voice exemplars
3. Preliminary hearings to determine probable cause to *detain*
4. Photo identifications or pre-charge investigative lineups

TRIAL

Applies

1. Felony trials
2. Misdemeanor trial if incarceration is actually imposed or if a suspended sentence is imposed
3. Guilty pleas

POST-TRIAL

Applies

1. Sentencing hearings
2. Appeals as a matter of right and appeals of guilty or nolo contendere pleas

Does Not Apply

1. Discretionary appeals (except of pleas of guilt or nolo contendere)
2. Post-conviction proceedings (*e.g.,* habeas corpus)
3. Parole and probation revocation

CMR
APPROACH CHART

2. **Stages at Which Not Applicable**
(i) Blood sampling; (ii) taking of handwriting or voice exemplars; (iii) precharge or investigative lineups; (iv) photo identifications; (v) preliminary hearings to determine probable cause to detain; (vi) brief recesses during the defendant's testimony at trial; (vii) discretionary appeals; (viii) parole and probation revocation proceedings; and (ix) post-conviction proceedings.

3. **Offense Specific**
The Sixth Amendment is offense specific. Thus, even though a defendant's Sixth Amendment rights have attached regarding the charge for which he is being held, he may be questioned regarding *unrelated*, *uncharged* offenses without violating the Sixth Amendment right to counsel (although the interrogation might violate the defendant's Fifth Amendment right to counsel under *Miranda; see* below). Two offenses will be considered different if each requires proof of an additional element that the other crime does not require.

4. **Waiver**
The Sixth Amendment right to counsel may be waived. The waiver must be knowing, voluntary, and intelligent. However, the waiver does not necessarily require the presence of counsel, at least if counsel has not actually been requested by the defendant but rather was appointed by the court.

5. **Remedy**
At *nontrial* proceedings (such as post-indictment interrogations), the *harmless error* rule applies to deprivations of counsel. But if the defendant was entitled to a lawyer at *trial*, the failure to provide counsel results in *automatic reversal of the conviction*, even without a showing of specific unfairness in the proceedings. Similarly, erroneous disqualification of privately retained counsel at trial results in automatic reversal.

6. **Impeachment**
A statement obtained in violation of a defendant's Sixth Amendment right to counsel, while not admissible in the prosecution's case-in-chief, may be used to impeach the defendant's contrary trial testimony. This rule is similar to the rule that applies to *Miranda* violations. (*See* D.4.a., *infra.*)

D. FIFTH AMENDMENT PRIVILEGE AGAINST COMPELLED SELF-INCRIMINATION

1. *Miranda* **Warnings**
For an admission or confession to be admissible under the Fifth Amendment privilege against self-incrimination, a person in custody must, prior to interrogation, be informed, in substance, that:

   (i)   He has the right to *remain silent*;

   (ii) Anything he says *can be used against* him in court;

   (iii) He has the right to presence of an *attorney*; and

   (iv) If he cannot afford an attorney, one will be *appointed* for him if he so desires.

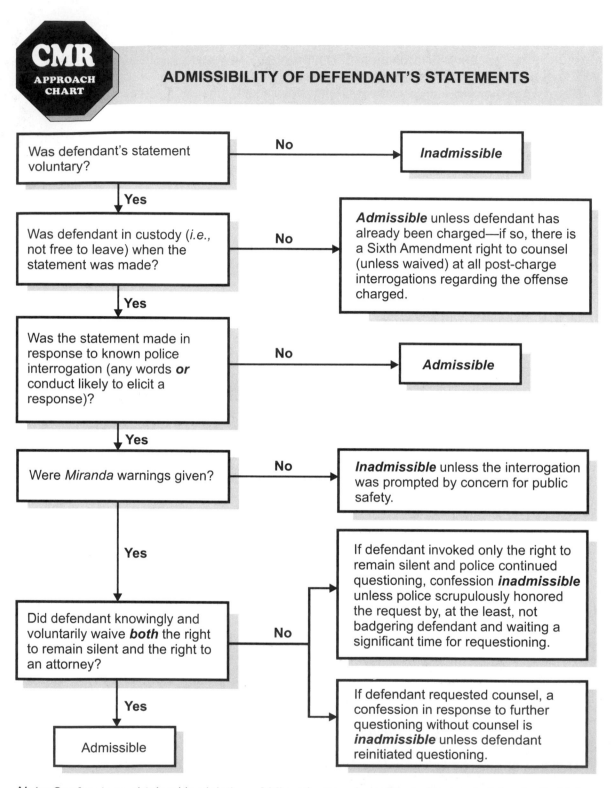

CMR APPROACH CHART

ADMISSIBILITY OF DEFENDANT'S STATEMENTS

Was defendant's statement voluntary?
— No → **Inadmissible**
— Yes ↓

Was defendant in custody (*i.e.*, not free to leave) when the statement was made?
— No → **Admissible** unless defendant has already been charged—if so, there is a Sixth Amendment right to counsel (unless waived) at all post-charge interrogations regarding the offense charged.
— Yes ↓

Was the statement made in response to known police interrogation (any words *or* conduct likely to elicit a response)?
— No → **Admissible**
— Yes ↓

Were *Miranda* warnings given?
— No → **Inadmissible** unless the interrogation was prompted by concern for public safety.
— Yes ↓

Did defendant knowingly and voluntarily waive **both** the right to remain silent and the right to an attorney?
— No →
- If defendant invoked only the right to remain silent and police continued questioning, confession **inadmissible** unless police scrupulously honored the request by, at the least, not badgering defendant and waiting a significant time for requestioning.
- If defendant requested counsel, a confession in response to further questioning without counsel is **inadmissible** unless defendant reinitiated questioning.

— Yes ↓

Admissible

Note: Confessions obtained in violation of *Miranda* are admissible to **impeach** defendant's trial testimony.

And note: If inadmissible confessions are erroneously admitted into evidence, a resulting conviction need not be reversed if there is other overwhelming evidence of guilt (the "harmless error" test).

CMR **Exam Tip** Despite the fact that the *Miranda* warnings mention a right to counsel, the failure to give the warnings violates a defendant's **Fifth Amendment** right to be free from compelled self-incrimination, not his Sixth Amendment right to counsel. Thus, do not be fooled by an answer choice that states such failure is a violation of defendant's Sixth Amendment rights.

2. **When Required**

Anyone in the custody of the government and accused of a crime must be given *Miranda* warnings **prior** to interrogation by the police.

a. **Governmental Conduct**

Generally, *Miranda* warnings are necessary only if the defendant **knows** that he is being interrogated by a **government agent**.

b. **Custody Requirement**

Whether a person is in custody depends on whether the person's freedom of action is denied in a significant way based on the **objective** circumstances (*e.g.,* an arrest constitutes custody; a routine traffic stop does not constitute custody).

c. **Interrogation Requirement**

"Interrogation" includes any words or conduct by the police that they should know would **likely elicit a response** from the defendant. Thus, *Miranda* warnings are not required before spontaneous statements are made by a defendant. Note that routine booking questions do not constitute interrogation.

d. **Waiver**

A suspect can waive his *Miranda* rights, but the prosecution must prove that the waiver was knowing, voluntary, and intelligent.

e. **Types of Statements**

Miranda applies to both inculpatory statements and exculpatory statements (*e.g.,* "I didn't shoot V, you did").

f. **Inapplicable at Grand Jury Hearing**

The *Miranda* requirements do not apply to a witness testifying before a grand jury, even if the witness was compelled by subpoena to be there.

3. **Right to Terminate Interrogation**

The accused may terminate police interrogation any time prior to or during the interrogation by invoking either the right to remain silent or the right to counsel.

a. **Right to Remain Silent**

If the accused indicates that he wishes to remain silent, the police must scrupulously honor this request by not badgering the accused, although the Supreme Court has allowed later questioning to occur on an unrelated crime.

b. **Right to Counsel**

If the accused **unambiguously** indicates that he wishes to speak to counsel, **all questioning must cease** until counsel has been provided unless the accused then waives his

right to counsel (*e.g.*, by reinitiating questioning). The request must be specific (*i.e.*, indicate that the defendant desires assistance in dealing with interrogation). Allowing defendant to consult with counsel and then resuming interrogation after counsel has left generally does not satisfy the right to counsel—counsel must be present during the interrogation unless defendant has waived the right.

CMR Exam Tip Note the difference here depending on what the defendant asks: If the defendant indicates that he wishes to remain silent, the police probably may requestion him about a different crime after a break if fresh warnings are administered. If the defendant requests counsel, the police may not resume interrogating defendant until counsel is provided or the defendant initiates the questioning.

4. Effect of Violation

Generally, evidence obtained in violation of the *Miranda* rules is inadmissible at trial under the exclusionary rule.

a. Use of Confession for Impeachment

Statements obtained in violation of the *Miranda* rules may be used to impeach the ***defendant's*** trial testimony, but may not be used as evidence of guilt.

b. Warnings After Questioning and Confession

If the police obtain a confession from a defendant without giving him *Miranda* warnings and then give the defendant *Miranda* warnings and obtain a subsequent confession, the subsequent confession will be inadmissible if the "question first, warn later" nature of the questioning was intentional (*i.e.*, the facts make it seem like the police used this as a scheme to get around the *Miranda* requirements). However, a subsequent valid confession may be admissible if the original unwarned questioning seemed unplanned and the failure to give *Miranda* warnings seemed inadvertent.

c. Nontestimonial Fruits of an Unwarned Confession

If the police fail to give *Miranda* warnings and during interrogation a suspect gives the police information that leads to nontestimonial evidence, the evidence will be suppressed if the failure was purposeful, but if the failure was not purposeful, the evidence probably will not be suppressed.

5. Public Safety Exception

The Supreme Court has allowed interrogation without *Miranda* warnings where it was reasonably prompted by a concern for public safety (*e.g.*, to locate a hidden gun that could have caused injury to innocent persons).

V. PRETRIAL IDENTIFICATION

A. SUBSTANTIVE BASES FOR ATTACK

1. Sixth Amendment Right to Counsel

A suspect has a right to the presence of an attorney at any ***post-charge*** lineup or showup. An accused does ***not*** have a right to counsel at photo identifications or when police take physical evidence, such as handwriting exemplars or fingerprints, from him.

Exam Tip Recall that the right to counsel *before* trial is very limited and does not cover procedures where defendant is not personally confronted by the witness against him (as in photo identification).

2. **Due Process Standard**

    A defendant can attack an identification as denying due process if the identification is *unnecessarily suggestive* and there is a *substantial likelihood of misidentification*.

 Exam Tip Since a lineup does not involve compulsion to give "testimonial" evidence, a suspect's Fifth Amendment right against compelled self-incrimination does not apply. Thus, the defendant may not refuse to participate in a lineup on this basis.

B. THE REMEDY

The remedy for unconstitutional identifications is exclusion of the in-court identification.

1. **Independent Source**

    A witness may make an in-court identification despite the existence of an unconstitutional pretrial identification if the in-court identification has an independent source. The most common independent source is opportunity to observe at the time of the crime (*e.g.*, the witness viewed the defendant close up for 40 minutes during commission of the crime).

2. **Hearing**

    Admissibility of identification evidence should be determined at a suppression hearing in the absence of the jury, but exclusion of the jury is not constitutionally required. The government bears the burden of proving that: (i) counsel was present; (ii) the accused waived counsel; or (iii) there is an independent source for the in-court identification. The defendant must prove an alleged due process violation.

VI. PRETRIAL PROCEDURES

A. PRELIMINARY HEARING TO DETERMINE PROBABLE CAUSE TO DETAIN

A defendant's liberty can be restricted only on a finding of probable cause. If probable cause has already been determined (*e.g.*, the arrest was pursuant to a warrant or a grand jury indictment), no preliminary hearing to determine probable cause need be held. If probable cause has not already been determined and there are *significant constraints on an arrestee's liberty* (*e.g.*, jail or bail, but not release on recognizance), a preliminary hearing to determine probable cause must be held within a reasonable time (*e.g.*, 48 hours). The hearing is an informal, nonadversarial proceeding. There is no real remedy for a denial of the hearing, but evidence discovered as a result of the unlawful detention can be excluded under the exclusionary rule.

B. PRETRIAL DETENTION—BAIL

Most state constitutions create a right to be released on bail unless the charge is a capital one. Generally, bail can be set no higher than is necessary to assure the defendant's appearance at trial. Refusal to grant bail or the setting of excessive bail may be appealed immediately; however, the Supreme Court has upheld portions of the federal Bail Reform Act that allow arrestees to be held without bail if they pose a danger or would fail to appear at trial.

 Exam Tip Since the Supreme Court has never held that the Eighth Amendment provision for bail applies to the states, the Eighth Amendment is not a very strong argument against a state's denial of bail. If, however, a state provides for bail (and most states do), arbitrary denials of bail will violate *due process*—detainees must be given the opportunity to prove eligibility.

1. **Defendant Incompetent to Stand Trial**

   Standards for commitment and subsequent release of defendants incompetent to stand trial must be essentially identical with those for commitment of persons not charged with a crime; otherwise there is a denial of equal protection.

C. GRAND JURIES

1. **Use of Grand Jury**

   The Fifth Amendment right to indictment by grand jury has not been incorporated into the Fourteenth Amendment, but some state constitutions require grand jury indictment. Most states east of the Mississippi and the federal system use the grand jury as a regular part of the charging process. Western states generally charge by filing an information—a written accusation of the crime prepared and presented by the prosecutor.

2. **Grand Jury Proceedings**

   a. **Secrecy and Defendant's Lack of Access**

      Grand jury proceedings are conducted in secret. The defendant has *no right* to notice that the grand jury is considering an indictment against him, to be present and confront witnesses at the proceeding, or to introduce evidence before the grand jury.

   b. **No Right to Counsel or to *Miranda* Warnings**

      A witness subpoenaed to testify before the grand jury does not have the right to receive *Miranda* warnings, nor is he entitled to a warning that he is a "potential defendant" when called to testify before the grand jury. Witnesses have no right to have an attorney present.

   c. **No Right to Have Evidence Excluded**

      A grand jury may base its indictment on evidence that would be inadmissible at trial, and an indicted defendant may not have the indictment quashed on the ground that it is based on illegally obtained evidence.

    Exam Tip For purposes of the Multistate Bar Exam, keep in mind these major differences between grand jury proceedings and criminal trials:

   - The "defendant" (grand jury witness) has no right to have counsel present during his grand jury testimony;

   - The grand jury may consider evidence that would be excluded at the criminal trial (*e.g.,* illegally obtained evidence or hearsay); and

   - The "defendant" (grand jury witness) must appear if called, although he can refuse to answer specific questions on the grounds that they may incriminate him.

   d. **No Right to Challenge Subpoena**

      There is no right to challenge a subpoena on the Fourth Amendment grounds that the grand jury lacked "probable cause"—or any reason at all—to call a witness for questioning.

e. Exclusion of Minorities

A conviction resulting from an indictment issued by a grand jury from which members of a minority group have been excluded will be reversed *without regard* to harmlessness of error.

CMR **Exam Tip** For purposes of the Multistate Bar Exam, exclusion of minorities is about the only defect sufficient to quash a grand jury indictment.

D. SPEEDY TRIAL

1. Standards

A determination of whether a defendant's Sixth Amendment right to a speedy trial has been violated is made by an evaluation of the *totality of the circumstances*. Factors considered are the length of delay, reason for delay, whether defendant asserted his right, and prejudice to defendant. The remedy for a violation of the right to speedy trial is dismissal with prejudice.

2. When Right Attaches

The right to speedy trial does not attach until the defendant has been *arrested or charged*. If the defendant is charged and is incarcerated in another jurisdiction, reasonable efforts must be used to obtain the presence of the defendant. Also, it is a violation of the right to speedy trial to permit the prosecution to indefinitely suspend charges.

Note: The defendant does not need to know of the charges for the speedy trial rights to attach.

CMR **Exam Tip** When a speedy trial issue is raised in a question, first check the timing—has the defendant been arrested or charged? If not, there is no right to a speedy trial.

E. PROSECUTORIAL DUTY TO DISCLOSE EXCULPATORY INFORMATION AND NOTICE OF DEFENSES

1. Prosecutor's Duty to Disclose Exculpatory Evidence

The government has a duty to disclose material, exculpatory evidence to the defendant. Failure to disclose such evidence—whether willful or inadvertent—violates the Due Process Clause and is grounds for reversing a conviction if the defendant can prove that: (i) the evidence is *favorable* to him because it either impeaches or is exculpatory; and (ii) *prejudice has resulted* (*i.e.*, there is a *reasonable probability* that the result of the case would have been different if the undisclosed evidence had been presented at trial).

2. Notice of Alibi and Intent to Present Insanity Defense

If the defendant is going to use an alibi or insanity defense, he must notify the prosecution. If an alibi is to be used, the defendant must give the prosecution a list of his witnesses. The prosecution must give the defendant a list of the witnesses it will use to rebut the defense. The prosecutor may not comment at trial on defendant's failure to produce a witness named as supporting the alibi or on failure to present the alibi itself.

F. COMPETENCY TO STAND TRIAL

1. Competency and Insanity Distinguished

Insanity is a defense to a criminal charge based on the defendant's *mental condition at the time he committed the charged crime*. A defendant acquitted by reason of insanity may not be retried and convicted, although he may be hospitalized under some circumstances. *Incompetency* to stand trial, on the other hand, is not a defense to the charge, but rather is a bar to trial. It is based on the defendant's *mental condition at the time of trial*. If defendant later regains his competency, he can then be tried and convicted.

2. Due Process Standard

A defendant is incompetent to stand trial if he either (i) lacks a rational as well as factual understanding of the charges and proceedings, or (ii) lacks sufficient present ability to consult with his lawyer with a reasonable degree of understanding. The state may place on the defendant the burden of proving incompetency by a preponderance of the evidence, but requiring the defendant to show incompetency by "clear and convincing" evidence is unconstitutional.

3. Detention of Defendant

A defendant who has successfully asserted the insanity defense may be confined to a mental hospital for a term longer than the maximum period of incarceration for the offense. However, the defendant cannot be indefinitely committed after regaining sanity merely because he is unable to prove himself not dangerous to others.

G. PRETRIAL PUBLICITY

Excessive pretrial publicity prejudicial to the defendant may require change of venue or retrial.

VII. TRIAL

A. BASIC RIGHT TO A FAIR TRIAL

1. Right to Public Trial

The Sixth and Fourteenth Amendments guarantee the right to a public trial, but the right varies with the stage of the proceeding involved.

a. Pretrial Proceedings

Preliminary probable cause hearings are presumptively open to the public and press, as are *pretrial* suppression hearings, although the latter may be closed to the public under limited circumstances (*e.g.,* the party seeking closure has an overriding interest likely to be prejudiced by disclosure and there is no reasonable alternative besides closure).

b. Trial

The press and public have a First Amendment right to attend the *trial itself*, even when the defense and prosecution agree to close it. The state may constitutionally permit televising criminal proceedings over the defendant's objection.

2. Right to Unbiased Judge

Due process is violated if the judge is shown to have *actual malice* against the defendant or to have had a *financial interest* in having the trial result in a guilty verdict.

3. **Must Judge Be Lawyer?**
A defendant in a minor misdemeanor prosecution has no right to have the trial judge be a lawyer if upon conviction the defendant has a right to trial de novo in a court with a lawyer-judge, but for serious crimes, the judge probably must be law-trained.

4. **Other Due Process Rights**
Due process is violated if:

(i) The trial is conducted in a manner making it *unlikely that the jury gave the evidence reasonable consideration*;

(ii) The state compels the defendant to stand trial in *prison clothing*;

(iii) The state compels the defendant to stand trial or appear at penalty phase proceedings *visibly shackled*, unless the court finds the shackling justified by concerns about courtroom security or escape; or

(iv) The jury is exposed to *influence favorable to the prosecution*.

Due process does not require the police to preserve all items that might be used as exculpatory evidence at trial, but does prohibit bad faith destruction.

B. RIGHT TO TRIAL BY JURY

1. **Right to Jury Trial Only for "Serious" Offenses**
There is no constitutional right to jury trial for petty offenses, but only for serious offenses. An offense is serious if imprisonment for *more than six months* is authorized. Also, there is no right to jury trial in juvenile delinquency proceedings.

   a. **Contempt**
   For civil contempt proceedings, there is no jury trial right. For criminal contempt proceedings, cumulative penalties totaling more than six months cannot be imposed without affording the defendant the right to a jury trial. If a judge summarily imposes punishment for contempt *during trial*, penalties may aggregate more than six months without a jury trial.

      1) **Probation**
      A judge may place a contemnor on probation for up to five years without affording him the right to a jury trial, as long as revocation of probation would not result in imprisonment for more than six months.

2. **Number and Unanimity of Jurors**
There is no constitutional right to a jury of 12, but there must be at least six jurors to satisfy the right to a jury trial. The Supreme Court has upheld convictions that were less than unanimous, but probably would not approve an 8-4 vote for conviction. Six-person juries must be unanimous.

3. **Right to Venire Selected from Representative Cross-Section of Community**
A defendant has a right to have the jury selected from a representative cross-section of the

community. He need only show the underrepresentation of a distinct and numerically significant group in the venire to show his jury trial right was violated. Note that a defendant does not have the right to proportional representation of all groups on his *particular jury*.

a. **Use of Peremptory Challenges for Racial and Gender-Based Discrimination**
Although generally a prosecutor may exercise peremptory challenges for any reason, the Equal Protection Clause forbids the use of peremptory challenges to exclude potential jurors solely on account of their race or gender. An equal protection-based attack on peremptory strikes involves three steps: (i) The defendant must show *facts or circumstances that raise an inference* that the exclusion was based on race or gender. (ii) Upon such a showing, the prosecutor must come forward with a *race-neutral explanation* for the strike (even an unreasonable explanation is sufficient, as long as it is race-neutral). (iii) The judge then determines whether the prosecutor's explanation was the genuine reason for striking the juror, or merely a pretext for purposeful discrimination. If the judge believes that the *prosecutor was sincere*, the strike may be upheld.

4. **Right to Impartial Jury**

a. **Right to Questioning on Racial Bias**
A defendant is entitled to questioning on voir dire specifically directed to racial prejudice whenever race is bound up in the case or he is accused of an interracial *capital* crime.

b. **Juror Opposition to Death Penalty**
In capital punishment cases, a state may not automatically exclude for cause all those who express a doubt or scruple about the death penalty; it must be determined whether the juror's views would prevent or substantially impair performance of his duties in accordance with his instructions and oath. A death sentence imposed by a jury from which a juror was improperly excluded is subject to automatic reversal.

c. **Juror Favoring Death Penalty**
If a jury is to decide whether a defendant is to be sentenced to death, on voir dire the defendant must be allowed to ask potential jurors if they would automatically give the death penalty upon a guilty verdict. A juror who answers affirmatively must be excluded for cause because such a juror cannot perform his duties in accordance with instructions as to mitigating circumstances.

d. **Use of Peremptory Challenge to Maintain Impartial Jury**
If a trial court refuses to exclude for cause a juror whom the court should exclude, and the defendant uses a peremptory challenge to exclude the juror, there is no constitutional violation.

5. **Inconsistent Verdicts**
Inconsistent verdicts (*e.g.*, finding defendant guilty and co-defendant not guilty on the same evidence) are *not* reviewable.

6. **Sentence Enhancement**
If substantive law provides that a sentence may be increased beyond the statutory maximum

for a crime if additional facts (other than prior conviction) are proved, proof of the facts must be *submitted to the jury* and proved beyond reasonable doubt; the defendant's right to jury trial is violated if the judge makes the determination. The same general rule applies to sentencing enhancements after guilty pleas. In deciding whether to overturn a sentence for failure to submit a sentencing factor to the jury, the harmless error test is applied.

a. Distinguish—Judge May Decide Whether Sentences Run Consecutively
A state legislature may give to its judges (rather than the jury) the power to decide whether sentences for multiple crimes are to run consecutively or concurrently, even though the decision is based on the facts of the case.

C. RIGHT TO COUNSEL
A defendant has a right to counsel. Violation of this right *at trial*, including erroneous disqualification of defendant's privately retained counsel, requires reversal. For nontrial denials, the harmless error test is applied.

CMR **Exam Tip** Remember that the right to counsel is available in misdemeanor cases only if imprisonment is actually imposed. Thus, if an exam question involves a nonfelony and defendant asks for counsel, is denied, and is convicted, whether the right to counsel has been violated depends on defendant's sentence: if he receives no imprisonment, his right has not been violated; if he receives prison time, his right has been violated.

1. Waiver of Right to Counsel at Trial and Right to Defend Oneself
A defendant has a right to defend himself at trial if, in the judgment of the judge, his waiver is *knowing and intelligent* and, based on the trial judge's consideration of the defendant's emotional and psychological state, he is *competent* to proceed pro se. Note that a defendant does not have a right to self-representation on appeal.

2. Indigence and Recoupment of Cost
The state generally provides counsel in close cases of indigence, but may then seek reimbursement from those convicted defendants who later become able to pay.

3. Effective Assistance of Counsel
The Sixth Amendment right to counsel includes the right to *effective* counsel. This right extends to the first appeal. Effective assistance of counsel is *generally presumed*.

a. Circumstances Constituting Ineffective Assistance
An ineffective assistance claimant must show:

(i) *Deficient performance* by counsel; and

(ii) But for the deficiency, the *result of the proceeding would have been different* (*e.g.,* defendant would not have been convicted or his sentence would have been shorter).

The defendant must point out specific deficiencies and cannot base the claim on inexperience, lack of time to prepare, the gravity of the charges, the complexity of defenses, or accessibility of witnesses to counsel.

b.   **Circumstances Not Constituting Ineffective Assistance**
Circumstances *not* constituting *ineffective* assistance include trial tactics and the failure to raise a constitutional defense that is later invalidated.

4.   **Conflicts of Interest**
Joint representation is not per se invalid. However, if an attorney advises the trial court of a resulting conflict of interest at or before trial, and the court refuses to appoint separate counsel, the defendant is entitled to automatic reversal.

a.   **Conflict with Attorney**
A defendant's conflict of interest with his attorney is rarely a ground for relief.

b.   **No Right to Joint Representation**
A defendant has no right to be jointly represented with his co-defendants if the government can show a potential conflict of interest.

5.   **Right to Support Services for Defense**
Where a defendant has made a preliminary showing that he is likely to be able to use the insanity defense, the state must provide a psychiatrist for the preparation of the defense.

6.   **Seizure of Funds Constitutional**
The right to counsel does not forbid the seizure of drug money and property obtained with drug money, even where defendant was going to use such money or property to pay an attorney.

7.   **Right Limited While Testifying**
A defendant has no right to consult with her attorney while testifying, and may be sequestered from her attorney during short breaks (*e.g.,* 15 minutes as opposed to overnight).

D.   **RIGHT TO CONFRONT WITNESSES**
The Sixth Amendment grants to a defendant in a criminal prosecution the right to confront adverse witnesses. The right is not absolute: Face to face confrontation is not required when preventing such confrontation serves an important public purpose (*e.g.,* protecting child witnesses from trauma). Also, a judge may remove a disruptive defendant, and a defendant may voluntarily leave the courtroom during trial.

1.   **Introduction of Co-Defendant's Confession**
If two persons are tried together and one has given a confession that implicates the other, the right of confrontation prohibits use of that statement, even where the confession interlocks with the defendant's own confession, which is admitted. However, such a statement may be admitted if:

a.   All portions referring to the other defendant can be *eliminated*;

b.   The ***confessing defendant takes the stand*** and subjects himself to cross-examination with respect to truth or falsity of what the statement asserts; or

c.   The confession of the nontestifying co-defendant is being used ***to rebut the defendant's claim that his confession was obtained coercively***.

2. **Prior Testimonial Statement of Unavailable Witness**
    Under the Confrontation Clause, prior testimonial evidence (*e.g.,* statements made at prior judicial proceedings) may not be admitted unless (i) the declarant is unavailable and (ii) the defendant had an *opportunity to cross-examine* the declarant at the time the statement was made.

    a. **What Is Testimonial?**
        The Court has not provided a comprehensive definition of the term "testimonial," but has held that it includes, at a minimum, statements from a preliminary hearing, a grand jury hearing, a former trial, or police interrogation conducted to establish or prove *past acts*. However, statements from police interrogations intended to aid the police in responding to an *ongoing emergency*—such as answering a 911 operator's question while reporting a crime in progress—are not testimonial.

        1) **Results of Forensic Lab Testing**
            The results of forensic laboratory testing are testimonial in nature. Therefore, a lab report is not admissible into evidence at trial under the Confrontation Clause unless the technician who produced the test report is unavailable and the defendant had an opportunity to cross-examine him.

    b. **Forfeiture by Wrongdoing**
        A defendant can be held to have forfeited a Confrontation Clause claim by wrongdoing. However, the Court will not find a forfeiture by wrongdoing unless the wrongdoing was *intended to keep the witness from testifying* (*e.g.,* a statement made to the police by a victim who was later killed by defendant cannot be admitted in defendant's murder trial absent evidence that defendant murdered the victim to keep her from testifying).

E. **BURDEN OF PROOF AND SUFFICIENCY OF EVIDENCE**
    The Due Process Clause requires in all criminal cases that the *state* prove guilt beyond a reasonable doubt. The presumption of innocence is a basic component of a fair trial. However, the state may generally impose the burden of proof upon the defendant in regard to an affirmative defense, such as insanity or self-defense.

    1. **Presumptions**
        A mandatory presumption or a presumption that shifts the burden of proof to the defendant violates the Fourteenth Amendment's requirement that the state prove every element of the crime beyond a reasonable doubt.

VIII. GUILTY PLEAS AND PLEA BARGAINING

A. **TAKING THE PLEA**

    1. **Advising Defendant of the Charge, the Potential Penalty, and His Rights**
        The judge must determine that the plea is *voluntary and intelligent.* This must be done by addressing the defendant personally in open court *on the record*. Specifically, the judge must be sure that the defendant knows and understands things like:

      (i)   *The nature of the charge* to which the plea is offered and the *crucial elements* of the crime charged;

      (ii) The *maximum possible penalty* and any *mandatory minimum*; and

      (iii) That he has a *right not to plead guilty* and that if he does plead guilty, he *waives the right to trial*.

a. Attorney May Inform Defendant
The judge need not personally explain the elements of each charge to the defendant on the record; it is sufficient that the record reflects that the nature of the charge and the elements of the crime were explained to the defendant by his own counsel.

2. Remedy
The remedy for a failure to meet the standards for taking a plea is withdrawal of the plea and pleading anew.

B. COLLATERAL ATTACKS ON GUILTY PLEAS AFTER SENTENCE
Those pleas that are seen as an intelligent choice among a defendant's alternatives are immune from collateral attack. But a plea can be set aside for (i) involuntariness (failure to meet standards for taking a plea), (ii) lack of jurisdiction, (iii) ineffective assistance of counsel, or (iv) failure to keep the plea bargain.

C. PLEA BARGAINING
A plea bargain will be enforced against the prosecutor and the defendant, but not against the judge, who does not have to accept the plea. A guilty plea is not involuntary merely because it was entered in response to the prosecution's threat to charge defendant with a more serious crime if he does not plead guilty. There is no prosecutorial vindictiveness in charging a more serious offense when defendant demands a jury trial.

D. COLLATERAL EFFECTS OF GUILTY PLEAS
A guilty plea conviction may be used as a conviction in other proceedings when relevant (*e.g.*, as the basis for sentence enhancement). However, a guilty plea neither admits the legality of incriminating evidence nor waives Fourth Amendment claims in a subsequent civil damages action.

IX. CONSTITUTIONAL RIGHTS IN RELATION TO SENTENCING AND PUNISHMENT

A. PROCEDURAL RIGHTS IN SENTENCING
A defendant has a *right to counsel* during sentencing. The usual sentence may be based on hearsay and uncross-examined reports (*i.e.*, defendant has *no right to confrontation or cross-examination*). However, where a magnified sentence is based on a statute that requires new findings of fact to be made (*e.g.*, defendant is mentally ill), those facts must be found in a context that grants a right to confrontation and cross-examination.

1. Capital Sentencing
A defendant in a death penalty case must have more opportunity for confrontation than need be given a defendant in other sentencing proceedings.

B. RESENTENCING AFTER SUCCESSFUL APPEAL AND RECONVICTION

If a greater punishment is imposed on a defendant who has been reconvicted after a successful appeal than was imposed at the first trial, the judge must set forth in the record the reasons for the harsher sentence. This ensures that the defendant is not vindictively penalized for exercising his right to appeal.

1. Exceptions

A judge need not give reasons if the greater sentence was imposed upon a de novo trial or in a state that uses jury sentencing, unless the second jury was told of the first jury's sentence.

C. SUBSTANTIVE RIGHTS IN REGARD TO PUNISHMENT

The Eighth Amendment prohibits *cruel and unusual punishment*. A penalty that is grossly disproportionate to the seriousness of the offense committed is cruel and unusual. State appellate courts do not have to compare the death sentence imposed in a case under appeal with other penalties imposed in similar cases.

1. Death Penalty

a. For Murder

The death penalty can be imposed only under a statutory scheme that gives the judge or jury reasonable discretion, full information concerning defendants, and guidance in making the decision. The statute cannot be vague. Moreover, it must allow the sentencing body to consider all mitigating evidence.

1) Based on Prior Convictions

If the death sentence is partly based on the aggravating factor of defendant's prior conviction, the sentence must be reversed if the prior conviction is invalidated.

2) Standard of Review

A death sentence that has been affected by a vague or otherwise unconstitutional factor can still be upheld, but only if all aggravating and mitigating factors involved are reweighed and death is still found to be appropriate.

b. For Rape or Felony Murder

The Eighth Amendment prohibits imposition of the death penalty for the crime of raping an adult woman or a child if the rape was neither intended to result in nor did result in death. *Rationale:* The penalty is disproportionate to the offense. Also, the same logic precludes the death penalty for felony murder unless the felony murderer's participation was major and he acted with reckless indifference to the value of human life.

c. Sanity Requirement

The Eighth Amendment prohibits executing a prisoner who is insane at the time of execution, even if he was sane at the time the crime was committed.

d. Mental Retardation

It is cruel and unusual punishment to impose the death penalty on a person who is mentally retarded.

e. **For Minors**

Execution of persons who were under 18 years old at the time they committed their offense (including murder) violates the Eighth Amendment.

f. **Lethal Injection**

The mere possibility that the three-drug lethal injection protocol used by many states to carry out executions *might* be administered improperly and thus cause the condemned unnecessary pain does not make the procedure cruel and unusual punishment. It would be cruel and unusual only if the condemned can prove that there is a serious risk of inflicting unnecessary pain or that an alternative procedure is feasible, may be readily implemented, and in fact significantly reduces substantial risk of severe pain.

2. **Status Crimes**

A statute that makes it a crime to have a given "status" violates the Eighth Amendment because it punishes a mere propensity to engage in dangerous behavior. However, it is permissible to make criminal specific activity related to a certain status (*e.g.,* driving while intoxicated).

3. **Considering Defendant's Perjury**

In determining the sentence, the trial judge may take into account a belief that the defendant committed perjury while testifying at trial on his own behalf.

4. **Imprisonment of Indigents for Nonpayment**

Where aggregate imprisonment exceeds the maximum period fixed by statute and results directly from involuntary nonpayment of a fine or court costs, there is an impermissible discrimination and violation of the Equal Protection Clause.

X. CONSTITUTIONAL PROBLEMS ON APPEAL

A. **NO RIGHT TO APPEAL**

There is no federal constitutional right to an appeal.

B. **EQUAL PROTECTION AND RIGHT TO COUNSEL ON APPEAL**

If an avenue of post-conviction review is provided, conditions that make the review less accessible to the poor than to the rich violate equal protection. Thus, indigents must be given counsel at state expense during a first appeal granted to all *as a matter of right* and for appeals of guilty pleas and pleas of nolo contendere.

In a jurisdiction using a two-tier system of appellate courts with discretionary review by the highest court, an indigent defendant need not be provided with counsel during the second, discretionary appeal.

C. **RETROACTIVITY**

If the Supreme Court announces a new rule of criminal procedure (*e.g.,* one not dictated by precedent) in a case on direct review, the rule must be applied to all other cases on direct review.

XI. COLLATERAL ATTACK UPON CONVICTION

A. AVAILABILITY OF COLLATERAL ATTACK

After appeal is no longer available or has proven unsuccessful, defendants may generally still attack their convictions collaterally.

B. HABEAS CORPUS PROCEEDING

An indigent has no right to appointed counsel at a habeas corpus proceeding. Petitioner has the burden of proof by *preponderance of evidence* to show an unlawful detention. The state may appeal the grant of a writ of habeas corpus. A defendant generally may bring a habeas petition only if the defendant is in custody. Generally, this includes anyone who has not fully served the sentence about which he wishes to complain.

XII. RIGHTS DURING PUNISHMENT

A. RIGHT TO COUNSEL AT PAROLE AND PROBATION REVOCATION

If revocation of probation also involves imposition of a new sentence, the defendant is entitled to representation by counsel in all cases in which she is entitled to counsel at trial. If, after probation revocation, an already imposed sentence of imprisonment springs into application, or if the case involves parole revocation, the right to counsel is available *only if representation is necessary* to a fair hearing (*e.g.,* defendant denies commission of alleged acts, or issues are otherwise difficult to present and develop).

B. PRISONERS' RIGHTS

Prisoners' rights issues rarely appear on the Multistate Bar Exam, and when they do appear they usually involve the same constitutional analysis as set out in the general constitutional law outline. The most important rules peculiar to criminal procedure are:

1. **Due Process**

    Prison regulations impinge on due process rights only if the regulations impose "*atypical and significant hardship*" in relation to the ordinary incidents of prison life.

2. **No Fourth Amendment Protection in Cells**

    Prisoners have no reasonable expectation of privacy in their cells and so have no Fourth Amendment protection with respect to searches of their cells.

3. **Right of Access to Courts**

    Prisoners must be given reasonable access to the courts.

4. **First Amendment Rights**

    Prisoners' First Amendment rights of freedom of speech, association, and religion may be burdened by regulations *reasonably related to penological interests* (*e.g.,* running a safe and secure prison). Note that *incoming* mail can be broadly regulated, but outgoing mail generally cannot be regulated. Note also that a federal statute prohibits states from interfering with a prisoner's religious practices absent a compelling interest.

5. Right to Adequate Medical Care
Prisoners have a right to adequate medical care under the Eighth Amendment prohibition against cruel and unusual punishment.

C. NO RIGHT TO BE FREE FROM DISABILITIES UPON COMPLETION OF SENTENCE
A person convicted of a felony may be unable to vote in state elections, and this disability can constitutionally continue beyond the term of her sentence.

XIII. DOUBLE JEOPARDY

A. WHEN JEOPARDY ATTACHES
Under the Fifth Amendment, a person may not be retried for the same offense once jeopardy has attached. Jeopardy attaches in a jury trial at the empaneling and swearing of the jury. In bench trials jeopardy attaches when the first witness is sworn. Commencement of a juvenile proceeding bars a subsequent criminal trial for the same offense. Jeopardy generally does not attach in civil proceedings other than juvenile proceedings.

B. EXCEPTIONS PERMITTING RETRIAL
Certain exceptions permit retrial of a defendant even if jeopardy has attached:

1. A state may retry a defendant whose first trial ends in a ***hung jury***.

2. A trial may be discontinued and the defendant reprosecuted for the same offense when there is ***manifest necessity*** to abort the original trial or when termination occurs at the behest of the defendant on any ground not constituting acquittal on the merits.

3. A state may retry a defendant who has ***successfully appealed*** a conviction unless the ground for reversal was insufficient evidence to support a guilty verdict. Retrial is permitted when reversal is based on the ***weight*** (rather than sufficiency) of the evidence. However, on retrial, a defendant ***may not be tried for a greater offense*** than that for which he was convicted. A harsher sentence may be imposed for reasons other than vindictiveness for taking an appeal, but if the jury found that the death penalty was not appropriate in the first trial, a death sentence may not be imposed at the second trial.

4. Charges may be reinstated after a defendant ***breaches*** her ***plea bargain***.

C. SAME OFFENSE

1. General Rule—When Two Crimes Not the Same Offense
Two crimes are the same offense unless ***each crime requires proof of an additional element*** that the other does not require, even though some of the same facts may be necessary to prove both crimes.

2. Cumulative Punishments for Offenses Constituting the Same Crime
Even if two crimes constitute the same offense under this test, multiple punishments are permissible if there was a ***legislative intent*** to have the cumulative punishments (*e.g.*, a defendant can be sentenced both for robbery and using a weapon during the commission of a crime if statutes so provide).

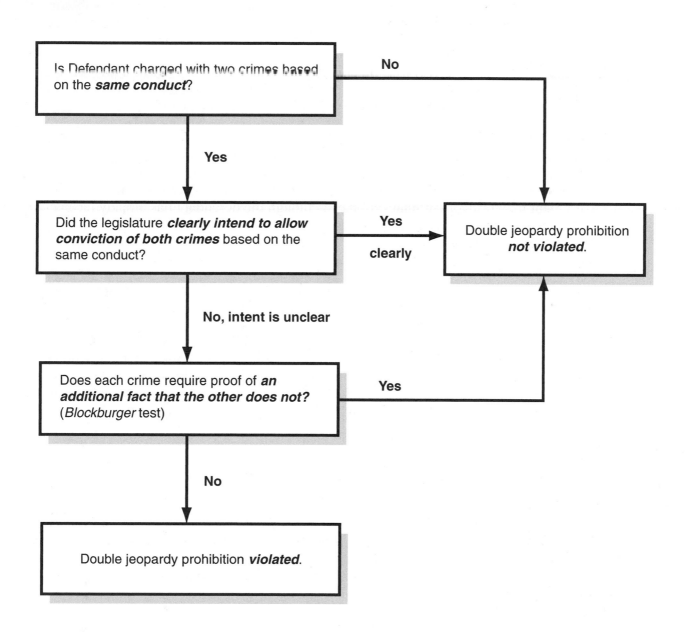

CMR
APPROACH
CHART

"SAME OFFENSE" UNDER DOUBLE JEOPARDY CLAUSE

Is Defendant charged with two crimes based on the **same conduct**?

No

Yes

Did the legislature **clearly intend to allow conviction of both crimes** based on the same conduct?

Yes

clearly

Double jeopardy prohibition **not violated**.

No, intent is unclear

Does each crime require proof of **an additional fact that the other does not?** (*Blockburger* test)

Yes

No

Double jeopardy prohibition **violated**.

3. Lesser Included Offenses

Attachment of jeopardy for a greater offense bars retrial for lesser included offenses. Attachment of jeopardy for a lesser included offense bars retrial for a greater offense, except that retrial for murder is permitted if the victim dies after attachment of jeopardy for battery. A state may continue to prosecute a charged offense despite defendant's guilty plea to a lesser included or "allied" offense stemming from the same incident.

a. Exception—New Evidence

An exception to the double jeopardy bar exists if unlawful conduct that is subsequently used to prove the greater offense (i) has not occurred at the time of prosecution for the lesser offense or (ii) has not been discovered despite due diligence.

4. Conduct Used as a Sentence Enhancer

The Double Jeopardy Clause is not violated when a person is indicted for a crime the conduct of which was already used to enhance the defendant's sentence for another crime.

5. Subsequent Civil Actions

The Double Jeopardy Clause prohibits only repetitive *criminal* prosecutions. Thus, a state generally is free to bring a civil action against a defendant even if the defendant has already been criminally tried for the conduct out of which the civil action arises. Similarly, the government may bring a criminal action even though the defendant has already faced civil trial for the same conduct unless it is clear from the statutory scheme that the purpose or effect of the statute is to impose a criminal penalty.

D. SEPARATE SOVEREIGNS

The constitutional prohibition against double jeopardy does not apply to trials by separate sovereigns. Thus, a person may be tried for the same conduct by both the state and federal governments or by two states, but not by a state and its municipalities.

CMR | **Exam Tip** | Double jeopardy questions on the MBE occasionally raise the separate sovereign issue. The rule is simple: Separate sovereigns *can* try a defendant for the same offense. Beware of facts that try to divert you from this easy issue (*e.g.,* statements about juries being empaneled or witnesses sworn in—things that go to attachment). Attachment does not matter if there are two separate sovereigns.

On the other hand, remember that municipalities are considered part of the state, and so both a state and its municipality *cannot* validly try a defendant for the same offense.

E. APPEALS BY PROSECUTION

Even after jeopardy has attached, the prosecution may appeal any dismissal on defendant's motion that does not constitute an acquittal on the merits. Also, the Double Jeopardy Clause does not bar appeals by the prosecution if a successful appeal would not require a retrial. There is no bar to a government appeal of a *sentence* pursuant to statute permitting such review. However, if the jury fails to impose the death penalty, the prosecution may not seek the death penalty on retrial after successful appeal.

F. COLLATERAL ESTOPPEL

Under the doctrine of collateral estoppel, a defendant may not be tried or convicted of a crime if a prior prosecution by that sovereignty resulted in a factual determination inconsistent with one required for conviction.

XIV. PRIVILEGE AGAINST COMPELLED SELF-INCRIMINATION

A. WHO MAY ASSERT THE PRIVILEGE
Only natural persons may assert the privilege, not corporations or partnerships. The privilege is personal and so may be asserted by a defendant, witness, or party only if the answer to the question might tend to incriminate him.

B. WHEN PRIVILEGE MAY BE ASSERTED
A person may refuse to answer a question whenever his response might furnish a link in the chain of evidence needed to prosecute him. The privilege must be claimed in civil proceedings to prevent the privilege from being waived for a later criminal prosecution. Thus, if an individual responds to questions instead of claiming the privilege during a civil proceeding, he cannot later bar that evidence from a criminal prosecution on compelled self-incrimination grounds.

C. METHOD FOR INVOKING PRIVILEGE
A *criminal defendant* has a right not to take the witness stand at trial and not to be asked to do so. In any other situation, the privilege does not permit a person to avoid being sworn as a witness or being asked questions. Rather, the person must listen to the questions and specifically invoke the privilege rather than answer the questions. *Note:* Merely being required to furnish one's name after a *Terry* stop (*see* III.B.3.a.1), *supra*) generally does not violate the Fifth Amendment because disclosure of one's name generally poses no danger of incrimination.

D. SCOPE OF PROTECTION

1. Testimonial but Not Physical Evidence
The Fifth Amendment privilege protects only testimonial or communicative evidence and not real or physical evidence. For a suspect's communication to be considered testimonial, it must relate a factual assertion or disclose information.

2. Compulsory Production of Documents
A person served with a subpoena requiring production of documents tending to incriminate him generally has no basis in the privilege to refuse to comply, because the act of producing the documents does not involve testimonial self-incrimination.

3. Seizure of Incriminating Documents
The Fifth Amendment does not prohibit law enforcement officers from searching for and seizing documents tending to incriminate a person.

4. When Does Violation Occur?
A violation of the Self-Incrimination Clause does not occur until a person's compelled statements are used against him in a criminal case.

CMR   **Exam Tip**   For purposes of the Multistate Bar Exam, two of the most important things to remember about the Fifth Amendment self-incrimination privilege are:

- Only *testimonial* evidence is protected. Thus, a defendant has no self-incrimination basis to object to a lineup or other identification procedure—even if he is asked to say certain words (*e.g.,* "Your money or your life!"). This procedure does not involve testimonial evidence; the words are used for identification purposes and not as testimony.

- Likewise, only *compelled* testimonial evidence is privileged. Thus, if the defendant produced a writing of his own free will (*e.g.,* took incriminating notes of a meeting), the police may seize this writing, or the defendant may be compelled to produce it by subpoena, because he was not compelled to make the statement originally.

E. PROHIBITION AGAINST BURDENS ON ASSERTION OF PRIVILEGE

1. Comments on Defendant's Silence

A prosecutor may not comment on a defendant's silence after being arrested and receiving *Miranda* warnings. Neither may the prosecutor comment on a defendant's failure to testify at trial. However, a defendant, upon timely motion, is entitled to have the judge instruct the jury that they may not draw an adverse inference from the defendant's failure to testify. Moreover, the judge may offer this instruction sua sponte, even over the defendant's objection.

a. Exception

A prosecutor can comment on a defendant's failure to take the stand when the comment is in response to defense counsel's assertion that the defendant was not allowed to explain his side of the story.

b. Harmless Error Test Applies

When a prosecutor impermissibly comments on a defendant's silence, the harmless error test applies.

2. Penalties for Failure to Testify

The state may not chill exercise of the Fifth Amendment privilege against compelled self-incrimination by imposing penalties for failure to testify.

F. ELIMINATION OF PRIVILEGE

1. Grant of Immunity

A witness may be compelled to answer questions if granted adequate immunity from prosecution.

a. "Use and Derivative Use" Immunity Sufficient

"Use and derivative use" immunity guarantees that the witness's testimony and evidence located by means of the testimony will not be used against the witness. However, the witness may still be prosecuted if the prosecutor shows that the evidence to be used against the witness was derived from a source independent of the immunized testimony.

b. Immunized Testimony Involuntary

Testimony obtained by a promise of immunity is coerced and therefore involuntary. Thus, immunized testimony may not be used for impeachment of a defendant's testimony at trial. However, any immunized statements, whether true or untrue, can be used in a trial for perjury.

c. Use of Testimony by Another Sovereign Prohibited

Federal prosecutors may not use evidence obtained as a result of a state grant of immunity, and vice versa.

2. **No Possibility of Incrimination**
    A person has no privilege against compelled self-incrimination if there is no possibility of incrimination (*e.g.*, statute of limitations has run).

3. **Scope of Immunity**
    Immunity extends only to the offenses to which the question relates and does not protect against perjury committed during the immunized testimony.

G. WAIVER OF PRIVILEGE

A criminal defendant, by taking the witness stand, waives the privilege to the extent necessary to subject him to any cross-examination. A witness waives the privilege only if he discloses incriminating information.

XV. JUVENILE COURT PROCEEDINGS

A. RIGHTS THAT MUST BE AFFORDED

The following rights must be given to a child during trial of a delinquency proceeding: (i) written *notice* of charges, (ii) *assistance of counsel*, (iii) *opportunity to confront* and cross-examine witnesses, (iv) the *right not to testify*, and (v) the right to have *"guilt" established by proof beyond reasonable doubt*.

The Supreme Court has held that there is *no* right to trial by jury in delinquency proceedings. Pretrial detention of a juvenile is allowed where it is found that the juvenile is a "serious risk" to society, as long as the detention is for a strictly limited time before trial may be held.

B. DOUBLE JEOPARDY

If the juvenile court adjudicates a child a delinquent, jeopardy has attached and the prohibition against double jeopardy prevents him from being tried as an adult for the same behavior.

XVI. FORFEITURE ACTIONS

A. INTRODUCTION

Actions for forfeiture are brought directly against property and are generally regarded as quasi-criminal in nature. Certain constitutional rights may exist for those persons whose interest in property would be lost by forfeiture.

B. RIGHT TO PRE-SEIZURE NOTICE AND HEARING

The owner of *personal* property (and others with an interest in it) is not constitutionally entitled to notice and a hearing before the property is seized for purposes of a forfeiture proceeding. A hearing is, however, required before final forfeiture of the property. Where *real property* is seized, notice and an opportunity to be heard is required before the seizure of the real property unless the government can prove that exigent circumstances justify immediate seizure.

C. MAY BE SUBJECT TO EIGHTH AMENDMENT

1. **General Rule**

   The Supreme Court has held that the Excessive Fines Clause of the Eighth Amendment applies only to fines imposed as punishment; it does not apply to civil fines. Thus, *penal* forfeitures are subject to the Clause, but *civil* forfeitures are not. Even if the Clause applies, the forfeiture will not be "excessive" unless *grossly disproportionate* to the gravity of the offense.

2. **Compare—Nonpunitive Forfeiture**

   a. **Civil In Rem Forfeitures**

      Civil in rem forfeitures generally are *not* subject to the Excessive Fines Clause.

   b. **Monetary Forfeitures**

      Monetary forfeitures (*e.g.*, forfeiture of twice the value of illegally imported goods) brought in civil actions generally are *not* subject to the Eighth Amendment.

D. PROTECTION FOR "INNOCENT OWNER" NOT REQUIRED

The Due Process Clause does *not* require forfeiture statutes to provide an "innocent owner" defense (*e.g.*, a defense that the owner took all reasonable steps to avoid having the property used by another for illegal purposes), at least where the innocent owner *voluntarily entrusted* the property to the wrongdoer.

EVIDENCE

TABLE OF CONTENTS

EVIDENCE

I. GENERAL CONSIDERATIONS

A. SOURCES OF EVIDENCE LAW

There are three sources of evidence law: (i) state common law and miscellaneous state statutes, (ii) comprehensive state evidence codes, and (iii) the Federal Rules of Evidence.

CMR   **Exam Tip**   The Federal Rules govern on the Multistate Bar Examination ("MBE"). Beware of answer choices stating the correct common law rule, rather than the Federal Rule.

B. THRESHOLD ADMISSIBILITY ISSUES

Generally, relevant evidence is admissible if it is competent. Under the Federal Rules, "relevant evidence" tends to prove (probativeness) any fact of consequence to the action (materiality). Evidence is competent if it does not violate any exclusionary rule (*e.g.,* the hearsay rule).

C. DIRECT AND CIRCUMSTANTIAL EVIDENCE

Direct evidence involves no inferences. It is testimony or real evidence that speaks directly to a material issue in the case. Circumstantial evidence is indirect and relies on inference. It is evidence of a subsidiary or collateral fact from which, alone or in conjunction with other facts, the existence of the material issue can be inferred.

D. LIMITED ADMISSIBILITY

Evidence may be admissible for one purpose but not another, or admissible against one party but not another. In these situations, the court must, upon request, restrict the evidence to its proper scope and instruct the jury accordingly.

II. RELEVANCE

CMR   **Exam Tip**   Relevance questions should be approached in two steps. *Step 1*: Determine whether the evidence is relevant (*i.e.,* tends to prove or disprove a material fact). *Step 2*: If relevant, determine whether the evidence should nonetheless be excluded based on: (i) judicial discretion (*i.e.,* probative value outweighed by prejudice, etc.), or (ii) public policy (*e.g.,* insurance, subsequent repairs).

A. DETERMINING RELEVANCE

Evidence is relevant if it tends to make the existence of any fact of consequence to the outcome of the action more probable than it would be without the evidence.

1. **General Rule—Must Relate to Time, Event, or Person in Controversy**

   Generally, the evidence must relate to the time, event, or person involved in the ***present*** litigation; otherwise, it is not relevant.

   When considering the relevance of evidence relating to a time, event, or person other than the one at issue, an important factor is its proximity in time to the current events.

2. **Exceptions—Certain Similar Occurrences Are Relevant**

   Previous similar occurrences may be relevant if they are probative of a material issue and that probativeness outweighs the risk of confusion or unfair prejudice. The following are examples of relevant similar occurrences:

DETERMINING ADMISSIBILITY OF EVIDENCE

CMR APPROACH CHART

STEP 1

Is the evidence *relevant* ?

STEP 2

Is there a proper *foundation* (*e.g.*, has the competency of the witness, the authenticity of the evidence, or the reliability of the scientific test been established)?

STEP 3

Is the evidence in the proper *form* (*e.g.*, questions are properly phrased, answers are within the requirements for lay and expert opinion, and documents comply with the best evidence rule)?

STEP 4

Is the evidence beyond the application of, or within an exception to, one of the following *exclusionary rules* ?

- Discretionary exclusion for prejudice (Rule 403)
- Policy-based exclusions (*i.e.*, subsequent remedial measures, settlement negotiations)
- Privilege
- Hearsay
- Parol evidence

ADMISSIBLE

a. **Causation**

Complicated issues of causation may be established by evidence concerning other times, events, or persons (*e.g.,* damage to nearby homes caused by D's blasting is relevant to prove D's blasting damaged P's home).

b. **Prior False Claims or Same Bodily Injury**

Evidence that a person has previously filed similar tort claims or has been involved in prior accidents is generally inadmissible to show the invalidity of the present claim. But evidence that the party has made previous similar false claims or claims involving the same bodily injury is usually relevant to prove that: (i) the present claim is likely to be false, or (ii) the plaintiff's condition is attributable in whole or in part to the prior injury.

c. **Similar Accidents or Injuries Caused by Same Event or Condition**

Evidence of prior accidents or injuries caused by the same event or condition is admissible to prove: (i) the *existence* of a dangerous condition, (ii) that the defendant had *knowledge* of the dangerous condition, and (iii) that the dangerous condition was the *cause* of the present injury.

 1) **Absence of Similar Accidents**

 Many courts are reluctant to admit evidence of the *absence* of similar accidents to show absence of negligence or lack of a defect. However, evidence of the absence of complaints is admissible to show the defendant's lack of knowledge of the danger.

d. **Previous Similar Acts Admissible to Prove Intent**

Similar conduct previously committed by a party may be introduced to prove the party's present motive or intent when such elements are relevant (*e.g.,* history of school segregation admissible to show motive for current exclusion of minorities).

e. **Rebutting Claim of Impossibility**

The requirement that prior occurrences be similar to the litigated act may be relaxed when used to rebut a claim of impossibility (*e.g.,* defendant's claim that car will not go above 50 m.p.h. can be rebutted by showing occasions when car went more than 50 m.p.h.).

f. **Sales of Similar Property**

Evidence of sales of similar personal or real property that are not too remote in time is admissible to prove value. Prices quoted in mere offers to purchase are not admissible. However, evidence of unaccepted offers by a party to the action to buy or sell the property may be used against him as an admission.

g. **Habit**

Habit describes a person's *regular response* to a specific set of circumstances. In contrast, character describes one's disposition in respect to general traits. Under Federal Rule 406, evidence of the habit of a person is relevant to prove that the conduct of the person on a particular occasion was in conformity with the habit.

CMR **Exam Tip** Watch for words such as *"instinctively"* and *"automatically"* in a question's fact pattern. These words indicate habit.

CHARACTER EVIDENCE VS. HABIT EVIDENCE

Character Evidence	Habit Evidence
"Sally is always in a hurry."	"Sally always takes the stairs two at a time."
"Bart is a drunk."	"Bart stops at Charlie's tavern every night after work and has exactly four beers."
"Jeff is a careless driver."	"Jeff never slows down for the YIELD sign at the end of the street."
"Lara is very conscientious about the maintenance of her car."	"Lara checks the brakes on her car every Sunday before church."

h. Industrial or Business Routine

Evidence that a particular business had an established business routine is relevant as tending to show that a particular event occurred.

i. Industry Custom as Evidence of Standard of Care

Industry custom may be offered to show adherence to or deviance from an industry-wide standard of care. However, industry custom is not conclusive on this point; *e.g.,* an entire industry may be acting negligently.

B. DISCRETIONARY EXCLUSION OF RELEVANT EVIDENCE

A trial judge has broad discretion to exclude relevant evidence if its *probative value is substantially outweighed* by the danger of unfair prejudice, confusion of issues, misleading the jury, undue delay, or waste of time.

CMR **Exam Tip** Under the Federal Rules, *unfair surprise* is *not* a valid ground upon which to exclude relevant evidence.

C. EXCLUSION OF RELEVANT EVIDENCE FOR PUBLIC POLICY REASONS

Certain evidence of questionable relevance is excluded by the Federal Rules because public policy favors the behavior involved. Subsequent repairs, for example, are not admissible to show negligence because society wishes to encourage the immediate repair of dangerous conditions. Evidence excluded for public policy reasons includes the following:

1. Liability Insurance

Evidence of insurance against liability is *not admissible to show negligence or ability to pay* a substantial judgment. However, it may be admissible: (i) to prove ownership or control, (ii) to impeach, or (iii) as part of an admission.

ADMISSIBILITY OF RELEVANT EVIDENCE

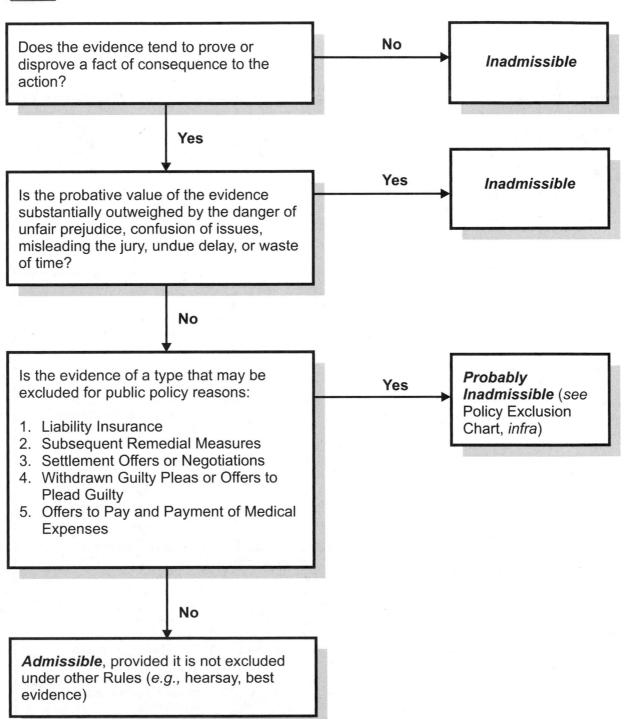

2. Subsequent Remedial Measures

Evidence of repairs or other precautionary measures made following an injury is **not admissible** to prove negligence, culpable conduct, a defect in a product or its design, or a need for a warning or instruction. However, it may be admissible to: (i) prove ownership or control, (ii) rebut a claim that the precaution was not feasible, or (iii) prove that the opposing party has destroyed evidence.

3. Settlement Offers and Withdrawn Guilty Pleas

Evidence of compromises or offers to compromise is **not admissible to prove liability for, or invalidity of, a claim that is disputed as to validity or amount**. Not even direct admissions of liability during compromise negotiations are admissible. Likewise, withdrawn guilty pleas and offers to plead guilty are inadmissible.

CMR **Exam Tip** For the exclusionary rule to apply to settlement negotiations, there must be some indication that a party is going to **make a claim** (although the party need not have actually filed suit). Furthermore, the claim must be **in dispute** as to liability or amount.

4. Offers to Pay Medical Expenses

Payment of or offers to pay the injured party's medical expenses are inadmissible. However, unlike the situation with compromise negotiations, admissions of fact accompanying offers to pay medical expenses are admissible.

CMR
SUMMARY CHART

EVIDENCE THAT MAY BE EXCLUDED FOR POLICY REASONS		
Evidence	**Inadmissible**	**Admissible**
Liability Insurance	To prove negligence or ability to pay	To prove ownership or control, as impeachment, or as part of an admission
Subsequent Remedial Measures	To prove negligence, culpable conduct, a defect in a product or its design, or a need for a warning or instruction	To prove ownership or control, to rebut a claim that precautions were impossible, or to prove destruction of evidence
Settlement Offers or Negotiations	To prove liability or invalidity of a claim that is disputed as to validity or amount	For all other purposes
Withdrawn Guilty Pleas and Offers to Plead Guilty	For nearly all purposes	Not admissible
Offers to Pay and Payment of Medical Expenses	To prove culpable conduct	For all other purposes (Admissions of fact accompanying an offer to pay medical expenses are admissible)

D. CHARACTER EVIDENCE—A SPECIAL RELEVANCE PROBLEM

Character evidence may be offered as substantive, rather than impeachment, evidence to: (i) prove character when it is the *ultimate issue* in the case, or (ii) serve as *circumstantial evidence* of how a person probably acted. The latter is more heavily tested and is the focus of the following discussion.

1. Means of Proving Character

Depending on the jurisdiction, the purpose of the offer, and the nature of the case, one or all of the following methods of proving character may be available:

a. Evidence of *specific acts*;

b. *Opinion testimony* of a witness who knows the person; and

c. Testimony as to the person's general *reputation* in the community.

2. Generally Not Admissible in Civil Cases

Unless character is directly in issue (*e.g.,* defamation), evidence of character offered by either party to prove the conduct of a person in the litigated event is generally not admissible in a civil case. For example, a plaintiff in a suit involving a car accident may not introduce evidence that the defendant is usually a reckless driver to prove that she was negligent at the time in question, nor may the defendant introduce evidence that she is generally a cautious driver.

3. Accused in Criminal Case—Generally Only Accused Can Initiate

The prosecution cannot initiate evidence of bad character of the defendant merely to show that she is more likely to have committed the crime. (Although the prosecution may introduce evidence of prior misconduct for reasons other than propensity to commit the crime. *See* 5., below.) The accused, however, may introduce evidence of her good character to show her innocence of the alleged crime.

a. How Defendant Proves Character

Under the Federal Rules, a witness for the defendant may testify as to the defendant's good *reputation* for the trait in question and may give his personal *opinion* concerning that trait of the defendant.

CMR | **Exam Tip** | Remember that a defendant does not put his character in issue merely by testifying. Taking the stand places the defendant's *credibility* (as opposed to character) in issue; *i.e.,* the prosecution is limited to impeachment evidence rather than substantive character evidence.

b. How Prosecution Rebuts Defendant's Character Evidence

Once the defendant opens the door by introducing character evidence, the prosecution may rebut it by:

1) *Cross-examining the character witness* regarding the basis for his testimony, including whether he knows or has heard of specific instances of the defendant's misconduct.

CMR | Exam Tip | *Any* misconduct, including prior arrests, may be inquired about while cross-examining a defendant's character witness. Remember, however, that the prosecutor is limited to inquiry of the witness; she *may not introduce any extrinsic evidence* of the misconduct. Be careful to distinguish asking a *character* witness whether he is aware of the *defendant's* prior arrests, which is proper, and impeaching a witness with the *witness's* arrests, which is improper. (*See* VI. E. 3. d., *infra.*)

> 2) *Calling qualified witnesses* to testify to the defendant's bad reputation or give their opinions of the defendant's character.

4. Victim in Criminal Case

Except in rape cases, the defendant may introduce reputation or opinion evidence of a bad character trait of the alleged crime victim when it is relevant to show the defendant's innocence. Once the defendant has introduced evidence of a bad character trait of the victim, the prosecution may counter with reputation or opinion evidence of (i) the victim's *good* character, or (ii) the *defendant's* bad character for the *same trait*.

a. Rape Victim's Past Behavior Generally Inadmissible

In any civil or criminal proceeding involving alleged sexual misconduct, evidence offered to prove the sexual behavior or sexual disposition of the victim is generally inadmissible.

1) Exceptions in Criminal Cases

In a criminal case, a victim's sexual behavior is admissible to prove that someone other than the defendant is the source of semen, injury, or other physical evidence. Also, specific instances of sexual behavior between the victim and the accused are admissible by the prosecution for any reason and by the defense to prove consent.

2) Exceptions in Civil Cases

In a civil case, evidence of the alleged victim's sexual behavior is admissible if it is not excluded by any other rule and its probative value substantially outweighs the danger of harm to the victim and of unfair prejudice to any party. Evidence of an alleged victim's reputation is admissible only if it has been placed in controversy by the victim.

5. Specific Acts of Misconduct

Evidence of a person's other crimes or misconduct is inadmissible if offered solely to establish a criminal disposition or bad character.

a. Admissible If Independently Relevant

Evidence of other crimes or misconduct is admissible if these acts are *relevant to some issue other than the defendant's character or disposition* to commit the crime or act charged. Such issues include motive (*e.g.,* burn building to hide embezzlement), intent (*i.e.,* guilty knowledge, lack of good faith), absence of mistake or accident, identity (*e.g.,* stolen gun used or "signature" crimes), or common plan or scheme. In a criminal case, the prosecution must, upon request, provide reasonable notice prior to trial of the general nature of any of this type of evidence it intends to introduce.

CMR **Exam Tip**   A convenient way to remember the issues for which evidence of prior acts of misconduct is admissible is through the mnemonic device "MIMIC":

*M*otive
*I*ntent
*M*istake (absence of)
*I*dentity
*C*ommon plan or scheme

1) **Requirements for Admissibility**
To be admissible: (i) there must be sufficient evidence to support a jury finding that the defendant committed the prior act, *and* (ii) its probative value must not be substantially outweighed by the danger of unfair prejudice (or the judge, in her discretion, may exclude it).

b. **Prior Acts of Sexual Assault or Child Molestation**
Evidence of a defendant's prior acts of sexual assault or child molestation is admissible in a case where the defendant is accused of committing an act of sexual assault or child molestation. The party intending to offer this evidence must disclose it to the defendant 15 days before trial (or later with good cause).

III. JUDICIAL NOTICE

A. JUDICIAL NOTICE OF FACT
Judicial notice is the recognition of a fact as true without formal presentation of evidence.

1. Facts Appropriate for Judicial Notice
Courts take judicial notice of *indisputable facts* that are either matters of *common knowledge* in the community (notorious facts) or *capable of verification* by resort to easily accessible sources of unquestionable accuracy (manifest facts). Courts have increasingly taken judicial notice of scientific principles as a type of manifest fact. Judicial notice of such facts may be taken at any time, whether or not requested.

2. Procedural Aspects of Judicial Notice
If a court does not take judicial notice of a fact on its own accord, a party must formally request that notice be taken of the particular fact. Judicial notice may be taken for the first time on appeal. The Federal Rules provide that a judicially noticed fact is conclusive in a civil case but not in a criminal case. In a criminal case, the jury is instructed that it may, but is not required to, accept as conclusive any judicially noticed fact.

3. "Adjudicative" and "Legislative" Facts
The Federal Rules, and thus their requirements, govern only judicial notice of "adjudicative" facts (*i.e.,* those that relate to the particular case). "Legislative" facts (*i.e.,* those relating to legal reasoning and lawmaking), such as the rationale behind the spousal privilege, need not be of common knowledge nor capable of indisputable verification to be judicially noticed.

B. JUDICIAL NOTICE OF LAW—MANDATORY OR PERMISSIVE
Courts *must* take judicial notice of federal and state law and the official regulations of the forum state and the federal government. Courts *may* take judicial notice of municipal ordinances and private acts or resolutions of Congress or of the local state legislature. Laws of foreign countries may also be judicially noticed.

IV. REAL EVIDENCE

A. IN GENERAL
Real or demonstrative evidence is actual physical evidence addressed directly to the trier of fact. Real evidence may be direct, circumstantial, original, or prepared (demonstrative).

B. GENERAL CONDITIONS OF ADMISSIBILITY
Real evidence must be relevant and meet the following legal requirements:

1. Authentication
The object must be identified as what the proponent claims it to be, either by:

a. *Testimony* of a witness that she *recognizes* the object as what the proponent claims it is (*e.g.,* witness testifies that a gun is the one found at the crime scene); or

b. Evidence that the object has been held in a *substantially unbroken chain of possession* (*e.g.,* blood taken for blood-alcohol test).

2. Condition of Object
If the condition of the object is significant, it must be shown to be in substantially the same condition at trial.

3. Balancing Test—Legal Relevance
Some auxiliary policy or principle may outweigh the need to admit the real evidence. Such policies include physical inconvenience of bringing the object into the courtroom, indecency or impropriety, or undue prejudice.

C. PARTICULAR TYPES OF REAL PROOF

1. Reproductions and Explanatory Real Evidence
Relevant photographs, diagrams, maps, or other reproductions are admissible if their value is not outweighed by the danger of unfair prejudice. However, items used entirely for explanatory purposes are permitted at a trial, but are usually not admitted into evidence (*i.e.,* they are not given to the jury during its deliberations).

2. Maps, Charts, Models, Etc.
Maps, charts, models, etc., are usually admissible for the purpose of illustrating testimony, but must be authenticated (testimonial evidence that they are faithful reproductions of the object or thing depicted).

3. Exhibition of Child in Paternity Suits
In paternity suits, almost all courts permit exhibition of the child to show whether she is the

race of the putative father. The courts are divided with respect to the propriety of exhibition for the purpose of proving physical resemblance to the putative father.

4. **Exhibition of Injuries**

Exhibition of injuries in a personal injury or criminal case is generally permitted, but the court has discretion to exclude this evidence if unfair prejudice would result.

5. **Jury View of the Scene**

The trial court has discretion to permit the jury to view places at issue in a civil or criminal case. The need for the view and changes in the condition of the premises are relevant considerations here.

6. **Demonstrations**

The court, in its discretion, may permit experiments or demonstrations to be performed in the courtroom. Demonstrations of bodily injury may not be allowed where the demonstrations would unduly dramatize the injury.

V. DOCUMENTARY EVIDENCE

A. **IN GENERAL**

Documentary evidence must be relevant in order to be admissible. In the case of writings, the authenticity of the document is one aspect of its relevancy.

B. **AUTHENTICATION**

As a general rule, a writing or any secondary evidence of its content will not be received in evidence unless the writing is authenticated by proof that shows that the writing is what the proponent claims it is. The proof must be *sufficient to support a jury finding* of genuineness.

1. **Authentication by Pleadings or Stipulation**

The genuineness of a document may be admitted by the pleadings or by stipulation.

2. **Evidence of Authenticity**

The following are examples of proper authentication:

a. **Admissions**

A writing may be authenticated by evidence that the party against whom it is offered has either admitted its authenticity or acted upon it as authentic.

b. **Eyewitness Testimony**

A writing can be authenticated by testimony of one who sees it executed or hears it acknowledged. The testimony need not be given by a subscribing witness.

c. **Handwriting Verifications**

A writing may be authenticated by evidence of the genuineness of the handwriting of the maker. This evidence may be the opinion of a *nonexpert with personal knowledge* of the alleged writer's handwriting or the opinion of an *expert who has compared* the writing to samples of the maker's handwriting. Genuineness may also be determined by the *trier of fact through comparison of samples*.

 Exam Tip Remember that a nonexpert without personal knowledge of the handwriting cannot become familiar with it for purposes of testifying.

d. **Ancient Documents**
A document may be authenticated by evidence that it:

1) Is at least *20 years old*;

2) Is in such *condition* as to be free from suspicion as to authenticity; and

3) Was found in a *place* where such a writing would likely be kept.

Exam Tip In contrast to the rule in many jurisdictions, the ancient document provision of the Federal Rules applies to all writings, not just dispositive instruments.

e. **Reply Letter Doctrine**
A writing may be authenticated by evidence that it was written in response to a communication sent to the claimed author.

f. **Photographs**
Generally, photographs are admissible only if identified by a witness as a portrayal of certain facts relevant to the issue and verified by the witness as a correct representation of those facts. Ordinarily, it is not necessary to call the photographer to authenticate the photograph; a witness familiar with the scene is sufficient.

1) **Unattended Camera—Proper Operation of Camera**
If a photograph is taken when no person who could authenticate the scene is present, the photograph may be admitted upon a showing that the camera was properly operating at the relevant time and that the photograph was developed from film obtained from that camera.

g. **X-Ray Pictures, Electrocardiograms, Etc.**
Unlike photographs, an X-ray cannot be authenticated by testimony of a witness that it is a correct representation of the facts. It must be shown that the process used is accurate, the machine was in working order, and the operator was qualified to operate it. Finally, a custodial chain must be established to assure that the X-ray has not been tampered with.

3. **Compare—Authentication of Oral Statements**
When a statement is admissible only if said by a particular person (*e.g.*, admission by a party), authentication as to the *identity of the speaker* is required.

a. **Voice Identification**
A voice may be identified by the opinion of anyone who has heard the voice at *any time*, including after litigation has begun for the sole purpose of testifying.

b. **Telephone Conversations**
Statements made during a telephone conversation may be authenticated by one of the parties to the call who testifies that: (i) he recognized the other party's voice; (ii) the

speaker had knowledge of certain facts that only a particular person would have; (iii) he called a particular person's number and a voice answered as that person or that person's residence; or (iv) he called a business and talked with the person answering the phone about matters relevant to the business.

4. **Self-Authenticating Documents**
Certain writings are said to "prove themselves." Extrinsic evidence of authenticity is not required for the following: (i) certified copies of public records, (ii) official publications, (iii) newspapers and periodicals, (iv) trade inscriptions, (v) acknowledged documents, (vi) commercial paper and related documents, and (vii) certified business records.

C. BEST EVIDENCE RULE
This rule is more accurately called the "*original document rule*." To *prove the terms* of a writing (including a recording, photograph, or X-ray), the original writing must be produced if the terms of the writing are material. Secondary evidence of the writing (*e.g.,* oral testimony) is admissible only if the original is unavailable.

1. **Applicability of the Rule**
The rule applies to two classes of situations, namely where: (i) the writing is a *legally operative or dispositive instrument*; or (ii) the *knowledge of a witness* concerning a fact results from having read it in the document.

2. **Nonapplicability of the Rule**
The best evidence rule does not apply in the following circumstances:

   a. **Fact to Be Proved Exists Independently of Writing**
   The rule does not apply where the fact to be proved has an existence independent of any writing. Many writings record details of essentially nonwritten transactions. Oral testimony of these facts may be given without the original writings recording the event.

   b. **Writing Is Collateral to Litigated Issue**
   The rule does not apply where the writing is of minor importance (*i.e.,* collateral) to the matter in controversy.

   c. **Summaries of Voluminous Records**
   The rule does not apply to summaries of voluminous records. It would be inconvenient to examine a voluminous collection of writings in court, and so the proponent may present their contents in the form of a chart or summary.

   d. **Public Records**
   The rule does not apply to copies of public records that are certified as correct or testified to as correct.

3. **Definitions of "Writings," "Original," and "Duplicate"**
The Federal Rules govern *writings*, *recordings*, *and photographs*, and they are broadly defined. An original is the writing itself or any duplicate that is intended by the person executing it to have the same effect as an original. A duplicate is an *exact copy* of an original, such as a carbon copy. Duplicates are admissible in federal courts unless the authenticity of the original is challenged or unfairness would result.

BEST EVIDENCE RULE

Best Evidence Rule Applies

Party seeks to prove the contents of a deed through witness testimony or other secondary evidence.

Party seeks to prove the contents of a contract through witness testimony or other secondary evidence.

Party seeks to prove the contents of a will through witness testimony or other secondary evidence.

In breach of warranty case, a witness seeks to testify to the contents of the written warranty, which she read.

Nurse seeks to testify regarding the content of a medical record that she read.

In an obscenity or copyright trial for a book, movie, photograph, etc., party seeks to introduce a newspaper review or witness testimony.

In a case where P claimed D defrauded her by selling her a gown she claimed was an original "Halvenchy," P seeks to testify that she found a label in the arm of the gown stating that it was made by L-Mart.

Radiologist seeks to testify regarding the extent of P's injuries he found in X-rays he took, without producing the X-rays.

Best Evidence Rule Does Not Apply

If D denies having made a contract with P, P may introduce secondary evidence to prove that a contract exists—but not its contents.

Witness may testify that he is 30 years old and married, without producing the respective certificates.

Witness may testify to testimony he heard at a prior proceeding, without producing a transcript.

Witness may testify that he is a real estate broker without producing his license (if not material to the case).

Nurse who took vital signs may testify to them without producing medical record.

Party may introduce chart summarizing the personnel records of 500 employees.

Party may introduce a certified copy of a certificate of incorporation, the original of which is on file with the secretary of state.

W may testify about a plane crash she witnessed, despite the fact that the crash was captured on home video.

P may testify that D delivered a deed to her by handing it to her.

CMR **Exam Tip** It is important to distinguish photocopies and copies made by hand. Photocopies are duplicates and, thus, are treated the same as originals. In contrast, handwritten copies are considered secondary evidence and are admissible only if the original or a duplicate is unavailable.

4. **Admissibility of Secondary Evidence of Contents**

   If the proponent cannot produce the original writing in court, he may offer secondary evidence of its contents (handwritten copies, notes, oral testimony) if a satisfactory explanation is given for the nonproduction of the original.

   a. **Satisfactory Foundation**

      Valid excuses justifying the admissibility of secondary evidence include:

      1) *Loss or destruction* of the original.

      2) The original is in possession of a third party *outside the jurisdiction* and is *unobtainable*.

      3) The original is *in the possession of an adversary* who, after due notice, fails to produce the original.

   b. **No Degrees of Secondary Evidence**

      Upon satisfactory foundation, the Federal Rules permit a party to prove the contents of a writing by any kind of secondary evidence, thus abolishing degrees of secondary evidence.

   c. **Testimony or Written Admission of Party**

      A proponent may prove the contents of a writing, recording, or photograph through the testimony, deposition, or written admission of the party against whom it is offered, and need not account for the nonproduction of the original.

5. **Functions of Court and Jury**

   Ordinarily, it is for the *court* to make determinations of fact regarding *admissibility* of duplicates, other copies, and oral testimony as to the contents of an original. However, the Federal Rules reserve the following questions of preliminary fact for the jury:

   a. Whether the original ever existed;

   b. Whether a writing, recording, or photograph produced at trial is an original; and

   c. Whether the evidence offered correctly reflects the contents of the original.

D. **PAROL EVIDENCE RULE**

   If an agreement is reduced to writing, that writing is the agreement and hence constitutes the only evidence of it. Prior or contemporaneous negotiations or agreements are merged into the written agreement, and they are inadmissible to vary the terms of the writing.

   1. **When the Rule Does Not Apply**

      The parol evidence rule does not apply to exclude evidence of prior or contemporaneous agreements in the following circumstances:

a. **Incomplete or Ambiguous Contract**
Parol evidence is admissible to complete an incomplete contract or explain an ambiguous term.

b. **Reformation of Contract**
The parol evidence rule does not apply where a party alleges facts (*e.g.,* mistake) entitling him to reformation.

c. **Challenge to Validity of Contract**
Parol evidence is admissible to show that the contract is *void or voidable*, or was made subject to a valid *condition precedent* that has not been satisfied.

2. **Subsequent Modifications**
The rule applies only to negotiations prior to, or at the time of, the execution of the contract. Parol evidence is admissible to show subsequent modification or discharge of the written contract.

VI. TESTIMONIAL EVIDENCE

A. COMPETENCY OF WITNESSES

Witnesses must pass tests of basic reliability to establish their competency to give testimony, but they are generally presumed to be competent until the contrary is established. Witnesses must possess to some degree four basic testimonial attributes: the capacity to observe, to recollect, to communicate, and to appreciate the obligation to speak truthfully.

1. **Federal Rules of Competency**
The Rules do not specify any mental or moral qualifications for witness testimony beyond these two limitations:

(i) The witness must have *personal knowledge* of the matter about which he is to testify; and

(ii) The witness must *declare he will testify truthfully*.

If a witness requires an interpreter, the interpreter must be qualified and take an oath to make a true translation.

2. **Modern Modifications of the Common Law Disqualifications**
Most jurisdictions and the Federal Rules have removed the common law witness disqualifications for lack of religious belief, conviction of a crime, and interest in the lawsuit.

a. **Infancy**
The competency of an infant depends on the capacity and intelligence of the particular child as determined by the trial judge.

b. **Insanity**
An insane person may testify, provided he understands the obligation to speak truthfully and has the capacity to testify accurately.

c. **Judge and Jurors**

The presiding judge may not testify as a witness. Likewise, jurors are incompetent to testify before the jury in which they are sitting.

3. **Dead Man Acts**

Most states have Dead Man Acts, which provide that a party or person interested in the event is incompetent to testify to a personal transaction or communication with a deceased, when such testimony is offered against the representative or successors in interest of the deceased. A person is "interested" if he stands to gain or lose by the judgment or the judgment may be used for or against him in a subsequent action. A predecessor in interest of the interested party is also disqualified.

CMR **Exam Tip** There is no Dead Man Act in the Federal Rules, but a state Act will apply in federal cases where state law, under the *Erie* doctrine, provides the rule of decision (*e.g.,* diversity cases).

B. **FORM OF EXAMINATION OF WITNESS**

The judge may exercise reasonable control over the examination of witnesses in order to aid the ascertainment of truth, to avoid wasting time, and to protect witnesses from harassment.

1. **Leading Questions**

Leading questions (*i.e.,* questions that suggest the answer desired) are ***generally improper on direct*** examination. However, they are permitted:

a. On cross-examination;

b. To elicit preliminary or introductory matter;

c. When the witness needs aid to respond because of loss of memory, immaturity, or physical or mental weakness; or

d. When the witness is hostile.

2. **Improper Questions and Answers**

Questions that are misleading (cannot be answered without making an unintended admission), compound (requiring a single answer to more than one question), argumentative, conclusionary, cumulative, unduly harassing or embarrassing, call for a narrative answer or speculation, or assume facts not in evidence are improper and are not permitted. Answers that lack foundation (the witness has insufficient personal knowledge) and answers that are nonresponsive (do not answer the specific question asked) may be stricken.

3. **Use of Memoranda by Witness**

A witness ***cannot read her testimony*** from a prepared memorandum. However, a memorandum may be used in certain circumstances.

CMR **Exam Tip** Any time you encounter an exam question in which a witness consults a writing, keep in mind the differences between refreshing and recorded recollection. The fact patterns are very similar and could be confusing if you have not thoroughly memorized the distinguishing features.

a. **Present Recollection Revived—Refreshing Recollection**

A witness may use any writing or thing for the purpose of refreshing her present

recollection. She usually may not read from the writing while she actually testifies because the writing is not authenticated and not in evidence.

b. **Past Recollection Recorded—Recorded Recollection**
Where a witness states that she has insufficient recollection of an event to enable her to testify fully and accurately, even after she has consulted a writing given to her on the stand, the writing itself may be *read into evidence* if a proper foundation is laid. The foundation must include proof that:

1) The witness at one time had *personal knowledge* of the facts in the writing;

2) The writing was *made by the witness* or under her direction, or it was *adopted* by the witness;

3) The writing was *timely made* when the matter was fresh in the witness's mind;

4) The writing is *accurate*; and

5) The witness has *insufficient recollection* to testify fully and accurately.

c. **Inspection and Use on Cross-Examination**
Whenever a witness has used a writing to refresh her memory on the stand, an adverse party is entitled to have the writing produced at trial, to cross-examine the witness thereon, and to introduce portions relating to the witness's testimony into evidence.

CMR COMPARISON CHART

PRESENT RECOLLECTION REFRESHED VS. PAST RECOLLECTION RECORDED

Present Recollection Refreshed	Past Recollection Recorded
Any writing may be used to refresh a witness's memory. (Things other than a writing may also be used, *e.g.,* a photograph.)	Only a *writing* that meets several *foundational requirements* (*e.g.,* timely made by witness; witness cannot remember the events after reading the writing) may be used.
The witness cannot read from the writing while testifying.	The writing itself is read into evidence.
There is *no hearsay problem*, because the writing is not offered into evidence.	This is *hearsay*, but it falls within a specific *exception* to the hearsay rule.

C. OPINION TESTIMONY

The general policy of the law is to prohibit admissibility of opinion evidence except in cases where the courts are sure that it will be necessary or at least helpful.

1. Opinion Testimony by Lay Witnesses

a. General Rule of Inadmissibility

Opinions by lay witnesses are generally inadmissible. However, there are many cases where no better evidence can be obtained. In most jurisdictions and under the Federal Rules, opinion testimony by a lay witness is admissible when it is: (i) rationally based on the witness's perception, (ii) helpful to a clear understanding of his testimony or helpful to the determination of a fact in issue, and (iii) not based on scientific, technical, or other specialized knowledge.

b. Situations Where Opinions of Lay Witnesses Are Admissible

An opinion of a lay witness is generally admissible with respect to:

1) The *general appearance or condition* of a person;

2) The *state of emotion* of a person;

3) Matters involving *sense recognition*;

4) *Voice or handwriting identification*;

5) The *speed* of a moving object;

6) The *value of his own services*;

7) The *rational or irrational nature* of another's conduct; and

8) *Intoxication* of another.

c. Situations Where Opinions of Lay Witnesses Are Not Admissible

Opinions of lay witnesses are not admissible with regard to whether one acted as an agent or whether an agreement was made.

2. Opinion Testimony by Expert Witnesses

An expert may state an opinion or conclusion, provided:

(i) The *subject matter* is one where scientific, technical, or other specialized knowledge would *assist the trier of fact* (an opinion will assist the trier of fact if it is relevant and reliable);

(ii) The *witness is qualified* as an expert (*i.e.,* possesses special knowledge, skill, experience, training, or education);

ADMISSIBLE OPINIONS OF LAY WITNESSES

1. **General Appearance or Condition of a Person**

   "He was about 80 years old."
   or
   "She seemed ill."

2. **State of Emotion**

   "She was angry."
   or
   "He was distraught."

3. **Matters Involving Sense Recognition**

   "The suitcase was heavy."
   or
   "He smelled of garlic."

4. **Voice or Handwriting Identification**
   (Foundation required)

   "It sounded like Mark."
   or
   "That's Fran's handwriting."

5. **Speed of Moving Object**

   "The truck was going very fast" or (if experienced in estimating rates of speed), "The truck was going at least 60 miles per hour."

6. **Value of Own Services**

   "My time is worth $50 per hour."

7. **Rational or Irrational Nature of Another's Conduct**

   "He was acting crazy."

8. **Intoxication**
   (Foundation may be required)

   "She was slurring her words and smelled of gin. She was drunk."

(iii) The expert possesses *reasonable probability regarding his opinion*; and

(iv) The opinion is supported by a *proper factual basis*. The expert's opinion may be based on one or more of three possible sources of information: (i) personal observation, (ii) facts made known to the expert at trial, or (iii) facts not known personally but supplied to him outside the courtroom and of a *type reasonably relied upon by experts* in the particular field.

a. Opinion on Ultimate Issues

Under the Federal Rules, an expert may render an opinion as to the ultimate issue in the case. However, in a criminal case in which the defendant's mental state constitutes an element of the crime or defense, an expert may not, under the Federal Rules, state an opinion as to whether the accused did or did not have the mental state in issue.

b. Authoritative Texts and Treatises

An expert may be cross-examined concerning statements contained in any publication established as reliable authority either by the testimony of this expert or another expert, or by judicial notice. Under the Federal Rules, these texts and treatises can be used not only to impeach experts, but also as substantive evidence, subject to the following limitations:

1) An *expert must be on the stand* when an excerpt is read from a treatise; and

2) The relevant portion is *read into evidence* but is not received as an exhibit.

D. CROSS-EXAMINATION

Cross-examination of adverse witnesses is a matter of right in every trial of a disputed issue of fact, but the scope of cross-examination is frequently a matter of judicial discretion.

1. Restrictions on Scope

Cross-examination is generally limited to: (i) the scope of direct examination, including all reasonable inferences that may be drawn from it, and (ii) testing the credibility of the witness.

2. Collateral Matters

The cross-examiner is generally bound by the answers of the witness to questions concerning collateral matters. Thus, the response may not be refuted by extrinsic evidence. However, certain recognized matters of impeachment, such as bias, interest, or a conviction, may be developed by extrinsic evidence because they are sufficiently important. The trial court has considerable discretion in this area.

E. CREDIBILITY—IMPEACHMENT

Impeachment means the casting of an adverse reflection on the veracity of the witness.

1. Accrediting or Bolstering

Generally, a party may not bolster or accredit the testimony of his witness (*e.g.,* by introducing

a prior consistent statement) until the witness has been impeached. However, in certain cases, a party may prove the witness made a timely complaint or a prior statement of identification. The prior identification may also serve as substantive evidence that the identification was correct.

2. Any Party May Impeach

Under the Federal Rules, a witness may be impeached by any party, including the party calling him.

 Exam Tip When a question involves a party impeaching his own witness, be sure to avoid the following **wrong answer choices** reflecting the traditional rule, which prohibits impeaching your own witness unless the witness:

(i) Is an **adverse party** or identified with an adverse party;

(ii) Is **hostile** and affirmatively uncooperative;

(iii) Is one whom the party is **required by law** to call; or

(iv) Gives **surprise testimony** that is affirmatively harmful to the party calling him.

3. Impeachment Methods—Cross-Examination and Extrinsic Evidence

A witness may be impeached either by cross-examination (by eliciting facts from the witness that discredit his own testimony) or by extrinsic evidence (by putting other witnesses on the stand who will introduce facts discrediting his testimony). Certain grounds for impeachment require that a foundation be laid during cross-examination before extrinsic evidence can be introduced. Other grounds allow impeachment to be accomplished only by cross-examination and not by extrinsic evidence. (*Note:* The term "cross-examination" is used for convenience because it is usually an adverse witness who is impeached. But remember that a party may impeach his own witness, which would be on direct or redirect examination.) The traditional impeachment devices follow.

a. Prior Inconsistent Statements

A party may show, by cross-examination or extrinsic evidence, that the witness has, on another occasion, made statements inconsistent with his present testimony. To prove the statement by extrinsic evidence, a proper foundation must be laid and the statement must be relevant to some issue in the case.

1) Foundation for Extrinsic Evidence

Extrinsic evidence can be introduced to prove a prior inconsistent statement only if the witness is, at some point, given an opportunity to explain or deny the statement. The exception to the rule is that inconsistent statements by hearsay declarants may be used to impeach despite the lack of a foundation. Under the Federal Rules, foundation requirements may be dispensed with where the interests of justice require (*e.g.,* witness unavailable when inconsistent statement is discovered).

CMR Exam Tip Remember the MBE follows the Federal Rules. Under the Rules, the opportunity to explain or deny need not come before introduction of a prior inconsistent statement.

2) Evidentiary Effect of Prior Inconsistent Statements

Usually, prior inconsistent statements are hearsay, admissible only for impeachment purposes. If, however, the statement was made under oath at a prior proceeding, it is admissible nonhearsay and may be admitted as substantive evidence of the facts stated.

b. Bias or Interest

Evidence that a witness is biased or has an interest in the outcome of a suit tends to show that the witness has a motive to lie.

1) Foundation for Extrinsic Evidence

Before a witness can be impeached by extrinsic evidence of bias or interest, he must first be asked about the facts that show bias or interest on cross-examination.

CMR Exam Tip Watch for facts indicating that the foundation requirement for extrinsic evidence of bias or interest has been fulfilled. Evidence that is otherwise inadmissible (*e.g.,* arrests, liability insurance) may be introduced if relevant for these impeachment purposes, provided the proper foundation is laid.

c. Conviction of Crime

A witness may be impeached by proof of a *conviction* (arrest or indictment is not sufficient) for certain crimes. A pending review or appeal does not affect the use of a conviction for impeachment.

1) Type of Crime

a) Any Crime Involving Dishonesty

A witness may be impeached by any crime, felony or misdemeanor, requiring an act of dishonesty or false statement. The court has *no discretion* to bar impeachment by these crimes.

b) Felony Not Involving Dishonesty

A witness may also be impeached by a felony that does not involve dishonesty, but the court has *discretion to exclude* it if:

(1) The witness being impeached is a *criminal defendant*, and the *prosecution has not shown* that the conviction's probative value outweighs its prejudicial effect; or

(2) In the case of all other witnesses, the *court determines* that the conviction's probative value is substantially outweighed by its prejudicial effect.

2) Remote, Juvenile, and Constitutionally Defective Convictions Not Admissible

Generally, if more than 10 years have elapsed since the date of conviction or the

date of release from confinement (whichever is later), the conviction is inadmissible. Juvenile convictions are similarly inadmissible. A conviction obtained in violation of the defendant's constitutional rights is invalid for all purposes, including impeachment.

3) Effect of Pardon
A conviction may not be used to impeach a witness if the witness has been pardoned and: (i) the pardon is based on innocence, or (ii) the person pardoned has not been convicted of a subsequent felony.

4) No Foundation Required for Extrinsic Evidence
A prior conviction may be shown either by cross-examination of the witness or by introducing a record of the judgment. No foundation is necessary.

d. Specific Instances of Misconduct—Bad Acts
Under the Federal Rules, subject to discretionary control of the trial judge, a witness may be interrogated upon cross-examination with respect to an act of misconduct only if the act is *probative of truthfulness* (*i.e.,* is an act of deceit or lying). However, the cross-examiner must inquire in good faith.

1) Extrinsic Evidence Not Permitted
Extrinsic evidence of "bad acts" to prove misconduct is not permitted. A specific act of misconduct, offered to attack the witness's character for truthfulness, can be elicited only on cross-examination of the witness.

CMR **Exam Tip** Keep in mind that asking about specific instances of misconduct does not include inquiring about arrests. An arrest itself is not a bad act. Thus, it is permissible to ask a witness whether he embezzled money from his employer. It is not permissible to ask him whether he was *arrested* for embezzlement.

e. Opinion or Reputation Evidence for Truthfulness
A witness may be impeached by showing that he has a poor reputation for truthfulness. This may include evidence of reputation in business circles as well as in the community in which the witness resides. Under the Federal Rules, an impeaching witness may state his own opinion as to the character of a witness for truthfulness.

f. Sensory Deficiencies
A witness may be impeached by showing, either on cross-examination or by extrinsic evidence, that his faculties of perception and recollection were so impaired as to make it doubtful that he could have perceived those facts. A witness may also be impeached by showing that he had no knowledge of the facts to which he testified.

4. Impeachment on Collateral Matter
Where a witness makes a statement not directly relevant to the issue in the case, the rule against impeachment on a collateral matter applies to bar his opponent from proving the statement untrue either by extrinsic evidence or by a prior inconsistent statement.

5. Impeachment of Hearsay Declarant
Under the Federal Rules, the credibility of someone who does not testify but whose out-of-court

statement is introduced at trial may be attacked (and if attacked, may be supported) by evidence that would be admissible if the declarant had testified as a witness. The declarant need not be given the opportunity to explain or deny a prior inconsistent statement. In addition, the party against whom the out-of-court statement was offered may call the declarant as a witness and cross-examine him about the statement.

CMR
SUMMARY
CHART

METHODS OF IMPEACHMENT

Impeachment Method	Means of Proof	Foundation
Prior Inconsistent Statements	• Cross-examination • Extrinsic evidence (if not a collateral matter)	Witness must be given opportunity to explain or deny the inconsistent statement. (Exception for hearsay declarants)
Bias or Interest	• Cross-examination • Extrinsic evidence	Witness must be asked on cross-examination about facts showing bias or interest before extrinsic evidence is allowed. If these facts are admitted on cross-examination, admissibility of extrinsic evidence is within court's discretion.
Conviction of Crime— Must be a **felony** or crime involving **dishonesty**	• Cross-examination • Record of judgment	None required
Specific Instances of Misconduct (Bad Acts)	• Cross-examination only	Not applicable
Opinion or Reputation for Truthfulness	• Calling other witnesses	None required
Sensory Deficiencies	• Cross-examination • Extrinsic evidence	None required

---

6.   **Rehabilitation**
      A witness who has been impeached may be rehabilitated by the following methods:

      a.   **Explanation on Redirect**
            The witness on redirect may explain or clarify facts brought out on cross-examination.

b. Good Reputation for Truthfulness

When the witness's character for truth and veracity has been attacked, other witnesses may be called to testify to the good reputation for truthfulness of the impeached witness or to give their opinions as to the truthfulness of the impeached witness.

c. Prior Consistent Statement

A party may not ordinarily rehabilitate a witness by showing a prior consistent statement. This is true even when the witness has been impeached by showing a prior inconsistent statement. But if the testimony of the witness has been attacked by an express or implied charge that the witness is *lying or exaggerating* because of some motive, a previous consistent statement is admissible to rebut this evidence. This previous statement also is substantive evidence of the truth of its contents, whether or not made under oath.

F. OBJECTIONS, EXCEPTIONS, AND OFFERS OF PROOF

1. Objections

Objections at trial should be made after the question, but before the answer, if the question calls for inadmissible matter. Otherwise, a motion to strike must be made as soon as an answer emerges as inadmissible. At a deposition, objections to the form of a question, or to a testimonial privilege, should be made when the question is asked or it may be waived. Objections based on the substance of a question or answer may be postponed until the deposition is offered in evidence.

 Exam Tip Failure to object is deemed a waiver of any ground for objection. Thus, if no objection is made, otherwise inadmissible evidence will be admitted.

a. Specificity of Objections

1) General Objections

A sustained general objection (one that does not state the grounds of the objection) will be upheld on appeal if there was any ground for the objection. An overruled general objection will be upheld on appeal unless the evidence was not admissible under any circumstances for any purpose.

2) Specific Objections

A sustained specific objection, which states the reason for the objection, will be upheld on appeal only if the ground stated was correct or if the evidence excluded was not competent and could not be made so.

b. "Opening the Door"

One who introduces evidence on a particular subject thereby asserts its relevance and cannot complain if his adversary thereafter offers evidence on the same subject.

c. Introducing Part of Transaction

Where part of a conversation, act, or writing is introduced into evidence, the adverse party may require the proponent of the evidence to introduce any other part that ought in fairness to be considered.

d. Motion to Strike—Unresponsive Answers

Examining counsel may move to strike an unresponsive answer, but opposing counsel may not.

2. **Exceptions**

It is not necessary for a party to "except" from a trial ruling in order to preserve the issue for appeal in most states.

3. **Offers of Proof**

An offer of proof may be made, disclosing the nature, purpose, and admissibility of rejected evidence, to persuade the trial court to hear the evidence and to preserve the evidence for review on appeal. It may be made by witness testimony, a lawyer's narration, or tangible evidence marked and offered.

G. **TESTIMONIAL PRIVILEGES**

Testimonial privileges permit one to refuse to disclose, and prohibit others from disclosing, certain confidential information in judicial proceedings.

1. **Federal Rules—No Specific Privilege Provisions**

The Federal Rules have no specific privilege provisions; privilege in federal courts is governed by common law principles as interpreted by the courts. The federal courts currently recognize the attorney-client privilege, the privilege for spousal communications, and the psychotherapist/social worker-client privilege. In *diversity* cases, the state law of privilege applies.

2. **General Considerations**

a. **Persons Who May Assert Privilege**

A privilege is personal to the holder; *i.e.,* it generally may be asserted only by the holder. Sometimes the person with whom the confidence was shared may assert the privilege on the holder's behalf.

b. **Confidentiality**

To be privileged, a communication must be shown or presumed to have been made in confidence.

c. **Comment on Privilege Forbidden**

Neither counsel for the parties nor the judge may comment on a claim of privilege.

d. **Waiver**

Any privilege is waived by: (i) failure to claim the privilege; (ii) voluntary disclosure of the privileged matter by the privilege holder; or (iii) a contractual provision waiving in advance the right to claim a privilege.

CMR **Exam Tip** A privilege is not waived when someone wrongfully discloses information without the privilege holder's consent. Similarly, a waiver by one joint holder does not affect the right of the other holder to assert the privilege.

e. **Eavesdroppers**

A privilege based on confidential communications is not abrogated because it was overheard by someone whose presence is unknown to the parties. Under the modern view, in the absence of negligence by the one claiming privilege, even the eavesdropper would be prohibited from testifying.

3. **Attorney-Client Privilege**

Communications between an attorney and client, made during professional consultation, are privileged from disclosure. The important elements of this privilege are:

a. **Attorney-Client Relationship**

The client must be seeking the professional services of the attorney at the time of the communication. Disclosures made before the attorney accepts or declines the case are covered by the privilege.

   1) **Corporate Clients**

   Corporations are "clients" within the meaning of the privilege, and statements made by corporate officials or employees to an attorney are protected if the employees were authorized by the corporation to make such statements.

b. **Confidential Communication**

To be protected, the communication must be confidential (*i.e.,* not intended to be disclosed to third parties), but representatives of the attorney or client may be present without destroying the privilege; otherwise, communications made in the known presence and hearing of a stranger are not privileged.

   1) **Communications Through Agents**

   Communications made to third persons (*e.g.,* secretaries, messengers, accountants) are confidential and covered by the privilege if necessary to transmit information between the attorney and client.

> **CMR** **Exam Tip** A favorite exam topic involves communications between a client and a doctor during an examination made at the attorney's request. Be careful—the physician-patient privilege (*infra*) does not apply because no treatment is contemplated. The attorney-client privilege will apply, however, as long as the doctor is not called as an expert witness.

   2) **No Privilege Where Attorney Acts for Both Parties**

   Where an attorney acts for both parties to a transaction, no privilege can be invoked in a lawsuit between the two parties, but the privilege can be claimed in a suit between either or both of the two parties and third persons.

c. **Client Holds Privilege**

The client holds the privilege, and she alone may waive it. The attorney's authority to claim the privilege on behalf of the client is presumed in the absence of contrary evidence.

d. **Privilege Applies Indefinitely**

The attorney-client privilege applies indefinitely. The privilege even continues to apply after the client's death.

e. **When the Privilege Does Not Apply**

There are three significant exceptions to the attorney-client privilege. There is no privilege:

   1) If the attorney's services were sought to aid in the planning or commission of something the ***client should have known was a crime or fraud***;

2) Regarding a communication relevant to an issue between *parties claiming through the same deceased client*; and

3) For a communication relevant to an issue of breach of duty in a *dispute between the attorney and client*.

f. Attorney's Work Product

Although documents prepared by an attorney for his own use in a case are not protected by the privilege, they are not subject to discovery except in cases of necessity.

g. Limitations on Waiver of Attorney-Client Privilege and Work Product Rule

A voluntary disclosure of privileged material operates as a waiver of the attorney-client privilege or work product protection *only with respect to the disclosed material*. Undisclosed privileged material is subject to the waiver only if the waiver is *intentional*, the disclosed and undisclosed material concern the *same subject matter*, and the material should be considered together *to avoid unfairness*. There is no waiver if the disclosure was *inadvertent* and the holder took reasonable steps to prevent disclosure and rectify the error.

CMR | **Exam Tip** | Look for fact patterns on an exam where a party discloses, *e.g.*, documents during discovery that would ordinarily be privileged under the attorney-client privilege or work product rule. If the disclosure is the result of an *innocent mistake*, then there is *no waiver*. However, if the documents were *voluntarily disclosed*, then a waiver is effective with respect to *those documents only*, unless the disclosing party intentionally waived protection of other privileged material that concerns the same subject matter and of which disclosure is necessary to prevent unfairness to the opposing party.

4. Physician-Patient Privilege

The physician-patient privilege belongs to the patient, and he may decide to claim or waive it. Confidential communications between a patient and his physician are privileged, provided that:

(i) A *professional relationship* exists;

(ii) The information is acquired while attending the patient in the *course of treatment*; and

(iii) The information is *necessary for treatment*. (Nonmedical information is not privileged.)

a. When the Privilege Does Not Apply

The physician-patient privilege does not apply (or is impliedly waived) if:

1) The *patient puts his physical condition in issue* (*e.g.*, personal injury suit);

2) The physician's assistance was sought to *aid wrongdoing* (*e.g.*, commission of crime or tort);

3) The communication is relevant to an issue of breach of duty in a *dispute between the physician and patient*;

4) The patient **agreed** by contract (*e.g.,* insurance policy) to waive the privilege; or

5) It is a **federal case applying the federal law of privilege**.

b. Criminal Proceedings
In some states, the privilege applies in both civil and criminal cases. In a number of others, it cannot be invoked in criminal cases generally. In still other states, the privilege is denied in felony cases, and in a few states, it is denied only in homicide cases.

 Exam Tip Remember that when a psychiatrist is the doctor involved, the applicable privilege is the psychotherapist-client privilege (below), which is more widely accepted in all proceedings than is the physician-patient privilege.

5. Psychotherapist/Social Worker-Client Privilege
The United States Supreme Court recognizes a federal privilege for communications between a psychotherapist (psychiatrist or psychologist) or licensed social worker and his client. Thus, the federal courts and virtually all of the states recognize a privilege for this type of confidential communication. In most particulars, this privilege operates in the same manner as the attorney-client privilege (*supra*).

6. Husband-Wife Privilege
There are two distinct spousal privileges.

a. Spousal Immunity
When the privilege of spousal immunity is invoked, a married person whose spouse is a defendant in a **criminal** case may not be called as a witness by the prosecution. Moreover, a married person may not be compelled to **testify** against his spouse in **any criminal proceeding**, regardless of whether the spouse is the defendant. There must be a valid marriage for the privilege to apply, and the privilege lasts only during the marriage.

1) Who Holds the Privilege
In federal court, the privilege belongs to the witness-spouse. Thus, the witness-spouse cannot be compelled to testify, but may choose to do so. (In some state courts, the privilege belongs to the party-spouse.)

b. Privilege for Confidential Marital Communications
In any civil or criminal case, confidential communications between a husband and wife during a valid marriage are privileged. For this privilege to apply, the **marital relationship must exist** when the communication is made. Divorce will not terminate the privilege, but communications after divorce are not privileged. In addition, the communication must be **made in reliance upon the intimacy** of the marital relationship (confidential).

c. When Neither Marital Privilege Applies
Neither privilege applies in actions between the spouses or in cases involving crimes against the testifying spouse or either spouse's children.

HUSBAND-WIFE PRIVILEGE

Spousal Immunity	Confidential Marital Communications
One spouse **cannot be compelled to testify** against the other spouse in any **criminal** proceeding.	**Communications** made in reliance upon the intimacy of the marital relationship are privileged. The privilege applies in both **civil and criminal** proceedings.
Only the **witness-spouse** may invoke spousal immunity (*i.e.,* the party-spouse cannot prevent the witness-spouse from testifying).	**Both spouses** have the privilege not to disclose, and to prevent the other from disclosing, a confidential marital communication.
The privilege can be claimed **only during marriage**, but covers information learned before and during the marriage.	The privilege **survives the marriage**, but covers only statements **made during marriage**.

7. **Privilege Against Self-Incrimination**
   Under the Fifth Amendment to the Constitution, a witness cannot be compelled to testify against himself. Any witness compelled to appear in a civil or criminal proceeding may refuse to give an answer that ties the witness to the commission of a crime.

8. **Clergy or Accountant Privilege**
   A privilege exists for statements made to a member of the clergy or an accountant, the elements of which are very similar to the attorney-client privilege.

9. **Professional Journalist Privilege**
   There is no constitutional right for a professional journalist to protect his source of information, so any privilege in this area is limited to individual state statutes on the subject.

10. **Governmental Privileges**
    Official information not otherwise open to the public or the identity of an informer may be protected by a privilege for the government. No privilege exists if the identity of the informer is voluntarily disclosed by a holder of the privilege.

H. **EXCLUSION AND SEQUESTRATION OF WITNESSES**
   Upon a party's request, the trial judge will order witnesses excluded from the courtroom. The judge may also do this on his own motion. The judge, however, may not exclude: (i) a party or a designated officer or employee of a party, (ii) a person whose presence is essential to the presentation of a party's case, or (iii) a person statutorily authorized to be present.

VII. THE HEARSAY RULE

A. STATEMENT OF THE RULE

The Federal Rules define hearsay as "a statement, other than one made by the declarant while testifying at the trial or hearing, offered in evidence to prove the truth of the matter asserted." If a statement is hearsay, and no exception to the rule applies, the evidence must be excluded upon appropriate objection. The reason for excluding hearsay is that the adverse party was denied the opportunity to cross-examine the declarant.

CMR **Exam Tip** An out-of-court statement that incorporates other hearsay within it ("hearsay within hearsay" or "double hearsay") is admissible only if *both* the outer hearsay statement and the inner hearsay statement fall within an exception to the hearsay rule.

1. "Statement"

For purposes of the hearsay rule, a "statement" is: (i) an oral or written assertion, or (ii) nonverbal conduct intended as an assertion (*e.g.,* nod of the head).

2. "Offered to Prove the Truth of the Matter"

If the out-of-court statement is introduced for any purpose other than to prove the truth of the matter asserted, there is no need to cross-examine the declarant; so the statement is not hearsay. The following out-of-court statements are *not hearsay*:

a. *Verbal acts or legally operative facts* (*e.g.,* words of contract; defamatory words);

b. Statements offered to show their *effect on the hearer or reader* (*e.g.,* to prove notice in negligence case); and

c. Statements offered as *circumstantial evidence of declarant's state of mind* (*e.g.,* evidence of insanity or knowledge).

CMR **Exam Tip** Do not confuse statements offered as circumstantial evidence of declarant's state of mind, which are almost always offered as evidence of insanity or knowledge, with statements that reflect directly on declarant's state of mind, which are usually offered to establish intent. The former is not hearsay, while the latter is hearsay subject to a specific exception.

CMR **Exam Tip** In deciding whether evidence is hearsay, ask yourself whether we are relying on the declarant's credibility; *i.e.,* does it matter whether the declarant is telling the truth? If not, the evidence is not hearsay.

3. Nonhuman Declarations

There is no such thing as *animal* or *machine* hearsay; there must be an out-of-court statement by a *person*. Thus, testimony about what a radar gun "said" or what a drug-sniffing dog did is not hearsay (but still must be relevant and authenticated to be admitted).

B. STATEMENTS THAT ARE NONHEARSAY UNDER THE FEDERAL RULES

Despite meeting the common law definition of hearsay, the following statements are not hearsay under the Federal Rules and are, therefore, admissible as substantive evidence:

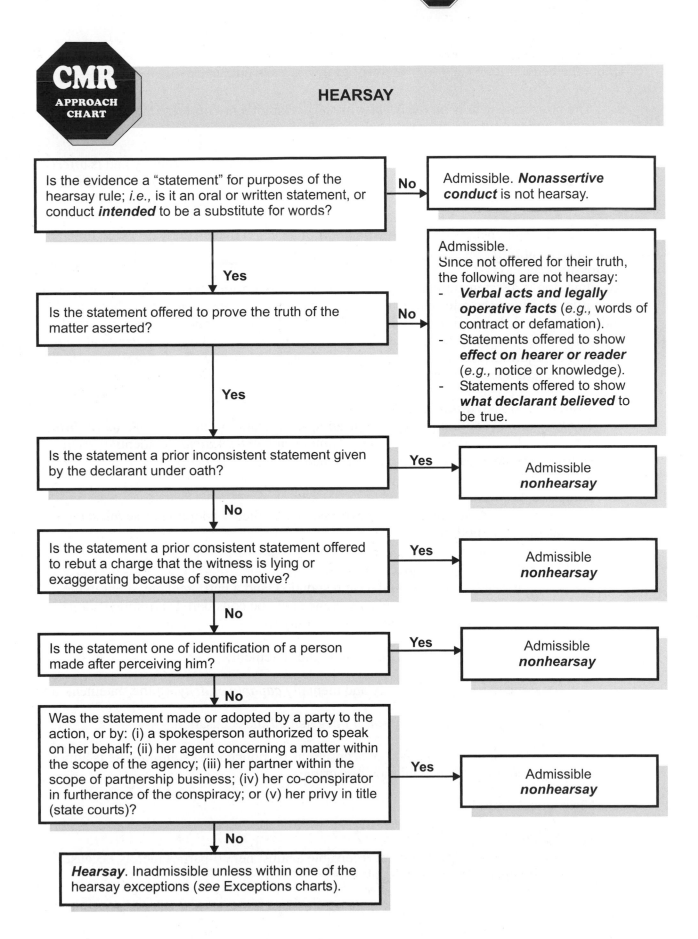

CMR
APPROACH CHART

HEARSAY

Is the evidence a "statement" for purposes of the hearsay rule; *i.e.,* is it an oral or written statement, or conduct **intended** to be a substitute for words?

No → Admissible. **Nonassertive conduct** is not hearsay.

↓ **Yes**

Is the statement offered to prove the truth of the matter asserted?

No → Admissible.
Since not offered for their truth, the following are not hearsay:
- **Verbal acts and legally operative facts** (*e.g.,* words of contract or defamation).
- Statements offered to show **effect on hearer or reader** (*e.g.,* notice or knowledge).
- Statements offered to show **what declarant believed** to be true.

↓ **Yes**

Is the statement a prior inconsistent statement given by the declarant under oath?

Yes → Admissible **nonhearsay**

↓ **No**

Is the statement a prior consistent statement offered to rebut a charge that the witness is lying or exaggerating because of some motive?

Yes → Admissible **nonhearsay**

↓ **No**

Is the statement one of identification of a person made after perceiving him?

Yes → Admissible **nonhearsay**

↓ **No**

Was the statement made or adopted by a party to the action, or by: (i) a spokesperson authorized to speak on her behalf; (ii) her agent concerning a matter within the scope of the agency; (iii) her partner within the scope of partnership business; (iv) her co-conspirator in furtherance of the conspiracy; or (v) her privy in title (state courts)?

Yes → Admissible **nonhearsay**

↓ **No**

Hearsay. Inadmissible unless within one of the hearsay exceptions (*see* Exceptions charts).

1. **Prior Statements by Witness**
Under the Federal Rules, a prior statement by a witness is not hearsay if:

   a. The prior statement is *inconsistent* with the declarant's in-court testimony and was *given under oath* at a prior proceeding;

   b. The prior statement is *consistent* with the declarant's in-court testimony and is *offered to rebut* a charge that the witness is *lying or exaggerating* because of some motive (and the statement was made before any motive to lie or exaggerate arose); or

   c. The prior statement is one of *identification* of a person made after perceiving him.

2. **Admissions by Party-Opponent**
An admission is a statement made or act that amounts to a prior acknowledgment by one of the parties of one of the relevant facts. Admissions of a party-opponent are not hearsay under the Federal Rules. To be an admission, the statement need not have been against the declarant's interest when made, and may even be in the form of an opinion. Personal knowledge is not required; the admission may be predicated on hearsay. The following types of admissions merit special attention.

   a. **Judicial and Extrajudicial Admissions**
   Formal judicial admissions (*e.g.,* in pleadings, stipulations, etc.) are conclusive. *Informal* judicial admissions made during testimony and *extrajudicial* (evidentiary) admissions are not conclusive and can be explained.

   b. **Adoptive Admissions**
   A party may make an admission by expressly or impliedly adopting or acquiescing in the statement of another.

      1) **Silence**
      If a reasonable person would have responded, and a party remains silent in the face of accusatory statements, his silence may be considered an implied admission. Silence is treated as an admission only if:

         (i) The party *heard and understood* the statement;

         (ii) The party was physically and mentally *capable of denying* the statement; and

         (iii) A *reasonable person would have denied* the accusation.

      Note that silence in the face of accusations by police in a *criminal case* is almost never considered an admission of a crime.

   c. **Vicarious Admissions**

      1) **Co-Parties**
      Admissions of a party are not receivable against her co-parties merely because they happen to be joined as parties.

2) **Authorized Spokesperson**

The statement of a person authorized by a party to speak on its behalf (*e.g.*, statement by company's press agent) can be admitted against the party as an admission.

3) **Principal-Agent**

Statements by an agent concerning any matter within the scope of her agency, made while the employment relationship exists, are not hearsay and are admissible against the principal.

4) **Partners**

After a partnership is shown to exist, an admission of one partner relating to matters within the scope of the partnership business is binding upon her co-partners.

5) **Co-Conspirators**

Admissions of one conspirator, made to a third party in furtherance of a conspiracy to commit a crime or civil wrong at a time when the declarant was participating in the conspiracy, are admissible against co-conspirators. However, testimonial admissions of a conspirator are admissible against another conspirator only if there was an opportunity to cross-examine the hearsay declarant.

6) **Privies in Title and Joint Tenants—State Courts Only**

In most state courts, admissions of each joint owner are admissible against the other, and admissions of a former owner of real property made at the time she held title are admissible against those claiming under her (grantees, heirs, etc.). These statements are not considered admissions under the Federal Rules, but may be admissible under one of the hearsay exceptions (*e.g.*, statement against interest).

7) **Preliminary Determinations**

Before admitting a hearsay statement as a vicarious admission, the court must make a preliminary determination of the declarant's relationship with the party against whom the statement is offered. In making such a determination, the court *must consider the contents of the statement*, but the statement alone is not sufficient to establish the required relationship.

C. HEARSAY EXCEPTIONS—DECLARANT UNAVAILABLE

There are five important exceptions to the hearsay rule that condition admissibility of the hearsay statement on the present unavailability of the declarant to testify.

1. **"Unavailability"**

A declarant is unavailable if he:

a. Is exempt from testifying because of *privilege*;

b. *Refuses to testify* concerning the statement despite a court order;

c. Testifies to *lack of memory* of the subject matter of the statement;

d. Is unable to testify due to *death or physical or mental illness*; or

e. Is *absent* (beyond the reach of the court's subpoena), and the proponent is unable to procure his attendance by reasonable means.

2. Former Testimony

The testimony of a now-unavailable witness, given at another hearing or deposition, is admissible if:

a. The party against whom the testimony is offered or (in a civil case) the party's predecessor in interest was a *party in the former action* ("predecessor in interest" includes grantor-grantee and other privity relationships);

b. The former action involved the *same subject matter* (causes of action need not be identical);

c. The testimony was given *under oath*; and

d. The party against whom the testimony is offered had an *opportunity at the prior proceeding to develop the declarant's testimony* (*i.e.,* by direct, cross, or redirect examination).

CMR **Exam Tip** Because grand jury proceedings do not provide an opportunity for cross-examination, the *grand jury testimony* of an unavailable declarant is not admissible against a defendant under the former testimony exception to the hearsay rule. Be careful not to confuse this with a prior inconsistent statement given under oath by a witness currently testifying. Grand jury testimony is admissible in that case, both as impeachment and substantive evidence.

3. Statements Against Interest

The statement of a person, now unavailable as a witness, against that person's pecuniary, proprietary, or penal interest *when made*, as well as collateral facts contained in the statement, is admissible under the statement against interest exception to the hearsay rule. The declarant must also have had personal knowledge of the facts, and must have been aware that the statement was against her interest when she made it.

a. Risk of Criminal Liability

Note that when a criminal defendant wishes to show her innocence by introducing another's statements admitting the crime, *corroborating circumstances* indicating the trustworthiness of the statements are required.

b. "Statement" Means Single Remark

If a person makes a declaration containing statements that are against his interest (*e.g.,* "I sold the drugs") and statements that are not (*e.g.,* "X runs the drug ring"), the exception covers only those remarks that inculpate the declarant, not the entire extended declaration.

ADMISSIONS VS. STATEMENTS AGAINST INTEREST

Admissions by Party-Opponent	Statements Against Interest
Statement need not have been against interest when made.	Statement must have been against interest when made.
Declarant need not have personal knowledge of facts.	Declarant must have personal knowledge of facts.
Declarant need not be unavailable.	Declarant must be unavailable.
Declarant must be a party.	

4. **Dying Declarations—Statements Under Belief of Impending Death**
In a ***homicide prosecution or a civil action***, a statement made by a now unavailable declarant is admissible if:

   a. The declarant ***believed his death was imminent*** (he need not actually die); and

   b. The statement concerned the ***cause or circumstances*** of what he believed to be his impending death.

CMR **Exam Tip** The bar exam will likely require you to distinguish the Federal Rule on dying declarations from the traditional rule. Beware of answer choices reflecting the traditional rule, which required that the declarant ultimately die of the injury and restricted the statement's use to homicide prosecutions.

5. **Statements of Personal or Family History**
Statements by a now unavailable declarant concerning births, marriages, divorces, relationship, genealogical status, etc., are admissible provided that:

   a. The declarant is a ***member of the family*** in question or intimately associated with it; and

   b. The statements are based on the declarant's ***personal knowledge*** of the facts or her knowledge of family reputation.

6. **Statements Offered Against Party Procuring Declarant's Unavailability**
The statement of a person (now unavailable as a witness) is admissible when offered against a party who has engaged or acquiesced in wrongdoing that ***intentionally procured the declarant's unavailability***.

HEARSAY EXCEPTIONS— **UNAVAILABILITY REQUIRED**	
Former Testimony	Statement made *under oath* at same or at other proceeding at which the party against whom it is offered had *motive and opportunity to develop testimony*.
Statement Against Interest	Statement against declarant's *pecuniary, proprietary, or penal interest when made*.
Dying Declaration	Statement made while declarant *believed death was imminent, concerning the cause* or circumstances of the impending death.
Statement of Personal or Family History	Statement of personal or family history (*e.g.,* birth, death, marriage) *made by family member* or one intimately associated with the family.
Statement Offered Against Party Procuring Declarant's Unavailability	Statement of unavailable declarant *offered against party who procured* declarant's unavailability.

D. HEARSAY EXCEPTIONS—DECLARANT'S AVAILABILITY IMMATERIAL

The following exceptions to the hearsay rule do not require that the declarant be unavailable.

1. Present State of Mind

A statement of a declarant's then-existing state of mind, emotion, sensation, or physical condition is admissible. It is usually offered to establish a person's intent or as circumstantial evidence that the intent was carried out. Except as to certain facts concerning the declarant's will, however, a statement of memory or belief is not admissible to prove the truth of the fact remembered or believed.

2. Excited Utterances

An out-of-court statement *relating to a startling event*, made while under the stress of the excitement from the event (*i.e., before the declarant had time to reflect* upon it), is admissible.

3. Present Sense Impressions

Comments made concurrently with the sense impression of an event that is not necessarily exciting may be admissible. There is little time for a calculated misstatement, and the contemporaneous nature of the statement makes it reliable.

4. **Declarations of Physical Condition**

    a. **Present Bodily Condition—Admissible**
        A spontaneous declaration of present bodily condition is admissible as an exception to the hearsay rule even though not made to a physician.

    b. **Past Bodily Condition—Admissible If to Assist Diagnosis or Treatment**
        Generally, declarations of past physical condition are inadmissible hearsay. Under the Federal Rules, however, these declarations are admissible if made to medical personnel to assist in diagnosing or treating the condition. Even declarations about the cause or source of the condition are admissible if pertinent to diagnosis or treatment.

        CMR | **Exam Tip** | Remember that, contrary to the majority state view, declarations of past physical condition made to a doctor employed to testify are *admissible* under the Federal Rules.

5. **Business Records**
    Any writing or record made as a memorandum of any act or transaction is admissible in evidence as proof of that act or transaction. Under the Federal Rules and modern statutes, the main requirements for admissibility are as follows:

    a. **"Business"**
        "Business" includes every association, profession, occupation, or calling of any kind, whether or not conducted for profit.

    b. **Entry Made in Regular Course of Business**
        To be admissible, it must appear that the record was made in the course of a regularly conducted business activity, and that it was customary to make the type of entry involved (*i.e.,* the entrant had a duty to make the entry). Self-serving accident reports prepared primarily for litigation usually are inadmissible.

    c. **Personal Knowledge**
        The business record must consist of matters within the personal knowledge of the entrant or within the knowledge of someone with a *duty* to transmit such matters to the entrant.

        CMR | **Exam Tip** | Watch for fact patterns involving police reports containing the statements of witnesses. While police reports may qualify as business records under some circumstances, remember that generally witnesses, or even parties, are not under a business duty to convey information to the police. Therefore, a report containing their statements cannot qualify as a business record, although it may be admissible under another exception (*see* 7., *infra*) or as an admission.

    d. **Entry Made Near Time of Event**
        The entry must be made at or near the time of the transaction.

    e. **Authentication**
        The authenticity of the record must be established. This can be accomplished by the custodian (i) *testifying* that the record is a business record, or (ii) *certifying in writing* that the record is a business record.

 Exam Tip Business records may be used to prove the nonoccurrence or nonexistence of a matter if it was the regular practice of the business to record all such matters.

6. Past Recollection Recorded

If the witness's memory cannot be revived, a party may introduce a memorandum that the witness made at or near the time of the event. For admissibility requirements, *see* VI.B.3.b., *supra*. The writing itself is not admissible; it must be read to the jury.

7. Official Records and Other Official Writings

a. Public Records and Reports

The following are admissible: records setting forth the activities of the office or agency; recordings of matters observed pursuant to a duty imposed by law (except police observations in criminal cases); or in civil actions and *against the government in criminal cases*, records of factual findings resulting from an investigation authorized by law. The writing must have been made by and within the scope of the duty of the public employee, and it must have been made at or near the time of the event.

CMR **Exam Tip** Police reports that do not qualify as business records may be admitted under the public records and reports exception. Even the officer's opinions and factual (not legal) conclusions would be admissible under this exception. Be careful, however, to test the statements of others contained in the report to make sure they are admissible under a hearsay exception; otherwise, those statements will be excluded even if the report is admitted.

CMR **Exam Tip** Remember that public records and reports generally are *not admissible against the defendant in a criminal case*. This means that investigative reports by the police, FBI, and other agencies are inadmissible in this situation.

b. Records of Vital Statistics

Records of vital statistics are admissible if the report was made to a public officer pursuant to requirements of law.

c. Statement of Absence of Public Record

Evidence in the form of a certification or testimony from the custodian of public records that she has diligently searched and failed to find a record is admissible to prove that the matter was not recorded, or inferentially that the matter did not occur.

d. Judgments

A certified copy of a judgment is always admissible proof that such judgment has been entered.

1) Prior Criminal Conviction—Felony Conviction Admissible

Under the Federal Rules, judgments of felony convictions are admissible in criminal and civil actions to prove any fact essential to the judgment. In a criminal case, however, the government may use the judgment for this purpose only against the accused; it may be used only for impeachment purposes against others.

HEARSAY EXCEPTIONS—AVAILABILITY IMMATERIAL

State of Mind	Statement of **then-existing state of mind, emotion, sensation, or physical condition**. (Usually introduced to establish **intent**. Admissible when state of mind is a material issue or to show subsequent acts of declarant.)
Excited Utterance	Statement made while **under stress of excitement of startling event**.
Present Sense Impression	Statement made **concurrently with perception** of event described.
Medical Diagnosis or Treatment	Statement made to **medical personnel** for the purpose of diagnosis or treatment.
Recorded Recollection	**Writing by witness who cannot now remember** the facts, made while the facts were fresh in her mind.
Business Records or Absence Thereof	Writing made in the **regular course of business**, consisting of matters within the **personal knowledge** of one with a **business duty** to transmit. Lack of such writing may be used to show nonoccurrence of event.
Public Records and Reports or Absence Thereof; Records of Vital Statistics	Records and reports of **public agencies** regarding their activities, and records of **births, deaths, marriages,** etc. Absence of public record is admissible to show nonexistence of matter.
Judgments	A copy of a judgment of a **prior felony conviction** is admissible to prove any fact essential to the judgment. In a criminal case, it may be used for this purpose only against the accused.
Ancient Documents	Documents **20 years old** or more.
Documents Affecting Property Interests	Statements in a document affecting an interest in a property (*e.g., deed, will*).
Learned Treatises	Statements from **authoritative works** admitted if called to attention of expert witness and **established as reliable** authority.
Reputation	Reputation evidence concerning a person's **character**, a person's **personal or family history**, land **boundaries**, or a community's **general history**.
Family Records	Statements of fact found in **family Bibles, jewelry engravings, tombstones,** etc.
Market Reports	Market reports and public compilations **generally relied on by the public** or persons of a particular occupation.

      2) Prior Criminal Acquittal—Excluded
      The exclusionary rule is still applied to records of prior acquittals.

      3) Judgment in Former Civil Case
      A civil judgment is clearly inadmissible in a subsequent criminal proceeding and generally inadmissible in subsequent civil proceedings.

8. Ancient Documents and Documents Affecting Property Interests
Under the Federal Rules, statements in any authenticated document *20 years old or more* are admissible, as are statements in *any document affecting an interest in property*, regardless of age.

9. Learned Treatises
Treatises are admissible as substantive proof under the Federal Rules if:

a.   Called to the attention of, or relied upon by, an expert witness; and

b.   Established as reliable authority by the testimony of that witness, other expert testimony, or judicial notice.

10. Reputation
Reputation evidence is admissible, under several exceptions to the hearsay rule, as evidence of the following: (i) character; (ii) personal or family history; (iii) land boundaries; and (iv) a community's general history.

11. Family Records
Statements of fact concerning personal or family history contained in family Bibles, jewelry engravings, genealogies, tombstone engravings, etc., are admissible.

12. Market Reports
Market reports and other published compilations are admissible if generally used and relied upon by the public or by persons in a particular occupation.

E. RESIDUAL "CATCH-ALL" EXCEPTION OF FEDERAL RULES
For a hearsay statement that is not covered by a specific exception to be admitted, the Federal Rules provide a catch-all exception, which requires:

1.   That the hearsay statement possess circumstantial guarantees of *trustworthiness*;

2.   That the statement be strictly *necessary*; and

3.   That *notice* be given to the adversary as to the nature of the statement.

F. CONSTITUTIONAL ISSUES
Because the use of hearsay evidence in a criminal case may violate the Confrontation Clause, prior testimonial evidence is inadmissible against a criminal defendant unless the hearsay declarant is unavailable, and the defendant had an opportunity to cross-examine the hearsay declarant at the time the statement was made. However, the defendant forfeits his right of confrontation if he committed a wrongful act that was intended to keep the witness from testifying. In addition, hearsay rules and other exclusionary rules cannot be applied where such application would deprive the accused of her right to a fair trial or deny her right to compulsory process.

CMR SUMMARY CHART

ADMISSIBLE OUT-OF-COURT STATEMENTS

NONHEARSAY

1. Nonassertive Conduct

2. Statement Not Offered for Its Truth

3. Prior Inconsistent Statement Made Under Oath

4. Prior Consistent Statement Offered to Rebut Charge that Witness Is Lying or Exaggerating

5. Prior Statement of Identification

6. Admission of Party-Opponent (including vicarious admission)

HEARSAY EXCEPTIONS

Unavailability Required

1. Former Testimony

2. Dying Declaration

3. Statement Against Interest

4. Statement of Personal or Family History

5. Statement Offered Against Party Procuring Declarant's Unavailability

Availability Immaterial

1. State of Mind

2. Excited Utterance

3. Present Sense Impression

4. Physical Condition (Medical Diagnosis or Treatment)

5. Recorded Recollection

6. Business Records or Absence Thereof

7. Public Records and Reports

8. Records of Vital Statistics

9. Judgments of Prior Convictions

10. Ancient Documents

11. Documents Affecting a Property Interest

12. Learned Treatises

13. Reputation

14. Family Records

15. Market Reports

VIII. PROCEDURAL CONSIDERATIONS

A. BURDENS OF PROOF

The burden of proof encompasses the burden of producing or going forward with the evidence, and the burden of persuasion.

1. Burden of Producing Evidence

The party who has the burden of pleading usually has the burden of producing or going forward with evidence sufficient to make out a prima facie case (*i.e.,* create a fact question of the issue for the trier of fact). Once the party has satisfied the burden of going forward with evidence, it is incumbent upon the other side to come forward with evidence to rebut the accepted evidence.

2. Burden of Persuasion (Proof)

After the parties have sustained their burden of production of evidence, the question is whether the party with the burden of persuasion has satisfied it. The burden of persuasion for civil cases is usually by a preponderance of the evidence (more probably true than not true), although some civil cases require proof of clear and convincing evidence (high probability). The burden of persuasion for criminal cases is beyond a reasonable doubt.

B. PRESUMPTIONS

A presumption is a rule that requires that a particular inference be drawn from an ascertained set of facts. It is a form of substitute proof in that proof of the presumed fact is rendered unnecessary once evidence has been introduced of the basic fact that gives rise to the presumption.

1. Effect—Shift Burden of Production

A presumption operates, until rebutted, to shift the burden of production to the party against whom the presumption operates.

CMR | **Exam Tip** | Remember that a presumption *does not shift the burden of persuasion*. The burden of persuasion remains on the same party throughout a trial.

2. Rebutting a Presumption

A presumption is overcome or destroyed when the adversary produces some evidence contradicting the presumed fact. Once sufficient contrary evidence is admitted, the presumption is of no force or effect.

3. Distinguish True Presumptions from Inferences and Substantive Law

True presumptions are the rebuttable type discussed above. Be careful not to confuse them with inferences and rules of substantive law.

a. Permissible Inferences

A permissible inference may allow the party to meet his burden of production (*e.g.,* establish a prima facie case), but does not shift the burden to the adversary. Examples include the inference of negligence arising from res ipsa loquitur, the inference that destroyed evidence was unfavorable to the spoliator, and the inference of undue influence when a will's drafter is also the principal beneficiary.

b. **"Presumptions" in Criminal Cases**

The presumption of innocence in criminal cases is merely a permissible inference. The burden of production never shifts to the accused.

CMR **Exam Tip** Special considerations apply when true presumptions arise in the criminal context. The judge cannot instruct the jury that it *must* find a presumed fact against the accused; he must instruct them that they *may* regard the basic facts as sufficient evidence of the presumed fact.

CMR **Exam Tip** If, in a criminal case, a presumed fact establishes guilt, is an element of the offense, or negates a defense, it must be proved beyond a reasonable doubt.

c. **Conclusive Presumptions**

Because it cannot be rebutted, a conclusive presumption (*e.g.,* that a child under age seven cannot commit a crime) is really a rule of substantive law.

4. **Specific Presumptions**

The following are common rebuttable presumptions:

a. **Legitimacy**

Every person is presumed to be legitimate.

b. **Against Suicide**

When cause of death is in dispute, there is a presumption in civil cases that it was not suicide.

c. **Sanity**

Every person is presumed sane in civil and criminal cases until the contrary is shown.

d. **Death from Absence**

If a person is unexplainably absent for a continuous period of seven years and he has not been heard from, he is presumed dead.

e. **Ownership of Car—Agent Driver**

Proof of ownership of a motor vehicle creates the presumption that the owner was the driver or that the driver was the owner's agent.

f. **Chastity**

Every person is presumed chaste and virtuous.

g. **Regularity**

It is presumed that persons acting in an official office are properly performing their duties.

h. **Continuance**

Proof of the existence of a person or condition at a given time raises a presumption that it continued for as long as it is usual with things of that nature.

i. **Mail Delivery**

A letter, properly addressed, stamped, and mailed, is presumed to have been delivered.

j. Solvency
A person is presumed solvent, and every debt is presumed collectible.

k. Bailee's Negligence
Proof of delivery of goods in good condition to a bailee and failure of the bailee to return the goods in the same condition create the presumption that the bailee was negligent.

l. Marriage
Upon proof of a marriage ceremony, a marriage is presumed valid.

5. Conflicting Presumptions
When two or more conflicting presumptions arise, the judge should apply the presumption founded on the weightier considerations of policy and logic.

6. Choice of Law Regarding Presumptions in Civil Actions
Under the Federal Rules, state law governs the effect of a presumption concerning a fact that is an element of a claim or defense to which, under the *Erie* doctrine, the rule of decision is supplied by state law.

C. RELATIONSHIP OF PARTIES, JUDGE, AND JURY

1. Allocation of Responsibilities
In our adversarial adjudicative process, the focus is on the party's responsibility to frame the issues in a litigation and to assume the burden of proving the issues he has raised. The trial judge's primary responsibility is to superintend the trial fairly. As a general rule, questions of law are for the trial judge to determine and questions of fact are for the jury.

2. Preliminary Determination of Admissibility
In most cases, the existence of some preliminary or foundational fact is an essential condition to the admissibility of proffered evidence. The Federal Rules distinguish preliminary facts to be decided by the jury from those to be decided by the judge on the ground that the former questions involve the relevancy of the proffered evidence, while the latter questions involve the competency of evidence that is relevant.

a. Preliminary Facts Decided by Jury
Examples of preliminary facts to be decided by the jury include agency, authenticity of a document, credibility of a witness, and personal knowledge.

b. Preliminary Facts Decided by Judge
Facts affecting the competency of the evidence must be determined by the trial judge. Requirements for hearsay exceptions, privileges, and expert testimony, as well as mental competence, must also be decided by the judge.

1) What Evidence May Be Considered
The Federal Rules permit the trial judge to consider any relevant evidence even though not otherwise admissible under the rules of evidence. Most state courts, however, hold that the rules of evidence apply in preliminary fact determinations as much as in any other phase of the trial; thus, only admissible evidence may be considered.

2) **Presence of Jury**
Whether the jury should be excused during the preliminary fact determination is generally within the discretion of the trial judge.

c. **Testimony by Accused Does Not Waive Privilege Against Self-Incrimination**
An accused may testify on any preliminary matter (*e.g.*, circumstances surrounding an allegedly illegal search) without subjecting herself to testifying at trial.

d. **Judicial Power to Comment upon Evidence**
A judge may comment on the weight of the evidence in federal courts, but generally not in state courts.

e. **Power to Call Witnesses**
A judge may call and interrogate witnesses on her own initiative.

f. **Rulings**
A trial judge has an obligation to rule promptly on counsel's evidentiary objections and, upon request, to state the grounds for her rulings.

g. **Instructions on Limited Admissibility of Evidence**
A judge will restrict evidence to its proper scope and instruct the jury accordingly.

REAL PROPERTY

TABLE OF CONTENTS

REAL PROPERTY

I. ESTATES IN LAND

A. PRESENT POSSESSORY ESTATES

A present possessory estate is an interest that gives the holder the right to present possession.

1. Fee Simple Absolute

A fee simple absolute is the largest estate recognized by law. It can be sold, divided, devised, or inherited and has an indefinite or potentially *infinite duration*. Today, a fee simple is presumed in the absence of express contrary intent (words of inheritance are no longer necessary).

2. Defeasible Fees

Defeasible fees are fee simple estates (*i.e.,* of uncertain or potentially infinite duration) that can be terminated upon the happening of a stated event.

a. Fee Simple Determinable (and Possibility of Reverter)

A fee simple determinable terminates upon the happening of a stated event and *automatically reverts* to the grantor. It is created by durational language, such as "for so long as," "while," "during," or "until." A fee simple determinable can be conveyed, but the grantee takes subject to the estate's being terminated by the specified event.

CMR **Exam Tip** Remember that statements of motive or purpose do not create a determinable fee. To create a fee simple determinable, words limiting the *duration* of the estate must be used. Watch for grants such as "for the purpose of" and "to be used for"; they are merely expressions of motive.

1) Correlative Future Interest in Grantor—Possibility of Reverter

Whenever a grantor conveys a fee simple determinable, he *automatically* retains a possibility of reverter, which is a reversionary future interest. A possibility of reverter is transferable, descendible, and devisable.

b. Fee Simple Subject to Condition Subsequent (and Right of Entry)

A fee simple subject to a condition subsequent is an estate in which the grantor *reserves the right to terminate* the estate upon the happening of a stated event; *i.e.,* the estate does not automatically terminate—the grantor must take some action. The estate is created by use of conditional words, such as "upon condition that," "provided that," "but if," and "if it happens that."

1) Correlative Future Interest in Grantor—Right of Entry

The right to terminate, reserved by the grantor, is called a right of entry. It must be *expressly reserved*; in contrast with a possibility of reverter, it does not arise automatically. Some courts hold that rights of entry are not transferable inter vivos, but most states agree they are devisable and all states agree they are descendible.

CMR **Exam Tip** A conveyance that contains both durational language *and* a power of termination will likely be construed as creating a fee simple subject to a condition subsequent, because the forfeiture is *optional* at the grantor's election rather than automatic. Policy disfavors forfeiture of estates.

c.   Fee Simple Subject to an Executory Interest
If a fee simple estate terminates upon the happening of a stated event (because it is determinable or subject to a condition subsequent) and then passes to a third party rather than reverting to the grantor or giving the grantor a right to terminate, the third party has an executory interest.

Examples: 1) "To A and his heirs for so long as liquor is not sold on the premises; in that event, to B." B has an executory interest.

2) "Blackacre to XYZ Church, but if it is used for anything other than church purposes, then to B." B has an executory interest.

3.   Fee Tail
The fee tail is an estate where **_inheritability is limited to lineal heirs_**. It is created by the words "to A and the heirs of his body." Most jurisdictions have abolished the fee tail, and an attempt to create one results in a **_fee simple_**.

4.   Life Estate
A life estate is one **_measured by the life_** or lives of one or more persons. It may be created by operation of law (*e.g.,* dower) or by conveyance.

a.   Life Estates by Marital Right (Legal Life Estates)
Dower and curtesy were the common law interests of a spouse in the real property of the other spouse. These interests could not be defeated by conveyance or by creditors. Most states have abolished dower and curtesy in favor of a statutory right to a portion of a spouse's estate.

b.   Conventional Life Estates

1)   For Life of Grantee
The usual life estate is measured by the life of the grantee (*e.g.,* "to A for life"). This type of life estate may be implied from language such as "to B after the life of A."

2)   Life Estate Pur Autre Vie (Life of Another)
A life estate "pur autre vie" is measured by a life **_other than the grantee's_** (*e.g.,* "to A for the life of B"). A life estate pur autre vie also results when the **_life tenant conveys_** his life estate to another (*e.g.,* if A, the holder of a life estate, conveys his interest to B, B has a life estate for the life of A).

CMR **Exam Tip**   Although a life estate is usually indefeasible (*i.e.,* it ends only when the life tenant dies), it is possible to create life estates that are defeasible in the same ways that fee estates can be defeasible. A life estate can be determinable, subject to a condition subsequent, and subject to an executory interest (*e.g.,* "to A for life so long as alcohol is not used on the premises" or "to A for life, but if A is divorced, to B").

c.   Rights and Duties of Life Tenant—Doctrine of Waste
A life tenant is entitled to any **_ordinary_** uses and profits of the land, but cannot do anything that injures the interests of a remainderman or reversioner. A future interest holder may sue for damages or to enjoin such acts.

PRESENT POSSESSORY ESTATES

Present Estate	Examples	Duration	Correlative Future Interest in Grantor	Correlative Future Interest in Third Party
Fee Simple Absolute	"To A & his heirs"	Forever	None	None
Fee Simple Determinable	"To A & his heirs for so long as . . ." until . . ." while . . ." during . . ."	As long as condition is met, then **automatically** to grantor	Possibility of Reverter	(*See* Fee Simple Subject to an Executory Interest, below)
Fee Simple Subject to Condition Subsequent	"To A & his heirs, but if . . ." upon condition that . . ." provided that . . ."	Until happening of named event **and** reentry by grantor	Right of Entry	(*See* Fee Simple Subject to an Executory Interest, below)
Fee Simple Subject to an Executory Interest	"To A & his heirs for so long as . . ., and if not . . ., to B"	As long as condition is met, then to third party	(*See* Fee Simple Determinable, above)	Executory Interest
	"To A & his heirs, but if . . ., to B"	Until happening of event	(*See* Fee Simple Subject to Condition Subsequent, above)	Executory Interest
Fee Tail	"To A & the heirs of his body"	Until A and his line die out	Reversion	None (but remainder is possible)
Life Estate (may be defeasible)	"To A for life," **or** "To A for the life of B"	Until the end of the measuring life	Reversion	None (*but see* below)
	"To A for life, then to B"	Until the end of the measuring life	None	Remainder
	"To A for life, but if . . ., to B"	Until the end of the measuring life **or** the happening of the named event	Reversion	Executory Interest

1) **Affirmative (Voluntary) Waste—Natural Resources**
Exploitation of natural resources (*e.g.,* minerals) by a life tenant is generally limited to situations when: (i) necessary for *repair or maintenance* of the land; (ii) the land is *suitable only for such use*; or (iii) it is expressly or impliedly *permitted by the grantor*. Under the open mines doctrine, if mining was done on the land prior to the life estate, the life tenant can continue mining—but is limited to the mines *already open*.

2) **Permissive Waste**
Permissive waste occurs when a life tenant fails to protect or preserve the land. A life tenant is obligated to: (i) preserve the *land and structures in a reasonable state of repair*; (ii) pay *interest* on mortgages (not principal); (iii) pay *ordinary taxes* on the land; and (iv) pay *special assessments* for public improvements *of short duration* (improvements of long duration are apportioned between the life tenant and future interest holder). A life tenant is *not* obliged to insure the premises for the benefit of remaindermen and is not responsible for damages caused by a third-party tortfeasor.

3) **Ameliorative Waste**
Ameliorative waste is a change that *benefits* the property economically. This waste was actionable at common law, but now a life tenant may alter or even demolish existing buildings if:

(i) The market value of the future interests is not diminished; and *either*

(ii) The remaindermen do not object; *or*

(iii) A substantial and permanent change in the neighborhood conditions (*e.g.,* change from residential to 90% industrial) has deprived the property in its current form of reasonable productivity or usefulness.

a) **Compare—Leasehold Tenant**
Leasehold tenants remain liable for ameliorative waste even if the neighborhood has changed and the market value of the premises was increased.

b) **Compare—Worthless Property**
If the land is practically worthless in its present state, the life tenant may seek a partition sale, the proceeds of which are put in trust with income paid to the life tenant.

d. **Renunciation of Life Estate**
If a life tenant who receives the estate by will or intestacy renounces his interest, the future interest following the life estate is generally accelerated so that it becomes immediately possessory.

5. **Estate for Years, Periodic Estate, Estate at Will, Tenancy at Sufferance**
These present estates are considered in the next chapter, which concerns the landlord-tenant relationship.

B. FUTURE INTERESTS
A future interest gives its holder the right or possibility of *future* possession of an estate. It is a *present*, legally protected right in property.

1. Reversionary Interests—Future Interests in Transferor

    a. Possibilities of Reverter and Rights of Entry
    These interests are discussed *supra* in connection with defeasible fees.

CMR COMPARISON CHART

POSSIBILITY OF REVERTER VS. RIGHT OF ENTRY

	Possibility of Reverter	Right of Entry
Correlative Present Interest	Fee Simple Determinable	Fee Simple Subject to Condition Subsequent
Example	"To A so long as alcohol is not used on the premises"	"To A on condition that if alcohol is used on the premises, O shall have the right to reenter and retake the premises"
Rights of Grantor	Estate *automatically* reverts to grantor upon occurrence of stated event	Estate does not revert automatically; *grantor must exercise his right of entry*
Alienability	Transferable, descendible, and devisable	Descendible and devisable, but some courts hold not transferable inter vivos

    b. Reversions
    A reversion is the estate left in a grantor who conveys less than she owns (*e.g.*, O conveys "to A for life"; O has a reversion). It arises by operation of law; it does not have to be expressly reserved. A reversion is alienable, devisable, and inheritable. Its holder can sue for waste and for tortious damage to the reversionary interest.

CMR **Exam Tip** All reversionary interests are *vested* and, thus, not subject to the Rule Against Perpetuities.

2. Remainders
A remainder is a future interest *in a third person* that can become possessory on the *natural expiration* of the preceding estate. It cannot divest a prior estate, and it cannot follow a time

gap after the preceding estate. A remainder must be *expressly created* in the instrument creating the preceding possessory estate.

Examples: 1) O conveys "to A for life, then to B and his heirs"; B has a remainder.

2) O conveys "to A for life, then to B and his heirs one day after A's death"; B does *not* have a remainder (because there is a gap).

CMR Exam Tip Because a remainder cannot "cut short" a preceding estate, it can *never follow a fee simple* estate, which is of potentially infinite duration. Executory interests are the future interests that cut short preceding estates or follow a gap after them.

a. Indefeasibly Vested Remainder

A vested remainder is one created in an *existing and ascertained* person, and *not subject to a condition precedent*. The remainderman has a right to immediate possession upon normal termination of the preceding estate. An *indefeasibly* vested remainder is a vested remainder that is not subject to divestment or diminution.

b. Vested Remainder Subject to Open

This is a vested remainder created in a class of persons (*e.g.,* "children") that is certain to become possessory, but is *subject to diminution*—by the birth of additional persons who will share in the remainder as a class.

Example: O conveys "to A for life, then to the children of B." A and B are living and B has one child, C. C has a vested remainder subject to open.

c. Vested Remainder Subject to Total Divestment

This is a vested remainder that is subject to a *condition subsequent*.

Example: O conveys "to A for life, then to B and his heirs; but if B dies unmarried, then to C and his heirs." B has a vested remainder subject to complete divestment by C's executory interest.

CMR Exam Tip Where language is ambiguous, the preference is for vested remainders subject to divestment rather than contingent remainders or executory interests. Policy favors early vesting of estates.

d. Contingent Remainder

Contingent remainders are those created in *unborn or unascertained* persons, or *subject to a condition precedent*.

1) Subject to Condition Precedent

A condition is precedent if it must be satisfied before the remainderman has a right to possession.

Examples: 1) O conveys "to A for life, then to B and his heirs *if* B marries C." B's remainder is contingent because he must marry C before he can take possession.

2) O conveys "to A for life, then to B and his heirs if B marries C, otherwise to D and his heirs." B and D have *alternative contingent remainders*.

Compare: O conveys "to A for life, then to B and his heirs; but if B marries C, then to D and his heirs." B has a vested remainder (because no condition precedent) subject to divestment by D's executory interest.

2) Unborn or Unascertained Persons

A remainder created in unborn or unascertained persons is contingent because until the remainderman is ascertained, no one is ready to take possession if the preceding estate ends.

Example: O conveys "to A for life, then to the children of B." If B is childless at the time, the remainder is contingent.

3) Destructibility of Contingent Remainders

At common law, a contingent remainder was destroyed if it failed to vest before or upon the termination of the preceding freehold estate.

Example: O conveys "to A for life, then to B if she reaches age 21." If A dies before B reaches age 21, B's remainder is destroyed.

Most states have abolished the destructibility rule. In those states, B's interest in the above example would be converted to an executory interest upon A's death because it will divest O's reversionary estate when B turns 21.

a) Related Doctrine of Merger

When one person acquires all of the present and future interests in land except a contingent remainder, under the common law, the contingent remainder is destroyed.

Example: O conveys "to A for life, then to B's children." If, before B has any children, O purchases A's life estate, O will have a life estate pur autre vie and a reversion. These interests merge, and the contingent remainder in B's unborn children is destroyed.

CMR   **Exam Tip**   When considering whether estates merge to destroy a contingent remainder, remember that if the life estate and the next vested interest were ***created by the same instrument***, there is no merger. (This would defeat the grantor's obvious intent.) Merger ***may*** occur only as in the example above, when one person later acquires immediately successive estates.

e. Rule in Shelley's Case (Rule Against Remainders in Grantee's Heirs)

At common law, if the same instrument created a life estate in A and gave the remainder only to A's heirs, the remainder was not recognized, and A took the life estate ***and*** the remainder.

Example: O conveys "to A for life, then to B for life, then to the heirs of A." The Rule transforms the remainder in A's heirs into a remainder in A. (No merger, however, because the remainder for life in B is ***vested***.)

The Rule in Shelley's Case has been abolished in most states.

f. Doctrine of Worthier Title (Rule Against Remainders in Grantor's Heirs)

Under the Doctrine of Worthier Title ("DOWT"), a remainder in the grantor's heirs is invalid and becomes a reversion in the grantor.

Example: O grants Blackacre "to A for life, then to the heirs of O." Under DOWT, A has a life estate, and O has a reversion.

DOWT is generally treated as a ***rule of construction*** (*i.e.,* it does not apply if an intent to create a remainder in heirs has been clearly manifested). DOWT applies only to inter vivos transfers (not wills), and only if the word "heirs" is used.

CMR SUMMARY CHART — TECHNICAL RULES OF THE COMMON LAW

	Destruction of Contingent Remainders	Rule in Shelley's Case	Doctrine of Worthier Title
Rule	Contingent remainders are destroyed if not vested at time of termination of preceding estate.	A remainder in a life tenant-grantee's heirs is deemed to be in the life tenant herself.	A remainder in the grantor's heirs is ineffective, so grantor has a reversion.
Example	"To A for life, remainder to A's children who reach 21."	"To A for life, then to A's heirs."	"To A for life, then to my heirs at law."
Result	If A has no children who are at least 21 at time of her death, property reverts to grantor.	A has a fee simple.	A has a life estate; grantor has a reversion.
Modern Status	Abolished in most jurisdictions.	Abolished in most jurisdictions.	Generally treated as rule of construction only.
Modern Result	Property reverts to grantor; A's children have a springing executory interest.	A's heirs have a contingent remainder.	Grantor's heirs have a contingent remainder.

3. **Executory Interests**

Executory interests are future interests in third parties that either ***divest*** a transferee's preceding freehold estate ("shifting interests"), or ***follow a gap*** in possession or ***cut short*** a grantor's estate ("springing interests").

Examples: 1) In a grant from O "to A and his heirs when A marries B," A has a ***springing*** executory interest because it divests the grantor's estate.

2) In a grant from O "to A for life, then to B and his heirs; but if B predeceases A, then to C and his heirs," C has a ***shifting*** executory interest because it divests a transferee's preceding estate.

Executory interests are not considered vested and thus are subject to the Rule Against Perpetuities, but executory interests are not destructible.

CMR | **Exam Tip** | Remember that if the future interest does not follow the natural termination of the preceding estate, it must be an executory interest; only an executory interest can follow a fee simple estate.

4. **Transferability of Remainders and Executory Interests**

Vested remainders are fully transferable, descendible, and devisable. At common law, contingent remainders and executory interests were not transferable inter vivos, but most courts today hold that they are freely transferable. Contingent remainders and executory interests are descendible and devisable, provided survival is not a condition to the interest's taking.

CMR | **Exam Tip** | Any future interest that is transferable is subject to involuntary transfer; *i.e.,* it is reachable by creditors.

5. **Class Gifts**

A "class" is a group of persons having a common characteristic (*e.g.,* children, nephews). The share of each member is determined by the number of persons in the class. A class gift of a remainder may be vested subject to open (where at least one group member exists) or contingent (where all group members are unascertained).

a. **When the Class Closes—The Rule of Convenience**

Under the rule of convenience, in the absence of express contrary intent, a class closes (*i.e.,* no one born after that time may share in the gift) *when some member of the class can call for distribution* of her share of the class gift.

Examples: 1) T's will devises property to W for life, then to A's children. At the time the will is executed, A has two children, B and C. A then has another child, D. T dies. A has child E, then W dies. After W's death, A has another child, F. The class closed at W's death because it was time to make the distribution. Thus, B, C, D, and E share the property, and F is excluded.

2) T's will devises the residue of his estate "to those of A's children who attain age 21." If any of A's children is 21 at T's death, the class closes at that time. Otherwise it closes when one of A's children reaches age 21. But remember, if it had been a future gift (*i.e.,* "to A for life, then to such of A's children who attain age 21"), the class would remain open until the life tenant's death even if some of the class members had reached the stated age at T's death.

CMR | **Exam Tip** | Recall that persons in gestation at the time the class closes are included in the class.

b. **Survival**

Survival of a class member to the time of closing is usually unnecessary to share in

FUTURE INTERESTS IN TRANSFEREES

Future Interests	Example	Alienability	Subject to Rule Against Perpetuities?
Indefeasibly Vested Remainder	"To A for life, then to B."	Transferable, descendible, and devisable	No
Vested Remainder Subject to Total Divestment	"To A for life, and on A's death, to B; but if B predeceases A, then to C."	Transferable, descendible, and devisable	No
Vested Remainder Subject to Open	"To A for life, then to A's children in equal shares."	Transferable, descendible, and devisable	Yes—as long as the class remains open
Contingent Remainder	"To A for life, then to B if B marries C." *or* "To A for life, then to A's surviving children."	Transferable in most states (not at common law), descendible, and devisable	Yes
Shifting Executory Interest	"To A for life, remainder to B and her heirs; but if B predeceases A, then to C and his heirs."	Transferable in most states (not at common law), descendible, and devisable	Yes
Springing Executory Interest	"To A when and if he becomes a doctor." *or* "To A for life, then two years after A's death, to B."	Transferable in most states (not at common law), descendible, and devisable	Yes

a future gift—*unless* survival was made an express condition (*e.g.,* "to A for life and then to his *surviving* children"). However, certain terms are construed to create *implied* survivorship conditions (*e.g.,* widow, issue, heirs, next of kin).

CMR **Exam Tip** Generally, when the instrument creating a gift of a future interest in an open class becomes effective, existing class members have a vested remainder subject to open. But watch for a condition precedent, which will prevent the remainder from vesting. For example, "to A for life, remainder to those of B's children who survive A" creates a contingent remainder in B's children even if they are in existence—and even if B is dead—because the remainder is contingent on surviving A.

C. TRUSTS

A trust is a fiduciary relationship with respect to specific property (*res*) wherein the *trustee* holds legal title to the property subject to enforceable equitable rights in a *beneficiary*. The creator of a trust is the *settlor*, who must own the property at the time of trust creation and must have had the *intent* to create the trust.

1. Application of Rule Against Perpetuities
The Rule Against Perpetuities applies to the equitable future interests of the beneficiaries in a private trust just as it does to "legal" future interests.

2. Creation of Trusts
A trust can be created by will (testamentary trust), inter vivos transfer of the trust res, or inter vivos declaration that the settlor is holding property in trust. All trusts of real property must be in writing. Note that a settlor may bequeath (by will) property to a trust created during his lifetime—*i.e.,* he may "pour it over" into the trust.

3. Charitable Trusts
A charitable trust must have a charitable purpose. The rules governing charitable trusts differ from those applicable to private trusts in three important ways: (i) a charitable trust must have *indefinite beneficiaries*; (ii) it may be *perpetual* (*i.e.,* the Rule Against Perpetuities does not apply); and (iii) the *cy pres doctrine*, which allows a court to select an alternative charity when the purpose of the settlor becomes impracticable or impossible, applies. Charitable trusts may be enforced by an action of the attorney general of the state.

CMR **Exam Tip** Remember that the Rule Against Perpetuities does apply to a shift from a private to charitable use or a charitable to private use.

D. THE RULE AGAINST PERPETUITIES
No interest in property is valid unless it must vest, if at all, not later than *21 years after some life in being* ("measuring life") at the creation of the interest. If there is *any possibility* that the interest might vest more than 21 years after a life in being, the interest is void. The Rule applies to contingent remainders, executory interests, vested remainders subject to open (class gifts), options to purchase (not attached to a leasehold), rights of first refusal, and powers of appointment.

1. **When Perpetuities Period Begins to Run**
   The time the interest is created and the perpetuities period begins to run depends on the instrument and the interest created: For interests granted by *will*, it runs from the date of the *testator's death*; for *deeds*, it is the date of *delivery*. The period runs on an *irrevocable trust* from the date it is *created*; it runs on a *revocable trust* from the date it *becomes irrevocable*.

2. **"Must Vest"**
   An interest vests for purposes of the Rule when it becomes: (i) possessory, or (ii) an indefeasibly vested remainder or a vested remainder subject to total divestment.

   CMR | **Exam Tip** | In analyzing Rule Against Perpetuities problems, keep in mind that the key is when the interest *could possibly vest*—not when it is likely to vest or even when it did. You must examine the grant as of the time of its *creation* and be sure that if the interest vests it will be within the period of the Rule (*i.e.,* life in being plus 21 years). If there is *any* possibility that it could vest beyond the period, it is void.

3. **"Lives in Being"**
   Unless other measuring lives are specified, one connected with the vesting of the interest is used. Any lives may be denominated measuring lives, provided they are *human* and of reasonable number.

4. **Interests Exempt from Rule**
   Except for vested remainders subject to open, the Rule Against Perpetuities does not apply to vested interests. Thus, other vested remainders, reversions, possibilities of reverter, and rights of entry are not subject to the Rule. Moreover, there is a *charity-to-charity* exception to the Rule (*i.e.,* the Rule does not apply to any disposition over from one charity to another), and an exception for options to purchase *held by a current tenant*.

   CMR | **Exam Tip** | Remember that the Rule Against Perpetuities applies *only* to *contingent* remainders, *executory interests*, vested remainders *subject to open*, and in most states, *options to purchase*. Thus, the *grantor's interests* (reversions, possibilities of reverter, rights of entry) are safe from the Rule; you don't need to consider them.

5. **Consequence of Violating Rule—Offensive Interest Stricken**
   Violation of the Rule destroys only the offending interest. The exception is the rare case of "infectious invalidity" where the testator would probably have preferred the entire gift to fail.

6. **The Rule in Operation—Common Pitfall Cases**

   a. **Executory Interest Following Defeasible Fee**
      Generally, an executory interest that follows a defeasible fee (*e.g.,* "to A for so long as no liquor is consumed on the premises, then to B") violates the Rule Against Perpetuities, and the executory interest is stricken. (An executory interest following a defeasible fee is valid only if the condition is specific to the fee holder or expressly limited to the perpetuities period.)

Exam Tip   When a void interest is stricken, the interests are classified as if the void interest were never there. For example, if O conveys "to A for as long as no liquor is consumed on the premises, then to B," B's interest would be stricken, A would have a fee simple determinable, and O would have a possibility of reverter. In contrast, if O conveys "to A, but if liquor is ever consumed on the premises, then to B," B's interest and the condition are stricken, and A has a fee simple absolute.

b.   Age Contingency Beyond Age Twenty-One in Open Class
A gift to an open class conditioned on members surviving beyond age 21 violates the Rule.
Example: "To A for life, then to those of A's children who attain the age of 25." The remainder in A's children violates the Rule and is void.

Some states have enacted perpetuities reform legislation that reduces such age contingencies to 21.

c.   Fertile Octogenarian
A woman is conclusively presumed to be capable of bearing children, regardless of her age or medical condition.
Example: "To A for life, then to A's children for life, then to A's grandchildren in fee." The remainder in A's grandchildren is invalid despite the fact that A is 80 years old.

Some states have enacted perpetuities reform statutes that raise a presumption that women over a certain age (*e.g.,* 55) cannot bear children. Also, medical testimony regarding a woman's childbearing capacity is admissible in these states.

d.   Unborn Widow or Widower
Because a person's widow (or widower) is not determined until his death, it may turn out to be someone who was not in being at the time of the disposition.
Example: O conveys "to A for life, then to A's widow for life, then to A's surviving *issue* in fee." In the absence of a statute to the contrary, the gift to A's issue is invalid because A's widow might be a spouse who was not in being when the interest was created.

Compare: A remainder "to A's *children*" would be valid because, unlike issue, they would be determined at A's death.

Where necessary to sustain a gift, some state statutes raise a presumption that any reference to a person's spouse, widow, or widower is to a person in being at the time of the transfer.

e.   Administrative Contingency
A gift conditioned on an administrative contingency (*e.g.,* admission of will to probate) violates the Rule.
Example: A gift "to my issue surviving at the distribution of my estate" is invalid because the estate might be administered beyond the period of the Rule.

Some state reform statutes eliminate this problem by raising a presumption that the transferor intended that the contingency should occur, if at all, within 21 years.

f.   Options and Rights of First Refusal
Generally, an option to purchase or right of first refusal that is structured so that it might be exercised later than the end of the perpetuities period is void. *Exception:* The Rule Against Perpetuities does not apply to options to purchase held by the current lessee.

Example: When O conveys Blackacre to A, he includes a clause in the deed that states, "A, his heirs, and assigns promise that upon finding a ready, willing, and able buyer for Blackacre, Blackacre will be offered to O, his heirs, or assigns on the same terms." This right of first refusal can be exercised well beyond a life in being plus 21 years, and thus violates the Rule.

CMR **Exam Tip**   Watch for a fact pattern on the exam where a tenant has an option to purchase beyond the perpetuities period. Remember that the Rule does not apply to such an option held by a *current* tenant or his assignee, but it does apply to a former tenant and to any party to whom the current tenant might transfer the option separately from the lease (in jurisdictions permitting such a transfer).

7.   Application of the Rule to Class Gifts

a.   "Bad-as-to-One, Bad-as-to-All" Rule
If the interest of any class member may vest too remotely, the whole class gift fails. For the class gift to vest, the *class must be closed* and *all conditions precedent must be satisfied* for every member.

b.   "Gift to Subclass" Exception
Each gift to a subclass may be treated as a separate gift under the Rule.

Example: "Income to A for life, then to A's children for their lives. Upon the death of each of A's children, the corpus is to be distributed to that child's issue, per stirpes." The gifts to each of A's children's issue are considered separately. Thus, the gifts to issue of A's children living at the time of the disposition are good, but the gifts to the issue of afterborn children of A violate the Rule and are void.

c.   Per Capita Gift Exception
A gift of a fixed amount to each member of a class is not treated as a class gift under the Rule.

Example: "$1,000 to each of my great-grandchildren, whether born before or after my death." This creates gifts to individuals, each of whom is judged separately under the Rule.

8.   Statutory Reforms
In most states, statutes modify the Rule Against Perpetuities. "Wait and see" statutes determine an interest's validity upon the termination of the preceding life estate—if the interest *actually* vests or fails within the perpetuities period, it is good; if it does not, it is void. Some states have statutes dealing with the common pitfall cases (*see supra*). Other statutes provide alternative vesting periods (*e.g.,* 90 years), and some allow court reformation of invalid interests to carry out the donor's general intent (*e.g.,* cy pres). These reforms are irrelevant for bar exam purposes unless referred to in the question.

INTERESTS UNDER THE RULE AGAINST PERPETUITIES

Valid Interests	Void Interests
"To A for life, then to A's children for their lives; and upon the death of the last survivor, to B." (B's interest is vested.)	"To A for life, then to A's children for their lives; and upon the death of the last survivor, to A's grandchildren." (A may have a child after this interest is created, so she could have grandchildren beyond the perpetuities period.)
"To B for life, remainder to those of B's siblings who reach age 21." (B's parents can be used as measuring lives.)	"To A for life, then to such of A's children who attain age 25." (Age contingency beyond age 21 in an open class.)
"To XYZ Orphanage for so long as it is used to house orphans; if it ceases to be so used, then to the American Red Cross." (This falls within the charity-to-charity exception.)	"To Amnesty International for so long as the premises are used for Amnesty International purposes; when they cease to be so used, then to Jane Webb." (This gift passes from a charity to a private person and so does not fall within the charity-to-charity exception.)
"To A for life, and on his death to his wife, W, for life; upon W's death, to A's children then living." (No unborn widow problem because the gift is to W, a life in being.)	"To A for life, then to his widow for life, then to A's surviving descendants." (Unborn widow problem.)
"To A for life, then to B; but if at her death B is not survived by children, then to C." (B is the measuring life.)	"To A for life, then to A's children for their lives, then to A's grandchildren in fee." A is 80 years old and has had a complete hysterectomy. (Fertile octogenarian problem.)
"To A, but if alcohol is served on the premises during Z's lifetime or within 21 years of Z's death, to B." (B's interest will vest, if at all, within a life in being plus 21 years.)	"To A, but if alcohol is ever served on the premises, then to B." (Future interest following a defeasible fee.)
"Trust income to Polo Club. At the death of the survivor of A, B, C, D, and E (all babies born on this date at Obie Hospital), the trust will terminate and the corpus will be distributed to Z, his heirs, successors, or assigns." (Saving clause.)	"The residue of my estate to my descendants who are living when my estate is distributed." (Administrative contingency problem.)
"To A for life, then to A's children for their lives, then to B if B is then living, and if B is not then living, to C." (B is the measuring life. B's and C's interests will vest or fail within B's lifetime.)	"To B for life, then to such of B's children who become lawyers." (B may have a child born after the disposition who becomes a lawyer more than 21 years after B's death.)

E. THE RULE AGAINST RESTRAINTS ON ALIENATION

Generally, any restriction on the transferability of a legal (as opposed to equitable) interest is void.

1. Types of Restraints on Alienation

There are three types of restraints on alienation: (i) *disabling* restraints, under which attempted transfers are ineffective; (ii) *forfeiture* restraints, under which an attempted transfer forfeits the interest; and (iii) *promissory* restraints, under which an attempted transfer breaches a covenant.

2. Restraints on a Fee Simple

All absolute restraints on fee simple estates are void; thus, the grantee may freely transfer the property. However, restraints on fee simple estates for a *limited time* and *reasonable purpose* are likely to be upheld (*e.g.*, a restraint limited to the joint lifetimes of co-owners as a reasonable way to ensure that neither will have to reside with a stranger).

a. Discriminatory Restraints

Judicial enforcement of restraints prohibiting the transfer or use of property to or by a person of a specified racial, religious, or ethnic group is *discriminatory state action* forbidden by the Fourteenth Amendment. Discriminatory restrictions may also violate the Fair Housing Act.

3. Restraints on a Life Estate

Forfeiture and promissory restraints on life estates are valid, but disabling restraints are void.

CMR | **Exam Tip** | Remember that the Rule Against Restraints on Alienation applies only to legal interests. Restraints on the alienation of *equitable* interests (*e.g.,* spendthrift clauses in trust instruments) are valid.

4. Other Valid Restraints on Alienation

The following are valid restraints on alienation:

a. Forfeiture restraints on transferability of future interests;

b. Reasonable restrictions in commercial transactions;

c. Rights of first refusal; and

d. Restrictions on assignment and sublease of leaseholds (*e.g.,* requiring landlord's consent).

F. CONCURRENT ESTATES

An estate in land can be held concurrently by several persons, all of whom have the right to enjoyment and possession of the land.

1. Joint Tenancy

A joint tenancy's distinguishing feature is the *right of survivorship*. When one joint tenant dies, the property is *freed* from her concurrent interest (her survivors do not succeed to it).

a. **Creation**

The common law requires four unities—*time, title, interest, possession*—to create a joint tenancy; *i.e.,* the interests of joint tenants must be *equal* in every way. They must take *identical* interests, at the *same time*, by the *same instrument*, with the *same right to possession*. Thus, all interests in a joint tenancy must be equal shares. If there are three joint tenants, they each own an undivided one-third interest. In a tenancy in common, by contrast, equal shares are presumed, but are not required. In a tenancy in common held by three parties, one tenant may own a two-thirds undivided interest while each of the other two tenants holds an undivided one-sixth share. In addition, modern law requires a clear expression of a right of survivorship; otherwise a conveyance to two or more persons is *presumed to be a tenancy in common*.

CMR **Exam Tip** If the bar examiners tell you in the question that the parties are joint tenants, take it as given that they are joint tenants with right of survivorship. In this situation, *do not* apply the presumption that any conveyance to two or more persons is a tenancy in common. The bar examiners are not testing your knowledge of that presumption unless the fact pattern actually gives you the quoted language of the grant creating the concurrent estate and asks you about the type of tenancy involved.

b. **Severance**

Under certain circumstances, the right of survivorship is severed (*i.e.,* terminated) and a tenancy in common results.

1) **Inter Vivos Conveyance**

A voluntary or involuntary conveyance by a joint tenant of her undivided interest destroys the joint tenancy. The transferee takes as a tenant in common. When there are more than two joint tenants, conveyance by one destroys the joint tenancy only to the extent of the conveyor's interest. Severance may not occur where one joint tenant does not transfer her entire interest.

a) **Judgment Liens**

Usually when a plaintiff obtains a money judgment against a defendant, that judgment becomes a lien on the defendant's real property in the county where the judgment is docketed. The lien runs with the land, burdening it until the judgment is paid or the lien expires (usually 10 years). If such a lien is acquired against a joint tenant, it does not sever the joint tenancy until it is actually sold at a foreclosure sale.

b) **Mortgages**

In most states, a mortgage is a lien on title and does not sever a joint tenancy. Severance occurs only if the mortgage is foreclosed and the property is sold. The execution of a mortgage in title theory states, however, does sever a joint tenancy.

c) **Leases**

States are split as to whether one joint tenant's lease of her interest causes a severance.

2) **Contract to Convey**

Severance results if one joint tenant contracts to convey her interest, but the courts are split on whether an executory contract by *all* joint tenants works a severance.

CONCURRENT OWNERSHIP

Type of Tenancy	Definition	Creation	Termination
Joint Tenancy	Each tenant has an undivided interest in the whole estate, and the surviving co-tenant has a right to the whole estate (*right of survivorship*).	"To A and B as joint tenants with the right of survivorship." (Without survivorship language, it may be construed as a tenancy in common.) Joint tenants must take: (i) identical interests; (ii) from the same instrument; (iii) at the same time; (iv) with an equal right to possess (the four unities).	The right of survivorship may be severed, and the estate converted to a tenancy in common, by: a conveyance by one joint tenant, agreement of joint tenants, murder of one co-tenant by another, or simultaneous deaths of co-tenants. A joint tenancy can be terminated by partition (voluntary or involuntary).
Tenancy by the Entirety	Husband and wife each has an undivided interest in the whole estate and a *right of survivorship*.	"To H and W." Some states presume a tenancy by the entirety in any joint conveyance to husband and wife where the four unities (above) are present.	The right of survivorship may be severed by death, divorce, mutual agreement, or execution by a joint creditor. Tenancy by the entirety cannot be terminated by involuntary partition.
Tenancy in Common	Each tenant has a distinct, proportionate, undivided interest in the property. There is *no right of survivorship*.	"To A and B" or, sometimes, "To A and B as joint tenants." Only unity required is possession.	May be terminated by partition.

3)   **Testamentary Disposition Has No Effect**
A will is ineffective to work a severance because at death the testator's interest vanishes.

4)   **Effect of One Joint Tenant's Murdering Another**
Conceptually, a joint tenant who murders the other joint tenant should not lose her right of survivorship. In some jurisdictions, statutes change this result; in others, a constructive trust is imposed for the decedent's estate.

2.   **Tenancy by the Entirety**
A tenancy by the entirety is a *marital* estate akin to joint tenancy. In some common law jurisdictions, it arises presumptively in any conveyance to a husband and wife. Only death, divorce, *mutual* agreement, or execution by a joint creditor of *both* the husband and wife can sever a tenancy by the entirety. An individual spouse cannot convey or encumber tenancy by the entirety property. A deed or mortgage executed by only one spouse is ineffective.

3.   **Tenancy in Common**
A tenancy in common is a concurrent estate with no right of survivorship. Tenants can hold different interests in the property, but each is entitled to possession of the whole. Interests are alienable, devisable, and inheritable. Today, multiple grantees are *presumed* to take as tenants in common, not as joint tenants.

4.   **Rights and Duties of Co-Tenants**

a.   **Possession**
Each co-tenant has the right to possess all portions of the property but has no right to exclusive possession of any part. A co-tenant out of possession cannot bring a possessory action unless she is *"ousted"* (*e.g.,* another co-tenant claims right to exclusive possession).

b.   **Rents and Profits**
In most states, a co-tenant in possession has the right to retain profits from her own use of the property; *i.e.,* she need not share profits with other co-tenants absent ouster or an agreement to the contrary. She must, however, share net rents from third parties and net profits gained from exploitations of land, such as mining.

c.   **Effect of One Concurrent Owner's Encumbering the Property**
A joint tenant or tenant in common may encumber her interest (*e.g.,* by mortgage or judgment lien), but may not encumber the interests of other co-tenants. If, *e.g.,* one tenant in common mortgages her interest, the mortgagee can foreclose only on the mortgaging co-tenant's interest. If a joint tenancy is involved, a mortgage (in a lien theory state) or lien does not sever the joint tenancy, but a foreclosure sale will. Note, however, that in the case of a joint tenancy, a mortgagee or lienor runs the risk that the obligated co-tenant will die before foreclosure, extinguishing the mortgagee's or lienor's interest.

d.   **Remedy of Partition**
Any co-tenant has a right to judicial partition, either *in kind* (physical division of land among co-tenants) or *by sale and division of the proceeds*. Courts prefer partition in kind but will permit partition by sale when a fair and equitable physical division of the

property cannot be made. Although generally this right may be exercised at any time, restraints on partition by co-tenants are valid, provided they are limited to a *reasonable time*.

e. Expenses for Preservation of Property—Contribution

1) Repairs
A co-tenant who pays more than her pro rata share of *necessary* repairs is entitled to contribution from the other co-tenants, provided she has notified the other co-tenants of the need for repairs.

2) Improvements
There is no right of contribution for the cost of improvements unless there is a partition.

3) Taxes and Mortgages
Contribution can be demanded for taxes or mortgage payments paid on the entire property. However, reimbursement to a co-tenant in sole possession is limited to the extent that expenditures exceed the rental value of her use.

f. Duty of Fair Dealing
A confidential relationship exists among co-tenants; *e.g.*, one co-tenant's acquisition of an outstanding title or lien that may affect the estate is deemed to be on behalf of other co-tenants. It is difficult for one co-tenant to adversely possess against other co-tenants.

II. LANDLORD AND TENANT

A. NATURE OF LEASEHOLD
A leasehold is an *estate in land*, under which the tenant has a present possessory interest in the leased premises and the landlord has a future interest (reversion).

1. Tenancies for Years
A tenancy for years continues for a *fixed* period of time (*e.g.,* L rents to T for two years).

a. Creation
Tenancies for years are usually created by written leases. Under the Statute of Frauds, a writing is required if the lease is for more than one year.

b. Termination
A tenancy for years ends *automatically* at its termination date.

1) Breach of Covenants
In most leases, the landlord reserves a *right of entry*, which allows him to terminate the lease if the tenant breaches any of the lease's covenants.

a) Failure to Pay Rent
In many jurisdictions, a landlord may, by statute, terminate the lease upon the tenant's failure to pay the promised rent—even in the absence of a reserved right of entry.

2) Surrender

A tenancy for years may also terminate if the tenant surrenders the tenancy and the landlord accepts. The same formalities required for creation of the leasehold are required for surrender (*e.g.,* if unexpired term exceeds one year, surrender must be in writing).

2. Periodic Tenancies

A periodic tenancy continues for successive periods (*e.g.,* month to month) until terminated by proper notice by either party.

a. Creation

A periodic tenancy can be created by:

(i) **Express agreement** (*e.g.,* L leases to T from month to month);

(ii) **Implication** (*e.g.,* L leases to T at a rent of $1,000 payable monthly); or

(iii) **Operation of law** (*e.g.,* T remains in possession after the lease expires, and L treats it as a periodic tenancy; or the lease is invalid, but T goes into possession).

b. Termination

A periodic tenancy is **automatically renewed** until proper notice of termination is given. Usually, the notice must be one full period in advance (*e.g.,* one month's notice for a month-to-month tenancy) and timed to terminate the lease at the end of a period (*e.g.,* the usual month-to-month tenancy can end only on the 30th or 31st, not the 15th). For a year-to-year lease, six months' notice is required.

3. Tenancies at Will

A tenancy at will is terminable at the will of either the landlord or the tenant.

a. Creation

Generally, a tenancy at will must be created by an express agreement that the lease can be terminated at any time. Absent such an agreement, periodic rent payments will cause a court to treat it as a periodic tenancy. If the lease gives only the landlord the right to terminate, a similar right will be implied in favor of the tenant. However, if only the tenant has a right to terminate, a similar right will not be implied in favor of the landlord.

b. Termination

A tenancy at will may be terminated **without notice** by any party with the power to do so, or it may be terminated by **operation of law** (*e.g.,* death, commission of waste, etc.).

4. Tenancies at Sufferance

a. Creation

A tenancy at sufferance arises when a tenant **wrongfully** remains in possession after the expiration of a lawful tenancy.

b. Termination

A tenancy at sufferance lasts only until the landlord takes steps to evict the tenant. No notice of termination is required.

LEASEHOLD ESTATES

Type of Leasehold	Definition	Creation	Termination
Tenancy for Years	Tenancy that lasts for some fixed period of time.	"To T for 10 years."	Terminates at the end of the stated period without either party giving notice.
Periodic Tenancy	Tenancy for some fixed period that continues for succeeding periods until either party gives notice of termination.	"To T from month to month." *or* "To T, with rent payable on the first day of every month." *or* L elects to bind hold-over T for an additional term.	Terminates by notice from one party at least equal to the length of the time period (*e.g.,* one full month for a month-to-month tenancy). *Exception:* Only six months' notice is required to terminate a year-to-year tenancy.
Tenancy at Will	Tenancy of no stated duration that lasts as long as both parties desire.	"To T for and during the pleasure of L." (Even though the language gives only L the right to terminate, L or T may terminate at any time.) *or* "To T for as many years as T desires." (Only T may terminate.)	Usually terminates after one party displays an intention that the tenancy should come to an end. May also end by operation of law (*e.g.,* death of a party, attempt to transfer interest).
Tenancy at Sufferance	Tenant wrongfully holds over after termination of the tenancy.	T's lease expires, but T continues to occupy the premises.	Terminates when landlord evicts tenant or elects to hold tenant to another term.

5. **The Hold-Over Doctrine**

If a tenant continues in possession after his right to possession has ended, the landlord may: (i) *evict* him, or (ii) bind him to a *new periodic tenancy*. Generally, the terms and conditions of the expired tenancy govern the new one. *Nonresidential* tenants may be held to a new year-to-year tenancy if the original lease term was for *one year or more*, or a periodic term based on the frequency of rent payments (*e.g.,* month to month) if the original term was for *less than one year*. *Residential* tenants, however, are generally held to a new month-to-month tenancy, regardless of the original term. If the landlord notifies the tenant *before* the lease expires that occupancy after the termination will be at increased rent, the tenant, by holding over, is held to have acquiesced to the new terms (even if the tenant actually objected to the new terms).

CMR Exam Tip There are exceptions to the hold-over doctrine. Watch for situations where: (i) the tenant remains in possession for *only a few hours* after termination or leaves a few articles of personal property, (ii) the delay is *not the tenant's fault* (*e.g.,* severe illness), or (iii) it is a *seasonal lease*. In these cases, the landlord cannot bind the tenant to a new tenancy.

B. LEASES

A lease is a contract that governs the landlord-tenant relationship. Covenants in the lease are generally *independent*; *i.e.,* if one party breaches a covenant, the other party can recover damages but must still perform his promises and cannot terminate the landlord-tenant relationship. The doctrines of actual and constructive eviction and the implied warranty of habitability are exceptions to this rule. Also, many states have created a statutory exception allowing the landlord to terminate the lease for the nonpayment of rent.

C. TENANT DUTIES AND LANDLORD REMEDIES

1. **Tenant's Duty to Repair (Doctrine of Waste)**

A tenant cannot damage (*i.e.,* commit waste on) the leased premises. The rules governing waste in the leasehold context are much like those governing waste in the life estate context.

   a. **Types of Waste**

   There are three types of waste:

   1) *Voluntary (affirmative) waste* results when the tenant intentionally or negligently damages the premises or exploits minerals on the property.

   2) *Permissive waste* occurs when the tenant fails to take reasonable steps to protect the premises from damage from the elements. The tenant is liable for all *ordinary* repairs, excluding ordinary wear and tear. If the duty is shifted to the landlord (by lease or statute), the tenant has a duty to report deficiencies promptly.

   3) *Ameliorative waste* occurs when the tenant alters the leased property, thereby increasing its value. Generally, the tenant is liable for the cost of restoration. There is a modern exception to this rule, however, which permits a tenant to make this type of change if he is a long-term tenant and the change reflects changes in the neighborhood.

   b. **Destruction of Premises Without Fault**

   If the leased premises are destroyed without the fault of either the landlord or the

tenant, no waste is involved. In the absence of lease language or a statute to the contrary, neither party has a duty to restore the premises, but the tenant has a duty to continue paying rent. In most states, statutes or case law now give the tenant the option to terminate the lease in this situation, even in the presence of an explicit covenant to repair.

c. Tenant's Liability for Covenants to Repair

If a *residential* tenant covenants to repair, the landlord usually remains obligated to repair (except for damages caused by the tenant) under the nonwaivable "implied warranty of habitability" (*see* D.3., *infra*). However, a *nonresidential* tenant's covenant to repair is enforceable, and a landlord may be awarded damages for breach based on the property's condition when the lease terminates compared with its condition when the lease commenced. A tenant who covenants to repair is *not* usually liable to rebuild after structural damage or casualty destruction, unless the covenant *expressly includes* these types of repairs. In the absence of a specific reference to ordinary wear and tear, a covenant to repair usually *includes* such repairs. However, repair covenants frequently *exclude* ordinary wear and tear.

2. Duty to Not Use Premises for Illegal Purpose

If the tenant uses the premises for an illegal purpose, the landlord may terminate the lease or obtain damages and injunctive relief. Occasional unlawful conduct by the tenant does not breach this duty.

3. Duty to Pay Rent

At common law, rent was due at the end of the leasehold term. However, leases usually contain a provision making rent payable at some other time (*e.g.,* "monthly in advance"). Most states today have statutes providing that if the leasehold terminates before the time originally agreed upon, the tenant must pay a *proportionate amount* of the agreed rent.

a. Rent Deposits

The landlord is not permitted to retain a *security deposit* beyond the damages actually suffered. If a rent deposit is denominated a *"bonus,"* the landlord can retain it after the tenant is evicted.

b. Termination of Rent Liability—Surrender

If a tenant effectively conveys (surrenders) his leasehold interest back to the landlord, his duty to pay rent ends.

4. Landlord Remedies

a. Tenant on Premises But Fails to Pay Rent—Evict or Sue for Rent

At common law, a breach of the lease, such as failure to pay rent, resulted only in a cause of action for money damages; a breach did not give rise to a right to terminate the lease. Most modern leases, however, give the nonbreaching party the right to terminate. Thus, if a tenant is on the premises and fails to pay rent, the landlord may bring suit for rent due or may evict the tenant under the state's *unlawful detainer* statute. The *only* issue in an unlawful detainer proceeding is whether the tenant has the right to possession; the tenant cannot raise counterclaims.

b. **Tenant Abandons—Do Nothing or Repossess**

If the tenant *unjustifiably* abandons the property, the majority view is that the landlord has a duty to mitigate damages by seeking to relet the premises. If the landlord repossesses and/or relets, the tenant's liability depends on whether the landlord has *accepted the surrender*. If surrender is not found, the tenant is liable for the difference between the promised rent and the fair rental value of the property (in cases of reletting, between the promised rent and the rent received from the reletting). If surrender is found, the tenant is free from any rent liability accruing after abandonment. Note that the landlord's resumption of possession for himself constitutes acceptance of surrender.

D. LANDLORD DUTIES AND TENANT REMEDIES

Subject to modification by the lease, a statute, or the implied warranty of habitability, the general rule is that a landlord has *no duty to repair or maintain* the premises.

1. Duty to Deliver Possession of Premises

Statutes in most states require the landlord to put the tenant in *actual* possession of the premises at the beginning of the leasehold term; *i.e.,* the landlord is in breach if he has not evicted a hold-over tenant by the beginning of the lease term.

2. Quiet Enjoyment

Every lease has an implied covenant that neither the landlord nor a paramount title holder (*e.g.,* a prior mortgagee who forecloses) will interfere with the tenant's quiet enjoyment and possession of the premises. This covenant may be breached in the following ways:

a. **Actual Eviction**

Actual eviction occurs when the landlord or a paramount title holder excludes the tenant from the *entire* leased premises. Actual eviction terminates the tenant's obligation to pay rent.

b. **Partial Eviction**

Partial actual eviction occurs when the tenant is physically excluded from only part of the leased premises. Partial eviction *by the landlord* relieves the tenant of the obligation to pay rent for the *entire* premises, even though the tenant continues in possession of the remainder. Partial eviction *by a third person* with paramount title results in an *apportionment* of rent; *i.e.,* the tenant is liable for the reasonable rental value of the portion she continues to possess.

c. **Constructive Eviction**

If the landlord does something (or, more often, fails to provide a service he has a legal duty to provide) that renders the property *uninhabitable*, the tenant may terminate the lease and seek damages. The conditions must be the result of the *landlord's actions* (not a neighbor's or other third party's), and the tenant *must vacate* the premises within a reasonable time.

3. Implied Warranty of Habitability

Most jurisdictions imply a covenant of habitability into *residential leases*. This warranty is *nonwaivable*. The landlord's duty is tied to standards of local housing codes. In the event of a breach, the tenant may: (i) *terminate* the lease; (ii) *make repairs and offset* the cost against future rent; (iii) *abate the rent* to an amount equal to the fair rental value in view of the defects; or (iv) remain in possession, pay full rent, and *sue for damages*.

 Exam Tip Keep in mind that the implied warranty of habitability does *not* apply to commercial tenants—only to residential tenants.

4. Retaliatory Eviction
In many states, a landlord may not terminate a lease or otherwise penalize a tenant in retaliation for the tenant's exercise of her legal rights, including reporting housing or building code violations. Many statutes presume a retaliatory motive if the landlord acts within, *e.g.,* 90 to 180 days after the tenant exercises her rights. To overcome the presumption, the landlord must show a valid, nonretaliatory reason for his actions.

E. ASSIGNMENTS AND SUBLEASES
Absent an express restriction in the lease, a tenant may freely transfer her leasehold interest, in whole or in part. A *complete* transfer of the entire remaining term is an *assignment*. If the tenant retains any part of the remaining term (other than a right to reenter upon breach), the transfer is a *sublease*.

 Exam Tip For bar exam purposes, a transfer will be considered a sublease, rather than an assignment, only when the original tenant reserves time for herself (*e.g.,* the last month of the lease).

1. Consequences of Assignment
An assignee stands in the shoes of the original tenant in a direct relationship with the landlord; *i.e.,* the assignee and the landlord are in *"privity of estate,"* and each is liable to the other on all covenants in the lease that "run with the land."

a. Covenants that Run with the Land
A covenant runs with the land if the original parties to the lease so intend and if the covenant *"touches and concerns"* the land (*i.e.,* benefits the landlord and burdens the tenant (or vice versa) with respect to their interests in the property).

b. Rent Covenants
Because a covenant to pay rent runs with the land, the assignee owes rent *directly* to the landlord. After assignment, the original tenant is no longer in privity of estate with the landlord but remains liable on the *original contractual obligation* to pay rent (*privity of contract*). If the assignee reassigns the leasehold interest, his privity of estate with the landlord ends, and he has no liability for the subsequent assignee's failure to pay rent.

2. Consequences of Sublease—Sublessee Not in Privity with Landlord
A sublessee is the tenant of the original lessee and usually pays rent to the original lessee, who then pays the landlord. A sublessee is not personally liable to the landlord for rent or for the performance of any of the covenants in the main lease unless the sublessee *expressly assumes* the covenants.

a. Landlord's Remedies
The landlord may terminate the main lease for nonpayment of rent or breach of other covenants if the lease so states or the power is given by statute. The sublease automatically terminates with the main lease. Also, many states allow a landlord who does not receive rent to assert a lien on personal property found on the premises; this applies to a sublessee's property as well as that of the original tenant.

ASSIGNMENT VS. SUBLEASE

	Assignment by Landlord	Assignment by Tenant	Sublease by Tenant
Consent	Tenant's consent not required.	Landlord's consent may be required by lease.	Landlord's consent may be required by lease.
Privity of Estate	Assignee and tenant are in privity of estate.	Assignee and landlord are in privity of estate.	Sublessee and landlord are not in privity of estate. Original tenant remains in privity of estate with landlord.
Privity of Contract	Assignee and tenant are not in privity of contract. Original landlord and tenant remain in privity of contract.	Assignee and landlord are not in privity of contract. Original tenant and landlord remain in privity of contract.	Sublessee and landlord are not in privity of contract. Original tenant and landlord remain in privity of contract.
Liability for Covenants in Lease	Assignee liable to tenant on all covenants that run with the land.	Assignee liable to landlord on all covenants that run with the land.	Sublessee is not personally liable on any covenants in the original lease and cannot enforce the landlord's covenants.
	Original landlord remains liable on *all* covenants in the lease.	Original tenant remains liable for rent and *all* other covenants in the lease.	Original tenant remains liable for rent and *all* other covenants in the lease and can enforce the landlord's covenants.

b. **Rights of Sublessee**

A sublessee cannot enforce any covenants made by the landlord in the main lease, except a residential sublessee may be able to enforce the implied warranty of habitability against the landlord.

3. **Covenants Against Assignment or Sublease**

Lease covenants restricting assignment and sublease are strictly *construed against the landlord*. (Thus, a covenant prohibiting assignment does not prohibit subleasing and vice versa.)

a. **Waiver**

A valid covenant against assignment is considered waived if the landlord was aware of the assignment and did not object (*e.g.,* by knowingly accepting rent from the assignee). Once the landlord consents to one transfer, he waives the covenant as to future transfers unless he expressly reserves it.

b. **Transfer in Violation of Lease**

If a tenant assigns or sublets in violation of a lease provision, the transfer is not void. The landlord, however, usually may terminate the lease or sue for damages.

4. **Assignments by Landlords**

A landlord may assign the rents and reversion interest he owns. This is usually done by deed when the landlord conveys a building to a new owner. The tenants' consent is *not* required.

a. **Rights of Assignee Against Tenants—Attornment**

Once tenants are given reasonable notice of the assignment, they must recognize and pay rent to the new owner as their landlord. The benefit of all tenant covenants that touch and concern the land runs with the landlord's estate to the new owner.

b. **Liabilities of Assignee to Tenants**

The burden of the landlord's covenants that touch and concern the land runs with the landlord's estate to the assignee; thus, the assignee is liable for the performance of those covenants. *The original landlord also remains liable on all of the covenants he made in the lease.*

F. **CONDEMNATION OF LEASEHOLDS**

If the *entire leasehold* is taken by eminent domain, the tenant's liability for rent is extinguished because both the leasehold and reversion have merged in the condemnor and there is no longer a leasehold estate. The lessee is entitled to compensation. However, if the taking is *temporary* or *partial*, the tenant is *not* discharged from the rent obligation, but is entitled to compensation (*i.e.,* a share of the condemnation award) for the taking.

G. **TORT LIABILITY OF LANDLORD AND TENANT**

1. **Landlord's Liability**

At common law, a landlord had *no duty* to make the premises safe. Today, there are six exceptions.

a. **Concealed Dangerous Condition (Latent Defect)**

If, at the time the lease is entered into, the landlord knows (or should know) of a dangerous condition that the tenant could not discover by reasonable inspection, the landlord must *disclose* (not repair) it. Otherwise, the landlord will be liable for any injuries resulting from the condition. If the tenant accepts the premises after disclosure, she assumes the risk for herself and others; the landlord is no longer liable.

b. **Common Areas**

The landlord has a duty of reasonable care in maintaining common areas (*e.g.*, halls, elevators).

c. **Public Use**

A landlord is liable for injuries to members of the public if, at the time of the lease, he:

1) Knows (or should know) of a *dangerous condition*;

2) Has reason to believe the tenant *may admit the public before repairing* the condition; and

3) *Fails to repair* the condition.

d. **Furnished Short-Term Residence**

A landlord who rents a fully furnished premises for a short period (*e.g.,* summer cottage) is under a stricter duty. He is liable for injuries resulting from *any* defect whether or not he knew of the defect.

e. **Negligent Repairs by Landlord**

Even if a landlord has no duty to make repairs, a landlord who actually attempts to repair is liable if an injury results because the repairs are done *negligently* or give a *deceptive appearance of safety*.

f. **Landlord Contracts to Repair**

If the landlord covenants to repair, he is liable for injuries resulting from his failure to repair or negligent repair.

2. **Modern Trend—General Duty of Reasonable Care**

Many courts are now holding that a landlord owes a general duty of reasonable care toward residential tenants, and will be held liable for injuries resulting from *ordinary negligence* if he had *notice* of a defect and an opportunity to repair it.

a. **Defects Arising After Tenant Takes Possession**

A landlord generally is held to have notice of defects existing before the tenant took possession but is *not liable* for defects arising after the tenant takes possession *unless* the landlord knew or should have known of them.

b. **Legal Duty to Repair**

If the landlord has a statutory duty to repair (*e.g.*, housing codes), he is liable for injuries resulting from his failure to repair or negligent repair.

    c.   **Security**
        Some courts hold landlords liable for injuries to tenants inflicted by third-party crimi-
        nals where the landlord failed to comply with housing code provisions dealing with
        security, maintain ordinary security measures, or provide advertised extraordinary
        security measures (*e.g.*, surveillance cameras).

3. Tenant's Liability
    The duty of care owed by a tenant, as an occupier of land, to third persons is discussed in
    the Torts outline.

III. FIXTURES

A. IN GENERAL
A fixture is a chattel that has been so affixed to land that it has ceased being personal property
and has become part of the realty. A fixture passes with the ownership of the land.

B. CHATTELS INCORPORATED INTO STRUCTURE
When items are incorporated into the realty so that they lose their identity (*e.g.*, bricks, concrete),
they are fixtures, as are items that are identifiable but whose removal would cause considerable
damage (*e.g.*, plumbing, heating ducts).

C. COMMON OWNERSHIP CASES
A common ownership case is one in which the person who brings the chattel to the land owns
both the chattel and the land (*e.g.*, X installs a furnace in his home). An item is a "fixture" if the
objective intention of the party who made the "annexation" was to make the item part of the
realty. This intention is determined by: the ***nature of the article***, the ***manner of attachment***, the
amount of damage that would be caused by its removal, and the ***adaptation*** of the item to the
use of the realty.

    1. Constructive Annexation
        An article of personal property that is so uniquely adapted to the real estate that it makes no
        sense to separate it (*e.g.*, keys to doors, custom curtain rods) may be considered a fixture
        even if it is not physically annexed to the property.

D. DIVIDED OWNERSHIP CASES
In divided ownership cases, the chattel is owned and brought to the realty by someone other than
the landowner (*e.g.*, tenant, licensee, or trespasser).

    1. Landlord-Tenant
        An ***agreement*** between the landlord and tenant is controlling on whether an annexed chattel
        is a fixture. Absent an agreement, a tenant is deemed to lack the intent to permanently
        improve the property, and thus may remove his annexed chattels if removal would not
        damage the premises or destroy the chattel. Annexed chattels must be removed ***by the end of***
        the lease term (or within a reasonable time after the termination of an indefinite tenancy),
        and the tenant is responsible for repairing any damage caused by the removal.

2. **Life Tenant and Remainderman**

The same rules apply in the life tenant-remainderman context as in landlord-tenant situations, except that the life tenant must remove annexations *before the end of his tenancy*.

3. **Licensee or Trespasser and Landowner**

Licensees are treated much like tenants, whereas trespassers normally lose their annexations. Thus, absent a statute, an adverse possessor or good faith trespasser cannot remove fixtures (*e.g.*, house erroneously constructed on a parcel that possessor believed she owned). Some courts, however, allow a good faith trespasser recovery measured by the value added to the land (not construction costs).

E. THIRD-PARTY CASES

1. **Third-Party Lien on Land to Which Chattel Affixed**

Generally, the mortgagee has no greater rights than the mortgagor. Thus, chattels annexed by the mortgagor's tenant are generally not within the lien of the mortgagee *except* where the mortgage is made after the lease and the mortgagee is without notice of the tenant's rights.

2. **Third-Party Lien on Chattel Affixed to Land**

Suppose a landowner affixes a chattel to the land. The seller of the chattel retains a security interest in the chattel, and the landowner mortgages the land. If the landowner then defaults on both chattel and mortgage payments, as between the seller and the mortgagee, the general rule is that the first to record his interest wins. However, under the U.C.C., a seller wins if the "fixture filing" is recorded within 20 days after the chattel is affixed to the land. The seller must compensate the mortgagee for damage or repair caused by removal.

IV. RIGHTS IN THE LAND OF ANOTHER—EASEMENTS, PROFITS, COVENANTS, AND SERVITUDES

A. IN GENERAL

Easements, profits, covenants, and servitudes are *nonpossessory* interests in land, creating a right to *use land possessed by someone else*.

B. EASEMENTS

1. **Introduction**

An easement holder has the right to use another's tract of land for a special purpose (*e.g.*, to lay pipe, to access a road or lake), but has no right to possess or enjoy that land. An easement is presumed to be of *perpetual duration* unless the grant specifically limits the interest.

a. **Types of Easements**

Most easements are *affirmative*, which means the holder is entitled to make affirmative use of the servient tenement. *Negative* easements, which entitle the holder to compel the possessor of the servient tenement to refrain from engaging in an activity on the servient estate (*e.g.,* building a structure in excess of three stories), are generally confined to only four types of easements: (i) for *light*, (ii) for *air*, (iii) for lateral and subjacent *support*, and (iv) for *flow* of an artificial stream.

 Exam Tip Negative easements are really restrictive covenants. Thus, for exam purposes, a restriction relating to light, air, support, or flow of an artificial stream can be either a negative easement or a restrictive covenant. Restrictions relating to anything else, however, are considered restrictive covenants.

b. Easement Appurtenant

An easement is appurtenant when it benefits the holder in his physical use or enjoyment of another tract of land. Thus, for an easement to be appurtenant, there must be *two tracts*: the *dominant* tenement (the estate benefited by the easement), and the *servient* tenement (the estate subject to the easement right). An easement appurtenant passes with the transfer of the benefited land, regardless of whether it is mentioned in the conveyance. The burden of the easement also passes automatically with the servient estate unless the new owner is a bona fide purchaser with no actual or constructive notice of the easement.

 Exam Tip It is important to remember that the easement appurtenant *passes with the benefited land*. Don't be fooled by questions that make you think it must be specifically mentioned in the deed. Similarly, recall that an easement appurtenant cannot be conveyed apart from the dominant tenement (unless it is conveyed to the owner of the servient tenement to *extinguish* the easement).

c. Easement in Gross

The holder of an easement in gross acquires a right to use the servient tenement independent of his possession of another tract of land; *i.e.,* the easement benefits the holder rather than another parcel. An easement in gross for the holder's personal pleasure (*e.g.,* right to swim in the pond on Blackacre) is not transferable, but one that serves an economic or commercial interest (*e.g.,* right to erect billboards on Blackacre) is transferable.

2. Creation of Easements

The basic methods of creating an easement are: express grant or reservation, implication, and prescription.

a. Express Grant

Any easement must be in writing and signed by the holder of the servient tenement unless its duration is brief enough (commonly one year or less) to be outside a particular state's Statute of Frauds' coverage. A grant of easement must comply with all the formal requisites of a deed (*see* VI.B.1., *infra*).

b. Express Reservation

An easement by reservation arises when a grantor conveys title to land, but reserves the right to continue to use the tract for a special purpose.

 Exam Tip Watch for fact patterns in which a grantor reserves an easement for someone else. Under the majority view, an easement can be reserved only for the *grantor*. An attempt to reserve an easement for anyone else is *void*.

c. Implication

An easement by implication is created by operation of law; it is an exception to the Statute of Frauds. There are three types of easements by implication:

1) Easement Implied from Existing Use ("Quasi-Easement")

An easement may be implied if:

(i) *Prior to the division* of a single tract;

(ii) An *apparent and continuous* use exists on the "servient" part;

(iii) That is *reasonably necessary* for the enjoyment of the "dominant" part; and

(iv) The court determines that the parties *intended* the use to continue after division of the land.

2) Easement Implied Without Any Existing Use

In two limited situations, easements may be implied without preexisting use.

a) Subdivision Plat

When lots are sold in a subdivision with reference to a recorded plat or map that also shows streets leading to the lots, buyers of the lots have implied easements to use the streets to access their lots.

b) Profit a Prendre

The holder of the profit a prendre (*see* C., *infra*) has an implied easement to pass over the surface of the land and to use it as reasonably necessary to extract the product.

3) Easement by Necessity

An easement by necessity arises when a landowner sells a portion of his tract and by this division deprives one lot of access to a public road or utility line. The owner of the servient parcel has the right to locate the easement.

d. Prescription

Acquiring an easement by prescription is analogous to acquiring property by adverse possession. To acquire a prescriptive easement, the use must be:

(i) *Open and notorious* (*i.e.,* discoverable upon inspection);

(ii) *Adverse* (*i.e.,* without the owner's permission); and

(iii) *Continuous and uninterrupted*;

(iv) For the *statutory period*.

Generally, prescriptive easements cannot be acquired in public land.

3. Scope

In the absence of specific limitations in the grant, courts assume that the easement was

intended to meet both present and future needs of the dominant tenement (*e.g.,* easement may widen to accommodate new, wider cars). If, however, the dominant parcel is subdivided, the lot owners will not succeed to the easement if to do so would unreasonably overburden the servient estate.

CMR **Exam Tip** When confronted with an exam question involving overuse or misuse of an easement, remember that such use *does not terminate* the easement. The appropriate remedy for the servient owner is an injunction against the misuse.

a. Use of Servient Estate—Repairs
The servient owner generally may use her land in any way she wishes so long as her conduct does not interfere with performance of the easement. The easement holder has the duty to make repairs to the easement if he is the sole user; but if both parties are using the easement, the court will apportion the repair costs.

4. Termination of Easements
An easement can be terminated in the following ways:

a. Stated Conditions
The original easement grant may specify when or under what conditions the easement will terminate.

b. Unity of Ownership (Merger)
If the same person acquires ownership of both the easement and the servient estate, the dominant and servient estates merge and the easement is destroyed. Even though there may be later separation, the easement will not be automatically revived. The unity must be complete (*e.g.,* the holder of the easement must acquire an interest in the servient tenement of *equal or greater duration* than the duration of the easement privilege).

c. Release
An easement (including an easement in gross, which is otherwise inalienable) can be terminated by a deed of release from the owner of the easement to the owner of the servient tenement.

d. Abandonment
An easement is extinguished when its holder demonstrates by physical action (*e.g.,* building a structure that blocks access to easement on adjoining lot) an intent to permanently abandon the easement. Merely expressing a wish to abandon does not extinguish the easement; neither does mere nonuse.

e. Estoppel
Oral expressions of an intent to abandon do not terminate an easement unless committed to writing (release) or accompanied by action (abandonment). But if the owner of the servient estate changes his position in reasonable reliance on the representations made or conduct by the owner of the easement, the easement terminates through estoppel.

f. Prescription
To terminate an easement by prescription, there must be an adverse, continuous interruption of the use for the prescriptive period (typically 20 years).

g. **Necessity**
Easements created by necessity expire as soon as the necessity ends.

h. **Condemnation and Destruction**
Condemnation of the servient estate extinguishes all easements. Courts are split as to whether easement holders are entitled to compensation. Involuntary destruction of a structure in which there is an easement extinguishes the easement; voluntary destruction of such a structure does not.

5. **Compare—Licenses**
Licenses privilege their holders to go upon the land of another. But unlike an easement, a license is not an interest in land; it is merely a privilege, *revocable* at the will of the licensor. A license is personal to the licensee and, thus, inalienable. Any attempt to transfer a license results in revocation by operation of law.

CMR **Exam Tip** A failed attempt to create an easement results in a license. Thus, if a grantor orally grants an easement for more than one year, it is unenforceable because it is not in writing. The grantee does not have a valid easement but does have a license.

a. **Irrevocable Licenses**
A license becomes irrevocable in the following circumstances:

1) **Estoppel**
If a licensee invests substantial amounts of money or labor in reliance on the license, the licensor is estopped to revoke. The license becomes an easement by estoppel, which lasts until the holder receives sufficient benefit to reimburse him for his expenditures.

2) **License Coupled with an Interest**
A license coupled with an interest is irrevocable as long as the interest lasts. For example, the vendee of a chattel may enter the seller's land to remove the chattel, and a future interest holder may enter and inspect the land for waste.

C. **PROFITS**
Profits entitle the holder of the benefit to take some resources (*e.g.,* soil, timber, materials, fish) from the servient estate. Implied in every profit is an easement entitling the benefit holder to enter the servient estate to remove the resources. All of the rules governing creation, alienation, and termination of easements are applicable to profits. In addition, a profit may be extinguished through *surcharge* (misuse that overly burdens the servient estate).

D. **COVENANTS RUNNING WITH THE LAND AT LAW (REAL COVENANTS)**
A real covenant, normally found in a deed, is a *written promise* to do something on the land (*e.g.,* maintain a fence) or a promise not to do something on the land (*e.g.,* not build a multi-family dwelling). Real covenants run with the land at law, which means that subsequent owners may enforce or be burdened by the covenants.

1. **Requirements for Burden to Run**
If the following requirements are met, any successor in interest to the burdened estate will be bound by the covenant as if she had herself expressly agreed to it:

a. **Intent**

The covenanting parties must have **intended** that successors in interest to the covenantor be bound by the terms of the covenant. This intent may be inferred from circumstances surrounding the creation of the covenant, but is usually found in the language of the conveyance itself.

b. **Notice**

Under modern recording acts (*see* VI.E., *infra*), to be bound by a covenant, a subsequent purchaser for value must have had actual, inquiry, or record notice of the arrangement at the time of purchase.

CMR **Exam Tip** Because the notice requirement arises under the recording acts, remember that it will protect **only purchasers for value**. Someone who does not give value may be bound by a covenant at law (not equity) even if he has no actual or constructive notice of the covenant.

c. **Horizontal Privity**

At the time the promisor entered into the covenant with the promisee, the two must have shared **some interest** in the land independent of the covenant (*e.g.,* grantor-grantee, landlord-tenant, mortgagee-mortgagor).

CMR **Exam Tip** Horizontal privity concerns only the **original** parties. Even if successors in interest are trying to enforce the covenant, you must look only to the original covenanting parties to determine horizontal privity.

d. **Vertical Privity**

To be bound, the successor in interest to the covenanting party must hold the **entire durational interest** held by the covenantor at the time he made the covenant.

e. **Touch and Concern**

Negative covenants touch and concern the land if they restrict the holder of the servient estate in his **use of that parcel** of land. Affirmative covenants touch and concern the land if they require the holder of the servient estate to **do something**, which increases his obligations in connection with his enjoyment of the land.

2. **Requirements for Benefit to Run**

If the following three requirements are met, the promisee's successor in interest may enforce the covenant:

a. **Intent**

The covenanting parties must have **intended** that the successors in interest to the covenantee be able to enforce the covenant.

b. **Vertical Privity**

The benefits of a covenant run to the assignees of the **original estate or any lesser estate**; *i.e., **any** succeeding possessory estate may enforce the benefit.

CMR **Exam Tip** Horizontal privity is not required for the benefit to run. Thus, where horizontal privity is lacking, the promisee's successors can enforce the covenant against the promisor, but not against the promisor's successors.

c. **Touch and Concern**

The benefit of a covenant touches and concerns the land if the promised performance benefits the covenantee and her successors in their use and enjoyment of the benefited land.

3. **Specific Situations Involving Real Covenants**

Generally, promises to *pay money* to be used in connection with the land (*e.g.,* homeowners' association fees) and covenants *not to compete* run with the land. Racially restrictive covenants are unenforceable.

4. **Remedy—Damages Only**

A breach of a real covenant is remedied by an award of money damages, collectible from the defendant's general assets. If an injunction is sought, the promise must be enforced as an equitable servitude (*see* below) rather than a real covenant.

5. **Termination**

As with all other nonpossessory interests, a covenant may be terminated by: (i) a written *release*, (ii) the *merger* of the benefited and burdened estates, or (iii) the *condemnation* of the burdened property. (*See* B.4., *supra.*)

CMR COMPARISON CHART

DISTINGUISHING CHARACTERISTICS OF REAL COVENANTS AND EQUITABLE SERVITUDES

	Real Covenants	Equitable Servitudes
Creation	Writing is *always* required	Writing is *usually* required but may arise by *implication* from common scheme of development of a residential subdivision
Running of Burden	Horizontal privity (shared interest in land, apart from the covenant, by *original* covenanting parties; *e.g.,* mortgagor-mortgagee, landlord-tenant) *and* vertical privity (successor holds entire interest held by covenanting party) required	No privity required
Running of Benefit	Vertical privity required	No privity required
Remedy	Damages	Injunction

E. **EQUITABLE SERVITUDES**

An equitable servitude is a covenant that, regardless of whether it runs with the land at law, equity will enforce against the assignees of the burdened land who have *notice* of the covenant. The usual remedy is an injunction.

 Exam Tip The crucial difference between real covenants and equitable servitudes is the *remedy sought*. If money damages are sought, you must use the real covenant analysis. If a party seeks an injunction, you must consider whether the requirements for enforcement as an equitable servitude have been met. A single promise can create both a real covenant and an equitable servitude.

1. Creation

Generally, as with real covenants, equitable servitudes are created by *covenants* contained in a *writing* that satisfies the Statute of Frauds. There is *one exception*: Negative equitable servitudes may be implied from a common scheme for development of a residential subdivision. Thus, if a developer subdivides land, and some deeds contain negative covenants while others do not, the negative covenants will be binding on all parcels provided there was a common scheme of development and notice of the covenants.

a. Common Scheme

Reciprocal negative servitudes will be implied only if, at the time that sales in the subdivision began, the developer had a plan that all parcels would be subject to the restriction. The scheme may be evidenced by: (i) a *recorded plat*, (ii) a *general pattern* of restrictions, or (iii) *oral representations* to early buyers.

 Exam Tip If the scheme arises after some lots are sold, no implied servitude can arise with respect to the lots already sold without express covenants. So remember, if Lots 1 through 5 are sold without a restrictive covenant and the deeds to Lots 6 through 50 contain one, the covenant cannot be enforced as a servitude against the owners of Lots 1 through 5.

b. Notice

To be bound by a covenant not in her deed, a grantee must have had notice of the covenants in the deeds of others in the subdivision. Notice may be *actual* (direct knowledge of covenants), *inquiry* (neighborhood appears to conform to common restrictions), or *record* (prior deed with covenant in grantee's chain of title).

2. Requirements for Burden to Run

A successor of the promisor is bound if:

a. The covenanting parties *intended* that the servitude be enforceable by and against assignees;

b. The successor of the promisor has *actual*, *inquiry*, *or record* notice of the servitude; and

c. The covenant *touches and concerns* the land (*i.e.,* it restricts the holder of the servient estate in his use of that parcel).

3. Requirements for Benefit to Run

The benefit of an equitable servitude runs with the land, and thus is enforceable by the promisee's successors, if: (i) the original parties so *intended*, and (ii) the servitude *touches and concerns* the benefited property.

In contrast to real covenants, which require vertical and horizontal privity of estate for burdens to run, and vertical privity for benefits to run, *no privity of estate is required* for an equitable servitude to be enforceable by and against assignees.

CMR
SUMMARY CHART

CHECKLIST OF REQUIREMENTS FOR THE RUNNING OF BENEFITS AND BURDENS

	Covenants		Equitable Servitudes	
	Benefit	Burden	Benefit	Burden
Intent	✓	✓	✓	✓
Notice		✓*		✓
Touch & Concern	✓	✓	✓	✓
Horizontal Privity		✓		
Vertical Privity	✓	✓		

* Under recording acts

4. **Equitable Defenses to Enforcement**
   A court will not enforce an equitable servitude if:

   a. The person seeking enforcement is violating a similar restriction on his own land (***unclean hands***);

   b. A benefited party ***acquiesced*** in a violation of the servitude by one burdened party;

   c. A benefited party acted in such a way that a reasonable person would believe the covenant was abandoned (***estoppel***);

   d. The benefited party fails to bring suit against the violator within a reasonable time (***laches***); or

   e. The ***neighborhood has changed*** so significantly that enforcement would be inequitable.

5. **Termination**
   Like other nonpossessory interests, an equitable servitude may be extinguished by: (i) ***written release*** from the benefit holders, (ii) ***merger*** of the benefited and burdened estates, or (iii) ***condemnation*** of the burdened property. (*See* B.4., *supra*.)

NONPOSSESSORY INTERESTS

	Easement	License	Profit	Real Covenant/ Equitable Servitude
Definition	A grant of an interest in land that allows someone to use another's land	Permission to go onto another's land	Right to take resources from another's land	Promise to do or not to do something on the land
Example	Owner of parcel A grants owner of parcel B the right to drive across parcel A	O allows the electrician to come onto his land to fix an outlet	O allows A to come onto O's land to cut and remove timber	O conveys an adjoining parcel to A. A promises not to build a swimming pool on the property
Writing	Generally required. *Exceptions:* Less than one year Implication Necessity Prescription	Not required. *Note:* An invalid oral easement is a license	Required	Required. *Exception:* Equitable servitude may be implied from common scheme of development of residential subdivision
Termination	Stated conditions Release Merger Abandonment Estoppel Prescription End of necessity	Usually revocable at will. May be irrevocable if coupled with an interest or if licensor estopped by licensee's expenditures	Same as easement	Release Merger Condemnation Also equitable defenses may apply to enforcement of servitude

F. PARTY WALLS AND COMMON DRIVEWAYS

Courts will treat a wall erected partly on the property of each of two adjoining landowners as belonging to each owner to the extent it rests upon her land. Courts will also imply mutual *cross-easements of support*, with the result that each party can use the wall or driveway and neither party can unilaterally destroy it.

1. Creation

A *written agreement* is required by the Statute of Frauds for the express creation of a party wall or common driveway agreement, but an "irrevocable license" can arise from detrimental reliance on a parol agreement. Party walls and common driveways can also result from *implication* or *prescription*.

2. Running of Covenants

If party wall or common driveway owners agree to be mutually responsible for maintaining the wall or driveway, the burdens and benefits of these covenants run to the successive owners of each parcel.

V. ADVERSE POSSESSION

A. IN GENERAL

Title to real property may be acquired by adverse possession. Title by adverse possession results from the operation of the statute of limitations for trespass. If an owner does not, within the statutory period, take action to eject a possessor who claims adversely to the owner, the title vests in the possessor.

B. REQUIREMENTS

To establish title by adverse possession, the possessor must show (i) an *actual entry* giving *exclusive possession* that is (ii) *open and notorious*, (iii) *adverse* (hostile), and (iv) *continuous* throughout the statutory period.

1. Running of Statute

The statute of limitations begins to run when the true owner can first bring suit. Filing a suit will not stop the period from running, however; the suit must be pursued to judgment.

2. Actual and Exclusive Possession

An adverse possessor will gain title only to land she actually occupies. In some cases, actual possession of the entire parcel claimed is not necessary. If an adverse possessor actually occupies a reasonable portion of the parcel, and her occupation is under *color of title* to the entire parcel, then she will be deemed to have constructively possessed the *entire* parcel, with the same result as if she had actually occupied the entire parcel. "Exclusive" means that the possessor is not sharing with the true owner or the public. Two or more people may obtain title by adverse possession; they take title as tenants in common.

3. Open and Notorious Possession

Possession is open and notorious when it is the kind of use the owner would make of the land. The adverse possessor's occupation must be *sufficiently apparent* to put the true owner on *notice* that a trespass is occurring.

4. Hostile

The hostility requirement is satisfied if the possessor enters *without the owner's permission*.

The adverse possessor's state of mind is irrelevant; *i.e.,* it does not matter whether she believes the land to be her own or knows she is trespassing. When possession starts permissively (*e.g.,* by lease), possession does not become adverse until the possessor makes clear to the true owner the fact that she is claiming "hostilely."

a. Co-Tenants—Ouster Required
Possession by one co-tenant is usually not adverse to his co-tenants because each co-tenant has the right to possession of all the property. A co-tenant must oust others or make an explicit declaration that he is claiming exclusive dominion to create adverse possession.

b. Grantor Stays in Possession—Permission Presumed
Where a grantor stays in possession of land after her conveyance, she is presumed to be there with permission of the grantee. (Likewise, if a tenant remains in possession after the expiration of the lease, he is presumed to have permission of the landlord.)

5. Continuous Possession
An adverse claimant's possession must be continuous throughout the statutory period. Intermittent periods of occupancy are *not* sufficient. However, constant use by the claimant is not required as long as possession is of a type that the usual owner would make. Also, there need *not* be continuous possession by the same person; an adverse possessor can *tack* her own possession onto the periods of adverse possession of her predecessors, but *privity* is required.

6. Payment of Property Taxes Generally Not Required
Most states do *not* require the adverse possessor to pay taxes on the property, but consider such payment good evidence of a claim of right.

C. DISABILITY
The statute of limitations does not begin to run if the true owner was under some disability to sue *when the cause of action first accrued*. (Typical disabilities: minority, imprisonment, insanity.) Only the disability of the *owner* existing at the time the cause of action arose is considered.

D. ADVERSE POSSESSION AND FUTURE INTERESTS
The statute of limitations does not run against a holder of a future interest until the interest becomes *possessory*.

CMR **Exam Tip** The event or condition giving rise to a grantor's right of entry (*e.g.,* "To Grantee on condition that if alcohol is ever used on the premises, Grantor shall have the right to reenter and retake the premises") does not trigger the statute of limitations for purposes of adverse possession. The statute does not begin to run until the right is *asserted by the grantor* because, until that time, the grantee's continued possession of the land is proper.

E. EFFECT OF COVENANTS IN TRUE OWNER'S DEED
If an adverse possessor uses the land in violation of a restrictive covenant in the owner's deed for the limitations period, she takes free of the restriction. If, however, the possessor's use complies with such a covenant, she takes title subject to the restriction.

F. LAND THAT CANNOT BE ADVERSELY POSSESSED
Title to government-owned land and land registered under a Torrens system cannot be acquired by adverse possession.

VI. CONVEYANCING

A. LAND SALE CONTRACTS
Contracts of sale precede most transfers of land.

1. Statute of Frauds Applicable

A contract must be in writing and contain the signature of the party to be charged and the essential terms (*e.g.*, parties, description of land, price). Part performance (*e.g.,* possession, substantial improvements, payment of purchase price) can take a contract out of the statute.

2. Doctrine of Equitable Conversion

Under this doctrine, once a contract is signed, equity regards the buyer as the owner of the *real property*. The seller's interest (the right to the proceeds of sale) is considered *personal property*. The bare legal title that remains in the seller is considered to be held in trust for the buyer. The right to possession follows the bare legal title, however; thus, the seller is entitled to possession until closing.

a. Risk of Loss

If property is destroyed (without fault of either party) before closing, the majority rule places the risk on the *buyer*. Some states, however, have enacted the Uniform Vendor and Purchaser Risk Act, which places the risk on the seller unless the buyer has title or possession at the time of loss.

CMR **Exam Tip** Even though the risk of loss is on the buyer, if the property is damaged or destroyed, the seller must credit any fire or casualty insurance proceeds he receives against the purchase price the buyer is required to pay.

b. Passage of Title on Death

Under the doctrine of equitable conversion, if a party to a land sale contract dies before the contract is completed, the seller's interest passes as personal property and the buyer's interest passes as real property. Thus, if the seller dies, bare legal title passes to his heirs or devisees, but they must give up title to the buyer at closing. If the buyer dies, his heirs or devisees can demand conveyance of the land at closing.

CMR **Exam Tip** If the property is specifically devised by will, check to see whether the ademption rules (*see* F.1., *infra*) change the result of the equitable conversion doctrine.

3. Marketable Title

Every contract contains an implied warranty that the seller will provide marketable title (*i.e.,* title reasonably free from doubt) at closing. It need not be perfect title, but must be free of questions that present an unreasonable risk of litigation.

a. Defects in Record Chain of Title

Title may be unmarketable because of a defect in the chain of title (*e.g.,* variation in land description in deeds, defectively executed deed, evidence that a prior grantor lacked capacity to convey).

1) Adverse Possession

On the Multistate Bar Exam, title acquired by adverse possession is ***unmarketable***, despite the fact that most modern cases are contra.

2) Future Interests Held by Unborn or Unascertained Parties

While most states consider all types of future interests transferable, when a holder of a future interest is unborn or unascertained it is impossible to convey marketable title. Courts will not appoint a guardian ad litem to represent the unborn or unascertained parties for the purposes of conveying land.

b. Encumbrances

Generally, mortgages, liens, restrictive covenants, easements, and *significant* encroachments render title unmarketable. A beneficial easement, however, if visible or known to the buyer, does not impair the marketability of title.

CMR Exam Tip Remember that a seller has the right to satisfy a mortgage or lien *at closing* with the proceeds of the sale. Thus, the buyer cannot claim that title is unmarketable because it is subject to a mortgage prior to closing, if the closing will result in marketable title.

c. Zoning Restrictions

Zoning restrictions do not affect marketability, but an *existing violation* of a zoning ordinance does render title unmarketable.

d. Time of Marketability

If the seller has agreed to furnish title at the date of closing, the buyer cannot rescind prior to that date on grounds that the seller's title is not marketable. Note that in an installment land contract, the seller need not provide marketable title until the buyer has made his last payment.

CMR Exam Tip Avoid answer choices referring to the implied warranty of marketability of title if the closing has already occurred. Once the closing occurs and the deed changes hands, the seller is *no longer liable* on this contractual warranty. The seller is then liable only for promises made *in the deed*.

e. Remedy If Title Not Marketable

The buyer must notify the seller that his title is unmarketable and give him reasonable time to cure the defects. If the seller fails to cure the defects, the buyer's remedies include rescission, damages, specific performance with abatement, and a quiet title suit. But if closing occurs, the contract and deed merge, and the seller's liability on the implied contractual warranty ends.

CMR Exam Tip Don't be fooled into choosing the answer that lets the seller off the hook for title defects because the contract calls for a quitclaim deed. A quitclaim deed does not in any way affect the warranty to provide marketable title.

4. Time of Performance

Courts presume that time is not "of the essence" in real estate contracts. Thus, the closing date is not absolutely binding, and a party late in tendering her own performance can still enforce the contract if she tenders within a *reasonable time* (*e.g.,* two months) after the closing date.

CMR
TIMELINE CHART

THE SALE OF LAND

This chart represents the chronological progression from contract through recording.

Parties Enter into Land Sale Contract →	Time Between Contract and Closing →	Closing →	Recordation →
1. Contract must be in writing (Statute of Frauds).	1. Buyer investigates Seller's title. If defective, Buyer must notify Seller and give him an opportunity to cure.	1. Title passes if deed is validly executed and delivered. Valid execution requires a writing signed by the grantor containing an adequate description of the parcel. Valid delivery requires intent by the grantor to immediately part with legal control.	Buyer records deed to protect her title against a subsequent purchaser for value.
2. Presumption that time is not of the essence unless so stated.	2. During this time, the risk of loss is on Buyer.	2. When title passes, the land sale contract is extinguished (along with the implied warranty of marketability).	
3. Implied warranty of marketability arises.		3. The only basis for a suit by Buyer after title passes is an express covenant, if any, in the deed. There are six possible covenants: Seisin Right to Convey Encumbrances Quiet Enjoyment Warranty Further Assurances	

a. **When Presumption Overcome**

Time is of the essence if: (i) the *contract* so states, (ii) the circumstances indicate that was the parties' *intent*, or (iii) one party gives the other *notice* that time is of the essence.

b. **Liability**

If time is of the essence, a party who fails to tender performance on the closing date is in breach and may not enforce the contract. Even if time is not of the essence, a party who is late in tendering performance is liable for incidental losses.

5. **Tender of Performance**

The buyer's obligation to pay and the seller's obligation to convey are *concurrent conditions*. Thus, neither party is in breach until the other tenders performance (even if the closing date passes). If neither party tenders performance, the closing date is extended until one of them does so.

a. **When Party's Tender Excused**

A party need not tender performance if the other party has *repudiated* the contract or it is *impossible* (*e.g.,* unmarketable title that cannot be cured) for the other party to perform.

6. **Remedies for Breach of Sales Contract**

The nonbreaching party is entitled to *damages* (difference between contract price and market value on date of breach, plus incidental costs) or, because land is unique, *specific performance*. Note that if the buyer wishes to proceed despite unmarketable title, she can usually get specific performance with an abatement of the purchase price.

a. **Liquidated Damages**

Sales contracts usually require the buyer to deposit "earnest money" with the seller, and provide that if the buyer defaults in performance, the seller may retain this money as liquidated damages. Courts routinely uphold the seller's retention of earnest money if the amount appears to be reasonable in light of the seller's anticipated and actual damages.

7. **Seller's Liabilities for Defective Property**

a. **Warranty of Fitness or Quality—New Construction Only**

Contracts of sale and deeds of real property carry no implied warranty of quality or fitness for purpose. However, a majority of courts now recognize a warranty of fitness or quality in the sale of a new house by the builder.

b. **Negligence of Builder**

A person may sue a builder for negligence in performing a building contract. Some courts permit the ultimate vendee to sue the builder despite lack of privity.

c. **Sale of Existing Land and Buildings—Liability for Defects**

The seller of existing buildings (not new construction) may be liable to the purchaser for defects such as a leaky roof, flooding basement, or termite infestation, on any of several different theories:

1) **Misrepresentation (Fraud)**
The seller is liable for defects about which he *knowingly or negligently* made a false statement of fact to the buyer if the *buyer relied* on the statement and it *materially affected* the value of the property.

2) **Active Concealment**
The seller will be liable for defects, even *without making any statements*, if he took steps to *conceal the defects* (*e.g.,* wallpapering over water damage).

3) **Failure to Disclose**
Most states hold a seller liable for failure to disclose defects if: (i) he *knows or has reason to know* of the defect; (ii) the defect is *not apparent*, and the seller knows that the buyer is unlikely to discover it upon ordinary inspection; and (iii) the defect is *serious* and would probably cause the buyer to reconsider the purchase if known. Factors increasing the likelihood that liability will be imposed in these cases include whether the property is a personal residence, whether the defect is dangerous, and whether the seller created the defect or made a failed attempt to repair it.

d. Disclaimers of Liability
A general disclaimer in the sales contract (*e.g.,* "property sold as is" or "with all defects") is *not* sufficient to overcome a seller's liability for fraud, concealment, or (in the states that recognize it) failure to disclose. If the disclaimer identifies *specific* types of defects (*e.g.,* "seller is not liable for any defects in the roof"), it will likely be upheld.

8. Real Estate Brokers
Real estate brokers are the seller's agents, but should disclose material information about the property if they have actual knowledge of it. Traditionally, agents earned their commissions when they produced a buyer who was ready, willing, and able to purchase the property. Therefore, the commission was owed regardless of whether the deal actually closed. The growing trend, however, is to award the commission only if the sale actually closes or if it fails to close because of the fault of the seller.

B. DEEDS—FORM AND CONTENT
Deeds transfer title to an interest in real property.

1. Formalities
A deed must be *in writing*, be *signed by the grantor*, and *reasonably identify the parties and land*. Most other formalities (*e.g.,* seal, consideration, attestation, and acknowledgment) are generally unnecessary. Thus, a deed may validly convey real property by *inter vivos gift* so long as the following requirements are met: (i) donative intent, (ii) delivery, and (iii) acceptance (*see* C., *infra*).

CMR **Exam Tip** Note that if a deed is delivered with the *name of the grantee* left blank, the court presumes that the person taking delivery has authority to fill in the name of the grantee. If the person fills in a name, the deed is valid. If, however, the *land description* is left blank, the deed is void unless the grantee was explicitly given authority to fill in the description.

2. Defective Deeds
A *void* deed will be set aside by the court even if the property has passed to a bona fide purchaser, but a *voidable* deed will be set aside only if the property has *not* passed to a bona

fide purchaser. Void deeds include those that are forged, were never delivered, or were obtained by fraud in the factum (*i.e.*, the grantor was deceived and did not realize that she was executing a deed). Voidable deeds include those executed by minors or incapacitated persons, and those obtained through fraud in the inducement, duress, undue influence, mistake, and breach of fiduciary duty.

CMR **Exam Tip** Watch for a situation in which a joint owner attempts to convey property by forging the signature(s) of the other owner(s). Such a conveyance would be valid as to the interest of the owner whose signature is genuine but void as to the other owner(s). Thus, if one joint tenant executes a deed for the entire property with his own signature and the forged signature of the other joint tenant, the conveyance works a severance; the buyer would hold as a tenant in common with the joint tenant whose signature was forged.

3. Fraudulent Conveyances

Even when a deed complies with the required formalities, it may be set aside by the grantor's creditors if it was made: (i) with actual intent to hinder, delay, or defraud any creditor of the grantor; or (ii) without receiving a reasonably equivalent value in exchange for the transfer, and the debtor was insolvent or became insolvent as a result of the transfer. However, the deed will not be set aside as against any grantee who took in good faith and paid reasonably equivalent value.

4. Description of Land Conveyed

A description is sufficient if it provides a *good lead* to the identity of the property (*e.g.*, "all my land in Stockton"). If it is too indefinite, the grantor retains title (but reformation of the deed is a possible remedy). Parol evidence is generally admissible to resolve patent or latent ambiguities if the description gives a good lead, but may not be admissible where the description is inadequate.

a. Rules of Construction

Where descriptions are inconsistent or conflicting, these methods of description are given the following order of priority: natural monuments (*e.g.*, oak tree); artificial monuments (*e.g.*, stakes, buildings); courses (*e.g.*, angles); distances (*e.g.*, feet, yards); name (*e.g.*, Blackacre); and quantity (*e.g.*, 300 acres).

b. Boundary Cases

Presumptively, title to land passes to the *center* of a right-of-way or water boundary. This presumption can be rebutted by language in the deed. In variable boundary line cases (*i.e.*, water boundary) the *slow and imperceptible change* in the course of a river or stream operates to change the legal boundary; *accretion* (slow deposit of soil on land abutting water) belongs to the abutting owner. *Avulsion* (sudden change of watercourse) does not change ownership rights. Fixed boundaries are not changed by encroachment of water.

c. Reformation of Deeds

A deed will be reformed if it does not represent the parties' agreement because of: (i) *mutual mistake*, (ii) a *scrivener's error*, or (iii) a unilateral mistake caused by *misrepresentation* or other inequitable conduct.

C. DELIVERY AND ACCEPTANCE
A deed is not effective unless it has been delivered and accepted.

CMR **Exam Tip** Remember that a deed to a dead person is void and conveys no title. The fact that the grantor was unaware of the grantee's death is irrelevant. Title remains in the grantor.

1. Delivery—In General
Delivery refers to the grantor's **intention** to make a deed **presently** effective even if possession is postponed. Delivery may be satisfied by manual delivery, notarized acknowledgment by the grantor, recording, or anything else showing the grantor's intent to deliver. Parol evidence is admissible on the issue of intent to deliver, but not to show that delivery was conditional.

CMR **Exam Tip** Title passes upon delivery. It cannot be canceled or taken back. Thus, if a fact pattern has the grantee returning a deed to the grantor, this has no effect; it is not a cancellation or a reconveyance. To return title to the grantor, the grantee must draw up a new deed and deliver it to the grantor.

2. Retention of Interest by Grantor or Conditional Delivery
Retention of control or interest by the grantor (*e.g.,* right to revoke) indicates a lack of intent to pass title. Thus, if a grantor executes a deed but does not deliver it during his lifetime, no title passes. Failure to record a delivered deed does not affect the passage of title even if the parties believe that the deed is ineffective until recording.

a. Express Condition of Grantor's Death
A properly executed and delivered deed that provides that title will not pass until the grantor's death is valid and creates a future interest in the grantee.

b. Conditions Not Contained in Deed
If a deed is absolute on its face but delivered with an oral condition, the condition is disregarded and the delivery is absolute.

3. Where Grantor Gives Deed to Third Party
Here, conditional delivery is permissible.

a. Transfer to Third Party with No Conditions
If the grantor gives a deed to a third party with instructions to give it to the grantee, there is a valid delivery. If the grantor fails to give instructions, the validity of the delivery depends on whether the third party could be considered the grantor's agent. If so, there is no delivery.

b. Transfer to Third Party with Conditions (Commercial Transaction)
A valid conditional delivery occurs when a grantor gives a deed to a third party with instructions to give it to the grantee when certain conditions occur (*e.g.,* if grantee pays purchase price before a certain date). Parol evidence is admissible to show that delivery is conditional. (Remember that the rule is contra where the grantor gives the deed **directly** to the grantee; *see* 1., *supra.*)

1) Grantor's Right to Recover Deed
A grantor can revoke only if: (i) the condition has not yet occurred, and (ii) there is no enforceable written contract to convey.

2) Breach of Escrow Conditions

If a grantee wrongfully acquires the deed from the escrow holder prior to performance of the condition, title does not pass and the grantee cannot give good title to a subsequent purchaser.

3) "Relation Back" Doctrine

Title usually passes when the condition occurs, but if justice requires it (*e.g.*, grantor dies or becomes incompetent) and there is an enforceable contract to convey, title may "relate back" to the time when the grantor gave the deed to the third party. Rights of intervening bona fide purchasers are protected.

c. Transfer to Third Party with Conditions (Donative Transaction)

When a grantor gives a deed to a third party to give to a *donee* when a condition occurs, the main issue is whether the grantor can revoke the deed before the condition occurs. Where the condition is not the grantor's death, delivery is irrevocable and creates a springing executory interest in the donee. Where the condition is the grantor's death, most courts follow the same reasoning, but some hold deeds revocable unless there is an enforceable contract to convey (*i.e.*, same as true escrow cases, above).

4. Acceptance

Acceptance by the grantee is required in order to complete a conveyance. Most states *presume* acceptance. Acceptance relates back to the date the deed was delivered into escrow (unless this would defeat the rights of intervening third parties).

5. Dedication

Land may be transferred to a public body (*e.g.*, city, county) by dedication. An offer may be made by written or oral statement, submission of a map or plat showing the dedication, or opening the land for public use. To be effective, a dedication must be accepted, which may be done by formal resolution, approval of map or plat, or actual assumption of maintenance or improvements.

D. COVENANTS FOR TITLE AND ESTOPPEL BY DEED

There are three types of deeds used to convey property interests other than leaseholds: the *general warranty* deed, the *special warranty* deed, and the *quitclaim* deed. The difference among these deeds is the scope of title assurance (*i.e.*, covenants for title).

 Exam Tip Be careful not to confuse covenants for title with real covenants (written promises to do or not do something on the land). They are completely different. Real covenants do not relate to title.

1. Covenants in General Warranty Deed

a. Usual Covenants

The following are the usual covenants for title contained in a general warranty deed.

1) Covenant of Seisin

The grantor covenants that she has the estate she purports to convey. She must have both title and possession at the time of the grant.

2) **Covenant of Right to Convey**

The grantor covenants that she has the authority to make the grant. Title alone will satisfy this covenant.

3) **Covenant Against Encumbrances**

The grantor covenants against the existence of physical (*e.g.,* encroachments) or title (*e.g.,* mortgages) encumbrances.

4) **Covenant for Quiet Enjoyment**

The grantor covenants that the grantee will not be disturbed in possession by a third party's *lawful* claim of title.

5) **Covenant of Warranty**

The grantor agrees to defend against reasonable claims of title by a third party, and to compensate the grantee for any loss sustained by the claim of superior title.

CMR **Exam Tip** The covenant for quiet enjoyment and the covenant of warranty are generally considered to be identical covenants for title.

6) **Covenant for Further Assurances**

The grantor promises to perform acts reasonably necessary to perfect title conveyed. (This covenant is *not* one of the usual covenants, but is frequently given.)

b. **Breach of Covenants**

Three of the covenants (seisin, right to convey, against encumbrances) are breached, if at all, *at the time of conveyance*. Quiet enjoyment, warranty, and further assurances are future covenants and are breached *only upon disturbance of the grantee's possession*.

c. **Damages and Remote Grantees**

If there are successive conveyances by general warranty deed and the last grantee is evicted by lawful claim of title, he may sue *anyone* up the line. Some states allow him to recover to the extent of consideration *received* by a defendant-covenantor. Other states limit recovery to the *lesser* of what he paid or what the defendant-covenantor received.

2. **Statutory Special Warranty Deed**

In many states, use of the word "grant" in a deed creates by implication two limited assurances against acts of the grantor (not her predecessors): (i) that the grantor has not conveyed the same estate or any interest therein to anyone other than the grantee; and (ii) that the estate is free from encumbrances made by the grantor.

3. **Quitclaim Deeds**

A quitclaim deed releases *whatever interest* the grantor has. No covenants of title are included or implied.

4. **Estoppel by Deed**

If the grantor purports to convey an estate in property that she does not then own, her subsequent acquisition of the estate will *automatically* inure to the benefit of the grantee. This doctrine applies where the conveyance was by warranty deed, or where the deed purported to convey a *particular* estate. It is not usually applicable to quitclaim deeds.

a. Rights of Subsequent Purchasers

Most courts hold that title inures to the benefit of the grantee only as against the grantor. Thus, if the grantor transfers her after-acquired title to a bona fide purchaser for value ("BFP"), the BFP will prevail over the original grantee.

b. Remedies of Grantee

The original grantee can accept title or sue for damages for breach of covenant.

E. RECORDING

At common law, if a grantor conveyed the same property twice, the grantee *first in time* generally prevailed. The recording acts change that outcome under certain circumstances.

1. Recording Acts—In General

Recording acts generally protect all BFPs from *secret* interests previously created and provide a mechanism for "earlier" grantees to give notice through recordation. These statutes require a grantee to record his deed to put subsequent purchasers on notice of his interest. Recording is not essential to the validity of the deed between the grantor and grantee, but can be essential to protect the grantee against a BFP. Proper recordation gives *constructive notice* of the first conveyance to everyone, so there can be no subsequent BFPs. Any instrument creating or affecting an interest in land can be recorded, provided it is acknowledged by the grantor before a notary public.

2. Types of Recording Acts

Recording acts are in effect in every state. There are three major types, but under all three, the burden is on the subsequent taker to prove that he qualifies for protection under the statute.

a. Notice Statutes

Under a notice statute, a subsequent BFP (person who pays value and has no notice of the prior instrument) prevails over a prior grantee who failed to record. The key is that the subsequent purchaser had *no actual or constructive notice at the time of the conveyance*.

Example: O conveys to A on January 1. A does not record. O conveys to B on January 15 for valuable consideration. B has no notice of the conveyance to A. B prevails over A. It is irrelevant whether A recorded after January 15 and before B recorded, because B had no notice *at the time he took*. (This distinguishes notice and race-notice statutes.)

CMR | **Exam Tip**   Remember that under a notice statute, the subsequent BFP is protected regardless of whether she records at all.

b. Race-Notice Statutes

Under a race-notice statute, a subsequent BFP is protected only if she takes without notice *and* records before the prior grantee.

Example: O conveys to A on January 1. A does not record. O conveys to B on January 15 for valuable consideration. B has no notice of the conveyance to A. A records on January 18. B records on January 20. A prevails over B because B did not record first.

c. **Race Statutes**

Under a pure race statute, whoever records first wins. Notice is irrelevant. Very few states have such statutes.

CMR
EXAMPLE CHART

Type of Statute	Typical Language	Effect
Notice	"No conveyance or mortgage of an interest in land is valid against any subsequent purchaser for value without notice thereof, unless it is recorded."	Subsequent ***bona fide purchaser*** (*i.e., for value,* without notice) prevails.
Race	"No conveyance or mortgage of an interest in land is valid against any subsequent purchaser whose conveyance is first recorded."	Grantee ***who records first*** prevails.
Race-Notice	"No conveyance or mortgage of an interest in land is valid against any subsequent purchaser for value without notice thereof whose conveyance is first recorded."	Subsequent ***bona fide purchaser*** (*i.e.,* for value, without notice) ***who records first*** prevails.

RECORDING STATUTES

3. **Who Is Protected by Recording Acts**

Only BFPs are protected from the claims of a prior transferee under "notice" and "race-notice" statutes. To be a BFP, a person must be a purchaser, without notice (actual, constructive, or inquiry), and pay valuable consideration.

a. **Purchasers**

All statutes protect purchasers (of the fee or lesser estate). Mortgagees for value are purchasers. Donees, heirs, and devisees are *not* protected because they do not give value.

1) **Purchaser from Donee, Heir, or Devisee**

A purchaser from a donee, heir, or devisee of the record owner is protected against prior unrecorded conveyances of the record owner.

2) **Judgment Creditors**

Most states permit a plaintiff who obtains a money judgment to place a judgment lien on the defendant's real property by filing the judgment in the appropriate county office. The majority, however, hold that such a judgment creditor is *not* protected by the recording statute against a prior unrecorded conveyance by the defendant.

3) Transferees from Bona Fide Purchaser—Shelter Rule

A person who takes *from* a BFP will prevail against any interest the transferor-BFP would have prevailed against. This is true even if the transferee had actual notice of a prior unrecorded conveyance. This rule does not, however, help a transferee who previously held title; she cannot "ship through" a BFP to get good title.

4) Purchaser Under Installment Land Contract

In most states, a purchaser under an installment land contract is protected only to the extent of payment made. In a dispute with a prior claimant, the court may award the purchaser: (i) a share of the property as a tenant in common equal to the proportion of *payments made*; (ii) a lien on the property to the extent of the *amount paid*; or (iii) the entire property, subject to a lien on the property to the extent of the *balance still owed*.

b. Without Notice

"Without notice" means that the purchaser had no actual, constructive (record), or inquiry notice of a prior conveyance at the time she paid consideration and received the interest.

 Exam Tip   In determining who is a BFP for purposes of protection of the recording statutes, remember that the purchaser must be without notice *at the time of conveyance*. It does not matter if she learns of an adverse claim after the conveyance but before recording.

1) Actual Notice

Actual notice includes knowledge obtained from any source (*e.g.,* newspaper, word-of-mouth).

2) Record Notice—Chain of Title

A subsequent purchaser will be held to have record notice only if the deed in question is recorded "in the chain of title," which means that it is recorded in a manner that a searcher could reasonably find it.

Exam Tip   Although *no one has a legal duty* to perform a title search, a subsequent purchaser will be charged with the notice that such a search *would* provide, whether or not she actually searches.

a) "Wild Deeds"

A "wild deed" is a recorded deed that is not connected to the chain of title. It does not impart constructive notice because a subsequent purchaser could not feasibly find it.

Example: O conveys Blackacre to A. A does not record. A conveys it to B, and B records. O conveys Blackacre to C. C does not have notice of B's claim.

b) Deeds Recorded Late

A deed recorded *after* the grantor is shown by record to have parted with title through another (subsequent) instrument is not constructive notice in most states (but is in some "race-notice" jurisdictions).

Example: O conveys to A on March 1. O conveys to B on April 1. B records on April 10. A records on April 15. B conveys to C on May 1. If C has no actual or inquiry notice of the O-A deed, he will prevail. Most states would hold that A's deed was recorded late and was not in C's chain of title.

c) Deeds Recorded Before Grantor Obtained Title
There is a split of authority on whether a recorded deed, received from a grantor who had no title when conveyed but who afterwards obtains title, imparts constructive notice to subsequent purchasers. Most courts say it does not, and a BFP will win on the grounds that the deed is not in his chain of title. The minority view protects the prior grantee over the BFP on an estoppel by deed theory (*see* D.4., *supra*).

d) Deed in Chain Referring to Instrument Outside Chain
Reference to another instrument in a recorded document that is in the chain of title may impart constructive notice of the instrument referred to—even if it is unrecorded or not itself in the chain of title.

e) Restrictive Covenants—Deeds from Common Grantor
Courts are split on whether deeds to adjacent lots or lots in a subdivision, executed by the same grantor and containing restrictions and easements involving the subject lot, are within the chain of title of the subject lot. The better view is that they are not.

3) Inquiry Notice
Under certain circumstances, a purchaser is required to make reasonable inquiries. He is charged with knowledge of whatever the inquiry *would have revealed*, even if in fact he made none. References in recorded instruments to unrecorded transactions, unrecorded instruments in the chain of title (*e.g.,* grantor's title documents are not recorded), and possession unexplained by the record put a purchaser on inquiry notice. The mere fact that a quitclaim deed was used does not charge the purchaser with inquiry notice.

c. Valuable Consideration
To be protected by the recording statute, the subsequent grantee must prove that he is a purchaser, not a donee. The consideration need not be adequate, but it must be of some pecuniary value (*i.e.,* love and affection is not valuable consideration). Note that property received as security for an antecedent debt is insufficient.

CMR **Exam Tip** A purchaser is protected by a recording statute only from the time consideration is paid. Thus, even if the deed was delivered and recorded before the consideration was paid, a purchaser will not prevail over deeds recorded subsequently but before the consideration was paid.

4. Title Search
In a *tract index* jurisdiction, the searcher looks at the page indexed by block and/or lot describing the property and any instruments affecting it. In a *grantor and grantee index* jurisdiction, the searcher establishes a chain of title by searching back in time in the grantee-grantor

index. From that point, he then searches forward in time in the grantor-grantee index to see if any grantor conveyed an interest to someone outside of the backward chain.

5. Effect of Recordation

Recordation gives prospective subsequent grantees constructive notice of the existence and content of recorded instruments. It also raises a ***presumption*** of valid delivery and authenticity. However, it does not validate an invalid deed or protect against interests arising by operation of law (*e.g.*, dower, title by adverse possession); to this extent, BFPs are still in jeopardy.

a. Recorder's Mistakes

An instrument is considered recorded when filed with the recorder's office, regardless of whether it is thereafter properly indexed. A subsequent purchaser is charged with notice of a misindexed instrument, but has a cause of action against the recorder's office.

b. Effect of Recording Unacknowledged Instrument

Because an unacknowledged instrument is not entitled to recordation, it does ***not*** give constructive notice. A subsequent grantee must have actual notice of a deed (*e.g.*, discover it in a title search) to be bound by it. *Compare:* Where acknowledgment is ***defective*** for reasons ***not apparent on the face*** of the instrument, the better view is that it imparts constructive notice.

F. CONVEYANCE BY WILL

Another way of conveying property is by will.

1. Ademption

If property is specifically devised or bequeathed in the testator's will, but the testator no longer owns it at the time of death, the gift *fails*. Ademption applies only to specific bequests, which can be satisfied only by the delivery of a ***particular item***; they cannot be satisfied by money. A gift of land is always a specific devise. If the testator specifically devises property and then sells or gives away a part of that property, only that portion is adeemed; the remainder passes to the devisee.

a. Land Under Executory Contract

Most state statutes do not apply the ademption doctrine to the proceeds of a contract for sale of land that was executory at the time of the testator's death; *i.e.,* the devisee gets the proceeds in place of the land. These statutes take precedence over the equitable conversion doctrine. In addition, ademption does not apply when the contract is entered into by the representative of an incompetent testator.

b. Other Proceeds Not Subject to Ademption

When property is damaged or destroyed before the testator's death but the casualty insurance proceeds are not paid until after the testator's death, ademption does not usually apply. The beneficiary of the specific bequest takes the insurance proceeds. Similarly, ademption usually does not apply to property condemned by the government where the taking was before death but the condemnation award was paid after death.

2. **Exoneration**

At common law and in many states, the devisee of specific property is entitled to have the land "exonerated" by the payment of liens and mortgages from the testator's residuary estate. However, there is a growing trend toward abolition of the exoneration doctrine.

3. **Lapse and Anti-Lapse Statutes**

A lapse occurs when the beneficiary of a gift in a will *dies before the testator*. Under the common law, if a lapse occurred, the gift was void. However, nearly all states now have statutes that prevent lapse by permitting the gift to pass to the predeceasing beneficiary's living descendants under certain circumstances. These statutes vary as to the scope of beneficiaries covered by the statute.

a. **Degree of Relationship to Testator**

Many of the anti-lapse statutes apply only when the named beneficiary is a descendant of the testator. Others apply if the beneficiary is more remotely related, such as a descendant of the testator's grandparent. Others apply to any relative, and still others apply to any beneficiary at all.

1) **Descendants Are Substitutes**

The anti-lapse statute does not save the gift for the predeceasing beneficiary's estate; rather, it substitutes the beneficiary's descendants for the beneficiary. Thus, property will never pass under the anti-lapse statute to a predeceasing beneficiary's spouse.

b. **Inapplicable If Beneficiary Dead When Will Executed**

If the beneficiary is already dead when the will is executed, the anti-lapse statute usually does not apply, and the gift will lapse and fail.

c. **Application to Class Gifts**

If a class member within the coverage of an anti-lapse statute predeceases the testator leaving surviving issue, the statute will apply and the issue will take the deceased class member's share of the gift.

d. **Anti-Lapse Statute Does Not Apply If Contrary Will Provision**

The anti-lapse statute does not apply if there is a contrary will provision; *e.g.*, the gift is contingent on the beneficiary's surviving the testator.

4. **Abatement**

If the estate assets are not sufficient to pay all claims against the estate and satisfy all devises and bequests, the gifts are abated (*i.e.*, reduced). Absent a contrary will provision, estates in most states abate in the following order: (i) property passing by intestacy, (ii) the residuary estate, (iii) general legacies, and (iv) specific devises and bequests.

G. **CROPS (EMBLEMENTS)**

Generally, the conveyance of land includes all crops growing on it. However, exceptions exist for (i) crops that have already been harvested or severed from the land, and (ii) crops planted by a tenant during the term of the tenancy. For title to crops to remain in a tenant, the tenancy must have been of *uncertain duration* and have terminated *without fault* on the part of the tenant.

VII. SECURITY INTERESTS IN REAL ESTATE

A. TYPES OF SECURITY INTERESTS
Of the five types of security interests in real estate, the first three are the most important.

1. Mortgage
The debtor/notemaker is the mortgagor. The lender is the mortgagee. On default, the lender can realize on the mortgaged real estate only by having a judicial foreclosure sale conducted by the sheriff.

2. Deed of Trust
The debtor/notemaker is the trustor. He gives a deed of trust to a third-party trustee, who is usually closely connected to the lender (the beneficiary). On default, the lender instructs the trustee to foreclose the deed of trust by sale.

3. Installment Land Contract
An installment purchaser obtains legal title only when the full contract price has been paid off. Forfeiture clauses, allowing the vendor upon default to cancel the contract, retake possession, and retain all money paid, are common.

4. Absolute Deed
An absolute deed, if given for security purposes, can be treated by the court as an *"equitable" mortgage* to be treated as any other mortgage (*i.e.*, creditor must foreclose by judicial action).

5. Sale-Leaseback
A landowner may sell her property for cash and then lease it back from the purchaser for a long period of time. Like an absolute deed, this may be treated as a disguised mortgage.

B. TRANSFERS BY MORTGAGEE AND MORTGAGOR
All parties to a mortgage or deed of trust may transfer their interests. The note and mortgage must pass to the *same person* for the transfer to be complete.

1. Transfer by Mortgagee

a. Transfer of Mortgage Without Note
Some states hold that the transfer of the mortgage automatically transfers the note as well, unless the mortgagee-transferor expressly reserves the rights to the note. In these states, the transferee of the mortgage can then file an equitable action and compel a transfer of the note as well. Other states hold that, because the note is the principal evidence of the debt, a transfer of the mortgage without the note is void.

b. Transfer of Note Without Mortgage
The *note can be transferred without the mortgage*, but the mortgage will automatically follow the properly transferred note, unless the mortgagee-transferor expressly reserves the rights to the mortgage. No separate written assignment of the mortgage is necessary.

1) Methods of Transferring the Note
The note may be transferred either by indorsing it and delivering it to the transferee,

or by a separate document of assignment. Only if the indorsement and delivery method is used can the transferee become a *holder in due course*. To be a holder in due course of the note, the following requirements must be met:

a) The note must be *negotiable in form* (payable "to bearer" or "to the order of" the named payee, with a promise to pay a sum certain, and no other promises).

b) The original note must be *indorsed* and signed by the named payee.

c) The original note must be *delivered* to the transferee.

d) The transferee must take the note in *good faith* (no notice that it is overdue, has been dishonored, is subject to any defense by the maker) and must pay *value* for it.

2) Benefits of Holder in Due Course Status
A holder in due course takes the note free of any personal defenses of the maker (*e.g.*, failure of consideration, fraud in the inducement, waiver, estoppel, and payment), but is still subject to real defenses (*e.g.*, infancy, other incapacity, duress, illegality, fraud in the execution, forgery, discharge in insolvency, and any other insolvency).

CMR **Exam Tip** Remember that if possession of the note has been transferred by the original mortgagee, any payment to that mortgagee will not count. The holder of the note can still demand payment—even if the mortgagor had no notice of the transfer. For example, X borrows $10,000 from Y, giving Y a note secured by a mortgage on Farmacre. Later Y assigns the note to Z, but does not tell X. X pays the $10,000 to Y. Z may still demand payment of the $10,000, and may foreclose the mortgage on Farmacre if payment is not forthcoming. The payment to Y is no defense.

2. Transfer by Mortgagor—Grantee Takes Subject to Mortgage
A grantee of mortgaged property takes subject to the mortgage.

a. Assumption
If the grantee signs an assumption agreement, he becomes *primarily* liable to the lender, while the *original* mortgagor is secondarily liable as a *surety*. If no assumption agreement is signed, the grantee is not personally liable on the loan, and the original mortgagor remains primarily and personally liable. However, if the grantee does not pay, the loan may be foreclosed, wiping out the grantee's investment.

CMR **Exam Tip** Remember that once a grantee has assumed a mortgage, any modification of the obligation by the grantee and mortgagee discharges the original mortgagor of all liability.

b. Due-on-Sale Clauses
Due-on-sale clauses, which appear in most modern mortgages, allow the lender to demand full payment of the loan if the mortgagor transfers any interest in the property without the lender's consent.

C. DEFENSES AND DISCHARGE OF THE MORTGAGE
Because a mortgage is granted to secure an obligation, defenses in an action on the underlying

obligation (*e.g.*, failure of consideration, duress, mistake, fraud) are defenses against an action on the mortgage. A mortgagee's right to foreclose is precluded by a discharge of the mortgage—*e.g.*, payment of the debt secured, merger of the legal and equitable interests, or the mortgagee's acceptance of a deed in lieu of foreclosure tendered by the mortgagor.

D. POSSESSION BEFORE FORECLOSURE

When a mortgagor defaults on his debt, the mortgagee can foreclose on the mortgage. A mortgagee may wish to take possession of the property, or begin receiving the rents from the property, before foreclosure.

1. Theories of Title

The mortgagee may have a right to take possession before foreclosure, depending on the theory the state follows. Most states follow either the lien or the title theory.

a. The Lien Theory

According to the lien theory, the mortgagee is considered the ***holder of a security interest only*** and the mortgagor is deemed the owner of the land until foreclosure. The mortgagee may ***not*** have possession before foreclosure.

b. The Title Theory

Under the title theory, ***legal title is in the mortgagee*** until the mortgage has been satisfied or foreclosed, and the mortgagee is entitled to possession upon demand at any time.

c. The Intermediate Theory

In the few states that follow the intermediate theory, legal title is in the mortgagor until default, and upon default, ***legal title is in the mortgagee***. The mortgagee may demand possession when a default occurs. There is little practical difference between this theory and the title theory.

2. Mortgagor Consent and Abandonment

The mortgagee may take possession if the mortgagor gives consent to do so, or if the mortgagor abandons the property.

3. Risks of Mortgagee in Possession

Most mortgagees do not wish to take possession because of the risks of liability. These risks involve the duty to account for rents, the duty to manage the property in a prudent manner, and potential tort liability for those injured on the property.

4. Receiverships

Most mortgagees attempt to intercept the rents before foreclosure by getting a receiver appointed by the court to manage the property. Courts will generally appoint receivers for rental property upon showing that: (i) waste is occurring, (ii) the value of the property is inadequate to secure the debt, and (iii) the mortgagor is insolvent.

E. FORECLOSURE

Almost all states require foreclosure by sale, under which the property is sold to satisfy the debt in whole or part. While all states allow ***judicial sale***, some states allow nonjudicial sale under a ***power of sale*** (usually with respect to deeds of trust). Foreclosure sales are usually conducted by auction, and the lender is permitted to bid at the sale.

REAL ESTATE FINANCING AND FORECLOSURE

Financing

Buyer finances purchase of land using the land as collateral. Usually done by giving lender a mortgage on the property, although it could be done with deed of trust, installment land contract, absolute deed, or sale-leaseback.

↓

Default

Mortgagor-borrower defaults. Mortgagee has right to foreclose. Up until the foreclosure sale, borrower may redeem by paying off mortgage and accrued interest (equitable redemption).

↓

Foreclosure

Foreclosure must be by sale, usually judicial sale.

Proceeds distributed according to priorities of security interests.

↓

Post-Foreclosure

If proceeds of sale are insufficient to satisfy debt, mortgagee can bring personal action against borrower for deficiency.

About one-half of states give borrower a right to redeem for a fixed period (*e.g.*, six months) after foreclosure by paying sale price (statutory redemption).

1. **Redemption**

    a. **Redemption in Equity**
        At *any time prior to the foreclosure sale*, the mortgagor may redeem the property by paying the amount due. If the note or mortgage contains an acceleration clause, the full balance of the note or mortgage must be paid to redeem. This right cannot be waived in the mortgage itself.

    b. **Statutory Redemption**
        About half the states allow the mortgagor to redeem the property for some fixed period (*e.g.,* six months) *after the foreclosure sale* has occurred.

2. **Priorities**
    A mortgage's priority is usually determined by the time it was placed on the property. Foreclosure does not destroy any interests senior to the interest being foreclosed. It generally destroys all junior interests, but failure to include a junior interest holder in a foreclosure action results in preservation of that party's interest.

    a. **Modification of Priority**
        Although priority among mortgages is generally determined by chronology, this priority may be changed by: (i) the operation of the recording statute if a *prior mortgagee fails to record*; (ii) a *subordination agreement* between a senior and junior mortgagee; (iii) a *purchase money mortgage*; (iv) the *modification of a senior mortgage* (junior mortgage has priority over the modification); or (v) the *granting of optional future advances* by a mortgagee with notice of a junior lien (junior lien has priority over advances).

    b. **Purchase Money Mortgages**
        A purchase money mortgage ("PMM") is a mortgage given in exchange for funds used to purchase the property. PMMs are given either to the seller as part of the purchase price or to a third-party lender. PMMs have priority over *prior* non-PMMs, even if such mortgages or liens are recorded first. However, *subsequent* mortgages or liens may defeat PMM priority by operation of the recording acts. As between two PMMs, a seller's mortgage has priority over a third party's. If there are two third-party PMMs, priority is determined by chronological order. Usually two PMMs have notice of the other's existence; thus, the recording acts are of no use in determining priority.

3. **Proceeds of Sale**
    Proceeds are applied first to the expenses of the sale, attorneys' fees, and court costs; then to the principal and accrued interest on the *foreclosed loan*; next to any other *junior interests* in the order of their priority; and finally to the *mortgagor*.

4. **Deficiency Judgments**
    If the proceeds are insufficient to satisfy the mortgage debt, the mortgagee retains a personal cause of action against the mortgagor for the deficiency.

F. **INSTALLMENT LAND CONTRACTS**
    Most installment contracts provide for forfeiture rather than foreclosure as the vendor's remedy for default, but courts use the following theories to avoid that harsh result:

1. **Equity of Redemption**
    Several states give the contract purchaser a grace period to pay the accelerated full balance of the contract and keep the land after default.

2. **Restitution**
    A number of decisions, while granting forfeiture, have required the vendor to refund to the purchaser any amount by which his payments exceed the vendor's damages.

3. **Treat as a Mortgage**
    A few states treat installment contracts as mortgages, thus requiring a judicial foreclosure sale.

4. **Waiver**
    Many cases hold that a vendor's pattern of accepting late payments constitutes a waiver of the right of strict performance. To reinstate strict performance, the vendor must send the purchaser a notice of his intention to do so and must allow a reasonable time for the purchaser to make up any late payments.

5. **Election of Remedies**
    The vendor must choose only one remedy (damages or specific performance) and forgo all others.

VIII. RIGHTS INCIDENTAL TO OWNERSHIP OF LAND (NATURAL RIGHTS)

A. IN GENERAL
An owner of real property has the exclusive right to use and possess the surface, the airspace, and the soil of the property.

B. RIGHTS TO LATERAL AND SUBJACENT SUPPORT OF LAND

1. **Lateral Support**
    Ownership of land includes the right to have the land supported in its *natural state* by adjoining land.

    a. **Support of Land in Natural State**
        A landowner is *strictly liable* if his excavation causes adjacent land to subside (*i.e.,* slip or cave in).

    b. **Support of Land with Buildings**
        An adjacent landowner is strictly liable for damage to land and buildings caused by excavation only if it is shown that the land would have collapsed in its natural state. Otherwise, he is liable for such damage only if his excavation was done *negligently*.

2. **Subjacent Support**
    An underground occupant of land (*e.g.,* a mining company) must support the surface and buildings existing on the date the subjacent estate was created. Liability for subsequently erected buildings requires *negligence*.

C. WATER RIGHTS
Different rules apply to watercourses, groundwater, and surface waters.

1. Watercourses (Streams, Rivers, and Lakes)
There are two major systems for determining allocation of water in watercourses: the riparian doctrine and the prior appropriation doctrine.

a. Riparian Doctrine
Under this doctrine, the water belongs to those who own the land bordering the watercourse. Riparian rights attach to all contiguous tracts held by the same owner as long as one abuts the water. Riparian owners can use water only in connection with the riparian parcel.

1) Natural Flow Theory
Under this theory, a riparian owner's use resulting in substantial or material diminution of the water's quantity, quality, or velocity is enjoinable.

2) Reasonable Use Theory
Under this theory, which is the most common, all riparians share the right of "reasonable use" of the water (*i.e.*, one owner's use is not enjoinable unless it substantially interferes with the use of other riparian owners). In determining "reasonable" use, courts balance the utility of the owner's use against the gravity of the harm. Six factors are helpful in making this determination: alteration of flow, purpose of use, pollution, extent of use, destination of water taken, and miscellaneous conduct that may give rise to litigation.

3) Natural vs. Artificial Use
Under either theory, natural uses (human uses, *e.g.*, consumption, gardening) prevail over artificial uses (*e.g.*, irrigation, manufacturing).

b. Prior Appropriation Doctrine
Under this doctrine, individuals acquire rights by actual use. Appropriative rights are determined by priority of beneficial use. If there is a decrease in flow, priority is accorded in terms of time of appropriation. An appropriative right can be lost by abandonment.

2. Groundwater (Percolating Water)
Four doctrines determine rights in diffuse underground water recovered through wells.

a. Absolute Ownership Doctrine
This doctrine is followed by about 12 eastern states. The owner of overlying land can take all the water she wishes, for any purpose, including export.

b. Reasonable Use Doctrine
About 25 states follow this doctrine. It is like absolute ownership, but exporting is allowed only if it does not harm other owners who have rights in the same aquifer.

c. Correlative Rights Doctrine
In California, owners of overlying land own the underground water basin as joint tenants, and each is allowed a reasonable amount for his own use.

barbri

    d.   Appropriative Rights Doctrine

         This doctrine is followed in some western states. Priority of use (not ownership of overlying land) is determinative.

3.   Surface Waters

A landowner can use surface water (*i.e.,* water without a channel that passes over land, such as rainfall, seepage, etc.) within her boundaries for any purpose she desires. Questions on surface water usually concern liability for changing natural flow by dikes, drains, etc. Liability depends on which theory the state follows.

    a.   Natural Flow Theory

         Under this theory, followed by half the states, owners cannot alter natural drainage patterns. This rule has been "softened" in most states to allow "reasonable changes."

    b.   Common Enemy Theory

         Under this theory, followed by most of the other states, an owner can take any protective measures to get rid of the water (*e.g.,* dikes). The rule has been modified by many courts to prohibit unnecessary damage to others' lands.

    c.   Reasonable Use Theory

         There is a growing trend to apply this theory, which involves balancing the utility of the use against the gravity of the harm.

CMR | **Exam Tip** | Remember that the above theories apply to redirecting surface water. A landowner can *capture* (*e.g.,* by a dam or in barrels) as much surface water as he wishes. Surface water can be diverted to any purpose on or off the land. Owners below have no cause of action unless the diversion was malicious.

D. RIGHTS IN AIRSPACE

The right to airspace above a parcel is not exclusive, but the owner is entitled to freedom from excessive noise.

E. RIGHT TO EXCLUDE—REMEDIES OF POSSESSOR

The possessor of real property has the right to exclude others. His remedies for invasions include actions for:

1. *Trespass* (land invaded by *tangible* physical object);

2. *Private nuisance* (land invaded by *intangibles* such as odors or noise);

3. *Continuing trespass* (land repeatedly invaded by trespasser); and

4. *Ejectment or unlawful detainer* to remove a trespasser or tenant. This action can be joined with a demand for money damages.

IX. COOPERATIVES, CONDOMINIUMS, AND ZONING

A. COOPERATIVES

In a cooperative, title to the land and buildings is held by a corporation that leases individual

apartments to its shareholders. Because of their economic interdependence and because the individual owners are regarded as tenants, a direct restraint on the alienation of an individual interest is valid.

B.   CONDOMINIUMS

In a condominium, each owner owns the interior of his individual unit plus an undivided interest in the exterior and common areas. Because condominium unit ownership is treated as fee ownership, the ordinary rules against restraints on alienation apply.

C.   ZONING

The state may enact statutes to reasonably control the use of land for the protection of the *health*, *safety*, *morals*, *and welfare* of its citizens. The zoning power is based on the state's police power and is limited by the Due Process and Equal Protection Clauses of the Fourteenth Amendment, and the "no taking without just compensation" clause of the Fifth Amendment. Cities and counties can exercise zoning power only if so authorized by a state enabling act. These terms should be remembered:

1.   Nonconforming Use

A use that exists at the time of passage of a zoning act that does not conform to the statute cannot be eliminated at once.

2.   Special Use Permit

A special use permit is one that must be obtained even though the zoning is proper for the intended use. It is often required for hospitals, funeral homes, drive-in businesses, etc.

3.   Variance

A variance is a departure from the literal restrictions of a zoning ordinance granted by administrative action.

CMR | **Exam Tip** | Zoning ordinances are generally invalid if they have no reasonable relation to public welfare, are too restrictive, are discriminatory as to a particular parcel, are beyond the grant of authority, violate due process, or are racially discriminatory.

4.   Unconstitutional Takings and Exactions

A zoning ordinance may so reduce the value of real property that it constitutes a taking under the Fifth and Fourteenth Amendments. If the ordinance constitutes a taking, the local government must pay damages to the landowner equal to the value reduction. If the ordinance regulates activity that would be considered a nuisance under common law principles, it will not be a taking even if it leaves the land with no economic value.

a.   Denial of *All* Economic Value—Taking

A regulation that deprives the owner of *all* economic use of his land constitutes a taking (unless the use was prohibited by nuisance or property law when the owner acquired the property).

b.   Denial of *Nearly All* Economic Value—Balancing Test

If a regulation leaves property with *very little economic value*, to determine if there was a taking the court will balance: (i) the *social goals* of the regulation, (ii) the *diminution in value* of the property, and (iii) the owner's ***reasonable expectations*** for use of the property.

c. **Unconstitutional Exactions**

Local governments often demand, in exchange for zoning approval for a new project, that the landowner give up some land for a public purpose, such as street widening. However, such demands are unconstitutional under the Fifth and Fourteenth Amendments unless the government proves: (i) the government demands are ***rationally connected*** to an additional burden the project will place on public facilities or rights (essential nexus); and (ii) the dedication is reasonably related in ***nature*** and ***extent*** to the impact of the proposed development (rough proportionality).

d. **Remedy**

If a regulation constitutes a taking, the government will be required either to compensate the owner for the property or to terminate the regulation and pay the owner damages for the temporary taking.

TORTS

TABLE OF CONTENTS

TORTS

I. INTENTIONAL TORTS

A. PRIMA FACIE CASE
To establish a prima facie case of intentional tort, plaintiff must prove:

1. Act by Defendant
The act required is a *volitional movement by* defendant.

2. Intent
Intent may be either (i) *specific* (the goal in acting is to bring about specific consequences) or (ii) *general* (the actor knows with "substantial certainty" that these consequences will result)

a. Transferred Intent

1) General Rule
The transferred intent doctrine applies when the defendant intends to commit a tort against one person but instead (i) commits a different tort against that person, (ii) commits the same tort as intended but against a different person, or (iii) commits a different tort against a different person. In such cases, the intent to commit a certain tort against one person is transferred to the tort actually committed or to the person actually injured for purposes of establishing a prima facie case.

2) Limitations on Use of Transferred Intent
Transferred intent may be invoked only if both the tort intended and the tort that results are one of the following:

a) Assault;

b) Battery;

c) False imprisonment;

d) Trespass to land; or

e) Trespass to chattels.

CMR **Exam Tip** Everyone is "capable" of intent. Incapacity is not a good defense. Thus, young children and persons who are mentally incompetent will be liable for their intentional torts.

3. Causation
The result must have been legally caused by defendant's act or something set in motion by him. Causation is satisfied if defendant's conduct was a *substantial factor* in bringing about the injury.

B. PRIMA FACIE CASE—INTENTIONAL TORTS TO THE PERSON

1. **Battery**
   Elements of the prima facie case:

   (i) *Harmful* or *offensive contact*;

   (ii) To plaintiff's person;

   (iii) Intent; and

   (iv) Causation.

   a. **Harmful or Offensive Contact**

      1) **Judged by Reasonable Person Standard**
         Harmfulness and offensiveness are judged by a reasonable person standard.

       Exam Tip Contact is considered offensive only if it has not been consented to. However, consent will be *implied* for the ordinary contacts of everyday life (*e.g.,* minor bumping on a crowded bus).

      2) **Direct or Indirect Contact**
         Contact can be direct (*e.g.,* striking plaintiff) or indirect (*e.g.,* setting a trap for plaintiff to fall into).

   b. **Plaintiff's Person**
      Plaintiff's person includes anything connected to the plaintiff (*e.g.,* clothing or a purse).

2. **Assault**
   Elements of the prima facie case:

   (i) An act by defendant creating a *reasonable apprehension* in plaintiff;

   (ii) Of *immediate harmful or offensive contact* to plaintiff's person;

   (iii) Intent; and

   (iv) Causation.

   a. **Distinguish Fear**
      Apprehension should not be confused with fear or intimidation (*e.g.,* a weakling can cause apprehension and thus assault a bully).

   b. **Apparent Ability Sufficient**
      If defendant has the *apparent ability* to commit a battery, this will be enough to cause a reasonable apprehension.

   c. **Effect of Words**
      Words alone are not sufficient. For the defendant to be liable, the words must be coupled

with conduct. However, words can *negate* reasonable apprehension (*e.g.,* the defendant shakes her fist but states that she is not going to strike the plaintiff).

    d.   Requirement of Immediacy
Plaintiff must be apprehensive that she is about to become the victim of an immediate battery.

3.   False Imprisonment
Elements of the prima facie case:

    (i)   An act or omission on the part of defendant that *confines or restrains* plaintiff;

    (ii) To a *bounded area*;

    (iii) Intent; and

    (iv) Causation.

    a.   Sufficient Methods of Confinement or Restraint
Sufficient acts of restraint include: (i) physical barriers, (ii) physical force, (iii) threats of force, (iv) failure to release, and (v) invalid use of legal authority.

    b.   Insufficient Methods of Confinement or Restraint
Insufficient acts of restraint include: (i) moral pressure and (ii) future threats.

    c.   Time of Confinement
It is irrelevant how short the period of the confinement is.

    d.   Awareness of Confinement
Plaintiff must *know* of the confinement or be *harmed* by it.

    e.   What Is a Bounded Area?
For an area to be "bounded," freedom of movement must be limited in all directions. There must be no *reasonable* means of escape *known* to plaintiff.

4.   Intentional Infliction of Emotional Distress
Elements of the prima facie case:

    (i)   An act by defendant amounting to *extreme and outrageous conduct*;

    (ii) Intent or recklessness;

    (iii) Causation; and

    (iv) Damages—*severe* emotional distress.

a. **Extreme and Outrageous Conduct**
This is conduct that transcends all bounds of decency. Conduct that is not normally outrageous may become so if:

1) It is continuous in nature;

2) It is directed toward a certain type of plaintiff (children, elderly persons, pregnant women, supersensitive adults if the sensitivities are known to defendant); or

3) It is committed by a certain type of defendant (common carriers or innkeepers may be liable even for mere "gross insults").

b. **Requisite Intent**
Unlike for other intentional torts, *recklessness* as to the effect of defendant's conduct will satisfy the intent requirement.

c. **Damages**
Actual damages (severe emotional distress), not nominal damages, are required. Proof of physical injury is not required. The more outrageous the conduct, the less proof of damages is required.

CMR **Exam Tip** Intentional infliction of emotional distress is the only intentional tort to the person that requires damages.

d. **Causation in Bystander Cases**
When the defendant intentionally causes physical harm to a third person and the plaintiff suffers severe emotional distress because of it, the plaintiff may recover by showing *either* the prima facie case elements of emotional distress *or* that (i) she was present when the injury occurred, (ii) she is a close relative of the injured person, and (iii) the defendant knew facts (i) and (ii).

CMR **Exam Tip** Intentional infliction of emotional distress is a fallback tort position. Thus, if another alternative in your exam question is a tort that will also allow plaintiff to recover, it should be chosen over this alternative.

C. PRIMA FACIE CASE—INTENTIONAL TORTS TO PROPERTY

1. **Trespass to Land**
Elements of the prima facie case:

(i) *Physical invasion* of plaintiff's *real property*;

(ii) Intent; and

(iii) Causation.

a. **Physical Invasion**
The invasion may be by a person or object (*e.g.,* throwing a baseball onto plaintiff's land is a trespass). If *intangible matter* (*e.g.,* vibrations or odor) enters, the plaintiff may have a case for nuisance.

b. **Real Property**

Real property includes not only the surface, but also airspace and subterranean space for a reasonable distance.

c. **Intent**

Defendant need intend only to enter on that particular piece of land (he need not know that the land belonged to another).

d. **Potential Plaintiffs**

Anyone in actual or constructive possession of the land may maintain this action.

2. **Trespass to Chattels**

Elements of the prima facie case:

(i) An act by defendant that *interferes with plaintiff's right of possession* in a chattel;

(ii) Intent;

(iii) Causation; and

(iv) Damages.

a. **Two Types of Interference**

The interference may either be an intermeddling (*i.e.,* directly *damaging* the chattel) or a dispossession (*i.e.,* depriving plaintiff of his lawful right of *possession* of the chattel).

b. **Damages**

Actual damages—not necessarily to the chattel, but at least to a possessory right—are required.

3. **Conversion**

Elements of the prima facie case:

(i) An act by defendant that *interferes with plaintiff's right of possession* in a chattel;

(ii) The interference is *so serious* that it warrants requiring defendant to pay the chattel's full value;

(iii) Intent; and

(iv) Causation.

a. **Acts of Conversion**

Acts of conversion include wrongful acquisition (theft), wrongful transfer, wrongful detention, and substantially changing, severely damaging, or misusing a chattel.

b. **Seriousness of Interference**

The longer the withholding period and the more extensive the use, the more likely it is to be conversion. A less serious interference is trespass to chattels.

c. **Subject Matter of Conversion**
Only tangible personal property and intangibles that have been reduced to physical form (*e.g.*, a promissory note) are subject to conversion.

d. **Potential Plaintiffs**
Anyone with possession or the immediate right to possession of the chattel may maintain an action for conversion.

e. **Remedies**
Plaintiff may recover ***damages*** (fair market value at the time of conversion) ***or possession*** (replevin).

CMR
COMPARISON CHART

TRESPASS TO CHATTELS VS. CONVERSION

	Trespass to Chattels	Conversion
Act by Defendant	An interference with plaintiff's right of possession of chattel (either intermeddling or dispossession)	An interference with plaintiff's right of possession so **serious** as to warrant that defendant pay the chattel's full value
Intent	Intent to do the act that brings about the interference	Intent to do the act that brings about the interference
Remedy	Recovery of actual damages from harm to chattel or loss of use (if dispossession, damages based on rental value)	Damage award of fair market value of chattel at time of conversion (*i.e.*, forced sale of chattel). May instead recover chattel (replevin)

D. DEFENSES TO INTENTIONAL TORTS

1. **Consent**
Plaintiff's consent to defendant's conduct is a defense, but the majority view is that one ***cannot*** consent to a ***criminal act***. Any consent fact pattern raises two inquiries:

(i) Was there a valid consent (*e.g.*, no fraud)?

(ii) Did the defendant stay within the boundaries of the consent (*e.g.*, not use a gun in a boxing match)?

a. **Express (Actual) Consent**
Defendant is not liable if plaintiff expressly consents to defendant's conduct. Exceptions: (i) mistake will undo express consent *if* defendant knew of and took advantage of the mistake; (ii) consent induced by fraud will be invalidated if it goes to an essential matter, but not a collateral matter; and (iii) consent obtained by duress will be invalidated unless the duress is only threats of future action or future economic deprivation.

b. **Implied Consent**
Apparent consent is that which a reasonable person would infer from custom and usage or plaintiff's conduct, *e.g.,* normal contacts inherent in body-contact sports, ordinary incidental contact, etc. *Consent implied by law* arises when action is necessary to save a person's life or some other important interest in person or property.

c. **Capacity Required**
Individuals without capacity are deemed incapable of consent, *e.g.,* incompetents, drunken persons, and very young children.

CMR **Exam Tip** This requirement of capacity differs from the rule for the intent element of intentional torts, where incapacity is no defense; *i.e.,* everyone (even a young child) has the capacity to *commit* a tort, but not everyone has the capacity to *consent* to a tort.

d. **Exceeding Consent Given**
If defendant exceeds the scope of consent and does something substantially different, he may be liable.

2. **Self-Defense, Defense of Others, and Defense of Property**
When a question involves the defense of self, others, or property, ask the following three questions:

(i) Is the privilege available? The tort must now be or about to be committed. Already committed torts do not qualify.

(ii) Is a mistake permissible as to whether the tort being defended against (battery, trespass, etc.) is actually being committed?

(iii) Was a proper amount of force used?

CMR **Exam Tip** Keep your parties clear. In questions involving these defenses, the conduct of the defendant was prompted by the commission or apparent commission of a tort by the plaintiff. That tort is not at issue, however; the issue is whether the defendant's response itself constituted a tort against the plaintiff (usually battery, trespass to land, or trespass to chattels) or instead was privileged by one of these defenses.

a. **Self-Defense**
When a person *reasonably believes* that she is being or is about to be attacked, she may use such force as is reasonably necessary to protect against injury.

1) When Is Defense Available?

a) One need not attempt to escape, but the modern trend imposes a duty to retreat before using deadly force if this can be done safely, unless the actor is in her home.

b) Self-defense is generally not available to the initial aggressor.

c) Self-defense may extend to third-party injuries (caused while the actor was defending herself). An actor might be liable to a third person if she deliberately injured him in trying to protect herself.

2) Is Mistake Allowed?
A reasonable mistake as to the existence of the danger is allowed.

3) How Much Force May Be Used?
One may use only that force that reasonably appears to be necessary to prevent the harm (including deadly force). If more force than is reasonably necessary is used, the defense is lost.

b. Defense of Others

1) When Is Defense Available?
One may use force to defend another when the actor *reasonably believes* that the other person could have used force to defend himself.

2) Is Mistake Allowed?
A reasonable mistake as to whether the other person is being attacked or has a right to defend himself is permitted.

3) How Much Force May Be Used?
The defender may use as much force as he could have used in self-defense if the injury were threatened to him.

c. Defense of Property

1) When Is Defense Available?
One may use reasonable force to prevent the commission of a tort against her real or personal property. A request to desist or leave must first be made unless it clearly would be futile or dangerous. The defense does not apply once the tort has been committed; however, one may use force in *hot pursuit* of another who has tortiously dispossessed the owner of her chattels because the tort is viewed as still being committed.

CMR **Exam Tip** Remember that this defense is *not available against one with a privilege*. Whenever an actor has a privilege to enter on the land of another because of necessity, recapture of chattels, etc., that privilege will *supersede* the privilege of the land possessor to defend her property.

2) **Is Mistake Allowed?**

A reasonable mistake is allowed as to whether an intrusion has occurred or whether a request to desist is required. A mistake is *not* allowed as to whether the entrant has a privilege (*e.g.,* necessity) that supersedes the defense of property right, unless the entrant conducts the entry so as to lead the defendant to reasonably believe it is not privileged (such as by refusing to say what the necessity is).

3) **How Much Force May Be Used?**

Reasonable force may be used. However, one may *not* use force causing death or serious bodily harm unless the invasion of property also entails a serious threat of bodily harm.

CMR **Exam Tip** There is a common misperception that deadly force may be used to protect one's home. This is not strictly true. Many of the "home defense" cases are really self-defense cases. Thus, deadly force can only be used when a person, not just property, is threatened.

d. **Reentry onto Land**

At common law, one could use force to reenter land only when the other came into possession tortiously. Under modern law, there are summary procedures for recovering possession of real property. Hence, resort to self-help is no longer allowed.

e. **Recapture of Chattels**

The basic rule is the same as that for reentry of land at common law: when another's possession began lawfully (*e.g.,* a conditional sale), one may use only peaceful means to recover the chattel. Force may be used to recapture a chattel only when in hot pursuit of one who has obtained possession wrongfully, *e.g.,* by theft.

1) **When Is Defense Available?**

a) **Timely Demand Required**

A timely demand to return the chattel is first required unless clearly futile or dangerous.

b) **Recovery Only from Wrongdoer**

The recapture may be only from a tortfeasor or some third person who knows or should know that the chattels were tortiously obtained. One may not use force to recapture chattels in the hands of an innocent party.

    c)   Entry on Land to Remove Chattel

        (1) On Wrongdoer's Land
        When chattels are located on the land of the wrongdoer, the owner is privileged to enter onto the land and reclaim them at a reasonable time and in a reasonable manner, after first making a demand for their return.

        (2) On Land of Innocent Party
        Similarly, when the chattels are on the land of an innocent party, the owner may enter and reclaim her chattel at a reasonable time and in a peaceful manner when the landowner has been given notice of the presence of the chattel and refuses to return it. (As noted above, the chattel owner's right of recapture supersedes the landowner's right to defend his property.) However, the chattel owner will be liable for any actual damage caused by the entry.

        (3) On Land Through Owner's Fault
        If the chattels are on the land of another through the owner's fault (*e.g.,* negligently letting cattle wander), there is no privilege to enter onto the land. They may be recovered only through legal process.

  2) Is Mistake Allowed?
  Generally, no mistake regarding defendant's right to recapture the chattels or enter on the land is allowed. However, ***shopkeepers*** may have a privilege to detain for a reasonable period of time individuals whom they reasonably believe to be in possession of shoplifted goods.

  3) How Much Force May Be Used?
  Reasonable force, not including force sufficient to cause death or serious bodily harm, may be used to recapture chattels.

3. Privilege of Arrest
Depending on the facts, the actor may have a privilege to make an arrest of a third person.

  a. Invasion of Land
  The privilege of arrest carries with it the privilege to enter another's land for the purpose of effecting the arrest.

  b. Subsequent Misconduct
  Although the arrest itself may be privileged, the actor may still be liable for subsequent misconduct (*e.g.,* failing to bring the arrested party before a magistrate, unduly detaining the party in jail).

  c. Mistake

1) **Misdemeanor**

If the arrest is for a misdemeanor, it is privileged only if for a breach of peace and if the action takes place in front of defendant. (Most state statutes grant police officers a broader privilege.)

2) **Felony**

For a felony arrest, a ***police officer*** may make a reasonable mistake. Citizens may make a reasonable mistake regarding the identity of the felon, but not regarding whether the felony occurred.

CMR
COMPARISON CHART

ARRESTS WITHOUT A WARRANT

	Felony Arrest by Police Officer	Felony Arrest by Private Citizen	Misdemeanor Arrests
When Privileged	The officer must reasonably believe that a felony has been committed and that the person he arrests has committed it	The felony in fact must have been committed and the citizen must reasonably believe that the person he arrests has committed it	The misdemeanor must be a breach of peace and committed in the arresting party's presence
Force Allowed	That degree of force reasonably necessary to make the arrest; deadly force only when the suspect poses a threat of ***serious harm***	That degree of force reasonably necessary to make the arrest; deadly force only when the suspect poses a threat of ***serious harm***	That degree of force reasonably necessary to make the arrest, but ***never*** deadly force

4. **Necessity**

A person may interfere with the real or personal property of another when it is reasonably and apparently necessary to avoid threatened injury from a natural or other force and when the threatened injury is substantially more serious than the invasion that is undertaken to avert it. There are two types of necessity: (i) public—when the act is for the public good; and (ii) private—when the act is solely to benefit a limited number of people. Under private necessity, the actor must pay for any injury he causes (unless the act was to benefit the property owner).

CMR **Exam Tip** Necessity is a defense only to property torts.

5. **Discipline**

A parent or teacher may use reasonable force in disciplining children.

II. HARM TO ECONOMIC AND DIGNITARY INTERESTS

A. DEFAMATION

The law of defamation is divided into two parts: the common law elements and the constitutional requirements.

The elements of common law defamation are:

(i) *Defamatory language*;

(ii) *"Of or concerning"* the plaintiff;

(iii) *Publication* thereof by defendant to a third person; and

(iv) Damage to plaintiff's reputation.

If the defamation involves a *matter of public concern*, the Constitution requires the plaintiff to prove two additional elements:

(v) *Falsity* of the defamatory language; and

(vi) *Fault* on the part of defendant.

 Exam Tip   In a common law case, plaintiff does not have to prove falsity as part of the prima facie case. Rather, defendant can offer truth of the statement as a defense.

1. Defamatory Language
Defamatory language is defined as language tending to adversely affect one's reputation. A statement of opinion is actionable only if it appears to be based on specific facts, and an express allegation of those facts would be defamatory. Name-calling is insufficient.

a. Inducement and Innuendo
If the statement is not defamatory on its face, plaintiff may plead additional facts as "inducement" to establish defamatory meaning by "innuendo."

b. Living Person Requirement
Any living person may be defamed. Defamation of a deceased person is not actionable. In a limited sense, a corporation, unincorporated association, or partnership may be defamed (*e.g.,* by remarks as to its financial condition, honesty, integrity, etc.).

2. "Of or Concerning" Plaintiff
The plaintiff must establish that a reasonable reader, listener, or viewer would understand that the defamatory statement referred to the plaintiff.

a. Colloquium
If the statement does not refer to plaintiff on its face, extrinsic evidence may be offered to establish that the statement refers to the plaintiff. This is known as pleading "colloquium."

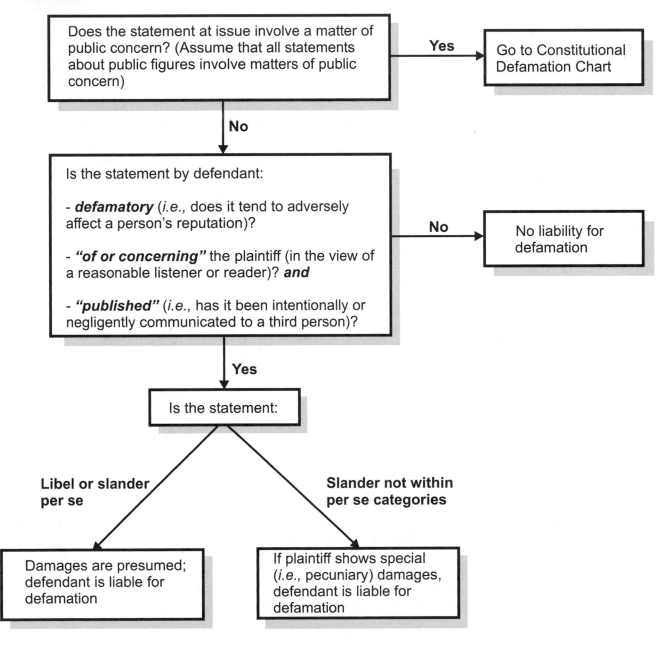

COMMON LAW DEFAMATION

Does the statement at issue involve a matter of public concern? (Assume that all statements about public figures involve matters of public concern)

Yes → Go to Constitutional Defamation Chart

No ↓

Is the statement by defendant:

- *defamatory* (*i.e.,* does it tend to adversely affect a person's reputation)?

- *"of or concerning"* the plaintiff (in the view of a reasonable listener or reader)? *and*

- *"published"* (*i.e.,* has it been intentionally or negligently communicated to a third person)?

No → No liability for defamation

Yes ↓

Is the statement:

Libel or slander per se

Damages are presumed; defendant is liable for defamation

Slander not within per se categories

If plaintiff shows special (*i.e.,* pecuniary) damages, defendant is liable for defamation

b. Group Defamation

1) If the defamatory statement refers to **all** members of a **small** group, each member may establish that the statement is "of and concerning" him by alleging that he is a group member (*i.e.*, everyone wins!).

2) If it is a **large** group, **no** member can prove that the statement is "of and concerning" him (*i.e.*, no one wins!).

3) If the statement only refers to **some** members of a **small** group, plaintiff can recover if a reasonable person would view the statement as referring to plaintiff.

3. Publication

Publication means communication of the defamation to someone other than the plaintiff. Such publication can be made either intentionally or negligently. It is the intent to publish, not the intent to defame, that is the requisite intent. Each repetition is a separate publication. However, for magazines, newspapers, etc., most states have adopted a "single publication" rule under which all copies are treated as one publication.

 Exam Tip An exam favorite is the situation where a defamatory statement about plaintiff is made only **to plaintiff**. As a general rule, there is **no** publication and thus no defamation.

a. Who May Be Liable?

Primary publishers (*e.g.*, newspapers, TV stations, etc.) are liable to the same extent as the author or speaker. One who repeats a defamation is liable on the same general basis as the primary publisher (even if she states the source or makes it clear that she does not believe the defamation). One selling papers or playing tapes is a secondary publisher and is liable only if he knows or should know of the defamatory content.

4. Damage to Plaintiff's Reputation

The type of damages plaintiff must prove depends on the type of defamation (libel or slander) involved. In some slander cases, plaintiff must prove that she suffered special damages—that is, she must have suffered some pecuniary loss in order to recover anything. But once plaintiff has proved special damages, she may recover general damages as well.

a. Libel

Libel is the written or printed publication of defamatory language. Plaintiff does not need to prove special damages and general damages are presumed. The minority position distinguishes between libel per se and libel per quod (not defamatory on its face).

b. Slander

Slander is spoken defamation. Plaintiff must prove special damages, unless defamation falls within slander per se categories; *i.e.*, defamatory statements that:

1) Adversely reflect on one's conduct in a business or profession;

2) One has a loathsome disease;

3) One is or was guilty of a crime involving moral turpitude; or

4)   A woman is unchaste.

c.   **Radio and Television Broadcasts Are Libel**
Radio and television programs are treated by most courts today as libel.

5.   **First Amendment Concerns**
When the defamation involves a ***matter of public concern***, plaintiff must prove, in addition to the common law elements:

(i)   Falsity of the statement, and

(ii)   Fault on the part of defendant.

a.   **Falsity**
In cases where plaintiff is constitutionally required to prove some type of fault, plaintiff also has the burden of proving falsity.

CMR   **Exam Tip**   If a statement of public interest is true, plaintiff has no cause of action for defamation. However, if you see this type of statement on the exam, consider whether plaintiff may have a cause of action for intentional infliction of emotional distress or invasion of right to privacy (unless plaintiff is a public figure).

b.   **Fault on Defendant's Part**
The type of fault that a plaintiff must prove depends on the plaintiff's status.

   1)   **Public Official or Figure Must Prove Malice**
Under the *New York Times v. Sullivan* rule, malice must be proved in defamation cases brought by public officials and public figures.

     a)   **What Constitutes a Public Figure?**
A person becomes a "public figure" by achieving pervasive fame or notoriety or by voluntarily assuming a central role in a particular public controversy.

     b)   **Definition of Malice**
Malice (as defined by *New York Times v. Sullivan*) is:

       (i)   ***Knowledge*** that the statement was false, or

       (ii)   ***Reckless disregard*** as to whether it was false.

       This is a subjective test. Defendant's spite or ill will is not enough to constitute malice. Deliberately altering a quotation may constitute malice if the alteration causes a ***material change*** in the meaning conveyed by the quotation.

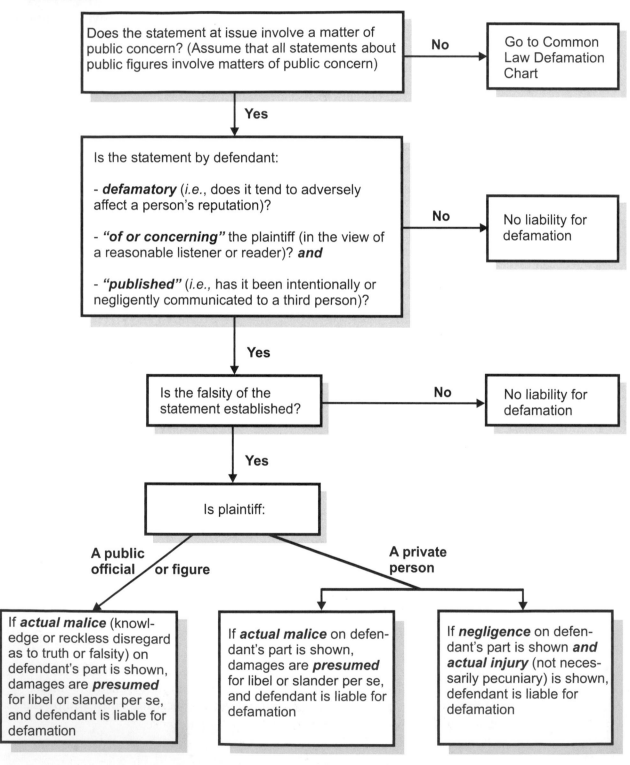

CONSTITUTIONAL DEFAMATION

Does the statement at issue involve a matter of public concern? (Assume that all statements about public figures involve matters of public concern)

No → Go to Common Law Defamation Chart

Yes

Is the statement by defendant:

- *defamatory* (*i.e.*, does it tend to adversely affect a person's reputation)?

- *"of or concerning"* the plaintiff (in the view of a reasonable listener or reader)? *and*

- *"published"* (*i.e.*, has it been intentionally or negligently communicated to a third person)?

No → No liability for defamation

Yes

Is the falsity of the statement established?

No → No liability for defamation

Yes

Is plaintiff:

A public official or **figure**

A private person

If *actual malice* (knowledge or reckless disregard as to truth or falsity) on defendant's part is shown, damages are *presumed* for libel or slander per se, and defendant is liable for defamation

If *actual malice* on defendant's part is shown, damages are *presumed* for libel or slander per se, and defendant is liable for defamation

If *negligence* on defendant's part is shown *and actual injury* (not necessarily pecuniary) is shown, defendant is liable for defamation

2) **Private Persons Need Not Prove Malice**

Under *Gertz v. Welch*, where a private person is the plaintiff, only ***negligence*** regarding the falsity must be proved if the statement involves a matter of "public concern." (If not a matter of public concern, constitutional restrictions do not apply.) Where the defendant is negligent, only "actual injury" damages are recoverable. However, where malice is found, damages may be presumed, and punitive damages allowed.

CMR **Exam Tip** Note that the status of the plaintiff (public figure or private person) is relevant ***only*** for the degree of fault required; the element of falsity must be proved regardless of the status of the plaintiff as long as a matter of public concern is involved (and you should assume that a matter of public concern is involved whenever the plaintiff is a public figure).

CMR SUMMARY CHART **FAULT AND DAMAGES RULES IN CONSTITUTIONAL DEFAMATION ACTIONS**

Type of Plaintiff/Defamation	Fault Required	Damages Recoverable
Public official or public figure	Actual malice (knowledge of falsity or reckless disregard as to truth or falsity)	Presumed damages under common law rules (and punitive damages where appropriate)
Private person/matter of public concern	At least negligence as to statement's truth or falsity	Damages only for proved "actual injury" (If plaintiff proves actual malice, presumed and punitive damages may be available)
Private person/matter of private concern	No fault as to truth or falsity need be proved	Presumed damages under common law rules (and punitive damages where appropriate)

6. **Defenses to Defamation**

a. **Consent**

Consent is a complete defense. The rules relating to consent to intentional torts apply here.

b. **Truth**

Where plaintiff does not need to prove falsity (*i.e.,* the statement is about a purely private matter), defendant may prove truth as a complete defense.

CMR **Exam Tip** Remember that falsity and fault are prima facie case elements only in a *constitutional* defamation case. Plaintiff does not need to prove falsity in a *common law* defamation case because defamatory statements are presumed to be false; defendant has the burden to prove truth as a defense.

c. Absolute Privilege—Can Never Be Lost

Defendant may be protected by an absolute privilege for the following: remarks made during judicial proceedings, by legislators during proceedings, by federal executive officials, in "compelled" broadcasts, and between spouses.

d. Qualified Privilege—Can Be Lost Through Abuse

Sometimes the speaker may have a qualified privilege for the following: reports of official proceedings; statements in the interest of the publisher—defense of one's actions, property, or reputation; statements in the interest of the recipient; and statements in the common interest of the publisher and recipient.

The qualified privilege may be lost if (i) the statement is not within the scope of the privilege, or (ii) it is shown that the speaker acted with malice. Defendant bears the burden of proving that a privilege exists.

7. Mitigating Factors

Mitigating factors (*e.g.,* no malice, retraction, anger of the speaker provoked by plaintiff) may be considered by the jury on the damages issue; they are not defenses to liability.

B. INVASION OF RIGHT TO PRIVACY

1. Four Branches

This tort includes four kinds of wrongs:

a. Appropriation of Plaintiff's Picture or Name

It is necessary to show *unauthorized use* of plaintiff's picture or name for defendant's *commercial advantage*. Liability is generally limited to advertisements or promotions of products or services. Mere economic benefit to defendant (not in connection with promoting a product or service) by itself is not sufficient.

b. Intrusion on Plaintiff's Affairs or Seclusion

The act of *prying or intruding* must be *objectionable to a reasonable person*. Furthermore, the thing into which there is an intrusion must be "*private*." Photographs taken in public places are not actionable.

c. Publication of Facts Placing Plaintiff in False Light

"False light" exists where one attributes to plaintiff views he does not hold or actions he did not take. The false light must be something *objectionable to a reasonable* person under the circumstances. For liability to attach, there must be publicity.

      1)   **First Amendment Limitation**
           If the matter is in the public interest, *malice* on the defendant's part must be proved.

    d.   **Public Disclosure of Private Facts About Plaintiff**
        This wrong involves public disclosure of *private information* about plaintiff (*e.g.,* matters of public record are not sufficient). The public disclosure must be *objectionable to a reasonable person* of ordinary sensibilities. Liability may attach even though the actual statement is true. First Amendment limitations probably apply if the matter is of legitimate public interest.

2.   **Causation**
The invasion of plaintiff's interest in privacy (under any of the four kinds) must have been proximately caused by defendant's conduct.

3.   **Proof of Special Damages Unnecessary**
Plaintiff need not plead and prove special damages. Emotional distress and mental anguish are sufficient damages.

4.   **Defenses**
Some defenses to the right of privacy actions are consent and the defamation privilege defenses. Truth generally is *not* a good defense; nor is inadvertence, good faith, or lack of malice.

5.   **Right of Privacy—Miscellaneous**
The right of privacy is a *personal right* and does not extend to members of a family, does not survive the death of the plaintiff, and is not assignable. The right of privacy is not applicable to corporations.

C.   MISREPRESENTATION

1.   **Intentional Misrepresentation (Fraud, Deceit)**
Prima facie case:

    (i)   *Misrepresentation* of a material fact (no duty to disclose and opinion not actionable unless rendered by someone with superior skill in the area). Silence is generally not enough; one must make affirmative misrepresentations;

    (ii)   *Scienter, i.e.,* when defendant made the statement, she *knew* or *believed* it was false or that there was no basis for the statement;

    (iii)   *Intent* to induce plaintiff to act or refrain from acting *in reliance* upon the misrepresentation;

    (iv)   *Causation* (actual reliance);

    (v)   *Justifiable reliance* (generally, reliance is justifiable only as to a statement of fact, not opinion); and

(vi) **Damages** (plaintiff must suffer **actual pecuniary loss**).

There are no defenses to intentional misrepresentation.

2. **Negligent Misrepresentation**
Prima facie case:

(i) **Misrepresentation** by defendant in a **business or professional capacity;**

(ii) **Breach of duty** toward a particular plaintiff;

(iii) **Causation;**

(iv) **Justifiable reliance;** and

(v) **Damages.**

Generally, this action is confined to misrepresentations made in a **commercial setting**, and liability will attach only if reliance by the **particular** plaintiff could be contemplated.

D. **INTERFERENCE WITH BUSINESS RELATIONS**
Prima facie case: (i) existence of a **valid contractual relationship** between plaintiff and a third party **or valid business expectancy** of plaintiff; (ii) defendant's **knowledge of the relationship or expectancy**; (iii) **intentional interference** by defendant inducing a breach or termination of the relationship or expectancy; and (iv) **damages**.

1. **Privileges**
Defendant's conduct may be privileged where it is a proper attempt to obtain business for itself or protect its interests. A privilege is more likely to be found if defendant: (i) interfered only with plaintiff's prospective business rather than with existing contracts; (ii) used commercially acceptable means of persuasion rather than illegal or threatening tactics; (iii) is a competitor of plaintiff seeking the same prospective customers; or (iv) has a financial interest in or responsibility for the third party, or is responding to the third party's request for business advice.

E. **WRONGFUL INSTITUTION OF LEGAL PROCEEDINGS**

1. **Malicious Prosecution**
Prima facie case: (i) **institution of criminal proceedings** against plaintiff (*e.g.*, filing a complaint with the police); (ii) **termination in plaintiff's favor**; (iii) **absence of probable cause** for prior proceedings (insufficient facts for a reasonable person to believe that plaintiff was guilty, or defendant, in fact, did not actually believe plaintiff to be guilty); (iv) **improper purpose** (*i.e.,* something other than bringing a person to justice); and (v) **damages**. Prosecutors are immune from liability.

a. **Wrongful Civil Proceedings**
Most jurisdictions have extended the malicious prosecution action to cover civil cases.

2. **Abuse of Process**
Prima facie case: (i) **wrongful use** of process for an ulterior purpose, and (ii) definite **act or threat** against plaintiff in order to accomplish an ulterior purpose.

III. NEGLIGENCE

A. PRIMA FACIE CASE
Elements of the prima facie case:

(i) A ***duty*** on the part of defendant ***to conform to a specific standard of conduct*** for protection of plaintiff against an unreasonable risk of injury;

(ii) A ***breach*** of that duty by defendant;

(iii) The breach is the ***actual and proximate cause*** of plaintiff's injury; and

(iv) ***Damage***.

B. DUTY OF CARE
A duty of care is owed to all foreseeable plaintiffs. The extent of the duty is determined by the applicable standard of care. Therefore, when confronted with a negligence question, always ask:

(i) Was the plaintiff foreseeable?

(ii) If so, what is the applicable standard of care?

1. Foreseeable/Unforeseeable Plaintiffs
A duty of care is owed only to foreseeable plaintiffs. However, a problem arises where defendant breaches a duty to one plaintiff ("P1") and also causes injury to another (possibly unforeseeable) plaintiff ("P2"). There are two possible outcomes:

a. Cardozo View (Majority)—Foreseeable Zone of Danger
P2 can recover only if she can establish that a reasonable person would have foreseen a risk of injury to her under the circumstances; *i.e.,* she was located in the foreseeable zone of danger.

b. Andrews View (Minority)—Everyone Is Foreseeable
P2 may establish the existence of a duty extending from defendant to her by a showing that defendant has breached a duty owed to P1.

2. Specific Situations

a. Rescuers
A rescuer is a foreseeable plaintiff where defendant negligently put himself or a third person in peril (*i.e.,* danger invites rescue). However, firefighters and police officers may be barred by the "firefighter's rule" from recovering for injuries caused by the risks of a rescue.

b. Prenatal Injuries
A duty of care is owed to a viable fetus. In cases of failure to diagnose a congenital defect or properly perform a contraceptive procedure, the child may not recover for "wrongful life," but the parents may recover damages in a "wrongful birth" or "wrongful pregnancy" action for any additional medical expenses and for pain and suffering from labor; ordinary child rearing expenses, however, cannot be recovered.

c. **Intended Beneficiaries of Economic Transactions**
A third party for whose economic benefit a legal or business transaction was made (*e.g.,* a beneficiary of a will) may be a foreseeable plaintiff.

3. Standards of Care

a. **Basic Standard—The Reasonable Person**
The reasonable person standard is an *objective* standard, *i.e.,* one's conduct measured against what the average person would do. A defendant's *mental* deficiencies and inexperience are not taken into account (*i.e.,* stupidity is no excuse). However, the "reasonable person" is considered to have the same *physical* characteristics as defendant (but remember, one is expected to know one's physical handicaps and to exercise the care of a person with such knowledge—*e.g.,* a blind person should not fly a plane).

b. **Particular Standards of Conduct**

1) **Professionals**
A professional or someone with special occupational skills is required to possess the knowledge and skill of a member of the profession or occupation in good standing in similar communities. Medical specialists will be held to a national standard of care.

   a) **Duty to Disclose Risks of Treatment**
   A doctor has a duty to disclose the risks of treatment to enable a patient to give an informed consent.

2) **Children**
Children are held to the standard of a child of *like age*, *education*, *intelligence*, *and experience*. This is a *subjective* test. A child under four is usually without the capacity to be negligent. Children engaged in adult activities may be required to conform to an "adult" standard of care.

3) **Common Carriers and Innkeepers**
Common carriers and innkeepers are held to a very high degree of care; *i.e.,* they are liable for slight negligence.

CMR | **Exam Tip** | For the higher common carrier and innkeeper standards to apply, the plaintiff *must* be a passenger or guest.

4) **Automobile Driver to Guest**
A guest in an automobile is owed a duty of ordinary care. In the few guest statute states, one is liable to nonpaying passengers only for reckless tortious conduct.

5) **Bailment Duties**

   a) **Duties Owed by Bailor**
   For a *gratuitous bailment*, the bailor must inform of known, dangerous defects in the chattel. For a *bailment for hire*, the bailor must inform of chattel defects of which he is or should be aware.

   b) **Duties Owed by Bailee**
   The bailee's standard of care depends on who benefits from the bailment:

(i) for a *sole benefit of the bailor* bailment, there is a low standard of care;
(ii) for a *sole benefit of the bailee* bailment, there is a high standard of care;
and (iii) for a *mutual benefit* bailment, there is the ordinary care standard.

6) Emergency Situations

A defendant must act as a reasonable person would under the same emergency conditions. The emergency is not to be considered, however, if it is of defendant's own making.

c. Owners and/or Occupiers of Land

The extent of the liability of owners and/or occupiers of land (and those in privity with the owner/occupier) depends on where the injury occurred and on the status of the plaintiff.

1) Duty of Possessor to Those Off Premises

There is no duty to protect one off the premises from *natural conditions* on the premises; however, there is a duty for unreasonably dangerous *artificial* conditions or structures abutting adjacent land. Also, one must carry on activities on property so as to avoid unreasonable risk of harm to others outside the property.

![CMR] **Exam Tip** In urban areas, the owner/occupier is liable for damage caused off the premises by trees on the premises (*e.g.*, falling branches). This has been an exam favorite in recent years.

2) Duty of Possessor to Those On Premises

In most states the duty owed a plaintiff on the premises for dangerous conditions on the land depends on the plaintiff's status as trespasser, licensee, or invitee.

a) Trespassers

No duty is owed to an *undiscovered* trespasser. As to *discovered* or *anticipated* trespassers, the landowner must: (i) warn of or make safe concealed, unsafe, *artificial conditions known to the landowner* involving risk of *death or serious bodily harm,* and (ii) use reasonable care in the exercise of "active operations" on the property. (No duty is owed for natural conditions or less dangerous artificial conditions.) Easement and license holders owe a duty of reasonable care to trespassers.

b) Attractive Nuisance Doctrine

Most courts impose on a landowner the duty to exercise ordinary care to avoid a reasonably foreseeable risk of harm to children caused by *artificial* conditions on his property. To establish the doctrine's applicability, plaintiff must show: (i) a dangerous condition on the land that the owner is or should be aware of, (ii) the owner knows or should know children frequent the vicinity of the condition, (iii) the condition is likely to cause injury, *i.e.,* dangerous because of child's inability to appreciate the risk, and (iv) the expense of remedying the situation is slight compared with the magnitude of the risk.

![CMR] **Exam Tip** For liability to attach, the four requirements above must be shown. The child *does not* have to be attracted onto the land by the dangerous condition, nor is the attraction alone enough for liability.

c) Duty Owed to Licensees

A licensee is one who enters on the land with the possessor's permission for her ***own purpose or business***, rather than for the possessor's benefit. The possessor has a duty to (i) warn of dangerous conditions (natural or artificial) known to the owner that create an unreasonable risk of harm to the licensee and that the licensee is unlikely to discover, and (ii) exercise reasonable care in the conduct of "active operations" on the property. The possessor has no duty to inspect or repair. (*Remember:* Social guests are considered licensees.)

d) Duty Owed to Invitees

Invitees enter land in response to an invitation by the landowner (*i.e.,* they enter for a purpose connected with the business of the landowner or enter as members of the public for a purpose for which the land is ***held open to the public***). The landowner or occupier owes the same duties owed to licensees ***plus*** a duty to make ***reasonable inspections*** to discover nonobvious dangerous conditions and, thereafter, make them safe. One will lose invitee status if she exceeds the scope of the invitation.

e) Duty Owed to Users of Recreational Land

A landowner who permits the general public to use his land for recreational purposes without charging a fee is not liable for injuries suffered by a recreational user, unless the landowner willfully and maliciously failed to guard against or warn of a dangerous condition or activity.

f) Modern Trend Rejects Status Rules

A strong minority of states reject the distinction between licensees and invitees (and, in a few states, trespassers as well), and simply apply a reasonable person standard to dangerous conditions on the land.

3) Duties of Lessor and Lessee of Realty

The lessee has a general duty to maintain the premises. The lessor must warn of existing defects of which he is aware or has reason to know, and which he knows the lessee is not likely to discover on a reasonable inspection. If the lessor covenants to repair, he is liable for unreasonably dangerous conditions. If the lessor volunteers to repair and does so negligently, he is liable.

CMR **Exam Tip** If the guest of a tenant is injured, the landlord may be liable as lessor of the premises. But don't stop there—remember that the tenant may also be liable to the guest because of the tenant's status as the owner/occupier of the premises.

4) Duties of Vendor of Realty

A vendor must ***disclose*** to the vendee concealed, unreasonably dangerous conditions of which the vendor knows or has reason to know, and which he knows the vendee is not likely to discover on a reasonable inspection.

d. Statutory Standards of Care

A statute's specific duty may replace the more general common law duty of due care if: (i) the statute provides for a ***criminal penalty***, (ii) the statute ***clearly defines the standard*** of conduct, (iii) plaintiff is ***within the protected class***, and (iv) the statute was ***designed to prevent the type of harm suffered*** by plaintiff.

1) **Excuse for Violation**

Violation of some statutes may be excused where compliance would cause more danger than violation or where compliance would be beyond defendant's control.

2) **Effect of Violation or Compliance**

Under the majority view, an unexcused statutory violation is negligence per se; *i.e.,* it establishes the first two requirements in the prima facie case—a *conclusive* presumption of duty and breach of duty. In contrast, even though violation of the applicable statute may be negligence, compliance with the statute will not necessarily establish due care.

CMR SUMMARY CHART — DUTY OF POSSESSOR OF LAND TO THOSE ON THE PREMISES

Status of Entrant	Duties Owed		
	Artificial Conditions	**Natural Conditions**	**Active Operations**
Undiscovered Trespasser	No duty	No duty	No duty
Discovered or Anticipated Trespasser	Duty to warn of or make safe known conditions if non-obvious and **highly** dangerous	No duty	Duty of reasonable care
Child (if presence on land foreseeable—attractive nuisance doctrine)	Duty to warn of or make safe if foreseeable risk to child outweighs expense of eliminating danger	No duty (unless child also qualifies as licensee or invitee)	Duty of reasonable care
Licensee (including social guest)	Duty to warn of or make safe known conditions if nonobvious and dangerous	Duty to warn of or make safe known conditions if nonobvious and dangerous	Duty of reasonable care
Invitee (e.g., member of public, business visitor)	Duty to make reasonable inspections to discover nonobvious dangerous conditions and warn of or make them safe	Duty to make reasonable inspections to discover nonobvious dangerous conditions and warn of or make them safe	Duty of reasonable care

4. Duty Regarding Negligent Infliction of Emotional Distress

The duty to avoid causing emotional distress to another is breached when defendant creates a foreseeable risk of physical injury to plaintiff, either by (i) causing a threat of physical impact that leads to emotional distress or (ii) directly causing severe emotional distress that by itself is likely to result in physical symptoms (limited to cases where a duty arises from a special relationship between plaintiff and defendant).

a. Zone of Danger Requirement

If plaintiff's distress is caused by threat of physical impact to her, most courts require that plaintiff be within the "zone of danger" to recover for her emotional distress.

1) Bystander's Distress from Seeing Injury to Another

Most courts now allow a bystander who is outside the "zone of danger" to recover for her distress from seeing defendant negligently injure another as long as (i) plaintiff and the person injured are closely related, (ii) plaintiff was present at the scene, and (iii) plaintiff observed or perceived the injury.

b. Physical Symptoms Requirement

Plaintiff can recover damages in most jurisdictions only if defendant's conduct caused some ***physical symptoms*** from the distress. While pure emotional distress may be insufficient, a severe shock to the nervous system that causes physical symptoms is sufficient. Two cases in which a physical injury is ***not*** required, however, are: (i) an erroneous report of a relative's death, and (ii) a mishandling of a relative's corpse.

CMR COMPARISON CHART

	INFLICTION OF EMOTIONAL DISTRESS	
	Intentional	**Negligent**
Conduct Required	Extreme and outrageous conduct by defendant	Subjecting plaintiff to threat of physical impact or severe emotional distress likely to cause physical symptoms
Fault Required	Intent to cause severe emotional distress or recklessness as to the effect of conduct	Negligence in creating risk of physical injury to plaintiff
Causation and Damages	Defendant's conduct must cause severe emotional distress	Defendant's conduct generally must cause physical symptoms from the distress
Bystander Recovery When Another Is Physically Injured	Plaintiff bystander must be present when injury occurs and be a close relative of the injured person, and defendant must know these facts when he intentionally injures the other person (or defendant must have intent to cause plaintiff distress)	Plaintiff bystander must (i) be closely related to the injured person, (ii) be present at the scene, and (iii) observe or perceive the injury

CMR **Exam Tip** Keep in mind that the torts for infliction of emotional distress are not the only means of recovering damages for emotional distress. If physical injury has been caused by commission of a tort, plaintiff can "tack on" damages for emotional distress as a "parasitic" element of his physical injury damages, without the need to consider the elements of the emotional distress torts.

5. **Affirmative Duties to Act**
Generally, one does not have a legal duty to act. Exceptions to this rule exist, however:

a. **Assumption of Duty by Acting**
One may assume a duty to act by acting (*e.g.*, once defendant undertakes to aid someone, he must do so with reasonable care).

Exception: Many states have enacted Good Samaritan statutes, which exempt doctors, nurses, etc., from liability for ordinary, but not gross, negligence.

b. **Peril Due to Defendant's Conduct**
One has a duty to assist someone he has negligently or innocently placed in peril.

c. **Special Relationship Between Parties**
A special relationship between the parties (*e.g.*, parent-child) may create a duty to act. Similarly, *common carriers*, *innkeepers*, *shopkeepers*, and others that gather the public for profit owe duties of reasonable care to aid or assist their patrons. In addition, places of public accommodation have a duty to prevent injury to guests by third persons.

d. **Duty to Control Third Persons**
Generally, there is no duty to prevent a third person from injuring another. An affirmative duty may be imposed, however, if one has the actual ability and authority to control a person's actions, and knows or should know the person is likely to commit acts that would require exercise of this control.

C. **BREACH OF DUTY**
Where defendant's conduct falls short of that level required by the applicable standard of care owed to the plaintiff, she has breached her duty. Whether the duty of care is breached in an individual case is a question for the trier of fact. The main problem relates to proof of the breach. Plaintiff may use one of the following theories:

1. **Custom or Usage**
Custom or usage may be used to establish standard of care, but does not control the question of whether certain conduct amounted to negligence. For example, although certain behavior is custom in an industry, a court may find that the entire industry is acting negligently.

2. **Violation of Statute**
Existence of a duty owed to plaintiff and breach thereof may be established as a matter of law by proof that defendant violated an applicable statute ("negligence per se"). Causation and damages must still be established by plaintiff.

3. **Res Ipsa Loquitur**
In some cases, the very occurrence of an event may tend to establish a breach of duty. The

doctrine of res ipsa loquitur requires plaintiff to show that (i) the accident causing the injury is a type that would not normally occur unless someone was negligent, and (ii) the negligence is attributable to defendant (*i.e.,* this type of accident ordinarily happens because of the negligence of someone in defendant's position). This can often be shown by evidence that the instrumentality causing the injury was in the exclusive control of defendant. (Plaintiff must also establish freedom from fault on his part.)

a. Effect of Res Ipsa Loquitur
Where res ipsa loquitur is established, plaintiff has *made a prima facie case* and no directed verdict may be given for defendant. Plaintiff can still lose, however, if the inference of negligence is rejected by the trier of fact.

 Exam Tip Questions testing on res ipsa loquitur often have the defendant making a *motion for a directed verdict*. These questions don't require you to memorize rules of civil procedure—all you need to remember is the following:

(i) *Deny* defendant's motion for directed verdict if plaintiff has established res ipsa loquitur or presented some other evidence of breach of duty (such as defendant's violation of a statute);

(ii) *Grant* defendant's motion if plaintiff has failed to establish res ipsa loquitur and failed to present some other evidence of breach of duty.

Occasionally, plaintiff may also move for a directed verdict. Plaintiff's motion should always be *denied* except in the rare case where plaintiff has established negligence per se through violation of an applicable statute *and* there are no issues of proximate cause.

D. CAUSATION
Once negligent conduct is shown (a breach of the standard of care owed a foreseeable plaintiff), plaintiff must show that the conduct was the cause of his injury. For liability to attach, plaintiff must show *both* actual cause and proximate cause.

1. Actual Cause (Causation in Fact)
Before defendant's conduct can be considered a proximate cause of plaintiff's injury, it must first be a cause in fact of the injury. Several tests exist:

a. "But For" Test
Act or omission is the cause in fact of an injury when the injury would not have occurred but for the act. This test applies where several acts (each insufficient to cause the injury alone) combine to cause the injury.

b. Joint Causes—Substantial Factor Test
Where several causes bring about injury, and any one alone would have been sufficient to cause the injury, defendant's conduct is the cause in fact if it was a substantial factor in causing the injury.

c. Alternative Causes Approach
This test applies when there are two acts, only one of which causes injury, but it is not known which one. The burden of proof shifts to defendants, and each must show that his negligence is not the actual cause. [Summers v. Tice]

CMR **Exam Tip** Distinguish these last two tests: Under the joint causes approach, both parties caused the harm. Under the alternative causes approach, although both parties acted negligently, only one caused the harm.

2. **Proximate Cause (Legal Causation)**
    In addition to being a cause in fact, the defendant's conduct must also be the proximate cause of the injury. Even though the conduct actually caused plaintiff's injury, it might not be deemed to be the proximate cause. Thus, the doctrine of proximate causation is a *limitation of liability* and deals with liability or nonliability for unforeseeable or unusual consequences of one's acts.

    a. **General Rule—Scope of Foreseeable Risk**
        A defendant generally is liable for all harmful results that are the normal incidents of and within the increased risk caused by his acts. This is a *foreseeability* test.

        CMR **Exam Tip** Questions raising proximate cause issues will not require you to make a judgment call on foreseeability in a close case. Often the call of the question will be whether one or both parties are entitled to summary judgment—which should be denied if there is any issue of foreseeability for the jury. In other cases, the facts in the question will be so clear-cut that common sense will tell you immediately whether the harm that occurred was foreseeable.

    b. **Liability in Direct Cause Cases**
        In a direct cause case, where there is an uninterrupted chain of events from the negligent act to plaintiff's injury, defendant is liable for all *foreseeable harmful results*, regardless of unusual manner or timing. Defendant is not liable for *unforeseeable harmful results* not within the risk created by defendant's negligence. Most harmful results will be deemed foreseeable in direct cause cases.

    c. **Liability in Indirect Cause Cases**
        In an indirect cause case, an affirmative intervening force (*e.g.*, an act by a third person, an act of God) comes into motion after defendant's negligent act and combines with it to cause plaintiff's injury.

        1) **Foreseeable Results Caused by Foreseeable Intervening Forces—Defendant Liable**
            Defendant is liable where his negligence caused a foreseeable harmful response or reaction from a dependent intervening force or created a foreseeable risk that an independent intervening force would harm plaintiff.

            a) **Common Dependent Intervening Forces**
                The following dependent intervening forces are *almost always foreseeable:* (i) subsequent medical malpractice, (ii) negligence of rescuers, (iii) efforts to protect the person or property of oneself or another, (iv) injuries caused by another "reacting" to defendant's actions, (v) subsequent diseases caused by a weakened condition, and (vi) subsequent accident substantially caused by the original injury.

            b) **Independent Intervening Forces**
                Independent intervening forces that are not a natural response or reaction to the situation created by the defendant's conduct may be foreseeable if

defendant's negligence increased the risk of harm from these forces. Independent intervening forces include (i) negligent acts of third persons, (ii) crimes and intentional torts of third persons, and (iii) acts of God.

2) **Foreseeable Results Caused by Unforeseeable Intervening Forces— Defendant Usually Liable**
Defendant is liable where his negligence increased the risk of a foreseeable harmful result and that result is ultimately produced by an unforeseeable intervening force. This rule does not apply where the unforeseeable intervening force was a crime or intentional tort of a third person.

3) **Unforeseeable Results Caused by Foreseeable Intervening Forces— Defendant Not Liable**
In the rare case where a totally unforeseeable result was caused by a foreseeable intervening force, most courts hold defendant not liable.

4) **Unforeseeable Results Caused by Unforeseeable Intervening Forces— Defendant Not Liable**
Intervening forces that produce unforeseeable results (results not within the increased risk created by defendant's negligence) are generally deemed unforeseeable and *superseding*. Superseding forces break the causal connection between defendant's initial negligent act and plaintiff's ultimate injury, thus relieving defendant of liability.

d. **Unforeseeable Extent or Severity of Harm—Defendant Liable**
In all cases, defendant takes his plaintiff as he finds him; *i.e.,* defendant is liable for all damages, including aggravation of an existing condition, even if the extent or severity of the damages was unforeseeable. This is also known as the "eggshell-skull plaintiff" rule.

CMR SUMMARY CHART

PROXIMATE CAUSE RULES

	Direct Cause Cases	Indirect Cause Cases	
		Foreseeable Intervening Force	**Unforeseeable Intervening Force**
Foreseeable Harmful Result	Defendant liable	Defendant liable	Defendant liable unless intervening force is crime or intentional tort
Unforeseeable Harmful Result	Defendant not liable	Defendant not liable	Defendant not liable; intervening force is *superseding*

E. DAMAGES

Damage is an essential element of negligence; thus, damage will not be presumed (and nominal damages are not available).

1. Personal Injury

Plaintiff is to be compensated for all his damages (past, present, and prospective), both special and general. Foreseeability of the extent of harm is generally irrelevant; *i.e.*, one takes one's plaintiff as one finds him.

2. Property Damage

The measure of damage is the reasonable cost of repair or, if the property is nearly destroyed, the fair market value at the time of the accident.

3. Punitive Damages

Plaintiff may recover punitive damages if defendant's conduct is "wanton and willful," reckless, or malicious.

4. Nonrecoverable Items

Nonrecoverable items include: (i) interest from the date of damage in a personal injury action, and (ii) attorneys' fees.

5. Duty to Mitigate

As in all cases, plaintiff has a duty to take reasonable steps to mitigate damages (*e.g.*, seek appropriate treatment).

6. Collateral Source Rule

Damages are not reduced just because plaintiff received benefits from other sources (*e.g.*, health insurance).

F. DEFENSES TO NEGLIGENCE

1. Contributory Negligence

Contributory negligence is negligence on the part of the plaintiff that contributes to her injuries. The standard of care for contributory negligence is the same as for ordinary negligence. Hence, a rescuer will not be deemed contributorily negligent without taking into account the emergency situation. Also, plaintiff's violation of an applicable statute may be used to establish his contributory negligence.

a. As Defense to Defendant's Violation of Statute

Contributory negligence is a defense to negligence proved by defendant's violation of an applicable statute unless the statute was designed to protect this class of plaintiffs from their incapacity and lack of judgment (*e.g.*, child injured after darting into street in school zone and getting hit by speeding car of defendant).

b. No Defense to Intentional Torts

Contributory negligence is not a defense to wanton and willful misconduct or intentional tortious conduct.

c. Effect of Contributory Negligence

Contributory negligence completely barred plaintiff's right to recovery at common law. Almost all jurisdictions now favor a comparative negligence system (*see infra*).

d. Last Clear Chance—An Exception to Contributory Negligence
Last clear chance permits plaintiff to recover despite her contributory negligence. Under this rule, the person with the last clear chance to avoid an accident who fails to do so is liable for negligence. (Last clear chance is essentially plaintiff's rebuttal to the defense of contributory negligence.)

1) Helpless Peril
In many states, where the plaintiff is in "helpless peril," defendant will be liable if he knew or should have known of plaintiff's predicament.

2) Inattentive Peril
In "inattentive peril" situations (*i.e.,* plaintiff could have extricated herself if attentive), defendant must actually have known of plaintiff's predicament.

3) Prior Negligence Cases
For the last clear chance doctrine to apply, defendant must have been able, but failed, to avoid harming plaintiff at the time of the accident. If defendant's only negligence occurred earlier, the doctrine will not apply.

e. Imputed Contributory Negligence
As a general rule, the contributory negligence of a third party will be imputed to a plaintiff (and bar her claim) only when the relationship between the third party and the plaintiff is such that a court could find the plaintiff vicariously liable for the third party's negligence. Negligence is imputed in employer-employee, partner, and joint venturer relationships. Negligence is not imputed between husband and wife, parent and child, and automobile owner and driver.

2. Assumption of Risk
Plaintiff may be denied recovery if she assumed the risk of any damage caused by defendant's act. Plaintiff must have (i) known of the risk and (ii) voluntarily proceeded in the face of the risk.

a. Implied Assumption of Risk
Knowledge may be implied where the risk is one that an average person would clearly appreciate. Plaintiff may *not* be said to have assumed the risk where there is no available alternative to proceeding in the face of the risk or in situations involving fraud, force, or an emergency. Also, common carriers and public utilities may not limit their liability by disclaimer, and members of a class protected by statute will not be deemed to have assumed any risk.

b. Express Assumption of Risk
The risk may be assumed by an express agreement.

c. No Defense to Intentional Torts
Assumption of risk is not a defense to intentional torts, but it is a defense to wanton and willful misconduct.

3. Comparative Negligence
In comparative negligence states, plaintiff's contributory negligence is not a complete bar to

recovery. Rather, the trier of fact weighs plaintiff's negligence and reduces damages accordingly (*e.g.,* if plaintiff is 10% at fault, her damages are reduced by 10%). A majority of states have adopted *partial* comparative negligence, which still bars plaintiff's recovery if his negligence was more serious than defendant's negligence (or in some states at least as serious as defendant's). States that have adopted *pure* comparative negligence allow recovery no matter how great plaintiff's negligence.

CMR **Exam Tip** On the MBE, you will be told to assume that pure comparative negligence applies unless the question states otherwise.

a. **Effect on Other Doctrines**

Last clear chance is not used in comparative negligence jurisdictions. Most comparative negligence jurisdictions have abolished the defense of implied assumption of risk but have retained the defense of express assumption of risk. In most states, plaintiff's negligence will be taken into account even though defendant's conduct was "wanton and willful" or "reckless," but not if it was intentional.

CMR COMPARISON CHART

	NEGLIGENCE DEFENSES			
	Contributory Negligence	**Implied Assumption of Risk**	**Pure Comparative Negligence**	**Partial Comparative Negligence**
Defined	Plaintiff's own negligence contributes to her injury	Plaintiff knew of a risk of injury and voluntarily assumed it	Plaintiff's own negligence contributes to her injury	Plaintiff's own negligence contributes to her injury
Effect	Plaintiff's claim completely barred	Plaintiff's claim completely barred	Plaintiff's damage award reduced by percentage of fault attributable to her	Plaintiff's damage award reduced if her fault is below the threshold level; otherwise, plaintiff's claim is barred
Defense Negated by Defendant's "Last Clear Chance"?	Yes	Not applicable	Not applicable	Not applicable
Defense Applies to Wanton or Reckless Tortious Conduct?	No	Yes	Yes	Yes

IV.   LIABILITY WITHOUT FAULT (STRICT LIABILITY)

A.   PRIMA FACIE CASE

For strict liability, the following elements must be shown: (i) existence of an *absolute duty* on the part of the defendant *to make safe;* (ii) *breach* of that duty; (iii) the breach of the duty was the *actual* and *proximate cause* of the plaintiff's injury; and (iv) *damage* to the plaintiff's person or property.

B.   LIABILITY FOR ANIMALS

1.   Trespassing Animals

An owner is strictly liable for reasonably foreseeable damage done by a trespass of his animals.

2.   Personal Injuries

a.   Strict Liability for Wild Animals

An owner is strictly liable to licensees and invitees for injuries caused by wild animals as long as the injured person did nothing to bring about the injury.

b.   No Strict Liability for Domestic Animals

An owner is not strictly liable for injuries caused by domestic animals unless he has knowledge of that particular animal's dangerous propensities that are not common to the species.

c.   Strict Liability Not Available to Trespassers

Strict liability will generally not be imposed in favor of trespassers in the absence of the owner's negligence. However, a landowner may be liable on intentional tort grounds for injuries inflicted by vicious watchdogs.

C.   ABNORMALLY DANGEROUS ACTIVITIES

Courts generally impose two requirements for finding an activity to be abnormally dangerous: (i) the activity must create a foreseeable risk of *serious harm even when reasonable care is exercised* by all actors; and (ii) the activity is *not a matter of common usage* in the community.

CMR **Exam Tip**   Exam questions testing on strict liability often include a statement in the facts or in an answer choice that the defendant exercised reasonable care. Remember that *no amount of reasonable care* on the part of the defendant will relieve him of liability in a strict liability situation.

D.   EXTENT OF LIABILITY

1.   Scope of Duty Owed

The duty owed is the absolute duty to make safe the normally dangerous characteristic of the animal or activity. It is owed to all foreseeable plaintiffs.

2.   Defenses

In *contributory negligence* states, contributory negligence is no defense if plaintiff has failed to realize the danger or guard against it. It is a defense if plaintiff knew of the danger and his unreasonable conduct was the very cause of the abnormally dangerous activity miscarrying. Assumption of the risk is a good defense to strict liability. Most *comparative negligence* states apply their comparative negligence rules to strict liability cases.

V. PRODUCTS LIABILITY

A. BASIC PRINCIPLES
Products liability refers to the liability of a supplier of a defective product to someone injured by the product.

1. Theories of Liability
There are five theories of liability that plaintiff may use: (i) intent, (ii) negligence, (iii) strict liability, (iv) implied warranties of merchantability and fitness for a particular purpose, and (v) representation theories (express warranty and misrepresentation).

CMR **Exam Tip** If the question does not indicate what theory of liability plaintiff is using, apply a strict liability theory because that is the easiest to prove.

2. Common Elements
To find liability under any products liability theory, plaintiff must show: (i) a *defect*, and (ii) existence of the defect *when the product left defendant's control*.

a. Types of Defects

1) Manufacturing Defects
If a product emerges from manufacturing different and more dangerous than the products made properly, it has a manufacturing defect.

2) Design Defects
When all products of a line are the same but have dangerous propensities, they may be found to have a design defect.

3) Inadequate Warnings
A product may be defective as a result of the manufacturer's failure to give adequate warnings as to the risks involved in using the product. For liability to attach, the danger must not be apparent to users.

b. Proving a Defect

1) Manufacturing Defects
For a manufacturing defect, defendant will be liable if plaintiff can show that the product failed to perform as safely as an ordinary consumer would expect (defendant must anticipate reasonable misuse). This test also applies to defective food products.

2) Design Defects
For a design defect, plaintiff usually must show that the defendant could have made the product safer, without serious impact on the product's price or utility.

3) Government Safety Standards
A product's *noncompliance* with government safety standards establishes that it is defective, while *compliance* with safety standards (including labeling requirements) is evidence—but *not* conclusive—that the product is not defective.

4) Scientifically Unknowable Risks
Defendant will not be held liable for dangers not foreseeable at the time of marketing.

5) Unavoidably Unsafe Products
Manufacturers will not be held liable for some dangerous products (*e.g.,* knives) if the danger is apparent and there is no safer way to make the product.

c. Existence of Defect When Product Left Defendant's Control
The defect must have existed when the product left defendant's control. This will be inferred if the product moved through normal channels of distribution.

 Exam Tip In virtually all products liability actions, the fact that there was no contractual *privity* between the plaintiff and defendant will not prevent plaintiff from recovering. Nevertheless, it is still a favorite *wrong choice* in products liability exam questions based on negligence or strict liability theories. Remember that any foreseeable plaintiff, including a bystander, can sue any commercial supplier in the chain of distribution regardless of the absence of a contractual relationship between them.

B. LIABILITY BASED ON INTENT
Defendant will be liable to anyone injured by an unsafe product if defendant intended the consequences or knew that they were substantially certain to occur. Products liability actions based on intent are not very common. If intent is present, the most likely tort is battery.

1. Who Can Sue?
Privity is not required, so any injured plaintiff can sue.

2. Damages
In addition to compensatory damages, punitive damages are available.

3. Defenses
The defenses are those available in other intentional torts cases.

C. LIABILITY BASED ON NEGLIGENCE
The prima facie case is the same as in any negligence case. Plaintiff must show (i) duty, (ii) breach, (iii) actual and proximate cause, and (iv) damages.

1. Duty of Care
A duty of care is owed to any foreseeable plaintiff.

a. Who Can Sue?
Privity with the defendant is no longer required, so any foreseeable plaintiff can sue. This includes:

1) Users;

2) Consumers; and

3) Bystanders.

   b.   **Who Can Be Held Liable?**
       Commercial suppliers such as manufacturers, wholesalers, and retailers can be held liable.

2.   **Breach of Duty**
    Breach of duty is shown by (i) *negligent conduct* of defendant leading to (ii) the supplying of a *defective product* (as defined above).

   a.   **Proof of Negligence**
       Negligence is proved the same as in a "standard" negligence case. The plaintiff may invoke res ipsa loquitur.

   b.   **Liability of Retailers and Wholesalers**
       It is very difficult to hold retailers and wholesalers liable for negligence because they can usually satisfy their duty through a cursory inspection.

3.   **Causation**
    An intermediary's (*e.g.,* wholesaler's) negligent failure to discover a defect does not supersede the original manufacturer's negligence unless the intermediary's conduct exceeds ordinary foreseeable negligence.

4.   **Nature of Damages Recoverable**
    Physical injury or property damage must be shown. (Recovery will be denied if the sole claim is for economic loss.)

5.   **Defenses**
    The defenses are the same as in a general negligence action.

D.   LIABILITY BASED ON STRICT TORT LIABILITY

The prima facie case: (i) a strict duty owed by a *commercial supplier* of a product; (ii) breach of that duty; (iii) actual and proximate cause; and (iv) damage.

1.   **Duty**
    Defendant has a duty to supply safe products.

   a.   **Who Can Sue?**
       Privity is not required—users, consumers, and bystanders can sue.

      1)   **No Substantial Alteration**
          For liability to attach, the product must reach plaintiff without substantial alteration.

      2)   **Does Not Extend to Services**
          Strict products liability applies only to products. Even where a product is provided incident to a service (*e.g.,* blood during an operation), there is no strict liability. Plaintiff may, however, sue in negligence.

   b.   **Who Can Be Held Liable?**
       Any commercial supplier can be held liable. Casual sellers will not be held strictly liable.

2. **Breach of Duty**
For breach of duty, plaintiff must show that the product is defective (as defined above). The defect must make the product unreasonably dangerous. Retailers may be liable even if they have no opportunity to inspect the product.

3. **Causation**
For actual cause, plaintiff must show that the defect existed when the product left defendant's control. If the defect is difficult to trace, plaintiff may be able to rely on an inference that this type of product failure ordinarily would occur only as a result of a product defect. Proximate cause is the same as in negligence cases.

4. **Nature of Damages Recoverable**
Physical injury or property damage must be shown. Recovery will be denied if the sole claim is for economic loss.

5. **Defenses**
In *contributory negligence* states, ordinary contributory negligence is no defense where plaintiff merely failed to discover the defect or guard against its existence, or where plaintiff's misuse was reasonably foreseeable. Assumption of the risk is a defense. In most *comparative negligence* states, courts will apply their comparative negligence rules.

6. **Disclaimers Ineffective**
Disclaimers are *irrelevant* in negligence or strict liability cases if personal injury or property damages occur.

E. **IMPLIED WARRANTIES OF MERCHANTABILITY AND FITNESS**
There are two warranties implied in every sale of goods that can serve as the basis for a suit by a buyer against a seller:

(i) *Merchantability*, which refers to whether the goods are of average acceptable quality and are generally fit for the ordinary purpose for which the goods are used; and

(ii) *Fitness for a particular purpose*, which arises when the seller knows or has reason to know the particular purpose for which the goods are required and that the buyer is relying on the seller's skill and judgment in selecting the goods.

1. **Who Can Sue?**
Most courts no longer require vertical privity. Most states adopted a narrow version of the horizontal privity requirement. This means the buyer, family, household, and guests can sue for personal injuries.

    a. **Bailee and Lessee**
    These warranties extend to bailments and leases as well as sales.

2. **What Constitutes Breach?**
If the product fails to live up to either of the above standards, the warranty is breached and the defendant will be liable.

    a. **Proof of Fault Unnecessary**
    Plaintiff does not have to prove any fault on the part of defendant.

3. **Causation**
   Actual cause and proximate cause are handled as in ordinary negligence cases.

4. **Damages**
   Personal injury and property damages, *and purely economic* loss, are recoverable.

5. **Defenses**
   Defenses include assumption of risk (using a product while knowing of breach of warranty) and contributory negligence to the same extent as in strict liability cases. Failure to give notice of breach is a defense under the U.C.C. (even in personal injury cases).

6. **Effect of Disclaimers**
   Disclaimers are generally rejected in personal injury cases but upheld for economic loss.

F. **REPRESENTATION THEORIES**
   In addition to the theory of implied warranties, a defendant may be liable when a product does not live up to some affirmative representation. The two representation theories are:

1. **Express Warranty**
   Any affirmation of fact or promise concerning goods that becomes part of the basis of the bargain creates an express warranty.

   a. **Who Can Sue?**
      Any consumer, user, or bystander can sue. If a buyer sues, the warranty must have been "part of the basis of the bargain." If plaintiff is not in privity (*e.g.,* bystander), she need not have relied on the representation as long as someone did.

      1) **Bailee and Lessee**
         This warranty extends to bailments and leases as well as sales.

   b. **Breach**
      Fault need not be shown to establish breach. Plaintiff need only show that the product did not live up to its warranty.

   c. **Causation, Damages, and Defenses**
      Causation, damages, and defenses are treated just as under implied warranties.

   d. **Disclaimers**
      A disclaimer will be effective only in the unlikely event that it is consistent with the warranty.

2. **Misrepresentation of Fact**
   A seller will be liable for misrepresentations of facts concerning a product where:

   (i) The statement was of a material fact concerning quality or uses of goods (mere puffery insufficient), and

   (ii) The seller intended to induce reliance by the buyer in a particular transaction.

   Liability is usually based on strict liability but may also arise for intentional or negligent misrepresentations.

PRODUCTS LIABILITY THEORIES

	Negligence	Strict Liability	Implied Warranties
Who Can Sue?	Any foreseeable plaintiff	Any foreseeable plaintiff	Purchaser and her family, household, and guests
Who Can Be Sued?	Any commercial supplier (*e.g.,* manufacturer, wholesaler, retailer)	Any commercial supplier	*Merchantability:* A merchant dealing in the kind of goods sold *Fitness for a Particular Purpose:* Any seller of the goods
What Constitutes Breach?	Negligent conduct that results in the supplying of a defective product	The supplying of a defective product	*Merchantability:* Sale of goods not generally acceptable or fit for ordinary purposes *Fitness for a Particular Purpose:* Sale of goods not fit for purpose that seller knows or has reason to know of (and knows that buyer is relying on seller's judgment)
What Damages Can Be Recovered?	Personal injury and property damage (no recovery for economic loss standing alone)	Personal injury and property damage (no recovery for economic loss standing alone)	Personal injury and property damage (recovery solely for economic loss also permitted)
What Defenses Are Available?	Assumption of the risk and any type of contributory negligence	*Contributory Negligence States:* Assumption of the risk and unreasonable misuse (failure to discover or guard against defect ***not*** a defense) *Comparative Negligence States:* Any type of fault (under state's comparative negligence rules)	*Contributory Negligence States:* Assumption of the risk, unreasonable misuse, and failure to give reasonable notice of breach *Comparative Negligence States:* Any type of fault (under state's comparative negligence rules)

a. **Justifiable Reliance**

Justifiable reliance is required (*i.e.,* the representation was a substantial factor in inducing the purchase). Reliance need not be the victim's (it may be a prior purchaser's). Privity is irrelevant.

b. **Causation and Damages**

Actual cause is shown by reliance. Proximate cause and damages are the same as for strict liability.

c. **Defenses**

Assumption of risk is not a defense if plaintiff is entitled to rely on the representation. Contributory negligence is the same as in strict liability, unless defendant committed intentional misrepresentation.

VI. NUISANCE

Nuisance is not a separate tort in itself. Rather, nuisances are a type of harm—the invasion of either private property rights or public rights by conduct that is tortious because it falls into the usual categories of tort liability (*i.e.,* intentional, negligent, strict liability). There are two types of nuisance: private and public.

A. PRIVATE NUISANCE

Private nuisance is a ***substantial***, ***unreasonable interference*** with another private individual's ***use or enjoyment*** of property that he actually possesses or to which he has a right of immediate possession.

CMR | **Exam Tip** | Nuisance questions on the MBE will often flag the correct choice with a key term from the definition of nuisance—*e.g.,* defendant is liable because the activity created a "substantial" (or "unreasonable") interference with plaintiff's use of her land.

1. Substantial Interference

Substantial interference is interference that is offensive, inconvenient, or annoying to the average person in the community. It is not substantial if it is merely the result of plaintiff's hypersensitivity or specialized use of his own property.

2. Unreasonable Interference

To establish unreasonable interference, required for nuisances based on intent or negligence, the severity of the inflicted injury must outweigh the utility of defendant's conduct. In balancing these respective interests, courts take into account that every person is entitled to use his own land in a reasonable way, considering the neighborhood, land values, and existence of any alternative courses of conduct open to defendant.

3. Trespass to Land Distinguished

In a trespass, there is an interference with the landowner's ***exclusive possession*** by a physical invasion; in a private nuisance, there is an interference with ***use or enjoyment***.

B. PUBLIC NUISANCE

Public nuisance is an act that unreasonably interferes with the ***health***, ***safety***, ***or property rights of***

the community, *e.g.,* using a building for criminal activities such as prostitution. Recovery by a private party is available for a public nuisance only if the private party suffered unique damage not suffered by the public at large.

C. REMEDIES

1. Damages
Plaintiff will usually be awarded damages.

2. Injunctive Relief
If the legal remedy of damages is unavailable or inadequate (*e.g.,* the nuisance will cause irreparable injury), injunctive relief will be awarded. In this case, the court will consider the relative hardships. However, hardships will not be balanced where defendant's conduct was willful.

3. Abatement by Self-Help
In the case of a private nuisance, self-help abatement is available after notice to defendant and his refusal to act. Only necessary force may be used. In public nuisance cases, only a public authority or a private party who has suffered some unique damage can seek an injunction or abatement.

D. DEFENSES

1. Legislative Authority
Legislative authority for "nuisance activity" (*e.g.,* zoning ordinance) is not an absolute defense but is persuasive.

2. Conduct of Others
No one actor is liable for all damage caused by concurrence of his acts and others.
Example: Ten steel mills are polluting a stream. Each steel mill is responsible only for the pollution it causes.

3. Contributory Negligence
Contributory negligence generally is no defense to nuisance unless plaintiff's case rests on a negligence theory.

4. Coming to the Nuisance
One may "come to a nuisance" (purchasing land next to an already existing nuisance) and, thereafter, pursue an action. It is generally not a bar to plaintiff's action unless she "came to the nuisance" for the sole purpose of bringing a harassing lawsuit.

VII. GENERAL CONSIDERATIONS FOR ALL TORT CASES

A. VICARIOUS LIABILITY
Vicarious liability is liability that is derivatively imposed. In short, this means that one person commits a tortious act against a third party and another person will be liable to the third party for this act. The basic situations that you should note for bar examination purposes are set out below.

1. **Doctrine of Respondeat Superior**

    A master/employer will be vicariously liable for tortious acts committed by her servant/ employee if the tortious acts occur within the *scope of the employment* relationship.

    a. **Frolic and Detour**

    An employee making a *minor* deviation from his employer's business for his own purposes is still acting within the scope of his employment. If the deviation in time or geographic area is substantial, the employer is not liable.

    b. **Intentional Torts**

    It is usually held that intentional tortious conduct by employees is not within the scope of employment. *Exceptions:*

    1) Force is authorized in the employment, *e.g.,* bouncer

    2) Friction is generated by the employment, *e.g.,* bill collector.

    3) The employee is furthering the business of the employer, *e.g.,* removing customers from the premises because they are rowdy.

    c. **Liability for Own Negligence**

    Employers may be liable for their own negligence by negligently selecting or supervising their employees. (This is *not* vicarious liability.)

2. **Independent Contractor Situations**

    In general, a principal will not be vicariously liable for tortious acts of her agent if the agent is an independent contractor. Two *broad exceptions* exist, however:

    (i) The independent contractor is engaged in inherently dangerous activities, *e.g.,* excavating next to a public sidewalk, blasting.

    (ii) The duty, because of public policy considerations, is simply nondelegable, *e.g.,* the duty to use due care in building a fence around an excavation site.

    a. **Liability for Own Negligence**

    The employer may be liable for her *own* negligence in selecting or supervising the independent contractor (*e.g.,* hospital liable for contracting with unqualified and incompetent physician who negligently treats hospital's patient). (This is not vicarious liability.)

3. **Partners and Joint Venturers**

    Each member of a partnership or joint venture is vicariously liable for the tortious conduct of another member committed in the *scope and course* of the affairs of the partnership or joint venture.

4. **Automobile Owner for Driver**

    The general rule is that an automobile owner is not vicariously liable for the tortious conduct of another person driving his automobile. In some jurisdictions, courts employ theories other than vicarious liability to hold an automobile owner liable.

a. **Family Car Doctrine**

In many states, the owner is liable for tortious conduct of immediate family or house-hold members who are driving with the owner's express or implied permission.

b. **Permissive Use**

A number of states have now gone further by imposing liability on the owner for damage caused by anyone driving with the owner's consent.

c. **Negligent Entrustment**

An owner may be liable for her *own* negligence in entrusting the car to a driver. Some states have also imposed liability on the owner if she was present in the car at the time of the accident, on the theory that she could have prevented the negligent driving, and hence was negligent herself in not doing so. (This is not vicarious liability.)

5. **Bailor for Bailee**

Under the general rule, the bailor is not vicariously liable for the tortious conduct of his bailee.

a. **Negligent Entrustment**

As above, the bailor may be liable for her *own* negligence in entrusting the bailed object. (This is not vicarious liability.)

6. **Parent for Child**

A parent is not vicariously liable for the tortious conduct of the child at common law. Note, however, that most states, by statute, make parents liable for the willful and intentional torts of their minor children up to a certain dollar amount (*e.g.,* $10,000).

a. **Child Acting as Agent for Parents**

Courts may impose vicarious liability if the child committed a tort while acting as the agent for the parents.

b. **Parent Liable for Own Negligence**

The parent may be held liable for her own negligence in allowing the child to do something, *e.g.,* use a dangerous object without proper instruction. Further, if the parent is apprised of the child's conduct on past occasions showing a tendency to injure another's person or property, she may be liable for not using due care in exercising control to mitigate such conduct, *e.g.,* by allowing the child to play with other children he has a history of attacking.

7. **Tavernkeepers**

a. **Common Law**

No liability was imposed on vendors of intoxicating beverages for injuries resulting from the vendee's intoxication, whether the injuries were sustained by the vendee or by a third person as a result of the vendee's conduct.

b. **Modern Law**

Many states, in order to avoid this common law rule, have enacted Dramshop Acts. Such acts usually create a cause of action in favor of any third person injured by the intoxicated vendee. Several courts have imposed liability on tavernkeepers even in the absence of a Dramshop Act. This liability is based on ordinary negligence principles (the foreseeable risk of serving a minor or obviously intoxicated adult) rather than vicarious liability.

CMR | **Exam Tip** | When you see an MBE question on vicarious liability, recognizing whether the doctrine applies is only the first step in your analysis. Even where defendant is not vicariously liable, plaintiff may prevail if defendant personally was negligent in supervising the person causing the injury. Always look for this option among your answer choices.

CMR SUMMARY CHART

VICARIOUS LIABILITY

Party Committing Tortious Act	Vicarious Liability of Related Party
Employee/Servant	Employer/master vicariously liable if tortious act within scope of employment relationship
Independent Contractor	Employer of independent contractor *not* vicariously liable unless activity is inherently dangerous or duty is nondelegable on public policy grounds
Partner or Joint Venturer	Other partners or joint venturers vicariously liable if tortious act within scope and course of partnership or joint venture
Driver of Automobile	Owner of automobile *not* vicariously liable unless jurisdiction has family car doctrine or permissive use statute
Bailee of Chattel	Bailor *not* vicariously liable
Child	Parent *not* vicariously liable (except for limited statutory liability for willful and intentional torts)
Patron of Tavern	Tavernkeeper *not* vicariously liable in absence of Dramshop Act

Note: Even if the related party is not vicariously liable, she may be liable for her ***own negligence*** (*e.g.,* negligent selection of independent contractor, negligent entrustment of automobile, negligent supervision of child).

B. PARTIES—MULTIPLE DEFENDANT ISSUES

1. Joint and Several Liability

Where two or more negligent acts combine to proximately cause an indivisible injury, each negligent actor will be jointly and severally liable (*i.e.,* liable to plaintiff for the entire damage incurred). If the injury is divisible, each defendant is liable only for the identifiable portion.

a. Defendants Acting in Concert

Where two or more defendants act in concert and injure plaintiff, each is jointly and severally liable for the entire injury. This is so even if the injury is divisible.

b. Statutory Limitations

Many states have abolished joint liability either (i) for those defendants judged to be less at fault than plaintiff, or (ii) for all defendants regarding noneconomic damages. In these cases, liability will be proportional to defendant's fault.

2. Satisfaction and Release

a. Satisfaction

Recovery of full payment is a "satisfaction." Only one satisfaction is allowed. Until there is satisfaction, however, one may proceed against all jointly liable parties.

b. Release

At common law, a release of one joint tortfeasor was a release of all joint tortfeasors. A majority of states now provide that a release of one tortfeasor does not discharge other tortfeasors unless expressly provided in the release agreement.

3. Contribution and Indemnity

Contribution and indemnity are doctrines that determine how joint tortfeasors allocate between them the damages they must pay to a successful plaintiff.

CMR | **Exam Tip** | To keep these two doctrines separate in your mind, recall that generally, for *contribution* to apply, both defendants must have a *measurable degree* of culpability for the tort, but *indemnity* usually applies when one of the parties is *much more responsible* than the other. It is important to note that neither of these doctrines affects how much the *plaintiff* receives. Rather, they deal with how much of the total award *each defendant* ultimately must pay.

a. Contribution

The rule of contribution allows a defendant who pays more than his share of damages under joint and several liability to have a claim against other jointly liable parties for the excess; *i.e.,* it *apportions responsibility* among those at fault.

1) Limitations

The contribution defendant must be originally liable to the plaintiff. Also, contribution is not applicable to intentional torts.

2) Methods of Apportionment

a) Comparative Contribution

Most states have a comparative contribution system, whereby contribution is imposed in proportion to the *relative fault* of the various defendants.

b) Equal Shares

In a minority of states, apportionment is in *equal shares* regardless of degrees of fault.

b.   **Indemnity**

Indemnity involves *shifting the entire loss* between or among tortfeasors. Indemnity is available in the following circumstances: (i) by contract, (ii) in vicarious liability situations, (iii) under strict products liability, and (iv) in some jurisdictions, where there has been an identifiable difference in degree of fault (*e.g.*, retailers who negligently rely on a product's condition may receive indemnification from the manufacturer who negligently manufactured it; one whose liability is based on a secondary duty may recover indemnification from a person who had a primary duty; one who is passively negligent may recover indemnification from a joint tortfeasor who is actively negligent).

c.   **Comparative Contribution**

As noted above, most comparative negligence states have adopted a comparative contribution system where contribution is in proportion to the relative fault of the various defendants. This approach *also* supplants indemnification rules based on identifiable differences in degree of fault.

C.   SURVIVAL AND WRONGFUL DEATH

1.   **Survival of Tort Actions**

Survival acts allow one's cause of action to survive the death of one or more of the parties. The acts apply to actions involving torts to property and torts resulting in personal injury. However, torts invading intangible personal interest (*e.g.*, defamation, invasion of right of privacy, malicious prosecution) expire upon victim's death.

2.   **Wrongful Death**

Wrongful death acts grant recovery for pecuniary injury resulting to the spouse and next of kin. A decedent's creditors have no claim against the amount awarded. Recovery is allowed only to the extent that the deceased could have recovered in action if he had lived (*e.g.*, deceased's contributory negligence reduces recovery in comparative negligence states).

D.   TORTIOUS INTERFERENCES WITH FAMILY RELATIONSHIPS

1.   **Husband-Wife**

Either spouse may bring an action for indirect interference with consortium and services caused by defendant's intentional or negligent tortious conduct against the other spouse.

2.   **Parent-Child**

A parent may maintain an action for loss of a child's services as a result of defendant's tortious conduct, whether intentional or negligent. A child, however, has no action in most states against one who tortiously injures the parent.

3.   **Nature of Action**

Actions for interference with family relationships are derivative. Hence, any defense that would prevent recovery by the injured family member also prevents recovery for interference with the family relationship.

E.   TORT IMMUNITIES

1. **Intra-Family Tort Immunities**

   Under the traditional view, one member of a family unit could not sue another in tort for personal injury. Most states have ***abolished husband-wife immunity***. A slight majority have also abolished parent-child immunity (but generally do not allow children to sue merely for negligent supervision). Those that retain it do not apply it (i) for intentional tortious conduct, and (ii) in automobile accident cases to the extent of insurance coverage.

2. **Governmental Tort Immunity**

   In varying degrees, federal, state, and municipal tort immunity has been eliminated. Where it survives, immunity attaches to ***governmental***, not proprietary, functions.

   a. **Federal Government**

      Under the Federal Tort Claims Act, the United States has ***waived immunity*** for tortious acts. However, immunity will still attach for (i) assault, (ii) battery, (iii) false imprisonment, (iv) false arrest, (v) malicious prosecution, (vi) abuse of process, (vii) libel and slander, (viii) misrepresentation and deceit, and (ix) interference with contract rights. Immunity is not waived for acts that are characterized as "discretionary," as distinguished from those acts termed "ministerial."

   b. **State and Local Governments**

      Most states have substantially waived their immunity to the same extent as the federal government; about half have also abolished municipal immunity to the same extent. Where municipal immunity has been abolished, the "public duty" rule provides that a duty owed to the public at large is not owed to any particular citizen absent a special relationship between the governmental body and the citizen. Where municipal immunity still exists, contrast "governmental" functions (*i.e.,* functions that could only be performed adequately by the government) and "proprietary" functions (functions that might as well have been provided by a private corporation). Courts limit application of sovereign immunity by ***not*** granting it for proprietary functions.

   c. **Immunity of Public Officials**

      Public officials carrying out official duties are immune from tort liability for discretionary acts done without malice or improper purpose. Liability attaches, however, for ministerial acts.

3. **Charitable Immunity**

   The majority of jurisdictions have eliminated charitable immunity.